MARKETING COMMUNICATIONS: PRINCIPLES AND PRACTICE

Philip J. Kitchen, Editor of *Marketing Communications: Principles and Practice*, has published many articles in UK, European and US journals on subjects pertaining to marketing communications, promotional management, public relations and corporate communications. Subsequent to a university degree in English and History, he attended the the University of Manchester, Institute of Science and Technology (UMIST), completing an MSc in Marketing. This was followed by an MBSc at Manchester Business School in 1987 and a PhD from Keele University in 1993.

Dr Kitchen was founder and director of the Strathclyde-based Research Centre for Corporate and Marketing Communications (1996–8). In 1996 he inaugurated the First International Conference on Corporate and Marketing Communications at Keele University; this is now an annual event, held in Belgium (1997) and Glasgow (1998). He is President of the Global Institute for Corporate and Marketing Communications.

Since March 1998, Professor Kitchen has held the Martin Naughton Chair in Business Strategy, Queen's University, Belfast specializing in teaching core marketing, marketing communications and corporate communications – mainly to postgraduate and post-experience students. He is also Director of the prestigious Queen's Executive MBA Programme.

MARKETING COMMUNICATIONS: PRINCIPLES AND PRACTICE

Philip J. Kitchen

Martin Naughton Chair in Business Strategy
Queen's University, Belfast

INTERNATIONAL THOMSON BUSINESS PRESS
I(T)P® An International Thomson Publishing Company

London • Bonn • Johannesburg • Madrid • Melbourne • Mexico City • New York • Paris
Singapore • Tokyo • Toronto • Albany, NY • Belmont, CA • Cincinnati, OH • Detroit, MI

Marketing Communications: Principles and Practice

Copyright © 1999 International Thomson Business Press

I(T)P® A division of International Thomson Publishing Inc.
The ITP logo is a trademark under licence

British Library Cataloguing-in-Publication Data
A catalogue record for this book is available from the British Library

First edition published 1999 International Thomson Business Press

Typeset in Baskerville by LaserScript, Mitcham, Surrey
Printed in the UK by TJ International, Padstow, Cornwall

ISBN 1–86152–196–0

International Thomson Business Press
Berkshire House
168–173 High Holborn
London WC1V 7AA
UK

http://www.itbp.com

CONTENTS

Preface   vii

1   INTRODUCTION AND OVERVIEW OF MARKETING COMMUNICATIONS   1

2   THE ROLE AND FUNCTION OF MARKETING COMMUNICATIONS IN
    ORGANIZATIONS   5

3   THE EVOLUTION OF MARKETING AND MARKETING COMMUNICATIONS:
    PRINCIPLES AND PRACTICE   18

4   PLANNING THE MARKETING COMMUNICATIONS PROCESS   39

5   THE NEED FOR ANALYSIS AS PART OF THE PLANNING AND IMPLEMENTATION
    PROCESS   57

6   THE ORGANIZATIONAL CONTEXT OF MARKETING COMMUNICATIONS   73

7   THE DRIVE FOR INTEGRATED MARKETING COMMUNICATIONS   89

8   AUDIENCE AND ENVIRONMENT: MEASUREMENT AND MEDIA   111

9   THE COMMUNICATIONS PROCESS AND THE SEMIOTIC BOUNDARY   135

10 CPM/HEM MODELS OF INFORMATION PROCESSING   156

11 THE ELABORATION LIKELIHOOD MODEL OF PERSUASIVE COMMUNICATION   172

12 ADOPTION AND DIFFUSION PROCESSES   189

13 ENVIRONMENTAL ISSUES IN MARKETING COMMUNICATIONS   214

14 MARKETING COMMUNICATIONS RENAISSANCE: A TIME FOR REFLECTION?   229

15 MARKETING COMMUNICATIONS ACTIVITIES   250

16 ADVERTISING   264

17 THE DYNAMIC ROLE OF SALES PROMOTION   289

18 DIRECT MARKETING   309

19 PERSONAL SELLING: MANAGEMENT AND ORGANIZATION   325

20   MARKETING PUBLIC RELATIONS   340

21   SPONSORSHIP   361

22   THE INTERNET (INTERNATIONAL CONTEXT)   381

23   RELATIONSHIP MARKETING   403

24   THE RELATIONSHIP AMONG ADVERTISERS, AGENCIES, MEDIA, AND TARGET
     AUDIENCES   422

25   THE ARGUMENT FOR ADVERTISING AGENCY REMUNERATION   442

26   MEASURING THE SUCCESS RATE: EVALUATING THE MARKETING
     COMMUNICATIONS PROCESS AND MARCOM PROGRAMMES   459

27   DEVELOPING A RESEARCH FRAMEWORK: HINTS AND GUIDES FOR
     DISSERTATIONS   477

28   ROLE AND FUNCTION: PRINCIPLES AND PRACTICE REVISITED   489

Bibliography   494
Index   528

PREFACE

There are many good textbooks on marketing communications, mostly American in origin. The rationale behind the emergence of *Marketing Communications: Principles and Practice* was a sense of annoyance that so few UK-based books attempted to portray the subject in a serious academic fashion with strong theoretical foundations. This book attempts to redress the balance in favour of theory, admittedly, but also draws on the opinions, views and conceptualizations of a large number of authors/contributors teaching marcoms across the United Kingdom and from other parts of the world. Various chapters have been drawn from recognized experts in the different areas marketing communications exemplifies. Notably, these contributors do not always agree in terms of subject content or context. My role as editor was to ensure a uniformity of style and form. For example, each chapter is accompanied by case vignettes, end-of-chapter cases and questions for seminar discussion, and extensive references drawing on the latest research available. Where there are differences in terms of emphasis or agreement or disagreement relating to a specific topic I have left these differential emphases alone deliberately. The rationale for this is that marketing communications is an area of exciting diversity and development. The last word has not been written on the subject of marketing communications nor its theoretical nor practical foundations. Indeed, for each area, there are many different viewpoints, and it is hoped that readers/students will take on board the idea of pluralistic perspectives and work within those perspectives.

Despite potential divergence in terms of perspective the contributing authors are ardent exponents in their disciplinary areas. They teach marcoms or a component thereof to ever-increasing numbers of undergraduate and postgraduate students. To each of the contributors I owe and acknowledge a significant debt of gratitude for taking the time, and for sharing their knowledge, in what was intended to be and has become a highly structured and interventionist editorial format. The authors are listed below in alphabetical order rather than the order in which they appear in the text.

- Val Clulow (Monash University) *Chapter 11*
- Fiona Cownie (Bournemouth University) *Chapter 23*
- Val Cox (Humberside University) *Chapter 12*
- Robin Croft (University of Lincolnshire & Humberside) *Chapter 8*

- Keith Crosier (Strathclyde University) *Chapters 16, 24, and 25*
- Christine Daymon (Bournemouth University) *Chapter 6*
- Janine Dermody (Bournemouth University) *Chapters 10 and 13*
- John Desmond (Herriott Watt University) *Chapter 4*
- Bill Donaldson (Strathclyde University) *Chapter 19*
- Douglas Eadie (Strathclyde University) *Chapter 26*
- Lynne Eagle (Massey University) *Chapter 5*
- Martin Evans (University of the West of England) *Chapter 18*
- Mark Gabbott (Monash University) *Chapter 11*
- Chris Hackley (Oxford Brookes University) *Chapter 9*
- Jim Hamill (Strathclyde University) *Chapter 22*
- Janet Hoek (Massey University) *Chapter 21*
- Graham Hughes (Leeds Metropolitan University) *Chapter 15*
- Andreas Laspadakis (Brand Manager) *Chapter 17*
- Andy Lowe (Strathclyde University) *Chapter 27*
- Ioanna Papasolomou (Keele University) *Chapter 20*
- Graham Spickett-Jones (Humberside University) *Chapter 12*

The text is intended for students and practitioners who wish to develop knowledge and skills in marketing communications.

The book is needed. At a time when courses in marketing communications and promotional management are multiplying, i.e. not only the typical CAM course and CIM Marketing Diploma modules, but also many other courses offered at UK institutions at both undergraduate and postgraduate levels, it is time for a good quality UK-generated textbook to be made available in order to satisfy student demand. The new approach, adopted in this text, has been indicated above. There has been a determination throughout to use the latest research findings from the marcoms domain and to present these in an attractive and readable format to students who are required to read, understand and apply the principles involved.

The book is designed with the following groups in mind:

- CAM (Communications, Advertising, Marketing (and Education)) Foundation Diploma students (CAM Diploma in Marketing)
- CIM (Chartered Institute of Marketing) students considering or studying the marketing communications subject
- undergraduate students studying for a BA/BSc in Marketing or courses in which Marketing Communications plays a prominent role, either as a stream of study, or as a specialist option
- postgraduate students studying for a direct qualification in Marketing (MA, Mphil, MSc) or for courses where Marketing Communications is offered as a specialist stream or as an elective (i.e. MA, MSc, MPhil, MBA or other functional management courses)
- as additional reading for students registered for PhDs in the Marketing Communication field
- also suitable for practitioner reading.

ACKNOWLEDGEMENTS

No book of this length and diversity could do justice to the subject of marketing communications without building on the foundations of many previous authors, whether from a practitioner or academic perspective. As Editor I gratefully acknowledge the debt owed to these previous writers. Also, I acknowledge and thank the many organizations and writers who have extended permission for their work to be cited in this book and the contributing authors who have sought and gained permission for these citations to be used. Given that a number of case vignettes are accessed from *Campaign* and *PR Week* I acknowledge that these are 'reproduced with the kind permission of the copyright owner, Haymarket Marketing Publications Ltd'.

Professor Philip J. Kitchen
Queen's University, Belfast

This book is dedicated to my wife Diane,
my partner and co-worker;
and children: Jared James and Emma Ruth

1

INTRODUCTION AND OVERVIEW OF MARKETING COMMUNICATIONS

Philip J. Kitchen

CHAPTER AIMS

- to provide readers with an outline and overview of the text

ILLUSTRATION: TESCO'S ONE-STOP SHOP

If you know a lot about your customers – and Tesco can tell you more about its customers than most – then the chances are you can target your marketing more effectively. According to received marketing wisdom, you can send customers targeted communications in the form of magazines, direct mail, or special offers applicable to their needs, begin to build a relationship, improve loyalty and increase product take-up.

It is also received wisdom that involvement in such relationship marketing is the preserve of the direct marketing or advertising agency – or at least those that practise one of those other 1990s marketing gospels: Integration. But Forward would beg to differ. If ever there was a pairing for which the term 'publishing agency' was coined it is that between Tesco and Forward. On behalf of Tesco, Forward produces, prints, and mails publications in four areas: *Clubcard, Baby Club, Recipe Collection* and *Vegetarian Collection*. These four titles will have a combined print run of 26 million copies in 1997.

Nor is this a straightforward publishing job. Take *Clubcard* magazine. As Hilary Ivory, Forward's editorial director on the Tesco account and a former consumer magazine managing editor at the National Magazine Company, explains: 'We're talking to a readership of six million people. It is hard to think of a single magazine that would be interesting to all of them all of the time. So we developed an innovative package.'

The package she refers to is not a single multi-targeted publication but five different ones, each corresponding to discrete segments of the vast Tesco Clubcard database, and all aiming their editorial output squarely at that target market. The five categories are: students; young adults without dependants; young families with children; those aged 40–60; and those aged 60 plus.

Similarly, Clubcard's most recent sibling, Tesco *Baby Club* magazine, is not one title but six, each corresponding to different stages of pregnancy and infancy. Some might say this is the future of ....?????

(*Source: Campaign*, Special Advertorial concerning Forward, 19 September 1997, see whole of the special issue; used with permission.)

* * *

INTRODUCTION

Marketing communications, which at this stage can be defined as communications by means of promotion within a target audience or market, is the subject of this text. As shown in the illustration it is necessary to *target customers in an integrated fashion* to inform, persuade and remind prospective and existing consumers and customers of the firm, its products and services and how these are differentiated to appeal to and satisfy targeted needs, wants and desires of target markets. Marketing communications is not a static subject, involving the continuous application of tried and tested techniques. Instead it is constantly moving and dynamic, not just in terms of messages, but also medias, monies expended, and changing consumer mindsets. It is also about creativity. When all is said and done, even the best products, priced well and distributed superbly, *need* to be promoted. And promotion – via advertising, sales promotion, marketing public relations, personal selling, direct marketing, sponsorship – has to be based firmly on understanding the dynamics of served (or to-be-served) markets, effective planning, implementation, and constant evaluation.

Marketing Communications: Principles and Practice is intended for students and practitioners who wish to develop a knowledge base, a skills base, and overall ability in the marcoms domain. Admittedly questions arise, and the questions are important. The answers, both creative and managerial, vary from firm to firm owing to different contexts, circumstances, firm positions and market needs. There are no 'pat' or 'easy' answers. But finding answers or effective approaches to marcoms activity is the essence of this book. The text is soundly anchored in strong theoretical foundations and draws on the opinions, views and expertise of theorists throughout the United Kingdom and overseas. The text draws various chapters from recognized experts and teachers in the marcoms domain. Each chapter comes complete with case materials and questions for seminar discussion.

Excellent marketing communications is the essence of effective marketing. It is an exciting and dynamic subject area. It is becoming the *sine qua non* underpinning all manner of exchanges in both the public and private sector. It is global in scope and it is an evolving (in a revolutionary sense) subject. Questions and issues abound, but the answers are within today's and tomorrow's practitioners and theorists. This is why students and practitioners of marketing communications are urged to adopt a critical perspective towards both the principles and practice of marketing communications. They should have this perspective because marcoms is a contemporary and inescapable part of human life, but also because it is dynamic and interesting from a managerial perspective.

The book is needed. At a time when courses in marketing communications and its derivatives are proliferating – that is, not only the typical CAM and CIM courses but also many other undergraduate and postgraduate courses throughout the UK – it is high time for a textbook such as this to satisfy student demand. As noted above, the text includes many case vignettes and discussion topics. There is a determination to use the very latest research findings from the academic and practitioner literature, but present it in such a way as to be comprehensible to students who are required to assimilate, interpret and potentially apply the principles and practices involved.

ORGANIZATIONAL ARCHITECTURE FOR THIS TEXT

The schema for marketing communications indicates the organizational architecture of this book.

Chapters 1 through 6 – Theoretical Foundations These chapters provide the theoretical foundations to marketing communications by considering its role and function within business organizations (C2); its evolution, particularly over the past ten to fifteen years (C3); planning the marcoms process (C4); analysing marcom dynamics as a prelude to planning and execution (C5); and considering marcoms from an organizational context (C6).

Chapters 7 through 14 – Change Engine Scenario These chapters are connected with the need to reconsider marketing communications from a consumer as opposed to organizational perspective. Thus the drive for IMC (C7) is predicated on the view that whatever terms marketers use, what consumers *perceive* is advertising or PR. Perception can be brought about in various ways and there is a strong underlying theme that messages through different medias need to be integrated from an audience/environmental context (C8), through elicitation of meaning (C9), and with consideration extended to rationality, emotion (C10) and the extent to which receivers are *involved* with particular messages (C11). Chapters 12 through 14 then consider these and other factors through the spectrum of adoption and diffusion processes, environmental issues, and whether in fact a renaissance of marcoms is taking (or has taken) place.

Chapters 15 through 23 – Functional Activities These chapters consider mainstream marcoms functions including advertising, sales promotion, direct marketing, personal selling, marketing public relations, sponsorship, new media (Internet), and relationship marketing.

Chapters 24 through 26 – Organizational Interactions These chapters consider how organizations interact with media agencies and also present a model for measuring the success rate in evaluating the overall communication process and individual marcoms programmes.

Chapter 27 – Research Dimensions This chapter offers a structured and dynamic approach as to *how* novice researchers could tackle research issues in the marcoms domain.

Chapter 28 – Summary and Conclusions This chapter offers a summary and conclusion to the marcoms text.

SUMMARY AND CONCLUSIONS

This chapter has sought to provide an outline of what readers might expect to find in the text. While marketing communications and promotional activities are exposed to dynamic flux and change, their ability to influence target audiences and markets is ubiquitous. Understanding marketing communications principles underpins successful management of marcoms practice. Change and variability in audience, environment, message, media, monies and measurement equate to marcoms as one of the most absorbing and vibrant fields of marketing activity, but also one of the most eclectic in business. It is hoped that by earnest study of this text and other readings, from the academic and practitioner literature, and by concerted application, readers will develop skill in the marcoms domain.

REFERENCES

'Special Advertorial concerning Forward Publishing', *Campaign*, 19 September 1997, 12 pp.; see whole of the special issue; Haymarket Publications Limited, London.

THE ROLE AND FUNCTION OF MARKETING COMMUNICATIONS IN ORGANIZATIONS

Philip J. Kitchen

CHAPTER AIMS

- to consider the role of marketing communications in modern business organizations
- to delineate the functions of marcoms from an organizational perspective
- to indicate a model for managing an integrated promotional planning programme, and a model for each function in the process
- to illustrate the role and functions by means of case vignettes, and point readers to detailed illustrations in the text

ILLUSTRATION: LEVI'S RETHINK SPAWNS REVIEW (BY EMMA HALE)

A decline in sales growth, a new client team, the loss of a senior agency figure – three familiar ingredients in the recipe for an advertising account review. But this time, the client is Levi Strauss and the agency is Foote, Cone & Belding. Over the duration of their 67-year relationship, all of the above scenarios (and more) must have cropped up.

Last week, Levi's announced it was reviewing its $90 million US account. Although the short list has not been specified, Levi's will be hard put to match the quality of the creative work spawned by its existing relationship. . . . It seems safe to assume that Bartle Bogle Hegarty, Levi's European agency, will willingly step into any breach that comes up as a result of the US trawl. TBWA/Chiat Day also looks likely to appear on the short list.

The review is the surprise result of an internal rethink at Levi's, prompted by slackening sales for the world's no. 1 clothing brand. Facing competition from designer ranges and own-label offerings, a new top management team felt it needed to know what was out there. FCB, with more than 100 people working on the account, has much to worry about.

Steve Goldstein, vice president for marketing and research for Levi's in the US, said: 'We know we have good advertising. It has nothing to with the current campaign, which I love. It's to do with the continued health and welfare of the Levi's brand.'

For many years the brand's overall welfare was largely entrusted to Mike Koelker, the FCB executive creative director who had a close relationship with the client until his death in 1995. Since then, it seems Levi's has lost the faith to keep all its eggs in one basket. Its interactive and direct marketing accounts have been farmed out to other agencies in the past year, and it looks as if Levi's will go the way of Nike – seeking fresh approaches and healthy competition by splitting its business between a handful of creative agencies.

(*Source*: 'Levi's Rethink Spawns Review', Hale, E., *Campaign*, 7 November 1997, p. 16; used with permission.)

INTRODUCTION

As illustrated in the opening vignette, marketing communications is very far from being a slow-moving monolithic subject (Shimp, 1997; Kitchen and Wheeler, 1997; Schultz and Kitchen, 1997). Instead, every facet of marcoms is encompassed by dynamic change, mainly caused by a host of environmental factors (see Chapters 3 and 14). Assuming that promotion is that part of marketing communications responsible for moving products and services forward, a number of factors have had and are having a significant effect within all organizations. The role and functions of marcoms in organizations are illustrated by another minor but telling vignette relating to Proctor & Gamble, once the bastion of the marketing concept:

VIGNETTE: P&G, SEEING SHOPPERS CONFUSED, OVERHAULS MARKETING

Proctor & Gamble Co., perhaps the world's pre-eminent consumer products company, discovered not long ago that it had forgotten someone: the consumer.

The average consumer in the company's home market is more often than not a woman and takes just 21 minutes to do her shopping. In that time she buys an average of 18 items, out of 30,000 to 40,000 choices. She has less time to browse; it is down 25% from five years ago. She isn't even bothering to check prices. She wants the same product, at the same price, in the same aisle, week after week. So why was P&G making 55 price changes a day across 110 brands, offering 440 promotions a year, tinkering with package size, colour, and contents?

'*We were confusing them*' admits Durk Jager, P&G's President and chief operating officer. P&G were also undermining brand loyalty which is crucial to the company. If you sell Ariel or Tide at full-price today and half-price tomorrow, shoppers get angry. So do retailers.

Result: Problems, Change, Opportunities, Threats

(*Source*: 'P&G, Seeing Shoppers Confused, Overhauls Marketing', by Raju Narisetti, *Wall Street Journal Europe*, 20 January 1997)

The two cases indicate that the promotion or marcoms role in organizations is strongly influenced by consumers' wants, needs, desires and product loyalties; by wider separation but greater visibility of companies and the consumers they ostensibly serve; by increased competition within and between industries and companies; by the ever-raging thirst by companies for market share; by greater financial risks for companies engendered by environmental turbulence; and by increased consumer sensitivities to company strategies and tactics. But what precisely is the role of marcoms and how does it function in organizations? Before tackling these questions it is first necessary to examine the importance of marcoms to organizations.

IMPORTANCE OF MARCOMS

Marketing communications has expanded immeasurably in importance since the 1950s. This growth, in one sense, is an inevitable corollary of the growth of marketing *per se* (Kotler, 1997; Cohen, 1991; Evans and Berman, 1994; Assael, 1993). The effectiveness of marketing has been cited by innumerable authors from virtually every country in the world. Marketing and marketing communications performance seem to be a robust and ongoing necessity to business and non-business organizations, particularly in the light of environmental turbulence occasioned by government deregulation (see opening vignette), escalating internationalization and globalization (see Chapter 14); interconnected economies; consumer concerns for health, vigour and vitality; use and pollution of the earth's resources; and collapsing time schedules. Coexisting with these readily identifiable trends, the image of nuclear families grouped around a cathode ray tube, consuming soap operas and advertisements, has already fossilized into past sedimentary strata and been replaced by modern buzz-words such as fractionalization, demassification and smudge (Kitchen, 1993). Result – marketing communications is more important now than at any previous stage in history. Doubtless, some may argue that corporate communications (see van Riel, 1995; van Riel and Balmer, 1997), identity and image are more important, but from a budgetary perspective alone, marcoms expenditures *dwarf* corporate communications expenditures.

THE MARCOMS ROLE

Organizations, generally business related, ceaselessly promote or present themselves to customers, prospective customers, or publics to achieve a variety of purposes (Shimp, 1997):

1 Informing prospective purchasers
2 Persuading people
3 Inducing action
4 Reaching and affecting a diversity of publics (see Kitchen, 1997)

The fourth factor is included to show the wider and necessary role of corporate image and identity, often beyond the need to create satisfactory exchanges necessitated by marketing. Notably, the role of marketing is characterized by a need to inform, persuade, remind, and induce action among potential buyers so that their purchase needs are directed toward particular organizational offerings. As already seen, however, organizational performance is affected by environmental turbulence. If it is assumed that competitors are inherently hostile and acting positively to create competitive differential advantage (see Cohen, 1991), then the role of promotion or marketing communications is to affect consumer or buyer behaviour. As will be seen in later chapters, consumers are not passive pawns on a marketer's chess board. They have power to listen or not listen, be exposed or not exposed to marcoms messages, pay attention or ignore, be involved or uninvolved, accept or reject, agree, disagree, or derogate sources.

Taking the role of marcoms a stage further, Volume 4.1 of the *Journal of Marketing Communications* (1998) is devoted to tackling issues related to new and technology-inspired developments in marcoms. All four papers touch on the issue of consumer power and initiative, thus underpinning radical sea change(s) in marketing communications. The article by van Raaij (1998) is particularly apposite and is cited with permission here.

Van Raaij indicates that the chain of delivery has reversed from producer → retailer → consumer to consumer → retailer → producer. The new model implies that consumers have the initiative when making purchases, and determine the where and how of distribution, and marcoms. Increasingly sellers will have to come to consumers rather than vice versa. Teleshopping, Internet shopping, home delivery systems are all indicative of a move to consumer-oriented information and delivery mechanisms (Olver and Farris, 1989). Typically, new consumers are impatient, erstwhile, difficult to reach, and generally try to determine which messages they are exposed to, and through which media. Van Raaij (1998) and Schultz and Schultz (1998) agree that the life-cycle stage in which this trend is pre-eminent could be described as early growth. Hence the middle chapters in this text focus extensively on consumer behaviour. The book can be neatly subdivided:

- Chapters 1 through 6: Background to marketing communications.
- Chapters 7 through 14: Change engine scenario: Consumer behaviour becomes the 'totem pole' around which various marcom functions perform their increasingly multi-interpretable, ambivalent, ironic and parodic interactions (see van Raaij, 1998; Gabriel and Lang, 1995).
- Chapters 15 through 23: Functional activities: Advertising, sales promotion, direct marketing, personal selling, marketing public relations, sponsorship, new media (Internet), relationship marketing.
- Chapters 24 through 26: Organizational interactions with media agencies.
- Chapter 27: An approach to conducting research in marcoms.
- Chapter 28: Marcoms – summary and conclusion to text.

The role of marcoms in a consumer-driven and consumer-focused society is still the responsibility to drive exchanges. In an age when products are increasingly similar, when price strategies display marked uniformities, when distribution shelf facings and organizational frontages have all the differentiation of a row of detergent packets on a supermarket shelf (see opening case vignette), promotion carries pole position. Thus the function of marketing communications is to use promotional techniques to underpin and support brand identity and accelerate or maintain behavioural loyalties or switching behaviour.

MARKETING COMMUNICATIONS – THE FUNCTIONS

Each of these is mentioned in greater detail in following chapters; here a brief overview will be presented.

As presented in this text, *two-way communication* is the essence of successful marketing and marketing communications. This implies a relationship between *senders* and *receivers* in which both parties are treated as equal partners. In other words, there has to be commonness of thought between senders and receivers. The short vignette following indicates how this works from the context of Anita Roddick (Body Shop) and her use of marketing public relations.

BODYSHOP

Anita Roddick opened her first shop in a Brighton back street in 1976. The name *Body Shop* was picked up by Roddick in her 'hippie phase' in 1960s USA. Whether by fortune or design, the minute premises were squeezed between two funeral parlours containing chapels of rest. Rest was certainly not enjoyed by the adjoining funeral parlour directors who did all in their power to ensure that the *Body Shop* did not survive. With minimal budget at her disposal, Roddick involved the local press by stating that 'mafia-style funeral operators were intimidating a poor little housewife who was contending to set up her first shop, selling face cream'. Publicity brought customers streaming into the shop and Roddick had learned her first lesson about marketing and marketing communications.

(*Source*: Bevan and Jay, 1989)

The two-way communications in this case involved consumers and an organization (small business). The shop and products alone were insufficient to create business. Consumers and organization needed to share meanings: about products, location, pricing, word-of-mouth, bigger business bullying, and so forth. Notably, had consumers not streamed into the Body Shop, or had their needs not been satisfied by the products sold, they would not have streamed back and Body Shop might have ended life rusting on the scrapheap of so many other failed businesses. However, public relations or marketing public relations is only one technique that can be deployed by a business. Other functions include the following.

Advertising

Advertising can be defined here (but see Chapter 16) as any paid-for form of non-personal presentation or promotion of ideas, goods and services, by an identifiable sponsor. Advertising is familiar, it is part of the cultural background noise within which all consumers throughout the world are immersed. Advertising is publicly presented (not privately), it is pervasive, it offers amplified expressiveness, and it is impersonal.

Advertising takes place via a multitudinous variety of media, the more common forms of which are television, radio, newspapers, magazines, posters, exhibitions and the Internet. Advertising has encountered problems (see Chapters 4, 11 and 14) but these are being tackled. Increasingly, advertising spearheads most other marcoms forms and in fact revitalized lethargic Levi's in the 1980s. Advertising has been affected by postmodernism in terms of the onus of responsibility transferring to receivers to decode or distil or retrieve meaning from advertisements (see van Raaij, 1993). Advertising, in its most modern form, is not just a delivery system, but a meaning retrieval system. As van Raaij (1998) puts it: 'You pick out what you want.'

Personal selling

Personal selling can be defined as oral presentation in a conversational form with one or more prospective purchasers with the intention of making sales (see Chapters 4, 14 and 19). For firms tackling large buyers, key account selling has become the norm. Selling is still, nonetheless, a key component of promotional activity. Selling is also a two-way street, for in order to be able to sell, sales representatives have to know how to market – in other words, to understand needs, wants, desires, buying motives, and scripts (their own and potential buyers') in order to create ongoing exchanges.

Sales promotion

Sales promotion can be defined as short-term incentives to encourage purchase of a good or service. But as Laspadakis makes clear in Chapter 17, sales promotion has become increasingly important for the following reasons: long-term environmental trends, growing retail concentration, maturity and gradual stagnation of most product categories, and decline in perceived effectiveness of traditional mass media advertising. Table 2.1 indicates how these trends are shaping the attractiveness of sales promotion, admittedly in terms of non-price-related promotional activities which tie in more with the IMC approach recommended in Chapter 7.

It can be argued (Jones, 1990a and 1990b) that sales promotion, if used predominantly in a price-related manner, can lead to a vicious cycle of promotion → commotion → demotion.

Marketing public relations

In a straitened publicity sense, this can be viewed as non-personal stimulation of demand for a product or service by planting commercially significant news about it in media likely to be read by a specified target audience, and which [ostensibly] is not paid for by the sponsor. However, MPR is wider ranging than publicity and Kotler (a leading guru of marketing) suggests:

> Marketing practitioners are very likely to increase their appreciation of PR's potential contributions to marketing the product because they are facing a real decline in the productivity of their other promotional tools. Advertising

Table 2.1 Sales promotion attractiveness criteria

Criterion	Causes
Mass media advertising not as effective	• High media cost • Growing media clutter • Audience fragmentation
Pre-purchase attraction	• Sales promotion works well short term • Due to changes in brand cost value • Due to changes in perceived brand value
Trade promotion dominates	• Need for tailor-made promotions • Targeted to store and customer criteria • Enhance long-term brand and company interest
Frequency of price promotion weakens	• Undermining of brand imagery • Regularity of price promotion weakens consumer loyalty and familiarizes consumers to deal loyalty • Loss of brand equity • Demotion of brands to commodities
Non-price promotion emergent as dominant form	• Ties into IMC approach • Supports brand values • Distinct, differentiated, well planned and organized • Reinforces consumer loyalty

Source: Laspadakis, A. (1997) Unpublished MSc dissertation, University of Strathclyde.

costs continue to rise while the advertising audience reached continues to decline. Furthermore, increasing advertising clutter reduces the impact of each ad. Sales promotion expenditures continue to climb and now exceed advertising expenditures two to one (NB, now three to one). Marketers spend money on sales promotion, now not out of choice, but out of necessity. Sales force costs continue to rise, in some cases costing firms over $300 a call. No wonder marketers are calling for more cost-effective promotional tools . . . . Here is where public relations techniques hold great promise. The creative use of news events, publications, social investments, community relations, and so on, offers companies a way to distinguish themselves and their products from their competitors (Kotler, 1989).

Notably, Harris (1993) goes a stage further than Kotler by indicating how today's top companies are using the new PR to gain a competitive edge. Harris cites a number of companies in Table 2.2.

Marketing public relations has battled its way successfully and permanently into the arsenal of marketing communications functions.

Direct marketing

This has been seen as a part of advertising. It can be viewed as seeking to evoke a direct response rather than a delayed one (see Chapters 4, 11, and 18). However, numerous differences between direct marketing and advertising were identified by Roberts and Berger (1989), see Table 2.3.

11

Table 2.2 The MPR explosion

Company	Brand strategy
Ford Motor Company	• Taurus and Sable Cars • 50% prelaunch awareness • 146 000 orders
Campbell Soup Company	• National Soup Month • 36% one-month sales increase
Coleco	• Cabbage Patch Kids • Featured on every major TV station and in every newspaper and magazine in USA
Nutrasweet	• Fat substitute – Simplesse • 30% brand awareness achieved overnight • Company swamped with orders

Source: Adapted from Harris (1993).

Table 2.3 Differences between advertising and marketing

Direct marketing	Indirect marketing
• Communicates directly through more targeted media	• Mass audience via mass media
• Personalizes marcoms	• Impersonal marcoms
• Relatively invisible to competitors	• Highly visible
• Promotion amount specified by budget	• Promotion amount specified by success
• Desired action usually delayed	• Immediate action enjoined (enquiry/purchase)
• Incomplete audience data sets	• Driven by database prospects
• Surrogate attempts to measure success (i.e. awareness/intent to buy)	• Easy to analyse, more measurable and controllable

From this table, it can ascertained that direct marketing is not simply another form of advertising, but offers singular advantages either as a stand-alone function or in terms of integration with other promotional functions. Notably, direct marketing is being replaced or buttressed by database marketing which again leads to a more integrative approach to marcoms.

Point-of-sales communications

This text does not deal with this particular area, but displays, signs, posters, merchandising, shelf facing, spacing, etc. are all designed to influence decisions at the point of sale (see McGoldrick, 1990 for more information).

Internet – form of electronic communications

The Internet can be described as a new medium that offers different approaches from all of the preceding functions. In particular, in its design form it is controlled by senders/designers, but accessed by receivers in their own time, and for their own reasons. Consumers have control over when and how content is accessed, the time period of exposure, and which information can be utilized (Hoffman and Novak, 1995; Croft *et al.*, 1996). Unlike the other tools of marcoms, the Internet is a global medium which implies coordination over marcoms in an integrated fashion on a global basis, a position which few companies would relish or are ready for (see De Mooij, 1994; Schultz and Schultz, 1998). From a large company perspective, few companies have developed a globally integrated strategy for the Internet and in fact many have Web sites managed nationally or internationally offering contradictory messages, designed in different ways, and operating in a relatively uncoordinated manner (see Burki, 1997). The Internet doubtless offers significant opportunities for the future, but for now most companies have a 'presence on the Net' but full development of the opportunities it offers may be some way in the future (see Chapters 14 and 22).

THE PROMOTIONAL MIX

Each of the preceding functions can be used alone or in combination in order to create meaningful exchanges with potential customers. The promotional mix, within the marketing mix, offers unique insights for looking at the entire marketing domain. But, apart from the Internet, there is really nothing new about the common promotional or communication functions. They have been around almost since modern marketing began. What is *new* is the contemporary environment in which these functions or tools are deployed and the promise of greater synergy and interaction afforded by the emergence of integrated marketing communications. It is argued later in the text that it is really only in the past 10–12 years that the promise of greater interaction and integration has become more mainstream, as driven by greater reliance on electronic technology (i.e. database management).

Integrated promotional management

The process of integrated promotional management consists of coordinating the promotional or marcom mix elements, setting objectives, establishing budgets, designing specific programmes, measuring results, and developing contingent tactics when results do not square with objectives. This process is depicted in Figure 2.1.

In Figure 2.1, the approach taken indicates that a sound understanding of the dynamics of served markets drives the promotional management process. This information is derived from marketing information systems, marketing decision support systems, and market research. Objectives, in stage 2, are marketing objectives – sales, profits, return on investment, market share, etc. The promotional budget is derived from marketing and will be linked to previous performance and current scenario planning. The objective and task method is recommended as the most appropriate approach (Kotler, 1993). The integrated promotional process implies that *all promotional activity* is approached from a dual perspective: one, the potential derivative meanings that need to be placed in an appropriate form desired by consumers; two, a conscious decision by marketing and those involved in

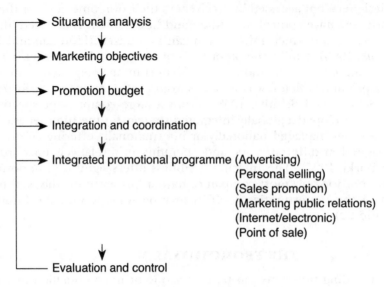

Figure 2.1 The integrated promotional management programme.
(*Source*: Adapted from Shimp, 1993)

communication to examine how and in what way(s) all marcoms functions interact, as well as evaluating how each individual component contributes to the whole. Each functional area, then, in addition to an overarching integrated perspective, also involves a microcosm of the integrated marketing communications process (see Figure 2.2).

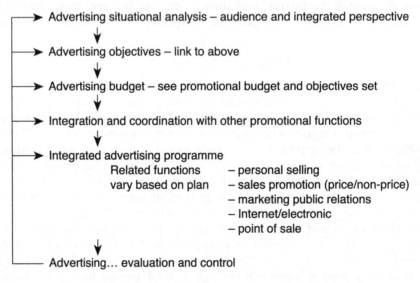

Figure 2.2 The integrated promotional management advertising programme.
(*Source*: Adapted from Shimp, 1993)

14

Though advertising is cited in Figure 2.2, marketing public relations, direct marketing, etc. could just as easily have been selected. Thus Figures 2.1 and 2.2 indicate a general promotional management process, *and* a more specific process dealing with each function in an integrated manner.

SUMMARY AND CONCLUSIONS

This chapter has indicated the role and function of marketing communications in modern business organizations. It is not a slow-moving, dinosaur-type subject. Marcoms has a distinct responsibility for moving products and services *forward* into the hands of paying recipients. Often, buyers are careful, cagey, contentious and sophisticated, and control over the when, how and where of marcoms appears to be moving in their direction. This implies greater understanding of the marcoms process/market dynamics/media involvement in an integrated and coordinated approach. The chapter contains several pointers to the greater detail of each subject in subsequent chapters.

DISCUSSION TOPICS

1 Accessing any secondary sources of information, assess how Levi's has progressed since this press article.
2 How and in what way(s) is marcoms influenced by consumers' wants, needs and desires?
3 Why did P&G overhaul their marketing? What does this signify for marcoms?
4 Why has the image of nuclear families fossilized into past sedimentary strata?
5 Discuss the concept of a reversal from producer→retailer→consumer to consumer→retailer→producer. Is there any evidence that this reversal is occurring?
6 What lesson concerning marketing and public relations did Anita Roddick learn with her first shop?
7 Are there any other functions which merit discussion, but have been omitted in this chapter? Can the omitted functions be placed under the more generic titles?
8 Is there anything new in the fact that meaning is neither in messages nor media, but in receivers? (It may be valuable to consider Hackley's argument in Chapter 9.)
9 Is MPR a new promotional discipline?
10 Compare and contrast the two models in Figures 2.1 and 2.2. Explore the interactions between them, and describe how these may be operationalized.

CASE STUDY – ASA CLEARS LEE JEANS WORK OF OFFENCE (BY JOHN TYLEE)

A jeans manufacturer and its agency have been cleared of glamorizing violence by ad watchdogs in a row over a poster showing a denim-clad woman resting her stiletto heel on a man's buttocks. Seventy-seven complaints were made to the Advertising

Standards Authority over the Grey poster for Lee Jeans which carried the headline, 'Put the boot in'.

But the ASA rejected claims the poster was offensive and promoted violence after Lee argued it presented the image of a woman in control and reflected the prevailing mood of 'girl power'.

At the same time, the ASA found the Japanese car maker, Nissan, not guilty of sexism and promoting violence in a poster featuring a man clutching his crotch in pain and carrying the headline, 'The Micra. Ask before you borrow it'. The authority ruled that the humour was slapstick and unlikely to cause serious offence. But, it has carpeted Panasonic and its agency McCann Erickson, for encouraging anti-social behaviour with an ad for a car stereo boasting it 'packs 200 watts of raw, ear-bleeding power'.

Meanwhile, Microsoft has been told to take greater care after a trade ad named alleged counterfeit software dealers before cases against two of them had been proven. The Euro RSCG Wnek Gosper ad showed a prison wall with barred windows with the headline, 'Counterfeit software dealers. Here's your version of windows'. The ad included a list of seven companies below the subheading 'Some companies we've taken action against'.

Microsoft said it had begun legal proceedings against all the companies named but admitted that cases against two of them were ongoing.

(Source: 'ASA Clears Lee Jeans Work of Offence' (by John Tylee) in Campaign,
14 November 1997, p. 6, used with permission.)

ACKNOWLEDGEMENTS

Grateful thanks are extended to <i>Campaign</i> and Haymarket Publications Limited for kind permission to include case vignettes. Similar gratitude is expressed to Fred van Raaij for permission to quote from his paper in <i>Journal of Marketing Communications</i> Volume 4.1, 1998.

REFERENCES

Assael, H. (1993) *Marketing: Principles and Strategy*, 2nd edn, Fort Worth: The Dryden Press, Harcourt Brace College Publishers.

Bevan, J. and Jay, J. (1989) *The New Tycoons: Becoming Seriously Rich at 40*, London: Simon and Schuster, 21.

Burki, P. (1997) *The Internet and International Marketing Communications*, unpublished MSc. dissertation, University of Strathclyde.

Cohen, W.A. (1991) *The Practice of Marketing Management*, New York: Macmillan.

Croft, R., Dean, D. and Gandersee, C. (1996) 'Interactive or hyperactive: advertising on the Internet' in *Proceedings of the 1st International Conference on Corporate and Marketing Communications*, edited by Kitchen, P.J., University of Keele, Keele, UK, April.

De Mooij, M. (1994) *Advertising Worldwide*, 2nd edn, New York: Prentice Hall.

Evans, J.R. and Berman, B. (1994) *Marketing*, New York: Macmillan.

Gabriel, Y. and Lang, T. (1995) *The Unmanageable Consumer*, London: Sage Publications, 7.

Hale, E. (1997) 'Levi's Rethink Spawns Review', *Campaign*, 7 November, 16.

Harris, T.L. (1993) *The Marketer's Guide to Public Relations*, New York: John Wiley & Sons, 3.

Hoffman, D.L. and Novak, T.P. (1995) 'Marketing in hypermedia computer-mediated environments: conceptual foundations', working paper, Vanderbilt University.

Jones, J.P. (1990a) 'Ad spending: maintaining market share', *Harvard Business Review*, Jan–Feb: 38–42.

Jones, J.P. (1990b) 'The double jeopardy of sales promotion', *Harvard Business Review*, Sept–Oct: 145–52.

Journal of Marketing Communications (1998) published by Routledge; volume 4.1 is devoted to new technology and developments in marketing communications.

Kitchen, P.J. (1993) 'Marketing communications renaissance', *International Journal of Advertising*, 12(4): 367–86.

Kitchen, P.J. (1997) 'Was public relations a prelude to corporate communications?' *Corporate Communications – An International Journal*, 2(1): 22–30.

Kitchen, P.J. and Wheeler, C. (1997) 'Issues influencing marcoms in a global context', *Journal of Marketing Communications*, 3(4): 243–59.

Kotler, P. (1989) 'Public relations vs marketing: dividing the conceptual domain and operational turf', Position paper prepared for the Public Relations Colloquium, San Diego, Jan 24, unpublished.

Kotler, P. (1993) *Marketing Management*, 6th edn, New Jersey: Prentice Hall.

Kotler, P. (1997) *Marketing Management*, 9th edn, New Jersey: Prentice Hall.

Laspadakis, A. (1997) 'The dynamic role of sales promotion in the Greek FMCG sector', University of Strathclyde, MPhil dissertation, unpublished, cited with permission, see also Chapter 17 of this text.

McGoldrick, P. (1990) *Retail Marketing*, London: Prentice Hall.

Nasuretti, R. (1997) 'P&G, seeing shoppers confused, overhauls marketing', *Wall Street Journal Europe*, 20 January.

Olver, J.M. and Farris, P.W. (1989) 'Push and pull: a one-two punch for packaged products', *Sloan Management Review*, Fall: 53–61.

Roberts, M.L. and Berger, P.D. (1989) *Direct Marketing Management*, Englewood Cliffs, NJ: Prentice Hall.

Schultz, D.E. and Kitchen, P.J. (1997) 'Integrated marketing communications: what is it, and why are companies working that way?' in *New Ways for Optimising Integrated Communications*, The Netherlands: ESOMAR, 1–24.

Schultz, D. and Schultz, H. (1998) 'Transitioning marketing communication into the 21st Century', *Journal of Marketing Communications*, 4(1).

Shimp, T.A. (1993) *Promotion Management and Marketing Communications*, 3rd edn, Fort Worth: Dryden Press, Harcourt Brace College Publishers.

Shimp, T.A. (1997) *Advertising, Promotion and Supplemental Aspects of Integrated Marketing Communications*, 4th edn, Fort Worth: Dryden Press, Harcourt Brace College Publishers.

Tylee, J. (1997) 'ASA clears Lee Jeans work of offence', *Campaign*, 14 November, 6.

van Raaij, W.F. (1993) 'Postmodern consumption', *Journal of Economic Psychology*, 14(2): 541–63.

van Raaij, W.F. (1998) 'Interactive communication and consumer power and initiative', *Journal of Marketing Communications*, 4(1).

van Riel, C. (1995) *Principles of Corporate Communication* London: Prentice Hall.

van Riel, C. and Balmer, J.M.T. (1997) 'Corporate identity: the concept, its measurement and management', *European Journal of Marketing*, 31(5 & 6): 340–55.

3

THE EVOLUTION OF MARKETING AND MARKETING COMMUNICATIONS: PRINCIPLES AND PRACTICE

Philip J. Kitchen

CHAPTER AIMS

- to consider the evolution of marketing in the twentieth century
- to indicate the interrelationship between marketing and marketing communications
- to describe how communication works, or is perceived to work
- to indicate the four mainstream areas of marcoms or promotion, namely advertising, sales promotion, personal selling and marketing public relations

ILLUSTRATION: CREATIVE MEDIA CAN SHIFT METAL

Consumers believe it's midsummer madness. Car manufacturers shrug their shoulders and accept it as a way of life. Media owners sit back and watch the money roll in. But, whichever way you look at it, car advertising has all the manifestations of a business out of control.

Take one Saturday in mid-July. The five quality broadsheets and the two mid-market tabloids carried nigh on 55 pages of car ads, ranging from small-space ads for the South Korean manufacturers, Daihatsu and Ssanyong, to spreads for the likes of Rover, Volvo, Peugeot and Citroën. Posters, radio, magazines and TV breaks are stuffed with car ads. In one day, the average consumer reading a newspaper, driving to the superstore, and watching, say, a couple of hours of TV, might have been exposed to £1–2 million worth of car advertising. Hardly, surprising, given that car manufacturers are expected to spend £500 million this year (1997–98) alone.

In this context, car marketing is less of a pure advertising business and more of a media proposition. Sure, it helps to have great creative work, but the biggest challenge is to get noticed – and that involves great creative strategies. The days when car manufacturers could rely on a great 60-second TV commercial, backed up with colour double-page spreads and a few mono price-and-finance-led ads, have long gone.

Indeed, some manufacturers have embraced the importance of this to the extent that their strategies are media-influenced. BMW led the way by taking the opening spread of any colour supplement, a media statement that underlined its premium appeal. The Nissan Micra used small space ads in unusual places to put forward the idea that the Micra was less a car than a cuddly friend. The Ford Maverick roadblocked editorial spreads to sell its four-wheel drive capability.

While media spend is rising at a double digit rate, so are the media options – which is just as well given the budgets to make an impact on TV. Most of the big manufacturers run customer magazines with circulations bigger than the specialist car press. Daewoo used interactive kiosks (no dreaded salesmen). Web sites are just beginning to take off. And that's before we get to interactive TV, which may be just the perfect medium for buying cars.

But, are there any 'golden rules'? TMD Carat client services director, who works on this Nissan account and handled the launches of the Primera and Almeira, says, 'It helps to have a good car. But the single most important thing *is the quality of the communication.*'

(*Source*: *Campaign Report*, 'Cars – the Ad Bonanza',
22 August 1997, pp. 3–4, used with permission)

Evidently, marketing and marketing communications play a very significant role in the UK and indeed worldwide car market. But where does the distinction between marketing and marketing communications lie? Which is *crucial* in creating exchanges that purport to satisfy individual needs while simultaneously fulfilling organizational objectives such as sales, profits and market share? Dominic Cadbury, addressing the Chartered Institute of Marketing, in May 1997 said, 'A fixation with advertising and advertising agencies makes it unsurprising that marketing has a struggle to be taken seriously in the boardroom and the notion of marketing as a source of competitive advantage is regarded with suspicion' (Schultz and Schultz, 1998). Marketing and marketing communications are under fire. The concept of marketing, however, is not under attack in this textbook.

Marketing communications is an integral part of marketing management. Presumably, and despite the quote from Dominic Cadbury, marketing is regarded as a needful practical and scholarly discipline. But, as indicated earlier, it is undergoing transition and has, in fact, transitioned or metamorphosed through various phases or orientations in response to environmental change (these issues are raised, in more detail, in Chapter 14). Latterly, and in response to environmental change, the four broadscale areas of marcoms activity, advertising, marketing public relations, sales promotion and personal selling, have all undergone developments in relation to achievement of cost-effective communication objectives.

INTRODUCTION

In order to grapple with the dynamics of marcoms, it is necessary to evaluate marketing in business organizations. Marketing is still perceived as a dynamic but relatively new subject. Within marketing, the communications or promotion mix is considered from the context of definition, development, and change over the past decade. These developments and changes are related in this chapter to firms in the packaged goods sector, though obviously possessing implications for other sectors.

EVOLUTION OF MARKETING

Marketing, as an academic and practical discipline, is a product of the twentieth century, and since its emergence in the early 1900s is now perceived as a legitimate and scholarly activity. Despite perceived legitimacy, there is no generally acceptable theory of marketing extant (Sheth *et al.*, 1988), though movement is being made toward such a theory. If such a theory were to emerge it would rest on two pillars: 'a thorough understanding of consumer needs and behaviour and a critical analysis of opportunities for competitive advantage' (Day, 1984; Bagozzi, 1986, cited in Sheth *et al.*, 1988). The argument adopted by Cutlip *et al.* (1985) is that marketing is bounded within those processes whose ultimate result is a market transaction, and it has to be said that Cutlip is not alone in this perspective; for example, Luck (1969) agrees with him. Against this perspective, however, is the so-called 'generic' concept of marketing, put forward by Kotler and Levy (1969) and Kotler (1972), which stipulated that: 'marketing is specifically concerned with how transactions are created, facilitated, stimulated, and valued. This is the generic concept of marketing'. Kotler (1972) then clarified the broadened boundaries of marketing: 'The core concept of marketing is the transaction. A transaction is the exchange of values between two parties. The things of value need not be limited to goods, services, and money; they include other resources such as time, energy, and feelings. Transactions occur not only between buyers and sellers, and organizations and clients, but also between any two parties.' While the purpose of this chapter is not theoretical, i.e. to discuss the nature and meaning of marketing, what these quotations illustrate is that questions such as what is marketing? may receive a diversity of answers depending on the perspective of those asked. For the purpose of this article the definition of the American Marketing Association (1985) will suffice that 'marketing is the process of planning and executing the conception, pricing, promotion, and distribution of ideas, goods, and services to create exchanges that satisfy individual and organizational objectives'.

Marketing, according to the above definition, involves anticipation, management, and satisfaction through exchange processes. Evans and Berman (1997) argue that marketing is now integrated in western society, that is, has developed contemporaneously in conjunction with economic and social development, and that it is of relevance to a diversity of organizations. They observe that 'the marketing concept is a consumer-oriented, integrated, goal-oriented philosophy for a firm, institution, or person'. A number of business orientations to fulfil demand have been utilized over time, of which marketing is one. These include production, product, sales, marketing, and societal marketing (Cohen, 1991). It appears self-evident that orientations to guide firms effectively in marketing products and services are dependent for their validity upon the underlying dynamics of served markets.

Marketing's origins are related to selling, from which it evolved and with which it is often confused (Levitt, 1960). The origins of marketing can be traced to individuals' use of the exchange process by barter, and then through the development of trading posts, travelling sales people, general stores, cities and national monetary systems. The Industrial Revolution marked the turning away from self-sufficiency and self-production to purchases wherein mass markets and mass production techniques started to emerge. Initially production was limited, demand high and competition scarce, and thus there was no real need for sophisticated consumer research, product modification or adaptation to consumer needs. The primary goal of business organizations was to increase production to keep pace with demand. The orientation in those early days was known as the 'production era of marketing'. However, as production schedules were maximized, business organizations employed larger sales forces and heavy advertising to persuade consumers to buy. In the sales orientation era, firms sold products without first determining consumer needs or desires. The role of advertising and selling was to make the desires, wants and needs of consumers fit manufactured product attributes. However, as competition grew, supply began to exceed demand. Marketing departments started to emerge. Initially, marketing departments were subordinate to other organizational functions. They carried out tasks such as market research, and advised management on product design, pricing, promotion and distribution of products. Some have termed this the 'department era of marketing' (Evans and Berman, 1988). A further orientation focused on the product itself and held that consumers favoured products that offered the most quality, performance and features. Organizations following this orientation focused energies on making good products and improving them over time. However, this orientation created 'marketing myopia' which focused undue concentration on products rather than needs. Metaphorically, firms could be accused of looking in a mirror rather than out of the window. Now the seeming centrality of marketing had been recognized, decisions were more likely to be successful if they were founded on the basis of thorough consumer research and carefully planned marketing management. This has to be the case in a highly competitive, turbulent environment. Consumers must be attracted and encouraged to remain loyal to firms' brands.

Marketing control, typified by Evans and Berman (1988), indicates that implementation of the marketing concept means that businesses must be consumer *and* profit-oriented and that marketing must be integrated throughout the organization (McKitterick, 1957). However, recent years have seen questions raised as to whether the marketing concept and orientation are appropriate in an age of environmental deterioration, population growth, world hunger and poverty, and neglected, under-funded and increasingly businesslike (profit-centred) social services (Feldman, 1971; Bell and Emery, 1971; Houston, 1986). This has led to a new stage of marketing, proclaimed by Kotler (1991) as the societal orientation, which is marketing 'in a way that preserves or enhances the consumer's and the society's well being'.

This type of orientation requires a three-pronged 'balancing act' by firms: company profits, consumer wants, satisfaction, *and* public interest. The latter ties in well to corporate public relations, but achievement of the first two provides a suitable backdrop to marcoms. Both profits and consumer want satisfactions are delivered by provision of appropriate products, in convenient locations, priced appropriately, and communicated in various ways. The Four Ps of marketing, ably popularized by McCarthy (1981), are the basis for effective marketing strategies and tactics. Each must be focused on the needs of target markets to be effective. In recognizing the interactive and synergistic nature of the four Ps, and in recognizing the role they all must play in communication *per se*, the discussion now focuses on marketing communications from the promotional perspective.

MARKETING COMMUNICATIONS

All elements of the marketing mix, of necessity, have a *communications* function. But only *promotion is charged with the responsibility to move products forward* (Shimp, 1997). But what is marketing communications? It is the process where commonness of thought and meaning is achieved or attempted between organizations (companies) and individuals (prospective customers and consumers). Notably, neither partner is dominant in the process of communication. Businesses are both senders and receivers of messages. As *senders*, businesses attempt to inform, persuade, remind and induce target market(s) to adopt courses of action compatible with organizational need to create exchanges. As *receivers*, businesses attune themselves to target market(s) in order to develop appropriate messages, adapt existing messages to changing circumstance, and spot emergent communication potentialities. Communication is thus *two-way*.

Marketing necessitates manufacturing appropriate products needed by target markets, pricing attractively and distributing conveniently, but also making markets aware of the product's existence and its benefits, over and above competitive alternatives. Promotion is needed to create brand awareness, inform of product improvements, introduce price changes, encourage distributors, reward loyalty, create/maintain image, or induce purchase. In today's dynamic and ever-changing environments, objectives of promotion might include increased market share (e.g. Halifax plc, following privatization in 1997), more frequent product use (wash, rinse, then repeat), attract new customers (e.g. First Direct's use of direct mail), or to influence perceptions or attitudes more favourably toward a company or its brands. But the key question may be: just how does communication work? Harold D. Laswell's robust model (1948) keeps on appearing in mainstream marketing texts, but does it really answer the question?

Figure 3.1, while indicating the basic elements of communication, implies a one-way communication street. Using the model may imply that audiences are passive recipients of promotional messages rather than active participants in a communications process. In other words, it is likely that for many messages there may be no appreciable audience reaction. But, as a basis, the model is useful for considering effective communications. All communications start with *marketing objectives* which in turn lead to development of marketing strategy. Part of marketing strategy includes

Who? →	Says what? →	How? →	To whom? →	With what effect?
(Source)	(Message)	(Channel)	(Audience)	(Reaction)

Figure 3.1 How communication works.

describing key characteristics of target markets which equate to audiences (*to whom*). Communication or promotion objectives and tasks can then be determined, media selected, and a process of coordination (integration), evaluation and control instigated. Laswell's model can be expanded into the model put forward by Wilbur Schramm (1971) in Figure 3.2.

The model has nine elements. Two elements represent major parties in communication: *sender and receiver.* Two represent major communication tools: *message and media;* four represent major communication functions: *encoding, decoding, response and feedback;* a further element represents *noise.* While message and media are the major focus of attention here, some explanation of the elements in Schramm's model is required:

- *Sender*: the party sending the message to another party
- *Encoding*: putting thought into symbolic form
- *Message*: the set of messages the sender sends
- *Media*: communication channels message is sent through
- *Decoding*: the process by which receivers assign meaning to the sender's transmitted symbols
- *Receiver*: the party receiving the message (audience)
- *Response*: set of reactions following exposure/reception of message
- *Feedback*: part of response transmitted back to sender
- *Noise*: unplanned static or distortion during process of communication

As shown in the model, communication becomes two-way as response and feedback mechanisms are built in and the sender or source may alter messages and media as necessary. What the sender may be aiming to do is to progress consumers/audiences through the cognitive, affective and conative stages as exemplified by the 'AIDA' (Strong, 1925), 'Hierarchy of Effects' (Lavidge and Steiner, 1961), 'Innovation-Adoption' (Rogers, 1962) or other communication models, all of which result in some type of action. However, messages may not be seen, viewed or heard, or may be decoded incorrectly because of selective exposure, distortion and retention (see Kotler, 1991; Cartwright, 1949).

Despite limitations, marketing communications often succeeds in establishing motivation or movement, in other words stimulating customers or audiences into action and/or facilitating more favourable perceptions toward companies or

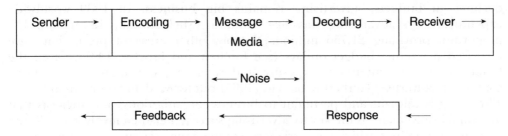

Figure 3.2 Elements in the communications process.
(*Source*: Kotler (1991) p. 568)

23

brands. A variety of elements can be deployed to fulfil this purpose. These include the four basic elements of advertising, personal selling, sales promotion and product publicity/marketing PR. Each element is now introduced and commented on, drawing upon appropriate literature, where possible, to illustrate changes caused by environmental turbulence.

ELEMENTS OF MARKETING COMMUNICATIONS

The marketing communications mix (sometimes referred to as the 'promotion mix') consists of four major tools. These are:

1 **Advertising**: any paid form of non-personal presentation and promotion of ideas, goods and services by an identified sponsor.
2 **Sales promotion**: short-term incentives to encourage purchase of a product or service.
3 **Personal selling**: oral presentation in a conversational form with one or more prospective purchasers for the purpose of making sales.
4 **Product publicity/marketing public relations**: a variety of programmes to improve, maintain, build or protect a company or product image.

These can be further subdivided into various components. But the key purpose is to develop effective communications, and for most business organizations the question is not whether to communicate but rather what to say, how to say it, through which media, to whom, and how frequently. Each of the preceding communication elements will now be explored in detail.

Advertising (see Chapter 16)

Advertising is a difficult and complex area in its own right. Despite the earlier bullishness associated with car advertising, news in the early 1990s spelt overall decline in advertising expenditure for the packaged goods sector owing to increased cost, media clutter, audience fragmentation and receptivity, and the attractiveness of available alternatives together with a move toward marketing public relations. A number of FMCG firms sliced their advertising budgets in 1989, according to a *Campaign* report (1989) (including Proctor & Gamble, down £3.5m; Mars, down £1.5m; Nestlé, down £1.5m; and Pedigree Petfoods, down £10m). Despite these declines in budgets, advertising remains big business. In 1989 worldwide expenditure on advertising was $240 billion (Micklethwait, 1990), the UK proportion providing £1,756 million. Notably, other areas of promotion have increased marketing budget outlays (see Kitchen and Proctor, 1991). Given the factors of selective attention, exposure and retention, why then do advertisers continue to advertise? Herbert Krugman (1965) put forward an argument as to why advertising is relevant and pertinent to business organizations, and suggests that 'personal involvement' is the key to advertising success. Personal involvement is 'the number of conscious bridging experiences, connections, or personal references per minute that the person makes between his or her own life and the stimulus' (Krugman, 1965).

According to Krugman's research, print media messages were found to be more involving than television, essentially because television is an easier form of communication (i.e. involving less effort). However, Krugman also argues for the need for repeated exposure which leads to 'behavioural completion' (Krugman, 1969, 1971):

> It requires repeated exposure to information that the consumer recognizes as present but to which they make no personally relevant connections; that is, remain uninvolved. However this repeated exposure can build a potential for the ability to see a product or brand differently. What is next required to release or trigger this potential is a behavioural opportunity such as in-store shopping.
>
> Behavioural completion is also required to release appropriate attitudes supportive and consistent with the shift in perceptual structure; that is, if the brand is then purchased, the new way of seeing it may then for the first time be expressed in words, for example, to 'explain' why it was selected.

What Krugman appears to be arguing for is a gradual shift in perceptual structure, aided by repetitive advertising in a low involvement medium (e.g. television), and followed at the time or later by a change in attitude (Aaker and Myers, 1982). If behavioural completion does not take place it may be because of some extraneous factor to do with selectivity. Krugman's argument relative to advertising is somewhat dated, but it does receive support in two more recent articles relative to advertising expenditure in relation to maintenance (Jones, 1990a) and growth of market share (Schroer, 1990). Such arguments, however, fly in the face of evidence of a possible decline in advertising expenditure for the aforementioned reasons – increased costs, media clutter, audience fragmentation and receptivity, and attractiveness of available substitutes.

Perhaps the most serious problem that seems to be affecting television advertising particularly may be that of rapidly rising costs. According to Shimp (1997), the cost of advertising has more than tripled over the past two decades. In one example quoted, the cost of a prime-time advertisement had increased sixfold for a 30-second commercial (i.e. from $110,000 to $650,000). Another problem is perhaps that of media clutter. Main advertisers now not only include the bedrock of FMCG firms but also consumer finance advertisers, new local advertisers, direct marketing businesses and a proliferation of small-scale advertisers (Admap, 1983). In addition, major sources of clutter perhaps also include television companies promoting their own programmes to stimulate audience viewing. All this may have the effect of disenchanting consumers toward the television medium and toward advertising in general (Webb and Ray, 1979; Gay, 1988). A further problem concerns audience fragmentation and receptivity, in particular the erosion of television audiences. Recent decades have seen the development of multi-set households, remote control television consoles, video recorders, teletext and Oracle, computers and television games, cable and satellite television, micro television, the WWW and Internet, touch key pads, and CD-ROMs, as well as the emergence of a multiplicity of other leisure and recreational pursuits and promotional activities. Even when consumers are watching television, their time may be spent in switching between channels (nipping), zipping through commercials when materials are prerecorded (Kneale,

1988), or zapping commercials by fast forwarding playback (Kitchen, 1986). Audiences could be becoming fractionalized, demassified and smudged; questions have been raised concerning the effectiveness of audience measurement devices, particularly in the UK, which measure programme, not advertisement, audiences. As Simon Broadbent (1979) points out: 'being rated does not mean "seeing an advertisement" but only "having a chance to see an advertisement"'. The focus so far has been on television advertising rather than radio or press. However, radio and press advertising are also considered.

Radio is weakened by its inability to use visualizations; however, like television, it may also be cluttered with competitive commercials and other forms of noise, interference and chatter. 'Nipping' also occurs in consumers owing to channel switching, sometimes seeking to avoid commercials. Moreover, radio advertising has shown a marked decline in expenditure over recent years, with a notable 40 per cent decrease in expenditure between 1988 and 1989 from £44 million to £26 million (*Marketing Pocketbook*, 1985–1990). Shimp (1997) points out that many advertisers use radio to supplement other media rather than using radio alone.

Print advertising has enjoyed increased expenditure over recent years with a 23 per cent increase in expenditure between 1988 and 1989 (*Marketing Pocketbook,* 1985–1990). Magazines suffer from a number of problems or limitations, including waste circulation (i.e. magazines may reach beyond an advertiser's target market) and lack of flexibility (i.e. long lead-in times). Newspapers, alternatively, are the largest advertising medium, but only 12 per cent of advertisements in this medium are national in scope (Goldman, 1988); the other 88 per cent is taken up by local retail advertising (50 per cent) and classifieds (38 per cent). Problems with newspapers include poor reproductive quality, buying space difficulties, higher rates for infrequent advertisers, and a lack of selectivity in audience criteria (i.e. newspapers can reach broad cross-sections of the population but may not be able to reach specific groups of consumers). Outdoor advertising generally has the following drawbacks: nonselectivity, short and fleeting exposure time, and difficulty in measuring the audience.

The main focus of this section on advertising has been to focus attention initially from the viewpoint of the benefit it provides to business organizations. At no time has it been suggested that advertising is unnecessary or not of value to such organizations. But it is fair to say that advertising seems to have encountered problems in recent years, notably related to media cost and clutter, audience fragmentation and receptivity. The attractiveness of available substitutes, or to phrase this in a more sophisticated fashion, the attractiveness of tools to work alongside advertising, has been left aside until now. Such substitutes are discussed in the sections on sales promotion and marketing public relations.

Sales promotion (see Chapter 17)

Each year, business organizations spend millions of pounds, beyond advertising and personal selling, to motivate and enthuse channel members and offer incentives to consumers (Schultz, 1987). Procter & Gamble, a major FMCG company, spends approximately $120 million on couponing, sampling and other vehicles (Quelch,

1982; East and Wilson, 1989). To accomplish these tasks, marketers use a wide variety of techniques known as sales promotion. The definition given of sales promotion is 'a short-term incentive to encourage purchase of a good or service', and this incentive can be developed as either a 'push' or a 'pull' strategy. Push strategies involve promotion directed toward trade members, encouraging them to handle products. Pull strategies suggest a backward tug from consumers to retailers. The 'pull' is the result of a manufacturer's successful advertising and sales promotion effort directed at the consumer. One could say that successful marketing involves a mixture of push through the trade and pull from consumers and thus the two areas are not mutually exclusive. Young and Greyser (1982) commented:

> Promotion . . . properly integrated . . . plays a growing role in the marketing mix, a tactical counterpoint to the strategic brand-sell advertising . . . and it will be a frequent tie-breaker . . . requiring a marketing generalist who can orchestrate promotion with the advertising (and personal selling) for optimum harmony.

While this quotation is somewhat dated, it illustrates the way in which sales promotion was perceived in 1982. The balance of power or influence between advertising and sales promotion moved significantly in favour of the latter during the 1980s. For example, Frey (1988) calculated the split between advertising and sales promotion was 42 per cent versus 58 per cent in 1977; 38 per cent versus 62 per cent in 1982; and 35 per cent versus 65 per cent by 1987. A recent estimate of below-the-line (Baker, 1985) expenditure is 69 per cent (Jones, 1990b). Major developments leading to the growth in sales promotion have been, first: the balance of power transfer between manufacturers and retailers; initially, manufacturers held the power. As the power of television seems to have waned in terms of communication effectiveness, the birth of optical scanning equipment ensured that retailers knew which products were selling (Towsey and Strickland, 1975). Retailers were able to demand terms of sale rather than accepting manufacturer offerings. The result is that every pound spent on promotion to support retailers' advertising and merchandising functions means a pound less to spend on advertising. A second factor concerned increased similarities between brands and price sensitivity, coupled with reduced consumer brand loyalties. Without real or significant product differentiation, consumers have become more reliant on price or price-related incentives (coupons, pence-off deals, refunds, give-aways and competitions). Sales promotion offers temporary advantages over competitors (Frankel and Phillips, 1986). A third factor contributing to the development of sales promotion may be demassification and fractionalization of markets, coupled with rising media costs; these were reviewed in the previous section. A fourth factor has been the concentration on brand management organizational structures which lends itself to short-term sales response rather than long-term growth. A fifth and final factor illustrating the development of sales promotion has been consumer responsiveness. Many consumers participate on a regular basis in some form of sales promotion (Hume, 1988).

Sales promotion seems to have undergone significant development during the 1980s and 1990s, although it is well nigh impossible to get at accurate data on expenditure. The 1980s were typified, at least in the consumer goods sector, by mature and stagnating markets which has forced manufacturers to seek improved profitability and tougher policies. According to Jones (1990b), the strategies shown in Table 3.1 were plainly evident in the 1980s and underpinned the development of sales promotion.

Market fragmentation and saturation, coupled with the desire for market share by many companies, have been among the major underlying causes behind any shift in emphasis and expenditure between advertising and sales promotion. But is this shift likely to continue? East and Wilson (1989) argue that it will continue based upon retailer pressure, rapidity of results and better returns from sales promotion than advertising. But evidence is starting to emerge that perhaps the long-term effect of sales promotion to consumers is to weaken the added value produced by advertising (Ogilvy, 1987; Broadbent, 1989). Their argument (see also Chapter 17) is that repeated price promotions are in effect price reductions and will diminish the perceived value of the brand and eventually market share. Trade promotions in particular lack the stress on building the consumer franchise that features product benefits or that builds warm non-rational associations with it. Jones (1990b) makes telling points against sales promotions (see Table 3.2).

While it may prove difficult to counter such arguments, it is evident that there are currently two schools of thought in relation to sales promotion. The first posits rapid growth and development of sales promotion in the 1980s and 1990s and calls upon the evidence of retailer concentration coupled with technological innovation, audience demassification and fragmentation, rising media costs, and other factors. The second school focuses on the negative effect of sales promotions in terms of its impact on long-term profits and sales performance. Sales promotion is doubtless currently a major component of the communications mix, and has enjoyed significant expansion and growth during the 1980s and 1990s. Moreover, it is a tactical tool that, while enjoying interaction with other communication mix elements, is not a substitute for them. However, its value as a brand-building tool is questioned from the price-promotion perspective.

Table 3.1 Strategies leading to the use of sales promotion

Strategies	Results
Fight for market share	Use of promotion as main tactical tool
Seeking small but growing segments of static markets via brand extensions	Market fragmentation and a multiplicity of brands
Exploring untraditional product categories	Backfiring of strategy; consumer misgivings
Searching for more business overseas	Birth and expansion of global marketing, questions of standardization vs adaptation
Pruning costs	Reduced R&D expenditure
Embarking on mergers and acquisitions	Search for scale economies and diversification, despite steeply rising costs

Table 3.2 Effects of long-term sales promotions

- *Evidence suggests that consumer sales effects are limited to the time period of the promotion itself; promotions bring volatile demand compared to advertising which brings stable demand*
- *Development of a 'mortgaging effect', i.e. bring forward sales from a later period. This lowers full-price sales and prolongs the period when the manufacturer is paying a heavy promotional subsidy to consumers.*
- *Promotions fan the flames of competitive retaliation far more than other marketing communication activities. Over time this allows strong brands to degenerate into virtually unbranded and unprofitable commodities.*
- *Promotions devalue the image of promoted brands in the consumers' eyes as a result of promotional 'wars' with other brands.*
- *As a general rule, promotions can never improve a brand or help stability of consumer franchises. Promotion tends to lead to a vicious circle of promotion, commotion and demotion.*

Personal selling (see Chapter 19)

Personal selling is a highly selective form of communications that permits sellers to tailor and adapt persuasive messages to suit the needs of individual buyers (see Chapter 19). It is adaptable to changing buyer–seller circumstances and develops an interaction between parties, leading to satisfactory exchanges in relation to buying needs. In relation to promotional strategies, personal selling varies widely from firm to firm and industry to industry. IBM, for example, marketing computers to large and medium-size companies, would place supreme emphasis on verbal, face-to-face interaction or selling. Alternatively, it would be expected that FMCG manufacturers, e.g. Kelloggs or Cadbury, would place promotional emphasis on advertising, sales promotion and public relations but would also put forward a significant personal selling effort. One part of the sales force would call on national and regional headquarters of major supermarkets and other chains to introduce new products, gain support for planned promotional programmes, and ensure satisfaction with existing and future purchase relationships. Another part of the sales force may well fulfil a merchandising function – checking inventories, setting up displays, stocking shelves, and seeking to build support and goodwill among store management (Govoni *et al.*, 1986). Personal selling provides the 'push' (as in push strategy) needed to get customers to carry new products, increase purchasing amounts and devote more effort to appropriate shelf facing or merchandising and promoting products and brands. In relation to today's retail sector sales, representatives may act as account managers requiring management teams to support an interface with key account customers or when major sales are at stake (Pegram, 1972; Hanan, 1982). The development of key account selling is a crucial criterion to both size and disposition of FMCG sales forces in the UK. The past three decades have witnessed both the growth of vertical marketing systems and concentration in the retail grocery trade. Vertical marketing systems refer to marketing channels being professionally managed and organized; this would include centralization and control of the purchase function, and effective monitoring of sales via electronic barcode scanning. As large retail organizations extend their control over marketing channels, independent small stores are squeezed out. Thus over time there would be fewer customers to actually call upon and the sheer volume and size of customers would ensure the need, not for a salesman to call, but for a team supporting a key account manager to be developed. Put another way, there are simply fewer customers and this has led to a contraction in sales force size over time, and this supports earlier commentary concerning a shift in the balance of power from manufacturer to retailer. Major concentration in the grocery sector took place between 1961 and 1981 (see Nielsen, 1982; Clark, 1981; Kitchen, 1993). Retail concentration is being focused in fewer and fewer hands in the western world, being particularly marked in the United Kingdom. Over time this has led to a significant contraction in the sales force, coupled with development of new relationships with powerful customers who control a significant proportion of market share for manufactured goods (see Chapter 19).

Marketing public relations/product publicity (see Chapter 20)

This section seeks to develop the concept of marketing public relations by describing the interactive relationship between corporate and marketing PR, and then considering product publicity and finally marketing PR, drawing upon appropriate strands of literature.

Historically, it can be said that advertising was the main communication function in business organizations because of budget size. As has been pointed out, the dominant role of advertising may be starting to slip toward sales promotion and public relations in a marketing sense and toward a diversity of tools in a corporate sense. Today, large-scale budgets for PR are not uncommon. In a marketing sense the reaction of consumers to a company's products may be becoming a function of their attitude toward the corporate parent (Bernstein, 1988). Thus from a corporate viewpoint public relations may seek to create relations with appropriate sections of the public and, in effect, also to prepare the ground in which marketing can fulfil its function of creating exchanges that satisfy individual and organizational objectives.

From a marketing perspective any company would seek to maximize the coordination of its marketing programme. This would include personal selling, sales promotion, advertising, and also product publicity or marketing PR. Product publicity can be defined as the activity 'for securing editorial space, as divorced from paid space, in all media read, viewed, or heard by a company's customers and prospects, for the specific purpose of assisting in sales goals' (Black, 1952). Product publicity was treated as a 'marketing stepchild' in the 1970s (Merims, 1972), i.e. it played a lesser role in the communications mix. The old name for marketing PR was publicity. But, according to Kotler (1991), marketing PR may go beyond simple publicity: it can assist in the launch of new products (e.g. Cabbage Patch Kids), assist in repositioning mature products (e.g. Glasgow – City of Culture), build interest in product categories (e.g. milk, egg, cheese consumption), influence specific target groups (e.g. sponsorship of local community activities), defend products that have encountered public problems (e.g. Johnson and Johnson and Tylenol), and build corporate image in a way that reflects favourably on products (e.g. Lee Iaccoca and the image of Chrysler Corporation). In each of these areas, what is put in may be 'marketing PR' but what comes out is 'product publicity'.

It has already been illustrated that as the power of advertising seemingly weakens owing to cost, clutter, and audience receptivity, and as criticism may be levelled at sales promotions in terms of sales effects and profits, and as sales forces diminish in size owing to retail concentration and key account selling, so firms may start to consider marketing public relations alongside the more traditional communication mix tools. Recent articles by PR practitioners, which could be viewed askance, have posited the development of marketing public relations. Edelman (1989), for example, states that 'public relations has the unique advantage of presenting messages in the context of today's news; the story is told in greater depth; it can have enormous impact'. The point was reinforced by another PR practitioner – Dilenschneider (1989) – who stated:

> Marketing is indeed warfare intended to win consumer commitment and awareness. When network TV could deliver more than 90% of homes in prime time, it was the weapon of choice. We have now entered the era of strategic marketing, and the choices are different. Advertising remains an important, but no longer an overriding, element of the marketing mix . . . and public relations has sharply ascending importance to successful marketing.
>
> (Dilenschneider, 1989)

However, as has already been mentioned, this comment was made by a PR practitioner seeking to market PR as opposed to practising it, and the downside to marketing PR usage has been the fact that advertising is perceived as measurable in terms of reach, frequency and cost per thousand criteria, unlike public relations. Gradually these questions may be being set aside as marketers consider this 'new' element in the communications mix (Cushman, 1988). According to Cushman the major rationale for marketing PR's development is credibility and cost-effectiveness.

Credibility for PR could be achieved in one way via the disinterested third-party endorsement of the media vehicle and thus be responsible for consumer and trade motivation to create sales (Gage, 1981). Public relations could use a variety of media methods to catch attention, including news releases, feature or human interest stories, photo pages, broadcast public service announcements, pre-packaged talk and television shows, broadcast clips, and staged media events (including sponsorships). Cost-effectiveness may be achieved because of the money not spent on advertising or agencies, and various mechanisms have been put forward measuring PR's contribution in relation to what it would have cost for the same amount of space for advertising (Merims, 1972; Kotler, 1991). But is there any real evidence that marketing public relations is being utilized in a UK context? The answer to this as yet cannot be ascertained with any degree of confidence. Quite a number of American examples are available; however, UK examples, though few and far between, have been seen in the trade literature, though virtually no academic articles have been discovered.

In the USA, Compton Public Relations sought to boost awareness and use of Bacardi Puerto Rican rum. This was achieved by creating food and dessert recipes calling for use of the rum. Recipes were sent, together with camera-ready articles and photographs, to newspaper editors, women's magazines, and special magazine editions highlighting recipes. As a result, the first half of 1980 witnessed an estimated 27 million impressions, receiving 4,600 column inches, and reaching 4.9 million people. Sales leaped from 11.7 million cases in 1979 to 14 million cases in 1980 (Gage, 1981). Another US company, with a $250,000 PR budget, realized $3.5 million-worth of television exposure through a carefully planned marketing-orientated PR programme (Cushman, 1988). Perhaps the best known example was that of Coleco's Cabbage Patch Kids. Launched in 1983 with a paltry advertising budget ($500,000), Coleco launched a massive publicity campaign; the result: in their first year Coleco's sales shot to $20 million (Forkan, 1983).

In the United Kingdom, examples are sparse (see Chapter 20) but show that marketing public relations has in a few instances been put to good use alongside traditional marcoms tools or alone. Barbican, the UK's first non-alcoholic beer, was repositioned following failure to penetrate the market despite heavy advertising. The new positioning was put forward in briefings to the trade press and samples of Barbican were hand-delivered to 200 newspapers and magazines in 1983. Sampling opportunities were arranged in conjunction with local health education bodies, by means of Barbican stands at health and road safety exhibitions. Tapes were made for local radio. A supporting activity was a consumer quiz competition with prizes of Barbican-branded sports goods. Sales developed from a very low point in 1983 to sales of around £16 million in 1986 (Kreitzman, 1986). Similarly, sales of the Rubik cube were stimulated by accessing media likely to be read or viewed by children.

For example, product stories appeared on LWT's Six-O'Clock Show, Thames Splash, TV-am, and BBC1's Saturday Superstore, and in the teen press. Matchbox claimed to have sold out its entire production line in three weeks. A third and final example was the rebuilding and positioning of Britvic 55 in 1984–5. A major trade press effort, including both news and feature material, was launched together with the television sponsorship of the Britvic 55 trophy for ITV's 'Survival of the Fittest'. Grocery sterling distribution rose from 33 per cent in 1985 to 58 per cent in 1986; sales increased by 140 per cent from 1984 to 1985, and showed a further 40 per cent increase in 1986 (Kreitzman, 1986). Furthermore, marketing PR has been used successfully for products such as sanitary towels, tampons, condoms and other 'unmentionable' products (Thomas, 1986).

Interviews with Beecham Toiletries (a subdivision of SmithKline Beecham) indicated that Brylcream was relaunched and repositioned initially via marketing public relations, without advertising (Kitchen, 1993). These examples are given to illustrate that marketing public relations can be used either alone or in conjunction with other communications mix tools to achieve marketing objectives. However, at this stage widespread evidence for the use of marketing public relations in UK firms is simply not available.

Toward integration of MPR in the promotional mix

Evidence presented thus far is fragmentary in terms of widespread usage or development of marketing public relations. What the evidence presented from the academic literature appears to amount to is that marketing public relations may be developing, albeit slowly. The slowness is basically because over the past half century advertising has been the dominant, potent and working force in marketing communications. Advertising slipped from its pre-eminent position during the 1970s and early 1980s as sales promotion was developed. Questions are now starting to be raised concerning sales promotion. In the meantime, some firms have utilized public relations in a marketing sense usually by working with and alongside highly experienced PR agencies. The key point to be derived from this is that marketing public relations in some firms appears to be working alongside or in a complementary manner to other elements in the communications mix. It is also noticeable that there may be some interaction with its more important relation: corporate public relations. However, practically all of the articles produced were written by PR practitioners, but there is some evidence for marketing PR development as put forward by Kotler (1991) and others (Cohen, 1991; Evans and Berman, 1990), though inclusion in their (American) textbooks is fairly recent.

MPR could seemingly work together with other elements of the communications mix in order to achieve marketing communication goals. It seems as if in the past these marketing communications elements have operated somewhat independently of each other. But the separation could be breaking down and integrated marketing communications is growing. Advantages of such integration include (Novelli, 1988):

- Increased effectiveness of adopting common strategies and delivering consistent, uniform messages to audiences.
- Integrated planning and centralized responsibility can lead to better ROI.
- Communications should stem from common strategies and the total programme, involving various tactics, should speak with one voice.
- Integration should improve ability to protect product equity and personality.
- Marketing communication partners should be better at identifying and capitalizing on new business communication opportunities.
- Time and money savings can be realized from well-coordinated marketing activities.

SUMMARY AND CONCLUSIONS

This chapter has sought to illustrate the development and evolution of marketing, marketing communications, and the various elements contained within marketing communications. Such development in marketing has taken place through various phases or orientations, and the majority of business organizations could be regarded currently as having the 'marketing orientation' with some moving into the 'societal marketing orientation'. This latter orientation links well into corporate PR and suggests that social responsibility may be a focus of firms in order to present and sustain favourable images. It was pointed out that firms not enjoying favourable imagery would also not enjoy appropriate sales. Marketing communications was described as an interactive process between buyer and seller, and models of marketing communication were presented. However, consumers may not receive or comprehend messages for reasons of selectivity; thus while sense organs may receive messages, such messages may be twisted or distorted to fit attitudinal predispositions.

The elements of marketing communications, including advertising, sales promotion, personal selling and marketing PR/product publicity, were explored in some detail. The focus was not to describe each element in detail but rather to mention issues and problems affecting them. The integration of marketing public relations with other communication mix elements was discussed.

In conclusion, marketing, marketing communications and its elements seem to have undergone significant change. As markets have matured competition has intensified. Technological breakthroughs have taken place, leading to fragmentation and demassification of mass markets. Consumers have become more sophisticated, more perceptive, and an as yet unexplored, negative consumer reaction to advertising appears to be taking place. When this scenario is coupled with rising media costs and media clutter, then business organizations may be considering and utilizing other communication mix tools in addition to the more straightforward ones of advertising, personal selling and sales promotion. While some evidence has been presented concerning the development of marketing public relations, it has to be concluded that evidence for the emergence of this tool, and its integration in a complementary way to other communication mix elements, is as yet fragmentary in the United Kingdom.

The main thrust of this chapter has been to review pertinent literature concerning marketing and marketing communications in a broad macro sense. Promotion is that element of marcoms charged with a specific responsibility for informing, persuading and inducing action in target audiences so that their purchase behaviour is ultimately directed toward the firm's offering.

DISCUSSION TOPICS

1 Why have the days 'long gone' when manufacturers could rely on one major television ad, supplemented to a minor extent?
2 Explore the interaction between marketing and marketing communications.
3 Are marketing communications and promotion synonyms?
4 Is the societal marketing orientation merely 'window dressing' for an expansionist marketing?
5 Compare and contrast Figures 3.1 and 3.2. What noticeable differences exist between them?
6 Using any element of the promotional mix, explain its usage for a firm of your choice.
7 Is there any evidence today that advertising is being replaced by other promotools?
8 Words like 'properly integrated', 'orchestrate' and 'optimum harmony' are merely ways of saying that sales promotion on its own is next to useless. Critique this statement.
9 You decide to set up a small firm. How important is promotion with reference to your chosen product strategy?

10 Focus on the two schools of thought in relation to sales promotion. Are you convinced by either school? Why or why not?

CASE STUDY – HOW TO GET CONTRACT PUBLISHING OUT OF THE DARK AGES (MARK JONES)

In the 1970s the following joke used to do the rounds of London advertising agencies. A client rings three agencies to ask the time. He rang Colletts and they told him to sod off. Then he rang Allen, Brady and Marsh, and they put it into a jingle and sang it to him. Finally he rang McCann-Erickson, who said, 'what time would you like it to be, sir?'.

Let me apologise at once to McCanns, who are much less supine than they used to be, and any youthful readers who do not know that Allen, Brady and Marsh was a singing dancing agency famous in its time for setting slogans to tunes. But the joke says just about all you need to know about the history of British advertising over the past 25 years. Once the world was dominated by huge US agencies, pack-shots, the hard sell, the prejudices of the chairman's wife and an approach to client service that would have struck Louis XIV as sycophantic. Then the world was shaken up by a small bunch of independent spirits led by Colletts, who had a pride and passion in their creative work and weren't afraid to say so. They slaughtered the pack-shots overnight and sent the chairman's wife grumbling back to her Women's Institute Committee.

Actually, these new spirits were as committed to client service as the old lot. They just didn't see why that precluded them from sticking up for their work, and from treating their audience as humans. One by one, encouraged by the experience of Gallaher, Whitbread and others, the clients began to agree. *Now the renegades and their followers run the top agencies in the land.*

The point is, compared with the ad industry, contract publishing is about in 1975.

(*Source: Campaign Report,* 12 September 1997, p. 12. Used with permission.)

ACKNOWLEDGEMENT

Grateful thanks are extended to *Campaign* and Haymarket Publications Limited for permission to include the opening and closing case vignettes in this chapter.

The material on which this chapter was based first appeared in Kitchen, P.J. (1993) 'Marketing Communications Renaissance', *International Journal of Advertising,* Volume 12, 4, pp. 367–86. Grateful acknowledgement is extended to the Journal for permission to use this material.

REFERENCES

Aaker, A. and Myers, D. (1982) *Advertising Management,* 2nd edn, Englewood Cliffs, NJ: Prentice Hall, 296.
Admap (1983) 'Editorial', January: 40–41.
American Marketing Association (1985) 'AMA board approves new definition', *Marketing News,* 1 March.

Bagozzi, R.P. (1986) *Principles of Marketing Management.* Chicago: Science Research Associates.

Baker, M.J. (1985) *Dictionary of Advertising and Marketing,* London: Macmillan.

Bell, M.L. and Emery, C.W. (1971) The faltering marketing concept', *Journal of Marketing,* 35(3), October: 37–42.

'Below-the-line': the line is an imaginary boundary between those advertising media which pay commission to advertising agencies and those who do not. Above-the-line media are: newspapers, magazines, television, radio, posters, and cinema. For example, directories, yearbooks, matchbooks, public relations and sales promotions are below-the-line. *Source:* Adapted and extended from Baker, M.J. (1985) *Macmillan Dictionary of Marketing and Advertising,* Basingstoke: Macmillan, 1.

Bernstein, J. (1988) 'PR in top communication role', *Advertising Age,* 7 November, 28.

Black, G. (1952) *Planned Industrial Publicity,* Chicago: Putnam Publishing, 3; as quoted in Merims (1972).

Broadbent, S. (1979) *Spending Advertising Money,* London: Business Books, 90.

Broadbent, S. (1989) *The Advertising Budget: The Advertiser's Guide for Budget Determination,* Henley: NTC Publications.

Campaign (1989) 'Report on top advertisers and brands', 4 May, 5.

Campaign Report (1997) 'Cars – the ad bonanza', 22 August, 3–4.

Campaign Report (1997) 'How to get contract publishing out of the Dark Ages' by Mark Jones, 12 September, 12.

Cartwright, D. (1949) 'Some principles of mass persuasion', *Human Relations,* 2(1): 253–67.

Clark, T.M. (1981) *The Distributive Trades in the Common Market,* London: HMSO.

Cohen, W. A. (1991) *The Practice of Marketing Management,* 2nd edn, Basingstoke: Macmillan, 7–9.

Cushman, A. (1988) '"New" element in marketing mix makes headway', *Marketing News, 19* December, 10–11.

Cutlip, S. M., Center, A. H. and Broom, G. M. (1985) *Effective Public Relations,* 7th edn, New Jersey: Prentice Hall International, 6–7.

Day, G.S. (1984) *Strategic Marketing Planning: The Pursuit of Competitive Advantage,* St Paul: Minnesota West Publishing Company.

Dilenschneider, R. (1989) 'PR on the offensive: bigger part of marketing mix', *Advertising Age,* 13 March, 20.

East, R. and Wilson, G. (1989) 'Sales promotion versus advertising: the debate sharpens'. Published in the *Annual Proceedings of the MEG Conference,* ed. L. Moutinho, 346–53.

Edelman, D. (1989) 'PR on the offensive: we can do better than ads', *Advertising Age,* 13 March, 20.

Evans, J.R. and Berman, B. (1988) *Marketing,* 3rd edn, London: Collier Macmillan, 12–13.

Evans, J.R. and Berman, B. (1990) *Marketing,* 4th edn, London: Maxwell Macmillan, 1–36.

Evans, J.R. and Berman, B. (1997) *Marketing,* 7th edn, New York: Macmillan Publishing Co.

Feldman, L.P. (1971) 'Societal adaptation: a new challenge for marketing', *Journal of Marketing,* July, 34(2): 54–60.

Forkan, J. (1983) '. . . Along with toys', *Advertising Age,* 5 December.

Frankel, B. and Phillips, J.W. (1986) 'Escaping the parity trap', *Marketing Communications,* November: 93–100.

Frey, N. (1988) 'Ninth annual advertising and sales promotion report', *Marketing Communications,* August.

Gage, T.J. (1981) 'PR ripens role in marketing', *Advertising Age,* 5 January, S–10–11.

Gay, V. (1988) 'Clutter is ad pollution', *Advertising Age,* 10 October, 56.

Goldman, T. (1988) 'Big spenders develop newspaper strategies', *Marketing Communications,* January, 24.

Govoni, N., Eng, R. and Galper, M. (1986) *Promotional Management,* Englewood Cliffs: Prentice Hall International, 294–95.

Hanan, M. (1982) *Key Account Selling*, New York: AMACOM.

Houston, F.S. (1986) 'The marketing concept: what it is, and what it is not', *Journal of Marketing*, April, 48(1): 81–7.

Hume, S. (1988) 'Coupons score with consumers', *Advertising Age*, 15 February, 40.

Jones, J.P. (1990a) 'Ad spending: maintaining market share', *Harvard Business Review*, January–February: 38–42.

Jones, J.P. (1990b) 'The double jeopardy of sales promotions', *Harvard Business Review*, September–October: 145–52.

Kitchen, P.J. (1986) 'Zipping, zapping, and nipping', *International Journal of Advertising*, 5(4): 343–52.

Kitchen, P.J. (1993) 'Marketing communications renaissance', *International Journal of Advertising*, 12(3): 386.

Kitchen, P.J. and Proctor, R.A. (1991) 'The increasing importance of public relations in fast moving consumer goods firms', *Journal of Marketing Management*, 7(4): 357–70.

Kneale, D. (1988) 'Zapping of TV ads appears pervasive', *Wall Street Journal*, 25 April, 21.

Kotler, P. (1972) 'A generic concept of marketing', *Journal of Marketing*, 36(2), April: 48–57.

Kotler, P. (1991) *Marketing Management, Analysis, Planning, Implementation and Control*, 7th edn, Englewood Cliffs: Prentice-Hall International, 26–27.

Kotler, P. and Levy, S.J. (1969) 'Broadening the concept of marketing', *Journal of Marketing*, 33(3), January: 10–15.

Kreitzman, L. (1986) 'Balancing brand building blocks', *Marketing*, 13 November, 43–46.

Krugman, H. (1965) 'The impact of television advertising: learning without involvement', *Public Opinion Quarterly*, 29: 353.

Krugman, H. (1969) 'The learning of consumer likes, preferences, and choices', in F.M. Bass (ed.) et al., *Applications of the Sciences in Marketing Management*, New York: J. Wiley and Sons, 224.

Krugman, H. (1971) 'Brain wave measures of media involvement', *Journal of Advertising Research*, 11, February: 8.

Laswell, H.D. (1948) *Power and Personality*, New York: Norton, 37–51.

Lavidge, R.J., and Steiner, G.A. (1961) 'A model for predictive measurements of advertising effectiveness', *Journal of Marketing*, 24, October: 61.

Levitt, T. (1960) 'Marketing myopia', *Harvard Business Review*, July/August: 45–56.

Luck, D.J. (1969) 'Broadening the concept of marketing – too far', *Journal of Marketing*, 33, July: 53–5.

Marketing Pocketbook (1985, 1986, 1987, 1988, 1989, 1990) Contain *Campaign*'s data, compiled by MEAL, The Advertising Association.

McCarthy, E.J. (1981) *Basic Marketing: A Managerial Approach*, 9th edn, New York: Richard D. Irwin.

McKitterick, J.B. (1957) 'What is the marketing management concept?', in F.M. Bass, (ed.), *The Frontiers of Marketing Thought and Action*, American Marketing Association, 71–82.

Merims, A.M. (1972) 'Marketing's stepchild product publicity', *Harvard Business Review*, November/December: 107–13.

Micklethwaite, J. (1990) 'A survey of the advertising industry: the proof of the pudding', *The Economist*, 9 June, 1–20.

Nielsen, A.C. (1982) *Nielsen Researcher. Annual Reviews of Grocery Trading*, London: Nielsen.

Novelli, W.D. (1988) 'Stir some PR into your communications mix', *Marketing News*, 5 December, 19.

Ogilvy, D. (1987) 'Sound the alarm', *International Journal of Advertising*, 6(1): 81–4.

Pegram, R.M. (1972) *Selling and Servicing the National Account*, New York: Conference Board.

Quelch, J.A. (1982) *Trade Promotion by Grocery Products Manufacturers: A Managerial Perspective*, Report No.82–106, Cambridge, Mass: Marketing Science Institute, August.

Rogers, E.M. (1962) *Diffusion of Innovations*, New York: Free Press, 79–86.

Schramm, W.D. (1971) 'How communication works', in W.D. Schramm, and D.F. Roberts, (eds), *The Process and Effects of Mass Communication,* Urbana: University of Illinois Press, 4.

Schroer, J.C. (1990) 'Ad spending: growing market share', *Harvard Business Review,* January–February: 44–48.

Schultz, D.E. (1987) 'Above and below the line: Growth in sales promotion in the United States', *International Journal of Advertising,* 6(1): 17–27.

Schultz, D.E. and Schultz, H. (1998) 'Transitioning marketing communications into the 21st century, *Journal of Marketing Communications,* 4(1): 1–26.

Sheth, J.N., Gardner D.M. and Garrett, D.E. (1988) *Marketing Theory: Evolution and Evaluation,* New York: John Wiley and Sons, 1–33.

Shimp, T.A. (1997) *Advertising, Promotion and Other Supplemental Aspects of Integrated Marketing Communications,* 4th edn, Dryden Press.

Strong, E.K. (1925) *The Psychology of Selling,* New York: McGraw Hill, 9.

Thomas, H. (1986) 'A modest success', *Marketing,* 13 November, 5–53.

Towsey, R. and Strickland, G. (1975) 'EDP systems in retailing, the practice and the philosophy', *Retail and Distribution Management,* January/February.

Webb, P.H. and Ray, M.L. (1979) 'Effects of TV clutter', *Journal of Advertising Research,* 19 June: 7–12.

Young, R.F. and Greyser, S.A. (1982) *Cooperative Advertising: Practices and Problems.* Cambridge, Mass: Marketing Science Institute, X3.

4

PLANNING THE MARKETING COMMUNICATIONS PROCESS

John Desmond

CHAPTER AIMS

- to discuss the ways in which planning has been and is conceptualized by academics and practitioners
- to evaluate the evidence for the usefulness of planning as a means for developing effective marketing communications strategies
- to discuss more specifically the role which planning may have for marketing communications

ILLUSTRATION

In 1985 planners at the UK-based Midland Bank recognized several problems stemming from the bank's external environment. The domestic market was saturated with financial institutions offering the same product; in particular, current accounts were seen to be generic, leading to the use of the 'Model T' Ford analogy by bank planners to describe the situation. The number of players was increasing whereas market potential was not. The number of customers overdrawing was in decline (which was bad news for banks!); the bank's overall share was declining; there was a net monthly loss in accounts. Finally, the recent introduction of free-if-in-credit banking and interest-bearing accounts had resulted in a transfer of value to the customer. Managers at Midland decided that something had to be done quickly. In order to maintain share, a decision was made to focus on the bank's main product, the current account. This was a valuable source of income in its own right which was also perceived to be the key to sales of other profitable products and to the relationship with the bank.

Branding was seen as the key to successful differentiation. But how could this be achieved? A researcher was commissioned to carry out research which could form the basis for effective segmentation of the consumer market. Findings indicated that bank customers could be segmented along two dimensions: the degree of confidence in dealing with the bank and the attitude towards the bank relationship. Initially this yielded up four segments: Opportunists, Traditionalists, Minimalists and New Bankers. An initial decision was made to focus on 'Opportunists', that segment who were confident in their dealings with banks but had very little respect for them. Research showed that opportunists tended to borrow at will without permission, yet became annoyed when 'hassled' by the bank. They were willing to pay for the service but wanted a minimum amount of hassle and wanted to be in control of whatever was agreed. Within the bank a product was devised which offered a current account with interest interlinked to a savings account, a cash card, credit card, fixed fee per month for money overdrawn up to £250 or up to £1,000 at a special rate, and finally one statement to cover all transactions. In May 1986, image consultants Fitch were asked to research names for the new product. Following a detailed investigation the name Vector was chosen.

Prior to developing any advertising concepts, qualitative research was conducted amongst the target audiences. Research findings indicated that the campaign should build on the existing corporate image 'Listening Bank' (corporate) campaign, yet should be strongly differentiated from this, more serious and less frivolous. The products must not be seen as money-making gimmicks. The first ad for Vector was developed on the basis of qualitative research. It became clear that the final ad would hinge on the character of the bank manager as much as that of the customer. The bank manager had to:

- look like everyone's idea of a bank manager
- be in some control of the situation but 'listen'
- emerge from the ad as a wiser, improved bank manager.

The customer should reflect the ideal profile of the 'Opportunist': clever, confident, with a lack of respect for banks. These features were incorporated into the research brief for the advertising agency.

Vector was launched in 1987, as a 'money transmission' product aimed at Opportunists. Subsequently two other brands were launched: Orchard, the mortgage product, and Meridian, a savings product. However, following the launch of the brands, managers began to change their perceptions of what these brands would be about. The main change was deceptively simple, involving a change of emphasis from the product to the customer. As one manager said, a Vector person would be a self-confident opportunist in many other walks of life and would act similarly with respect to many other products that they might wish to buy. Why restrict the 'Vector' person to a money transmission product? Why not offer a mortgage and savings and loan scheme as well? The concept of multi-service accounts was developed from this concept and it was decided to relaunch Vector with its sister brands, Orchard and Meridian, in September 1989. However, because of the launch of a rival product, the date was brought forward to January. The multimedia campaign which followed was the biggest the bank had ever undertaken.

The immediate effect of the campaign showed that 15 per cent of the total sample who were aware of new or improved current accounts spontaneously recalled Vector. Among Midland customers the respective level of awareness was 31 per cent. Some 6 per cent of Midland customers expressed interest in holding a Vector account. By December 1990 the Vector brand awareness average, at 62 per cent, was just behind the leader, Liquid Gold from the Leeds.

INTRODUCTION

From the illustration it would appear that Midland Bank's personnel developed the bank's marketing and communications strategy in a manner which is consistent with a classic textbook approach. Yet there are crucial differences. First of all, branding was conceived of as *the* strategy – alternatives were not really considered. Secondly, a fundamental reformulation of strategy (the development of multi-service accounts) took place after the launch of Vector. Thirdly, the 1991 decision by new chief executive Brian Pearse to shelve both Vector and Orchard which came as a surprise even to Midland marketing director Kevin Gavaghan[1] smacks of political and not just rational motives. Planning is thus far from a neutral, value-free and objective description of events. Rather it can act as a powerful normative force to structure accounts in such a way that the eventual story emerges as a purposive, rational, linear sequence of events, which effectively masks or at best glosses over the dynamic tensions, complexity and contradictions which occur in everyday reality. The danger derives in large part from the academic legacy of planning whereby economists and psychologists have taken a predominantly left-brain (Mintzberg, 1994) approach which stresses sequential, rational and analytical processing to such an extent that right-brain functions such as dreams, spatial perception, emotion and intuition have become all but erased. Mintzberg believes that there is a need for a major readjustment of the way in which we *think* about planning processes:

> To draw from one extreme (where we believe that planning has always been) toward the middle, one has to pull from the far end (much as in trying to balance a seesaw with all the weight on one end, one has to put weight on the other end; not in the middle.
>
> (Mintzberg, 1994: 324)

While some marketing practitioners might tend to reduce planning to a formula, there are many who believe that 'magic' is essential for the creation of effective marketing communications programmes. This latter approach is not either or, analysis *or* magic; it is both, analysis *and* magic. This chapter does not attempt to sow seed where there already has been a bumper harvest. A number of excellent books have described the communications planning process in a much more illuminating and detailed way than could be achieved here. Rather the intention is to demonstrate firstly that planning can mean different things to different people, between different 'academics' and different 'practitioners'; secondly, to show that planning is context dependent; it can be a drawback if it is used in a ritualistic, formulaic way as a crutch, or as a means of retrospectively rewriting history; a benefit in providing direction, control and coordination. It is not so much a way of reducing uncertainty, but rather provides a means for living with uncertainty.

PLANNING: AN ACADEMIC VIEW

Nowadays it is difficult to imagine a time when planning did not appear high on the organizational agenda (see Knights and Morgan, 1991). Planning is touted for its ability to fill the gaps that other approaches fail to fill; for example Young and

Steilsen (1996) have argued that the use of planning scenarios can replace 'spec' presentations in advertising agency selection; Dwek (1997) talks of the nascent role of the communications strategy expert whose role includes finding solutions which integrate the roles of human resource directors, corporate affairs directors and marketing directors.

Given the ubiquity of planning discourse, it is difficult to believe that the current conception of planning is the product of a particular time (the 1940s) and place (the USA). For example, Thomas (1919), which was one of the first books devoted to commercial advertising, contains no reference to plans. How then can planning be understood? Simon (1957) draws the powerful metaphor of a tree:

> If we are to find a common conceptual roof under which both economic man and administrative man can live, that roof can only include ( ) the 'tree' of future possible behaviours (the idea of representing possible future behaviours as a 'tree' with branches radiating from each point so that the individual must select at each point the appropriate branch to follow).
>
> (Simon, 1957: xxxiii–xxxiv)

While one may trace a preoccupation with planning back to von Clausewitz (1832), the modern conception of formal planning may be traced to the publication in 1944 of von Neumann and Morgenstern's *Theory of Games and Economic Behaviour* and the subsequent attacks on this viewpoint made by Herbert Simon (1957). There is indeed a fundamental difference in outlook between the two views. Von Neumann and Morgenstern focused on strategy as a rational game where (it was assumed) decision makers used Bayesian theory to estimate subjective expected utilities; there was also an assumption that planners identify and evaluate all options prior to selecting a course of action. Simon argued that von Neumann and Morgenstern's approach was 'fundamentally wrongheaded' (1957b: 202) and set out his own approach which views strategic thinking as a form of information processing, in a series of books and articles. Simon (*ibid.*) argued that because of information processing and memory constraints, it is impossible for the planner to compute and evaluate probabilities for all potential courses of action. He suggested that in real life planners get round this problem by means of heuristics (rules of thumb) such as means–ends analysis. This basically means that with some ill-defined problems, the decision maker splits the problem down into manageable chunks which can be solved and then uses the solutions to these sub-problems as means for redefining the nature of the original. Simon's information processing perspective was powerful enough to mould the first major academic contribution to planning in management (Ansoff, 1965) and continues to influence marketing planning (e.g. McDonald, 1984) and marketing communications scholars (e.g. Rossiter and Percy, 1987) to this day. Figure 4.1 illustrates the relations between the problem-solving process and planning.

What comes to mind when considering the role of the planner? Perhaps this conjures up a picture of a conclave of senior managers who have been spirited away to a corporate retreat for a weekend where they huddle together in a room to develop a sense of mission and purpose for the organization; next to define objectives; then perform a 'gap' analysis to determine the difference between where

Situation analysis	Initial state
Objectives	Goal state
Strategies	Operators
Constraints	Operator restrictions

Figure 4.1 Mapping Planning as a Rational Problem-Solving Process

the organization is now and where it wants to be; next to develop and evaluate bold new strategies to fill the planning gap; finally to consider tactics and the implementation programme. If this is indeed the kind of picture which came to mind then you are in good company. This more or less corresponds to the way in which strategic planning has been described and taught in boardrooms and classrooms over the past 40 years.[2] Competence in planning is seen as essential in all contemporary works on marketing communications. This is seen as a *sine qua non* by authors such as Yeshin (1997) Aaker and Myers (1992), Ray (1982), Rossiter and Percy (1987), Shimp (1997) and Schultz (1984). Assumptions made in the marketing communications literature are the following:

- Planning is a rational activity which involves the operation of sequential processes of formulation (thinking) and implementation (doing). Communications plans thus encompass a series of steps of goal setting, analysis, evaluation, selection and planning of implementation to achieve an optimal long-term direction for the firm. Not only should the process be rational, it should also be comprehensive. For example Aaker and Myers (1992: 32) stress the point that: 'A complete situation analysis will cover all marketing components and involve finding answers to dozens of questions about the nature and extent of demand, competition, environmental factors, product, costs, distribution and the skills and financial resources of the firm.'
- The aim of the planning process is to develop and implement strategy.
- Communications plans are built on the base of marketing plans which are in turn constructed on the foundation of the corporate plan. Most authors suggest that the communications plan should be closely tied to the marketing plan. The communications plan itself is usually presented as a linear sequence of actions which result in implementation of the plan and its subsequent evaluation and contribution to the attainment of marketing objectives.
- From the previous two points, planning is assumed to be a top-down process; formulators are not necessarily the same people as implementers.
- Planning is assumed to be (naturally) a good thing.

RESEARCH EVIDENCE: DO ORGANIZATIONS PLAN?

What is the evidence for planning? It may be difficult to imagine but, despite the amount of attention devoted to the topic, little quality research has been devoted to the issue of planning generally.[3] Despite this, a range of research evidence suggests that in practice the way in which organizations plan diverges quite sharply from the normative academic model. These are discussed briefly below.

Formulation/implementation

One important assumption that is made by the normative model is that first managers think (formulate the problem); then they act (implement the solution). This contention is often attributed to Herbert Simon whose problem-solving scheme has had a marked influence in both psychology and management. At one stage Simon was of the view that intelligence activity should be carried out prior to the others. More recently he has modified this view:

> On some early occasions when I was asked to advise companies about the acquisition of a computer, my advice was that, before they made any decision or commitment, they should make a careful determination of whether they needed a device and how they would use it. I soon realized that this was poor advice – that a company only acquired the ability to make sound decisions about computers (or almost any other novel technology) by hands-on experience with them
>
> (Simon, 1977: 43)

Thus Simon suggests that best results can come about as the outcome of learning and active experimentation. The belief that there should be some form of split between formulation and implementation is also contradicted by the findings of management researchers who suggest that both processes are carried out in parallel (Quinn, 1980; Mintzberg and McHugh 1985; Johnson, 1988). In any case, many planning situations are framed the other way round, where the plan is someone's pet idea, a classic case of a solution chasing a problem, the 'garbage can' approach outlined by Cohen (1979). Nutt (1984) found that a large number of processes were similar to the 'garbage can' model. This occurred when the availability of new technology drove the decision-making process or where executives with pet ideas created a situation where solutions were looking for problems.

Role of the leader

Frequently magazine and other articles impute strategy to the General Manager. When Microsoft acts, it is because Bill Gates has made a strategy. As Mintzberg (1989: 29) points out, this attribution bias masks the real complexity and confusion that get swept under this assumption.

Evaluation of alternative solutions

Research disputes the idea that planners move purposefully and act logically and rationally in evaluating a number of alternative solutions. Field studies such as that carried out by March and Olsen (1976) have shown that decision-making processes were characterized by flight and oversight rather than by active specification of alternatives. Evidently managerial decision makers may willingly obscure some alternatives when they already have a solution in mind.

Systematic development of strategy?

This aspect of planning has been researched by a number of authors. It is well known that small firms exhibit a reluctance to engage in formal planning (Hogarth-Scott *et al.*, 1996) However, findings from several studies show that even for larger firms there is little evidence to suggest that strategies are developed systematically and emerge fully fledged from the planning process (see, for example, Quinn, 1980; Nutt, 1984; Mintzberg and McHugh, 1985; Johnson, 1988). For example, Nutt (*ibid.*) found that implementers tend to find uncertainty intolerable. As a result, nothing even remotely resembling normative methods was carried out in real situations. The sequence of problem definition/alternative generation/refinement and selection was not used and instead ideas drove the process. Mintzberg and McHugh (1985) noted that in the entrepreneurial organization which they studied, the owner had developed the strategy well in advance of the plan. The role of the plan in this case was to help to formalize and codify the strategy and to ensure coordination and control. In a later study, Mintzberg and McHugh (1985) suggested that the classic planning model, with its distinction between formulation and implementation and its formal stages of problem recognition, search, evaluation and implementation, describes processes found most often in stable machine bureaucracies. However, they argued that the machine bureaucracy is not the typical organizational structure of the modern era but rather that the project structure or 'adhocracy' is the structure of contemporary industry (1985: 161). In one adhocracy, the National Film Board of Canada, they found that the process of formulation followed by implementation was 'hardly pervasive' (1985: 188). Thus the pattern observed by several researchers is that the process of strategy development is not rational comprehensive but generally accords with Charles Lindblom's (1959) account of 'muddling through'.[4] Authors described the process of strategy formulation as incremental although each author advances different reasons for this incrementalism. Quinn (1980) described the approach to strategy development as a form of logical incrementalism by which managers consciously and skilfully guide streams of actions and events incrementally towards strategies 'embodying many of the structural principles of elegant formal strategies'. (1980: 44). Top executives rarely built overall strategies within the formal planning cycle, choosing instead a series of incremental processes which built strategies at more disaggregated levels and then integrating these subsystem strategies step by step for the total organization. Quinn uses Herbert Simon's (1957a) problem-solving metaphor to explain why in his view this is the case. Strategic decisions are 'soft data' (ill-defined) problems which cannot be fully analysed using formal financial analysis or quantitative modelling techniques. He suggested that no single analytical process could handle all of these strategic variables simultaneously. Precipitating events over which managers had no control would precipitate urgent, piecemeal interim decisions which inexorably shape a company's strategic posture. On the other hand Pettigrew (1977) focuses more on the issue of organizational political processes as a reason for incrementalism.

Johnson (1988) extended this view to build his own explanation of the organizational paradigm. Basically this refers to the dominant organizational world-view of paradigm, which Johnson argued can become so detached from reality that 'strategic drift' ensues. While Quinn's logical incremental view of strategy development is adaptive, Johnson shows how this can be maladaptive.

The illustration which describes the development of the Midland Bank brands describes an incremental rather than a synoptic process. The case also provides an interesting opportunity to further explore Johnson's concept of the organizational paradigm. The key assumption made by planners (supported by research) was that customers wanted a relationship with the bank. On the other hand the Midland Bank direct banking operation First Direct, which was launched in October 1989, just nine months after the Midland Bank brands, was guided by the *opposite* logic. This may explain why the direct banking initiative was not set up as part of the bank's central operation and also why its launch reportedly created much mirth in the other clearing banks. In early 1993 First Direct management had to pull a TV advertising campaign because staff could not cope with the demand created by press advertising and a mailshot, which was three times greater than that anticipated. First Direct did not return to promotions until 1995. What happened? The campaign had been well researched and the conclusions had reinforced the 'paradigm': that most customers prefer relationships and that the up-take on the new brand would be small. Managers had to conclude that in this instance customers said one thing but did another. First Direct claimed to have learned from the experience. Amanda Richards of *Marketing* noted that 'In most sectors poor projections such as these have caused many a senior marketer to lose his or her job. But not at First Direct. "We got it wrong. Maybe we could have projected it better. But we have learned", he (First Direct CEO Kevin Newman) says.' (*Source: Marketing*, 27 October 1994: 26). The organization ensured that it had the ability to cope with a major upsurge in demand following its next major communications campaign in 1995.[5]

Finally one might comment that authors do not seem to be in agreement as to where particular pieces of the plan should come in the process (maintaining for a moment the fiction that this really is a linear process). It is impossible to adequately demonstrate the divergence between different views in just a few lines. Taking one or two examples, several authors discuss the determination of the communications budget at length, often placing this item after the definition of the marketing or communications objectives. However, White (1993: 18) says that with respect to budgets, theory and practice are far apart and pragmatically admits that often the budget comes first as it is predetermined. More recently authors have differed as to the position of marketing objectives, with authors such as Schultz pushing these quite far down the planning process.

Emergence of bold and innovative strategies?

Research also suggests that innovative strategies rarely emerge from the planning process. Nutt (1984) found that in only 15 per cent of the cases which he examined were normative aspirations confirmed, the nova processes where companies struck out to find an innovative solution. Nutt found that the classic planning approach (which he described as Problem Evoked) was in only 45 per cent of the cases which followed the 'traditional' planning approach, i.e. identify problems, search for information, evaluate alternatives and find solutions. His conclusions were that, first, there was very little use of nova processes. Rather there is a tendency to copy the ideas of others. This finding is borne out by those of other researchers (Mintzberg, 1994). The decision to launch brands by Midland Bank reported here *was* a bold decision as it was the first ever major attempt at such a venture. However, it will probably never be known whether this bold approach was derived from the strategic planning process or whether it had always been the 'pet idea' of a well-placed executive. In their earlier, more succinct work, Schultz and Martin (1979: 9) point out the following false syllogism:

(a) A carefully written and well-presented plan precedes great advertising campaigns.
(b) Great advertising campaigns have a solid research foundation.
(c) Therefore, solid research and careful planning will result in great advertising.

As the authors point out, there is no magic recipe: it is in the application of knowledge that the true genius works; the 'magic' is added by the brilliance of the marketers. One might imagine that following a formula-based checklist approach to planning is more likely to result in a series of outcomes which are more or less the same. Pascale (1984) reports how Japanese managers ferreted out the formulae of their concept-driven American competitors and then used this knowledge to exploit their inflexibility.

Evidence of a logical 'cascade' of plans: from corporate to marketing and communications?

No studies were found which specifically explored this dimension. Most case studies in the area are written 'as if' this were the case. However, the case study genre tends to stamp the logic of planning rationality onto its material and so one must be careful whether these can be taken as reliable guides. The examples of Midland Bank's brands and First Direct indicate that there is a more dynamic and iterative relationship between the two, where the communications planning process may result in further refinement or even gross transformation of the marketing strategy. The Daewoo case (Duckworth, 1997) provides more evidence. When Daewoo arrived in the UK the company had no marketing strategy; however, management were innovative and were willing to think beyond the boundaries of traditional car marketing. Daewoo had stated the intention to try to gain a 1 per cent share of the UK market within three years, which represented a most ambitious target. The advertising agency staff realized that a radical solution was called for and on the basis of research suggested that Daewoo focus on building a trusting relationship and not just a sale. Daewoo's response to the agency's recommended brand positioning was to consider dispensing with dealers entirely. This then led to a 'torrent' of innovation and brainstorms resulting in the creation of a brand package. The communications campaign was based on convincing a cynical audience that the company really was different.

Can planning be bad for the organization?

The reader should now be getting the feeling that it is not so much planning *per se*, as a particular approach to planning which may be the problem. Thus as Tversky and Kahneman (1974) report, a planning culture may contribute to the illusion of control. Citing Air Canada as an example, Mintzberg *et al.* (1995) found such an obsessive emphasis on a culture built on planning and control that the company stuck to the plan to the extent that they missed a major reorientation of strategy. An obsession with planning is not just the province of practitioners. Pascale's (1984) work is a devastating indictment of consultants and academics at Harvard and UCLA who reworked (and over-rationalized) history to attempt to show that Honda's entry into the US market was a classic example of careful planning. Pascale quotes Soichoro Honda who said that 'In truth we had no strategy other than the idea of seeing if we could sell a car in the US.' Pascale notes the disturbing tendency that:

> Western consultants, academics and executives express a preference for oversimplifications of reality and cognitively linear explanations of events. We tend to impute coherence and rationality to events when the opposite may be closer to the truth. How an organization deals with miscalculation, mistakes and serendipitous events outside its field of vision is often crucial to success over time.
>
> (Pascale, 1984)

Nowotny (1989) draws similar conclusions. In a discussion of planning in crisis management communications, she cautions that people should not allow themselves to be lulled into security by the existence of a plan, as unanticipated events require fast decisive action. The implication is that while planning is no doubt useful, what is crucial is the organization's ability to react quickly and effectively to unforeseen circumstances.

Another difficulty with the planning approach is that despite their best intentions, authors are still haunted by the ghost of the Sender–Message–Channel–Receiver Model, whereby the customer is conceived of as a target, or at best a territory to be occupied (Ries and Trout, 1986). As a result, the planning mentality tends to undervalue the creative power of the active audience. For example, while Rossiter and Percy (1987) build in a view of the 'active' consumer generally via the concept of 'involvement', the main preoccupation of the book is concerned with communications 'effects'. This is not surprising, given that the book is guided by a planning framework, where the stated intention is to influence behaviour. However, given the bald fact that no one actually knows precisely how planned communications achieve their effects, the focus on 'effects' can orient the planner towards an over-simplistic approach. Many books on communications planning still work with conceptions such as AIDA, DAGMAR and related approaches (Colley, 1961; Lavidge and Steiner, 1961), although for many years authors have cautioned that the reality is much more complex (Franzen, 1994: 6). In particular, authors could do more to build on research which shows that advertising does not just 'work'; it is actively 'worked on' by the audience. For example, in a range of articles, O'Donohoe (most recently 1997) has explored the ways in which young adults in Scotland construe advertising. She found that they were highly

48

advertising literate and generally found that ads were a source of entertainment. The informants drew on a great deal of knowledge of the world beyond advertising in interpreting ads. Ads were not viewed in isolation but were related to each other. For example, Gold Blend ads featuring the 'yuppie couple' were considered to be the same sort of idea as the Cointreau ads. Informants were also aware of earlier executions, recognizing the use of parody in current campaigns which spoofed older ones. In discussing ads, informants mentioned how they fed back into popular culture via television shows which parodied advertising and others which are largely dedicated to ads, such as Clive James. Also, given that current views of the consumer still tend to be dominated by psychological accounts, stressing 'involvement', one might wish to see more attention given to accounts which focus on social and cultural contexts. For example, Elliott and Ritson (Brown, 1997) and Davidson (1992) have focused on a subcultural context where the individual operates a radical oppositional code which literally inverts the dominant code present in the ad. While current 'planning' approaches emphasize analysis of factors such as 'involvement', or 'attitude', such factors represent an impoverished (and therefore partial) view of a rich tableau. There is thus a need, as Alan Cooper suggests (1997: xv), not only to figure the relationship between the person and the brand but to build a more holistic view of the consumer as a complete person.

AN ALTERNATIVE APPROACH: PLANNING AS THE CODIFICATION OF STRATEGY

Mintzberg flatly contradicts the notion that effective strategies can emerge only as the result of the strategic planning process. Counterposed to the planning 'tree' described by Simon, Mintzberg talks of strategies growing like weeds. In this view strategies are often deliberate; however, they can also emerge, that is, patterns can develop over time in the absence of intentions or even despite them. For this reason it is important that strategists seek to evaluate intended and unintended strategies. From the above discussion there appears to be some support for Mintzberg's (Mintzberg *et al.*, 1976; Mintzberg, 1978; Mintzberg and Wates 1982) view of strategy as emergent. Thus one can conceive a role for planning, not so much to create strategies as to codify strategies which already exist – to elaborate and operationalize the consequences of those strategies formally and to evaluate the impact of strategies. From Figure 4.2 it can be seen that there several points for evaluation and control built into the process.

Thus strategy is not so much the end point or consequence of planning but its start point; planning properly belongs to implementation of strategy, not its formulation; the need to programme strategy is for better coordination.

Mintzberg (1987, 1989) attempts to redress what he sees as the predominantly left-brain approach to strategy by reconceptualizing it as a craft process:

At work the potter sits before a lump of clay on the wheel. Her mind is on the clay, but she is also aware of sitting between her past experiences and her future prospects. She knows exactly what has and what has not worked for her in the past. She has an intimate knowledge of her work, her capabilities and her markets. As a craftsman she senses rather than analyses these things; her

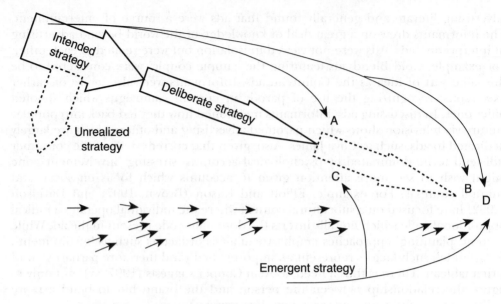

A Control of planned performance
B Control of implementation
C Control of realization
D Control of strategic performance

Figure 4.2 Relating Intended/Deliberate/Emergent and Realized Strategies
(*Source*: Mintzberg and Waters, 1982)

knowledge is 'tacit'. All this is working on her mind as her hands are working on the clay. The product that emerges on the wheel is likely to be in the tradition of her past work. But she may break away and embark on a new path. Even so, the past is no less present, projecting itself into the future.

(Mintzberg, 1989: 27).

The metaphor of crafting strategy encapsulates the relations between thinking and acting, of knowledge and feeling. It integrates knowledge and analysis with feelings of involvement, intimacy and harmony with materials.

PRACTITIONERS' VIEWS

What of 'practitioners' views of the usefulness or otherwise of planning? Account planners have been a feature of UK advertising agencies for 30 years; more recently they have begun to appear in PR, Direct Marketing and Design agencies. When viewed against the role of the creative, the planner perhaps exemplifies best the 'left-brain' of the organization. How do planners conceive of their role and the role of planning generally in communications? Books by Cooper (1997) and Duckworth (1997) provide a range of views written by planners. This material was supplemented by separate conversations held between the author and four account planners and one freelance design consultant. While obviously not 'scientific', nevertheless this does provide some insight into contemporary views of planning.

Left-brain/right-brain

The formal espoused view of planners is very similar to the rational analytic approach described earlier. For example, this forms the basis for Leslie Butterfield's account of the planning process in Cooper (1997). However, this more formal approach was tempered by the views of one informant who said that:

> the planning process is about thinking, feeling, intuiting – information is fast, available, cheap, it is thinking that is important. The 'Advertising Works' cases tend to be written by planners. That is a left brain thing, but when you read them you see the right brain thing, the 'leap'.
>
> (Cooper, 1997)

This latter view was backed by another informant who said that it would be a grave mistake to see the planning process as strictly logical and rational. One also needed to be aware of the dynamics of the situation which involves people, politics and power. Another said 'there is a place for magic and you need to leave space for that to happen'.

It is also interesting to note that in the lore of planning (eloquently described by M.T. Rainey in Cooper, 1997: 3), the planner role evolved as a response to the growth of a mechanistic US 'test to destruction' culture. By contrast the planner role is to stand between the client and the creative as the representative of the customer. This may seem banal to outsiders, but Rainey claims that it shook agency culture to its foundations (1997: 6). The planner was to be an expert in the consumers' relationship with brands. To do so she had to use research, not just do it. Thus planners have encouraged their clients to adopt a more sophisticated view of their customers than might otherwise be the case. In this respect one might add that practitioners seem to have been ahead of most academics.[6]

As planners came to be associated with the view of the customer, they quickly became involved in issues relating to evaluation, in particular the pre-testing of advertisements (to bring a more sophisticated understanding to bear than 'day-after' recall). Several planners are wary of clients' perceived need to rely on simplistic measures which may provide them with reassurance (a crutch, as one said), but are unlikely to reflect the complexities of the true response, nor to result in effective communications. One planner candidly said that smarter clients know that the only proper test is a real test; marketing is about doing it; testing is about *not* doing it. Shelbourne and Baskin (Cooper 1997: 96) suggest that pre-testing should not be carried out according to some formula. Instead the role of the planner is to get all parties to focus on the questions of:

- How do we think advertising works?
- What do we expect this particular ad to do in this case?
- Which type of research method will give us the most appropriate guidance?

Given concerns with DAGMAR (Colley, 1961) and the development of a more sophisticated understanding of communications' effects (Franzen, 1994: 6), one would imagine that the above reflects good common sense.

Planners reflect on the tensions between different groups within both client and agency – will the creative win the coveted DNAD award?; will the planner get to win an IPA award?; power relations between agencies and clients and within agencies, the 'which account are you working on?' syndrome. People become emotionally attached to their roles and the campaigns that they create. This can create problems. Take, for example, the issue of pre-testing. One planner stated: 'Planners will usually write the brief; if you have developed the brief and then they say they want to take it away and test it then you want to hang onto your baby and make sure it isn't messed about with.' At rock bottom it is these issues which tend to be squeezed out of retrospective accounts of a [presumed] rational planning process.

IMPLICATIONS FOR THE PROCESS

The foregoing discussion is not an attempt to subvert the usefulness of planning for marketing communications; indeed there appears to be a strong level of support from practitioners for this. Thus the intention has not been to play on the strengths of planning: those occasions where it does enable people to cope with unforeseen contingencies; the proven ability of a well-communicated plan to create a framework for action and to build goodwill; the necessity of crafting a process which a number of different parties can readily understand and buy into; as a coordination and control device and a means for resource allocation. The aim here has been to expose the various ways in which a planning mentality can be maladaptive. In this respect this chapter traces the concerns expressed by Mumby and Putnam (1992), who wish to see the development of a less psychological and more social and emotional approach, and by Brownlie and Spender (1995) who recognize that marketing planning processes do not do what they set out to do, which is reduce uncertainty. They ask 'Should we abandon analysis and depend on intuition?' The short answer with respect to marketing communications planning is 'no; we should rely on analysis *and* intuition'. Recent developments which have barely been touched on here, the media 'explosion', audience fragmentation and calls for integrated communications, will press home this need.

SUMMARY

It would seem from the above that:

- Formulation and implementation of plans are not sequential processes, they are closely intertwined.
- Plans are often created to justify pre-existent strategies.
- Sometimes strategies emerge rather than develop as the result of planning processes.
- Following planning processes can lead to the development of 'me-too' strategies.
- In practice it is quite possible for cogent communications plans to emerge prior to corporate and marketing plans – and still win awards.

- In some contexts, a focus on planning can be a bad thing. It may feed the 'illusion of control'; via case studies it tends to tidy messy realities retrospectively; finally it can result in customers being viewed as targets and not partners.
- Following from the above there needs to be more of an acceptance that analyses and formulae can never be a substitute for managerial judgement and that 'right brain' activities should be built into the overall picture.

DISCUSSION TOPICS

1 Herbert Simon characterizes the planning process as a 'tree'. Mintzberg describes how strategies can grow like 'weeds'. What are the implications of these views for the proper role of planning within communications?
2 Evaluate the likely benefits and also the pitfalls of adopting a planning culture.
3 Outline the differences between rational comprehensive and incremental approaches to planning. What is the evidence for each view?
4 Outline the different reasons which explain why strategy development in reality tends to be piecemeal and incremental.
5 In ideal circumstances, should a corporate plan precede a marketing plan which in turn precedes a marketing communications plan?
6 Evaluate the differences and similarities between academic and practitioner views of the role of the communications planner.
7 What is meant by an emergent strategy? What implications does this have for how one might view the planning process?
8 Name three different theories which purport to explain how advertising works.
9 Why is it important for the communications planner to have some theory of how planned communications work?
10 Are planning and creativity mutually exclusive concepts within the marketing communications context or can they work together? How can this be achieved?

CASE STUDY – RECENT ARTICLES

Two recent articles reinforce points made in this chapter. Laura Mazur (1996) seeks to define the traits which define good business leadership. She suggests that leaders such as Bill Gates, Peter Wood and Sir Ian McLaurin share common traits such as being driven, innovative and commercially keen. They also know the benefit of good marketing. Mark Whelan (1996) suggests that youths have 'zero' interest in banks' messages. Why? Because banks are all the same. He goes on to suggest that for too long banks have pushed weak products backed by boring advertising:

> We all know that weak products can't hide behind advertising, particularly when dealing with a group who grew up in the 1980's – a period where there was more bull flying around than the French Farmer's protests. They (consumers) see and know too much to respond to old formulae, but they do respond to good ideas, and good ideas start before an advert is made.
>
> (Whelan, 1996)

From a planning perspective, much still needs to be done to attract new customers. Old, staid or outdated approaches seem to cut little ice with today's high-spending youth markets. Will banks become innovative in relation to this lucrative segment?

NOTES

1 *Source: Marketing*, 8 August 1991, p. 2. It was announced that Vector had attracted only 230 000 new account holders despite high levels of awareness.
2 It also parallels the actual description of a planning retreat for TRW described by Sheehan (in Ansoff, 1965).
3 See, for example, Mintzberg (1994) for a review. A search of the marketing communications literature for this chapter yielded up a similar disappointing result. With respect to research on planning in general, Starbuck (1985) criticized the use of mail surveys using seven-point scales and also authors' attempts to generalize on the basis of response rates averaging 20 per cent. Another difficulty noted by Daft and Buenger (1990: 91) is that researchers' belief in the concept is so strong that this can mask alternative explanations.
4 Although Quinn (1980) would distance himself from this to an extent in that he believed that the process is still rational.
5 References consulted include Richards (1995), Cramp (1996) and Yates (1996).
6 The planning function developed in the UK during the 1970s. Despite pathbreaking theory and research by Katz and Lazarsfield (1955), Riley and Riley (1959) and Eco (1986), it was not until much later that academics working in marketing communications fully appreciated the concept of the active audience (see O'Donohoe, 1997). Simon Clemmow in Cooper (1997) points out that as early as 1967 Timothy Joyce wrote about the difficulties of using AIDA as a model for measuring effectiveness.

REFERENCES

Aaker, D.A. and Myers, J.G. (1992) *Advertising Management*, 4th edn, Englewood Cliffs: Prentice Hall.

Ansoff, I. (1965) *Business Strategy*, London: Penguin.

Brownlie, D. and Spender, J. (1995) 'Managerial judgement in strategic marketing: some preliminary thoughts', *Management Decision*, 33(6): 39–51.

Clausewitz, C. von (1832, 1968 edn) *On War* (trans. Col. J.J. Graham), ed. Col. F.N. Maude, London: Penguin.

Cohen, M.D., March, J.G. and Olsen, J.P. (1972) 'A garbage can model of organizational choice', *Administrative Science Quarterly*, 17: 1–25.

Colley, R.H. (1961) *Defining Advertising Goals for Measuring Advertising Results*, New York: Association of National Advertisers.

Cooper, A. (ed.) (1997) *How to Plan Advertising*, London: Cassell.

Cramp, B. (1996) 'Reading your mind', *Marketing*, 22 February: 33–34.

Daft, R.L. and Buenger, V. (1990) 'Hitching a ride on a fast train to nowhere: the past and future of strategic management research', In J.W. Frederickson (ed.) *Perspectives on Strategic Management*, New York: Harper and Row.

Davidson, M.P. (1992) *The Consumerist Manifesto: Advertising in Postmodern Times*, London: Routledge.

Duckworth, G. (1997) *Advertising Works 9: Papers from the IPA Advertising Effectiveness Awards*, Institute of Practitioners in Advertising, 1996, Henley-on-Thames: NTC Publications.

Dwek, R. (1997) 'So is this evolution or revolution?', *Marketing*, 27 February, 2–4.

Eco, U. (1986) 'Towards a semiological guerilla warfare', in *Travels in Hyperreality*, trans. W. Weaver, London: Pan Books.

Elliott, R. and Ritson, M. (1997) 'Poststructuralism and the dialectics of advertising: discourse, ideology, resistance', in S. Brown and D. Turley (eds.) *Consumer Research: Postcards From the Edge*, London: Routledge.

Franzen, G. (1994) *Advertising Effectiveness: Findings From Empirical Research*, Henley-on-Thames: NTC Publications.

Hogarth-Scott, S. Wilson, K. and Wilson, N. (1996) 'Do small businesses have to practice marketing to survive and grow?', *Market Intelligence and Planning*, 14(1) (January): 6–19.

Johnson, G. (1988) 'Rethinking incrementalism', *Strategic Management Journal*, 9: 75–91.

Katz, E. and Lazarsfield, P.F. (1955) *Personal Influence*, Glencoe: Free Press.

Knights, D. and Morgan, G. (1991) 'Strategic discourse and subjectivity: towards a critical analysis of corporate strategy in organisations', *Organization Studies*, 12(2): 251-274.

Lavidge, R.J. and Steiner, G.A. (1961) 'A model for predictive measurements of advertising effectiveness', *Journal of Marketing*, 24 (October): 59–62.

Lindblom, C.E. (1959) 'The science of muddling through', *Public Administration Review*, 19 (Spring): 79–88.

March, J.G. and Olsen, J.P. (1976) *Ambiguity and Choice in Organization*, Universitetforlaget, Bergen: Norway.

Mazur, Laura (1996) 'Follow the leader', *Marketing*, 29 Feb, 20–22.

McDonald, M.B. (1984) *Marketing Plans: How to Prepare Them: How to Use Them*, Oxford: Chartered Institute of Marketing, Heinemann.

Meller, P. (1991) 'Midland takes a simpler tack', *Marketing*, 8 August, 2.

Mintzberg, H. (1978) 'Patterns in strategy formulation', *Management Science*, 24(9): 934–48.

Mintzberg, H. (1987) 'Crafting strategy', *Harvard Business Review*, July/August.

Mintzberg, H. (1989) *Mintzberg on Management: Inside Our Strange World of Organizations*, New York: The Free Press, McMillan.

Mintzberg, H. (1994) *The Rise and Fall of Strategic Planning*, New York, London: Prentice Hall.

Mintzberg, H. and McHugh, A. (1985) 'Strategy formation in an adhocracy', *Administrative Science Quarterly*, 30: 160–197.

Mintzberg, H. and Waters, J.A. (1982) 'Tracking strategy in an entrepreneurial firm', *Academy of Management Journal*, 6: 465–499. See also Mintzberg, H., and Waters, J.A. (1985) 'Of strategies, deliberate and emergent', *Strategic Management Journal*, 6: 257–272.

Mintzberg, H., Quinn, J.B. and Ghoshal, S. (1995) *The Strategy Process*, European edn, London: Prentice Hall.

Mintzberg, H. Raisinghani, D. and Theoret, A. (1976) 'The structure of unstructured decision processes', *Administrative Science Quarterly*, 21: 246–75.

Mumby, D.K. and Putnam, L.L. (1992) 'The Politics of Emotion: A Feminist Reading of Bounded Rationality', *Academy of Management Review*, 17(3): 465–486.

Neumann J. von and Morgenstern, O. (1944) *The Theory of Games and Economic Behaviour*, Princeton: Princeton University Press.

Novotny, M. (1989) 'Best laid plans vs. reality', *Public Relations Journal*, 5(9) September: 17–19.

Nutt, P.C. (1984) 'Types of organizational decision processes', *Administrative Science Quarterly*, 29: 414–450.

O'Donohoe, S. (1997) 'Raiding the postmodern pantry: advertising intertextuality and the young adult audience', *European Journal of Marketing*, 31(3/4), 234–254.

Pascale, R.D. (1984) 'The real story behind Honda's success', *California Management Review*, XXVI(3): 47–72.

Pettigrew, A. (1977) 'Strategy formulation as a political process', *International Studies of Management and Organization*, VII(2): 78–87.

Quinn, J.B. (1980) *Strategies for Change*, Homewood, Ill: Irwin.

Ray, M.L. (1982) *Advertising and Communication Management,* London: Prentice Hall.

Richards, A. (1995) 'First Direct set for a TV return', *Marketing,* 26 January: 4.

Ries, A. and Trout, J. (1986) *Marketing Warfare,* New York: Mcgraw-Hill Marketing Series, International Edition.

Riley, M.W and Riley, J.W. (1959) 'Mass communication and the social system', in R.K. Merton, L. Broom and L. Cottrell (eds) *Sociology Today: Problems and Prospects,* New York: Harper.

Rossiter, J.R. and Percy, L. (1987) *Advertising and Promotion Management,* New York: McGraw-Hill.

Schultz, D.E. and Martin, D.G. (1979) *Strategic Advertising Campaigns,* Chicago: Crain Books.

Schultz, D.E., Martin, D.G. and Brown, W. (1984) *Strategic Advertising Campaigns,* Chicago: Crain Books.

Sheehan, R. (1965) 'The way they think at TRW', in Igor, A. (ed.) *Business Strategy,* London: Penguin.

Shimp, T.A. (1997) *Advertising, Promotion, and Supplemental Aspects of Integrated Marketing Communications,* Fort Worth: The Dryden Press, Harcourt Brace.

Simon, H.A. (1957a) (1965 edn) Administrative Behaviour, New York: Free Press, McMillan.

Simon, H. (1957b) *Models of Man: Social and Rational,* New York: John Wiley; London: Chapman & Hall.

Simon, H. (1977) *The New Science of Management Decision,* Englewood Cliffs, NJ: Prentice Hall.

Starbuck, W.H. (1985) 'Acting first and thinking later: theory versus reality in strategic change', in J.M. Pennings and Associates, *Organizational Strategy and Change,* San-Fransisco: Jossey-Bass, 336–372.

Thomas, R. (1919) *Commercial Advertising,* LSE Studies of Economic and Political Science, London and New York: G.P. Putnam's and Sons Ltd.

Tversky, A. and Kahneman, D. (1974) 'Judgement under uncertainty: heuristics and biases', *Science,* 185: 1124–31.

Whelan, M. (1996) 'Why youths have zero interest in banks' messages', *Marketing,* 12 December: 6.

White, R. (1993) *Advertising: What it is and How to Do it,* London: McGraw-Hill.

Yates, K. (1996) 'First Direct reveals humorous film', *Campaign,* 30 August: 7.

Yeshin, T. (1997) *Marketing Communications Strategy 1996-97,* The Chartered Institute of Marketing, Oxford: Butterworth–Heinemann.

Young, M. and Steilen, C. (1996) 'Strategy based advertising selection: an alternative to "spec" presentations', *Business Horizons,* 39(6), (November/December): 77–81.

5

THE NEED FOR ANALYSIS AS PART OF THE PLANNING AND IMPLEMENTATION PROCESS

Lynne Eagle

CHAPTER AIMS

- to examine the role of analysis in marcoms planning and implementation
- to highlight the potential consequences of decisions based on inadequate analysis
- to review sources of data for analysis and to assess problems confronting marketing communications planners
- to examine the changing marcoms environment and the implications of changes for marcoms planning and analysis

ILLUSTRATION: NZ CHEESE PROMOTIONS

'If you wanna make
'em smile, Say Cheese'

NZ Cheese Promotions faced a declining domestic market (down 19 per cent over 1987–92), no control over pricing, distribution (cheese was, however, found in 96 per cent of all homes), or the product (controlled by individual brands). A generic cheese marketing communications programme to increase *per capita* cheese consumption was based on a thorough analysis of consumers' purchase, use of and attitude towards cheese. Analysis included perception of cheese as a food product and customers' frequency of purchase and usage of cheese. Cheese was revealed to be perceived as boring, 'the unexciting yellow brick'. Of particular concern was the fact that consumers' views were also shared by retailers and the food service industry. Consumers were still buying cheese, but less of it, as other foods that were perceived as more innovative, dynamic and contemporary attracted more of grocery expenditure. Further analysis showed that there were a number of perceived attributes which could be used as the basis for promotional activity – cheese, although boring, was also versatile, tasty, healthy and economical! The resultant integrated marketing communications campaign brought these attributes 'from the back of people's minds to the front', with an integrated campaign which demonstrated cheese's versatility, taste, value and health properties. 'If you wanna make 'em smile, Say Cheese' was born . . . and saw an increase in sales of 32 per cent from 1992 to 1996 through a repositioning of cheese in the hearts and minds of consumers.

(*Source*: Duffy and Eagle, 1997; NZ Cheese Promotions logo reproduced with permission.)

INTRODUCTION

Marketing communications are a key element of marketing management. Effective marketing management depends on the identification of sustainable competitive advantage over competitors in the minds of consumers. The primary goal of marketing communications is to add value for the consumer (Stewart, 1996). This is increasingly important for marketers for two major reasons. Firstly, many markets are comprised of a number of brands which are similar in terms of benefits and features. Few brands have 'unique' features which cannot be readily and rapidly copied by competitors. Secondly, there has been an increased focus since the mid-1990s on the effectiveness and efficiency of marketing communications elements, particularly advertising. This focus has arisen as a result of increasing clutter in main media and escalating media costs (e.g. Kiely, 1993). An additional concern has been that advertisements spend less time promoting product attributes and, while they may entertain, they may not achieve the persuasive goals set for the advertising campaign overall – they strive to be different rather than relevant. Figure 5.1 highlights the major environmental factors which have influenced the growth of, and therefore increased focus on, promotional activity.

Given the competitive marketplace, it therefore becomes increasingly important to obtain adequate data to allow a thorough understanding of not only your own customers and why, how, where and when they buy, but also who makes the buying decision and what is purchased. Bradmore (1996) advocates that it is also necessary to understand competitors in order to develop and implement more effective marketing plans.

A caution: in determining why customers buy, attention is often focused on determining their wants and needs. Wants and needs represent internal drives and motives and are hence difficult to observe and measure. Guiltinan and Paul (1994) note that the concept of benefits (functional and psychological benefits that buyers hope to receive) is used as a means of reflecting these underlying factors. This must be taken into account at all stages of analysis planning and implementation of marcoms activity. Analysis is a key weapon in developing competitive advantage, not just in the planning stage, but also as a part of a continuous monitoring of a plan's implementation in order for marcoms programmes to be adjusted to reflect changes in the competitive market. As will be shown in later sections of this chapter, the process is far from simple.

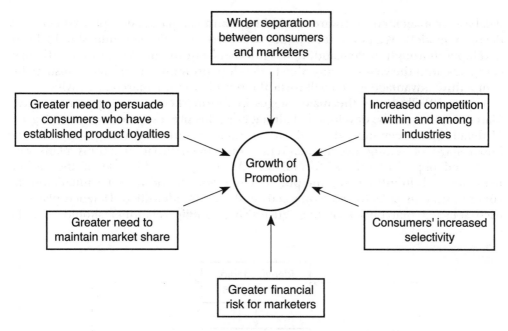

Figure 5.1 Environmental factors influencing promotional activity.
(*Source*: Burnett, 1993)

WHY ANALYSE

Analysis: the division of a physical or abstract whole into its constituent parts to examine or determine their relationship

(*Collins English Dictionary*)

This definition suggests a move from simple descriptive information to a detailed focused review of all controllable and non-controllable factors which may impact on marketing communication (marcoms) programmes. Effective marcoms programmes, be they advertising, public relations, sales promotions or any other (or combination of) marcoms tools available, should be based on sound planning, starting from an analysis of the past and the present. Historical analysis can then be used to provide a projection of the likely future. From this comes the development of both organizational and marketing objectives and the development of plans for the strategies and tactics to be implemented in order for the objectives to be achieved.

The planning process centres around analysis of available data, collection of additional data needed to inform decisions and analysis of available courses of action in order to select the course and to develop appropriate strategies and tactics most likely to achieve the identified objectives. Analysis is centred on a combination of qualitative and quantitative techniques, increasingly drawing on a range of database management software, including statistical packages, spreadsheets and decision models. Whatever techniques are used, the ultimate aim should be to develop a thorough understanding of customers and the market in which the firm competes, with the view of being able to develop, promote and protect a sustainable competitive advantage which will form the foundation for marcoms activity.

Figure 5.2 illustrates the major stages in the marketing management process. Marcoms plans will be developed at all stages in this process, and in various degrees of detail. Plans seemingly depend on the same careful analytical process. At the initial stage of setting overall marketing objectives, broad marcoms plans with associated objectives will be formulated. At this point, the role of the various marcoms tools in influencing the purchase decision should be determined and the communications tasks for marcoms activity should be identified. Detailed plans for each selected marcoms tool (e.g. advertising, public relations) should then be

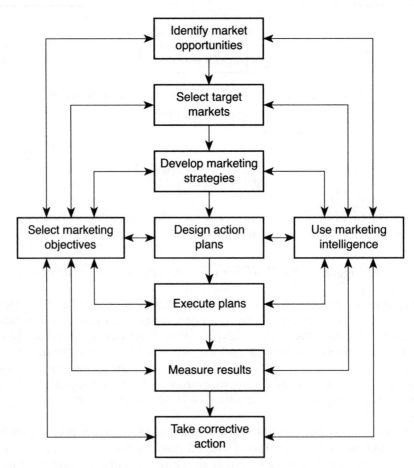

Figure 5.2 Marketing management steps.
(*Source*: Burnett, 1993)

60

developed, drawing on the data analysis already undertaken and adding specialist information relating to the specific marcoms area. These plans will have specific objectives and appropriate strategies and tactics established from the objectives.

Whatever marcoms tools are used, the objectives upon which each plan is based should be:

- output oriented (stating the desired result of a planned activity);
- time specific;
- realistic and achievable, given the resources available and the competitive marketplace environment (thus they should also be cost-effective – some desirable objectives may simply be unachievable/unaffordable);
- measurable;
- specific (eliminating problems in the post-campaign analysis stage of what was to be measured);
- consistent with objectives set for all marcoms elements and with overall marketing objectives (e.g. Parente *et al.*, 1996).

The quality of these objectives is totally dependent on the quality of analysis which has been undertaken to develop them. Broadbent (1997) cautions that both the purpose and the 'how' of communications should be spelt out explicitly: asserting that 'individuals cannot be accountable unless standards have been set in advance'. Marketers are seeking greater accountability from marketing communications planners, making thorough and competent analysis the essential foundation for all stages of the planning and implementation process.

SUSTAINABLE COMPETITIVE ADVANTAGE

Bradmore (1996) identifies marketing-oriented managers as seeing the satisfaction of customer wants and needs as *the* primary competitive weapon and proposes that customers will consistently favour goods and services which most precisely match their needs and wants. He advocates market research as the foundation for identifying these needs and wants, for identifying the market segments whose needs can be satisfied by your product better than by competitors. In-depth analysis of data allows products and services to be positioned and promoted as different from (and presumably of more value than) competitors' products and services.

The difference should be defendable and not readily copied by competitors. It should be able to be communicated to (and understood by) customers, and should be consistent with organizational and marketing goals. All too often, marcoms programmes attempt to establish an up-market quality image for a product or service – which is then heavily discounted at retail level, conflicting with the marcoms message. Price reductions may devalue a brand's image and lessen customers' valuation of the brand. Significant promotional investment may then be required to restore the perceived brand value and pricing to former levels.

Competitive advantage should become self-sustaining – and financially rewarding for the firm itself. By delivering superior value to customers consistently over time, the firm should obtain superior returns – which will allow the firm to reinvest in and reinforce the attributes which allow it to offer sustainable competitive advantage,

61

thus reinforcing and strengthening its market position. By defining sustainable competitive advantage, an organization has the genesis of a base for developing effective marcoms strategies.

Development of a sustainable competitive advantage starts with a thorough understanding of the customer and of competitors. Appropriate marketing strategies and tactics (which may include pricing decisions) will develop from this understanding and enable marcoms programmes to be developed which are internally consistent and correspond with broader organizational goals.

UNDERSTANDING THE CUSTOMER

There are numerous models in existence which allow consumer behaviour to be analysed. For example, Dickson (1994) reviews a number of 'mental models' and market segmentation options based on alternatives such as consumer benefit, lifecycle and lifestyle, product usage, consumer beliefs, choice rules, brand loyalty and price sensitivity.

The selection of the most useful segmentation option is rarely obvious, needing to be evaluated on the option's ability to identify market segments for which different strategies could be pursued. Aaker (1995) notes the increased use of benefit segmentation, with emphasis on what motivates customers to buy and use products or services, what attributes of the offering are important and what objectives are sought by the customer. Importantly, he identifies this analysis as being a dynamic and ongoing process, with a focus on changes in customer motivation, which may be occurring or likely to occur, forming a key element of ongoing analysis. In addition, he extends the potential analysis to include unmet needs, customer satisfaction and analysis of problems identified by existing customers.

Having determined the consumer's wants and needs, there may be several constraining factors which inhibit a company's ability to match their products and services to those desired by the consumer. These constraints include financial and production resources (including managerial and technological expertise). Planners should also consider (of course!) relevant regulations and legislation which may influence what can be undertaken with marcoms activity. There is also increasing awareness of, and interest in, environmental and ethical issues in marketing communications (e.g. Shimp, 1997; Engel *et al*, 1994).

A further constraint is the change in distribution channels which has been driven by the growth in direct response marketing and, increasingly, the Internet. Not only must planners understand (through careful analysis) what motivates customers to buy, when and how often – but also where they buy from. Changes to distribution channels may warrant changes in promotional programmes.

UNDERSTANDING COMPETITORS

As with analysing consumers, there are numerous methods of analysing competitors. Brandenburge and Nalebuff (1995) suggest the use of game theory to shape strategy development. Bradmore (1996) provides a useful review of more conventional techniques for analysing competitors' offerings. However, he extends the analysis beyond such conventional factors as their objectives, strategies and tactics to include competitors' assumptions, strengths, weaknesses, and competitive advantage relative to one's own competitive advantage. He includes analysis of competitive reaction patterns (and predictions of future patterns based on historical information) as a key planning element. Bradmore proposes that detailed analysis of such factors allows strategic decisions to be made regarding which competitors should be attacked or avoided and what market position may be appropriate for a specific product or service.

Whatever system of competitor intelligence and analysis is put in place, it should be ongoing, in order to allow a company to modify its own strategies and tactics to adjust to changing market conditions. Identifying new and emerging competitors and evaluating their impact on one's own activity is an additional challenge facing analysts. Such activity is, however, vital in ensuring a solid foundation upon which to develop marcoms (and all marketing) programmes.

DANGERS OF NOT FULLY UNDERSTANDING CUSTOMERS OR OF NOT INTEGRATING MARCOM PROGRAMMES

It should no longer be necessary to convince people of the need for integrated marketing communications planning but rather to concentrate on the benefits of such activity. Kitchen and Schultz (1997) posit that integrated marketing communications potentially has significant value for organizations, particularly in lowering costs and offering greater client control over marcoms programmes, a view supported by Duncan and Everett (1993) who suggest that the benefits of using integrated marketing communications extend further, to include gaining a competitive edge for marketers (consistent with the philosophy of sustainable competitive advantage).

While the benefits appear to be self-evident, problems of not effectively integrating marcoms programmes appear to offer potentially severe penalties. Schultz *et al.* (1992) consider that 'mixed up, mass directed, incompatible communications stem from manufacturers' wishes rather than from customer needs'. They further say that too little effort is spent on understanding the consumers and their needs – and on demonstrating how the product or service can solve the consumers' problems. Schultz (1996) warns that communications technology and the wider technological revolution will continue to drive integrated marketing communication and that concepts such as market homogeneity and linear market communications models (such as the hierarchy of effects model) must be rethought.

Schultz further states that the consumer integrates the marketer's and advertiser's communication whether the marketing or advertising organization does or not! He warns that this may mean that messages are put together in unexpected ways – which may even be harmful to the brand. This view is supported by Englis and Solomon (1996) who warn that, if there is not a systematic effort to coordinate the messages consumers receive, the result can be inconsistencies among messages sent – with resulting problems for both the product and/or the organization. Schultz (1996) further warns that manufacturer and retailer efforts must be aligned and that, in fact, the whole communications flow needs to be organized around the fact that consumers are no longer dependent on the manufacturer to supply information. Consumers will request information as needed or desired, and will make their purchase decisions at places and times convenient to *them*. Effective integration of marcoms activity implies that the messages used in individual marcoms elements are psychologically similar or consistent, even if they do not look or sound alike (e.g. Parente *et al.*, 1996), ensuring that consumers receive consistent messages across the marcoms programme.

Stewart (1996) warns that 'marketers may manage and coordinate, but they cannot make consumers pay attention to, process or integrate communications'. He suggests that the essence of successful IMC is not simply a matter of coordinating messages sent via different marketing communications channels – which most marketers would claim to do as a matter of course. He proposes that IMC programmes can be successful if a 'market back' approach is used. This implies starting with the value being created for the customer as the unit of analysis, and organizing the firm's activities around the customer, not the product or business function, with continuous feedback from the market being essential to building successful relationships with customers (Stewart, 1996). It is this subtle distinction between coordinating existing marcoms efforts, and using a strategic planning approach which starts with the customers and understanding their wants and needs, that makes IMC an advancement on existing marcoms thinking – and analysis a key tool for effective marcoms programme implementation.

DATA SOURCES

Many companies maintain they cannot afford comprehensive market research, particularly on an ongoing basis. They ignore the substantial amount of data readily and cheaply available within their own organizations or from other 'public' sources. Kalitka (1996) states that up to 80 per cent of marketing intelligence information is available from public sources. While many (usually large) firms invest in complex market information gathering systems, customers, suppliers, retailers and one's own sales force can also provide valuable competitive data (e.g. Cohen, 1991). In addition, syndicated research organizations such as A.C. Nielsen can provide considerable 'off-the-shelf' data – usually relating to sales trends or market category aggregate purchaser profiles. While sources such as these can provide valuable 'background' and trend data, they generally provide minimal data on consumer beliefs and motivation. Beware of the timeliness of 'public domain' data – there is often a significant time delay between the collection and publication of data released through public channels (e.g. official government or industry statistics), lessening their usefulness as an analytical tool.

Stewart (1996) laments the lack of research on how the goals and purposes of consumers influence their attention to, and use of, information, and suggests that such goals are often established by the researcher – not the consumer! He advocates research relating to 'what consumers want to know, the form they want the information and when they want the information' as being 'minimum requirements for designing marketing communications in an environment in which consumers increasingly control information flows'.

It is important to determine what data is required – and that, where new data is sought, the 'right' questions are asked in order to obtain it. Research techniques should be appropriate for the research task – and management should have the skills to be able to interpret the data adequately. Similarly, whether the data measures what was intended (validity), how accurately it measures it, and whether repeated studies would give similar results (reliability) are also factors to be given close consideration.

Decisions made on the basis of comprehensive data analysis depend on the quality of the data used. Serious errors can result in serious misinformation and faulty decision making. Obviously, data which is biased, or which has been drawn from a sample which does not reflect the characteristics of the wider population from which it is drawn, will provide a poor foundation for analysis and decision making. Interpretation of data can also cause problems. A correlation between two variables does not imply one causes the other; there may be alternative explanations for reported behaviour – accepting the most obvious may be extremely dangerous.

For a more detailed discussion of these aspects of marcoms development, consult a reputable market research text.

IMPLEMENTATION: MONITORING AND ANALYSIS ARE ONGOING

Ongoing monitoring and analysis of the (competitive) market is important in order to ensure that customers receive the communications as intended, that they interpret the marcoms message as intended and that adjustments to the marcoms programmes can be made on the basis of this analysis and of analyses of competitive activity and changes in the overall market. Stewart (1996) emphasizes the importance of continuous feedback from the market as 'a guide to adjusting structures, systems, procedures and information flows that add or subtract value for the customer'.

Having decided on what objectives are to be achieved and therefore where an organization wants to position its products or services in the market, ongoing monitoring and analysis is the only way of determining if the organization is achieving what is intended, and of identifying (and, hopefully, rectifying) factors which may be hindering this achievement. Engel *et al.* (1994) provide a useful review of techniques for the 'measurement of promotional effectiveness' but, in common with many texts, concentrate largely on advertising measurement rather than on broader promotional measurement.

Media audits are an underused marcom tool. They perform several functions, starting with whether the marcoms activity appeared as planned and whether (particularly in relation to television) it performed as expected in terms of ratings, reach and frequency levels compared to original estimates. It can also provide valuable data on performance achieved relative to competitors. A database can be built up over time which will provide substantial information on competitors. Scheduling and targeting strategies can be evaluated, expenditure and rating levels can be monitored and media buying efficiencies/space achieved compared.

Over a period of time, sufficient data can be gathered to allow competitive activity trends to be identified and, often, to be predicted. It is at this point that weaknesses in competitive strategies, if identified, can be exploited. Planners must look for ways to outmanoeuvre competitors and to seek to minimize the effects of competitive clutter. Activity should be continuously fine-tuned to take into account any changes within the media environment itself and in competitive strategies.

It is possible to combine audit data with other sales/tracking data to cross-tabulate marcom expenditure or rating data against sales, awareness, recall or other significant marketing trend data and thus to gain deeper insights into the impact of marketing management decisions. The expansion of in-store scanning and the growth of single-source data are continually improving the sophistication of data available for analysis and decision making. Duncan (1995) suggests that effective database management 'makes it possible for companies to become learning organizations', continually seeking to understand and meet the needs of current and potential customers.

The establishment of effective analytical structures and resources in order to control the flow of data and ensure accurate, timely and competent analysis which is available for decision makers to act upon is a crucial factor in marketing management. The tasks involved are far from simple and the following section demonstrates that there are a number of problems in establishing what data may be relevant and what possible models of marketing communications usage may be relevant as analytical and predictive planning tools.

PROBLEMS CONFRONTING IMC PLANNERS

Franzen (1994) describes present-day society as 'the communications society' and notes that communications consumption has its limits in that *per capita* consumption of communication is increasing, but at a far lower rate than is communication supply. He cautions that consumers are being supplied with 30 times more information than they process, that they are becoming increasingly selective in what receives their attention, break off contact with communications more readily, and process communications at a more superficial level. This presents a major challenge to marcoms planners to ensure that communications are interesting and relevant to the target group in order to gain and retain attention.

Measuring the impact of various marcoms forms presents another hurdle for planners. Lutz (1996) suggests that measuring IMC effects is a major challenge due to the complexities of evaluating and comparing marcoms exposures from a range of communication channels. A number of writers (e.g. Hansen, 1995; Solomon and Englis, 1994; Benedixen, 1993) have proposed various theoretical models of how marcoms (particularly advertising) works. Such writers are critical of the historical dependence on hierarchy of effects models, two of which are reproduced here (Figures 5.3 and 5.4).

Kincaid states that the model's foundation (Figure 5.3) is an assumption that, 'since all promotion is persuasive communication, each advertisement must reflect the steps through which one goes in being persuaded', and that the model has been used historically in developing sales presentations in personal selling. He then asserts that 'since persuasion is the goal in advertising as well as in personal selling, the essence of

66

| Attention ---- } | Interest ---- } | Desire ---- } | Action |

Figure 5.3 AIDA model.

(*Source*: Kincaid, 1985)

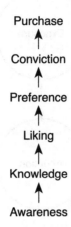

Purchase

Conviction

Preference

Liking

Knowledge

Awareness

Figure 5.4 Hierarchy of effects model.

(*Source*: Lavidge and Steiner (1961), cited by Kincaid (1985))

the model is equally appropriate in creating an advertisement'. Figure 5.4 shows an earlier model. It suggests that people go through a series of steps in arriving at their decision to buy and that advertising can be a force that moves them up these steps.

There are two problems with models such as these. Firstly, they focus only on advertising and not the wider marcoms mix. Secondly, the straight progression of hierarchical stages in processing marketing communications must be questioned.

Lannon (1996) states that too much emphasis is still placed on the measurement of advertising alone, even with modern models (e.g. Broadbent, 1997) – and on an outdated question of 'How does advertising work?' whereas the question should now be 'How and why do all the other forms of communication work?' . . . and, turning it round to the consumer viewpoint: 'How do consumers use these different forms of commercial communications?'.

Franzen (1994) proposes that there is no longer a definitive succession of stages and that 'there is more likely to be a constant, more or less simultaneous, interaction between existing knowledge, attitudes and behaviour on the one hand, and the perception and processing of advertisements on the other. If some succession does exist, the sequence of effects may well differ from the one on which hierarchy-of-effects models were based originally'.

He illustrates this with a model of complex, constant interactions between existing knowledge, attitudes and behaviours and the perceptions and processing of advertisements (Figure 5.5). The complex interactions highlight the need for thorough understanding of the processes involved. This understanding can only be based on detailed analysis of all the underlying factors illustrated – the model can readily be extended to incorporate all marketing communications elements, not just advertising.

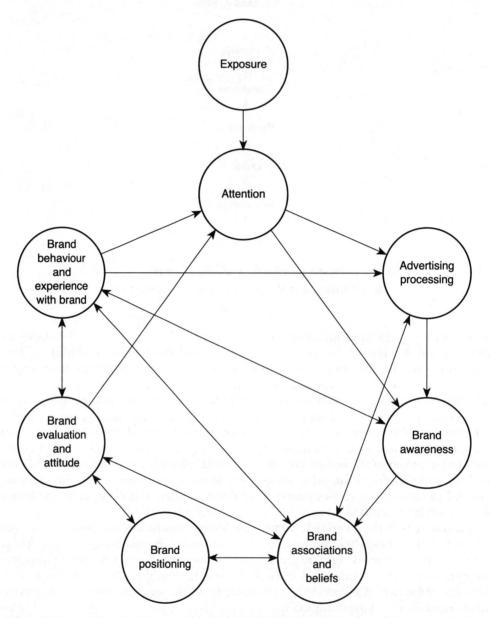

Figure 5.5 Interactions between knowledge, attitudes and behaviours and the perceptions and processing of advertisements.

(*Source*: Franzen (1994))

The marketing communications environment continues to change and evolve. The advent of (200 or more) digital television channels, interactive services and video-on-demand will have a major impact on media consumption patterns – experts are debating whether digital will create fragmentation or segmentation (e.g. McIntosh and Wheble,1997). New measurement systems are needed, especially as convergent technologies use television screens for purposes other than the viewing of television channels (e.g. Meredith and Twyman, 1997).

The advertising industry has implemented a series of advertising effectiveness awards in many countries which recognize and reward advertising campaigns which can be shown to have produced measurable results. Advocates such as Fletcher (1997) state that advertising effectiveness awards are valuable – but in need of a change in focus to include profitability measurement. Nowhere does he consider the role of advertising as part of the wider marcoms arsenal and whether the awards concept itself should be re-examined in a broader context. Indeed, the obsession with advertising effectiveness alone may be hindering a focus on the wider issue of evaluating the effectiveness of both individual marcoms elements and the combined impact of marketing communications programmes overall.

Marcoms planners must continually evaluate and develop their analytical tools and techniques in order to be able to examine these concerns, to propose answers to current and future challenges and to keep pace with the changing marketplace they face. Effective and efficient analysis at all stages of marketing communications planning and implementation will remain the foundation no matter how much the marcoms environment itself changes.

SUMMARY

Analysis, while a crucial tool in marcoms planning and implementation, is dependent upon the quality of data available for the analytical task at hand and the skills of the analyst. Most products and services operate in dynamic and highly competitive markets and the need for accurate and timely data – and astute analysis – is increasingly important. Marcoms analysis is an evolving field which must keep pace with ever-developing technology and the demands of the vibrant and challenging marketplace. Long-established models of the marketing communications process may need to be re-examined and amended in the light of major changes to consumers' marketing communication consumption patterns. Evolving technology will also alter these consumption patterns, requiring new analytical approaches in order to allow planners to comprehend consumers and to develop and implement effective and efficient marketing communications programmes.

DISCUSSION TOPICS

1 Discuss the role of analysis in the initial marcoms planning stages.
2 What is the relevance of a sustainable competitive advantage to marcoms programmes?
3 Discuss, giving examples to illustrate your answer, the ways in which consumer behaviour data may be analysed for marcoms programme development.

4 Why should competitive analysis extend beyond an examination of objectives, strategies and tactics?

5 What dangers are there in not fully understanding customer behaviour?

6 Explain Schultz' statement that the consumer integrates marketing communications messages even if the organization does not.

7 What are the strengths and weaknesses of publicly available market research data for planning and implementation analysis purposes?

8 Why should monitoring and analysis be viewed as an ongoing activity?

9 Analyse Franzen's statements regarding the growth in communications. Why is an understanding of these factors important for marcoms planners?

10 Draw up a recommended marcoms audit programme for a large fast-moving consumer goods company and then for a social service of your choice. How do they differ and why?

CASE FOR DISCUSSION

Road safety campaigns present a special challenge for marketing communications. Many thousands of lives are lost internationally every year – at social costs of billions of dollars. While most people are shocked by the carnage on highways, irresponsible behaviour still exists, behaviour which has a direct influence on the road toll (in New Zealand, speeding and alcohol-impaired driving contributed to 68 per cent of all fatal crashes and 35 per cent of all injury crashes in 1996. (*Source*: New Zealand Land Transport Safety Authority statistics).

International experience has shown that the only effective way to reduce the road toll is to drive attitudinal and behavioural changes by making drivers aware of the consequences of irresponsible driving behaviour. Attempts to reduce the road toll through enforcement and 'mild' information campaigns have not proven effective.

The New Zealand 'tough' road safety campaign, similar in its approach to that used in several other countries, was based on the premise that changes in beliefs led to changes in attitude, intention and, ultimately, behaviour. The starting point of the campaign development was a detailed analysis of some of the common beliefs, attitudes and emotions towards road safety issues and the identification of 'illusions' such as speeding being safe depending on the driver's level of skill, experience and the road conditions.

The campaign was designed to emphasize the consequences, to tell it how it is with absolute realism, including the accident 'event', its cause, the aftermath, blame and consequences. Different propositions and messages were therefore developed for different parts of the target audience, based on the beliefs, attitudes and 'illusions' identified in the original analysis, such as 'speed kills' for older drivers and 'speeding could disfigure you for life' for young drivers, but all activity was integrated to ensure consistency of the overall themes such as emphasizing the link between speeding, drink driving and road crashes and the consequences, together with the awareness of the probability of getting caught.

Post-analysis included recall, attitude change – and a monitor of the number of road fatalities (which dropped by 30 from 1995 to 1996). (*Source*: Duffy and Eagle, 1997/NZ Road Transport Safety Authority.)

DISCUSSION

Consider the difficulties in other marcoms programmes which are aimed at significant behavioural change, especially when the objectives are to decrease rather than increase occurrences of 'undesirable' behaviour (e.g. drug usage, cigarette smoking). How do such campaigns differ from those for more conventional products and services such as fast-moving consumer goods, banking or travel? What forms of analysis would you recommend be undertaken to provide a foundation for the development of marcoms programmes?

Consider particularly the data available to measure 'effectiveness' – what measurements can be used in place of sales? What external environmental factors might have influenced 'results'?

REFERENCES

Aaker, D.A. (1995) *Strategic Marketing Management*, 4th edn, New York: John Wiley & Sons, 56.

Benedixen, M.T. (1993) 'Advertising effects and effectiveness', *European Journal of Marketing*, 27(10): 19–32.

Bradmore, D. (1996) *Competitive Advantage: Concepts and Cases*, Englewood Cliffs, NJ: Prentice Hall, 25–32.

Brandenburger A.M. and Nalebuff, B.J. (1995) 'The right game: use game theory to shape strategy', *Harvard Business Review*, July–August: 57–71.

Broadbent, S. (1997) *Accountable Advertising: A Handbook for Managers and Analysts*, Oxfordshire: AdMap Publications, 53.

Burnett, J.J. (1993) *Promotion Management*, Boston, MA: Houghton Mifflin Company, 8, 11.

Cohen, W.A. (1991) *The Practice of Marketing Management: Analysis, Planning and Implementation*, 2nd edn, New York: Macmillan Publishing.

Collins English Dictionary and Thesaurus (1993) Glasgow: Harper Collins Publishers, 40.

Dickson, P.R. (1994) Marketing Management, New York: Dryden Press, 82.

Duffy, M. F. and Eagle, L.C. (1997) *Inaugural Advertising Effectiveness Awards: Winners' Casebook*, Auckland, NZ: Profile Publishing & Advertising Agencies' Association of New Zealand/Association of New Zealand Advertisers.

Duncan, T. (1995) 'The concept and process of integrated marketing communication', *Integrated Marketing Communications Research Journal*, 1(1) Spring: 3–10.

Duncan, T.R. and Everett, S.E. (1993) 'Client perceptions of integrated marketing communications', *Journal of Advertising Research*, 33(3) May/June: 30–9.

Engel, J.F., Warshaw, M.R. and Kinnear, T.C. (1994) *Promotional Strategy: Managing the Marketing Communications Process*, Homewood IL: Richard D. Irwin Inc.

Englis, B. and Solomon, M.R. (1996) 'Using consumption constellations to develop integrated communications strategies', *Journal of Business Research*, 37(3): 183–91.

Fletcher, W. (1997) 'The IPA effectiveness awards – time to move forward?', *Admap*, 32 (8) Iss. 376, September: 55–7.

Franzen, G. (1994) *Advertising Effectiveness: Findings From Empirical Research*, Oxfordshire, UK: NTC Publishers/AdMap Publications, 3–21.

Guiltinan, J.P. and Paul, G.W. (1994) *Marketing Management: Strategies and Programs*, 5th edn, New York: McGraw Hill Inc, 69.

Hansen, F. (1995) 'Recent developments in the measurement of advertising effectiveness: the third generation', *Marketing and Research Today*, November: 259–69.

Kalitka, P. (1996) 'The equalizer versus competitive intelligence', *Competitive Intelligence Review*, Spring, 7(1): 83–6.

Kiely, M. (1993) 'Integrated marketing: way of the future or ghost from the past?', *Marketing (Australia)*, February: S1–S6.

Kincaid, W.M. Jnr (1985) *Promotion: Products, Services and Ideas*, 2nd edn, Columbus, Ohio: Charles E. Merrill Publishing Co.

Kitchen P.J. and Schultz, D.E. (1997) *Integrated Marketing Communications: What is it and Why are Companies Working That Way? New Ways for Optimizing Integrated Marketing Communications*, The Netherlands: ESOMAR, 1–24.

Lannon, J. (1996) 'Integrated communications from the consumer end,' *Admap*, 32(11), Iss. 379, February 23–6.

Lavidge, R.J. and Steiner, G.A. (1961) 'A model for predictive measurements of advertising effectiveness', *Journal of Marketing*, October: 61 (cited in Kincaid, W.M. Jnr (1985) *Promotion: Products, Services and Ideas*, 2nd edn, Columbus, Ohio: Charles E. Merrill Publishing Co.

Lutz, R.J. (1996) 'Some general observations about research on integrated marketing communications', in J. Moore and E. Thorsen (eds) *Integrated Communication: Synergy of Persuasive Voices*, New Jersey: Lawrence Erlbaum Associates, 362.

McIntosh, A. and Wheble, A. (1997) 'The myth of fragmentation', *Admap*, 32(11), Iss. 379, December: 26–9.

Meredith, W. and Twyman, A. (1997) 'BARB – wired for the future?', *Admap*, 32(11), Iss. 379, December: 29–31.

Parente, D., Vanden Berg, B., Barban, A. and Marra, J. (1996) *Advertising Campaign Strategy: A Guide to Marketing Communications Plans*, Orlando, FL: The Dryden Press.

Schultz, D.E. (1996) 'The inevitability of integrated communications', *Journal of Business Research*, 37(3): 139–46.

Schultz, D.E., Tannenbaum, S.I. and Lauterborn, R.F. (1992) *Integrated Marketing Communications: Pulling it Together and Making it Work*, Lincolnwood, IL: NTC Business Books, 65.

Shimp, T.A. (1997) *Advertising, Promotion and Supplemental Aspects of Integrated Marketing Communications*, 4th edn, New York: The Dryden Press.

Solomon, M.R. and Englis, B.G. (1994) 'Observations: The Big Picture: Product complementarity and Integrated Communications', *Journal of Advertising Research*, January–February: 57–61.

Stewart, D.W. (1996) 'Market-back approach to the design of integrated communications programmes: a change in paradigm and a focus on determinants of success', *Journal of Business Research*, 37(3): 147–53.

6

THE ORGANIZATIONAL CONTEXT OF MARKETING COMMUNICATIONS

Christine Daymon

CHAPTER AIMS

- to explore the organizational context in which marketing communications take place
- to explain the influence of organizational context on the nature and role of marketing communications
- to outline some of the conceptual frameworks for understanding behaviour and work activities in organizations

ILLUSTRATION

The following quotation identifies some of the influences on work activities in commercial organizations, that is, structure and culture; organizational systems such as budgets; and people, including leaders, staff and customers. Issues concerning these factors and their linkage to marketing communications are discussed in this chapter.

'What this business demands is lack of hierarchy. I don't go around and impose upon people my view of how things should be done; they come to me and say, "I want to do it this way." Providing it isn't a waste of money, I let them do it that way. We have a very long reputation of not over-spending on our programmes for our clients and that's due to the self-discipline of our staff, it's not due to me. What happens in this company is that the budget is an open system. The budget is available to anyone who wants to see it. I believe our system works. Everybody gets up in the morning wanting to succeed – it doesn't matter what they are doing, they want to succeed. . . . This company reflects the people within it, and that's what I want it to be like and that's what our clients like. When they come here, they are amazed at the enthusiasm of our people.

'I walk around, I spend my entire time walking around, I know everyone by their first names. Leading by example is what it's all about. The army is often used as a derogatory system but if you take the US Army, which is on the platoon system or what is known as the "buddy" system, you know who will be

the person in charge if there's a crisis. But up until that point, everybody's the same. If there is a crisis I will run ahead and deal with it, I will manage it.'
(Interview with senior partner of a television company. *Source*: Goffee and Scase, 1995: 33–5.
Used by permission.)

INTRODUCTION

Conventional literature has sought to enhance the practice of marketing and marketing communications by offering analytical techniques and models designed to achieve greater effectiveness. The many influences of organizational contexts where these activities take place rarely feature in these unidimensional prescriptions (see, for example, Shimp, 1997). Perhaps, therefore, it is not surprising that some empirical studies show that practice often falls short of the ideals espoused by prescriptive literature (Piercy and Morgan, 1990).

In contrast, this chapter sets out not to provide remedies for greater communication effectiveness, but to offer insights into what goes on in organizations, on the assumption that theories of marketing communication can be significantly enriched by being grounded in the realities of the organizational environment in which communication happens.

STRUCTURE

The shape an organization takes has implications for the practice and position of marketing communications. Whether managed communications take a strategic or tactical role, whether they are controlled centrally or are decentralized often depends upon the way an organization is structured. Structure refers not to physical characteristics but to the formal lines of accountability and interaction of people in organizations.

In most industries up until the late 1970s, the predominant organizational design was the hierarchical, integrated company. Characterized by multiple layers of management, functional specialization, integrated operations and clear distinctions between line and staff responsibilities, the pyramid shape is evident today in many manufacturing companies and in the public sector (Goffee and Scase, 1995). Organizations of this type endeavour to undertake all activities themselves, from product design, manufacture and distribution, to all support services including, for example, catering, security, training and publicity. On the whole, marketing in these organizations is a centralized operation, situated at corporate headquarters, with experienced, senior managers reviewing and directing the specialized work of junior members of staff (Webster, 1992). This arrangement allows for centralized control of marketing communications efforts for individual brands across national and international markets.

Because these organizations are large, many people are needed to handle, and specialize in, all elements of marketing communications. Bureaucratic communication processes are used to standardize procedures and to provide coordinating mechanisms across the many structural layers. Internal communication emphasizes written reports and memos. Training programmes act as communication channels to socialize members into management's preferred organizational culture. The many formal procedures and the multi-tiered nature of this organizational design result in cumbersome decision making that disadvantages innovation. Organizations of this type move slowly and are unsuited to fast-moving, competitive climates.

Where large organizations have recognized the need to adapt to changing market demands and greater competition, the more extreme bureaucratic practices have been dismantled and operations are decentralized. Although the vestiges of a corporate unit may exist to coordinate strategic communications, marketing communications are handled in separate units, focusing on products, geographical markets, different customer/institutional divisions, or a combination of these according to the strategic policy of the company (Kotler, 1997). Despite the advantages of getting closer to the customer through decentralized operations, the problem for marketing communicators in organizations of this type is that their large size results in slow responses and difficulty sometimes in controlling the quality of services rendered. Skolnik (1993) reports the problems faced by CI Group, a large public relations consultancy in New York.

> On a multi-office account with the head team in New York City and activity in three other countries, the account manager had to go through the CEO for Europe to interact with the other three offices. Coordinating with sister agencies of parent Grey Advertising meant going through the corporate CEO. Even the senior-most counselors in international offices had to go through the international president to work with each other.
>
> (Skolnik, 1993)

To eliminate issues of size when it is not accompanied by responsiveness and adaptability, some organizations over the past decade or so have reshaped by collapsing pyramid structures and shrinking into wheel-like shapes. A small, focused core at the hub contains highly experienced, permanent employees who work in multi-functional teams. On the periphery individuals and businesses cluster: strategic partners, wholly owned subsidiaries, licensees, franchisees, joint ventures, freelancers (some of them teleworkers) and subcontractors, all loosely linked to the core. In this way, companies concentrate on distinctive competences, and outsource or subcontract non-essential activities through loose confederations of suppliers and distributors.

This adaptable design allows organizations to fluctuate in size according to current project needs; only the appropriate levels of staff and expertise for each task or project are deployed. The flat, 'lean' shape of this 'flexible' organization promotes internal communication that is informal, personal and speedy because it is unfettered by hierarchy. Thus, creativity and innovation are encouraged (Mazur and Hogg, 1993). Vertical disintegration, therefore, is capable of providing operational efficiency and cost effectiveness with responsiveness and flexibility.

Scenario

In a leading hotel and leisure group, senior marketing communicators at the organization's core work closely with core corporate decision makers in formulating communications strategies aimed primarily at building longer-term relationships with all customers. They also provide direction and support for projects which include keeping all relationships in the network focused on the changing needs and expectations of customers. Operational activities stemming from marketing communications plans are outsourced to peripheral networks of freelance writers, designers, publicists, researchers and planners employed on a temporary basis just for the duration of specific campaigns. In addition, market research, advertising, public relations, sponsorship and direct marketing agencies are contracted for periods which often accord with the life of a product concept or market niche. Figure 6.1 illustrates a network of outsourcing arrangements for marketing communications.

Burns and Stalker (1961) were the first to identify organizations structured in this manner. They called them 'organic'. Since then, other writers have described them as 'networks' (Miles and Snow, 1986), 'alliances' (Ohmae, 1989), 'Shamrock' organizations (Handy, 1990), 'adhocracies' (Mintzberg, 1983) and 'flexible firms' (Atkinson, 1984). They are evident today in growth sectors such as tourism, advertising, publishing, public relations, the media industries, computing, telecommunications, and in more established sectors such as transport, engineering, chemicals, glass, hospital supplies, and fashion (Barnatt and Starkey, 1994; Goffee and Scase, 1995; Webster, 1992). Morris and Pitt predict that before long all businesses will operate in this way; there will be:

> flexible teams and partnerships consisting of individuals of varied backgrounds and representing multiple organizations . . . The only constant will be customer relationships, and the organization as a whole will continually put together novel packages of resources to grow these relationships and to capitalize on new opportunities.

(Morris and Pitt, 1994: 558–9)

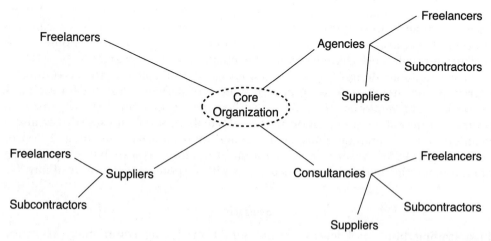

Figure 6.1 A network of outsourcing arrangements for marketing communications.

Suppliers and employees, then, are not the only ones encompassed within these wheel-like patterns of organization. Customers, too, are linked through a variety of relationships, such as in joint investment projects, joint exploration of new technologies, sharing resources and developing new products and markets together. Where once there was a clear distinction between a company and its external environment, this now has disappeared. Webster quotes one company's annual report which states:

> In a boundary-less company, suppliers aren't 'outsiders'. They are drawn closer and become trusted partners in the total business process. Customers are seen for what they are – the lifeblood of a company. Customers' vision of their needs and the company's view become identical, and every effort of every man and woman in the company is focused on satisfying those needs. In a boundary-less company, internal functions begin to blur. Engineering doesn't design a product and then 'hand it off' to manufacturing. They form a team, along with marketing and sales, finance, and the rest. Customer service? It's not somebody's job. It's everybody's job.
>
> (Webster, 1992: 12)

Within 'flexible' organizations, the abandonment of layers of management means that decision making is now devolved to those who directly interact with customers (Coulson-Thomas, 1991). Marketing communications planning emerges from team decision making, that is, from a group of core organizational members who include not only those directly involved in planned communications, but also those with ultimate responsibility for the organization's overall strategic policies. In this way, emphasis is laid upon the matching of strategic organizational aims with internal and external marketing objectives. This allows, too, for integrated communications programmes.

A key issue for internal communication activities is the difficulty of identifying who belongs and who does not to this organization with its fluctuating, fuzzy boundaries. Because electronic technology facilitates communication flows between core and periphery, this is an essential integrating mechanism. However, more subtle messages about operating beliefs and values of those at the organization's core are difficult to convey to individuals whose involvement is only transitory. In stable, hierarchical organizations, assimilation of members into the organization's patterns of working and expectations is achieved through communication mechanisms such as training and socialization programmes which acquaint staff with the organization's 'way of doing things', which, for staff communicators, involves appreciating the norms and expectations that the organization holds about marketing and communications. Those employed on temporary or part-time contracts (that is, those working on the organization's periphery, such as freelancers or suppliers) are rarely offered such programmes. What then are the ties that support these dynamic networks, and how can the process of planned communications be controlled when such a variety of individuals is involved?

The heritage of former shared work experiences and relationships, also industry training schemes or academic programmes (such as the many degrees now offered in advertising, public relations, marketing communications, etc.), mean that many working in a particular sector have developed similar understandings about how work should be practised and evaluated. The bonds of shared industry expectations, professional norms and values, and collegial relationships serve to loosely couple individuals and peripheral units in their beliefs about how work and relationships should be conducted. Gregory's (1983) study of Silicon Valley organizations shows that the values and expectations of occupational groups may transcend organizations. She suggests that organizations consist merely of multiple occupational subcultures which 'cross-cut' many organizations. If this is so, then it is likely that tensions may exist between the expectations of those on the periphery and those at the organization's core. Indeed, this reflects some of the conflict noted in empirical studies on organizational and professional/occupational values (for example, Dawson's (1994) study of law and medical organizations; Organ and Greene's (1981) research on engineers and scientists; and many studies of media organizations including Burns (1977), Daymon (1997) and Elliott (1977)).

Yet, underpinning these dynamic and sometimes contradictory patterns of relationships are stable mechanisms in the form of financial systems and planned communication programmes. Although 'flexible' organizations despise bureaucracy, to some extent it is systems operating on bureaucratic principles that prevent disintegration within and across their complex network of internal and external relationships. Coordination comes not only from external members' professional expertise, and from already established interpersonal relationships, but also from the linkage to core and peripheral members provided by systems such as marketing communications with its plans and preconceived strategies. Marketing communications, therefore, exists not only to promote the products and services of businesses, but also to hold the organization together through its focus on the development of mutually beneficial relationships.

In many cases, these relationships come together to provide customers with 'the whole experience', that is, unique combinations of products and services that are more attractive together than if purchased separately, such as the joint loyalty scheme, Smart, in Scotland. Shell, Menzies, Victoria Wine, Dixons, Currys, The Link, RAC, Commercial Union, Hilton Hotels and Vision Express cooperate in a scheme that allows members to collect and redeem more points faster because it can be used for more purchases (Mitchell 1997). Marketing communications in situations such as this are less concerned with targeting, segmenting and differentiating, than with connecting, unifying, networking and maintaining relationships in order that customers might be encouraged upwards on the customer loyalty ladder to become advocates and devotees of the company's products and services (Christopher, *et al.* 1991).

A further issue for marketing communicators situated in the core of 'flexible' organizations is in finding and retaining the right people to implement programmes. Because external network connections are loose, there is nothing to prevent the uncoupling of links from either side. In this case, security of supply can be a problem for organizations. Internal marketing communications are therefore vital in establishing strong connections and trust between all parties in order that relationships are maintained. In the television industry, a flourishing freelance sector in the early 1990s began to dry up in the middle of the decade, leaving experienced camera operators, designers, producers, directors, writers and other creative individuals in high demand by broadcasters and independent programme makers. The established reputations of certain broadcasters and interpersonal connections between core and periphery ensured that some organizations continued to attract freelancers and subcontractors who could deliver the appropriate quality products and services. On the other hand, the following example indicates problems for broadcasters when those relationships are disrupted: after recent changes in leadership and commissioning editors at Channel Four, Paula Milne, a respected freelance writer of a number of hugely popular Channel Four series, said: 'I am seriously reconsidering my position . . . I have never met [the new director of programmes]. I don't work for people I don't know.' (Brown, 1997).

The maintenance of good reputations and relationships is equally as important for those marketing communicators who choose to work on the periphery (that is, those who prefer 'insecurity and freedom' (Burns, 1977) to the stability offered at the core) because these help to sustain communicators' 'employability', a characteristic which guarantees continuous employment. Although the possession of essential skills indicates capability to do the job, this is often a less significant factor in organizational recruitment decisions than the ingredient of 'acceptability' (Brown and Scase, 1994). The prevalence of team working means that everyone, core and peripheral member, has to get along. Therefore, successful freelance communicators and suppliers develop extensive contacts and peer associations because these signal compatible social norms and values with those from whom they seek work.

Yet another issue for marketing communications in 'flexible' organizations is that peripheral businesses may be, simultaneously, customer, competitor and supplier as well as partner. Continuing the broadcasting industry example, a regional broadcaster may buy transmission services from another broadcaster, may supply programmes to that same broadcaster, both may directly compete for the same advertisers, both may jointly coordinate media promotions in order to publicize network programming, and both may be financially and creatively involved in the development of co-productions. In this instance, commercial confidentiality requires marketing communications to tread a delicate path of simultaneous symmetrical and asymmetrical communication. A dearth of research on the pressures and communication processes involved in maintaining these complex relationships means that this area is little understood.

LEADERSHIP

Today's 'flexible' forms of organization call for different behaviours from marketing communications managers because sustaining and coordinating relationships amongst all members of organization networks is critical to the viability of businesses. There is increasing emphasis on interpersonal management skills, on open-participative styles of management and on competencies in communicating informally. Yet, as the vignette above indicates, this is contingent upon each particular situation. In a crisis, for example, a more authoritarian style of leadership is needed; too much democracy and participation can lead to disarray. In traditional organizations, the directive approach is common because subordinates expect leaders to explain what, when, where and how tasks are to be carried out. Here the focus is primarily on getting the job done with less emphasis on interpersonal relationships.

Hersey and Blanchard (1988) have attempted to explain situational leadership by pointing out that leaders' behaviours need to fit with 'follower readiness', that is, the degree of ability, willingness and confidence in subordinates to undertake tasks. They suggest that, once follower readiness has been taken into account, leaders' behaviours should vary according to task or relationship needs – for example – from total delegation on the one hand to command and instruction communication on the other. Situational leadership, therefore, is a combination of styles which includes delegating, participating, selling and telling. In 'flexible' organizations, the norm is for delegation and participation at the core with sometimes a more directive style on the periphery because of the need to apply greater control mechanisms to freelance and temporary work. This applies less frequently when peripheral workers are experienced specialists used to working autonomously and coordinating through mutual adjustment.

Hersey and Blanchard's prescriptive approach has been criticized on a number of counts. Bryman (1986, 1996) notes that other factors besides 'followers' are also influential, such as pre-existing levels of trust, resource constraints, social, political and economic factors. Handy (1985) draws attention to the variety of work that is undertaken, the organization's structure and technology, and its culture. However, Hersey and Blanchard's primary contribution is in highlighting how leaders and managers need to be flexible in behavioural terms, as the initial vignette in this chapter illustrated.

LEADERSHIP AND CULTURE

In noting Handy's reference to organizational culture, attention now turns in this direction because of the inherent connections between leadership, culture and communication. Culture, according to Schein (1992), consists of shared underlying beliefs and values in organizations as well as the more visible signs such as common language or jargon, behaviour, rites, rituals, ceremonies and, to some extent, physical artefacts.

Many studies have suggested that managing culture is a central role of designated leadership (Dyer, 1985; Gagliardi, 1986; Lundberg, 1985; Pettigrew, 1979; Sathe, 1985; Schein, 1983, 1985, 1992). They consider that leaders knowingly use a set of beliefs (or a vision) as a guide to orient behaviour in a desired direction and, at the genesis of an organization, the founders have a particularly strong impact because they are:

> very strong-minded about what to do and how to do it. Typically, they already have strong assumptions about the nature of the world, the role their organization will play in that world, the nature of human nature, truth, relationships, time and space.

> (Schein, 1983: 17)

Writings of this nature depict designated leaders as managers of meaning where vision has a pivotal role in the formation of organizational culture (Bryman 1996). Sathe (1985) and Gagliardi (1986) highlight the significance of rewards by top managers for desired behaviours and outcomes because in this way cultural preferences are learned by employees and reinforced. Similarly, McDonald's (1991) case study of the Olympic Games Organizing Committee is illustrative of the symbolic role played by leaders and senior managers. Her research records the importance not only of managers' sayings but also their behaviours in communicating their intent and underlying assumptions about the nature of work and organization. For example, all new members of the committee were required to take a general knowledge test about the Olympic Games administered by the president, Peter Ueberroth. The impression given was that lack of preparation was grounds for immediate dismissal. Good results in the test resulted in personal congratulations from the president. What became known as the 'Peter test' communicated to Olympic Committee employees that they had to prepare and perform all their duties well in order to be effective team members.

Snyder's (1988) research into the Lockheed-California Company also focuses on the issue of leader-driven communications in the development of organizational culture. When organizational members are viewed as key customers, that is, essential components in the process of marketing (Varey, 1995), Snyder's findings illustrate a number of marketing communications techniques available to senior managers for the advancement of organizational goals and subsequent commercial effectiveness through culture development. They are:

1 Clear articulation of the desired vision and associated practices
2 Translation of that vision into simple, memorable language
3 Top management modelling of the desired practices
4 Building a team that embodies those desired practices
5 Working close to members of lower levels of the hierarchy in order to understand and 'reframe' their perceptions to fit organizational objectives
6 Engaging in other symbolic acts (such as engaging in rituals and ceremonies).

(Snyder, 1988: 205)

Both Snyder and McDonald, like the majority of management writers, believe that culture can be managed. Planned communication activities, as well as symbolic behaviours by top managers, send messages about management's preferred way of doing things which, as McKenna (1991) writes, is not always positive or innovative. He suggests that, because culture is the 'underlying and usually unspoken "social web" of management, it subtly but powerfully channels managers' behaviour into comfortable ruts' (page 94).

There are two main problems with this approach. First, culture is understood to be a unified whole, a characteristic of the total organization, something that can be changed from one entity into another to suit managerial goals. Cultures, from this perspective, comprise that which is shared organization-wide – language, behaviours, beliefs, values and underlying assumptions (Schein, 1992) – and conflict is not included. Yet, as Parker (1995) points out, conflict may be just as pronounced in organizations as consensus. Martin (1992: 68) argues that, because unanimous agreement is unlikely to be found in organizations, 'organization-wide consensus is bound to entail the imposition of someone's authority on someone else'. The writing of Deal and Kennedy (1982) illustrates:

> Modern managers who try to be humane may at the same time undermine the values upon which the culture of the institution rests. Modern heroes may need to be hard and 'insensitive' to keep a company consistent with its goals and vision – the very elements that made it strong in the first place . . . Humaneness is important, but the goals of the culture are paramount.
>
> (Deal and Kennedy, 1982: 56–57)

Morgan (1997: 150) is alarmed at emphasis such as this, writing that, 'The fact that such manipulation may well be accompanied by resistance, resentment and mistrust, and that employees may react against being manipulated in this way, receives scant attention.' Even Varey (1995) who, when writing about internal marketing for sustaining competitive advantage, makes nodding acquaintance with people and power issues in cultures, still bases his ideas on the fundamental premise that effectiveness stems from management-determined, unified values. Numerous other texts discuss how to change culture (sometimes by adapting marketing communications techniques) in order that employees will focus on the customer, that quality standards will prevail, or that the company will embrace more competitive values (two early, acclaimed examples are Deal and Kennedy (1982), and Peters and Waterman (1982)). What is overlooked is that there are many other influences which shape culture, including employees themselves with their differences in personal goals, aptitudes, personalities and motivations, as well as group influences. The notion of culture as a means of enhancing control disturbs Anthony (1994) who writes that culture, instead, should be thought of as representing a series of relationships rather than a commodity.

ORGANIZATIONAL MEMBERS AND CULTURE

Anthony's concerns are echoed in the writings of researchers who take an interpretive stance towards understanding culture. They dispute the dominance of leaders as culture creators and highlight difference instead of consensus (Bloor and Dawson, 1994; Martin, 1992; Martin *et al.*, 1985; Thompson and Luthans, 1990; Schumacher, 1997; Van Maanen and Barley, 1985; Ybema, 1997; Young, 1989). They draw attention to the active role that *every* member of the organization plays in the process of 'refining, sustaining or rejecting organizational culture' (Bloor and Dawson, 1994: 279), a process where intra- and intergroup relationships are developed in relation to organizational goals, for example in the formation of subcultures which support or are in conflict with organizational goals.

The predispositions of members, who bring attitudes and values from outside into an organization (such as professional communications norms), contribute to the ways in which those members interpret the meanings of new situations. This, in turn, determines which solutions and understandings go on to become accepted as part of the organization's culture. In Brown and Starkey's (1994) study of a UK confectionery company, for example, members' antipathy towards bureaucratic procedures contributes towards the 'under-development' of the company's management information systems. Instead, members encourage the use of *ad hoc* communication and the grapevine because these are perceived to offer more effective solutions to communication problems. These behaviours and attitudes characterize subcultural practices in Brown and Starkey's focal organization.

Brown and Starkey's study draws attention to more general communication issues; first, the way in which planned communication processes may be bypassed or supplemented with *ad hoc* forms of communication activity as organizational members shape organizational life according to their own needs and expectations (see also Ybema, 1997). Second, where planned communication provides the official version of events, informal channels allow individuals and groups to draw upon richer sources, some of them external to the organization. These informal networks, which exist alongside formal channels, often provide a faster route to information acquisition and interpretation (Katz and Kahn, 1978) as well as providing different interpretations of official communication content. If, as Brown and Starkey suggest, culture influences what is done in communication terms, and, in turn, communications also help to shape culture, what are the implications for marketing communications?

IMPLICATIONS FOR MARKETING COMMUNICATIONS

1 Leaders and senior managers are influential in shaping organizations' contexts and these contexts, in turn, constrain or promote various marketing communications practices.
2 But, messages may be misinterpreted or marketing intentions undermined within organizations because of differing subcultural values and beliefs held by organizational members.
3 Similarly, external norms and associations or the residue of former experiences may be influential in shaping marketing communications practices – and these sometimes may be at odds, sometimes in harmony with managerial thinking.
4 Organizations consist of real people with personal values and ethics, experiences, motivations and individual goals. Their behaviours, relationships and attitudes fundamentally shape organizational capabilities, especially with regard to planned communication. In many cases, their subtle adaptations of marketing communications practices have implications for the success or failure of programmes.
5 Marketing communications are a mechanism which aids coordination of diverse sets of internal and external network relationships.

SUMMARY

Whereas this chapter began by discussing structural constraints and opportunities for marketing communications, and revealed marketing communications' contribution to the coordination of the organization itself, it ends by pointing to the cultural dimension of organizations where structures and systems (such as marketing communications) are understood to be complex expressions of the differing beliefs and values of all organizational members, managers and employees alike. This chapter provides no prescriptions for making marketing communications more effective but offers explanation for why they work as they do, that is, diversely according to different organizational contexts.

DISCUSSION TOPICS

1 With reference to the organization in which you are working or studying:
   - Identify any influences which you consider affect the practice of marketing communications.
   - To what extent have marketing communications needs influenced what goes on in your organization?
2 Offer examples to support or challenge Schein's (1992) view that leaders play a crucial role in developing organizational culture, and thus an organization's communication activities.
3 How would you describe the culture of the department where you work or study? Does this differ from the culture of the organization as a whole? If so, why?
4 Compare the internal communication activities in your department with those in the overall organization. Explain the rationale for any differences.
5 Who are some of the peripheral workers and businesses involved with your organization? How might they influence the communication activities of the organization?
6 In your experience, should organizational culture be managed? If so, how? If not, why not? Explain the implications of this from a marketing communications perspective.
7 Why might the structure of an organization be influential in determining the position and role of marketing communications practitioners?
8 What might be some of the implications for marketing communications practice when organizations interact with peripheral companies which are simultaneously customer, competitor and supplier?
9 In what way might the values and norms of marketing communications professionals cross-cut organizational boundaries?
10 Critique Figure 6.1 and offer an explanation as to how outsourcing may impact on business-to-business marketing communications.

CASE STUDY – DELMA'S DECISION

Delma Scott knew she had a tough day ahead when she arrived at the offices of Stanpit Insurance. She'd worked there for six months as Head of Communications. Last week she sent a proposal to her boss, J.J. Dendle, chief executive, and had received only a stony silence. Today she'd have to write a further document and maybe lobby other senior colleagues to support her case.

Her idea was to scale down the size of the marketing communications department and subcontract some of its work outside to integrated communications agencies. She wanted to tap into the expertise of specialist copywriters and designers by employing them on a project basis. It would result in the loss of some of Stanpit's older employees who'd been with the company for many years, of course, but Delma considered it worth it for the fresh vision and creativity that youthful outsiders could bring to the company's communications campaigns. Naturally, she'd ensured her own role was securely built into the proposed new structure.

Delma crossed Stanpit's high-vaulted, marble-columned entrance lobby, was greeted by the uniformed guard and made her way in the lift to the fourth floor. She strode down the long corridor to the corner office, past the closed doors of the design unit, internal communications, advertising and marketing. Pondering on Dendle's obvious resistance to her proposals, she recalled how the company had a reputation for conservatism. 'More like stuck in a rut', she thought. Dendle always said the only way to do things well was to do them yourself – hence the company's lack of trust in outside suppliers.

Where marketing communications were concerned, the company spent heavily on press advertising. Traditionally this had been considered the best medium for communicating all those solid British values that Stanpit stood for. But there was no research budget and consequently no measurement of advertising effectiveness. Yet Delma had a hunch that potential customers had little awareness or interest in the company's products and services. She wanted to change all that. What was nagging her, though, was the company's ethos: conservatism and family values. 'Concern for the individual' was the motto on which the company was built and this was demonstrated by staff retention schemes and generous employee benefits. In return, staff were intensely loyal to Stanpit. What would happen to morale if the marketing communications department was suddenly down-sized and people either shunted into other departments or offered early retirement? On the other hand, could the company continue to ignore a changing marketplace with different communication expectations?

Delma closed the door and walked across the thick carpet to her desk. She couldn't help recalling the energy and frenetic pace of the small, theatre production company, Bright Ideas, where she'd worked last year. There'd been a 'buzz' about the place. Executives and secretaries had pulled together as a team. Deadlines were often impossible. When things got tough, Lottie Miller, founder-director, would say: 'We're the best. We can do it.' She'd set the business up with the aim of becoming the UK's top production business within ten years. She wasn't far off. Trophies for award-winning productions were displayed in the reception area. Together with theatre posters and photographs, they were evidence of employees' creative output.

Bright Ideas' offices were mostly open plan. Delma used to drop by colleagues' desks to bounce ideas around. And freelances too, employed to work on diverse projects, would just wander in and join the conversations. Although employed as a copywriter, Delma didn't have a traditional 'creative' role because Lottie liked employees to be adaptable. Instead, she got involved in other activities too: press conferences, hospitality management, client strategy meetings, budgeting, and building client and supplier relationships on her own. There wasn't any need to write reports or memos about conversations or plans; everyone just talked things through. Sometimes, though, it was hard to pin down freelance designers and writers. She couldn't always remember if she'd briefed them or not. Sometimes, too, it was annoying when people misinterpreted what she'd said, or forgot what had been decided, or got deadlines wrong. Delma's decision to change jobs happened on the spur of the moment during one of these times of frustration. She didn't have any qualms about leaving; other staff changed frequently.

Six months on, Delma sat at her desk at Stanpit and switched on her computer. Pondering her proposal to the chief executive, she wondered if it had been appropriate. Were activities that worked in Bright Ideas the best ones for Stanpit, its employees, its customers and its business? What should she say in her follow-up report?

REFERENCES

Anthony, P. (1994) *Managing Culture*, Buckingham: Open University Press.

Atkinson, J. (1984) 'Manpower strategies for flexible organizations', *Personnel Management*, August: 18–31.

Barnatt, C. and Starkey, K. (1994) 'The emergence of flexible networks in the UK television industry', *British Journal of Management*, 5(4) 251–60.

Bloor, G. and Dawson, P. (1994) 'Understanding professional culture in organizational context', *Organization Studies*,15(2): 275–95.

Brown, A. and Starkey, K. (1994) 'The effect of organizational culture on communication and information', *Journal of Management Studies*, 31(6), November: 807–828.

Brown, M. (1997) 'Long knives and high drama', *The Guardian*, 14 July, 4–5.

Brown, P. and Scase, R. (1994) *Higher Education and Corporate Realities*, London: UCL Press.

Bryman, A. (1986) *Leadership and Organizations*, London: Routledge and Kegan Paul.

Bryman, A. (1996) 'Leadership in organizations', in S. Clegg, C. Hardy and W. Nord (eds) *Handbook of Organization Studies*, London: Sage, 276–92.

Burns, T. (1977) *The BBC. Public Institution and Private World*, London: Macmillan.

Burns, T. and Stalker, G.M. (1961) *The Management of Innovation*. London: Tavistock.

Christopher, M., Payne, A., Ballantyne, D. (1991) *Relationship Marketing*, Oxford: Butterworth–Heinemann.

Coulson-Thomas, C. (1991) 'Customers, marketing and the network organization', *Journal of Marketing Management*, 7(3): 237–55.

Dawson, S. (1994) 'Changes in the distance: professionals reappraise the meaning of management', *Journal of General Management*, 20(1), Autumn: 1–21.

Daymon, C. (1997) *Making sense of Meridian. A cultural analysis of organizational life in a new television station*, unpublished PhD thesis, University of Kent at Canterbury.

Deal, T. and Kennedy, A. (1982) *Corporate Cultures. The Rites and Rituals of Corporate Life*, Reading, Mass: Addison-Wesley.

Dyer, W. (1985) 'The Cycle of Cultural Evolution in Organizations', in R. Kilmann, M. Saxton, Serpa and Associates (eds), *Gaining Control of the Corporate Culture*, San Francisco, C.A.: Jossey Bass, 200–229.

Elliott, P. (1977) 'Media organizations and occupations: an overview', in J. Curran, M. Gurevitch and J. Woollacott (eds) *Mass Communication and Society*, London: Edward Arnold.

Gagliardi, P. (1986) 'The creation and change of organizational cultures: a conceptual framework', *Organizational Studies*, 7(2): 117–134.

Goffee, R. and Scase, R. (1995) *Corporate Realities. The Dynamics of Large and Small Organizations*, London: Routledge.

Gregory, K. (1983) 'Native-view paradigms: multiple cultures and culture conflicts in organizations', *Administrative Science Quarterly*, 28: 359–376.

Handy, C. (1985) *Understanding Organizations*, 3rd edn, London: Penguin.

Handy, C. (1990) *The Age of Unreason*, London: Arrow Books.

Hersey, P. and Blanchard, K.H. (1988) *Management of Organizational Behavior: Utilizing Human Resources*, New Jersey: Prentice Hall.

Katz, D. and Kahn, R. (1978) *The Social Psychology of Organizations*, 2nd edn, New York: John Wiley.

Kotler, P. (1997) *Marketing Management. Analysis, Planning, Implementation and Control*, 9th edn, Englewood Cliffs, NJ: Prentice Hall.

Lundberg, C. (1985) 'On the Feasibility of Cultural Intervention'. In P. Frost, L. Moore, M.R. Louis, C. Lundberg and J. Martin (eds) *Organizational Culture*, Newbury Park, CA: Sage, 169–198.

Martin, J. (1992) *Cultures in Organizations: Three Perspectives*, New York: Oxford University Press.

Martin, J., Sitkin, S. and Boehm, M. (1985) 'Founders and the elusiveness of a cultural legacy', in P. Frost, L. Moore, M.R. Louis, C. Lundberg and J. Martin (eds) *Organizational Culture*, Beverly Hills, CA: Sage, 99–124.

Mazur, L. and Hogg, A. (1993) *The Marketing Challenge*, Wokingham: Addison-Wesley and The Economist Intelligence Unit.

McDonald, P. (1991) 'The Los Angeles Olympic Organizing Committee: developing organizational culture in the short run', in M. Jones, M. Moore and R. Snyder (eds) *Inside Organizations*, Newbury Park, CA: Sage, 165–78.

McKenna, R. (1991) 'Marketing is everything', *Harvard Business Review*, January–February: 65–79.

Miles, R. and Snow, C. (1986) 'Network organizations: new concepts for new forms', *California Management Review*, 28(3), Spring: 10–28.

Mintzberg, H. (1983) *Structure in Fives*, Englewood Cliffs, NJ: Prentice Hall.

Mitchell, A. (1997), 'Star gazing', *Marketing Business*, June: 32–5.

Morgan, G. (1997) *Images of Organization*, 2nd edn, Thousand Oaks, CA: Sage.

Morris, M. and Pitt, L. (1994) 'The organization of the future: unity of marketing and strategy', *Journal of Marketing Management*, 10(7): 553–60.

Ohmae, K. (1989) 'The global logic of strategic alliances', *Harvard Business Review*, 67 (March–April): 143-54.

Organ, D.W. and Greene, C.N. (1981) 'The effects of formalization of professional involvement: a compensatory process approach', *Administrative Science Quarterly*, 26(2): 237–52.

Parker, M. (1995) 'Working together, working apart: management culture in a manufacturing firm', *The Sociological Review*, 43(3), August: 518–47.

Peters, T. and Waterman, R. (1982) *In Search of Excellence*, New York: Harper and Row.

Pettigrew, A. (1979) 'On studying organizational cultures', *Administrative Science Quarterly*, 24(4): 570–81.

Piercy, N. and Morgan, N. (1990) 'Organizational context and behavioural problems as determinants of the effectiveness of the strategic marketing planning process', *Journal of Marketing Management*, 6(2): 127–43.

Sathe, V. (1985) *Culture and Related Corporate Realities*, Homewood, Illinois: Richard D. Irwin.

Schein, E. (1983) 'The role of the founder in creating organizational cultures', *Organizational Dynamics*, 12(1): 13–28.

Schein, E. (1985a) *Organizational Culture and Leadership*, San Francisco, CA: Jossey-Bass.

Schein, E. (1985b) 'How Culture Forms, Develops and Changes'. In R. Kilmann, M. Saxton, R. Serpa and Associates (eds) *Gaining Control of the Corporate Culture*, San Francisco, CA: Jossey-Bass, 17–43.

Schein, E. (1992) *Organizational Culture and Leadership*, 2nd edn, San Francisco, Calif: Jossey Bass.

Schumacher, T. (1997) 'West Coast Camelot: the rise and fall of an organizational culture', in S. Sackmann (ed.) *Cultural Complexity in Organizations. Inherent Contrasts and Contradictions*, Thousand Oaks: Sage, 107–132.

Shimp, T. (1997) *Advertising, Promotion, and Other Aspects of Integrated Marketing Communications*, 4th edn, Orlando, FL: The Dryden Press.

Skolnik, R. (1993) 'The emerging firm of the '90s', *Public Relations Journal*, March: 20–5.

Snyder, R. (1988) 'New frames for old. Changing the managerial culture of an aircraft factory', in M. Jones, M. Moore and R. Snyder (eds) *Inside Organizations. Understanding the Human Dimension*, Newbury Park, CA: Sage.

Thompson, K. and Luthans, F. (1990) 'Organizational culture: a behavioral perspective', in B. Schneider (ed.). *Organizational Climate and Culture*, San Francisco, CA: Jossey-Bass, 319–44.

Van Maanen, J. and Barley, S. (1984) 'Occupational communities: culture and control in organizations', in B. Staw and L. Cummings (eds) *Research in Organizational Behaviour*, Vol. 6. Greenwich, CT: JAI Press, 287–365.

Varey, R. (1995) 'A model of internal marketing for building and sustaining a competitive service advantage', *Journal of Marketing Management*, 11(1): 41–54.

Webster Jnr, F.E. (1992) 'The changing role of marketing in the corporation', *Journal of Marketing*, 56(4), October: 1–17

Ybema, S. (1997) 'Telling tales: contrasts and commonalities within the organization of an amusement park – confronting and combining different perspectives', in S. Sackmann (ed.) *Cultural Complexity in Organizations. Inherent Contrasts and Contradictions*, Thousand Oaks: Sage, 160–86.

Young, E. (1989) 'On the naming of the rose: interests and multiple meanings as elements of organizational culture', *Organization Studies*, 10(2): 187–206.

7

THE DRIVE FOR INTEGRATED MARKETING COMMUNICATIONS

Philip J. Kitchen

CHAPTER AIMS

- to analyse the emergence of integrated marketing communications (IMC)
- to provide theoretical and practical foundations for IMC
- to provide empirical evidence of current perceptions of IMC from UK ad agency executives
- to consider the extent to which IMC may be seen as a passing management fad

ILLUSTRATION: ORANGE BRAND INTEGRATION

Orange proposition – 'Orange Offers the Future Today'

Since Orange's launch in April 1994 it has maintained its brand image in both advertising and below-the-line marketing and has positioned itself as the mobile phone brand that owns the 'future' of telecommunications. As Orange was the fourth company into the market, it had to carve out a niche for itself. At the time the market was cluttered with many different and confusing messages about mobile phones. To cut through the clutter Orange's communication had to be consistent and motivating. While everyone else was talking about mobile phones, Orange talked about 'Wire Free Communication', in other words a clean world that is optimistic and uncluttered. This clean optimism is consistent in everything Orange does.

Wolff Olins created and have continued to develop and supervise Orange's corporate identity. WCRS are responsible for all above-the-line advertising and help coordinate activity with the other agencies as new campaigns are launched. Dutton Merrifield ensure that all copy and glossary of terms are consistent through-the-line and provide customer communication leaflets such as bill inserts. Option One provide Point-of-Sale and until recently WWAV was working on the Direct Marketing. All this is managed between the agencies and also through the Orange campaigns and design team.

Since launch, Orange has created a multi-media mix to ensure that synergy is felt across all sectors. Creative consistency and media phasing create a sense of ubiquity for the brand. The Orange audience are given a taste of a new campaign through the use of posters, which hint at the message but do not tell the whole story. TV and press then follow to start the campaign explanation. This is joined by shop displays, information leaflets, bill inserts and fulfilment information for enquirers.

The compounded effect is far more powerful than a disparate campaign that uses each marketing discipline independently. The end result ensures that the message is absorbed on several levels and so is more effective. This saves Orange money. Rather than [potentially] confusing consumers with independent creative work by sector, a powerful brand image is formed and maintained and Orange gets more out of each pound spent as messages and images are shared and remembered through-the-line.

(*Source*: *WCRS* 1997, used with permission)

INTRODUCTION

As noted in the Orange case vignette, the compounded effects of utilizing an integrated approach are more effective than campaigns which use disparate elements (e.g. advertising alone). But is or was the Orange campaign a one-off? To what extent are other corporations and agencies using IMC? Is IMC a passing fad? Is there any difference between the [presumed] integrated approach versus previous approaches? This chapter tackles these questions and also attempts to describe the development of *Integrated Marketing Communications* (IMC) from a theoretical and practical perspective and provide empirical evidence from an exploratory study of IMC within a judgement sample of UK advertising agencies (total estimated billings – £3.5 billion). The chapter considers what IMC is, why companies are working that way, and whether IMC offers significant value to advertising agencies and clients in the rapidly changing communications marketspace leading toward the next millennium.

IMC does not appear to be a managerial fad, nor is it simply a reformulation of existing theory or practice. Instead IMC is a clear response by advertising agencies and clients affected by a constellation of factors driven by new forms of information technology including development and usage of databases, media fragmentation, client desires for interaction/synergy, and global and regional coordination. The chapter concludes by offering two further case vignettes. IMC is a marked, fundamental, probably irreversible, shift in both the thinking and practice of clients and advertising agencies as reflected by advertising executives.

There seems little doubt that IMC is an emergent concept whose time seems to have arrived. IMC research commenced in 1991 at the Medill School of Journalism, Northwestern University, USA (Caywood *et al.*, 1991). This chapter extends knowledge on how the concept of IMC is diffusing by providing an initial analysis of data on how senior advertising agency executives perceive IMC use and development in the United Kingdom. It provides a perspective on the current state of IMC, and levels of implementation and usage in an important segment of the marketing communications landscape. As a note, further IMC studies with ad agencies and marketing organizations are taking place in the USA, India, New Zealand and Australia.

Empirical research in the UK was predicated on the dynamic that there may well be wide variation and differing views concerning what IMC conceptually represents.

Thus, implementation of an integrated approach by advertising agencies may well differ not only in thought but in practice. Thus this chapter neither has a consensual nor a conclusive mission; its overall aim is to explore the multiple dimensions of IMC, including what it means, how it works, and why companies are working that way, thus helping to move the subject forward.

BACKGROUND

Prior to the study conducted by Caywood *et al.* (1991), there appeared to be little or no formal discussion or even description of what is now being called Integrated Marketing Communications. While there doubtless had been practitioner discussions and trade press articles, the Northwestern study, funded by the American Association of Advertising Agencies (AAAA)(USA) and the Association of National Advertisers (USA) appears as the first formal, structured attempt to bring some understanding of the concept to the literature. Thus, most of the history of IMC thinking and discussion is generally less than a decade old. While there has been considerable debate and discussion of the subject, who does it, how it is done, etc., the formal presentation of research, theory development and other materials by either practitioners or academics has been slow in coming. Given its history, much of the IMC literature and learning has focused on the explanation of IMC in the marketplace, i.e. what it is, how it operates in the marketplace, rather than on theory building or understanding of the basic principles. These points must be kept in mind, for while the literature is sparse at this point, it is growing rather rapidly.

Schultz (1991) formalized the IMC discussion in the USA by arguing that nothing [in the USA] had received as much publicity, discussion at learned meetings, while seeing little real activity, as had the concept of IMC in 1990. At that time most manufacturers and marketing organizations in the USA were still trying to sort out the need for and value of IMC. What is evident now, some years later, is that the concept is still undergoing development.

A special issue of the *Journal of Marketing Communications* (1996) devoted to IMC found that virtually all the papers dealt with theory building and/or identification of key issues – in other words, IMC still appears to be in a pre-paradigm as opposed to a post-paradigm state (Mills, 1959; Kuhn, 1964; Crane, 1972). This is as expected for integration is not the norm in western cultures despite papers to the contrary (Kotler, 1972, 1986, 1997; Kitchen and Proctor, 1991; Kitchen, 1993, 1994, 1996; Kitchen and Moss, 1995; Duncan, 1993, 1995; Duncan and Everett, 1993; Novelli, 1989–90; Waterschoot and van Bulte, 1992). However, most mainstream marketing texts and more specialist texts on marketing communications have practically *all* adopted some type of integrated approach or perspective (Kotler, 1997; Zikmund and D'Amico, 1996; Shimp, 1997; Belch and Belch, 1995; Krugman *et al*, 1994) – a sure sign that IMC is progressing into acceptability and has become entrenched as perceived 'academic wisdom' in marketing generally.

While various authors and researchers have developed some type of IMC approach or concept for their teaching and research, each appears to have done so independently from the others, or at least each appears to have developed the concept from his or her own view (see, for example, Beard, 1996; Constanzo,1996).

There does not, at this point, appear to be any consistent or mutually agreed-upon definition, description or process to identify what IMC is, and what it isn't. Thus, while IMC is generally accepted in the marketing communications literature there are still many grey areas which are in need of clarification and this may act as a brake on IMC becoming mainstream (Schultz, 1996b).

Against this groundswell of academic opinion, ably supported by case study material (mainly US in origin), discordant voices can be heard asking 'what's new?' (Hutton, 1995; Wolter, 1993); or 'what does IMC actually mean?' (Phelps et al., 1994; Nowak and Phelps, 1994). The real issue expressed by many UK academics and practitioners (Kitchen, 1996) is that IMC may be no more than another management 'fad', no different from Total Quality Management (TQM) or re-engineering or Effective Customer Response (ECR). Indeed, these experts argue that IMC is simply another term to embrace many already well-known notions, or a minority concern by those anxious to differentiate themselves in some way, perhaps 'much ado about nothing'. However, it could be argued that these latter arguments are missing the point. Insofar as marketing communications is concerned, most activities in the past have been focused on breaking down concepts and activities into ever more finite specializations. Few marketing or communications approaches have involved integration or holistic thinking. It appears that much marketing thought is driven by the basics of segments and segmentation. So, despite the development of integrative or systems thinking, particularly in the area of marketing and marketing communications, this may not be reflected in companies practising communications or in advertising agencies servicing their needs. Indeed, generally, the decomposition of existing systems and processes underpins the nature of social science investigation, that is, to separate, reduce or individualize activities and events, the assumption apparently being that if the parts of the subject can be understood, the whole can be understood as well. So, the concept of integration, while conceptually sound, may be met with scepticism, challenge, even rejection by both academics and practitioners alike. Certainly specialists, say in advertising, may not want to see the whole, only their part of it.

Recent studies have tended to show that while IMC is welcomed, accepted and attempted elsewhere, its prevalence may not be as strong as in the USA (Rose, 1996). Its practice is still indeterminate in global communication strategies (Grein and Gould, 1996) despite the overarching integration of advertising and only advertising in global promotional campaigns (Keegan, 1995). Further, evidence (Duncan and Caywood, 1996) tends to support the view that IMC is contingent on the extensive use of behavioural (preferably individualized) databases (Jackson and Wang, 1994; Junu, 1993) which underpin the process of active organizational learning in order to develop increasingly sophisticated integrated marketing communication activities. Access to such databases may not be as prevalent or as well developed elsewhere as in the USA.

Since databases are considered to be so critical to the development and practice of IMC, it is worth considering how these are evolving on a global scale. To alleviate the concerns that a behavioural database is required for the practice of integrated marketing communications, an emerging concept of what a database is and what data is or may be needed to practise IMC in a less research-developed economy should be considered. Increasingly, the concept of a database is taken to include all the information which an organization can gather on both customers and consumers (Schultz, 1996). While there are often critical lacks of consumer or end-user data in channel-delivered systems, business-to-business and service organizations have considerable internal data which will allow the development of such behavioural databases. Indeed, even within fast-moving consumer goods organizations, there is substantial customer (channel) data which could provide the basis for the development of a consumer (end-user) database. Unfortunately, it is the lack of connection or cooperation between marketing, sales and research which prevents the use of this system-wide data. So, it may be that the lack of actual data is more a function of the lack of internal ability to gather existing data than it is one of lack of actual marketplace information (Schultz, 1996).

From this scenario two arguments arise. The first, in favour of integration, centres on rapidly diffusing information technologies which are impacting on the marketplace, consumers, media, and distribution of products and services (Shocker *et al.*, 1994). This argument has been particularly well advanced by Rayport and Sviokla (1994) whose approach to retailing as 'marketspace' rather than 'market-place' leads to a wide variety of supporting arguments for new forms of electronic communication which impact not only existing systems but evolve into new forms such as the World Wide Web and the nebulous Internet (Kitchen and Wheeler, 1997). These arguments, though led by US academics and practitioners with some inputs from Europe, are finding correspondence in literature, albeit embryonic and emergent, drawn from the international market. The second argument, against IMC, challenges the approach as being nothing more than traditional marketing and advertising dressed up in new clothes and given a new title. Such an argument suggests that integration is nothing new, that it revolves around an academic argument, and has few real managerial implications (Sloan, 1994). The latter would appear to be an argument that would find some correspondence in the United Kingdom. Therefore, included in this chapter is an exploratory academic study, tackling not companies, but advertising agencies in the United Kingdom. Findings of this study follow.

EXPLORATORY STUDY AND FINDINGS

The study was based upon the 'construct explication' approach. IMC was defined, both conceptually and operationally, and 'real world' measurements were then developed through a series of scaled questions. The conceptual definition of IMC used in this research was:

> IMC is a concept of marketing communications planning that recognizes the added value of a comprehensive plan that evaluates the strategic roles of a variety of communications disciplines (for example general advertising, direct response, sales promotion, and public relations) . . . and combines these disciplines to provide clarity, consistency, and maximum communications impact.
>
> (Schultz, 1993)

Operational exploration related to areas associated with this definition by analysing what IMC was, as viewed through the lens of ad agency executives. The original research instrument was developed to quantify perceived conceptual and operational aspects of IMC and was adapted from the original Northwestern University study (Caywood, *et al.*, 1991). Thus, some comparisons of the US adoption and development in 1990 and the diffusion of the concept in the UK in 1996 are possible.

The research instrument used was an 89-question, self-administered questionnaire (estimated completion time – 30 minutes). Questions were organized into three major topic areas each related to the three objectives (1. reaction to the definition; 2. personal and organizational demographics; 3. agreement or otherwise with contingent statements using a ten-point Likert scale (1 – strongly disagree to 10 – strongly agree)). The remainder of the questions were categorical, descriptive or open-ended. The questionnaire, originally developed by the faculty at Northwestern University, was adapted and extended. It was then pre-tested by submission to experts at the IPA (UK), and via screening by ten industry practitioners. Questionnaires were sent to a selected list of members of the IPA in the UK which was provided by that organization. Each questionnaire was accompanied by a cover letter from a senior member of the IPA (UK) encouraging participation. A postage-paid envelope was enclosed, and respondents could request a summary of the research findings. The questionnaire was posted first class to the IPA members in Summer, 1996. By the cut-off date 65 usable responses had been received, a response rate of 29 per cent. Thus perceptions of IMC as given relate purely to a judgement sample of advertising agency executives.

Empirical exploration of research findings

Demographic profiles

Responses were received from the following: Managing Director (19), Chairman (9), CEO (7), and the rest were in senior positions of authority in advertising agencies ranging from Media and Research Director to SBU Director. The average period of time respondents had spent with their firm was 10.2 years (standard deviation of 7 years). Educationally, 21 executives had been educated to 'O' level standard, 22 to 'A' level, 10 to HND equivalence, 34 graduates and 8 postgraduates.

Table 7.1 indicates the amount of time these executives estimated they devoted to IMC programmes on behalf of client firms.

As can be seen, approximately 50 per cent of those responding stated that they spent between 25 and 74 per cent of their time on IMC programmes for their client firms. Thus, while the development of IMC programmes is not dominant, it appears that it is receiving substantial time and attention from senior UK advertising agency executives.

Among the agencies, mean annual gross billings were £58.3 million which account for in excess of total billings of £3.5 billion (standard deviation 12.45m). Expectations, following a period of recession in the UK, were on average that increases in billings in 1996 would be in the order of 12.3 per cent (standard

Table 7.1 Amount of time devoted to IMC programmes for client firms

Amount of time (%)	Percentage Distribution
10 or Less	9
10–24	28
25–49	23
50–74	30
75 or more	9

deviation 1.3). The percentage of client budgets devoted to IMC programmes for clients through individual agencies was 42 per cent. Thus, there appears to be a strong correlation between the amount of time agencies are investing in IMC programmes and the IMC-related billings of those same agencies.

Table 7.2 illustrates how client budgets are allocated in the responding agencies. It is interesting to note that almost 50 per cent of the advertising agency billings are now in activities below the line, i.e. other than traditional advertising, with more than 20 per cent now in direct marketing. Client budget allocations among the four marketing communications functions are recorded in Table 7.2. Again, this distribution of functional billing seems to indicate that the agencies are indeed developing IMC and not concentrating their billing only on above-the-line activities.

Of the responding agencies, 36 are compensated by full commission, 35 by reduced commission, 52 by the fee system, 35 on a project basis, and 41 on a mix of commission and fee (total adds to more than 100 due to multiple responses). This would seem to verify the very diversified types of programmes which agencies are developing for their clients and which require more non-traditional compensation schemes.

Reactions to IMC definition

All the respondents agreed that companies should be integrated in terms of communication. This seems to demonstrate that even if IMC is nothing more than a current management fad, it is a well-accepted concept and area of interest for the agencies that responded. Qualitative exploration of this agreement indicated that

Table 7.2 Clients' budget allocations for 1996

Function	Mean	SD	Count	CL@95%*
Advertising	51.3	19.3	34	6.5
Sales promotion	21.0	12.3	32	4.3
Marketing PR	11.5	7.1	32	2.4
Direct marketing	21.6	15.7	31	5.5

Note: Means sum to more than 100%, not all respondents divulged this information.

client firms required greater synergy and consistency among all types of marketing communication because of the need for cumulative impact and effects, consistency and reinforcement, style, tone, content, and key measures, and that each element added value to communications expression. From a consumer perspective there was a perceived need to get reinforcement of the communication via many different channels using the same message. For clients and agencies, IMC was seen to offer a multi-disciplinary, multi-integrated and cost-effective solution to communication needs. However, amid this storm of affirmation the point was made repeatedly that the definition may imply that IMC = one agency with multi-disciplines as indicated in the qualitative responses. There is a struggle between what IMC is and how it might be practised.

Most agencies do not get the opportunity to control all communication programmes for clients, therefore the onus is on clients to develop and control integrated programmes. Given that client firms should have integrated communications the extent to which differential elements of communications were integrated was explored (Table 7.3). As will be shown, there is considerable area for development and clarification of the topic.

While integration may be desirable by client companies, the extent to which communication elements are integrated varies significantly. Advertising is furthest along the track toward integration, but the majority view is that communication elements are integrated to some extent, with public relations with its dual focus on corporate and marketing activities still with some way to go.

Of concern to practitioners and academics alike is whether IMC is being developed as an alternative to increasing budgets or simply trying to make better use of the funds available. In this study, 41 agencies expected client budgets to increase over the next three years (33 of these by up to 10 per cent p.a.), 21 agencies expected client budgets to remain the same, and the rest expected a decline. Given clients who had purportedly integrated, 33 agencies expected budgets to increase (26 by up to 10 per cent p.a.), 25 thought integrated firms' budgets would remain the same, and the rest expected a decrease of up to 10 per cent p.a.

Notably, for firms which have integrated, only 16 agencies expected client communications staff to increase, compared to 29 who envisioned the same staffing levels, and 20 who anticipated a decline in client communications staff.

Table 7.3 Extent to which differential communication elements are integrated

Communication	Fully integrated	To some extent	Not yet integrated
Advertising	30	31	–
Direct marketing	16	40	3
Sales promotion	12	35	9
Public relations	13	27	17
Other*	2	8	1

Other* includes sponsorship, exhibitions, Internet/interactive, point of purchase materials, employee/internal, and package design. Only four respondents indicated that these elements varied significantly client by client though this was the expected norm. Not all firms responded.

From these results, it is difficult to substantiate the often-stated view that IMC is a client-driven effort to reduce costs or budget. It appears at best that UK agencies believe that most of their clients will maintain the status quo or do no worse than meet market growth needs.

In Table 7.4, further reactions to the Schultz definition are given. As can be seen, the vast majority of the agencies responding agreed with the definition. Thus, despite the variety of views, the definition used in this study may well be quite acceptable to the UK agencies that responded. Again, the qualitative comments raise the issue of definition versus practice of IMC.

In summary, while the definition of IMC is acceptable, there is likely a need for constant review for greater salience from both a conceptual and an operational view.

Contingent issues

The findings from the research now break into several subcategories. The first of these relate to what IMC actually is perceived to be by detailing executive beliefs and considerations about IMC. Major aspects are summarized in Table 7.5.

Most agency executives indicated that IMC is a sound idea and has significant value for client organizations, not least of which are the idea of 'one voice' and 'one brand personality', increased impact of marcoms programmes and creative ideas, and greater communications consistency. Notably, IMC offers the promise of fewer staff meetings, potentially lowers costs, and offers greater client control over marcoms programmes. From the agency side, the issues are still positive with greater perceived professional expertise offered to clients, but not necessarily a basis for effective measurement, although IMC does contribute to decreased misconceptions between multiple agencies, presumably as the client has greater control over the design of messages, media choices, and setting and evaluating stipulated objectives.

It is interesting to evaluate the responses on a decreasing mean scale. It appears that Statements 1 through 5, which have the highest agreement, primarily involve

Table 7.4 Reactions to IMC definition

Statement	Mean	SD
Definition captures IMC meaning	7.68	1.84

Positive aspects
- the vast majority of executives agreed with the definition strongly, though some felt the definition could be expanded by
  - including strategic and tactical roles of IMC
  - inclusion of internal and external audiences
  - adding 'creativity'
  - including brand experiences, informative communications, and relationship marketing
  - adding key words: 'cost-efficient' and 'synergistic'

Negative aspects
- Definition says nothing about the 'how' and the 'why'
- Doesn't really indicate who does the coordinating (client or agency)

Table 7.5 What does IMC do? (Internal beliefs and considerations)

Abbreviated statement	Mean	SD
1 Provides greater communications consistency	9.25	1.02
2 Ensures increased impact	9.03	1.59
3 Enables more impact from creative ideas	9.03	1.59
4 Increases impact of marcoms programmes	8.92	1.24
5 Underlines increased importance brand personality, one voice	8.61	1.50
6 Enables greater client control over marcoms	7.85	2.04
7 Helps eliminate misconceptions between multiple agencies	7.62	2.39
8 Provides more client control	7.49	2.51
9 Provides client with greater professional expertise	7.28	1.98
10 Necessitates fewer meetings	7.14	2.31
11 Enables client consolidation of responsibilities	7.01	2.06
12 Reduces cost of marcoms programmes	6.87	2.06
13 Provides method for effective measurement	6.55	2.83
14 Agency can provide faster solutions	6.15	2.27

the product that advertising agencies produce, i.e. various forms of advertising and communication. Those in the mid-range of agreement, Statements 6 through 9, seem to focus on how to do IMC. The final group, statements 10 through 13, all revolve around the value of IMC to the agency. So, while not necessarily being designed to do so, the mean rankings of agreement with 'Internal Beliefs and Considerations About IMC' seem to indicate the varying values agencies put on the issues that IMC raises. Perhaps this reflects, to a certain extent, what agencies believe are their primary interests which they have then related to IMC. The least agreement occurred on the statement 'Agency can provide faster solutions' which may indicate that agencies believe integration takes more time or is more difficult to develop than traditional advertising-alone programmes.

Table 7.6 offers further insight into the perceived interaction of multiple agencies. It can be seen that there is an expectation by advertising agencies that clients will increasingly make use of integrated communications approaches; generally, though, these are perceived as directed from 'one-stop' suppliers as opposed to a series of unaffiliated agencies. This suggests again that IMC is more than a passing fad, but is likely to have considerable managerial implications for marcoms planning and strategy. The further point to note is that clients in the UK, not agencies, seem to have control when it comes to designing, implementing and measuring IMC programmes. While 'one-stop' shops seem a viable client-centred approach, disagreement (mean – 4.83) was expressed with the view that over the next three years client firms would use one advertising agency and its various divisions for their marcoms needs. Thus while 'one-stop' shops may be emergent it does not necessarily follow that they will be selected for clients' promotional needs. Rather the battle for consistency, creativity, continuity, imagery, and past

Table 7.6 Perceived interaction among differential communication agencies

Abbreviated statement	Mean	SD
1 Closer interaction between different marcoms agencies	7.97	1.96
2 Client firms reliance on external marcoms personnel	7.57	1.53
3 Agencies offer broader range of services beyond advertising	7.57	1.53
4 Closer interaction between DM and other marcoms agencies	7.31	3.29
5 Closer interaction between PR and other marcoms agencies	7.06	2.46
6 Closer interaction between SP and other marcoms agencies	6.70	2.96
7 Clients to work with variety of unaffiliated agencies	5.37	2.21

DM = direct marketing, PR = public relations, SP = sales promotion

performance of advertising and other agencies' activities in these areas will likely prove a useful barometer of future agency billings.

Again, if one compares agency executive responses on a decreasing mean scale in terms of agreement, it becomes clear that agencies believe their clients expect closer interaction of all communication elements and that both services and personnel are expected to support this need (Responses 1, 2 and 3). Comparing these results in Table 7.6 to those in Table 7.3, one can see how the perceptions of integration of the various specific disciplines such as sales promotion and public relations are reflected in the actual integration which is taking place.

The drive for IMC appears to be stemming from all areas of client functions, i.e. corporate management (mean = 6.94), marketing (7.72), advertising (6.67), and sales management (6.28). Notably, marketing management led the ranks for supporting IMC initiatives, ably seconded by corporate management. This appears to bode well for the development of IMC based on the senior management support which appears to be present.

Perhaps a major factor underpinning this management support relates to budgetary or measurement considerations. Based on this study, client budgets are likely to be centrally controlled over the next three years (mean = 7.57). In relation to measurement issues agreement was expressed with the view that IMC does appear to provide a basis for more effective measurement (see Table 7.5).

Table 7.7 indicates more details of IMC measurement issues. It shows that IMC measurement is neither simple nor straightforward, in a very similar way to measuring existent measurement of effectiveness for singular aspects of marcoms.

Table 7.7 IMC measurement/evaluation issues

Abbreviated statement	Mean	SD
IMC relies on measurements similar to those already used	6.16	2.09
IMC makes evaluation of marcoms effectiveness more difficult	4.41	2.81
IMC sidesteps the issue of measuring programme effectiveness	3.49	2.25

Figure 7.1 illustrates perceptions of the effectiveness or otherwise of IMC evaluation.

As can be seen, IMC measurement and evaluation still need further work, or further dissemination of appropriate evaluation techniques. While IMC is recognized as of significant value and importance to clients and agencies alike, the fact that no clear proposal of measurement or evaluation has been developed weakens conceptual application in a global sense. It may well be that the lack of capacity to measure the impact and effect of current individually planned and implemented functional elements such as advertising or public relations or sales promotion leads these agency executives to believe that perhaps IMC offers some new or innovative solution to these ongoing questions. That seems to be the case when the qualitative results are considered.

Factors derived from the literature were evaluated to see whether they constituted barriers to the adoption of IMC as a concept or IMC in terms of a programme for client firms. Table 7.8 indicates the level of agreement on barriers to IMC programmes.

In the responses to the questions on perceived barriers to IMC programmes, the agencies tended to agree with statements which suggested that clients would have difficulty with the development of integrated programmes (Responses 3, 5, 6, 7 and 8) while at the same time, they disagreed that the development of IMC would be a problem for them (Responses 12, 13, 14 and 15). Interestingly, agency executives

Neither 'simple nor straightforward'	Provides measurement method	Evaluation of marcoms effectiveness made more difficult by IMC
• It is a simple or as complex as you wish, specialists have a vested interest in perpetuating the myth that IMC measurement is complex • There is no simple or straightforward way of measuring the individual elements either • The level playing field of sales=impact doesn't exist • Strongly agree (n = 25) • It is no different, you still measure components • We haven't really begun to understand how to do this • For marcoms with a measurable ROI, it is relatively straightforward, measuring brand value is much more difficult • PR, direct marketing, sales promotion, advertising all use different measurement devices, question is how to integrate measurement/evaluation? • It is always going to be (a) what the client wants; and (b) whether there are clear objectives which can be evaluated systematically	• No basis for this claim • Depends on discipline, analysis, sophistication of measurement, and commitment • Very underdeveloped area • Exchange rate doesn't yet exist • No, the methods are no different than at present • Still need to measure individual components • Potentially, this is the case • How? • A single multimedia, multi-discipline campaign working to a common objective will make it easier to attribute measurable results • IMC is total marcoms programme not a method of measurement; nor at this time have any claims been made for it to provide a method of measurement • Depends upon clear objectives, and coordination across the board • Yes, but which part contributes the effectiveness?	• It was difficult without IMC; it hasn't really got any easier • It is easier to track IMC programmes, but how and where do you break down the individual elements? • As before, no common exchange rate • Each element needs to be measured in its own right, the objective(s) of each campaign, its communication, and the integrated outcomes will also have to be measured • Should be no more but no less difficult • The measurement techniques will need to be designed more sensitively, but it is to the benefit of the client to know which element is contributing most strongly • It will be more difficult at first, as it is new, but it is worth the struggle • Sales is the fundamental measure – and this is much easier to relate to IMC • IMC will/should allow client companies to have a greater understanding of this total marketing and sales activity

Figure 7.1 Views of IMC measurement.

Table 7.8 Perceived barriers to IMC programmes

Abbreviated statement	Mean	SD
1 IMC programme at one agency helps bring client SBUs together	6.98	1.67
2 Integrated agencies do not have talent in all marcom areas	6.87	2.51
3 IMC means client staff have to develop new skills	6.67	2.08
4 IMC gives a few individuals too much control	6.44	2.06
5 Requires client staff to be more generalist	6.43	2.25
6 Client staff lack expertise to undertake IMC programmes	6.25	1.75
7 Client organizational structures constrain IMC development	6.09	2.34
8 Client centralization difficulties	5.23	2.40
9 Clients decide the 'what' and 'how' of IMC programmes	5.03	2.08
10 Over-dependence on single suppliers	5.00	2.51
11 Goes against client's corporate culture	4.35	2.42
12 IMC implies additional staff to manage programmes	4.21	2.17
13 IMC programmes modification difficulties	3.94	2.26
14 Increased cost	3.77	2.28
15 Provides advertising agencies with too much control	3.49	2.45

most strongly agreed that IMC programmes at one agency could help bring client SBUs together. This would seem to indicate that clients would have problems developing and implementing IMC programmes but that agencies believe they can solve these problems.

While this seems to indicate that agencies believe they can help or even drive the IMC effort, the agency executives agreed that integrated agencies do not have talent in all marcoms areas. From responses to the question, it is difficult to determine if agency personnel were referring to their own agencies or other agencies which bill themselves as integrated or capable of integration, but it does reinforce the idea that most agencies believe they are very skilled at the development of advertising but are somewhat lacking in other promotional areas.

Table 7.9 appears to resolve the question of whether IMC is simply a management fad or a reflection of a major change in the field of marketing communications. From the responses to the questions regarding marketing communications criteria, it becomes clear that the advertising agency respondents see marketplace changes which are truly reflective of substantial change. For example, those statements such as 'Changes in media buying practices', (mean 7.74, s.d. 1.4), 'Fragmentation of media markets' (mean 7.07, s.d. 2.02), 'Changing role of advertising agencies' (mean 6.60, s.d. 2.42), 'Shift in marketplace power from manufacturers to retailers' (mean 6.56, s.d.2.00), 'Ongoing revolution changing rules of marketing' (mean 6.35, s.d. 2.30) and 'Lack of "rules of marketing"' (mean 5.82, s.d. 2.18) all appear to confirm that agencies perceive or have observed substantial change in the general structure of the marketplace and their role in it. Thus, they feel a need to respond to their clients' changing needs. In fact, respondents did not disagree with any of

Table 7.9 Marketing communication criteria

Abbreviated statement	Mean	SD
1 Call for synergy among promotional tools	7.75	1.59
2 Changes in media buying practices	7.74	1.59
3 Rapid growth and development of database marketing	7.52	1.85
4 Recognition that IMC for clients equates to further growth	7.49	1.82
5 Rapid growth in IMC importance	7.32	1.74
6 Emergence of a variety of compensation methods	7.20	2.20
7 Fragmentation of media markets	7.07	2.02
8 Changing role of advertising agencies	6.60	2.42
9 Shift in marketplace power from manufacturers to retailers	6.56	2.00
10 Ongoing revolution changing rules of marketing	6.35	2.30
11 Lack of 'rules of marketing'	5.82	2.18
12 Escalating price competition resulting in more price sensitivity	5.77	1.92
13 Shift in advertising £s to sales promotion	5.58	1.92
14 Traditional advertising too expensive and not cost-effective	5.30	2.31

the 14 statements which attempted to get at this question of whether IMC is a true change or simply a management fad or folly. There appears to be some slight dissonance with regard to whether advertising is perceived as too expensive and not cost-effective, compared to the shift in advertising £s toward sales promotion. Evidently, further research is needed on both these issues.

Discussion

The empirical research confirms that IMC is developing and/or of importance within firms served by UK advertising agencies. Also, it is of importance to the agencies themselves in the way(s) they conduct their business. As might be expected in an advertising agency context, advertising is being integrated more rapidly than other marcoms functions. From this perspective IMC is not a management fad as advertising agency staff are spending 25 per cent more of their time on integrated programmes. Moreover, the trend is toward more, not less, integration. IMC is being driven by fundamental changes in the marcoms business such as the development of databases, media fragmentation, and client desire for interaction, coordination and synergy. The agencies' concern is much more on practice and facilitation rather than an understanding of how or why IMC needs to be done. Measurement of integrated communications is of crucial significance to ad agencies and measurement of IMC is more readily comprehensible now than at any time in the past.

Tables 7.1 and 7.2 clearly show that a significant amount of time and budget is being devoted to integration. Agency executives spend a substantive amount of money and time on integrated activities. Referring to internal beliefs, agencies believed that clients have to develop IMC. Unless clients demand/require an integrated programme, with all that entails, integration is unlikely to take place. Agencies believe that they can do the coordination but not necessarily all the activities within the agency – i.e. the agencies see themselves as the general contractor, a position echoed in the case vignettes. Thus while they may not have all the skills in-house, from the planning standpoint they believe they could be helpful.

Following up the previous point, agencies could well be the vehicle whereby IMC becomes the norm, but it seems doubtful that individual agencies will be granted authority to develop integrated programmes on behalf of clients, simply because of the ceding of control by clients this would entail. Despite this perceived reluctance, the future of advertising agencies may well lie in their ability to work with other marcoms agencies, provide a broader range of services, and fulfil the coordination and the evaluation function. If this is the case, it changes the agency from a tactical implementor to a strategic partner. This, of course, raises major compensation issues (Table 7.9). Agencies currently have a variety of compensation methods (7.2 ranking on the scale of agreement) and these are likely to be further diversified.

The findings from the research with UK advertising agencies are endorsed by the two case vignettes derived from advertising agencies at the end of the chapter.

SUMMARY AND CONCLUSIONS

If the cases at the end of the chapter are compared with the Orange case at the start of this chapter, several characteristics become evident. In each case, development of a clear brand positioning statement is evident and needful. Secondly, there is a close degree of convergence and interaction, a long-term relationship of trust, between clients (brand owners) and agencies. Thirdly, a consumer perspective is always taken. And, marketing departments, in one case truncated in size, needed to liaise more closely with media and message intermediaries. Thus, the overall trend is one of increased compactedness of message design, interaction and synergy. Often advertising may be used as the 'spearhead' for an integrated campaign, but presumably the lead promotional function can just as well be direct marketing or sponsorship.

Summarizing the theoretical and practical contributions, it would appear that:

1 IMC is not a management fad, but is a fundamental and marked shift in thinking and practice of marketing communications of clients and advertising agencies as reflected by agency executives.
2 IMC is being taken very seriously and is being practised by an important group of marcoms practitioners who, while they may have wished to stay in the advertising function, are diversifying, expanding, and adopting a coordinative role in the current environment.
3 The critical issue concerning IMC is that of evaluation and measurement of integrated programmes. This issue, as yet, has not been soundly addressed by advertising agencies or clients, and still remains ambiguous among writers in this area. Part of the difficulty is that traditionally advertising, sales promotion, direct marketing and the public relations disciplines have developed separate and

distinct measurement approaches – the measurement of integrated programmes which can estimate the synergy between elements is a totally new field which remains relatively undeveloped. The main approaches seem to be tracking studies, and measurements focused on attitudinal criteria.

4 The primary value that agencies see with IMC is the consistency, impact and continuity which an integrated programme provides (see case vignettes).

5 This continuity aspect is to be expected of agencies since they generally have long-term and continuing relationships with clients, whereas sales promotion, direct marketing, and public relations are often handled on a project basis so it would be expected that agencies would focus more on communication continuity than on short-term projects. However, the case evidence provided indicates that other marcom functions than advertising are seen as equally valuable as media and markets continue to demassify and smudge.

6 Public relations is that part of marketing communications which is less integrated than other marcoms activities. While the reason for this may be the public relations boundary spanning role, integrated communications seems to require a more interactive approach with the promise of greater synergy.

7 A main barrier to IMC would appear to be the lack of synergy among promotional tools. The focus in the past has been on specialization but integration calls for generalists, i.e. the ability to consolidate and bring together all the specialisms but in a single, structured, comprehensive and measurable fashion. Generalists will need not a broad overview, but a deep appreciation of all communication disciplines; and, how to perceive their interactions from two angles: 1. the organizational context; and 2. the consumer dimension. Indeed, one might view this as a systems approach to the development of marketing communications similar to the systems approaches which have been developed in manufacturing and distribution. As seen in the case vignettes, this barrier is being overcome.

IMC is a new approach to marketing communications planning being driven by technology, customers, consumers, and by organizational desire to properly allocate finite resources. IMC is still an emerging discipline and integration is like a transition between the old historical product-driven outbound marketing systems versus the new information-driven interactive consumer focussed marketplaces of the twenty-first century.

Several research issues are highlighted by this chapter. First, while IMC is growing in use and popularity, there is really no clear definition of what it is nor what it encompasses. While the definition developed by Schultz (1993) and adopted by the AMA was used, it is clear that changes in approach, the marketplace and technology demand that the concept be further defined and refined. Until it can be agreed as to what IMC is or isn't, it is difficult to build much of a theoretical base. So, while IMC appears to be much like pornography (I will know it when I see it), it leaves much to be desired in terms of scholarly and thoughtful development of the concept and approach. Much of this likely stems from the practitioner community who appear to be saying it is not as important to understand and define IMC as it is to find ways to practise it, for that is the demand of the moment.

Second, an underlying theme centres on the need to find ways to measure the impact and effect of all types of marketing communications, not just IMC. Much of this no doubt comes from the frustration of both scholars and practitioners in finding suitable and effective methods of measuring the impact of various marketing communications functional activities such as advertising, public relations and sales promotion. It appears that many of the practitioners who responded to the survey believed that IMC would or could provide a new method or approach to marketplace effectiveness measurement. So, while the riddle of functional communication activity measurement remains unsolved, hope seems to spring eternal and that hope is based on some type of IMC measurement system or approach which will provide the (or a) solution. Present levels of IMC practice and understanding do not fully provide the answers to this. In other words, this is a substantial area for development.

Finally, IMC appears to be driven by new technology and new marketplace information such as that gathered or contained in databases and other repositories. Yet, there does not seem to be any consistent methodology or approach for developing or implementing an IMC plan. While management tools such as marketing and financial plans are well developed today, there appears to be no real system, concept or approach for developing an integrated communications plan that is acceptable and useful to clients and agencies. If IMC is to grow and mature as respondents to the survey indicated it must, IMC must have its own theoretical base, i.e. this is why one develops integrated programmes, this is how one goes about it, and this is how one evaluates whether or not the integrated plan or programme is strong or weak. It is this lack of intellectual support for IMC that sorely needs addressing. There must be more to IMC than simply taking a set of functional activities and trying to make them look alike or sound alike or, the current theme, 'one sight, one sound'. It is the need for theoretical development that is key. If the theoretical base can be developed, which depends to a great extent on definitional agreement, then the issue of measurement should be possible and practical.

DISCUSSION TOPICS

1 Explain the difference between fragmentation of promotion versus the move toward integrated marketing communications.
2 Is IMC likely to be applicable to companies of specific types? Why? (Examples required.)
3 What problems, if any, do you envisage in getting UK firms to consider and use IMC?
4 'Enter a new age in advertising: respectful, not patronizing; dialogue-seeking, not monologic; responsive, not formula driven.' Critique this statement from an IMC perspective.
5 Provide at least two scenarios where you think IMC has been deployed well, and at least two scenarios where you think IMC may not be appropriate.
6 Based on other chapters in this book, why do you think it is so hard to measure, accurately, the effectiveness of an integrated campaign? What barriers, if any, stand in the way?

7 Analyse the three case vignettes from this chapter. Identify and discuss any patterns of commonality.

8 Argue for or against the case that IMC is simply 'marketing and advertising dressed up in new clothes'.

9 IMC is 'a new way of looking at the whole, or realigning communications from the customer viewpoint – a flow of information from indistinguishable sources; . . . it is all 'one thing' at least to the customer who sees or hears it' (Schultz *et al.*, 1992). Discuss.

10 'Through-the-line communications is true marketing in action. But it needs to be created and implemented by the kind of agency which is committed to the concept, is fully equipped to deliver the strategy, and will do so with integrity. Right through the line' (Mosely, Managing Director, DMS Menzies, 1995). Discuss.

CASE STUDY – INTEGRATION IN MARKETING COMMUNICATIONS – AUDI

1. What is integration in marcoms

Essentially this is seen by Audi as a means by which to transmit different, appropriate messages to different, appropriate groups of people using a single, consistent, but multi-faceted brand personality.

2. How is it used?

Everyone, both within the Audi marketing department and within the many agencies they use, has a full and equal understanding of the personality and potential of the brand. Thus, while each discipline operates with a degree of autonomy within its own area of expertise, the start point is always the same.

In the case of a new car launch, positioning for the new car is developed and agreed between the team at Bartle Bogle Hegarty (BBH) and Audi marketing. This is then communicated to the other agencies and personnel involved in the launch. This, married to a sound brand understanding, means that each discipline can operate within its own area of expertise, using the most appropriate means of communication. In this way they avoid the 'matching luggage' syndrome, and achieve meaningful integration, without compromising the effectiveness of each strand of communication.

3. Why is it used?

The need for integration in marketing communications in Audi's case stems from the fact that they are small spenders within the huge car market. They recognize that all communications need to be consistent in order to maximize effectiveness. They are aware of facing an ever-increasing proliferation of media channels to choose from. Media are fragmenting rapidly and so are their traditional target groups. Simultaneously, head count within the marketing department is being reduced, and they are forced to use an increasing number of outside agencies. It is essential, then, to integrate efforts to retain consistency.

(*Source*: Bartle, Bogle, Hegarty, 1997, used with permission.)

CASE STUDY: INTEGRATION IN MARKETING COMMUNICATIONS: TEXAS INSTRUMENTS' NOTEBOOKS

Background

Texas Instruments have differing levels of market share and awareness throughout Europe. In some countries they are market leaders but in most they were, at best, fourth or 'top of the second division' behind Toshiba, IBM and Compaq. In some markets the difference between first and second division is significant. Texas Instruments' Notebooks compare very favourably, and sometimes outperform, competitive brands.

Objectives

The company objective is to be one of the top three market players by the year 2000. The task is to create and sustain positive awareness of Texas Instruments and position them as a leading player with superior, or at least comparable, product performance benefits. This cannot be achieved without building a strong Texas Instruments Brand with appropriate positive brand values. Consequently, the objective of all integrated marcoms activity is to build a Texas Instruments Brand – relevant to the corporate customer, the individual purchaser and the channel.

Existing marcoms properties

Texas Instruments own a specific promotional and merchandisable property – 'Start Doing Extraordinary Things'. This property is rightly perceived as a true corporate and user benefit in order to achieve total customer awareness.

Target audiences

- Senior decision makers within corporates
- Users who can influence product choice
- The SoHo market (small office, home office)
- All channel elements

Advertising

Developed to accentuate and use 'Start Doing Extraordinary Things'. The advertising and execution had to pertain to the target audience's needs and aspirations. This resulted in the 'Flying Man' campaign – with the strapline 'leave the rest behind'. This purposely positioned Texas Instruments as the Notebook that gave users significant advantages over competitors – individually or corporately. Other advertisements in the series targeted other user benefits – the 'clock advertisement' with the benefit of longer battery life, and a different 'floating man' advertisement with the benefit of lightness.

Extension strategy

All direct marketing/mailing picks up the main and initial campaign theme to carry to Corporates, users, and the channel. POS material in retail outlets, together with giveaways, reinforces core brand values.

Implementation

Campaign in its entirety or as key component parts now in UK, France, Italy, Netherlands, Nordic region, Austria, Switzerland and Eastern Europe.

Evaluation

Too early to tell. Planned research planned for validation of effectiveness. However, anecdotal evidence suggests that both users and the channel have received the campaign positively and favourably – in establishing the Texas Instruments Brand.

(*Source*: Carey Howells Jeans & Spira (CHJS), 1997, used with permission.)

ACKNOWLEDGEMENTS

Grateful thanks are extended to Bartle, Bogle, Hegarty, WCRS, and CHJS for their kind permission to utilise the case vignettes.

This Chapter was first presented as a paper at the ESOMAR Seminar 'New Ways for Optimising Integrated Communication', Paris, April 1997.

Permission for using this material has been granted by the European Society for Opinion and Marketing Research (E.S.O.M.A.R.) J.J. Viottastraat 29, 1071 JP, Amsterdam.

REFERENCES

Beard, F. (1996) 'Integrated marketing communications: new role expectations and performance issues in the client–agency relationship', *Journal of Business Research*, 37(3): 207–15.

Belch, G.E. and Belch, M.A. (1995) *Introduction to Advertising and Promotion: An Integrated Marketing Communications Perspective*, 3rd edn, Chicago, IL: Irwin.

Caywood, C., Schultz, D. and Wang, P. (1991) 'Integrated Marketing Communications: A survey of national goods advertisers', unpublished report, Medill School of Journalism, Northwestern University, June, 1–42.

Constanzo, P.J. (1996) 'Teach IMC technology to future marketers', *Marketing News*, 30(2), 15 January: 4.

Crane, D. (1972) *Invisible Colleges and Social Circle: A Sociological Interpretation of Scientific Growth*, Chicago: University of Chicago Press.

Duncan, T. (1993) 'Integrated marketing? It's synergy', *Advertising Age*, 64, 8 March: 22.

Duncan, T. (1995) 'The concept and process of integrated marketing communication', *Integrated Marketing Communications Research Journal*, 1, Spring: 3–10.

Duncan, T. and Caywood, C. (1996) 'The concept, process, and evolution of integrated marketing communications', in E. Thorson, and J. Moore, (eds) *Integrated Communications: Synergy of Persuasive Voices*, Hillsdale, NJ: Erlbaum, 13–34.

Duncan, T. and Everett, S.E. (1993) 'Client perceptions of integrated marketing communications', *Journal of Advertising Research*, 33, May–June: 30–9.

Grein, A.F. and Gould, S.J. (1996) 'Globally integrated marketing communications', *Journal of Marketing Communications*, 2(3): 141–58.

Hutton, J. (1995) 'Integrated marketing communications and the evolution of marketing thought', paper presented at the American Academy of Advertising Annual Conference, March, and forthcoming in the *Journal of Business Research.*

Jackson, R. and Wang, P. (1994) Strategic Database Marketing, Lincolnwood, IL: NTC Publishing.

Journal of Marketing Communications (1996) special edition devoted to Integrated Marketing Communications, 2(3), guest edited by Don Schultz.

Junu, B.K. (1993) 'Databases open doors for retailers', *Advertising Age*, 64, 15 February: 38–39.

Keegan, W.J. (1995) *Global Marketing Management*, 5th edn, Englewood Cliffs, NJ: Prentice Hall International, 553–78.

Kitchen, P.J. (1993) 'Marketing communications renaissance', *International Journal of Advertising*, 12(4): 367–86.

Kitchen, P.J. (1994) 'The marketing communications revolution: a Leviathan unveiled?', *Marketing Intelligence and Planning*, 12(2): 19–25.

Kitchen, P.J. (1996) Quotes from unpublished letters from leading UK academics, and CEOs in UK Public Limited Companies.

Kitchen, P.J. and Moss, D.A. (1995) 'Marketing and public relations: the relationship revisited', *Journal of Marketing Communications*, 1(2): 105–19.

Kitchen, P.J. and Proctor R.A. (1991) 'The increasing importance of public relations in UK FMCG firms', *Journal of Marketing Management*, 7: 357–91.

Kitchen, P.J. and Wheeler, C. (1997) 'Issues influencing marcoms in a global context', *Journal of Marketing Communications*, 3(4): 243–59.

Kotler, P. (1972) 'A generic concept of marketing', *Journal of Marketing*, 36(2): 46–50.

Kotler, P. (1986) 'Megamarketing', *Harvard Business Review*, 64(2): 117–24.

Kotler, P. (1997) *Marketing Management*, 9th edn, Englewood Cliffs, NJ: Prentice-Hall International, 603–35.

Krugman, D.M. *et al.* (1994) *Advertising: Its Role in Modern Marketing*, 8th edn, New York, Dryden Press.

Kuhn, T.S. (1964) *The Structure of Scientific Revolutions*, Phoenix: University of Chicago Press.

Mills, C.W. (1959) *The Sociological Imagination*, New York: Oxford University Press, 31–72.

Mosely, F. (1995) 'Whose line is it anyway?', *The Drum*, Glasgow, October: 15.

Novelli, W.D. (1989–90) 'One-stop shopping: some thoughts on integrated marketing communications', *Public Relations Quarterly*, Winter: 7–8.

Nowak, G. and Phelps, J. (1994) 'The integrated marketing communications' phenomenon: an examination of its impact on advertising practices and its implications for advertising research', *Journal of Current Issues and Research in Advertising*, 16(1): 49–66.

Phelps, J. Plumley, J. and Johnson, E. (1994) 'integrated marketing communications: who is doing what?' in K.W. King (ed.) *Proceedings of the 1994 Conference of the American Academy of Advertising*, University of Georgia, Athens, GA, 143–45.

Rayport, G.F. and Sviokla, J.G. (1994) 'Managing and marketspace', *Harvard Business Review*, November/December.

Rose, P.B. (1996) 'Practitioner opinions and interests regarding IMC in selected Latin American countries', *Journal of Marketing Communications*, 2(3): 125–39.

Schultz, D.E. (1991) 'Integrated marketing communications: the status of integrated marketing communications programs in the US today', *Journal of Promotion Management*, 1(1): 37–41.

Schultz, D.E. (1993) 'Integrated marketing communications: maybe definition is in the point of view', *Marketing News*, 18 January: 17.

Schultz D.E. (1996b) 'Integrating the organization's information resources', *Marketing News*, 30(15): 7.

Schultz, D.E. (1996a) 'Is IMC finally becoming mainstream?', *Marketing News*, 30(14), 1 July: 4.

Schultz, D.E. (1994) Tannenbaum, S.I. and Lauterborn, R.F. (1992) *Integrated Marketing Communications: Pulling It Together and Making It Work*, Illinois: NTC Business Books.

Shimp, T.A. (1997) *Advertising, Sales Promotion, and Other Aspects of Integrated Marketing Communications*, 4th edn, Orlando, FL: Harcourt, Brace, Jovanovich International Edition.

Shocker, A.D., Srivastava, R.K. and Ruekert, R.W. (1994) 'Challenges and opportunities facing brand management: an introduction', *Journal of Marketing Research*, Spring: 149–57.

Sloan, J.R. (1994) 'Ad agencies should learn the facts of life', *Marketing News*, 28 February: 4.

Waterschoot, W. and Bulte, C. (1992) 'The four P classification of the marketing mix revisited', *Journal of Marketing*, 56, October: 83–93.

Wolter, L. (1993) 'Superficiality, ambiguity threatens IMC's implementation and future', *Marketing News*, 27, 13 September: 12.

Zikmund W.G. and D'Amico, M. (1996) *Marketing*, 5th edn, New York: West Publishing Company, 482–515.

8

AUDIENCE AND ENVIRONMENT: MEASUREMENT AND MEDIA

Robin Croft

CHAPTER AIMS

- to introduce some of the conventional strategies used by advertisers in trying to position products and services in consumers' perceptions
- to illustrate some of the ways in which audiences have changed over the past 20–30 years
- to appraise critically some of the conventional theories relating to audience and environment
- to explore the ways in which modern consumers appear to defy attempts at classification
- to question some of the assumptions made about the ways in which consumers *use* advertising

ILLUSTRATION

The following section deals with one of the most elusive audiences of all – the youth market. Young people are attractive to brand owners as they have comparatively high levels of disposable income and can at times be almost obsessively brand-loyal. And in this relationship-centred era, companies are also anxious to try to attract young consumers in an attempt to make *lifetime customers* of them.

Segmenting the youth market – seventies-style

In 1979 Dick Hebdige of Goldsmith's College London produced a classification of young consumers, basing his profiles on the moods, needs and desires of British youth as reflected in the fashion statements they chose to make:

- *Teddy boys* he saw as excluded and temporarily detached from the respectable working class, while still being uncompromisingly proletarian and xenophobic.
- *Mods* were lower-class dandies, obsessed with the small details of dress.
- *Skinheads* were aggressively proletarian, puritanical and chauvinist.
- *Rastas* were the most political grouping, a style that proclaimed the alienation felt by many young black Britons.

- *Punks* represented nameless housing estates, anonymous dole queues and slums, they were blank, expressionless, rootless.

Generation X

Douglas Coupland's novel *Generation X* profiled a section of educated young Americans in the late 1980s. They opted out of well-paid, high-pressure working lives and into a transitory, apparently aimless existence. They consciously chose short-term, undemanding 'McJobs' while rejecting the urban consumer lifestyle. Tellingly, one chapter is titled 'I am not a target market', another 'Shopping is not creating'. Stephen Brown (1995), a leading authority on retailing and marketing, points out 'So accurate . . . is Coupland's summation of America's 25–35-year-old blank generation, those aware of and hostile to the machinations of marketing, that marketing practitioners and researchers now employ the term "Generation X" to describe this particular cohort of consumers.'

Nineties-style segmentation

Research by advertising agency Cowan Kemsley Taylor in 1993 said that young people were less materialistic, more creative and more media-literate than five years previously. Claiming that a million young people were going to licensed raves each week, the research claimed that their frame of reference had changed: according to Charlie Sampson, a director at the agency, 'They talk much more about how they feel about something rather than how it looks. They are less overtly image-conscious than they were four or five years ago'.

ROAR (Right of Admission Reserved) was a major survey of thousands of young people interviewed between August 1995 and January 1996, dealing with their consumption hates, jobs, incomes, loves, hates, hopes and dreams. It was commissioned by advertising agency BMP DDB Needham, and proposed the following groupings:

- *Bill and Ted* – passions in life: music, music and music. When they were not playing their collection of vinyl LPs, they were thinking up weird names for their newly formed bands.
- *Conservative careerists* – although they probably wouldn't vote Tory, their views were less liberal than many of their peers.
- *Moral fibres* – the members of this little group knew exactly what course they would do at university, and at what age they would get married. They excelled at their studies, were good at games and said 'no' to drugs.
- *Blairites* – they were proud to be politically correct and had no difficulty in reconciling their left-wing views with their love of cash. They were ambitious, materialistic and smiled all the time.
- *New modernists* – this group would rather be artistic than earn a lot of money. They stood up for their principles. In their early twenties, they were either at university or had just graduated. They were ambitious, creative and articulate, and picked up on new trends quickly.

- *Corporate clubbers* – young, free and single, living for the weekend, and were usually to be found at dawn in the Ministry of Sound.
- *Adolescent angst* – those who fell into this group were having a hard time of adolescence, even though many of them were in their twenties. They had spots, problems with the opposite sex, and really bad taste in everything.

> *Sources*: Rhys Williams (1993) 'Switched-on advertisers ready for the rave', *The Independent on Sunday,* 25 April, p. 8; Dick Hebdige (1979) *Subculture: The Meaning of Style,* London: Methuen; Armstrong, S. (1996) 'Catch 'em young', *The Sunday Times,* 12 May, Culture supplement p. 12; Douglas Coupland, (1991) *Generation X,* London: Abacus; Stephen Brown, (1995) *Postmodern Marketing,* London: International Thomson Business Press.

INTRODUCTION

From an audience and environmental context, messages and media choice, particularly concerning advertisements, appear deceptively simple. For example, target markets are segmented according to straightforward criteria – social, demographic, lifestyle and so on – and advertising is used persuasively in the final, positioning stage, creating and sustaining the competitive advantages of rival brands. Audiences are homogeneous, clearly defined: new technology and media enable these audiences to be reached more effectively than ever before. In other words, a straightforward process.

It can come as something of a shock, therefore despite Crosier's comments in Chapter 12, to find Stephen Brown's (1995) semi-apocalyptic descriptions of the environment in which marketing communications exists: citing the work some of the leading *postmodernists* of the age, Brown talks of a society characterized by

> a three-minute soundbite culture of bored, channel-hopping, MTV-watching couch potatoes; a congeries of restless, cynical, world-weary, self-obsessed hedonists demanding instant gratification and ever-escalating doses of stimulation; a 'moronic inferno of narcissists cretinized by television' for whom literacy and mathematical acumen are less important than an ability to set the video recorder and familiarity with the intricacies of the latest soap opera or computer game.
>
> (Brown, 1995: 80, citing Lasch, 1979; Bloom, 1987; Callinicos, 1989)

The advertising business, seemingly, is unperturbed: billings and margins are strong, and in the trade press Winston Fletcher (1996) robustly defends his industry and explodes a number of popular 'myths'. But there is underlying disquiet. Rapp and Collins (1994) suggest that 'the traditional methods . . . simply aren't working any more'. Significantly, a study of 'advertising avoidance' by agency Lowe Howard-Spink was entitled 'Advertising isn't working' (Archer, 1996b). Privately, many in the industry will admit to this and are uneasy at the way in which they see clients being cajoled into spending ever-increasing amounts on inappropriate *above-the-line* campaigns. Reporting the findings of a research project jointly financed by the

113

Institute of Practitioners in Advertising and accountants KPMG, *The Economist* (1996) observes 'Advertising remains woefully hit-or-miss.'

But one thing which advertising has always done effectively is to promote itself. As a result, the whole area is characterized by contradiction and confusion, and many writers of mainstream marketing communications texts have done little more than recycle ideas which are manifestly inappropriate at the end of the twentieth century. This chapter looks at some of the common treatments of the notion of audiences and environment, and invites critical re-examination. All is not as it seems.

THE AUDIENCE IN MARKETING COMMUNICATIONS

Market segmentation, targeting and positioning are the three crucial elements in strategic marketing management. The underlying philosophy is that it generally makes poor commercial sense to market goods or services in an undifferentiated way to a mass market. Instead, the key to profitability is tailoring offerings to particular needs and wants of certain groups. Marketing communications has a key role to play in this process, in particular in the third and final stage of *positioning*, where attempts are made to describe offerings in such a way that they come to be endowed, in the minds of target markets, with distinctive properties in relation to competitors.

In studying the evolution of modern marketing, the advertising business was one of the first marketing functions to employ the principles of market segmentation. Initially it used some of the crude demographic variables set out in Table 8.1.

But the two main demographic bases used by advertisers have become steadily less relevant as time has moved on. When age-based segmentation was first tried, the

Table 8.1 Audience demographics

The age groups normally used for advertising segmentation are:

- up to 15
- 15–24
- 24–35
- 35–55
- 55+ . . .

The other means of identification used in advertising is 'social grade'. This is a classification based on the occupation of the head of the household, and it indicates the household's spending power. The table below shows the special grades, the occupation to which they refer, and the approximate proportions of each grade in the total UK population:

A   Higher managerial, administrative and professional (3.0%)

B   Intermediate managerial, administrative and professional (19.3%)

C1   Supervisory/clerical and junior managerial, administrative and professional (27.1%)

C2   Skilled manual (22.5%)

D   Semi-skilled and unskilled manual (16.4%)

E   Casual labourers, state pensioners and the unemployed (11.7%)

(*Source*: Advertising Association, Student Briefing No 6, September 1996)

under-18s as a 'market' scarcely existed at all. Now it forms a massive segment in its own right, with a vast amount of spending power: young people also exert a major influence on other purchases in the home. This whole area is covered in more detail later in this chapter.

Similarly, socio-economic segmentation variables, as used by advertisers traditionally, are based on family-centred notions of households – yet the concepts of 'family' and 'household' have both changed fundamentally over the past 25 years. Even simple gender-based demographic segmentation has had to change: historically, advertisers were aware of the critical importance of addressing women – in their role as 'housewives' they had the major say in the purchase of staple *FMCGs* in the home. Now, as seen later in this chapter, women are increasingly targeted in their own right.

Old certainties in advertising are being eroded, as consumers and audiences continue to change and to defy understanding. The IPA, advertising's professional association, talks wryly of 'the spectre of media fragmentation leading to the antithesis of the homogeneous, tidy audiences, traditionally loved by advertisers'. It is an inescapable fact, though, that one of the main features of end-of-century marketing is fragmentation – of audiences, markets and media.

FRAGMENTATION OF FAMILY GROUPINGS

The socio-economic classifications used by advertisers were based originally on a notion of stable family living, centred on the household 'head' – invariably the bread-winning father – whose economic activity was used as the classification determinant. This whole notion, by the end of the 1990s, is increasingly questionable, and although advertisers no longer portray the clichéd versions of family life, which they did as recently as the 1970s, the notion of the nuclear family still affects the segmentation variables used.

Divorce and family breakdown have been one of the major contributors to the changing family landscape: around one-third of marriages in Britain end in divorce (the highest in Europe), and people are now starting to be comfortable settling into relationship patterns which would have been unthinkable in the 1960s (Wynne-Jones, 1997). Official government reports observe that nearly 28 per cent of all households contain just one person. The popular image of the family (one man, one woman and two children) accounted for just 10 per cent of the total. The future, though, appears more apocalyptic than ever:

> Less than half the adult population will be married in 20 years' time . . . more than one in 3 households will comprise one person . . . about 29% will be single, 13 per cent divorced and 9 per cent widowed . . . only 42% of households will comprise a married couple by 2016, compared with 71 per cent in 1971. There will be 8.5 million one-person households, compared to an estimated 5.9 million last year.
>
> (Brindle, 1997 based on *Social Trends* 27, HMSO)

Similarly, the whole concept of a classification based on a 'head-of-household' is now dubious (Lambert, 1993). Many families now have dual incomes, just as large-scale long-term male unemployment is now being recognized as a fact of life. With changing working patterns and the end of the job-for-life culture, more homes than ever are likely to have one or more partners out of work, if only short term. How relevant is the 'head-of-household' classification when women have taken most of the new jobs created in developed western economies, and when most of these have been part-time?

Perhaps as a consequence, that old staple of TV commercials – the family meal – has been replaced by the TV dinner: more than half of us now eat in front of the television (see Table 8.2). Even here, though, old certainties have gone: in the 1960s, 1970s and early 1980s the TV was the focal point of the home, and advertisers could rely on it for appealing to family groups. Now mass ownership is such that many homes have three TV sets or more, and increasingly people are viewing TV on their own.

But at the same time a new phenomenon of social viewing has grown up: young people, in particular, are starting to group together to watch particular favourites, especially TV soap operas and sports specials. The growth of social TV watching has been stimulated by the increasing incidence of satellite TV installations in pubs and clubs; but significantly, Henley Centre's researchers have noted that 50 per cent of people who enjoy televised pub sport could actually view it at home.

SOCIAL FRAGMENTATION

The self-styled 'futurologist' Faith Popcorn (1991) described the social isolationism that was a feature of the 1970s as 'cocooning' – where the family was the critical audience unit, tight-knit against the forces of the outside world. This has given way in the 1990s to 'socialized cocooning' where consumers group together in a phenomenon termed 'huddling and cuddling' – where the unit has been broadened to include a circle of like-minded friends and acquaintances. But, far from imitating neighbours, many consumers now display new individualism, a desire to 'keep away from the Joneses' (Brown 1995).

Table 8.2 The television society

- In the 15 years to 1997, 55 million televisions have been sold in the UK.
- 99% of homes now have televisions.
- In the early 1980s only one-third of households had more than one TV. Now on average there are 2.2 per household.
- There were an estimated 700,000 televisions sold in the UK during the 1997 Christmas shopping period alone.
- New house designs in the UK now typically feature three built-in TV aerial points – in the living room, kitchen and main bedroom.
- The family meal around the table is becoming a thing of the past: now half of us gather round the TV to eat our evening meal.
- In the UK we watch on average 3.76 hours of television per day: we spend more time on television than on any other leisure activity.

Based on *The Remote Controllers*, Channel 4 TV, 29 December 1997

As Waldrup (1994) observes, 'People are identifying themselves in smaller and smaller units', but these units are increasingly less likely to be family ones. 'People are putting walls around themselves . . . We've moved away from big mass audiences.' Just as audiences have fragmented into ever smaller and less accessible segments, so the number of offerings in existing product categories has proliferated: in 1950 the average Sainsbury store stocked 550 product lines; in 1997 an average superstore carries over 20 000 different products (McCann, 1997).

THE YOUTH MARKET

One of the most telling portrayals of the phenomenon of social fragmentation of the 1990s was Douglas Coupland's novel *Generation X*, referred to at the start of this chapter. The term 'Generation X' is commonly mis-applied by advertisers and media commentators to the youth market as a whole, something perhaps attributable to the huge cult following which Coupland's novel has achieved. But Generation X, as the book's sleeve notes point out, is now into its late twenties and thirties: its experiences are shaped by 'divorce, Watergate and Three Mile Island, and scarred by the 80s fall-out of yuppies, recession, crack and Ronald Reagan'.

The youth market is different again – far larger and more fragmented. The first real 'youth market' was the American 'baby boomers' – born just after World War II – who were identified as important consumers in their own right as they reached their teens in the early 1960s. The huge purchasing power of this group meant that it has become the target of consumer goods manufacturers and their advertisers ever since.

As witnessed at the start of the chapter, the youth market has been the subject of survey after survey. Advertisers are desperate to reach youth, not only because of their high levels of discretionary spending power, but because they hope to be able to influence purchasing patterns and brand preferences in later life. Youth, though, like Generation X, is a product of its environment: attitudes and beliefs are difficult to identify, track and (above all) influence. As one advertiser warned:

> If there is one thing that all the youth researchers polled agreed on, it is that young people are disillusioned, cynical, unsure of the future and living in a culture that moves faster and becomes more confusing every day. But the last thing they want is to face ceaseless attempts to define their world for them.
>
> (Armstrong, 1996)

The implications for advertising are that young people are notoriously sceptical as consumers. This is not a new phenomenon, though: work published by Robertson and Rossiter in 1974 suggested that children, by the ages of just 9 or 10, had developed a '"cognitive defense" against advertising persuasion, which is reflected in a more skeptical, less accepting reception of television commercials'. More recent research (Boush, *et al.*, 1994) reinforces the messages from the 1970s. More worrying for advertisers, perhaps, is the evidence that this mistrust continues throughout adulthood (Calfee and Ringold, 1994; Goldberg and Hartwick, 1990).

Clearly, today's youth, brought up on television, video and computer games, *uses* advertising quite differently to previous generations. According to the Futures director of one of London's leading advertising agencies, they are 'connoisseurs rather than mere recipients of communications'. Pointedly, though, he goes on to warn, 'If it's bollocks – they spot it instantly. Get it right, however, and they keep coming back for more.' (cited by Carter, 1997b).

How is the youth market developing? Is it as portrayed by ROAR at the start of this chapter, or are young people rediscovering community values? Educationalists in the US are claiming that:

> Interviews with undergraduates in America show that the Me Generation is ancient history and the notorious Generation X is fading fast. In its place is the We Generation and these young people are driven not by money or status but by idealism and the desire to give something back.
>
> (Treneman, 1997)

According to this view, pointing to the increasing numbers of students involved in community work and enrolling in teacher training courses, altruism is on the increase – like the youth generations of the 1960s and early 1970s, there is a belief that they can make a difference. And the new generation is even prepared to adopt some of the values of Generation X – opting out of the acquisitive, materialistic, self-interested rat-race.

WOMEN AND ADVERTISING

As we have seen, advertising traditionally targeted women in their capacity as notional 'housewives', just as their menfolk were 'heads of household'. Yet it is questionable whether such a stereotypical situation ever existed: back in 1971 Betty Friedan wrote how her research into the notion of the 'contented housewife' discovered that this type of person was a rarity, almost a myth.

As the British Social Attitudes report makes clear, 'the single long-term trend probably most responsible for changing the roles of men and women is the marked increase in women in the labour market' (cited in Lambert, 1993). Advertisers in the 1990s have woken up to the fact that women need to be understood better – not least because they now have considerable financial muscle in their own right, and they are in the majority in any case: 'The existence of high-earning, economically powerful women will register more strongly in the minds of manufacturers, advertisers and employers. Their views will be taken into account.'

But advertising still tends to define women by their personalities and their feelings, rather than by their roles (Wardle, 1995). And even now the industry is accused of demonstrating its male dominance in its products, moving from one outdated set of stereotypes to what Clifton (1995) calls a 'tyranny of typologies'. Advertisers' failure to understand and keep apace of the changes in which women live their lives is matched by the ways in which they fail to be participative with their female audiences.

Advertisers have been attempting to establish what women want: Wardle (1995) cites the findings of Saatchi & Saatchi's research to illustrate what women would like to see in advertising: ads which build female self-esteem, which reflect a female world view, and so on. Meanwhile, Ogilvy & Mather's research confirms that social change is destroying traditional segmentation and is making domestic life and the roles that women play individual and varied. As Le Boutiller (1995) puts it:

> the multidimensional sense of 'me' within women, [is] coloured by their previous experiences, and that is always there, however much it is currently suppressed . . . the key to targeting women successfully in communication terms is to access the 'me' within them that best reflects their relationship with the brand and the medium in question.'
>
> (cited in IPA Marketing Appraisal, Bulletin 561, February 1996)

AUDIENCE POWER

This discussion was prefaced by a consideration of the role of advertising in the key strategic tasks of segmentation, targeting and positioning. But marketers and their advertisers need to be clear about the critical difference in emphasis between the terms *target market* and *audience:* confusingly, the terms are often used interchangeably. The term *audience* is probably more helpful in marketing communications – partly because advertising is regularly *consumed* by people not in a specific target market, and partly because people appear to use advertising more in the way they would view entertainment than as information.

Related to this is the fact that marketing is now a mature phenomenon – a whole generation has now grown up with saturation exposure to TV advertising, taking advertising clutter (see Table 8.3) as a fact of life. Consumers have evolved strategies for coping with the ever-increasing amounts of marketing which are being pushed so vigorously. Many have become sceptical, antagonistic or worse. And although advertisers seek to understand the issues, advertising itself is a part of problem.

NOISE AND CLUTTER IN ADVERTISING

Advertising clutter is something which is regularly discussed, both by practitioners and theorists. Examples of clutter abound (see Table 8.3) although few authors bother to define the term. Perhaps the most common treatment of clutter involves discussing it in terms of *noise* in the communications process. Shimp (1993) talks of a sharing relationship between the sender and the receiver, and noise is referred to as 'extraneous and distracting stimuli that interfere with reception of a message in its pure and original form'. Theoretically, clutter is directly related to noise, in that the sheer proliferation of advertising messages reduces the impact of individual advertisements, by interfering with their reception and degrading the process of decoding the messages.

In practice, though, it can be argued that the concept of *noise* is unhelpful in any case. The traditional marketing communication model (Figure 8.1) was developed from Schramm's (1955) basic communications model, and adapted by Shannon and Weaver (1962) and Kotler (1991). The original model was designed to explain the flow patterns of telecommunications, how messages are transmitted by the sender, how they are translated by the receiver, and how interference can affect the quality and clarity of the message.

Table 8.3 Advertising clutter

- The average person will see 250 television advertisements per week, 350 poster sites and 400 press ads per week. Young people will see around 140 000 different ads between the ages of four and 18. The average British commuter sees 80 to 100 commercial messages between getting up and reaching their office each day.

- Advertising on eggs, in pub toilets or on petrol pump nozzles means that each day we are exposed to 1 300 commercial messages. Ads are to be found on fast-food take-away cartons. Radion ads on bus tickets were impregnated with a synthetic scent which smelled of freshly laundered washing.

- In total there are 11 000 television adverts broadcast every day in 1997, compared to 1987 when there were 500 shown a day. The British are being bombarded by so much commercial information that one-third of the population is now actively trying to avoid advertising.

- A study by agency Lowe Howard-Spink claimed that as much as £465 million spent on advertising in 1995 may have been wasted because of 'advertising avoidance': 44 per cent of us are zapping TV commercials, 56 per cent snubbing magazine ads, and 54 per cent ignoring posters.

- London and some other British cities allow advertising on taxi cabs. Advertisers can expect to pay between £7,000 and £8,000 for a cab painted out in their livery. Most of London's 17 000 taxicabs carry some advertising.

- So-called 'ambient ads' appear in places where perhaps you would least expect them. For example, during summer 1997 First Direct bank bought space on the barriers of certain car parks, presenting drivers with the message 'Banking without barriers 24 hours a day'.

- There is no advertising on the BBC, or is there? Both BBC radio and TV regularly promote BBC products – videos, cassettes, spin-off magazines and other merchandise. The BBC paid around £2 million for the acclaimed promotional video 'Perfect Day'.

- During a live international rugby match BSkyB viewers in the UK were treated to ads from a 'virtual hoarding' apparently at the ground in Sydney; viewers in other countries were spared the treatment – the ads were inserted digitally by the broadcaster for UK audiences only. Portuguese football fans, meanwhile, found the words 'Black & Decker' appearing in the penalty areas during a televised match between Benfica and Standard Liege.

Sources: Meg Carter 'Youth advertising? Just cool it', *The Independent*, 3 March 1997; Henley Centre, Media Futures Report, and Western Media (cited in McCann, P. 'Britons shun advertising overkill', *The Independent*, 18 October 1997, 2); Belinda Archer, 'Why consumers are switching off', *The Times*, 30 October 1996, 22; Nigel Cope, 'Black cabs make the switch to the colour of money', *The Independent*, 17 January 1994, Business & City, 29; Meg Carter, 'Zap! That's another £1 million down the tube', *The Independent*, 12 May 1993, Media Supplement, 17; Dave Hill, 'It's a mad, mad, ad world', *The Observer*, 28 December 1997, business supplement, 4.

Despite the ongoing presence of clutter, marcoms models can be a useful way to conceptualize the marketing communications process, but it can also deceive through over-simplicity. For example, different consumers decode advertising messages *differently* without the operation of extraneous *noise* factors. In his fascinating reflections of a whole career in advertising, David Ogilvy (1983) quotes the figure of 25 per cent of audiences misinterpreting typical advertisements, with some commercials being misunderstood by as many as 40 per cent of viewers.

A range of complex psychological and physiological factors affect the way consumers interpret all external stimuli, and it would seem to be a gross over-simplification to label the entire range as *noise*. While it it known, for example, that the human brain is able to isolate and block out repetitive sounds, what scientists term *habituation* is the process whereby people living near busy roads or airports no longer 'hear' what others would regard as intrusive, although they do notice silence. But when considering the fact that many shop assistants report that they are not even aware of the in-store radio or constant-running video demonstration units, there is a concern about whether repetitive advertising is received and decoded at all.

Just as it is perhaps over-simplistic to talk of *noise* in the communications process, perhaps the term *clutter* is a subjective one. Sheffield University's Professor of Journalism, Barry Gunter, points out that there is a vast array of content available to young people through visual, auditory and text media – often simultaneously: but whereas 'children and teenagers have these days learned to cope . . . older people find it a jungle.' (cited by Kudos, 1997). Channel 4's head of presentation talks of the station's efforts to reduce clutter but stresses that 'Television punctuation has changed immeasurably. . . Younger viewers especially can take in information more quickly, and lose interest more quickly' (cited in Carter, 1993). And Winston Fletcher (1996), one of the advertising industry's *enfants terribles*, is prepared to acknowledge the challenge posed by the increasingly sophisticated video-game-literate consumer, while insisting that clutter is not a factor.

On the other hand, Boutie (1994) maintains that advertising *is* cluttering the minds of consumers with useless information and as a result is causing brands to lose their function. Industry figures regularly voice their concern about 'audience fatigue', particularly where TV and radio companies bombard audiences with their own and their sponsors' promotional materials as well as the advertising. Speaking at an international industry conference in 1993, one said: 'Clutter in the ad breaks is costing us money and it could be damaging the effectiveness of the medium . . . The whole issue of whether the audience watches the commercials has been skilfully side-stepped by broadcasters.' (cited in Carter, 1993).

Perhaps, though, this is too extreme a view, and consumers, without deliberately avoiding ads, are actually unaware of much of the advertising around them; in other

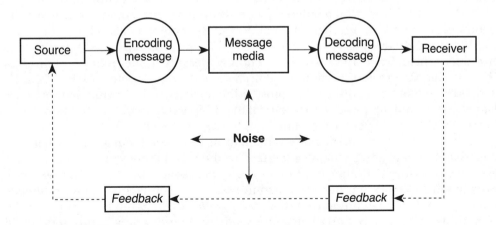

Figure 8.1 Simple communication model.

121

words, advertising is part of the landscape, similar to a form of moving wallpaper if over-exposure occurs. Observations such as Waldrup's (1994), that customers are 'bombarded with seemingly pointless messages', may therefore miss the point. It is a powerful argument, though, and one reinforced by Kitchen (1994), who warned that the proliferation of marketing communications risks becoming a new form of pollution, potentially damaging to consumers and society.

What is certain is that often there is a significant gap between intended meanings advertisers seek to convey and received meanings/decodings/interpretations made by audiences. If this is happening to any great extent, it could clearly be undermining the positioning strategies of a range of products and services. But conventional advertising research, being largely quantitative, tends to ignore *meaning* or interpretation and focus instead on accurate brand *recall* which is not the same thing at all. Work by Tavassoli *et al.* (1995) suggests that TV commercials placed during high-involvement programmes (such as major sporting events) can cause irritation among enthusiasts and actually be counter-productive in branding terms. Yet these same advertisements often score highly in recall tests.

The whole decoding process is far more complex than many advertisers are prepared to admit. Recent research by clinical psychologists (rather than advertisers themselves) has been studying implicit memory of advertising, and suggests that advertising effects can be strong where there is only average or limited brand recognition (Perfect and Heatherley, 1996). Brand personalities may be ingrained more strongly or weakly in audiences than the advertising industry's methodologies allow for.

CUSTOMIZATION AND CONTROL

The conventional communications model (Figure 8.1) depicts audiences or consumers in very much a passive role, decoding material pushed at them by advertisers. But audiences no longer are passive, and modern consumers in particular are prone to customize and control their own consumption of advertising. One of the critical developments in this process was the introduction of the remote control, first for TV and then video cassette recorders. The remote control enables the audience to *zap* to another channel during the commercials, while consumers can *zip* through the ads in pre-recorded videotapes. Shimp (1993) refers to a *Newsweek* article from 1988 which facetiously described the remote control as representing the greatest threat to capitalism since the development of Marxism. TV and video remote controls are the most visible examples, but manufacturers have launched equivalent devices for controlling hi-fi equipment in the home and instruments for in-car entertainment.

Audiences are often particularly vehement in their condemnation of what they regard as irritating ads, perhaps influenced by the fact that they often feel as if they are 'forced' to listen because at times they feel 'imprisoned' in a car or their place of work, unable to block out this unwanted intrusion. Earlier in this chapter reference was made to the research reported by Tavassoli *et al.* (1995) about how 'intrusive' TV advertising can actually impact negatively on the brand: many consumers would argue that the same applies to irritating radio commercials.

The importance of the remote control has been recognized by advertisers, programme makers and TV networks alike: with consumers in immediate control of their viewing, these organizations need to collaborate effectively to ensure that audiences are not lost to one party through the perceived deficiencies of another. The process has been recognized by manufacturers too, with electronics giant Phillips maintaining that 'Zapping has stimulated . . . this appetite of being in control of everything and not losing anything. . . zapping is the first step of personalizing the content of TV.' According to this view, the positive side is that there is a 'great opportunity of personalized entertainment of information media . . . the individual feels less manoeuvred, less under the power of an invisible power, more in control' (Stefano Marzano, Phillips Design, cited by Kudos). This implicit feeling of being in control was also identified as one of the emotional triggers in the successful penetration of TV-based home shopping channels (Dean *et al.*, 1997).

Television is a key area for consumer control:

> The BBC is piloting an interactive health and fitness programme in which you key in your weight, height, age and sex . . . Interactive digital TV . . . will increase the possibilities of getting involved and not just passively watching . . . in the case of the BBC's award-winning Science Zone Interactive, watching children could even recut the programme as they watch.
>
> (Karpf 1997)

Customization technology, it is claimed, is also finding its way into advertising, with the potential (according to industry *guru* Adam Lury) to 'shift the balance of power between producer and consumer, the latter no longer confined to the former's agenda. "There will be an opportunity to say what information you want about a product"' (cited by Karpf, 1997). This phenomenon is part of a new type of 'push' technology in hybrid TV-based systems, which will increasingly take the place of the 'pull' technology of the Internet. Where once we browsed and searched for the material we wanted, pulling it down to us, now only tailored information will be pushed at us, pre-sifted on our behalf, Lury maintains. In the feature of fragmented audiences, as a leading commentator notes, the effect of remote controls and new customization technology 'marks another stage in the transition from public to private . . . Come the millennium will there be no such thing as society, only the customised consumer?' (Karpf 1997).

THE SCEPTICAL CONSUMER

A major impact on advertising decoding comes from the fact that modern consumers consider that advertising is inherently untrustworthy. It is certain that the purpose of advertising is persuasion (Friestad and Wright, 1994) and as a result many have become sceptical of its methods and approaches (Boush, *et al.*, 1994).

Although earlier in this chapter it was observed that advertising was a part of the problem, it must be emphasized that it is not the only feature; as consumers, we live in an increasingly cynical age (Treneman, 1997), where there seems to be a marked loss of faith in the very institutions which [ostensibly] purport to govern lives – the police, the legal system, parliament, the press. Research carried out by the influential Henley Centre noted that 'consumers are becoming more and more cynical and distrusting of every corporate body and communication with whom they come in to contact' (Culligan, 1995; Griffith, 1997). A survey by advertising agency Ogilvy & Mather found that trust in some of Britain's major advertisers – British Gas, British Airways and Shell, for example – had fallen sharply over the early 1990s (Archer, 1996a); however, this is not necessarily attributable to advertising as Marks & Spencer, a comparatively small spender, had also suffered during the same period.

Consumer distrust appears to be extending from advertising to the traditional stalwarts of marketing campaigns, celebrity endorsers (Miller, 1994; Teather, 1995), although some studies appear to suggest that in economic terms, at least, they remain of value (Agrawal and Kamakura, 1995; Sanders, 1995). And as Waldrup (1994) observes, 'when consumers lose respect for media messages, ads lose credibility'. No longer is the public made up of 'passive and uninformed consumers'. The market is characterized by the 'adversarial consumer' with an 'adversarial mindset'.

THE NEED TO BE ENTERTAINED

This hostile mentality has probably been evolving in modern consumers over the past 50 years. It can be argued that to a large extent, marketing in general, and advertising in particular, is responsible for this evolution: the whole thrust of modern marketing has been to assure customers that they are *always* right (Iacobucci *et al*, 1994), while at the same time financing the proliferation of advertising messages outlined in Table 8.3. The audience feels omnipotent. As argued earlier, the conventional communication model (Figure 8.1) presupposes a largely passive audience, whereas in fact consumers are often highly involved and vocal in their consumption of advertising.

Potentially hostile consumers, armed with the ubiquitous remote control and soon multimedia and technological alternatives, no longer have to accept meekly what programmers and advertisers push out at them. The proliferation of communications channels has meant that programmers have had to redouble their efforts to attract and to keep audiences: as one TV scheduler put it, 'You have to make sure the people don't get bored and slip away . . . efforts are made during and between programmes to *invite* people to stay' (quoted by Kudos, 1997, our italics). Yet strangely, these very 'efforts' during and between programmes are often described in conventional advertising texts as 'noise' and industry figures are quick to label them as such; they point out that zapping is often triggered by poor programming. The TV industry, though, can counter with figures which show how ITV's peak-time audiences can fall by up to 18 per cent between the end of a programme and the commercial break (Carter, 1993). Satellite channel UK Gold allows only one commercial break in the middle of programmes in order to keep viewers, and Carlton is said to scrutinize the 'affinity' of the advertisements with the programmes themselves for the same reason.

Both advertisers and programmers now have a common purpose: indifferent or irritating advertising content can undermine a channel's carefully planned audience strategy by having viewers or listeners reaching for the remote control. A leading copywriter puts it like this:

> Advertisers and viewers have grown collaborative over the years. 'We know what you're up to,' said a man in research. 'Just don't patronise us.' In other words entertain us, treat us intelligently and we will allow charming, relevant, witty images to become part of your product.
>
> (Brignull,1996).

This message has been received and understood by many advertisers: entertainment is now largely what advertising is about – rather than being the dull, commercial filling in TV programmes or newspapers, ads can be newsworthy in themselves, whole TV series can be built around them, ads are interesting and collectable.

ADVERTISING AS INFORMATION

Advertisers have historically sought to define advertising in terms of marketing strategy and consumer response: the consumer *decoding* element has therefore to be understood in the context of the *positioning* element in an overall strategic plan. To this end, marketers have proposed a number of models of the advertising task in relation to consumer choice. Three so-called hierarchy of effects models are shown in Figure 8.2, and are commonplace in traditional treatments of advertising.

Each model is designed to explain in simple terms how advertising works, and to focus the attention of those who produce advertising on the strategic elements in the process. A further influential model, Roger's Product Adoption Model, is considered tangentially in Chapter 12. In this type of framework, the consumer is treated as a rational individual, using advertising as a source of information about products, services, objects, people, and possible outcomes in the 'real world'. Indeed, in research, consumers still tend to report that they use advertising to provide them with valuable information about products and services (Calfee and Ringold, 1994).

The advertising industry, while it now makes superb entertainment (see Table 8.4 below), still maintains that the old certainties hold good: a former leading J. Walter Thompson copywriter puts it thus: 'Advertisements work on two levels. First, they inform: they familiarise, remind and spread news' (*The Economist*, 1996).

Advertising appears both explicitly and implicitly in numerous renowned models of consumer buying behaviour, particularly in situations of extensive problem solving, where the strategic importance of personal or corporate purchases causes the buyer to seek out large amounts of data with which to come to a decision (for example, Howard and Sheth, 1969). However, the whole empirical basis of general models of consumer behaviour has been regularly called into question, for example by Foxall (1984). Similarly, it has been argued for more than 30 years that hierarchy models of advertising effects are flawed as few consumers actually pass through the stages listed; many consumers, for example, may actually purchase a product first and then use advertising later to convince themselves about its worth (Palda, 1966).

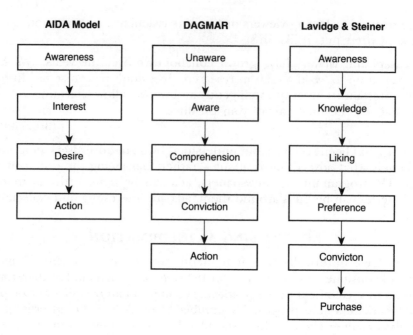

Figure 8.2 Hierarchy of Effects models. The origins of the AIDA model are obscure, but it was in use in advertising prior to World War II. DAGMAR is the acronym for defining advertising goals for measured advertising results, and was developed by Colley in 1961 and 1983; see Chapter 16.

ADVERTISING AS ENTERTAINMENT

As seen, consumers increasingly *use* advertising in quite different ways to those envisaged by advertisers. Advertisers are beginning to realize that they are dealing with *audiences* rather than *markets*. Here the emphasis in understanding the phenomenon is discovering that viewers and readers are now tending only to make the effort for advertising which entertains, amuses or intrigues them. So advertisers are setting out more to launch campaigns that appear quite deliberately to set out to shock indifferent audiences into noticing them, to get their advertisements talked about (Trapp 1993).

Advertising itself has become as interesting as the programmes or articles it helps to finance. As portrayed in Table 8.4, advertising's creations often have lives of their own outside the commercials. At election times, national press and TV turn out to witness the launch of new poster campaigns, just as they report on controversial new campaigns from Benetton or Club 18–30. Media speculation dominates the new celebrity endorsements by the stars of sport or popular music, and advertisers – mindful of the need for fully integrated marketing communications – build this into their strategies. The ads themselves are often talked about more than the products or services they promote (*The Independent*, 1994). Advertisements now promote advertisements: for example, SEGA was reported to have spent somewhere between £10 million and £15 million on the launch of the Mega CD games system, with a whole series of ads building up the launch of the actual commercial: their aim was 'to make the brand's name bigger than the product itself' (Carter, 1993).

Launching a new video for the Christmas 1996 market – a 72-minute compilation of 'classic' TV advertisements – a producer commented, 'A lot of people enjoy adverts more than they enjoy the programmes these days.' Another video, featuring the world's so-called sexiest ads, was launched in the same year. Industry journal *Campaign*'s editorial director was not surprised: 'Advertising is part of the popular culture now' (Midgley and Whitworth, 1996). There are entire TV programmes – documentary and entertainment – given up wholly or partly to advertisements.

Perhaps, though, this is less of a modern phenomenon than it first seems. David Ogilvy's insights into advertising include a discussion of the crucial need to create advertising with 'impact', a criterion he had already adopted by the 1960s. And the whole notion of advertising being 'consumed' as a cultural product is not a new one: Stephen Brown (1995) describes how as long ago as the 1930s, the celebrated literary historian F.R. Leavis railed against what he regarded as the culturally degenerative influence of advertising.

Official statutes and self-regulation, though, seek to emphasize advertising's distinct status in whichever medium it is placed: this is why press and advertisement releases which may resemble editorial material are headed up 'Advertisement' or 'Advertising Feature'. And despite audiences' preferences in terms of advertising and entertainment, the regulation of TV advertising seeks to subvert the relationship:

> The seven-minutes-per-hour advertising time limit on British TV is only one of the restrictions. Probably the most important rule is that it must be easy for the viewer to tell the programmes and the commercials apart. The commercial 'break' in fact, must be a real break. This is why there is always a short pause at the end of a programme before the advertisements start and why, if there is a break in the middle of a programme, a caption card announces the end of one part and the start of the next.
>
> (Advertising Association, Student Briefing No. 4, September 1996)

Advertising, especially TV advertising, as a cultural product is consumed by considerably larger numbers of people than 'conventional' cultural products such as literature, drama, painting or sculpture. Stephen Brown (1995) lists a whole series of marketing products and environments which are featured in popular culture, in particular in film: but more extraordinary, perhaps, is the independent success which many products of advertising have been able to achieve, often across a number of media (see Table 8.4).

In a topsy-turvy postmodern world, many of the products of marketing communications are appropriated by artists and audiences and used as cultural products. The cross-over between popular culture and advertising is a two-way traffic, though: just as many of the creations of advertising have achieved an independent cultural 'life' in books, jigsaws and computer games, so many creations of popular TV culture find their way into advertising (see Table 8.5)

But just as the boundaries between 'elite' and 'popular' culture become blurred, so too do those between advertising and other forms of mass entertainment – in particular the boundaries between TV commercials and the programming which

Table 8.4 Advertising's cultural creations

Gold Blend (Nestlé). A long-running advertising soap-opera has charted the life and loves of a young couple since 1987. The unfolding drama regularly makes the editorial pages of popular press, reflecting the fact that the saga has become a major talking-point for a whole sector of society. New ads were screened at prime time, with the run-up to these events featuring trailers on all the commercial TV channels and cross-media promotion in national newspapers. On one occasion the Gold Blend couple made the front page of the tabloid press, when *The Sun* discovered that a declaration of love was about to be made in the subsequent episode. In 1993 the story was ghost-written into novel format by Susannah James, with an initial print run of 350 000 copies, and reached No 4 in the bestseller charts. The author developed the characters over more than 300 pages, going as far as to give them names and dark secrets. The product has also spawned two compilation CDs.

Fly Fishing by J.R. Hartley. An advertisement for *Yellow Pages,* first screened in the early 1980s, featured the quest of a supposed author through second-hand book shops for a copy of his long-out-of-print work, *Fly Fishing.* In 1991, apparently by popular demand, this work was actually written up by Michael Russell, and went on to sell 100 000 copies in hardback. A sequel, *J.R. Hartley Casts Again,* was published in October 1992. Further extensions came in 1996 when software company ARL Developments released a computer game version.

Little Harry. Own-label branding can be extended too: in 1996 Safeway launched a range of tea-towels, mugs and badges based on the angel-faced toddler, Harry, from their commercials. In the same year Golden Wonder established a fan club for Terry, the star of their Pot Noodle commercials, and a range of merchandise. Tango were reputed to have sold 250 000 orange rubber men promoting the soft drink.

Peperami. TV commercials for this spicy sausage snack featured a manic, nameless character whose by-line was 'I'm a bit of an animal', with a voiceover from cult comedian Adrian Edmondson. Peperami was extended from advertising in 1996 when the computer game 'Animal' was launched by software firm Microtime. Peperami then entered the music business with a voiceover on a chart single. Peperami has its own interactive website, produced by Ammirati Puris Lintas, the advertising agency responsible for creating the character, together with a range of merchandise and its own perfume.

Sources: Andrew Gliniecki, 'Writer hopes to strike gold with tale of coffee lovers', *The Independent,* 8 February 1993, 3; Meg Carter, 'Zap! That's another £1 million down the tube', *The Independent,* 12 May 1997; Meg Carter, 'Youth advertising? Just cool it', *The Independent,* 3 March 1997; 'Instant coffee, instant fame', leader in *The Independent,* 8 February 1993, 16; Meg Carter, 'You saw the ad and bought the dress. But what about the hatchback?', *The Independent,* 7 September 1996, shopping supplement 12.

they help to finance. Although, as we have seen, regulators insist that advertisers distinguish their offerings from those of the medium, audiences 'find the distinction between the real and the fake to be *irrelevant or not useful,* and therefore choose products for other reasons (or for no reason)' (Grayson and Vehill, 1997). Consumers, therefore, are clearly aware of the differences between advertising and programme content, but tend to treat both in the same way. This means, according to Stern (1994), that we tend to treat advertisements as 'fictive discourse' – more akin to a film or play than to a piece of reference or information.

To demonstrate this, Grayson and Vehill's research shows how, paradoxically, audiences find advertisements featuring actors more credible than those using 'real consumers': this is explained by the fact that consumers treat advertising as entertainment – both have to follow certain conventions in terms of structure, treatment plot and dialogue. Where an advertisement does this (following the

Table 8.5 Life after television: fictional celebrity endorsements

Cult comedian Harry Enfield is no stranger to TV commercials, but his ads for Pillsbury Toaster Pockets (a flaky pastry snack) broke new ground. The product was promoted by one of Enfield's fictional TV characters, Kevin the Teenager. First screened in the UK early in 1997, the commercial became an overnight sensation for millions of consumers. As well as acting in the ad, Enfield wrote the script and directed the filming. Enfield was able to use the Kevin character as intellectual property rights are owned by his production company, Tiger Aspect, which also makes the comedy programmes as well as the advertisements.

British Telecom's advertising agency fell foul of copyright when they produced ads featuring characters from the BBC's EastEnders, headed by Letitia Dean, who formerly played Sharon: although the ads made no direct reference to the TV soap opera, the agency had to pay compensation to the BBC. Meanwhile, Pauline Quirke and Linda Robson, stars of long-running BBC comedy 'Birds of A Feather', have appeared in commercials for Unilever's detergent Surf since the 1980s. Although again there is no reference to the TV programme or its characters, audiences clearly make the connection.

Similarly, actor Richard Wilson, famous for his portrayal of crabby Victor Meldrew in the BBC comedy 'One Foot in the Grave', started promoting Flora Margarine in 1996. Although there is no specific reference to the programme, Wilson's characteristics within the commercial are indistinguishable from those of his fictional character.

Martin Clunes, typecast as the amoral Gary in 'Men Behaving Badly' has, astonishingly, appeared on radio promoting financial services products. Clunes is one of the most prolific celebrity advertisers, both in his own right and with fellow *MBB* star Neil Morrisey.

Sources: Scott Hughes, 'Good ad, bad ad', *The Independent*, 17 November 1997, media supplement, 8; Paul Walter and Scott Hughes, 'Good ad, bad ad', *The Independent*, 13 October 1997, media supplement, 7; Meg Carter, 'Youth advertising? Just cool it', *The Independent*, 3 March 1997.

conventions of 'fiction'), consumers seem prepared to suspend disbelief and to listen to the message. The appearance of 'real consumers', by contrast, creates turbulence in this world and causes the advertisement to lose credibility and impact.

Strangely, then, consumers 'seek information from advertisements much as they might seek information from a fable or a drama – they know it is not denotatively real, but they believe its messages to be useful to their real lives' (Grayson and Vehill, 1997). These findings bear out the observations of earlier research which suggested that advertising achieves at least some of its effects because of its power as a narrative (Deighton, 1992; Deighton, *et al.*, 1989; Wells, 1988). It is mistaken, therefore, to use criteria to judge advertising which are more properly applied to informationally oriented media: indeed the whole basis of the advertising industry's own voluntary code of conduct – 'honest, legal, decent and truthful' – is open to question. Just as consumers would not consider applying these same criteria to a film or to television drama, neither do they as audiences apply them to advertising.

This whole discovery has delicious overtones: advertising executives – particularly the *creatives* – have long seen themselves as media people, up alongside writers, dramatists, artists and film directors. Mere commercial considerations – 'yes, but does it sell product?' can be seen as something of an irritation or irrelevance. Personnel moves into and out of film and advertising reinforce their point. Now, it seems, the cross-over is more appropriate than ever: advertising is more entertainment than information, and entertainment itself contains more advertising than ever before.

Table 8.6 Advertising courts media stars, media stars court advertising

---

1 Cult US cinema director Spike Lee has formed a production partnership with advertising agency DDB Needham. Lee's first two commercials as part of the partnership were highly acclaimed ads for the 1997 Tyson–Holyfield boxing encounter. 'The new venture adds an aura of hipness to DDB, in the past considered a conservative firm.' Lee has collaborated with DDB before, producing commercials for Busch beer.

2 According to the Advertising Association, 'The demands of telling a compelling story in a short space of time have influenced the direction of films for the cinema, and it is no accident that one of the most successful film-directors, Alan Parker of 'Bugsy Malone', 'Midnight Express' and 'Shoot the Moon' fame, began in films as a director of TV commercials.'

3 'Harry Enfield spoofed the whole genre of splash-and-flash radio advertising brilliantly in an award-winning radio ad for the Armadillo and Dime Bar Warehouse.' He has appeared in ad campaigns for Hula Hoops, Worthington's bitter, Sekonda watches, British Gas, Mercury, Skol and Fab Ice Cream. . . Enfield worked with the advertising agency Lowe Howard-Spink to refine the Pillsbury script.

4 'Mel Smith and Griff Rhys Jones have appeared in, scripted and directed numerous radio ads and television commercials through their own production company. Rowan Atkinson has a long-running relationship with Barclaycard: although he does not direct the ads (that is left to his old friend and Blackadder collaborator John Lloyd) he does have a creative veto. Clive James and Chris Evans now work exclusively through their own production companies, Watchmaker Productions and Ginger Productions respectively. Meanwhile, television actors including Ian McShane, Jimmy Nail, Robson Green and Jerome Flynn have followed the example of Hollywood stars Jodie Foster, Tim Robbins and Sharon Stone by forming their own production companies.'

Sources: 1) Griffith, V., 'Black consumers enter the arena', *Financial Times*, 2 June 1997; 2) Advertising Association, Student Briefing No 4, September 1996; 3) Gardner, L., 'Wave riding, ads and lasses', *The Guardian*, April 5 1997, 7; 3) and 4) Meg Carter, 'Harry's game', *The Independent*, 4 February 1997, tabloid section, 14–15.

SUMMARY AND CONCLUSION

Notably, audience and environmental context has changed dramatically in the past three decades. With characteristic understatement the industry's professional body coyly admits 'People are decoding messages in very different ways' (IPA Marketing Appraisal, Bulletin 629, June 1996). Messages have had to become far more focused *and* sophisticated, even as media fragmentation means sub-segmentation and niche marketing is of ever-increasing prevalence. Despite many of the assertions made in this chapter, advertising (at least for the foreseeable future) will continue to be a dominant and expensive mechanism for communicating with and to target audiences. But (and again for the foreseeable future), it will operate alongside and in conjunction with many of the other promotional tools (i.e. an integrated approach), including the nebulous Internet. Ultimately, the juxtaposition of technology (i.e. television, telephone, computer, etc.) will mean that control over receptivity (dare it be said, *exposure*) is passed inexorably into the hands of consumers. Many of the themes addressed in this chapter will continue in the next on the communications process and the semiotic boundary.

DISCUSSION TOPICS

1 How and in what way(s) might communicators target messages at the groupings cited by DDB Needham (introductory case vignette)?
2 Explore the issue of compatibility between straightforward advertising strategy and that depicted in the semi-apocalyptic vision description by Brown (1995).
3 'Old certainties in advertising are being eroded, as consumers and audiences continue to change and to defy understanding.' Critically discuss.
4 Illustrate how audiences have changed over the past three decades. Is there any evidence to support the view of a slow-down in the rate of change?
5 Critically appraise or re-present some of the conventional theories relating to audience and environment. Surely, there is little wrong with these theories and they are still of relevance as we approach the twenty-first century?
6 'Consumers are easily classified and easy to reach.' Discuss.
7 Do consumers *use advertising*?
8 Discuss whether advertising (or indeed other forms of) clutter need to be taken seriously by advertisers.
9 Karpf (1997) suggests that in an interactive way 'watching children can even recut the programme as they watch'. Isn't this to the advantage of communicators? Why should it be seen as negative?
10 Using any of advertising's 'cultural creations' (see Table 8.4 or access the most current or recent), justify how advertisements may be seen as cultural noise, or a form of moving wallpaper.

CASE STUDY – 'TO THE ENDS OF THE EARTH AND THE TOP OF THE WORLD: ONLY TWO OF US HAVE MADE IT'

The above caption appeared above the picture of Erling Kagge who on 9 May 1994 became the very first man to achieve the impossible. However, he didn't make it alone! He was accompanied by his Rolex Explorer 11. The script for the newspaper advertisement stated:

> He had reached the North Pole with no outside help. He had reached the South Pole totally alone. And he had succeeded in conquering Mount Everest at his very first attempt.
>
> He [ostensibly] stated concerning his Rolex Explorer 11: 'It's the one piece of equipment I know I can trust. It's built to withstand almost anything, and its never once let me down.'
>
> Strength and reliability are the qualities that Erling Kagge values above all others: 'I never trust to luck', he says. 'But I've found the better your equipment, the luckier you get'.
>
> Maybe that's why he values his Rolex so highly!

(*Source: The Times*, Tuesday 12 March, 1998, p. 3)

REFERENCES

Agrawal, J. and Kamakura, W.A. (1995) 'The economic worth of celebrity endorsers: an event study analysis', *Journal of Marketing*, 59(3): 56–62.

Archer, B. (1996a) 'Reality v blue-chip advertising', *The Times*, 14 August, 16.

Archer, B. (1996b) 'Why consumers are switching off', *The Times*, 30 October, 22.

Armstrong, S. (1996) 'Catch 'em young', *The Sunday Times*, 12 May, Culture supplement, 12.

Bloom, A. (1987) *The Closing of the American Mind*, Harmondsworth: Penguin.

Boush, D.M., Friestad, M. and Rose, G.M. (1994) 'Adolescent skepticism toward TV advertising and knowledge of advertiser tactics', *Journal of Consumer Research*, 21 (June): 165–75.

Boutie, P. (1994) 'Who will save the brands?', *Communicaton World*, 11(7): 24–29.

Brignull, T. (1996) 'Big bang, little impact', *The Guardian*, 12 February, media supplement, 10–11

Brindle, D. (1997) 'Rise in single households takes toll on wedding bells', *The Guardian*, 30 January, 6.

Brown, S. (1995) *Postmodern Marketing*, London: International Thomson Business Press.

Calfee, J.E. and Ringold D.J. (1994) 'The seventy percent majority: enduring consumer beliefs about advertising', *Journal of Public Policy and Marketing*, 13 (Fall): 228–38.

Callinicos, A. (1989) *Against Postmodernism: A Marxist Critique*, Cambridge: Polity.

Carter, M. (1993) 'Zap! That's another £1m down the tube', *The Independent*, 12 May, 3.

Carter, M. (1996) 'You saw the ad and bought the dress. But what about the hatchback?', *The Independent*, 7 September, shopping supplement, 12.

Carter, M. (1997a) 'Harry's game', *The Independent*, 4 February, tabloid section, 14–15.

Carter, M. (1997b) 'Youth advertising? Just cool it', *The Independent*, 3 March.

Clifton, R. (1995) 'Do we need another article about women?', *Admap*, September.

Cope, N. (1994) 'Black cabs make the switch to the colour of money', *The Independent*, 17 January, 29.

Coupland, D. (1991) *Generation X, Tales for an Accelerated Culture*, London: Abacus.

Culligan, K. (1995) 'Word-of-mouth to become true measure of ads', *Marketing*, 9 February, 7.

Dean, D., Price, L. and Croft, R. (1997) TV-based retailing in Britain, *Proceedings of 2nd International Conference on Marketing & Corporate Communications*, RUCA Antwerp, April.

Deighton, J. (1992) 'The consumption of performance', *Journal of Consumer Research*, 19 (December): 362–72.

The Economist (1996) 'Which half? Which advertisements work?', 339, 8 June.

Fletcher, W. (1996) 'The end of advertising as we know it?', *Admap*, January.

Foxall, G.R. (1984) 'Consumers' intentions and behaviour: a note on research and a challenge to researchers', *Journal of the Marketing Research Society*, 26(3): 213–35.

Friedan, B. (1971) *The Feminine Mystique*, London: Gollancz.

Friestad, M. and Wright P. (1994) 'The persuasion knowledge model: how people cope with persuasion attempts', *Journal of Consumer Research*, 21 (June): 1–31.

Gardner, L. (1997) 'Wave riding, ads and lasses', *The Guardian*, 5 April, 7.

Gliniecki, A. (1993) 'Writer hopes to strike gold with tale of coffee lovers', *The Independent*, 8 February, 3.

Goldberg, M.E. and Hartwick J. (1990) 'The effects of advertiser reputation and extremity of advertising claim on advertising effectiveness', *Journal of Consumer Research*, 17 (September): 172–9.

Grayson, K. and Vehill, K. (1997) 'How does advertising mean what it does? The impact of "real consumers" in commercials', unpublished, London Business School Working Paper Series.

Griffith, V. (1997) 'Black consumers enter the arena', *Financial Times*, 2 June.

Hebdige, D. (1979) *Subculture: The Meaning of Style*, London: Methuen.

Hill, D. (1997) 'It's a mad, mad, ad world', *The Observer,* 28 December, *Business* supplement, 4.

Howard, J.A. and Sheth, J.N. (1969) *The Theory of Buyer Behaviour,* New York: Wiley.

Hughes, S. (1997) 'Good ad, bad ad', *The Independent,* 17 November, media supplement, 8.

Iacobucci, D., Grayson, K. and Ostrom, A. (1994) 'Customer satisfaction fables', *Sloan Management Review,* 35(4): 93–6.

The Independent (1993) 'Instant coffee, instant fame', 3 February, 16.

The Independent (1994) 'When you wish upon a star. . .', 27 December, media supplement, 12.

Karpf, A. (1997) 'Read all about me', *The Guardian,* 30 May, G2T supplement, 2.

Kitchen, P.J. (1994) 'The marketing communicatons revolution – a Leviathan unveiled', *Marketing Intelligence & Planning,* 12(2): 19–25.

Kotler, P. (1991) *Marketing Management, Analysis, Planning, Implementation and Control,* Englewood Cliffs: Prentice Hall International.

Kudos Productions (1997) 'The Remote Controllers', Channel 4 TV, 29 December.

Lambert, A. (1993) 'Woman as head of the house? Shock! Horror!', *The Independent,* 1 April, *Living* supplement, 24.

Lasch, C. (1979) *The Culture of Narcissism,* New York: Norton.

Lavidge, R.J. and Steiner, G.A. (1961) 'A model for predictive measurements of advertising effectiveness', *Journal of Marketing* October: 61 (cited in Kincaid, W.M. Jnr (1985) *Presentations: Products Services and Ideas,* 2nd edn, Columbus, Ohio: Charles E. Merrill Publishing Co.

Leavis, F.R. and Thompson, D. (1933) *Culture and Environment,* London: Chatto and Windus.

Le Boutiller, P. (1995) 'Creating car advertising for women', *Admap,* September.

McCann, P. (1997) 'Britons shun advertising overkill', *The Independent,* 18 October, 2.

Midgley C. and Withworth, D. (1996) 'Adverts take centre stage in Christmas video sales battle', *The Times,* 23 November, 7.

Miller, C. (1994) 'Celebrities hot despite scandal', *Marketing News,* 28(7): 1–2.

Ogilvy, D. (1983) *Ogilvy on Advertising,* London: Pan Books.

Palda, K.S. (1966) 'The hypothesis of a hierarchy of effects – a partial evaluation', *Journal of Marketing Research,* 3(1).

Perfect, T. and Heatherley, S. (1996) 'Implicit memory in print ads', *Admap,* January.

Popcorn, F. (1991) *The Popcorn Report,* London: Arrow Books.

Rapp, S. and Collins, T.L. (1994) *Beyond Maxi-marketing,* New York: McGraw-Hill.

Robertson, T.S. and Rossiter J.R. (1974) 'Children and commercial persuasion: an attribution theory analysis', *Journal of Consumer Research,* 1 (June): 13–20.

Rogers, E.M. (1983) *Diffusion of Innovations,* 3rd edn, New York: Free Press.

Sanders, S. (1995) 'Celebrity name game', *Discount Store News,* 34(10): A32–33.

Schramm, W. (1955) *The Process and Effects of Mass Communications,* Urbana IL: University of Illinois Press.

Shannon, C. and Weaver, W. (1962) *The Mathematical Theory of Communication,* Urbana IL: University of Illinois Press.

Shimp, T.A. (1993) *Promotion Management & Marketing Communications,* 3rd edn, Fort Worth TX: Dryden Press.

Stern, B. (1995) 'Consumer myths: Frye's taxonomy and the structural analysis of a consumption text', *Journal of Consumer Research,* 22 (September): 165–85.

Tavassoli, N.T., Shultz II, C.J. and Fitzsimons, G.J. (1995) 'Program involvement: are moderate levels best for ad memory and attitude toward the ad?', *Journal of Advertising Research,* September/October.

Teather, D. (1995) 'Stars bring unknown risk to endorsement', *Marketing,* 6 July, 6.

Times, The, Tuesday, March 12 1998, 3.

Trapp, R. (1993) 'Viewers drink in lager mystery', *The Independent on Sunday,* 12 September, Business supplement, 26.

Treneman, A. (1997) 'Why teaching is sexy in the States', *The Independent,* 26 March.

Waldrup, J. (1994) 'Advertising that counts', *American Demographics*', 16(5): 48–57.

Walter, P. and Hughes, S. (1997) Good ad, bad ad', *The Independent*, 13 October, media supplement, 7.

Wardle, J. (1995) 'The good, the bad, and the ugly', *Admap*, September.

Wells, W.D. (1988) 'Lectures and dramas', in P. Cafferata and A. Tybout, (eds.) *Cognitive and Affective Responses to Advertising*, Lexington, MA: D.C. Heath.

Williams, R. (1993) 'Switched-on advertisers ready for a rave', *The Independent on Sunday*, 25 April, 8.

Wynne-Jones, R. (1997) 'Rise of the pick'n'mix family', *Independent on Sunday*, 26 October, 5.

9

THE COMMUNICATIONS PROCESS AND THE SEMIOTIC BOUNDARY

Christopher E. Hackley

CHAPTER AIMS

- to introduce the concept of semiotics
- to describe and explain the origins, basic concepts and terminology of the discipline
- to set semiotics within the context of marketing communications by illustrating relevance and applications
- to offer a balanced view of the semiotic perspective by pointing out some controversies and debates within the discipline
- to demonstrate how the semiotic perspective can complement the communications science perspective within marketing communications
- to place the semiotic boundary in marketing communications within the broader cultural context of the twentieth-century marketing communications 'revolution'

ILLUSTRATION

In the following case vignette a regional sports shoe manufacturer seeks a promotional concept which will create powerful public meaning and recognition for his brand. In particular, he is seeking the same economy of message that the leading world brands such as Nike can generate with a single visual image. He wants a single sign to stand for his brand and all the values he feels the brand represents.

'Runners'

'Runners', a small manufacturer of sports shoes based in northern England, invited advertising agencies to pitch for a forthcoming campaign. The proprietor and marketing director of 'Runners', Oswald Daley, wanted to brand his shoes powerfully so that sales-led growth could generate the cash for major expansion. Daley was particularly fascinated by the Nike branding concept. How, he wondered, could a single image (the Nike 'swoosh') be so powerful as a meaningful symbol of value for millions of people? In the brief he sent out to agencies, Daley tried to explain that he sought the same kind of economy in his advertising messages that Nike could generate from their 'swoosh'. He wanted one image, word or sign that was loaded with layers of positive meaning for his potential consumers. He understood that this could mean time and a large promotional budget, but he was prepared for that. If a world brand was worth building, he thought, it was worth time and money. But the end result must be a universally meaningful sign or symbol that means something valuable to his consumers (actual and potential). Daley sat back and waited for the agencies to provide his solution.

INTRODUCTION

Some possible responses to the advertising brief for 'Runners' might already occur to readers. A stick drawing of a running athlete perhaps, or two footsoles in a running juxtaposition. Maybe two footprints on a sandy shore, filling up with sea water as the runner, long gone, speeds on. But these images would not do: the economy of reference and universality of application could only come from an image-message which could be transmitted via any promotional medium. The idea must be static so that it transfers to posters and press as well as being transmissible on moving media. In any case, how could Daley be sure that the image chosen will have deep significance for the market? It would seem that designing a sign which carries a powerful meaning for a target group of consumers is no easy business. Insight into how consumers interpret the marketing signs and messages to which they are exposed could assist in elucidating the 'Runners' marketing problem. But where does such an interpretation begin? How is it possible to analyse the process of how and in what ways consumers draw meanings from the marketing signs they encounter? This chapter seeks to introduce a possible basis for such analysis through the semiotic 'boundary'; in other words, between the design and delivery of marketing communications and advertising messages, and meaningful interpretations of such messages by consumers. The chapter begins with an introduction to the origins and scope of semiotics.

Semiotics is a field of study in its own right as well as a perspective on all other human sciences. It has its own vocabulary and even its own internal disagreements, and readers need some introduction to this in order to understand the value of the semiotic perspective to marketing communications. The analysis is then broadened by taking points of view from cultural studies of advertising promotions. These emphasize the culturally relative nature of meaning-making. In other words, in order to understand the systems of codes by and through which consumers interpret promotional signs and symbols as meaningful messages, it is necessary to understand the cultural context of promotional messages.

The chapter concludes by offering several brief sketches of UK promotional campaigns and attempts to show how a semiotic perspective can offer insights into how and why these campaigns were successful in making meaningful messages for their respective target audiences.

ORIGINS AND SCOPE OF SEMIOTIC STUDY

Semiotics (from the Greek *sema*, meaning marks or signs) is the study of signs and their meaning. Semiosis can be defined as the 'capacity for containing, replicating and extracting messages, and of extracting their significance' (Sebeok, 1985). A sign is broadly defined, following the more precise technical definition of Charles Pierce, as anything that can stand for something else. Signs may be visual, verbal, aural, electronic, chemical: in fact anything which can be detected through sense experience can be a sign to a human. An open window, a footprint in the snow, a bloodied knife: such signs, pregnant with meaning in particular contexts, are characteristic of detective stories. Danesi (1993) gives several examples of how the colour red can signal very different meanings depending on the context in which it is seen, for example in traffic lights ('stop'), on an armband in a political rally ('left wing'), or in a description of an emotional state ('she turned red with embarrassment'). 'Red' is a word-sign, the colour red is a point on a scale of light frequencies, but the meaning of red is given by its interpretation in a particular context. In marketing, consumers are accustomed to recognizing brand signs in the form of visual logos, musical phrases, the faces of particular sponsoring personalities, the colour schemes of package designs, and so on. Marketing messages seek to utilize signs to signify certain values to certain groups ('target segments') of people. Signs communicate and the subjective human world of meanings is, for the semiotician, a tapestry whose threads are individual semiotic interpretations of signs. The origins of semiotics can be traced back to the ancient medical techniques of Hippocrates and Galen. These techniques included the interpretative science of inferring medical conditions from the symptoms (verbal or non-verbal) reported by patients. For example, a reported symptom, such as dancing lights before the eyes, could be interpreted as an indicator of a medical condition, say, concussion. Alternatively, non-verbal signs such as dilated pupils or cold sweats can be interpreted as symptomatic of other underlying conditions. The symptom is here operating as a sign of an underlying physiological event. Since these beginnings, semiotics has been extensively developed as a perspective on many fields of human activity (for general (but sophisticated) introductions, see Eco, 1976; Barthes, 1968). For some semioticians, the legitimate scope of the discipline covers everything and anything that is made by humans (Danesi, 1993). For others (Sebeok, 1991), semiotics goes further since it may form part of an integrated science of communication which begins with study of the message-making of single cells.

'The subject matter of semiotics is often said to be "the communication of any messages whatever" (Jakobson, 1974), or the exchange of any messages whatever and of the system of signs which underlie them' (Sebeok, 1976, in Sebeok, 1991, p. 60).

The potential and actual scope of semiotics is indeed broad, although there is controversy as to whether semiotics should be superordinate to, or subsumed within, other human sciences. Sebeok (1991) refers to philosopher Charles Pierce who suggested that the entire universe is diffused with signs and this view is taken as a basis for regarding semiotics as superordinate and complementary to other human social sciences. To illustrate with a rather simplistic metaphor, semioticians could regard each living cell as a link in a chain of life, the fundamental essence of which is the sending and receiving of messages. Understanding this flow of messages is not considered a matter of devising a universal underlying context-free language, such as mathematics. It is considered a matter of understanding the universal activity of interpreting signs through an understanding of the codes used for interpretation in different communication contexts. This illustration hints at the deep philosophical issues with which semioticians must engage in order to ground the claims and insights of their science. The purpose of this chapter is less complex. It is to offer a necessarily brief introduction to the general principles of the discipline and suggest ways in which the techniques of semiotics might provide insight into how advertising and marketing communications can work, that is, how they might form messages which are meaningful to consumers.

SEMIOTIC TERMS AND CONCEPTS FOR MESSAGE- AND MEANING-MAKING

A brief introduction such as this should include some description of the basic concepts and terms of semiotic analysis. Organisms (and machines) send messages in encoded form. At the level of the cell, messages are electrical impulses. Humans form messages through biochemical activity about which little is known. However, what is known is that messages can be encoded in words or other visual or aural symbols. A medium, a channel and a receiver are then needed for communication to take place. The medium might be the vibrations of vocal apparatus, the microprocessor capacity of a computer's word processing package, or the marks on a piece of paper (writing). The channel refers to the characteristics of the medium, for example soundwaves produced by vocal apparatus can be transmitted through electronic channels in telephones or radio waves. Of course they can also be transmitted through the channel of the physical environment, person to person. The receiver of the message is, with the sender, a joint participant in the making of meaning. The sender might form the message in a language code and the receiver has to decode the meaning of the message through tapping into the same code. Communications can be hindered by noise in the channel or medium which inhibits message transmission. Literally, noise might be distortion of sound produced by static interference on a telephone transmission. Figuratively, noise can be any distraction to the concentration of the speaker or listener in verbal communication. Redundancy is a feature of the code that is being used which assists in the suppression of the noise effect. In verbal messages one might repeat certain words or phrases, or periodically ask for confirmation with expressions like 'know what I mean?'. Such parts of a code are redundant in the sense that they do not carry the meaning of the message but act as confirmatory devices to ensure that the message is received. Finally, this brief review around some of the main concepts of semiotics should include mention of 'entropy', that is unpredictable elements in message-making; and 'feedback' – the ways senders can monitor the success or otherwise of message sending and adapt if necessary.

According to Danesi (1993), following Pierce, signs may signify in three ways which are not mutually exclusive but which form overlapping facets of signification. These three categories of signification, it should be noted, are not uncontroversial in semiological study. Many authors have argued for different definitions of the basic terms sign, symbol, index, icon, with differing views on the relation each has with the others (see Leach, 1976: 10 for brief overview). The definitions taken here are adopted for clarity of exposition suitable for the current purpose. Taking Danesi's (1993) approach, the meaning of any given sign may emphasize its constitution as an icon, an index or a symbol. An icon is, put simply, like the thing it represents. Iconicity resides in this identity between, say, a Madonna and child and Christian holiness, or James Dean and western ideas of teenage rebellion. An index points to or indicates something else, such as a wavy line on a road sign pointing to bends in the road ahead. Indexicality has been extensively examined by philosophers of language who try to explain how a word symbol can refer to something in the world. Finally, semiosis can be achieved through symbolism, by which is meant a sign stands for something else, such as a red cross for compassionate medical care, a Nazi salute for National Socialism under Adolf Hitler, or the many uses of psychosexual symbolism in Freudian psychoanalysis. As mentioned above, these three divisions are not necessarily regarded (by, for example, Danesi, 1993) as mutually exclusive and the examples may be cumbersome, but the point worth emphasizing is that the use of a sign in any context will, on this view, entail a predominant emphasis on one of these three categories of semiosis. A sign is likely to engender semiosis through its function primarily as an index pointing to something (a silhouette of a man or woman on a toilet door), or as an icon which is an aspect of the thing it represents. Another example of iconic semiosis may be religious icons which are themselves treated as holy things because they embody the religion. Finally, semiosis may be generated through a symbol which stands for something else (a Chicago Bulls jacket stands for the basketball team, a red sports car symbolizes youth, vigour and the good life).

So far, the chapter has attempted to show the scope of semiotics and the main concepts of semiotic analysis. Marketing communications and advertising are a rich source of semiotic study and reflection. However, it is worth pointing out that while the study of communications is integral to semiotics, the semiotic perspective represents a distinctive tradition of scholarship which is separate from the study of marketing communications. Certainly, marketing in its communicative aspects attempts to make messages which will be meaningful for consumers. This function of marketing communications clearly falls within the scope of semiotic study. However, marketing communications, as a discrete focus of study, draws heavily on communication science (Buttle, 1995) and tends to emphasize the study of the process of message-making from the point of view of the sender (e.g. Berlo, 1960; Schramm, 1948). Semiotics, in turn, tends to seek answers to questions (or at least clarification of the questions) of how messages are interpreted by meaning-makers. This process of semiosis is the process which is undertaken by, in the marketing arena, marketing communications professionals and groups of targeted consumers. Understanding semiosis leads to kinds of insights which are complementary to, but distinct from, the perspectives of communications science *qua* communications science. For some semioticians (e.g. Sebeok, 1991), semiotics can be an overarching discipline which subsumes other forms of the study of communication, but the reverse is not true: much communications science is conducted on a cognitive science model which emphasizes the processes of message-making and encoding, rather than the interpretative processes of meaning-making through semiosis.

Different theoretical perspectives yield different forms of explanation and the semiotic perspective on marketing communications and advertising offers a distinctive view which stands apart from, but which is complementary to, other kinds of theoretical approach. The question of which field is superordinate to the other is one on which professionals and academics will not necessarily agree. However, the foregoing passage was intended to demonstrate some important distinctions in the respective research traditions of semiotics, communications science and marketing communications. Some understanding of these distinct but overlapping schools of thought can help readers make an informed judgement about which perspective or combination of perspectives might serve to illuminate a particular issue. The next section develops this integrative theme by describing some ways in which semiotic study has informed marketing thought.

SEMIOTICS AND MARKETING

Semiotic interest in marketing and advertising has a substantial tradition (see, for example, Sherry, 1987; Umiker-Sebeok, 1987; Umiker-Sebeok *et al.*, 1988). For Sebeok (1991) marketing messages are composed of 'strings of signs' (p. 146). These strings of signs constitute messages whose promotional success depends on how meaningful they are to targeted consumers. The growth in marketing culture, and the concomitant growth in technologies of communication in the twentieth century, raises many questions. How can the world of marketing signs which we encounter every day be interpreted? This is an environment which teems with commercial messages to a historically unprecedented degree (Hackley and Kitchen, 1996; Kitchen 1994). How can the effect of this culture be understood in the context of marketing messages on the ways consumers behave, think and make consumption decisions (Hackley and Kitchen, 1997)? What is the nature of codes utilized to make meaning from these messages and how do consumers decide what code or codes are appropriate in any given circumstances? What are the implications of this multitude of marketing messages, for marketing organizations, for individual marketing managers, for consumers, and for society? A deeper understanding of how marketing messages work through semiosis might afford some insights into large-scale questions such as these. However, marketing communications are a form of the broader set of human communications and the semiosis which confers meaning on these does not occur in isolation from the broader historical, social and cultural context. Marketing message-making must, in order to be meaningful to consumers, be placed within the consumers' cultural frame of reference.

INTERTEXTUALITY AND THE SEMIOTIC ANALYSIS OF MARKETING COMMUNICATIONS

Many semiotic studies are relevant to the study of marketing communications. The semiotics of, for example, the cinema (Metz, 1974), theatre and drama (Elam, 1988), and language (Eco, 1984) can contribute to semiotic studies of advertising (e.g. Berger, 1987; Fry and Fry, 1986; Collins, 1987; Bertrand, 1988; Geis, 1982). This section will take one of many possible semiotic views of marketing communications.

This is the view that marketing communications engender semiosis from within a cultural context, and that the analysis of semiosis in marketing communications is best undertaken from a cultural perspective. This view, adopted in this section and drawing on a particular genre of semiotic study, will be illustrated particularly by reference to Wernick (1991) since this work is a noted example of the cultural perspective on the semiotics of advertising which contains many useful illustrations of marketing communications and, particularly, advertising, at work. Other works which attempt a similarly culturally mediated semiotic study of advertising include O'Barr (1994) and Mueller (1996).

The semiotic perspective is, on this view, obtained on the boundary of cultural, historical and sociological analysis. Semiotic interpretants change over time, between cultures and between individuals and are never subject to hermeneutic closure. Interpretants themselves are signs which stand for an object, in infinite regress in Pierce's universe of signs. Wernick (1991) feels that: 'semiological approaches to advertising had eclipsed attention both to the historicity of promotional texts and to their contextual dimension' (p. 25).

On this view, the semiological (or semiotic) perspective had focused too narrowly on individual advertising signs as if they appeared in a cultural vacuum. Advertisements (and other forms of marketing communication) are meaningful in terms of their relation to other cultural products of the time and of preceding times, including other advertisements. That is, advertisements gain their meaning from their relation to other advertisements as well as to other cultural products to which they refer. This notion of intertextuality is popular in postmodernist critical literary theory and refers to the self-referential nature of discourses (such as marketing promotion). Promotional messages make use of cultural values and acquire meaning through reference not only to these but to other promotional messages. Consequently the semiosis through which promotional messages acquire their meaning for individuals occurs through and within a broader sign system which is historically located and culturally variable. The message here is that the interpretation of promotional signs is a complex phenomenon which needs to take account of historicity, cultural values and ideologies, and intertextuality.

Wernick (1991) uses examples of advertisements which refer to other products, e.g. Avis, Pepsi, and advertisements which refer, implicitly through subtle visual references, to earlier advertisements (sometimes for the same product, e.g. Cavalier, IBM, (pp. 92–4). Many recent television advertisements mimic film and cinematic styles (Volkswagen) and employ humorous or ironic intertextual references to other products of popular and commercial postmodern culture. An individual promotional message is seen as a text to be interpreted as a sign made up of an agglomeration of other signs. From a cultural perspective a promotional message presupposes certain forms of semiosis simply by virtue of its membership of the class of cultural objects 'promotional messages'. From an ideological standpoint, promotional messages themselves collectively promote values of [a]capitalistic marketing culture (and this may include messages from religious, environmental or state-sponsored agencies about human behaviour and beliefs). Therefore, the semiotic possibilities of any given promotional message need to be placed within the broader semiotic landscape of marketing culture.

141

However, notwithstanding this view, it is well established within semiological study that messages have meaning only by virtue of their relation to other messages. Just as word-sounds are linguistically meaningful because of the other word-sounds in a string of phonemes, meaningful non-verbal messages are also embedded within a landscape of message signs which frame the meanings which may be extracted in a given context. As the social anthropologist Edmund Leach (1976) put it:

> signs do not occur in isolation; a sign is always a member of a set of contrasted signs which functions within a specific cultural context; a sign only conveys information when it is combined with other signs and symbols from the same context . . . signs are always contiguous to other signs which are members of the same set
>
> (Leach, 1976: 13)

From this can be seen that semiotic analysis of marketing (or any other forms of communication) need not imply that a particular message be taken as a communication which stands alone. Indeed, meaningful communication cannot stand alone and promotions, and other forms of communication, are threads in a larger tapestry which give context and, through context, give meaning. The semiosis which takes place when advertisements and other marketing communications are apprehended by consumers is therefore necessarily a culturally embedded process. As Leach (1976) writes: 'we must know a lot about the cultural context, the setting of the stage, before we can even begin to decode the message' (p. 96).

DECONSTRUCTING CULTURALLY EMBEDDED MESSAGE CODES IN MARKETING COMMUNICATIONS

The deconstruction of message-meaning codes in advertising and marketing communications can take various analytical forms (e.g. Cleveland, 1989; Chapman and Egger, 1993; Berger, 1987). Taking the cultural perspective, Wernick (1991) offers many examples of marketing communications meaning-making through signification within a cultural context of advertising ideology. For example, the incidence of cigarette smoking among females grew considerably in the US between the 1950s and 1960s. Various reasons for this could be suggested, particularly the social equalizing that war made necessary and the concomitant loosening of male dominance over professional roles, education and income. US cigarette manufacturers wanted to tap into the growing female cigarette buying market and sought to do so through images which reflected the contradictions in the changing social status of women. Wernick (1991) writes of the 'symbolic' content of advertisements – the reader should note that he does not usually employ the distinctions of different forms of semiosis. These symbols included promotional images of women as a powerful gender yet also juxtaposed powerful images with subordinate ones, reflecting the ambivalence about woman's gender roles in society. So, for example, a woman cigarette smoker might have been depicted as a powerful business person, but the image would also conform to traditional (male) images of idealized femininity. Further ambivalent message codes used biblical symbols of temptation and illicit pleasure, with the woman as both temptress and symbol of (female) liberation. Such promotional images reflected the changing nature of social gender roles and the ambivalence felt by both men and women towards these changes, and tied cigarette smoking in with this cultural process of change. The image of female liberation is still used to sell cigarettes to women in the US, although the patronizing subtext of the ads remains: 'You've Come a Long Way Baby!' goes the copy of one campaign as a young woman flounces along the street, a cigarette dangling from glossy lips but, strangely, no ash on the business suit. Yeh, right on.

The symbolic content of promotional messages must, in order to be meaningful to the consumer, make use of the cultural currency of symbolic codes in contemporary use. Marketing communications may not conform to rational criteria of economic, political or ethical assessment. However, they must conform to a kind of cognitive rationality in tapping into the symbolic codes by which people constitute their social world.

> . . . it would be impossible to valorize products symbolically if the symbolism employed to that end were itself unintelligible or without ideological appeal. Symbolic ads, must therefore not only find effective pictorial and verbal devices by which to link the commodity with a significance. They must also build up significance from elements of an understood cultural code: and in such a way that the values in terms of which the product is endorsed are themselves endorsed by those to whom they make appeal.
>
> (Wernick, 1991: 37–8)

So, for example, advertisers might make use of celebrity endorsers who are currently popular. In the present day, it is sports stars who are mythologized in our popular culture and it is these people whom advertisers try to attract to associate with their products. There is little need for an explicit rational appeal to product quality or economic value: the association of the star with the product is enough. Semiosis in this case depends upon the human need for mythical heroes and the current (and transitory) mythical status of a particular celebrity. Few celebrity sportspeople have universal appeal: more usually, they may have mythological status in one country or region, but not another. And then this status may only obtain for groups or segments of the population, rather than the whole. A sports hero must, in order to sell product for an advertiser, constitute a sufficiently powerful image for a target group so that they will buy consumer products which remind them of him or her. Few celebrities have this kind of appeal, and advertisers are often wary of, as it were, putting all their promotional eggs in one celebrity basket. If the celebrity's life or career goes off course for a while, the product image will suffer, as Pepsi discovered when Michael Jackson was dropped as a celebrity endorser because of some difficult publicity about a court case and a young friend.

This chapter has so far attempted to show how semiotics might be used as a fruitful perspective through which to examine the ways promotional messages in marketing can be meaningful to consumers. The final section will discuss the visual semiosis of a selection of advertisements which were successful in the UK in the 1980s.

DECONSTRUCTING ADVERTISING CODES

There are two points to note before the discussion begins. The first is that codes by which promotional messages make meaning for consumers are often easier to spot if the promotional message was constructed in a different cultural context to that of current viewers. If images of advertising (or other media products) from the 1950s, 1960s and even 1970s [are seen] distinctive aspects of dress are easily recognizable as well as other visual codes. The images are perhaps amusing and dated now because they seem clichéd, hackneyed and anachronistic. It is the cultural distance from one's own cultural idiom that reveals these message codes. When messages are seen as part of one's current cultural milieu, it is often much harder to see the kinds of message codes that are at work. The 'strings of signs' which constitute marketing messages must, in order to be meaningful to target audiences, make use of symbols that are currently culturally meaningful. Well-constructed promotional messages make use of symbols which are so fundamental to the current way of understanding the cultural world that they are not even noticed.

For example, the TV comedian Harry Enfield has made much of the comedic potential of British cinema images which were, at the time, not considered funny at all. The greased-down hairstyles and plummy accents of the men, and the stereotypically feminine behaviour of the women, were a feature of broadcasting culture in the 1950s. Men had hair parted in the centre and lathered with barrels of Brylcreem, while women sat in the corner looking motherly and doing needlepoint. However, where a plummy upper-class English accent was [ostensibly] once (in Britain) a semiotic index of authority, education and good sense, in today's culture it can be taken to indicate a Jeeves and Wooster form of vacuous idiocy and pretension, a cultural anachronism. Enfield's character 'Tim Nice but Dim' is quintessentially upper class English, but a figure of ridicule rather than authority. In 1997, a television advertising campaign for the Almera car satirized one of the most popular TV series of the 1970s. Two characters do bad skits of John Thaw and his sidekick Denis Waterman (*The Sweeney* take-off). The way they spoke and behaved and the way other characters interrelated in the plots were considered cutting edge television by those consumers who were gripped by the series. The Parker duffle coats, flared trousers and 'page boy' haircuts were semiotic symbols of youth, power and glamour at the time. The frequent car chases were manic, with old sausage rolls and pork pies flying around inside the car as it mounted kerbs and usually crashed while the bad guys got away. Now, it all seems really funny. The Almera advertising is a bunch of thirtysomethings having a right old laugh at themselves. But thirtysomethings enjoy the campaign, remember the car, and appreciate the irony. The target audience understands the code of the message, while other groups may not. This campaign makes use of the important principle that cultural distance can reveal semiotic codes retrospectively. The Almera points this out in a satirically funny way which is engaging to a particular target group. While the irony of the message is clear, the subtext is also clear: people who used to watch *The Sweeney* can see it was funny, but they still think it was cool. If it wasn't cool then, it wouldn't be funny now. The strapline is 'Buy the All Action Almera'.

The second point alluded to is this: signs are always open to a variety of interpretations. While scientific semiotic study can isolate sign-meanings which predominate among the people of a cultural milieu, the purpose of this chapter is to offer an introduction which will enable readers to form their own semiotic perspective on marketing communications messages, including those in currency. It may assist readers to refer to the simplified guide (Table 9.1) which illustrates some of the things to look for in deconstructing the message codes of an advertisement.

The analyses below are therefore offered as possible interpretations of some advertisements. Finally, the examples drawn from 1980s UK advertising campaigns described in Channon (1989) are accessed because:

(a) they are close enough culturally for most readers to understand at least some of the symbolic message codes employed;
(b) they are sufficiently far away culturally to enable readers to more easily notice and be able to articulate aspects of these codes; and
(c) each example is described in detail in a widely available text so that readers can, if they wish, conduct their own semiotic analysis of these advertisements.

As consumers we are embedded in cultural codes so that semiosis often takes place unconsciously. Therefore, a series of successful 1980s advertising campaigns might reveal their semiotic codes more willingly than more recent examples. Four examples follow.

Table 9.1 Semiotic deconstruction of advertisements

Questions to ask	What does X signify to me?
	Why does X signify this to me?
	What might X signify for others?
	Why might X signify this for others?
Possible sources of X in a given advertisement:	
Objects: (visual semiosis)	For example, clothes, hairstyles, make-up styles, use of colour, texture, the ways objects are used by people, use of printed copy, typeface, use of logo/pictorial symbolic image, the spatial inter-relationships of objects
Gesture: (bodily semiosis)	For example, body types, facial types, interactive gestures, expressive gestures, facial expressions, posture, gaze, juxtaposition of bodies, juxtaposition of bodies and objects (i.e. the advertised product)
Speech: (verbal semiosis)	For example, use of idiomatic expressions, accent, use of metaphor/metonymy, tone/volume of delivery, pace of delivery, use of voiceover, use of humour, emphasis on particular words/ phonemes

"IF YOU WANT ME OUT YOU SHOULD HAVE THE RIGHT TO VOTE ME OUT."

Everyone's entitled to their view. The British constitution says you express it through the ballot box.

That's the law.

Unfortunately the Government doesn't like the law as it stands in relation to the GLC.

Today the first bill relating to the abolition of the GLC gets its second reading in the House.

It's devised to wipe out next year's GLC elections. Whether you're Labour, Tory, Liberal or SDP, you'll have no say.

Not since the last World War has your statutory right to vote been withdrawn in this way.

And it's a cynical dismissal of public opinion.

In a recent MORI poll 61% of Londoners of all political persuasions said no.

Only 22%, by the way, said yes.

In every straw poll, overwhelming public opinion has said no to abolition.

On 26th March Tom King the Conservative Secretary for Employment outlined in the House the elementary rights of people to register their vote without interference.

That was in relation to the Trade Union movement.

This Government steadfastly refuses to apply the same principles to the rights of 7 million Londoners.

You may hold the view of course,

that they were voted into power democratically and have the right to do as they wish.

But, nowhere in the Tory manifesto was there a mention of abolishing your right to vote in local elections.

Ask yourself why the Government is intent on doing away with the GLC in the first place.

There has not been a single proposition motivated by the desire to improve London.

What you might have heard have been outbursts.

"Red Ken spending our money on weirdos again."

(For the record less than half of one

per cent of GLC expenditure is allocated to all minorities.)

Don't let bigoted arguments of this kind blind you to the real issue.

This country's centuries old democratic tradition is at stake.

Local Government is one of the checks and balances which safeguard us against the abuse of central Government power.

And it would be an abuse of power for any Government to abolish a democratic institution such as a local authority, simply because it did not like the incumbent administration.

SAY NO TO NO SAY.

Figure 9.1 The GLC's Anti 'Paving Bill' Campaign.

Example 1: The GLC's Anti-Paving Bill Campaign

Ken Livingstone is currently a member of the British Parliament and occupies a political space to the left of the British Labour Party. At one time he was leader of the GLC (Greater London Council) and a controversial public figure. The poster employs an aspect of bodily semiosis: a direct and steady eye-to-eye gaze. It's a powerful semiotic device signalling a direct, open and personal communication. The effect is supported by the frank words beneath which appeal to an (almost) universal concern for democratic principles. Of course, eye-to-eye contact can mean different things in different contexts (such as aggression or sexual attraction), but it is clear that in this case a sincere, rational appeal is being made. The metaphor of personal communication, transmitted through a poster, might be powerful enough to get the public to read the argument in the small type. This is what the ad sets out to do but engaging semiotic codes (such as a frontal facial view with direct eye contact, no smile, no showbizzy hairdo or clothes and a direct quote) create association with honest personal communication. The fact that the person in the picture was distrusted by many people for his left wing views (he was known as Red Ken in some circles) makes the direct appeal more engaging. (*Source*: Channon, 1989)

Example 2: Birds Eye/Walls-Alphabites

The concept of children's food is historically recent. In many cultures childhood was considered merely a prelude to adulthood rather than a meaningful phase of human development in itself. Marketing potato as a children's food is an idea which chimes with the cultural tendency to glorify childhood as an idealized state which demands its own special rituals, of which eating is one. The advertiser seeks to employ non-verbal message codes to signify values which will appeal to the mother (or, exceptionally, the father) who buys and cooks the child's food. The semiotic power of music is employed to signify the idealized state of childhood: the visual semiosis of a fish finger sun (the sun is a powerful sign of life and vitality, as British newspaper proprietors know), the pictures of happy, pretty children, the nicely arranged meals (must be a caring Mum there) and the Birds Eye brand all together constitute a string of message-signs of which consumers would not normally be conscious, but which conspire to tap into cultural message codes to create a meaningful semiosis which is favourable to the product. (*Source*: Channon, 1989)

Example 3: Hofmeister Lager

The Hofmeister bear was the first time the author recalls alcohol being sold with a children's costume character. The target audience was 18–24-year-old male lager drinkers. Market research had seemed to indicate that Hofmeister tasted as good as other lagers but was bought less because it lacked a distinctive brand identity. The bear campaign sought to address this by making the lager cool, sophisticated, funny, irreverent. In the 1950s, alcohol and cigarette advertisements featured people who looked very grown up and acted in the kind of genteel manner lampooned by Harry Enfield today. Here, young adults were being told that drinking Hofmeister

Figure 9.2 Alphabites.

Bear: Life in a Bavarian forest was boring.
A big event was me and Ronnie Rabbit watching a leaf fall down.
Rabbit: (exitedly) a leaf! A leaf!
Bear: Hey . . .

Bear: Then one day I discovered Hofmeister lager with a picture of my Grandpa on it.
It had a cool cut on the back of the throat that was so good I decided to leave the forest.

And so I found . . . companionship.

I found the left hand screw to kiss onto the pink. (SFX kiss)
But most of all I found Hofmeister on draught.

The moral is: If you want poetry stand and stare

But if you want great lager – follow the bear, hey!

Figure 9.3 Hofmeister: A Study of Advertising in the Lager Market.

Bear: So the cold Hofmeister is sliding down like a dream

When this girl comes up and asks me what I do.

So I tell her I'm a dispensing chemist, which really impresses her for a bear,

And I'll read her prescription any time.

Sometimes I think the medical profession is misunderstood. I prescribe Hofmeister twice nightly, hey.

Hofmeister. For great lager – follow the bear.

Figure 9.3 Continued

would mean that they could be children rather than adults, and they liked it. Drinking and smoking once signified maturity and sophistication: now here is a campaign which seemed to be doing the reverse but in a subtle manner which carried [potentially] conflicting messages. The campaign employed a touch of postmodern irony (and whimsy) with the anthropomorphic bear a sign of fun, spontaneity and an irreverent sophistication which [were] in tune with the times. Today, many adult marketing appeals use signs once kept for children, such as cartoon or costume characters and mischievous humour. It is interesting to note that these kinds of advertising appeal would have been thought very strange indeed in the 1950s. (*Source*: Channon, 1989)

Example 4: Castlemaine Four X Lager

This campaign for Castlemaine XXXX lager (Australians wouldn't give a XXXX for anything else) was an advertising landmark in the use of postmodern ironic humour to carry a message of sophistication, individuality, self-expression, independence and indefatigability. The poster is a simple message using the famous slogan to remind consumers about the series of carefully produced television stories of Castlemaine culture in the outback. Australian men would find themselves having to choose between a can of lager and something less important, like their best friend's life. The advertisements were filmed with flair, ironic humour and high production values and succeeded in positioning Castlemaine favourably in the competitive UK lager market. Like the Hofmeister campaign, Castlemaine utilized cultural codes which emerged in the 1980s in order to create a meaningful semiosis through humour, whimsy, iconoclasm, irreverence, turning traditional conservative values upside down in a sophisticated way and positioning the brand as the superordinate sign for all these values. (*Source*: Channon, 1989)

Figure 9.4 Castlemaine XXXX Lager.

151

These four brief examples demonstrate the kinds of perspectives semiotics can offer. The chapter will have succeeded in its aims if readers are finding that they disagree with the above interpretations in favour of their own. Semiotic study is always open to alternative forms of interpretation: the position of this chapter is that the semiotic boundary always offers interesting perspectives on meaning-making in marketing communications.

SUMMARY AND CONCLUSIONS

This chapter has tried to describe some of the main concepts and principles of semiotics as the study of sign making, and has framed this discussion in the context of applied marketing communications studies. It began by attempting to set apart the semiotic boundary from other domains of analysis in the field of marketing communications. It developed the semiotic perspective in general and then placed this form of analysis in the cultural context of marketing communications. Finally, the chapter offered examples of what a semiotic perspective might offer students of marketing communications as part of an integrated approach to marketing communications from both a message and meaning-making perspective. The general position of the chapter is that the semiotic perspective is complementary to other perspectives in marketing communications since it focuses on the culturally embedded interpretation of message signs by consumers.

DISCUSSION TOPICS

1 Study the four examples given of advertising semiosis. Do you find the interpretations offered credible, or can you devise more detailed, more plausible ones?
2 Collect examples of marketing communications messages in various forms (TV storyboards, radio ads, scripts, press and poster ads, advertising copy, examples of product placement in movies, sponsorship and celebrity endorsement, brand logos, PR press releases, etc.). Discuss the process of semiosis which might be at work in each case. What is the nature of the cultural message code being employed? How successful is each example in tapping into this code to create a meaningful semiosis for the target consumers?
3 The semiotic position is often held that words evolved in humans as cognitive modelling devices first, communicative devices second. This view leaves non-verbal communication in a position of prime importance in marketing communications. What examples of non-verbal semiosis can you find in the examples of advertisements and marketing communications given in this chapter?
4 Explain and discuss the following semiotic terms. In each case, find an example from marketing communications to illustrate your definition of the meaning and semiotic function of each term.

- Symbol
- Index
- Icon
- Meaning
- Message
- Communication code
- Culture

5 Discuss the following statement: 'Messages have no meaning, instead people have meaning for messages.'

6 Disentangle the cultural meaning embedded in a cultural code of your choice (e.g. Nike 'swoosh').

7 Argue the case that marketing messages are composed of a 'string of signs'. From an integrated perspective, are the signs similar in transposition through the Four Ps of marketing?

8 From a semiotic perspective, how can signs be deconstructed? This should be approached from a historical and current perspective and provide evidence of deconstruction.

9 'Cultural meanings are detached from the culturally constituted world and attached to lesser objects.' Choose five brands and attempt to justify or negate this statement.

10 'Global communications is simply a non-sequitor.' Using some of the ideas from this chapter, critically discuss this statement.

CASE STUDY – THE UNION JACK

The British Tourist Authority has declared that it intends to replace the Union Jack flag as its logo or at least consider alternatives. The new logo is to be revealed at a future point. This proposal has been met with controversy among and from citizens. Of course, any issue to do with a national flag tends to be greeted with strong opinions because of the powerful symbolic value placed on it, and the associated values of national pride and belonging. However, the precise interpretation of the flag as a sign of something differs from individual to individual, and from context to context. The BTA argues along the lines that the Union Jack does not signify the particular features of Britishness that draw tourists. They argue that people from other countries visit Britain because of the rich contrasts of its culture, because of a certain quirky individualism with which Britishness is associated, and because the texture of British life is distinctively different from that elsewhere in the world. Some people have responded angrily to this view, saying that the Union Jack is a quintessential symbol of Britishness that it would be unpatriotic to abandon. Perhaps the BTA are responding to a sense of the post-colonial sensitivity of the idea of the British Empire. In any case, we can see that the Union Jack flag does mean something to people but the meaning is not the same for all people. (*Source:* BBC News, 13 August, 1997)

Related questions

1 Is the Union Jack flag an icon, an index or a symbol? Give examples to illustrate your answer.

2 What is the meaning of a national flag?

3 From memory, try to recall four national flags (sketching them briefly may help). What do these images mean to you? What do think they might mean to members of these or other countries? What are possible sources of these meanings?

4 To what extent is a flag a message?

5 How can a piece of cloth with an arrangement of colours on it engender such a wide range of semiosis among those who see it? List physical and emotional reactions to a flag. How may a semiotic perspective offer insight into these reactions?

ACKNOWLEDGEMENT

Grateful acknowledgement is extended for permission to use material from *20 Advertising Case Histories*, edited by Charles Channon, Cassell Educational, 1989.

REFERENCES

Barthes, R. (trans. 1968) *Elements of Semiology*, trans. Lavers, A., New York: Hill and Wang.

Berger, A. (1987) 'What is a Sign? Decoding Magazine Advertising, Semiotics of Advertisements', L. Henny (ed.), special issue of *International Studies in Visual Sociology and Visual Anthropology*, 1: 7(20).

Berlo, D.K. (1960) *The Process of Communication*, New York: Holt, Reinhart and Richardson.

Bertrand, D. (1988) 'The creation of complicity: a semiotic analysis of an advertising campaign for Black and White Whiskey', *International Journal of Research in Marketing*, 4(4): 273–89.

Buttle, F.A. (1995) 'Marketing communication theory: what do the texts teach our students?', *International Journal of Advertising*, 14(4): 297–313.

Channon, C. (ed) (1989) *20 Advertising Case Histories*, second series, London: Cassell.

Chapman, S. and Egger, G. (1983) 'Myth in cigarette advertising and health promotion', in H. Davis and P. Walton (eds.) *Language, Image, Media*, Oxford: Blackwell, 166–86.

Cleveland, C.E. (1989) 'Semiotics: determining what the advertising message means to the audience', *Advertising and Consumer Psychology*, (3): 227-41.

Collins, C.D. (1987) 'Ad images and iconography', in 'Semiotics of advertisements', L. Henny (ed.), special issue of *International Studies in Visual Sociology and Visual Anthropology*, 1, 21–39.

Danesi, M. (1993) *Messages and Meanings: An Introduction to Semiotics*, Toronto: Canadian Scholar's Press Inc.

Eco, U. (1976) *A Theory of Semiotics*, Bloomington: Indiana University Press.

Eco, U. (1984) *Semiotics and the Philosophy of Language*, London: Macmillan.

Elam, K. (1988) *The Semiotics of Theatre and Drama*, London: Routledge.

Fry, D., and Fry, V.L. (1986) 'A semiotic model for the study of mass communication', M. McLaughlin (ed.) *Communication Yearbook 9*, Beverly Hills: Sage, 443–61.

Geis, M.L. (1982) *The Language of Television Advertisng*, New York: Academic Press.

Hackley, C. and Kitchen, P. (1996) 'Ethical perspectives on the postmodern communications Leviathan', *Proceedings of the annual conference of the Marketing Education Group*, Strathclyde University, Scotland, UK, July (CD-ROM).

Hackley, C. and Kitchen, P.J. (1997) 'Ethical concepts for a phenomenology of marketing communications', in G. Moore (ed.) *Business Ethics: Principles and Practice*, Sunderland: Business Education Publishers, 99–112.

Jakobson, R. (1974) *Main Trends in the Science of Language*, New York: Harper and Row.

Kitchen, P.J. (1994) 'The marketing communications revolution – a Leviathan unveiled?', *Marketing Intelligence and Planning*, 12(2): 19–25.

Leach, E. (1976) *Culture and Communication: the logic by which symbols are connected – an introduction to the use of structuralist analysis in social anthropology*, Cambridge: Cambridge University Press.

Metz, C. (1974) *Film Language – a Semiotics of the Cinema*, New York: Oxford University Press.

Mueller, B. (1996) *International Advertising – Communicating Across Cultures*, California, London: Belmont.

O'Barr, W.M. (1994) *Culture and the Ad. – Exploring Otherness in the World of Advertising*, Boulder, Colorado: Westview Press.

Pierce, C.S. (1975) 'Some consequences of four incapabilities', *Journal of Speculative Philosophy*, 2: 140–51, in Pierce, C.S. (1975) C. Hartshon, P. Weiss and A.W. Burks (eds), *Collected Papers of Charles Sanders Pierce*, Cambridge: Harvard University Press.

Schramm, W. (1948) *Mass Communications*, Urbana, IL: University of Illinois Press.

Sebeok, T. (1976) *Contributions to the Doctrine of Signs*, Bloomington: Indiana University Press.

Sebeok, T. (1985) 'Pandora's box: how and why to communicate 10,000 years into the future', in M. Blonsky (ed.) *On Signs*, Baltimore: John Hopkins University Press, 448–66.

Sebeok, T.A. (1991) *A Sign is Just a Sign*, Bloomington and Indianapolis: Indiana University Press.

Sherry, J.F. (1987) 'Advertising as a cultural system', in J. Umiker-Sebeok (ed.), *Marketing and Semiotics*, Berlin: Mouton, 441–62.

Umiker-Sebeok, J. (ed.) (1987) *Marketing Signs: New Directions in the Study of Signs for Sale*, Berlin: Mouton.

Umiker-Sebeok, J., Cossette, C. and Bachand, D. (1988) 'Selected bibliography on the semiotics of marketing', *Semiotic Enquiry*, 8(3): 415–23.

Wernick, A. (1991) *Promotional Culture – Advertising, Ideology and Symbolic Expression*, London, Newbury Park: Sage.

10

CPM/HEM MODELS OF INFORMATION PROCESSING

Janine Dermody

CHAPTER AIMS

- to offer insight into consumer processing of marketing messages
- to evaluate consumer information processing within a hedonic and cognitive framework
- to examine the challenges facing the marketing communications industry in designing hedonic and cognitive appeals

ILLUSTRATION: 'SEX SELLS LEVI'S'

The setting is a café in the sun-baked landscape somewhere in the American Southwest. In comes an old man in overalls that hang loosely from his desiccated torso. He walks up to the counter, which is tended by a beautiful woman. Suddenly the view shifts to the side, where a staircase to the upper floor is marked with a 'Rooms To Let' sign. Down the stairs comes a ruggedly handsome young man. His shirt is open, and he is in his underpants. The old man looks at him in shock. The young woman looks at him longingly. He walks behind the counter, opens the refrigerator, takes out his jeans, and slowly slides into them, as the old man and two other old people look on with troubled expressions. Then he strides past them and out the door. With the young woman gazing after him, he mounts his motorcycle and drives off into the distance.

(British TV campaign for Levi's Jeans, Messaris, 1997)

INTRODUCTION

What sense might a consumer make of the Levi's campaign? The only words are in the song which stresses 'we are over 21'. The images are provocative in their sexuality. The body language of the young woman is pure desire, and for the man, pure macho maleness. So what is going on in an individual's mind when they consume this ad?

Bettman (1979) highlights a critical issue facing marketing communicators: how do consumers process their messages? The active way in which individuals process information has been recognized for some time (Petty *et al.* 1981; Festinger and Maccoby, 1964). What is less clear, however, is how consumers process the myriad of advertising messages, brand names, packaging cues and other forms of marketing communications relevant to their attitudes, beliefs, emotions, needs and wants. Does this involve a reasoned, logical approach, is it more emotionally based, or is it a mix of the two? This chapter will review two paradigms which attempt to explain the ways in which consumers process marketing information to make informed consumption choices. The first of these is the consumer processing model (CPM) which regards behaviour as 'rational, highly cognitive, systematic and reasoned' (Shimp, 1997). The second is the hedonic, experiential model (HEM) which perceives the pursuit of 'fantasies, feelings and fun' (Holbrook and Hirschman, 1982) to be the foundation of behaviour. It would be naive, however, to assume that these models embrace the diversity and complexity of consumer information processing. They represent two extremes, they are the antithesis of each other, so how can they both be right? It is more likely that behaviour results from both logic and emotion (Shimp, 1997). The models should therefore be regarded as operating on a spectrum embracing both rational and hedonic information processing in their purest sense and the varying gradients of the rational–emotional equation in-between. This spectrum is presented in Figure 10.1. The mix itself will be dependent on the characteristics of the consumer and the nature of the consumption decision to be made.

This chapter begins with an exploration of current thinking on the cognitive vs. hedonic debate. The discussion will then consider both perspectives within an information processing framework. Implications for marketing communications will be emphasized throughout. The chapter will conclude by highlighting key issues for consideration in designing persuasive messages and suggest a research agenda for the next millennium.

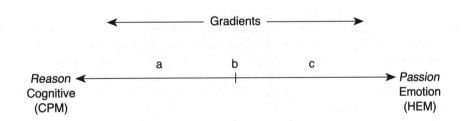

Key:
a: skewed towards reason with a small element of emotion
b: balance between reason and passion
c: skewed towards passion with a small element of reason
Note this is a simple illustration of three gradients; the spectrum itself will be more complex than this

Figure 10.1 The CPM/HEM spectrum.

COMMUNICATING WITH THINKING AND FEELING CONSUMERS

> Consumer researchers have devoted little attention to the underlying determinants of fun and playful activities even though it appears that consumers spend many of their waking hours engaged in events that can be explained on no other grounds.
>
> (Holbrook and Hirschman, 1982: 138)

People as thinkers have dominated consumer behaviour research for decades, (Holbrook, 1995; Perloff, 1993; Obermiller and Atwood, 1990). This perspective portrays people as actively searching for verbal and factual information consistent with their logical and cognitive characteristics. The cognitive paradigm emphasized the importance of consumer beliefs in information processing and elevated the processing of verbal information to the exclusion of other senses (Holbrook 1980). Where emotions were considered, research restricted itself to rating tangible product features (Holbrook, 1980). This emphasis on cognitive thinking was further strengthened by an economic view which regarded products as fulfilling utilitarian needs. While this may be appropriate for products whose attributes and functions are central to their value to the consumer, Hirschman amd Holbrook (1982) argue it is less valid for products selected to fulfil emotional needs, for example opera, music and sport. While products such as these are deemed to be inherently hedonic, any product can be emotionally arousing if consumers perceive it as such (Levy, 1980).

It was not until the early 1980s that the concept of the cognitive consumer was challenged, most notably by that of the 'hedonic (feeling) consumer'. Zajonc (1980) and Hirschman and Holbrook's (1982) claims concerning the independence and importance of emotional/hedonic responses to persuasive messages encouraged scholars to reassess the dominance of the cognitive paradigm. The hedonic perspective is attempting to redress the balance by recognizing the multisensory images, fantasies and emotions through which consumers respond to their world (Hirschman and Holbrook, 1982). 'This experiential perspective is phenomenological in spirit and regards consumption as a primarily subjective state of consciousness with a variety of subjective meanings, hedonic responses and aesthetic criteria' (Holbrook and Hirschman, 1982: 132).

In effect, what is being ignored by the cognitive perspective is consumption as play (leisure), sensory pleasure, daydreaming and aesthetically and emotionally fulfilling experiences. Fournier and Guiry (1993), for example, suggest that for some individuals longing for an object of their desire is filled with so many enjoyable fantasies, it virtually satisfies needs and wants in its own right. How might the cognitive paradigm make sense of this truly hedonic experience?

Further, the language and delivery of persuasive appeals will vary for cognitive and hedonic consumers. Cognitive consumers actively search for verbal information, hedonic consumers are less active, but when they do search, it will be for sensory information (Lofman, 1991; Venkatraman and MacInnis, 1985).

The underlying propositions of hedonic consumption have important implications for marketing communications. Firstly Maslow (1968) maintained that emotional desires can override functional motives in particular circumstances. For example, consumers' deductive reasoning based on economic criteria can be superseded by emotions such as love, hate or jealousy (Dichter, 1960). Marketing communicators therefore need to determine whether their messages should appeal to an audience's reason or emotion – a semantic vs. syntactic approach.

Secondly, it is generally accepted that individuals supplement the tangible features of a product with subjective meaning (Cowley, 1991; Holbrook, 1981). Campbell (1987) maintains that 'Individuals do not so much seek satisfaction from products, as pleasure from the self-illusory experiences which they construct from their associated meanings'.

This essentially falls into the domain of product symbolism – branding. From a hedonic perspective, communication professionals will be communicating the brand values – the symbolic, experiential dimensions. A cognitive style would be rooted in reason and logic, focusing on tangible product features.

Expanding on this, marketing communications must recognize the influence of individuals' imagination in the whole consumption experience. That individuals create their own realities cannot be denied (Lofman, 1991; Swanson, 1978; Singer, 1966). Hedonic consumption occurs within an individual's creation of a 'perfect world' which is typically far removed from reality (Holbrook and Hirschman, 1982; Dichter, 1960). For the consumer this is not an issue. For the communicator, however, matching the message to this 'perfect reality' can cause problems. This is one situation where research is vital. It is only by probing the mental imagery surrounding a product and exploring consumers' fantasies in consuming it that their subjective reality can begin to emerge (Swanson, 1978). An example of this subjective reality is our transformation into pop stars when we consume a new CD or music video of our favourite musicians. The Marlboro campaign depended heavily on individuals fantasizing about themselves as 'Marlboro Cowboys'. For some consumers the centrality of the message was about them being able to act out their fantasies as a Cowboy, rather than simply a 'macho Marlboro man image' (Holbrook and Hirschman, 1982).

> Emotionally, Marlboro owns the best. Whether it's a grizzled Cowboy shading his eyes from the burning ember as he lights his cigarette from the campfire, a round up of wild horses or simply a loving close-up of saddle and spur, there are few places in the world where the identifying brand name wouldn't immediately spring to mind. So potent is the symbolism that it allows the advertiser to 'tailor' his message according to the ever increasing degree of restriction prevalent in a particular country. You can't show someone smoking? You don't need to. The symbol says it all.
>
> (Clark, 1988)

In constructing persuasive messages, marketing communicators need to recognize that individuals are motivated to consume either through sensory-emotive or cognitive information stimulation (Hirschman 1982; Zuckerman, 1979). What makes persuasion more difficult is that mixes will vary. Some individuals may favour one more than the other, they may be equally weighted, or above or below average on both (Venkatraman and McInnis, 1985; Hirschman, 1982). Lacher (1994) and Lacher and Mizerski (1994) explored these ratios in relation to gender and hedonic

159

consumption and concluded that men and women respond differently to incoming stimuli. Lacher (1994) maintains that women typically respond to music in a sensorial way, often through dance, while men are more analytical, seeking cognitive stimulation through a hedonic experience. Bruell (1986) maintained that men are more masculine in their use of and receptiveness towards language, whereas women are more feminine. Inherent within this, Bruell (1986) argued that women are more expressive in their use of language. This is epitomized in the title of one of his papers: 'He: This is an okay (lovely) analysis (emotional investigation) of our words (deepest corridors of meaning)'. The language outside the parentheses is masculine and inside feminine. Followed to its logical conclusion, persuasion targeting women may be more effective if it is feminine and appeals to the senses, whereas for men it would have to be framed in a more cognitive, masculine style where pleasure can be determined through a cause and effect relationship.

Multicultural norms and values will also influence the ratio of cognitive vs. hedonic processing (Hirschman, 1982). This has implications for the development of international marketing messages. Communication professionals must recognize the extent to which international audiences are hedonically or cognitively inspired, as well as the extent to which cultural taboos impair emotional expression. Huang (1997) stresses that advertisers must distinguish between basic and social emotions in developing emotive appeals. Basic emotional messages are more suited to international communication because they are more common across cultures. Thus, 'happy appeals will be more appropriate than humorous appeals; loving appeals will be better than warm appeals; and sad appeals will be more effective than surprising appeals' (Huang, 1997).

Patai (1977) maintains that ethnic norms encouraged Jewish and Italian Catholics to express their emotions much more than was permitted among Protestants. Singer (1966) concluded that this same group fantasize much more frequently than Protestants and their fantasizes are richer – often erotic and sensual. It could well be that the increasing globalization of cultures since this research was conducted has weakened these differences. However, it is clear that both hedonic and cognitive consumption will be influenced by cultural differences and marketing communications must continue to recognize this.

It would appear, therefore, that human behaviour is both cognitively and experientially bound. The cognitive and hedonic perspectives are complementary and offer a much more insightful and holistic approach to our understanding of the ways in which audiences process persuasive messages. Marketing communications must recognize that consumers think and feel, feel and think in their responses to persuasion. Having established the parameters of the hedonic and cognitive paradigms, the discussion will move on to consider them within an information processing framework.

PROCESSING PERSUASIVE MESSAGES

If one had to identify the central fundamental question behind all psychological enquiry, it would be this: what is the relationship between mental processes and behaviour? What makes this a difficult question . . . is that behaviour is observable whereas mental processes can only be inferred . . . .

(Eiser, 1981)

From McGuire's typology of information processing, it would appear that the processing of marketing messages can be characterized by exposure, attention, comprehension and evaluation. This discussion will concentrate on the cognitive and hedonic dimensions of attention, comprehension and evaluation and the implications for decision making and behaviour. It will begin with an analysis of attention.

Selective attention

Attending to a message involves the consumer being aware of and reflecting on a message. Attention, however, is very selective; the human brain cannot cope with the multitude of messages to which it is exposed every day. In addition, the human brain acts in an ego-defensive manner to protect existing attitudes, beliefs and values, and hence self-identity (Katz, 1960). Selective attention therefore occurs as a result of limited mental ability to process information; ego-defence; the personal relevance of the information to which the individual is exposed; and limited motivation to process, perhaps because the message does not excite its audience.

Breaking through the barriers of selective attention can be difficult. Marketing communicators therefore need a variety of message styles to gain spontaneous attention. These include appeals based on cognitive and hedonic needs which can be expressed through the use of novel stimuli (Shimp, 1997). Consumers are receptive to messages which are cognitively engaging, thereby satisfying their informational goals (cognitive needs). They are also receptive to messages that they associate with pleasure, their fantasies and rewards (hedonic needs) (Holbrook and Hirschman, 1982). The hedonic perspective suggests that in order to gain attention and aid processing, messages should activate and arouse, through, for example, promises of pleasure (Holbrook and Hirschman, 1982; Kroeber-Riel, 1979). This moves the debate towards the rather contentious issue of 'right-brain' processing which is associated with emotion. While the validity of such research has been called into question (Ryan, 1980), it would seem that this has more to do with our ignorance of brain functioning rather than the left–right brain concept itself (Holbrook and Hirschman, 1982).

Sexual messages are an example of message themes appealing to pleasure, fantasy and play. The Joe Bloggs campaign theme, 'you only get a snog in a pair of Joe Bloggs', is a case in point. The Levi's campaign is another. Sexual messages are also used to sell food, for example the women office workers ogling the male construction worker who's drinking Diet Coke. But why is the link between food and sex so pervasive? Psychoanalysts have argued that for some people, this association is a feature of their sexual experiences. Patterson and Kim (1991) found that people fantasize about (and some allegedly practice) such acts as licking whipped cream off a sexual partner. From the cognitive perspective this theme would reinforce a consumer's cognitions towards the brand (sexual appeal), while from a hedonic perspective it would appeal through its promise of pleasure. This illustrates how cognitive and hedonic needs can run in unison. However, for some ad agencies the use of sexual metaphors for selling food has lost its edge, except perhaps through humour as the ad for Foster's illustrates:

> The commercial begins with a man and a woman in bed, feeding each other ice cream. The action heats up, the camera moves in for tighter close-ups, and the man pull off his shirt. But they have reached the bottom of the ice cream container. 'More,' the woman purrs. The man gets up, goes to the kitchen. He looks into the freezer compartment of the refrigerator, and we see another tub of ice cream. But then the camera travels to the shelves below, and a can of Foster's lager comes into view. Cut to the woman in the bedroom, waiting impatiently. Suddenly, from another part of the house, we hear the sound of a TV sports announcer. Seething with frustration, the woman turns to the viewer: 'Don't you just hate it when that happens?'
>
> (Foster's TV campaign, Messaris, 1997)

Novel stimuli tend to gain audience attention because they are unusual, distinctive and unpredictable, (Shimp, 1997). Consumers notice these types of messages because they stand out from the crowd of other stimuli which bombard them every day. An illustration of this is the use of colour in black and white print or vice versa. Sparkman and Austin (1980) found that sales of products can be increased by as much as 41 per cent where colour is employed in newspaper advertising.

While these techniques can assist marketing communicators in gaining audience attention, it must be recognized that this is not easy because of the criteria which make processing selective. Furthermore, an audience's world is very cluttered with competing messages and environments. Clutter in television advertising has been found to impair its effectiveness, (Webb, 1979; Webb and Ray, 1979). More low-rather than high-involvement ads appear to be screened out as a result, likewise ads placed later in a series of commercials. Psychologists refer to this as the recency and primacy effects.

Message comprehension and acceptance

Comprehension, or perception as it is sometimes referred to, is concerned with interpretation, essentially how consumers comprehend their world. This involves interpretation of meaning from stimuli and symbols. As the preceding discussion has indicated, it is important to recognize that we do not all see the same world. While there will be common elements, interpretations are personal (Lofman, 1991; Chapman, 1987; Swanson, 1978; Singer, 1966). Marketing communicators therefore need to understand these individual interpretations and ensure their messages reflect them. This is one of the most difficult and important areas of marketing communications.

The process of comprehension begins with perceptual encoding. This occurs at two levels, feature analysis and synthesis. The process is initiated with feature analysis which identifies and classifies messages. Synthesis is rather more complex; incoming messages are combined with the context in which they are received, and with audience characteristics including existing cognitions stored in memory, expectations, personality, and mood states (Fazio *et al.*, 1994; Loudon and Della Bitta, 1993). Existing cognitions include attitudes and beliefs; messages will be accepted or rejected on the basis of whether or not they are consistent with these cognition's, (Zimbardo and Leippe, 1991). Expectations relate to an individual's previous experiences, which results in a 'preconditioned set'. Information which fits into this set will be accepted. However, interestingly, information which contradicts an individual's expectations may be accepted, providing it is not too challenging (Perloff, 1993). Contradictory information is more acceptable to some personality types. Individuals with moderate self-esteem, for example, may be more susceptible to persuasion involving challenging messages (Janis, 1954). Dogmatic and authoritarian personality types are less likely to accept conflicting information unless the message is endorsed by a powerful and credible source (Perloff, 1993).

Sometimes messages are intentionally (but probably unconsciously) misinterpreted to preserve consistency with existing attitudes, values and beliefs which act as reference points guiding behaviour. Sherif and Sherif (1967) maintain that this judgemental distortion occurs through a process of assimilation and contrast. In assimilation, individuals interpret the meanings of acceptable messages as being closer to their own attitude position than they really are. Unacceptable messages, however, are subjected to the contrast effect whereby a greater difference is perceived between message meanings and attitudinal positions than exists in reality. It is therefore critical, in understanding information processing, to appreciate the attitudinal positions of consumers. Indeed Whittaker (1967) argues:

> Communicators must know the position or stands of individuals with whom they are communicating, at least if they are interested in changing attitudes. It is not enough to simply present one's own position. In fact, presentation of one's own position without regard for that of the listener may result in convincing the listener that he is right and the communicator wrong.
>
> (Whittaker, 1967)

Attitudinal position would therefore appear to be a powerful influence in the acceptance or rejection of persuasive messages. However, in addition to appealing to consumer attitudes, values and beliefs, the credibility of the message will further enhance its acceptance (Andrews and Shimp, 1990; Misra and Beatty, 1990; Kaikati, 1987).

Mood states can also influence receptiveness to persuasive messages. Gardner (1985) found that when individuals are feeling positive, they are more likely to retrieve happy memories, be more optimistic about events happening in their world and respond more favourably to stimuli. Marketing communications is therefore more likely to be successful if it can create or sustain positive mood states. This embraces the earlier discussion of right-brain processing.

Furthermore, communicators must recognize the extent to which their target market is influenced by group pressures, which in turn will impact on the acceptance or rejection of a message. Snyder (1987) refers to these individuals as high self-monitors. They are concerned with fitting into social situations and therefore look externally for cues on how they should behave, rather than referring to their own attitudinal stance. They will often adopt peer group norms and values, hence accepting a group identity which in turn influences the acceptance of messages which fit these norms and values and the rejection of those that do not. This is a particularly powerful determinant of the adoption of brands and consequently message themes need to portray brands in this way. For example, if the norms and values of European adolescents centre around the pursuit of pleasure and the fulfilment of fantasies, the communication of brands targeting them will need to be hedonically packaged, whether it's Coca-Cola, a nightclub or a new film release. Low self-monitors (Snyder, 1987), on the other hand, look internally to their attitude position to guide their processing of messages and subsequent behaviour. Therefore understanding individual attitudes, values and beliefs is far more important for these consumers. It is therefore critical for persuaders to profile their audiences psychographically in an attempt to identify individual and group influences on message acceptance and rejection. For example, to what extent is high and low self-monitoring linked with levels of self-esteem which facilitate or inhibit counterarguments?

Message retention, search and retrieval

Memory and learning are central to the retention, search and retrieval of information contained in campaigns, and as a result impact on consumer decisions and behaviour. Psychologists maintain that individuals' memories are structured to provide temporary storage of information through sensory and short-term memory (STM) into a more permanent, or certainly durable, long-term memory (LTM) store. If incoming message stimuli gain attention in sensory memory, they are transferred to STM where they are compared with existing cognitions in LTM and information from our sense organs. If the message is deemed to be acceptable, it is transferred to LTM and organized into schemata or knowledge structures, so in turn becoming a reference point for the analysis of future information (Mitchell, 1983). The retention of information would therefore appear to be very straightforward. However, it must be recognized that the STM can only process a limited amount of information at any one time; information overload will result in ineffective processing or the rejection of messages and will hamper recognition and recall of messages (Shiffrin and Atkinson, 1969).

The aim of marketing communicators is to ensure that their messages enter LTM, often by emphasizing benefits, where they can be retrieved to influence future decisions which will essentially involve the rejection of competitors' claims. In this respect, communicators are facilitating human learning through the translation of messages into consumer cognitions (Mitchell, 1983). Adolescents have learnt that wearing Levi jeans, Nike trainers and drinking Coca-Cola will make them more acceptable among their peers. 'Housewives' have learnt that Radion will deodorize and clean their families' clothes. Voters learnt that voting for 'New Labour' could make a difference to their lives. This process of learning essentially requires marketing communicators to reinforce links between their message and existing cognitions stored in memory so that association takes place. Repetition, creativity and unambiguous language can all aid this process. Learning and retrieval are further enhanced when the information being transferred into memory is tangible rather than abstract (concretization), for example the tangible benefits of a brand. Alternatively communications professionals can attempt to create new links between existing cognitions and the message, (Mitchell, 1983). This in turn aids retrieval of stored information which is improved when new cognitions are linked with familiar and readily accessible memories (Shimp, 1997).

While the cognitive perspective focuses on this knowledge structure of beliefs represented by memory schemata, hedonic explorations of information processing maintain that cognitions are inherently more private and subconscious than the cognitive paradigm would have us believe (Holbrook and Hirschman, 1982). Freud maintained that these latent cognitions are repressed because they are socially embarrassing and lead to anxiety. As a result they are expressed through visual imagery, fantasy and daydreams.

Visual imagery can be used by marketing communicators to facilitate persuasion, (Oliver, *et al.*, 1993; Burns, *et al.*, 1993; Miller and Marks, 1992; Rossiter, 1982). This relationship can be expressed in terms of dual-coding theory which maintains that pictures have a greater chance of being remembered and recalled because they can be stored in visual or verbal formats. Text on the other hand is rarely stored in any other format (Rossiter and Percy, 1978). Houston *et al.* (1987) maintain that the recall of product attributes is enhanced when the message includes pictures, compared with text alone. Visuals can also improve attention to messages, particularly where copy is low in imagery (Unnava and Burnkrant, 1991). Lutz and Lutz (1977) found that individuals' memory of company names improved significantly when they were related to meaningful pictures. This is not surprising since according to Shepard (1978) virtually everything that we feel and visualize is derived from what we see, with 70–80 per cent of learning being visual.

Marketing communicators can also use visual imagery to encourage consumers to fantasize about particular products. Communicators can use imagery to transform brands into subjective symbols of feelings, fantasies and fun; for example, the Haagen Daz campaigns which assist consumers in fantasizing about the pleasure of sensual experiences. In addition to visuals, imagery includes auditory, olfactory and tactile appeals. According to Fitzgerald-Bone and Jantrania (1992), appeals based on olfactory images (smells) can activate strong images of consumption contexts, brands and brand usage. In addition, they can gain consumers' attention; encourage them to process information; influence their memories and their evaluations of product-performance; and trigger their behaviour, (Fitzgerald-Bone and Jantrania,1992; Schab, 1991). It would therefore appear that the potential of imagery in marketing communications is tremendous; it can 'appeal to our senses and evoke images that activate emotions, influence cognition, and enhance memorability of marketing messages' (Shimp, 1997).

Consumer decision making and behaviour

So, having processed the information contained in marketing messages, one would assume that consumers simply refer to existing cognitions to direct them in their decision making. This is probably the case for simple decisions, but what about decisions relating to brands? It is likely that consumers have stored numerous 'facts' about different brands, some of which will be contradictory and incomplete. In order to assist decision making in these situations, consumers often rely on heuristics (strategies) to ease their choices. Ultimately what the consumer is attempting to do is to choose the 'best brand'. A number of heuristics can be adopted, including affect referral, compensation and conjunctive decisions.

Affect referral is a simple strategy whereby consumers retrieve from memory their attitudes towards alternative brands and choose the one with the most positive attitudes (Wright, 1975). However, it is rare for a choice to be so simple; a brand would have to be very superior in all attributes and benefits for this heuristic to work. What is more realistic is that brands will have different strengths and weaknesses and consumers must decide which attributes and benefits they rate most highly. This is the essence of the compensatory heuristic. For example, consumers may decide to trade the premium pricing of brand A for the lesser quality of brand B, depending on their ratings which determine their choice criteria. The Theory of Reasoned Action (Fishbein and Ajzen, 1975) provides a good illustration of this compensatory process. Alternatively, consumers may choose a non-compensatory strategy, for example a conjunctive heuristic. This involves consumers setting standards on all key choice criteria. A brand will only continue to be considered if it meets or exceeds these standards (Bettman, 1979). It is unlikely that these different heuristics operate independently of each other; a combined strategy is more likely (Bettman, 1979). For example, a consumer may start with a conjunctive heuristic and then progress to a compensatory heuristic once the brands have been reduced down to the select few. To illustrate, having purchased a motorbike, the buyer will be looking for reassurance, often to alleviate anxiety not just in terms of value for money and performance, but also in terms of brand values and a positive self-identity, (Belk,1988; Steele, 1988; Steele and Liu, 1983; Festinger 1957), and the promised fun, pleasure and fantasies (Hirschman and Holbrook, 1982).

These promises of fun, pleasure and fantasy expand heuristics into hedonic criteria which are somewhat different. Rather than focusing on issues such as quality and value for money, consumer criteria would be based on the fulfilment of fun and fantasy. These evocative experiential associations, linked together through experience, extend decision criteria beyond satisfaction to embrace the associations of pleasure that occur when an individual consumes (Holbrook and Hirschman, 1982; Klinger, 1971).

In conclusion, while decision making is an important aspect of the whole consumption process, it must be recognized that the pursuit of pleasure through multisensory gratification, arousing fantasies and heightened mood states is an objective in its own right (Holbrook and Hirschman, 1982). Further, as the preceding discussion has highlighted, purchase does not need to occur for consumers' hedonic desires to be satisfied (Fournier and Guiry, 1993).

SUMMARY AND CONCLUSIONS

The review has indicated the multiplicity of issues which marketing communicators need to take into account in designing and delivering persuasive messages. It would appear, however, that this design and delivery can be improved, providing communicators understand the processing strategies adopted by their target audience, both rational and experiential.

Message platforms need to satisfy both hedonic and cognitive consumer needs and wants: cognitive through the perceived value of the products functions and attributes, hedonic through the promise of pleasure, fantasy and emotional and aesthetic arousal. Both styles can break through the barriers of selective perception and assist message comprehension and acceptance, providing they are targeted appropriately. Targeting raises a number of considerations for marketing communicators considering hedonic and cognitive appeals. The preceding discussion has indicated gender and cultural receptiveness to different forms of persuasion. The acceptability of different message styles will be influenced by cultural norms, particularly in relation to hedonic appeals and their inherent sensuality. This has obvious implications for the design of international marketing communications, not only in terms of cultural taboos, but also processing styles of different nationalities.

With respect to gender, it would seem that women respond to hedonic appeals and men to cognitive ones. They could therefore be classified into feminine and masculine message styles. Communicators must recognize, however, that there will be exceptions to this and appeals can be a mix of the two. With consumers becoming more sophisticated and cynical in their attitudes towards advertising in particular, marketing communicators will increasingly need to avoid generalizing about their audiences and instead 'fine-tune' their communication to audiences, whether it is an emotional or rational appeal, or a mix of the two. Homosexuals, for example, may be more receptive to hedonic appeals.

Finally, communicators need to match hedonic and cognitive appeals with different language styles. Cognitive language will typically be verbal, factual and informative. Hedonic language will be visual, sensory and use imaginal symbolism. These perspectives essentially embrace semantic vs. syntactic styles. Hedonic appeals lead into the realms of semiotics where visual language enables signs and symbols to be decoded at a much faster rate than they otherwise might have been, thereby aiding consumers in their processing skills and marketing communicators in their persuasion skills.

The opportunities for successful persuasion are therefore very much enhanced by the cognitive and hedonic paradigms of information processing. While it is clear that human beings are thinking beings, it is clear that they are also hedonic. Marketing communicators must recognize the contribution that both these paradigms can make. It is not the case that one is better than the other; rather different styles will be appropriate for different communication objectives, brands and target audiences.

It must also be recognized that consumer behaviour researchers' understanding of hedonic processing is limited. There is certainly a need for further research into right- and left-brain processing; the psychobiological basis of consumer arousal; the receptiveness of different nationalities, genders and age groups to hedonic and rational appeals; matching personality types to experiential and rational communication, to name but a few. Further, the methodological difficulties involved in researching the hedonic consumer must not be underestimated.

DISCUSSION QUESTIONS

1 Explore the origins of the cognitive and hedonic information processing paradigms. How and in what way(s) have they shaped marketing communications?
2 Consider the merits and problems of developing sensory-emotive and cognitive-informative advertising appeals.
3 Using the principles of demographic, psychographic and lifestyle segmentation, develop a profile of (a) a hedonic consumer, (b) a cognitive consumer.
4 Design persuasive appeals based on your profiles developed in Question 3 for your home country and one international market.
5 How might your understanding of consumer needs and wants be facilitated by the hedonic experiential perspective? How can this be used in designing advertising appeals?
6 Review current understanding of the impact of sensual imagery on persuasion. What are the implications for marketing communications?
7 Examine how consumer mood states can enhance or inhibit receptiveness to marketing messages.
8 Consider how the hedonic experiential model can be used by brand managers to enhance communication of their brands.
9 Assess how the hedonic and cognitive perspectives can assist marketing communicators in overcoming consumer information processing barriers.
10 Is it appropriate for individuals to be regarded as thinking and feeling consumers? Consider the strategic importance of designing persuasive messages to appeal to both.

CASE STUDY – 'DIRTY ANGELS'

Music, Mud and Angels!!!

Our intrepid reporter reviews the UK's latest success story . . .

The crowd screamed for more, but the 'Angels' weren't having any of it; the last note died and the lights went out – the end of another successful gig. 'Dirty Angels' are the UK's latest success story. Their music is an awe-inspiring mix of rock, blues and folk music. The band have been playing in London's clubs and bars for the last four years and are about to hit the big time. Their latest single, 'Blowing the Clouds Away' (Anita Gabrielle (1998) song writer and musician), has just entered the UK charts and their new album is due for release in six weeks. The band's lead singer, with her flame red hair and cheeky grin, says their unique sound arose out of their love of American blues, Irish folk and the loud noise she made on her drums! Their sensual and upbeat lyrics promise a better world; their music is electrifying. Their philosophy is a mix of New Age and hedonism. Cool isn't the word for this band, they're hot and ready to set the music scene alight!

From your understanding of cognitive and hedonic processing, suggest how the band might be promoted.

REFERENCES

Andrews, J.C. and Shimp, T.A. (1990) 'Effects of involvement, argument strength, and source characteristics on central and peripheral processing of advertising', *Psychology and Marketing*, 7(3): 195–214.

Belk, R.W. (1975) 'Situational variables and consumer behaviour', *Journal of Consumer Research*, 2, December: 157–64.

Belk, R.W. (1988) 'Possessions and the extended self', *Journal of Consumer Research*, 15, Sept: 139–68.

Bettman, J.B. (1979) *An Information Processing Theory of Consumer Choice*, Reading, Mass: Addison-Wesley.

Bruell, E. (1986) 'He: this is an okay (lovely) analysis (emotional investigation) of our words (deepest corridors of meaning)', *Chicago Tribune*, 31 December, Sec. 7, 12.

Burns, A.C. Biswas, A., and Babin, L.A. (1993) 'The operation of visual imagery as a mediator of advertising effects', *Journal of Advertising*, 21, June: 71–85.

Campbell, C. (1987) *The Romantic Ethic and the Spirit of Modern Consumerism*, Oxford, UK: Basil Blackwell.

Cowley, D. (ed.) (1991) *Understanding Brands By Ten People Who Do*, London: Kogan Page.

Denes-Raj, V. and Epstein, S. (1994) 'Conflict between intuitive and rational processing: when people behave against their better judgement', *Journal of Personality and Social Psychology*, 66(5): 819–29.

Dichter, E. (1960) *The Strategy of Desire*, Garden City, NY: Doubleday.

Eiser, J.R. (1981) *Attitudes in Psychology*, Exeter University Press.

Fazio, R.H., Roskos-Ewoldsen, D.R. and Powell, M.C. (1994) 'Attitudes, perception, and attention', in P.M. Niedenthal and S. Kitayama (eds) *The Heart's Eye: Emotional Influences in Perception and Attention*, San Diego: Academic Press, 197–216.

Festinger, L. (1957) *A Theory of Cognitive Dissonance*, Stanford, CA: Stanford University Press.

Festinger, L. and Maccoby, N. (1964) 'On resistance to persuasive communications', *Journal of Abnormal and Social Psychology*, 68: 359–66.

Fishbein, M. and Ajzen, I. (1975) *Beliefs, Attitude, Intention, and Behaviour: An Introduction to Theory and Research*, Reading, Mass: Addison-Wesley.

Fitzgerald-Bone, P. and Jantrania, S. (1992) 'Olfaction as a cue for product quality', *Marketing Letters*, 3, July: 289–96.

Fournier, S. and Guiry, M. (1993) 'An emerald green Jaguar, a house on Nantucket, and an African safari: wish lists and consumption dreams in materialist society', *Advances in Consumer Research*, 20: 352–58.

Gardner, M.P. (1985) 'Mood states and consumer behaviour: a critical review', *Journal of Consumer Research*, 12, December: 281–300.

Hirschman, E.C. (1982) 'Ethnic variation in hedonic consumption', *Journal of Social Psychology*.

Hirschman, E.C. and Holbrook, M.B. (1982) 'Hedonic consumption: emerging concepts, methods and propositions', *Journal of Marketing*, 46, Summer: 92–101.

Holbrook, M.B. (1980) 'Some preliminary notes on research in consumer esthetics', *Advances in Consumer Research*, 7.

Holbrook, M.B. (1981) 'Integrating compositional and decompositional analyses to represent the intervening role of perceptions in evaluative judgements', *Journal of Marketing Research*, 18, February: 13–28.

Holbrook, M.B. (1995) *Consumer Research – Introspective Essays on the Study of Consumption*, CA: Sage.

Holbrook, M.B. and Hirschman, E.C. (1982) 'The experiential aspects of consumption: consumer fantasies, feelings, and fun', *Journal of Consumer Research*, 9, September: 132–40.

Houston, M.J. Childers, T.L. and Heckler, S.E. (1987) 'Picture-word consistency and the elaborative processing of advertisements', *Journal of Marketing Research*, 24, November: 359–69.

169

Huang, M.H. (1997) 'Exploring a new typology of emotional appeals: basic, versus social, emotional advertising', *Journal of Current Issues and Research in Advertising*, 19(2), Fall: 23–36.

Janis, I.L. (1954) 'Personality correlates of susceptibility to persuasion', *Journal of Personality*, 22: 504–18.

Kaikati, J.G. (1987) 'Celebrity advertising: a review and synthesis', *International Journal of Advertising*, 6: 93–105.

Katz, D. (1960) 'The functional approach to the study of attitudes', *Public Opinion Quarterly*, 24: 163–204.

Klinger, E. (1971) *Structure and Functions of Fantasy*, New York: Wiley-Interscience.

Kroeber-Riel, W. (1979) 'Activation research: psychobiological approaches in consumer research', *Journal of Consumer Research*, 5, March: 240–50.

Lacher, K.T. (1994) 'An investigation of the influence of gender on the hedonic responses created by listening to music', *Advances in Consumer Research*, 21: 354–59.

Lacher, K.T. and Mizerski, R. (1994) 'An exploratory study of the responses and relationships involved in the evaluation of, and intention to purchase new rock music', *Journal of Consumer Research*, 21, September: 366–81.

Levy, S.J. (1980) *The symbolic analysis of companies, brands, and customers*', Albert Wesley Frey Lecture, Graduate School of Business, University of Pittsburgh, PA.

Lofman, B. (1991) 'Elements of experiential consumption: an exploratory study', *Advances in Consumer Research*, 18: 729–35.

Loudon, D.L. and Della Bitta, A.J. (1993) *Consumer Behaviour*, McGraw-Hill.

Lutz, K.A. and Lutz, R.J. (1977) 'Imagery-eliciting strategies: review and implications of research', *Advances in Consumer Research*, 5: 611–20.

Maslow, A.H. (1968) *Toward a Psychology of Being*, 2nd ed, Princeton, NJ: Van Nostrand.

McGuire, W.J. (1976) 'Some internal psychological factors influencing consumer choice', *Journal of Consumer Research*, 4, March: 302–19.

Messaris, P. (1997) *Visual Persuasion, The Role of Images in Advertising*, CA: Sage.

Miller, D.W. and Marks, L.J. (1992) 'Mental imagery and sound effects in radio commercials', *Journal of Advertising*, 21, December: 83–93.

Misra, S. and Beatty, S.E. (1990) 'Celebrity spokesperson and brand congruence: an assessment of recall and affect', *Journal of Business Research*, 21: 159–73.

Mitchell, A.A. (1983) 'Cognitive processes initiated by advertising', in R.J. Harris (ed.) *Information Processing Research in Advertising*, Lawrence Erlbaum Associates.

Obermiller, C. and Atwood A. (1990) 'Feelings about feeling-state research: a search for harmony', *Advances in Consumer Research*, 17: 590–93.

Oliver, R.L., Robertson, T.S. and Mitchell, D.J. (1993) 'Imaging and analyzing in response to new product advertising', *Journal of Advertising*, 22, December: 35–50.

Patai, R. (1977) *The Jewish Mind*, New York: Charles Scribner's Sons.

Patterson, J. and Kim, P. (1991) *The Day America Told the Truth*, New York: Plume.

Perloff, R.M. (1993) *The Dynamics of Persuasion*, Lawrence Erlbaum.

Petty, R.E., Ostrom, T.M. and Brock, T.C. (1981) 'Historical foundations of the cognitive response approach to attitudes and persuasion', in R.E. Petty, T.M. Ostrom and T.C. Brock (eds) *Cognitive Responses in Persuasion*, Hillsdale, NJ: Lawrence Erlbaum Associates, 5–29.

Rossiter, J.R. (1982) 'Visual imagery: applications to advertising', *Advances in Consumer Research*, 9: 101–6.

Rossiter, J.R. and Percy, L. (1978) 'Visual imaging ability as a mediator of advertising response', *Advances in Consumer Research*, 5: 621–9.

Schab, F.R. (1991) 'Odor memory: taking stock', *Psychological Bulletin*, 109(2): 245–51.

Shepard, R.N. (1978) 'The mental image', *American Psychologist*, 33, February: 125–37.

Sherif, M. and Sherif, C.W. (1967) 'Attitude as the individual's own categories: the social judgement-involvement approach to attitude and attitude change', in C.W. Sherif and M. Sherif (eds) *Attitude, Ego-involvement, and Change*, New York: Wiley, 105–39.

Shiffrin, R.M. and Atkinson, R.C. (1969) 'Storage and retrieval processes in long-term memory', *Psychological Review*, 76, 23 March: 179–93.

Shimp, T.E. (1997) *Advertising, Promotion and Supplemental Aspects of Integrated Marketing Communications*, 4th edn, Fort Worth: Harcourt Brace College Publishers, Chapter Five.

Singer, J.L. (1966) *Daydreaming: An Introduction to the Experiential Study of Inner Experience*, New York: Random House.

Snyder, M. (1987) *Public Appearances/Private Realities: The Psychology of Self-Monitoring*, New York: W.H. Freeman.

Sparkman, Jr., N. and Austin, L.M. (1980) 'The effects on sales of colour in newspaper advertisement', *Journal of Advertising*, Fourth Quarter.

Steele, C.M. (1988) 'The psychology of self-affirmation: sustaining the integrity of the self', in L. Berkowitz (ed.) *Advances in Experimental Social Psychology*, 21, San Diego: Academic Press, 261–302.

Steele, C.M. and Liu, T.J. (1983) 'Dissonance process as self-affirmation', *Journal of Personality and Social Psychology*, 45: 5–19.

Swanson, G.E. (1978) 'Travels through inner space: family structure and openness to absorbing experiences', *American Journal of Sociology*, 83, January: 890–919.

Unnava, H.R. and Burnkrant, R.E. (1991) 'An imagery processing view of the role of pictures in print advertisements', *Journal of Marketing Research*, 28, May: 226–31.

Venkatraman, M.P. and MacInnis, D.J. (1985) 'The epistemic and sensory exploratory behaviours of hedonic and cognitive consumers', *Advances in Consumer Research*, 12: 102–7.

Webb, P.H. (1979) 'Consumer initial processing in a difficult media environment', *Journal of Consumer Research*, 6, December: 225–36.

Webb, P.H. and Ray, M.L. (1979) 'Effects of TV clutter', *Journal of Advertising Research*, 19, June: 7–12.

Whittaker, J.O. (1967) 'Resolution of the communication discrepancy issue in attitude change', in C.W. Sherif and M. Sherif (eds) *Attitude, Ego-involvement, and Change*, New York: Wiley, 159–74.

Wright, P.L. (1975) 'Consumer choice strategies: simplifying vs. optimizing', *Journal of Marketing Research*, 11, February: 60–7.

Zanjonc, R. (1980) 'Feeling and thinking: preferences need no inferences', *American Psychologist*, 35, February: 151–75.

Zimbardo, P.G. and Leippe, M.R. (1991) *The Psychology of Attitude Change and Social Influence*, McGraw-Hill.

Zuckerman, M. (1979) *Sensation-Seeking: Beyond the Optimal Level of Arousal*, Hillsdale, NJ: Lawrence Erlbaum.

11

THE ELABORATION LIKELIHOOD MODEL OF PERSUASIVE COMMUNICATION

Mark Gabbott and Val Clulow

CHAPTER AIMS

- to present the Elaboration Likelihood Model of persuasion
- to consider how routes to persuasion are formed and conceptualized
- to discuss the merits and demerits of the ELM model
- to explore the extent of applicability of ELM to marketing communications from a researcher and practitioner perspective

ILLUSTRATION: THE IRON CAMPAIGN

The Australian Meat and Livestock Corporation commissioned the advertising agency Campaign Palace to develop a campaign to address a clear marketing objective: to redress a general decline in red meat consumption.

A decision was made to target women, based on two factors. Firstly, research had suggested that women were responsible for 80 per cent of meat purchase decisions, and therefore directly influenced the patterns of household consumption of meat. Secondly, research suggested that younger women, more than any other demographic group, held the attitude that they should 'do without red meat in their diet'.

The advertising agency identified four 'mindsets' about red meat consumption in the female population of Australia. These were:

Appreciators	(17%)	'I enjoy red meat and it's essential to healthy living.'
Acceptors	(42%)	'I like red meat and it's hard to do without it – although there are foods I enjoy as much.'
Resistors	(29%)	'Meat's not essential to a healthy diet – there are other foods I enjoy more.'
Rejectors	(12%)	'Meat's bad for you, I don't really like it.'

(Source (percentages): Dangar Research Ltd)

The campaign targeted the resistors, generally younger women who were less inclined to consider red meat as an essential part of the diet. The objective was to persuade or influence these women that red meat was a positive feature of the diet.

Nutritional attributes of red meat were evaluated, in order to select an element to serve as the information trigger central to the campaign, which would then influence attitudes of the target market. Iron emerged as a powerful link between the target market and the persuasive message as women already recognized the need for dietary iron in relation to menstrual blood loss and related lethargy.

The issue was whether to present the message as a reasoned argument in which credible 'researched' information was presented about the health benefits of red meat, or whether to rely upon a single positive image repeated in different media. The images would be those such as a large red tick superimposed on a serving of red meat, or simple visual comparisons of equivalent iron contribution, or the portrayal of healthy activity associated with the meat.

As you read on, consider the decision about which message strategy to use in order to gain the greatest impact upon the attitudes of the target market. One of the campaign advertisements is reproduced here.

INTRODUCTION

Perhaps one of the most fundamental concerns for marketing communicators is how to design and deliver messages that will have the desired impact upon customer groups. At a more general level, this concern about communication effectiveness has a long and chequered history drawing from the early propaganda of the world wars to current media presentation of government policy. At the heart of this pursuit for effectiveness is a desire to persuade or influence message recipients to a particular point of view about a product, a political party, a place or an idea. This is in order to exert some influence over a behavioural outcome, be it a purchase decision, a decision on how to vote, the selection of a service provider, or in making a choice about which brand of margarine or which daily newspaper to buy. In this realm of consumer behaviour there are very few certainties for the marketer and the interaction between even commonly accepted constructs such as attitudes, beliefs and intentions have been called into question. This chapter reviews one of the main perspectives on the influence process developed by Petty and Cacioppo (1986) – the Elaboration Likelihood Model (ELM). Their approach suggests that there are two routes to persuasion. The first and central route is the cognitive processing of the message content with input from the recipient, called elaboration. The second peripheral and [perhaps more] subtle route involves the recipient responding instinctively to the communication, using cues associated with communicator, message content and medium and relying upon simple heuristic devices rather than expending energy on topic-relevant information. This model provides a coherent unifying framework for consideration of the persuasive communication process and the factors that contribute toward attitudinal and behavioural response.

ATTITUDES AND PERSUASION: THE ELM MODEL OF RECEIVER INVOLVEMENT

The study of influence, attitudes and the associated behavioural responses to messages have been at the centre of social psychology since the early part of the

122g grilled lean rump steak, one way to absorb half your daily iron needs.

1.75kg boiled English spinach, another way to absorb half your daily iron needs.

Figure 11.1

twentieth century (Ross, 1908). This work became increasingly important in the 1950s as government and policy makers began to explore issues associated with the identification of successful persuasive communications and the characteristics of persons most easily persuaded (Hovland, *et al.*, 1953). It soon became apparent that persuasion and influence were a complex area of study with very few general principles which could be used to link communication accurately with attitude change and via this route to subsequent behavioural change. After a considerable flourishing of research activity up to the early 1960s (see, for example, Allport, 1935; Frank, 1963; Poffenberger, 1925; Ross, 1908; Strong, 1925), interest began to wane as researchers became unsure about two central tenets of the persuasion model. The first was the questioning of whether attitudes were really capable of predicting behaviour, and if they didn't then attitudes may not be a productive route for exploring behavioural response to communications (Abelson, 1972; Wicker, 1971). The second issue was that if it was assumed that attitudes were an important mediating construct, and this position was the dominant one at the time, how best could they be changed? These two debates dominated the psychology literature from the early 1970s, and now marketers, and specifically advertising and communication professionals, began to examine the application of the various techniques associated with influence in marketing (see, for example, Wright, 1973). What they found was considerable confusion, and a persistent failure to validate the relationship between attitude and behaviour as well as a failure to address some of the environmental and emotional effects upon message acceptance. A summary of the literature at the time by Eagly and Himmelfarb (1974) supported the view that every independent variable studied had increased persuasion in some situations and not in others. Indeed, some even decreased persuasion in certain circumstances. With the parallel emergence of interest by social psychologists in the study of information processing, a more unifying framework was developing which coincided with the increasing focus by business on influencing consumer behaviour through persuasive communication.

While research continued to search for evidence of a generalizable and applicable model for effective persuasive communication, a number of authors presented variants upon a generalizable cognitive response theory (Greenwald, 1968). Cognitive response theory proposes a model of 'self-persuasion', a state produced by information which is processed by the recipient through reading, listening or anticipating both the content and the context of the communication. If the communication evokes thoughts supportive of the position being advocated, the individual is more likely to adopt that position. Equally, if the communication evokes unsupportive thoughts (such as counter-argument or derogation), the individual will remain at best unconvinced and may even rebound from the message and shift away from the position being advocated. This model also proposes that the success of persuasive communication is related to the ability and propensity of the recipient to generate counter-argument. This basic premise led to a number of validation studies as well as attempts to assess the importance of forewarning, and message innoculation (McGuire, 1964; Papageorgis and McGuire, 1961; McGuire and Papageorgis, 1961; Hass and Grady, 1975; Freedman and Sears, 1965; Petty and Cacioppo, 1977; McAlister *et al*, 1980; Cohen, 1980; Feshbach, 1980). At a general

175

level, cognitive response theory concentrated upon the processing of the message by the recipient and as such was instrumental in designing message strategies based upon two-sided communication (i.e. exposure of the recipient to both sides of an argument in order to avoid immediate counter-argument). However, despite the undoubted advance that the cognitive response model represented, it did not encompass a range of additional attributes of the message beyond the substantive argument. For instance, communication elements such as the communicator, the content of receipt, the number of arguments and additional cues associated with the graphical or visual impact of the message were not featured. Petty and Cacioppo's contribution to this debate was to suggest an alternative explanation based upon an extension of this approach using distinct persuasive routes. This approach forms the basis of the Elaboration Likelihood Model of attitude persistence.

THE ELABORATION LIKELIHOOD MODEL

The first exposition of the ELM model was published by Petty and Cacioppo in 1983, although the foundation of the model stems from earlier work by Petty dating from 1977. The underlying structure is to distinguish between two processing routes, which were subsequently termed 'routes to persuasion'. The major constituent of the model is the identification of two routes of persuasion, each characterized by a different likelihood of elaboration. Research in cognitive and social psychology had suggested that at times, people engage in deep and mindful analysis of stimuli and at other times their analysis is likely to be shallow, mindless and heuristically based (Craik, 1979; Eagly and Chaiken, 1984; Kahneman, *et al.*, 1982; Langer, 1978; Schneider and Shiffrin, 1977; Slater and Rouner, 1996). In keeping with these results, the model suggests a differential processing response to a persuasive communication. The 'central route' is described by Petty and Cacioppo as a process of persuasion involving 'a person's careful and thoughtful consideration of the true merits of the information presented in support of an advocacy' (1986:3). This central route to persuasion relies upon the individual elaborating upon the message and reaching a reflective and considered weighing of the evidence to come to an evaluated conclusion. If the message is persuasive then the conclusions reached will be those contained in the appeal. The 'peripheral route' occurs when the motivation or ability to elaborate are relatively low. In these circumstances the individual will rely upon a series of peripheral cues in his or her response to the message. The receiver may infer the validity of the message via the credibility of the source, for example, or other heuristics. The important distinction is that as elaboration decreases, the importance of peripheral cues to information increases, and the converse is true. The model had immediate intuitive appeal as it appeared to account for the many conflicting and contradictory findings from previous studies in this field (see, for instance, Greenwald, 1968). The mechanism for persuasive change in attitude consists of a key process called elaboration, a distinction between high and low elaboration routes of processing and finally, a series of variables which impact upon the process of elaborating upon a message.

Elaboration

In common language, elaboration refers to the embellishment of, or addition to, some core idea or source of information. In the context of this model, elaboration refers to the recipient's processing activities in adding to or embellishing a communicated message. This term is used as an umbrella for a range of cognitive and behavioural activities associated with what is referred to as the 'consideration of information relevant to the issue of the communication', or ' the extent to which a person thinks about issue relevant information' (Petty and Cacioppo, 1986:7). The degree of elaboration is closely associated with the extent to which the person is willing to engage such effort to enlarge their information resource. The authors do not delimit clearly the range of activity which they have in mind, referring to elaboration variously as 'thinking', 'searching', 'listing', 'consulting' and 'reworking'. As such, elaboration may also have a physical dimension in the acquisition of this issue-relevant information. At the other end of the scale, individuals may not engage in any issue-relevant thinking upon the receipt of a communication, for a variety of reasons. These may include the credibility of the source, the time involved, or their cognitive capacity at the time. The degree to which a person engages in elaboration forms a continuum from extremely high to cases of little or none. In the case of high elaboration an individual may attend to the communication appeal, attempt to access additional information from various sources, interpret and analyse the message, and draw conclusions about the merits of the argument. This will lead to the derivation of new arguments or personal translations of the new message, which may then be incorporated into the belief and attitude structure. The model incorporates the possibility for demographic, situational and emotional variance in the elaboration response, which has interesting possibilities for the extended application of this model in marketing. A variety of factors have been identified which have an impact upon the degree of elaboration and these can be grouped into three classes: those which relate to the motivation for elaboration, those which relate to the ability to elaborate and finally those which are associated with the individual receiver's predisposition or propensity. Although these factors do not act discretely and are essentially multifaceted, they are considered in turn.

Motivation to elaborate

In considering a person's motivation to elaborate upon the content of a message, a number of influences can be identified. These can be considered as task, context and difference variables. The two most important task-related variables on the motivation to elaborate are the personal relevance of the message, and perceived responsibility for evaluating the recommendation contained in the message. In the first case, personal relevance as a variable would describe a situation where an individual can immediately identify between the content of the message and their immediate situation, such that where the message is more relevant the motivation to elaborate is higher and the likelihood of attitude change is higher (Heppner et al., 1995; Andrews and Gutkin, 1994; Scott and Ambroson, 1994). Communications associated with smoking, for instance, would perhaps have a higher relevance to smokers than to non-smokers. Equally, personal relevance may include a valency weighting for smokers who are considering quitting rather than those who do not perceive their habit as a health risk. Allied to the issue of personal relevance is perceived responsibility to evaluate a message (White and Harkins, 1994). For instance, an employee tasked with the responsibility to make a subsequent recommendation based upon the argument would have a higher propensity to elaborate on the message because of the perceived responsibility to undertake a thorough analysis. Context variables include the number of sources which are congruent, for example the type and number of media used, the personal context in which the message is received and how the message is framed. It would also include the situation or physical context of the reception, which may in turn impact directly upon the extent of elaboration. This will be true especially for messages which are behaviourally based and received *in situ*, such as warnings or reminders. In the first case, congruence of sources, messages which are received from many different sources, assuming similar credibility, are likely to encourage higher levels of elaboration than those which emanate from a single source. The immediate physical situation is also likely to affect the degree of elaboration simply by the poignancy of the moment (Lord, *et al.*, 1995; Penner and Fritzsche, 1993). For instance, a speeding motorist already experiencing awareness of their excessive speed may have a greater propensity to elaborate on a slow-down message received via the car radio than in front of the television set that evening.

The final set of factors relevant here are those which describe individual differences of the receiver. This would include demographic effects (such as the differential processing ability of age groups), cultural differences in terms of elaboration effort and more intrinsic characteristics such as predisposition to elaborate messages in general and need for cognition. Consistent with information processing approaches to consumer behaviour this model also includes a set of individual difference variables designed to account for variation in response to the same stimuli. It is also possible to distinguish a difference between temporary and pervasive states, that is, a difference between emotion (Wegener and Petty, 1996) and information endowment as temporary states, versus personality, aptitude and belief structures which are pervasive.

Ability to elaborate

The second set of factors which influence elaboration have been classified as being associated with ability to elaborate. Within this categorization, distraction and prior knowledge have attracted particular attention (Baron *et al.*, 1973; Buller, 1986; Petty and Brock, 1981). Distraction refers to some additional stimulus which occurs at the same time as the persuasive message. From a research perspective, the distraction effect has been pursued with devices such as flashing lights, moving crosses, beep sounds and static (Petty and Brock, 1981). However, distraction outside the experimental laboratory could include the effect of other people during receipt, competing sensory demand and media used. As yet none of these distraction effects have been investigated but it is proposed that under conditions which would otherwise lead to high levels of elaboration, distracting stimuli should interfere with this process and cause lower elaboration levels. However, it should be noted that distraction can also be a promoter of elaboration where the individual would normally have unfavourable responses to the advocated position. The research is inconclusive, however. (For a more detailed debate on distraction effects see Baron, *et al.*, 1973; Buller, 1986; Petty and Brock, 1981). The second important area when considering ability to elaborate is the effect of prior knowledge. This refers to the amount of information that the receiver already holds concerning the persuasive topic (see Wood and Kallgreen, 1988). The argument presented holds that where a person who has extensive prior knowledge receives a message which is inconsistent with their position, they are better placed to generate counter-argument. Therefore the extent of prior knowledge and its form can impact directly upon elaboration, and indirectly upon the process of persuasion. For instance, a person who subscribes to a firmly held ideological belief would be better able to generate a counter-argument against the message promoted by an opposition party. As a consequence, they would be less likely to be persuaded than those who did not hold such firm ideological beliefs. When considering the degree of elaboration likelihood, it should be evident from the above that the range of possible variables in any particular communication context is very wide indeed. One could also conclude that the range of responses by the receiver to any particular message will cover a range of persuasive outcomes. The key construct here is the degree of elaboration likelihood, and the possible variation describes the essential component of the ELM approach to understanding persuasive pathways.

Elaboration mechanisms

So far, consideration has been extended to the factors affecting the extent of elaboration or 'mindful thinking' abut the message received. However, an important second stage in considering the model and its application to marketing communications is to review the mechanisms of elaboration, by which we mean how a receiver gains greater topic-relevant information and how different communication pathways affect message evaluation. Under a high‑elaboration scenario the outcome of a persuasive message is dependent upon the direction of the elaboration activity. Quite simply, if the message elicits a favourable response then the elaboration activity is also favourable and the chances of persuasive success (i.e. the move to the desired attitudinal position) are similarly positive. Equally, if the message does not elicit a favourable response then elaboration is likely to be counter-attitudinal and therefore the persuasive argument lost. The key thing to remember is that ELM is about persuading the receiver of a new attitudinal position which may often conflict with an attitude already held. One of the key determinants of elaboration direction and the corresponding shift in position is the strength of the argument presented (Andrews and Gutkin, 1994). In simple terms, 'strength' is a synonym for quality, such that when the argument is scrutinized by the recipient it is defensible and intuitively coherent but more importantly the response is mainly a favourable disposition, whereas a weak argument is of low quality, elicits either an ambivalent or negative response, and therefore has a low persuasive effect. Clearly, the scenario of high elaboration as described is not particularly helpful from a

179

practitioner perspective. Because of the lack of detail and the absence of any deconstruction of argument process, it provides no explicit guidance for argument design. It also suffers from a lack of direction in estimating the effects of prior knowledge, specifically whether the strength of the persuasive communication should be different for differently endowed customer groups, i.e. users versus non-users.

The second elaboration scenario is the low-level route, by which is meant that the outcomes of the persuasive message are not directly the result of what Petty and Cacioppo (1986) refer to as 'thoughtful consideration'. In the absence of cognitive reflection on the argument, it is suggested that consumers will rely upon simple heuristic devices to evaluate their response to the message. These heuristics are considered to be simple decision processes characterized in the form of rules. These heuristics can take many forms and may be activated by characteristics of the communication. An example of an heuristic in this context could be response to source, such as unconditional belief in the communicator's integrity, or response to brand in terms of past experience. Equally, the heuristic could be one based upon the perception of weight of opinion among others and therefore appeals based upon surveys and validation could trigger a favourable response.

HEURISTIC DEVICES

A number of distinct heuristic devices have been suggested to explain consumers' processing of peripheral cues in the self-persuasion process. It should be noted that the ELM model assumes that there are predictable patterns of cue effects associated with these heuristic devices. In itself this is a significant assumption, for it absolves the individual receiver from self-selection of cues. The most heavily evidenced heuristics are credibility, liking and consensus, although clearly there are many individualized responses that these generalized responses do not reflect (Chaiken, 1987).

Credibility

It has been suggested by Chaiken (1987) and Cialdini (1987) that in situations of low elaboration likelihood, the receiver is likely to give weight to the credibility of the communicator on the basis that the receiver can trust their message and avoid the need for further elaboration (Andrews and Gutkin, 1994; Zotos, et al., 1992). An important underlying mechanism of this heuristic is evidence from Rhine and Severance (1970) that as the receiver's involvement in a particular message or issue increases, the effects of communicator credibility diminish. As a consequence, credibility has a higher impact upon a persuasive outcome when elaboraration likelihood is low. For example, in a political context, a loyal party voter receiving a communication from the party he or she supports would rely more heavily on the endorsement of the party leader for credibility of the message rather than elaborating on the detail. Equally, in situations where there is a high elaboration likelihood, the use of a highly credible spokesperson would be less essential in terms of persuasive outcome.

Liking

A second and associated heuristic principle is the degree to which the receiver likes the communicator; we can distinguish credibility which is based upon trust and the perceived expertise of the source, from liking which is much more associated with issues such as reasonableness, attraction, identification, common values, etc. In low elaboration likelihood, liked sources would prove more persuasive. Therefore in a situation where a political party is selecting a spokesperson, the personal popularity of the candidate would be a good selection criterion. Of course the interplay of liking and credibility makes such a selection decision more complex. A spokesperson who is not liked could nevertheless be highly credible. The precise nature of the interplay between these two dimensions of the relationship would need to be carefully researched with target audiences. As in the case of credibility, the persuasive advantage of a liked communicator diminishes as receiver involvement increases (Petty, *et al.*, 1983 and extensions by Wood and Kallgreen, 1988). In summary, both the credibility and liking heuristics indicate an important role for the spokesperson in reaching persuasive outcomes. Personal attributes of the communicator can act independently of the message (Smith and Shaffer, 1995; Gelinas-Chebat and Chebat, 1992). For instance, a well-modulated voice could evoke both liking and credibility regardless of the identity of the communicator. Other message components, such as music, which are not necessarily associated with a person could also aid persuasive outcome in low elaboration situations. As yet there has been no research into the effects of heuristics associated with non-personal cues, although this would present an important extension of the ELM approach.

Consensus and compliance

The third heuristic which has been identified is associated with reactions of other people at the time that the message is communicated. This heuristic is based upon a belief that individuals will be more likely to be persuaded if those around them express favourable responses to the message. Conversely, studies have found that receivers are less persuaded when they overhear an audience expressing disapproval. This draws together a number of research threads associated with dissonance, the role of peer groups, self-esteem and personality in understanding the impact of others on message response. However, this heuristic makes a number of implicit assumptions which may or may not be tenable. The first of these is that the individual receiver is motivated to comply with others, which in turn may be related to personal attributes such as personality, self-confidence and experience as well as social status within the group. Although there is ample evidence of a consensus effect on persuasive outcome, in reality the effect is likely to be context specific and unpredictable in terms of message design.

A number of other factors have been suggested as possible heuristic devices in low elaboration situations. These could include the strength of the brand in an advertising message, the perceptions of the target audience, and the medium of delivery (Lord *et al.*, 1995). Little research has been undertaken to date into these other heuristics, and while they are clearly probable peripheral cues, as yet their impact cannot be substantiated.

DISCUSSION

While the elaboration likelihood model has received some critical acclaim it has also been the object of some criticism, both in terms of the mechanics of persuasion and related to the empirical validation of the model. However, this debate has been largely academic with practitioner involvement at a minimal level. It would appear that practitioners intuitively apply many of the principles embodied in the model but do not recognize it as a coherent approach to their marketing communications. For instance, there is an acceptance that many conscious and unconscious processes are at work in achieving behavioural change but that there is no single unifying model of the process. Indeed, it would be a worrying prospect to many if such a generalizable framework for persuasion existed. But before considering some of these wider ethical issues, the critical debate surrounding the model needs review.

The first set of criticisms emerges from the identification of two routes to persuasion, one well defined, the central route associated with issue relevant thinking, and the other, less distinct route relying upon peripheral cues. There has been considerable debate in the marketing literature concerning the use of cues to approximate missing or complex information, and within this literature there has been an acceptance of a broad distinction between intrinsic and extrinsic cues. Intrinsic relates to the central part of a message or product, and extrinsic relates to such attributes as brand, price and location which are merely contextualizers for the experience. Petty and Cacioppo make no reference to the way in which the cues they identify as important in the peripheral route actually operate, in particular from where they originate, how the receiver validates them over time and the interaction of the various cue classes in a particular message. It may be that a particualar message elicits a particular response to cues, making the influence on the persuasive outcome highly contextualized. More importantly perhaps from a practitioner perspective, no detailed examples are given of cues which are generalizable to different message contents. From the literature it is evident that the identification, use and validation of cues is very much a personal and individual process and as such difficult to assess, evaluate or much less to predict. As a consequence the practitioner/observer is really only left with a distinction between conscious or active reasoning as opposed to subconscious information processing which in real terms is a small progression in understanding.

The second source of criticism relates to the empirical evidence used to validate this model. As O'Keefe (1990) points out, there is a relatively small number of message topics used in ELM research, especially given the large number of studies undertaken. There is a predominance of studies using student examinations and tuition charges which have been described as highly rarefied communication environments. For a theory which purports to be representative of a general model of persuasion rather than a particular one (college exams), this concentration upon context in the literature is worrisome. One would expect to see some variety in persons, age groups and message forms to fully appreciate the applicability of the model, but there appears to be little enthusiasm for a wider validation exercise. It can be surmised that this concentration is a result of a desire to pre-test and screen the model components previous to a wider study, coupled with the desire for convenience on behalf of the researchers. Nevertheless, it might have been expected that a wider variety of topics would have emerged by now.

A wider issue that has received less attention in established literature on ELM is the ethical dimension of a general model of persuasion. It hits at the heart of the debate in marketing concerning the demand creation role for marketing communication as opposed to one of latent demand facilitation. This issue of whether the marketing profession serves to create demand or respond to it has long been debated, and offers a point of philosophical contention. The perception is widely held that there are ethical considerations in any situation where an individual's free will to choose is compromised by a persuasive message which employs psychologically based mechanisms designed to manipulate or control behaviour (Santilli, 1983). The issue is whether a persuasive message applies undue pressure toward counter-argument which is different to the receiver's natural response. For example, appealing to fear, sex-appeal or humour in an attempt to overcome resistance to purchase has been presented as a typical communication approach (Ray, 1982).

If the ELM model is truly a theory of persuasion that can be turned on and off at the behest of the communicator, the ethical dimension of this situation becomes paramount. While the model remains vague and indistinct in its practitioner-orientated detail, the ethical issues remain dormant, but the question of the morality of applying psychosocial theoretical constructs to marketing communication highlights another far-reaching debate. Some of the questions this raises which are more fully addressed in other chapters may be: 'Can application of the principles of persuasion, uncovered by models such as ELM, to an advertising message be immoral on the grounds that it manipulates (or intends to manipulate) individual behaviour?' 'What impact does advertising have on the values held by a society?' 'Is the engineering of a persuasive message directed at a particular demographic group morally acceptable?' Santilli (1983) hypothesized that persuasion undermines the rational cognitive processes by which people evaluate their needs. His perspective implies that all forms of persuasive advertising are immoral and that all forms of informative advertising are moral. His criterion for judging morality was the truthfulness of the content of the message, in style and content. This view is problematic, as in much advertising material it is difficult to distinguish between the elements of information and persuasion. Indeed, ELM proposes that the receiver takes an active role in determining the level of topic-related information elaboration in any case.

CONCLUSION

This chapter has illuminated the complexity of the persuasive process using one model of the process. As may be deduced from the material discussed in this chapter, the nature of persuasive communication is far from fully researched. The necessary inclusion of variables which emanate from the environment, the individual, and the communication of the message make the pursuit of a unifying theory a worthy cause but unlikely to appear. Equally, in this final section the undesirability of this outcome is highlighted even were it feasible. However, sensitivity to the contribution Petty and Cacioppo have made is enjoined, and to the intuitive appeal of the routes to persuasion approach. It is clear that cognition is one mechanism for attitudinal change and that is the basis of much of the traditional literature on the formation, structure and stability of attitudes. But it is also known that attitudinal positions are dynamic in many respects and that all change cannot be ascribed to conscious reasoning or differential exposure to counter-positional communications. The use and mechanisms associated with cues are still unknown and may remain obscure primarily because of their nature, but the ELM approach certainly establishes some relational parameters which may inform future research. Having now read about the Elaboration Likelihood Model, you may wish to consider the following Australia-wide advertising campaign and investigate the extent to which the principles encompassed by the ELM have been applied.

DISCUSSION TOPICS

1 Using material from this chapter indicate how messages can have a 'desired impact' on target groups.
2 What techniques were useful for explaining persuasion prior to Petty and Cacioppo's theory?
3 What are the main differences between the two routes to persuasion in ELM?
4 Suggest circumstances in which consumers might become heavily involved in a marketing communication message.
5 Indicate your reasons why so much of television advertising is essentially uninvolving.
6 How can a communicator increase the motivation to elaborate?
7 Suggest reasons why consumers may be motivated but yet lack ability to elaborate.
8 Critique the ELM model.
9 Suggest reasons why even when consumers may be involved in a message argument (i.e. be motivated, comprehend etc) they may still remain unchanged in terms of acceptance.
10 Choose two recent TV ads, as illustration for either of the two routes to persuasion.

CASE STUDY – QUIT – AUSTRALIAN NATIONAL TOBACCO CAMPAIGN

Around 18000 Australians die every year because of smoking-related illness. Treatment and care of patients with these diseases and associated expenses cost the Australian community an estimated AUD\$12.7 billion each year. The public awareness campaign designed to persuade the 25 per cent of Australians who smoke to quit draws on newly released medical evidence which illustrates three key issues. Firstly, health damage leading to serious disease starts immediately a person begins to smoke. Secondly, social research reviewed by the Ministerial Tobacco Advisory

Group found that 80 per cent of smokers want to quit and believe that they will some time in the future. Thirdly, the appeal was centred around the finding that the most common reason both smokers and reformed smokers gave for giving up smoking was their health.

The campaign focuses on the fact that every single cigarette damages the health of smokers and appeals to the large majority of smokers identified as wanting to quit one day; it attempts to move the 'quitting action' onto 'today's agenda'.

Research found that smokers want to be confronted with graphic portrayals of how smoking damages their health, how tobacco addiction escalates and some of the long-term benefits of giving up smoking. The campaign moved the strategic approach from informing smokers on the 'risks' associated with smoking (as research had found that many people were translating warnings into a calculated risk that they were prepared to take, not unlike buying a lottery ticket) to a concentration upon the certainty that '*every* cigarette is doing you damage'.

The campaign provides smokers with the information and motivation to put 'quitting' back onto their daily agenda, with a range of practical support services such as the 'Quitline' open to callers 24 hours a day.

The Quitline offers information on:

- The best way for you to quit
- Coping with withdrawal symptoms
- Quit courses and details of local organizations which provide individual help and counselling.

The advertisements use graphic images which confront and challenge smokers with a minimum of detailed argument but with a maximum of bold visual impact. Smokers have been shocked, disturbed, even frightened by their content but they are designed to influence and reinforce their latent desire to quit. This campaign differed from previous campaigns which assumed that the public would act to quit if they were better informed of the risks, in that they portrayed the certainty of the consequences of smoking rather than the severity of them. The key message was that 'every cigarette is doing you damage' and that smoking is not like a lottery that's drawn when you are 70 years old, rather more like building a pathway from imperceptible early damage to serious disease.

The Three Advertisements

The LUNG advertisement

This advertisement shows actual footage of the smoker lighting up in a typical situation, such as a work break, and literally follows the pathway of the smoke down the oesophagus and into the lungs. The visual clearly shows the discolouration and rotting process in the healthy lung tissue associated with smoke inhalation, with the tag that 'every cigarette is doing you damage'.

The ARTERY advertisement

The artery advertisement is an explicit depiction of a section of human artery. The visual shows a 'doctor' squeezing out the fatty substance built up in the artery through smoking.

The p53 advertisement

The p53 advertisement shows graphically how the p53 gene, found in every cell in the human body and the protector of DNA, can be damaged by cigarette smoke, for example by the carcinogen benzopyrene which is found in high concentrations in cigarette smoke, and increase the susceptibility to cancerous growth.

The key messages throughout the campaign, which covered television, radio, newspapers, buses, posters, etc., were simple:

- Every cigarette is doing you damage.
- It's not just a risk – it's a certainty that smoking will damage your health.
- Smoking clogs your arteries and damages your lungs.
- There is a nationally coordinated effort to help you quit.

Each message component was supported by the simple bold image with a minimum of textual or complex medical argument. The results of the campaign are being tracked through random telephone surveys every week of the three-week campaign. The data being collected is about 'awareness' of the campaign, recall of the slogan 'every cigarette is doing you damage', the percentage of smokers or recent ex-smokers who believe each advertisement is thought-provoking, believable and relevant, and the percentage of the sample for whom the campaign had provoked discussion about smoking in their household.

(with thanks to 'The National Tobacco Campaign, a Federal, State and Territory Health Initiative')

REFERENCES

Abelson, R. (1972) 'Are attitudes necessary?' in B.T. King and E. McGinnies (eds) *Attitudes, conflict, and social change*, New York: Academic Press.

Allport, G.W. (1935) 'Attitudes', in C. Murchison (ed) *Handbook of Social Psychology*, Vol. 2, Worcester, MA: Clark University Press.

Andrews, L.W. and Gutkin, T.B. (1994) 'Influencing attitudes regarding special class placement using a psychoeducational report: An investigation of the Elaboration Likelihood Model', *Journal of School Psychology*, 32(4): 321–37.

Baron, R.A., Baron, P. and Miller, N. (1973) 'The relation between distraction and persuasion', *Psychological Bulletin*, 80: 310–23.

Buller, D.B. (1986) 'Distraction during persuasive communication: A meta-analytic review', *Communication Monographs*, 53: 91–114.

Cacioppo, J.T., Petty, R.E., Kao, C.F. and Rodriguez, R. (1986) 'Central and peripheral routes to persuasion: An individual difference perspective', *Journal of Personality & Social Psychology*, 51(5): 1032–43.

Chaiken, S. (1987) 'The heuristic model of persuasion', in M.P. Zanna, J.M. Olson and C.P.

Herman (eds.) *Social Influence: The Ontario Symposium*, Vol. 5, Hillsdale, NJ: Lawrence Erlbaum, 3–39.

Cialdini, R.B. (1987) 'Compliance principles of compliance professionals: Psychologists of necessity', In M.P. Zanna, J.M. Olson and C.P. Herman (eds) *Social Influence: The Ontario Symposium*, Vol. 5, Hillsdale, NJ: Lawrence Erlbaum, 165–84.

Cohen, S. (1980) 'Training to understand TV advertising: Effects and some policy implications', Paper presented at the American Psychological Association convention, Montreal, September.

Craik, F.I.M. (1979) 'Human memory', *Annual Review of Psychology*, 30: 63–102.

Eagly, A.H. and Chaiken, S. (1984) 'Cognitive theories of persuasion', in L. Berkowitz (ed.) *Advances in Experimental Social Psychology*, Vol. 17, New York: Academic Press.

Eagly, A.H. and Himmelfarb, S. (1974) 'Current trends in attitude theory and research', in S. Himmelfarb and A. Eagly (eds) *Readings in Attitude Change*, New York: Wiley.

Feshback, N.D. (1980) 'The child as psychologist and economist: Two curricula', Paper presented at the Amercian Psychological Association convention, Montreal, September.

Frank, J.D. (1963) *Persuasion and Healing*, New York: Schocken Books.

Freedman, J.L. and Sears, D.O. (1965) 'Warning, distraction, and resistance to influence', *Journal of Personality and Social Psychology*, 1: 262–66.

Gelinas-Chebat, C. and Chebat, J-C. (1992) 'Effects of two voice characteristics on the attitudes toward advertising messages', *Journal of Social Psychology*, 132(4): 447–59.

Greenwald, A.G. (1968) 'Cognitive learning, cognitive response to persuasion, and attitude change', In A. Greenwald, T. Brock and T. Ostrom (eds) *Psychological foundations of attitudes*, New York: Academic Press, 148–70.

Hass, R.G. and Grady, K. (1975) 'Temporal delay, type of forwarning and resistance to influence', *Journal of Experimental Social Psychology*, 11: 459–69.

Heppner, M.J., Good, G.E., Hillenbrand-Gunn, T.L., Hawkins, A.K., *et al.* (1995) 'Examining sex differences in altering attitudes about rape: A test of the Elaboration Likelihood Model', *Journal of Counseling & Development*, 73(6): 640–7.

Hovland, C., Janis, I. and Kelley, H.H. (1953) *Communication and Persuasion*, New Haven: Yale University Press.

Kahneman, D., Slovic, P. and Tversky, A. (eds) (1982) *Judgement Under Uncertainty: Heuristics and Biases*, New York: Cambridge University Press.

Langer, E. (1978) 'Rethinking the role of thought in social interaction', in J. Harvey, W. Ickes and R. Kidd (eds) *New Directions in Attributional Research*, Vol. 2, Hillsdale, NJ: Erlbaum.

Lord, K.R., Lee, M-S., and Sauer, P.L. (1995) 'The combined influence hypothesis: Central and peripheral antecedents of attitude toward the ad', *Journal of Advertising*, 24(1): 73–85.

McAlister, A., Perry, C., Killen, J., Slinkard, L.A. and Maccoby, N. (1980) 'Pilot study of smoking, alcohol and drug abuse prevention', *American Journal of Public Health*, 70: 719–21.

McGuire, W.J. (1964) 'Inducing resistance to persuasion: Some contemporary approaches', in L. Berkowitz (ed.) *Advances in Experimental Social Psychology*, Vol. 1, New York: Academic Press.

McGuire, W.J. and Papageorgis, D. (1961) 'The relative efficacy of various types of prior belief-defense in producing immunity against persuasion,' *Journal of Abnormal and Social Psychology*, 62: 327–37.

O'Keefe, D.J. (1990) *Persuasion: Theory and Research*, London: Sage.

Papageorgis, D. and McGuire, W.J. (1961) 'The generality of immunity to persuasion produced by pre-exposure to weakened counterarguments', *Journal of Abnormal and Social Psychology*, 62: 475–81.

Penner, L.A. and Fritzsche, B.A. (1993) 'Magic Johnson and reactions to people with AIDS: A natural experiment', *Journal of Applied Social Psychology*, 23(13): 1035–50.

Petty, R.E. (1977) 'A cognitive response analysis of the temporal persistence of attitude changes induced by persuasive communications', Unpublished doctoral dissertation, Ohio State University, Columbus, OH.

Petty, R.E. and Brock, T.C. (1981) 'Thought disruption and persuasion: Assessing the validity of attitude change experiments', in R.E. Petty, T.M. Ostrom and T.C. Brock (eds) *Cognitive Responses in Persuasion*, Hillsdale, NJ: Lawrence Erlbaum, 55–79.

Petty, R.E. and Cacioppo, J.T. (1977) 'Forewarning, cognitive responding, and resistance to persuasion', *Journal of Personality and Social Psychology*, 35: 645–55.

Petty, R.E. and Cacioppo, J.T. (1983) 'Central and peripheral routes to persuasion: Application to advertising', in L. Percy and A. Woodside (eds), *Advertising and Consumer Psychology*, Lexington, MA: Lexington Books, D.C. Heath, 3–23.

Petty, R.E. and Cacioppo, J.T. (1986) *Communication and Persuasion: Central and Peripheral Routes to Attitude Change*, New York: Springer-Verlag.

Petty, R.E., Cacioppo, J.T., and Schumann, D. (1983) 'Central and peripheral routes to advertising effectiveness: The moderating role of involvement', *Journal of Consumer Research*, 10: 135–46.

Poffenberger, A.T. (1925) *Psychology in Advertising*, New York: Shaw.

Ray, M.L. (1982) *Advertising and Communication Managment*, Englewood Cliffs, NJ: Prentice Hall.

Rhine, R.J. and Severance, L.J. (1970) 'Ego-involvement, discrepancy, source credibility, and attitude change', *Journal of Personality and Social Psychology*, 16: 175–90.

Ross, E.A. (1908) *Social Psychology: An Outline and a Source Book*, New York: Macmillan.

Santilli, P.C. (1983) 'The informative and persuasive functions of advertising: A moral appraisal, *Journal of Business Ethics*, 2: 27–33.

Schneider, W. and Shiffrin, R.M. (1977) 'Controlled and automatic human information processing: Detection, search and attention', *Psychological Review*, 84: 1–66.

Scott, C.G. and Ambroson, D.L. (1994) 'The rocky road to change: Implications for substance abuse programs on college campuses', *Journal of American College Health*, 42(6): 291–96.

Slater, M.D. and Rouner, D. (1996) 'Value-affirmative and value-protective processing of alcohol education messages that include statistical evidence or anecdotes', *Communication Research*, 23(2): 210–35.

Smith, S.M. and Shaffer, D.R. (1991) 'Celerity and cajolery: Rapid speech may promote or inhibit persuasion through its impact on message elaboration', *Personality & Social Psychology Bulletin*, 17(6): 663–69.

Strong, E.K. (1925) *The Psychology of Selling and Advertising*, New York: McGraw-Hill.

Wegener, D.T. and Petty, R.E. (1996) *Effects Of Mood On Persuasion Processes: Enhancing, Reducing, And Biasing Scrutiny Of Attitude-Relevant Information*, Mahwah, NJ: Lawrence Erlbaum.

White, P.H. and Harkins, S.G. (1994) 'Race of source effects in the Elaboration Likelihood Model', *Journal of Personality & Social Psychology*, 67(5): 790–807.

Wicker, A. (1971) 'An examination of the 'other variable' explanation of the attitude-behavior inconsistency', *Journal of Personality and Social Psychology*, 19: 18–30.

Wood, W. and Kallgren, C.A. (1988) 'Communicator attributes and persuasion: Recipients' access to attribute-relvant information in memory', *Personality and Social Psychology Bulletin*, 14: 172–82.

Wright, P. (1973) 'The cognitive processes mediating acceptance of advertising', *Journal of Marketing Research*, 10: 53–62.

Zotos, Y., Lysonski, S., and Martin, P. (1992) 'Elaboration Likelihood Model and locus of control: Is there a connection?', *Psychological Reports*, 70(3, Pt 2), Spec Issue: 1051–56.

12

ADOPTION AND DIFFUSION PROCESSES

Val Cox and Graham Spickett-Jones

CHAPTER AIMS

- to consider the value of new product concepts and innovation
- to discuss the concepts of adoption and diffusion in relation to marketing communications (marcoms)
- to review the value of market modelling in relation to diffusion processes.
- to explore the value of diffusion and adoption in understanding communications processes within communications channels

ILLUSTRATION: A FAST-CHANGING WORLD

Change is one of the few things that can be predicted with confidence. Marketing is about turning change into 'organised rational innovation' (Ambler, 1996).

The sad news for anyone who bought a 'state of the art' computer six months ago is that it may already be dated by an even newer wave of technological innovation. The rate of new development in information technology rises constantly but it is only one area of a fast-evolving and competitive world in which consumers are regularly presented with new products and concepts. Everything – from the packaging of pet food with ring pull lids to purchasing groceries by means of the Internet – offers customers innovative new behavioural choices. Nor is this an area that just has marketing relevance for consumer products. Marketers need to understand how individuals/audiences/markets respond to marcoms and other stimuli and adopt ideas. For example, campaigns to change perceptions of social acceptability of drinking and driving and/or to encourage 'safe sex' (i.e. HIV avoidance) illustrate how marketers have needed to consider how best to introduce new concepts and encourage adoption of new behaviours.

(*Source*: authors)

INTRODUCTION

New product, idea, and brand launch occupies a vital place in marcoms activity. For example, US consumers were bombarded with a record number of product launches in 1996 (nearly 26 000), as packaged goods companies shifted product marketing efforts into overdrive in a bid to satisfy the consumer's increasing desire for innovations or manufacturers' need for shelf-space dominance. In what Castle (1997) referred to as an 'explosion of choice' new food, beverage, health and beauty, household and pet products were offered to an erstwhile market. Meanwhile in the UK (1996) nearly 3 000 new products were launched. Notably, *Marketing–Nielsen Biggest Brands Sixth Annual Survey* (in *Campaign*, 16 March 1995) reported that the five fastest-growing brands in the UK had all been launched within the previous four years.

However, no matter how appealing a new product may seem in development, whether consumers adopt determines commercial success. This chapter deals with the marcoms role in the new product (*pace* – also ideas and innovations). In particular, it considers sources of customer information, and how this information may be processed in purchase behaviour, and also explores how information is channelled and controlled in a social framework. Further, the chapter highlights the range of diffusion research, covering proposed models of *adoption* and *diffusion* that purport to explain these processes, and considers the usefulness of these models for marketing practitioners. It then explores the common elements of these processes and considers how these relate to marcoms. Marketers need to understand who is likely to respond, to which message, and when, as new product adoption spreads, or diffuses, through a market. They are then better equipped to know who to target, with what promotional effort, at the appropriate time and location for maximal impact.

New product introduction and innovation is an important mechanism for corporate success. Kay (1993), in analysing 'successful' companies, lists innovation as one of the few sources of competitive advantage while explaining that it is not easy to control, unless it can be patented or owned in some unique way (like a secret production process). To him, 'innovation is an obvious sources of distinctive capability, but it is less often a sustainable or appropriate source because successful innovation quickly attracts imitation'.

Staying ahead of imitators is one reason why new product development is important to leading companies, but for sustainable competitive advantage this means more than continued innovation – it requires careful management of the marketing processes by which new products are promoted and brought to market. Before determining suitable strategies and promotional campaigns, marketers must understand what different potential customers perceive as 'new', the likely appeal factors, how to create awareness, how to encourage persuasion leading to adoption, and when consumers are likely to consider adopting.

DIFFUSION OF INNOVATION

Innovation is a complex term that describes individual perception of something as being *new* or *different*, even if it is not new to others (i.e. mobile phones may be seen as innovations in markets that do not yet have such a facility). Innovation may also be applied to a wide range of consumer experiences, such as products, ideas, services, policies, lifestyles and beliefs. In that sense, the term may apply just as much to a new type of political ideology as to a new brand of soap powder. 'Diffusion of innovation' involves two processes: *adoption* considers the take-up of new ideas at the level of the individual (a micro-adoption process), and *diffusion* considers the way new ideas permeate society (a macro-diffusion process).

Manifestly, communication is integral to the concept of diffusion. Rogers (1995) defines diffusion as 'the process by which innovation is communicated through certain channels over time amongst members of a social system'.

Diffusion is a type of social communication process *(the diffusion process)*, in the sense that it is about how information which communicates new understanding spreads through elements of a population. However, adoption is defined as 'the process by which the individual becomes committed to the continued use and or repurchase of an innovation' (Rogers, 1995). Adoption, therefore, is dependent on the separate but related process *(the adoption process)* of each individual's decision making.

The breadth of diffusion research is revealed in an authoritative review of diffusion research literature by Rogers (1995) who lists nearly 4 000 studies covering 11 disciplines, including anthropology, sociology, education and geography as well as marketing. Marketing is a major research area, second only to rural sociology, with nearly 600 studies recorded. Thus, there is a body of research to guide development, some of which has been applied to predictive market modelling in the commercial world.

Newness implies a level of uncertainty and lack of knowledge. When presented with uncertainties it is not uncommon to turn to friends and trusted personal contacts for advice. Those who adopt something new relatively early have higher levels of innovativeness *(innovators* and *early adopters* (Rogers, 1962, *et al.*) or *pioneers*, (Ambler, 1996)). They may be able to tolerate higher levels of uncertainty than later adopters. For all adopters, one way to reduce uncertainty is to acquire more understanding, a process that requires the 'transfer of information', which can be another way to describe marcoms activity. The rate at which markets adopt new products typically rises dramatically at between 10 and 25 per cent of total market penetration (Rogers, 1995). At this point, interpersonal communication between adopters and potential adopters typically becomes an active part of the diffusion process. Here, some early adopters act as trusted personal contacts (opinion leaders) and inform or influence those who have still to adopt. Early selling to these opinion leaders has implications for marketing managers. Where these 'leaders' are thought to act as market catalysts, this influences the communications objectives at early stages of a new product's promotional campaign.

THE DIFFUSION PROCESS

The *diffusion process* deals with how new ideas are passed to and between members of a whole social group through communication contacts. With different types of new product, which have their own character and market potential, the diffusion process may involve different communications channels and happen at different speeds. For example, a new flavour of fresh vegetable soup may be adopted by a high proportion of the market for fresh soup in a few days (some supermarkets sell a 'Flavour of the Month' variety). However, a new type of vegetarian high-protein meat substitute, like 'Quorn', may take years to be widely accepted.

The *diffusion process* is a process of information exchange through a population, and is characterized by population features, such as average adoption time and adoption rate (the proportion of population adopting at a given time). Adoption at the individual unit level results from the separate process, the *adoption process*, followed to arrive at the personal adoption decision. When an individual's adoption process is similar to that of other individuals in a population, it might be expected to reveal similar characteristics (e.g. time taken to adopt).

The classical interpretation of the diffusion model suggests that the distribution of innovativeness (propensity to adopt early) in a population will follow a comparatively *normal* distribution pattern (Rogers, 1995). This type of population distribution can be described as falling within three standard deviations of either side of the mean value (see note 1). In his now famous model of categories of innovativeness, Rogers (1962) adopts points of *standard deviation* as boundaries to identify sub-populations with different adoption behaviour. Rogers identifies five different groups (1. *Innovators*, 2. *Early adopters*, 3. *Early majority*, 4. *Later majority*, 5. *Laggards*) that adopt innovation successively, according to the proportion of the population they represent, and their place along a scale of time taken to adopt (Figure 12.1).

After diffusion has happened, allocating which category adopters belong to is simple. Different innovativeness, revealed by adoption times, is also an indication of different decision-making *processes* by individuals. These may be influenced by factors such as information availability or willingness to seek out information. By distinguishing characteristics common to people that follow a similar decision-making *process* (other than innovativeness, as revealed by time), it may be possible to identify category membership prior to a new product being launched. If marketers know who early adopters are and what proportion of a population they form, it may

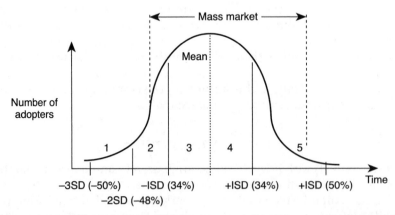

Figure 12.1 A standard distribution pattern of population innovativeness, (showing adopter categories, by time to adoption, using points of standard deviation * [SD]).

(adapted from Rogers, 1983).
(* Standard deviations can be calculated from the root value of the mean of the squares of the deviations from the common mean for a set of values.)

be possible to track their behaviour and use this to predict the likely behaviour of the whole population (giving an early estimate of market size and rates of penetration).

Rogers (1995) lists a range of characteristics which are likely to belong to those individuals found within his adopter categories. It must be accepted, however, that categorization into discrete groups is only a conceptual device to aid understanding. He offers five 'ideal types' abstracted from empirical research where there appears to be supporting evidence to claim useful distinctions, as shown in Table 12.1.

At some point in time there is likely to be a maximum number of people being converted to an innovation (a maximum rate of adoption). After that point the rate of adoption will fall away again as non-adopters become increasingly scarce, until the market is saturated. This can be illustrated using a graph to plot the accumulated total of adopters on an S-shaped curve (Figure 12.2).

Understanding who is likely to be in which adopter category means appropriate marcoms objectives can be set. This makes it possible to estimate when and how a promotional strategy needs to evolve and which messages and channels are most appropriate.

The standard diffusion concept describes a *centralized* process which may fit some successful innovations. Marketers should be aware this is a descriptive rather than prescriptive model. The original model draws on observations made across a range of disciplines, some of which are concerned with relatively pervasive changes in relatively standardized populations, like agriculture communities or primitive societies (Rogers, 1995).

Table 12.1 'Ideal' innovator types

Innovators (2.5%)	Ideas gatekeepers, tend to be obsessed with new ideas, are citizens of the world and fall into cliques of the similar-minded which can span national boundaries. They can be rash but have sufficient financial resources to absorb mistakes in their purchases and resolve to accept such mistakes, they have the technical knowledge to understand complex products and can cope with high levels of uncertainty. They may not be popular or respected by other members of a social system, but can play a useful role in adoption by importing innovations from outside boundaries of the social system
Early adopters (13.5%)	Respected within the social system, they may be sought for advice, giving some high degree of opinion leadership. They are typically communications targets for 'agents of change' who see them as potential missionaries in the social system, capable of promoting the diffusion process
Early Majority (34%)	A socially interactive group who deliberate and seek interpersonal advice before adoption; as a large group they provide interconnections in the diffusion process
Late Majority (34%)	Often sceptics under financial pressure, they require weight of system norms to be in place before it is safe to act; they adopt perhaps out of economic necessity or peer pressure when comfortable with the risk involved
Laggards (16%)	Suspicious traditionalists, often comparatively isolated in the social system, they look to the past for guidance and have sparse resources they must handle carefully

193

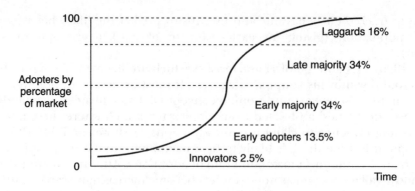

Figure 12.2 Accumulated totals of adopters (adapted from Rogers, 1983).

THE ADOPTION PROCESS

The *adoption process* is distinguished from other types of decision-making process in that it is usually concerned with *new* products, services or ideas (where the customer lacks previous knowledge or experience). Shortage of knowledge and experience makes this type of decision making inherently risky and hence encourages information-seeking and information-processing behaviours aimed at minimizing uncertainty. Different people will have different perceptions of risk, perceive relative advantages and disadvantages of an innovation differently, and may have differential access to information. This implies that there will be differences in the rate at which new products are adopted by different types of people.

Some people may have a personal disposition toward a type of innovation, may tolerate risk well, be skilled at acquiring information (to promote understanding and reduce risk), and may have access to special sources of information. Marketers can do little about consumer personal disposition, or their personality traits, drives and motivations. They can, however, help reduce risk by taking control of the marcoms process and provide information in appropriate ways to promote understanding and adoption.

In Rogers' model (1983) people move through a set of *behavioural type* stages in their adoption process. This involves a series of hierarchical stages (from cognitive to affective to behaviour modes) in five steps: knowledge, persuasion, decision, implementation, confirmation (see Figure 12.3). Diffusion across a population produces a range of adoption times that suggest each category of adopter has a different time scale for these steps, and promotional effort can be adapted accordingly, with early adopters meriting initial special attention to help harness their potential as opinion leaders and market catalysts.

MACRO MODELS, MICRO MODELS AND MARKETING

The classical interpretation of diffusion studies (Rogers, 1995) draws on two theoretical assumptions. Firstly, the micro-level adoption process takes place at different rates, depending on an individual's level of innovativeness, and leads to a sustained mode of behaviour. Secondly, the macro-level social diffusion process describes a pattern of communications relationships, promoting adoption, which affects a whole population over time. These describe marketing ideals rather than likely outcomes; the first can be related to a totally *loyal* customer and the second to full market *penetration*. To be able to draw on diffusion models, marketing needs to be aware of these and other limitations.

Diffusion – macro models and marketing

Adoption by a small group who have innovative tendencies is no guarantee of diffusion across wider markets, as the high failure rate of new products demonstrates (Urban and Hauser, 1993).

In developed markets diffusion can be a complex process. For example, even if an efficient electric car is developed its success might also inhibit adoption. It is not difficult to imagine the value of petrol cars being depressed by such an innovation. Devaluation of petroleum-based technology, by *new* electric power, may force people to extend purchase-cycle length and run their current petrol car for longer than normal between purchases, because the reduced value makes changing it less affordable.

Diffusion does not have to lead to adoption amongst a whole population to be successful in marketing terms. Those who seek to acquire status from prestige and exclusive luxury goods, for example, may rely on the idea of the status bequeathing qualities for these goods being diffused to a wider market than would seek to acquire them, so the wider market can confer this status. Designer sunglasses may convey status and support a high price because of a public acceptance of what they stand for, not because everyone will adopt them.

Diffusion need not be thought of as just a one-directional process. For markets, like telecommunication, during the process of diffusion, increasing adoption changes the value of adoption for those who have adopted early, as innovation capacity expands. Those who were first to have e-mail could make far less use of it prior to a wider market adopting it. The benefits of adoptions may therefore expand after adoption, thus redefining the innovation.

When marketing deals with new products and innovations in developed markets, many adoption choices are comparatively ephemeral and consumers are frequently involved in making judgements about conflicting choices and rival propositions that by no means guarantee a straightforward diffusion process. Diffusion studies are starting to appreciate this (Rogers, 1995) with the introduction of a continuum of *centralized* and *decentralized* diffusion systems. In the decentralized model, diffusion is not a 'trickle down' process through a vertical hierarchy of innovativeness in a population. Rather than treat the whole population as connected to innovativeness on a similar continuum, decentralized diffusion grants the adopter high levels of interpretative judgement and suggests that more horizontal diffusion takes place, often between individuals in discrete groups who operate in comparative isolation and where each group may adopt for different reasons. This raises the possibility of parallel adoption processes going on in a range of 'sub-populations' within

195

developed markets, all of whom might be exposed to some similar aspects of marcoms activity, but who might also have access to communications networks that are unique to that particular group. For example, in 1998, Cable and Wireless started to offer a set of new telephone service packages matched to a range of different customer uses. They encouraged diffusion through a reward-driven 'customer-get-customer' promotion that encourages each customer to act as an opinion leader amongst his or her very own 'technology-connected community', thereby using the very technology that is instrumental in the adoptive behaviour to promote diffusion of similar new telephone service packages.

Adoption – micro models and marketing

It is unreasonable to assume the all consumers go through a similar *process,* within degrees of innovativeness, that results in different times to complete adoption. The possible range of dynamic influences makes the concept of adoptions along one linear diffusion continuum unlikely for many of the subtle innovations marketing may be interested in promoting, as the notion of decentralized diffusion is starting to appreciate.

The diffusion model takes 'time' as a variable (to operationalize innovativeness) but to be a valid continuum that reveals a social phenomenon requires it to be measuring similar processes associated with individual adoption. Adoption, while common to human experience, is not necessarily born out of a common set of processing characteristics. It is conceivable that adoption could be responsive to different influences in different adopters, or it may be a symptom of different types of complex buyer behaviour. As people bring their personality traits, circumstances, socialization and communication networks to a given task there is no guarantee that a complex *range* of different processing behaviours is not involved in adoption for many new products.

It has also been possible to show that rates of adoption depend on which countries, cultures and communications systems are involved (Takada and Jain, 1991). Just as different members of a population may have different resistances to disease, so diffusion does not just depend on the innovation itself but on those who may adopt it. Products are often promoted in a social system with complex and interacting social norms, values and communications channels, not all of which can be shared equally. Such complexity makes one mode of adoption as likely as finding only one tightly cohesive social system in any developed marketplace. For example, freshly cooked chilled food may be adopted *inter alia* because of a disability causing problems with cooking tasks, because someone does not know how to cook, or because of a busy lifestyle of shift schedules, or perhaps because working couples do not wish to burden their partner with domestic chores. Two people may buy a microwave oven at the same time but for quite different reasons, or seeking different benefits.

Adoption processes have traditionally been looked at as a set of behavioural steps which take little note of the role of interpretation and judgements which potential adopters bring to a purchase decision. This fails to appreciate the interactive dynamics in modes of communication, whether through interpersonal or media channels. While some communications models may suggest otherwise, little communication activity is really one-way. While media messages lack many dimensions of interpersonal communication (body language cues, intonations of spoken language, etc.), consumers still bring a form of interactivity even to television ads. For example, recent research from the University of Leicester (*Campaign*, 21 November 1997) suggested that consumers 'move' toward media in ways that influence their interaction. Supporting the ELM model discussed elsewhere, higher levels of involvement in programme content around advertisements were reported to generate greater attitudinal change, while lower involvement was better at producing short-term recall.

The decision not to adopt does not necessarily imply active rejection but could be part of delayed acceptance that may or may not be converted into adoption at a later stage, perhaps at a change of circumstances. There is, therefore, a need to make a distinction between adoption, passive rejection (passive lack of adoption) and active rejection. Behaviour is typically more predictable when it is extreme (Argyle, 1972). Diffusion and adoption process models display the clearest evidence of useful application following adoption where comparatively stark choices apply in widely shared social circumstances, such as where new technology is introduced to a specific industry (Rogers, 1995). Such situations are not usually common in consumer marketing.

Adoption may not be a standard event. It may involve some element of reinvention as consumers turn products to new and sometimes unexpected roles, perhaps subverting the values and uses of a new product; an ice-cream machine may be a wedding present for one adopter or a lifestyle statement for another.

In marketing, consumer loyalty is a complex individual issue and full market penetration is an unlikely event. Different levels of consumer involvement and different product categories lead to different levels of loyalty in buyer behaviour. Individual decision making may lead to a range of behaviours, e.g. trial, rejection, adoption (with possible later rejection), non-adoption (with possible later adoption), adoption to a preference repertoire, etc. Companies may also be interested in not just adoption but adoption by special target customers, often those with high consumption potential.

Adoption does not have to originate outside the adopter. The evolution of *trade marketing* concerns itself with business-to-business relationships where added value can be forged between organizations. Innovations may be jointly shared, perhaps through shortening supply chains or sharing market information that enables technology to find new applications. This type of diffusion model is not about dissemination of ideas and solutions; instead, it implies that innovation and adoption become synonymous concepts which evolve out of shared understanding of problems, mutual cooperation, and goal convergence.

DIFFUSION ELEMENTS

Engel *et al.* (1993) identify four elements that influence the diffusion and adoption process: the *innovation* itself, *channels of communication* by which messages reach potential adopters, the *social system* in the population in which diffusion takes place, and the *time* involved to complete different stages of adoption and diffusion. By appreciating how these elements affect individual decisions and take-up of new ideas by markets, it is possible to understand some of the dynamics that marketers need to take account of when planning communications strategy.

1. Innovation

Not all innovations are of the same form. Some innovation can be ground-breaking (the digital camera), while others may be more incremental (coloured fridges). Redmond (1996) even describes an innovation in the process to 'disadoption' by looking at the behaviour of quitting smoking. It has also been suggested that many types of innovations can be classified on a continuum from minor line extensions, at one extreme, to major technological breakthroughs, at the other (Robertson *et al.*, 1984). Most new products change people's capacity to carry out tasks in some way; Robertson (1967) assessed the impact this has on behaviour to classify innovation types (Table 12.2).

There is an expectation that the more complex the innovation, or the more it involves a departure from established cultural norms, the more difficult it would be to communicate benefits, hence the slower the diffusion rate (e.g. dishwashers). Similarly, innovations which carry higher levels of perceived risk may be expected to lead to greater levels of customer resistance to adoption. Such risk factors may include potential social ridicule or great personal financial loss (arguably the failed 'Sinclair C5' electric car had both these problems).

A marketing truism states that: 'people don't buy products, they buy benefits'. Product attributes, therefore, need to be understood alongside tangible and intangible benefits potential adopters may perceive an innovation to offer before marketers can really know what or how to communicate. From the marketer's point of view, the important issue is the *consumer perspective*, i.e. the subjective judgemental basis. It is not enough for the product, service or idea to deliver in cold objective technical terms, it must be perceived as appropriate by potential buyers and users. An innovation must be 'of its time' and capable of being communicated effectively. The marketing task includes informing and educating customers and distribution

Table 12.2 Behavioural impact of innovations

Continuous	Involves little change in consumer behaviour. Innovation more by way of minor modification than radical invention, e.g. computer software, supermarket cook-chilled meals, or a new flavour of ice-cream
Dynamically continuous	Where consumer behaviour may undergo some adjustment such as via some alteration to the product, e.g. a new type of computer control like a joystick for games playing
Discontinuous	Where technology offers a periodic step change in the capacity of people to perform particular tasks or types of behaviour (these are less common). The Internet may be seen as this even in its current level of market penetration

channels about the benefits of relevant innovations while recognizing that their influence is limited. One example, which led to product withdrawal, was when in the late 1970s Colgate Palmolive launched liquid washing 'powder', for laundry use. The product was withdrawn when retailers helped confuse customers by displaying the product with washing-up liquid (author experience).

In an attempt to classify types of innovation, Rogers (1983) dealt with potential adopters' perceptions of benefits by looking at the impact of these from a consumer decision-making processual perspective. Under the heading of *persuasion*, Rogers looked at the characteristics of an innovation and classified these by their relative superiority over previous offerings and by the ease with which advantages could be appreciated and understood. This may be particularly appropriate to innovations that offer significantly different benefits to those previously available, such as when dealing with dramatic improvement in performance or capacity, or when introducing established technology to less developed cultures. Such situations are quite rare in marketing, where innovations are more typically subtle components of a complex product and are often incorporated into products with established brand identities and equities.

Marketing seeks to manage relationships and not just transactions. People have relationships with people, pets, places *and* brands. *Planning for Social Change* (Henley Centre, reported in *Marketing*, 1996) reported that consumers see *brands* as part of society and accord some of them high levels of trust. Kellogg and Cadbury, for example, were more trusted than the police and the church. Brand management has a central role in caring for customer relationships and maintaining brands as assets. Kapferer (1997) describes the brand as a potential 'prism' that can influence the way a product is seen, and as an 'amplifier', capable of adding synergy so as to echo and reinforce values (some values may be bound to core attributes creating benefits, e.g. safety features for 'Volvo', or they may be more abstract, e.g. a fair trade policy for coffee importers ('cafédirect').

An innovation does not have to lead to a new brand. The 1990s have witnessed a marked reversal in previous brand proliferation (Kapferer, 1997), along with rising management appreciation of brand values and equities. Managing brand investments involves caring for the value systems a brand evokes and new product development can play an important role in this management. Especially in categories where products are improved in small incremental ways (rather than via technological breakthroughs), adding appropriate and relevant innovations can help manage brands and their relationships with consumers, helping keep them fresh and contemporary. Thus, from an innovation perspective, of the nigh on 26 000 'new' products cited earlier in this chapter (Castle, 1997), only 6.7 per cent were truly innovative in the sense that they featured an innovation in formulation, positioning, packaging, technology or creating a new market. This low figure had decreased from previous years (1994 – 7.2 per cent, 1984 – 18.6 per cent).

An innovation introduced under the umbrella of an existing brand may be 'refracted' by consumers' brand perceptions; e.g. customers may expect higher levels of innovation from some brands, like Sony. Brands can therefore underwrite customers perceptions of risk with a new product but this will only be true if the type of innovation is compatible with and appropriate to a brand's identity. Strong brands, therefore, may be able to serve as trusted sources of advice about risk, similar to trusted personal contacts.

The corporate processes which generate new product ideas are likely to be better managed when they draw on marketing's carefully nurtured brand values *and* customers' perceptions of brand value and identity. If branded innovations need to be synergistic with core brand values, this might help explain why, as Kapferer (1997) claimed: 'weak brands do not succeed in capitalising on their innovations: they do not manage either to enhance the brand's meaning or create that all important resonance'. In other words, stronger brands can give innovations a greater chance of survival. Brands, too, can only be assured of survival if they constantly *renew* themselves via marketing to match changing needs while simultaneously remaining true to customers' expectations of core brand identity.

From a marcoms perspective, messages about *new* can be separated into introduction of:

- **low equity new product concepts** (require new adoption behaviour with high risk);
- **high equity new product concepts** (require new adoption behaviour with potentially lower risk – due to the equity of a known brand);
- **incremental new product concepts** (with little new adoption behaviour where innovations help existing brand concepts to retain or improve the status quo by managing brand equity).

New products, therefore, often arrive supported by the equity of some existing brand. In such situations, it can be important to consider 'newness' in terms of fit with established brand identities, and whether the character of an innovation extrapolates brand values or damages them. An innovation classification along branded lines should account for the perceived values of each brand by each market segment. 'Newness' would, therefore, need to be judged in the context of the trust and understanding potential customers attach to existing brands, against consumers' 'malleability' in both their behaviour toward an innovation and their conception of a brand's identity. For these reasons Rogers' (1983) model of adopter perceptions, below, has been modified to incorporate potential branding implications:

- **Relative advantage** – improved benefits along dimensions customers rate
- **Compatibility** – the match with the potential adopters' current modes
  - *brand synergy* – fit with existing brand equity
  - *zeitgeist* – malleability of the cultural context
- **Complexity** – the ease with which an innovation can be understood and used
- **Trialability** – how easily benefits can be sampled
- **Observability** – ease with which benefits can be demonstrated

Innovations that are perceived by potential adopters as having greater relative advantage, compatibility, trialability, etc. are likely to be more rapidly adopted. However, when it comes to adoption behaviour, customers' propensity to innovativeness is not necessarily a stable commodity. There is no guarantee that those who are attracted to one type of innovation will also be attracted to another, nor that a particular type of innovation would be attractive to potential adopters just because they have exhibited past innovator behaviour in a similar area. People are subject to changes in circumstances and personal development that may impact on selective attention and relevant interest in product categories.

2. Communication channels

One of the more valuable marketing insights from diffusion studies comes from the improved understanding of the communications processes. Beyond the more conspicuous forms of media communication, adopters can play an active personal part in the decision-making process of other adopters. Mass adoption, or diffusion through a population, is seen by Rogers (1995) as the result of a communications process, what he describes as:

> a particular type of communication in which the message content that is exchanged is concerned with a new idea. The essence of the diffusion process is the information exchange through which one individual communicates a new idea to one or several others.

> (Rogers, 1995)

In a developed market where marcoms has access to a range of communications channels, the notion that ideas should pass by individual contact can be extended to include media use as part of the social environment.

When an innovation is first introduced, the only source of information is the agent launching the innovation. At this stage the marketer has the greatest control over the message, effectively being what diffusionists call a 'change agent', the instigator that sets off a diffusion process. Typically, communication objectives may include announcing an innovation, creating awareness and understanding, promoting trial, and reinforcing the purchase decision. A key question in diffusion research is whether, and if so how, innovators and early adopters differ from later adopters, as this may inform communications strategy. As the innovation starts to be adopted, alternative non-managed communications channels often come into play and customer 'word-of- mouth' (WOM) takes on increasing importance. Foxall (1989) suggests that personal influence plays a much larger role in creating the market for new products than communication instigated and controlled by marketing managers. Thus, innovative and early adoptive buyers display new products to the less adventurous bulk of potential customers, who require reassurance of the acceptability of the product. In other words, they act as a source of social display and legitimization to later adopters.

Thus, aspects of communication can be considered by exploring possible information needs of potential adopters and how this information can best reach them. As recipients of a message, what do they need to know or understand if they are to move toward adoption of an innovation? Rogers (1983) version of the decision process steps can be used to illustrate how different types of marketing communication are better suited to reaching particular communications objectives more efficiently, as different communication channels are better suited to carrying different types of information (see Figure 12.3).

201

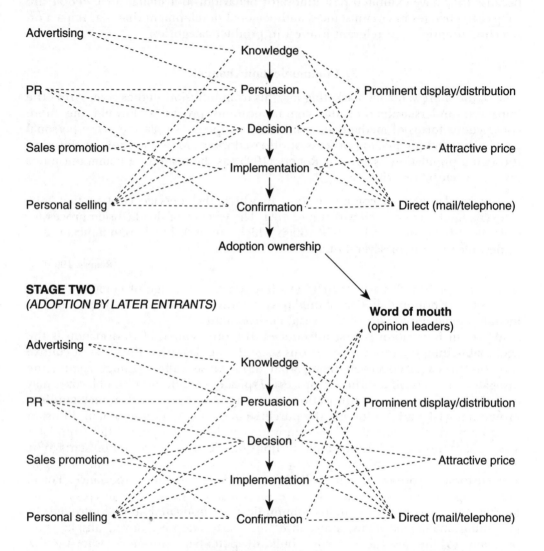

Figure 12.3 The two-stage communications processes (showing potential key influences in the decision making process for early and later adopters).

(*Source*: Rogers, 1983)

Conventionally, much marcoms activity involved in diffusion is viewed as a hypodermic-style process, with information flowing in a linear one-way *one-step* mode (from company to customer via messages typically broadcast through the media). Innovations found toward the discontinuous innovation end of the innovations continuum are likely to be further from the experience of customers and inherently perceived as more risky, and therefore a greater communications challenge when encouraging adoption. Mass media are not normally good at building the sort of interpersonal dialogue that is suited to conveying complex information. In these circumstances, a short media communications chain is not always influential enough to promote mass market adoption (Rogers, 1995).

A diffusion model insight introduces the concept of a *two-stage* or *multi-stage* communication process. From this perspective, messages from media sources will have reached and promoted adoption amongst the less risk-sensitive innovative (or early adoptive) consumers, some of whom may be opinion leaders. After they have adopted, opinion leaders may start to sway other potential adopters in a population, by communicating with them at an interpersonal level. This is a process of 'passing on', akin to the spread of a contagious disease through interpersonal contact. A range of literature (Rogers, 1996) supports the role of opinion leadership in the diffusion process and suggests that launching innovations, with their inherent risks (Cooper and Kleinschmit, 1987), deserves to be thought of as a special situation for marcoms activity. This potential step in the diffusion process, interpersonal communication between members of the population, or word-of-mouth (WOM), is normally outside direct marketing control, but not necessarily outside its influence (Figure 12.3).

Managing the communications tasks involved with introducing innovations requires the use of product or brand management strategies and, particularly when dealing with the larger parts of a potential market population, an appreciation of the role of WOM (word-of-mouth) communications in the way information is shared and spread. WOM communication is not something within direct marcoms control but it can ape some of its qualities through activities like database-driven interactive communications and loyalty-building schemes.

Much of the diffusion literature dates from a period before the modern media landscape was in place. In developed markets where the role of media in people's lives is evolving, many 'brand relationships' are managed by marcoms activities. Marcoms can, therefore, be used to harness a symbolic form of social relationship (it was reported, above, that the Cadbury brand has greater levels of consumer trust than the police). Some communications channels have the capacity to fulfil a social role and to carry information content that can substitute or mimic some features of interpersonal communication. Communication activity can also be devised to stimulate interpersonal communication, rather than just convey a message direct to a potential consumer.

By appreciating the dynamics of information flows which influence people in a communications infrastructure, marketing communicators are able to adapt to the tasks facing them more effectively, and draw on the synergy of integrated or combined communication approaches. This might include incorporating features normally found in less controllable channels (like interpersonal communication) into other communication forms (like direct mail). Alternatively, it might involve stimulating forms of less controllable 'informal' communication activity (e.g. WOM and media hype, where the presentation of information can help to generate 'SPIN' or 'bandwagon' effects that enter the public consciousness). Inspired creative devices, clever marketing public relations, or teaser or enigmatic advertising are typical devices for creating SPIN.

3. The social system

The binding forces holding together a *social system* come from the communications links that allow the sharing of values and meaningful references between units (whether individual units, family units or organizational units). These communications links help share the social norms that shape aspirations and expectations held within the social system, and which give it boundaries and a sense of entity. For marketers, the way these communications links are shared and the functions they have within a population help to define and segment target markets. It also suggests what values and references to include in commercial messages, to help make them more relevant and easily interpreted.

Relationships between the different units give a social system structure (whether rigid, formal and hierarchical, as in the armed forces, or informal and loosely structured, like a house party). Knowing how individuals (or units) interact and relate gives valuable information about social structure and allows the 'flow pattern' of communication to be predicted and managed with greater accuracy. Marketing can then take a flow pattern and use it to predict likely information exchanges and consequent adoption rates, and this can be used to anticipate problems in a communications chain.

Before new ideas can permeate a social system they must first enter it. *Change agents* describe instigators that can bring innovations into the social system, e.g. an individual who is first to adopt because he or she has contact with an innovation beyond the social system, or a firm seeking to introduce new products (marketing can, therefore, be a change agent).

Whether change agents also form good opinion leaders in a population is likely to depend on their level of connectedness to the social system. In a hierarchical social system, change agents might be an elite that the bulk population aspire to and will ape. By definition, though, those who adopt very early are exhibiting untypical behaviour, and in that sense are at the margins of the social system. This may mean their closeness of 'fit' to the norms and values of others is not high (*heterophily*). When this 'fit' is relatively dissimilar to the central values and norms of the population then this is likely to reflect on a low level of empathy with the bulk of the population, with consequent poor communication links (Engel, *et al.*, 1993) and a weak ability to influence others. In IT terms they might be seen as the computer nerds, or 'anoraks', who are known to possess knowledge but who are accorded little social respect.

An effective opinion-leading role, one that can generate good communications to those in a population's majority, requires a degree of relative *homophily*, or similarity between communications units. This comes from similar shared references: values systems, jobs, interests, etc. 'When they . . . (*two or more individuals*) . . . share common meanings, a mutual sub-cultural language, and are alike in personal and social characteristics, the communications of new ideas is likely to have greater effects in terms of knowledge gain, attitude formations and change, and overt behaviour change' (Rogers, 1995).

In classical diffusion models the very first to adopt may be weak at bringing influence to mass markets but they may have contact with those who are strong, i.e.

the socially mobile who can straddle a range of social values, some of whom may be 'opinion leaders'. Opinion leaders have relative homophily with the mass market and sufficient respect for their opinion to be sought. Rogers (1995) identifies the majority of opinion leaders as found in a group he classifies as '*early adopters*'. He also reveals that, relative to later adopters, they tend to share communication characteristics such as being more networked to outside influences, having relatively high contact with change agents, coming into contact with more media and interpersonal communications channels, and seeking and acquiring more information about innovations.

Shared interpretation is a key to good communication and the closer people are to similar frames of reference then the easier it is likely to be for them to facilitate effective information exchanges. The evidence suggests most interpersonal diffusion networks are largely homophilous (Rogers, 1995). Perfect homophily implies no need for diffusion, as knowledge of innovations would already be shared. Therefore, all adoption behaviour requires some degree of heterophily. Similarly, efficient communications is possible between the homophilous but it is also likely to be a barrier to adoption if they do not allow outside access from heterophilous sources of information. Hence the need for 'linking' communications mobility, between change agents and the mass market. This linking is classically performed by opinion leaders but marcoms activity can also perform this function by reaching communications targets with messages encoded with creative content that draws on the frames of reference familiar to the receiver (allowing homophilous-style interaction). However, the channels or messages may not carry the same authority as opinions offered through interpersonal communication.

For large populations, the decentralized diffusion concept suggests the possible existence of parallel sub-groups, or separate social systems, where each sub-group may be simultaneously going through adoption processes at different rates and employing behaviours that involve different processual factors. A proactive marketing effort can be planned to interact with a parallel set of simultaneous diffusions: the privatization of BT involved 'selling' an idea to the public, to politicians, the press and the City, simultaneously. Even within consumer markets, database marketing is starting to make it possible to isolate sub-markets and manage market penetration of parallel or isolated groups who might have subtle but important differences in the benefits they seek: new service-based products, like telephone banking, are offered to different social groups simultaneously using customized communications strategies (people are encouraged to enquire what services are available and are then offered service innovations matched to their claimed requirements and usage).

Classical diffusion models see the social system as consisting of 'interrelated units that are engaged in joint problem-solving to accomplish common goals' (Rogers, 1995). In an increasingly interactive integrated electronic and media-driven age, interrelationships can involve wide-ranging channels of communication. In a widely applied model, Bass (1969) suggested potential adopters can be influenced by two types of communications channels: word-of-mouth *and* mass media. In this model, adoption influenced by the media takes place throughout the whole diffusion process but is most impactful at the early stages, while WOM adopters (the majority of the population) gradually increase in adoption rate to a high point before gradually declining again (describing a 'normal' type of distribution). This model was investigated through the 1970s with some success (Rogers, 1995) but it fails to consider the modern media landscape and the influences a complex communications infrastructure (which includes a range of electronic and interactive media systems) might have on the communications process in a developed social system.

Nonetheless, WOM, as a trusted form of advocacy, provides an insight into the influences at work in the communications structure binding a social system. There are marketing implications from proposing that consumers are driven to seek trusted forms of advocacy when exposed to that which is beyond current experience, as when dealing with innovation. Marcoms activity can expect to have greater impact on mass markets when it harnesses the most powerful agents of influence for each adopter group, such as opinion leaders for the mass market, or when it uses controllable communication devices that effectively substitute 'advocacy' information found in communications channels normally beyond marketing control (like WOM). Ideally such substitute information should also be 'phrased' with familiar values and references to mimic homophily with the target audience.

In this age of fast-evolving mediascapes and changing social structures, it is evident that the status and authority of different modes of communication also change. The notion of different levels of media literacy in some cultures demonstrates this evolving status (Goodyear, 1991). Some modes of communication offer the capacity to substitute interpersonal aspects that give people a sense of community in their homophilous associations, a notion which could describe the objectives of relationship marketing. The strands in the communications infrastructure of the social environment are already partly composed of a media-made fabric. Thus, it can be hypothesized that introduction of innovations may rely less in the future, therefore, on the role of interpersonal communication, particularly when products appeal to more media active or media involved populations.

4. Time

In diffusion models time is taken as the main dimension for isolating different adopter categories. It assesses when adoption takes place for different types of adopter. This can assist marketers in categorizing target markets and identifying them in the population, so as to deploy target promotional efforts effectively.

At the individual level, time also identifies progress in how a particular consumer may be moving toward his or her own adoption decision. This can help marketers to determine what messages might be most appropriate at a given time, to move adopters through states, from unawareness toward confirmation.

Population characteristics are studied using time. It is the level of innovativeness reflected by proportions of the population at different times which helps to establish characteristic-like rates of adoption. Market saturation is more of an abstract concept than a marketing reality. The diffusion model assumes total adoption to establish population characteristics. In marketing terms, there is a poor likelihood of total market penetration. Most markets exhibit aspects of customer defection, disadoption and rejection and there are problems such as market decay and issues like replacement cycles (e.g. durable goods) to account for. Car driving, for example, has not been adopted by the whole market for cars. This pro-innovations bias is acknowledged by diffusionists (Rogers, 1995) but not addressed. Nevertheless, diffusion can have a valuable role in 'estimating' market characteristics that can help guide promotional activities and it can be used to 'judge' the penetration of markets and the effectiveness/success of promotional efforts.

Time is also a key to coordinating integrated proactive communications activity and planning how to capitalize on the synergy of combined aspects of a promotional campaign. In classical diffusion models, the time dimension prescribed a standard distribution of adoption behaviours, with late and early adopters lying approximately equally spaced about some mean time of adoption. However, marketing is often a competitive activity where players may seek the commercial benefits of early market share domination and, if successful, will soon be followed by rivals. It is plausible to envisage diffusion patterns sharply skewed toward the introduction end of the time scale, as companies compete with a particularly high level of promotional effort to win early advantage (see Figure 12.4).

MARKETING COMMUNICATIONS MANAGEMENT

The interest in diffusion models for marcoms was originally born out of a desire to understand the collective behaviour of groups of potential adopters. Such knowledge can help marketing to identify communications targets and to predict the likely outcome of the advertising and promotional (A&P) spend for new products. In the 1970s and 1980s the Bass 'market penetration' model and its variants were adopted as predictive devices, particularly for durable goods. These models were joined by a range of 'repeat purchase' type models that attempted to take account of product categories that require second purchase to distinguish adoption from trial purchase. The successful application of these models is mainly a commercially sensitive issue which Rogers (1995) considers to be dependent on

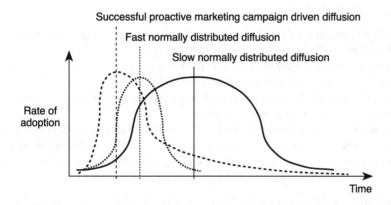

Figure 12.4 Different rates of market penetration (showing peaks of rate of diffusion).

market-specific factors. For example, established computer games companies have lost out in the mid-1990s because of Sony's success with their new 'PlayStation', which is as much to do with the adaptation to different market characteristics as it is to do with its launch and the technology itself (*The Guardian*, supplement section, 14 March 1998).

Predictive market modelling becomes more difficult as product life cycles shorten and the rate of introduction of new technology accelerates. Markets can be quite specific, and they do evolve. While a firm with some recent experience of successfully launching a new product in a defined field may be able to use this experience to model market penetration characteristics, there is no guarantee that the processes in adoption behaviour will have remained constant and will reoccur in the same way should they come to launch another product in a similar category. Nevertheless, market modelling is an important management tool and diffusion models offer valuable predictive and explanatory insights into the aggregated behaviour of consumers.

To help cope with different product categories and the potential influences involved in diffusion and adoption processes, a range of models has emerged. Tidd *et al.* (1997) identify a range of diffusion models that illustrate two focuses of classification: *demand-side,* adoption-type models which are mainly statistical, and *supply-side,* diffusion-type models which are mainly sociological.

Demand side models include:

- **Epidemic**: potential adopters in a population are similar and information is spread by personal contact;
- **Bass**: separates segments of early and later adopters (who are influenced by the early adopters); information is spread by personal contact and different communication strategies applying best to each segment;
- **Probit**: potential adopters can acquire understanding but their own decision-processing influences determine when they choose to adopt;
- **Baysian**: potential adopters have unequal understanding of an innovation and make their own different judgements about adoption value in isolation from others.

Supply-side models include:

- **Appropriability**: assumes that the superiority of the advantages an innovation is perceived to have will determine its adoption;
- **Dissemination**: assumes information is critical and concentrates on providing it in appropriate forms and communication channels;
- **Utilization**: deals with the challenges of explaining and understanding uses of innovations and how to go about adoption;
- **Communication**: concentrates on the exchange of information between potential adapter and supplier and is especially important for business-to-business situations where strategic alliances are forged and in bespoke consumer situations where new solutions are sought.

Most diffusion models fail to account for the sophistication of the media landscape and the role proactive marcoms can play in generating and managing informal communications channels which may involve interpersonal communication or media publicity and comment. However, valuable marcoms insight from the diffusion models comes from an appreciation of the power of relationships to influence in a social context.

Adoption of new products is normally interpreted as driven by interpersonal communication at a critical stage of diffusion. However, the body of evidence for this comes largely from a period that predates the modern media environment. Far from being beyond marketing control, the diffusion model accommodates the idea of how marcoms can be managed to promote adoption amongst markets that are sceptical of commercial messages or which require high levels of guidance and reassurance in their decision-making behaviour. Some marcoms efforts may take *formal* and easily controlled forms, like advertising and direct mail. Others can be interpreted as *informal* and less controllable, like WOM and media publicity. Marcoms can play a vital role in informal channels, e.g. creative advertising can become a talking point (Benetton, Blackcurrant Tango) and PR can create 'SPIN' (Virgin balloons); in combination or singly they can energize informal and interpersonal channels of communication.

Recent demonstrations of the 'art' of marcoms in the launch of new products can be found in examples where managing WOM is particularly successful. The Virgin group have managed to extend the range of their business interests across a broad sweep of consumer markets (from entertainment to travel to financial services). Most of this can be seen to be supported by a 'softly spoken' but 'deeply pervasive' communications effort that is led by inspired marketing public relations activity linked to other marcoms forms in an integrated fashion.

Marcoms efforts can take many forms and the synergy achieved through multiple channels of communication may create a magnified influence, compared to the use of single forms of communications device. The use of interactive communications effort and database-driven marketing is enabling marcoms to be customized for different types of consumer behaviour. This means potential adopters can be sent messages customized to match their own propensity to innovativeness, as predicted by past behaviour. Careful targeting can also help achieve different outcomes amongst different market segments at similar times. For those who still seek interpersonal reassurance, marcoms can be used to stimulate or simulate WOM rather than just adoption and this can be monitored by tracking and survey devices, so as to adjust communications strategy appropriately.

In short, the insight which comes from diffusion provides an appreciation of the role communication can play as a part of the social environment, both to stimulate secondary communication amongst individuals and to mimic and substitute the messages that would otherwise normally come from interpersonal communication. The media have entered into the social fabric of modern life and every organization that needs to communicate ideas needs to be aware of how to use it in effective and sometimes subtle ways, not just how to advertise product propositions. As John Butler said on his appointment to the post of Bishop of Southwark, 'the airwaves are our parish now' (Radio 4, 'Sunday' programme, 22 March 1998).

SUMMARY AND CONCLUSION

Diffusion and adoption have received considerable academic attention over 40 years and the models of diffusion have been taken up and applied by commercial marketing departments to help manage the introduction of new products. The success of commercial application is difficult to establish because of business-sensitive issues.

The classical centralized diffusion model deals with adoption across populations. It has been used to categorize market segments according to when potential consumers are likely to adopt new products. This has been particularly useful for marcoms as it has enabled key communications targets to be identified. One of the key communications targets had been 'opinion leaders', those consumers who are early to adopt a new product and who can influence later adopters.

Diffusion models have been criticized for not being sensitive enough to the conditions that apply in developed markets at the launch of many new products. In particular, they may fail to take sufficient account of the complex communications processes which can take place through channels of communications that include the media landscape within a developed social environment. Neither do they take account of the introduction of many innovations under existing brand names, which have already-existing values and expectations for potential adopters. Recent developments in diffusion models have started to appreciate that a decentralized diffusion process may exist. These developments promise to help address shortcomings in the centralized diffusion models, but there is a shortage of literature in the area.

Lessons from the processes of diffusion and adoption in this chapter might be summed up by the conclusion that relationships matter to people. If marcoms activity can promote or create the role of opinion leadership it can help engineer relationships that can give consumers a sense of reduced uncertainty, which can be important for adoption. Marcoms that is able to simulate or stimulate aspects that promote the diffusion process can start to manage aspects of diffusion that were previously considered to be beyond its control.

DISCUSSION QUESTIONS

1 Discuss the role of word of mouth in the diffusion process. How can it be stimulated by marketers?
2 How would you expect the diffusion of *Soft* to compare with *The Insult* and why?
3 Can authors be branded and how does this affect the adoption and diffusion of their work?
4 Why should diffusion research be considered important by marketing and marketing communicators?
5 Does 'categorization into discrete groups' act as a conceptual device to aid understanding? Justify your response.
6 How does understanding the Cable and Wireless (1998) vignette illustrate uncontrollable communication networks? How significant are these networks?
7 So many 'innovations' are not really 'new'. What, in your view, would constitute an innovation?

8 Using Figure 12.3, illustrate with examples Stage 1 or Stage 2 adoption by consumers.
9 Should marketers take social systems into consideration when planning marcom activities? Surely, in many cases, there is no need for very detailed evaluation?
10 Illustrate the value of marketing modelling from a marcom perspective.

CASE STUDY – SOFT

In March 1998, Bloomsbury published *Soft*, the latest Rupert Thomson novel. Thomson had already published four previous novels and had achieved the reputation of a cult figure. Bloomsbury evidently were hoping to build on previous success, and make *Soft* a bestseller.

Thomson's previous book *The Insult* had attracted significant critical acclaim. It was short-listed for the *Guardian* Fiction prize and featured in many 'fiction reviews of the year' in the quality press. The book was a popular success despite a lack of promotional support. The main publicity came from word-of-mouth. The publishing trade recognizes sales of 20 000 as the critical level for triggering word-of-mouth and bandwagon effects. At that point, the title was recognized as something special and went on to achieve sales of over 50 000.

In the absence of other promotional support, the cover was the principal vehicle for controlled marcoms. It invited readers to join Thomson's mailing list by writing to a PO Box number in London's Earl's Court. This gave a bedsit-land image that provided a useful storyline for journalists and also reinforced the idea of the author as a cult figure. Added to this was Thomson's book-jacket photograph which was described by one reviewer as 'looking like Anthony Perkins in *Psycho*.

The cover for *Soft* was similarly exploited both to give an indication of the book's content and to brand the author as a new-generation writer. For this book, however, there was a much fuller promotional campaign.

Bloomsbury's marketing manager defined the campaign objectives as

- to establish the book as a cult title,
- to attract people who would not normally read fiction, and
- to reposition Thomson from thriller writer to popular culture icon.

The novel tells the story of the launch of a new orange soft drink called 'Kwench!' and the communications campaign takes this as its central theme.

For the pre-launch trade campaign, Bloomsbury sent out canned orange drinks with dayglo orange 'Kwench!' labels which read 'Ingredients: 100% persuasion, 70% deception, 85.5% murder' and 'can help relieve the mind of tension only as a part of a controlled diet'. The teaser campaign in the trade press read 'The object of advertising is to change the behaviour of the consumer so that they purchase more of the product. The product is soft.' Building on the advertising theme of the novel, another strapline was '97% of all "Kwench!" drinkers said that "Kwench!" helped their decision making'.

Soft was featured as Bloomsbury's lead title for March 1998 in a full-page colour advertisement in the inside front cover of the leading trade publication, *The Bookseller's Buyer's Guide*.

Three thousand flyposters went up a week before launch in the London area, described by Bloomsbury's marketing manager Steve Blackburn as 'very in-your-face, yet leaving people so they are still not sure what it is'.

On the day of publication, every bookshop on the Charing Cross road covered all their windows with orange flyposters announcing the book. They also displayed hundreds of the labelled cans. The launch itself took place in a north London studio entirely coloured in orange.

The book's cover was luminous orange, giving maximum standout on the shelf and creating high-impact window displays. It featured a barcode as the main design element and had the legend 'Drink Me' embossed on the front. There was no dust jacket.

Bloomsbury's Web site carried a preview of *Soft* together with a piece by Thomson giving his reasons for writing the book. The book was reviewed in the national press (not entirely favourably in comparison with *The Insult*) and the author was also profiled as a personality outside the book review sections. Further exposure was gained through radio appearances, readings and signings.

Bloomsbury were hoping to emulate the success of such titles as Dava Sobel's *Longitude* which captured the public imagination and, after achieving peak sales of 35 000 plus during the 1997 Christmas period, continued to sell 3–4000 copies per month for a further year.

(*Sources*: David Flusfeder, 'The Soft Sell', *The Guardian Weekend*, 14 March 1998, 26–27; Ken Baker and Richard Knight, 'Keeping Track of the Titles', *The Bookseller*, 21 November 1998, 25; Douglas McCabe, 'The Future is (Dayglo) Orange', *The Bookseller*, 20 February 1998, 38; James Saynor, 'The Insult', *The Observer*, 28 January 1998, 15; Christopher Hawtree, 'Books: Visions with the lights off', *The Independent*, 10 February 1996, 11)

NOTES

1 The different times people take to adopt can be taken as a measure of innovativeness and used to describe the population behaviour on a continuum. The classical interpretation of the diffusion model suggests innovativeness will follow a comparatively *normal* distribution pattern (Rogers, 1995) where population records will be spread about the mean quite symmetrically, according to how close the various adoption times are to the mean and how dispersed they are (the proportion of adopters falling at different points along the time scale). This sort of *normal* population distribution can be described as falling, approximately, within three standard deviations of either side of the mean value (where each successive standard deviation from the mean describes a known area under the distribution curve).

REFERENCES

Ambler, T. (1996) *Marketing from Advertising to Zen*, London: Pitman.

Argyle, M. (1972) *The Psychology of Interpersonal Behaviour*, Harmondsworth: Penguin.

Bass, F.M. (1969) 'New product growth model for consumer durables', *Management Science*, 13(5): 215–17.

Campaign, 21 November 1997, reference to University of Leicester.

Castle, D. (1997) *Grocer*, 18 January, 15.

Cooper, R.G. and Kleinschmidt, E.J. (1987) 'New products: What separates the winners from the losers', *Journal of Product Innovation Management* , 4(3), September 1986, 169–84.

Engel J.F., Blackwell R.D. and Miniard P.W. (1993) *Consumer Behaviour*, Florida: Dryden Press: 792.

Foxall, G. (1989) 'Marketing innovations and customers', *The Quarterly Review of Marketing*, Autumn: 14–18.

Goodyear, M. (1991) 'Five stages of advertising literacy, why different countries respond to different levels of sophistication, *Admap*, 54(3), March: 19–21.

Guardian, The, Supplement Section, 14 March 1998.

Henley Centre: *Planning for Social Change*, cited in *Marketing*, 23 October 1996.

Kapferer, J.N. (1997) *Strategic Brand Management*, 2nd edn, London: Kogan Page, 56, 68.

Kay, J. (1993) *Foundations of Corporate Success*, Oxford: Oxford University Press.

Marketing (1995) 'Marketing–Nielsen Biggest Brands', 16 March, 3.

Marketing, see reference to Henley Centre, 23 October 1996.

Radio 4, *Sunday Programme*, 22 March 1998.

Redmond W. H. (1996) 'Product disadoption: quitting smoking as a diffusion process', *Journal of Public Policy and Marketing*, 15(1), Spring: 87–97.

Robertson, T.S. (1967) 'The process of innovation and the diffusion of innovation', *Journal of Marketing*, January: 14-19.

Robertson T.S., Zielinski, J. and Ward, S. (1984) *Consumer Behaviour*, Glenview, IL: Scott Foresman.

Rogers, E.M. (1962) *Diffusion of Innovations*, 1st edn, New York: Free Press.

Rogers, E.M. (1983) *Diffusion of Innovations*, 3rd edn, New York: Free Press.

Rogers, E.M. (1995) *Diffusion of Innovations*, 4th edn, New York: Free Press, 5, 12, 17, 19, 23, 100, 261, 273, 288, 364.

Rogers, E.M. (1996) *Communications Technology: The new media in society*, New York: Free Press.

Smith P.R. (1993) *Marketing Communications, An Integrated Approach* , London: Kogan Page.

Takada, H. and Jain, D. (1991) 'Cross-national analysis of diffusion of consumer durable goods in pacific rim countries, *Journal of Marketing*, 55(2), April: 48–54.

Tidd, J., Bessant, J. and Paritt, K. (1997) *Managing Innovations*, Chichester: Wiley.

Urban, C.L. and Hauser, J.R. (1993) *Design and Marketing of New Products*, 2nd edn, Englewood Cliffs, N.J: Prentice Hall.

13

ENVIRONMENTAL ISSUES IN MARKETING COMMUNICATIONS

Janine Dermody

CHAPTER AIMS

- to provide insight into environmental issues in marcoms
- to analyse these issues using as perspective the notion of 'green' advertising
- to explore differing philosophies underlying company responses to environmental issues
- to identify challenges facing the advertising industry in developing marcoms in the current environmental context

ILLUSTRATION: THE 'GREEN CON' AWARDS

Eastern Electricity were awarded first place in Friends of the Earth (FoE) 'green con' award for advising their customers to increase their use of electricity in order to reduce their personal contribution to global warming. The company informed customers that if they used fossil fuels directly they were accountable for the CO_2 emissions they generated; however, using electrical appliances in the home removed this personal accountability. FoE maintained that this is a very selective approach in communicating environmental benefits to consumers. While they agreed electricity does reduce CO_2 emission at the point of use, Eastern Electricity were negligent in the sense of ignoring emissions from power stations and in failing to endorse the recognisable fact that gas cooking and heating appliances resulted in significantly less CO_2 emissions than their electric equivalents. Scott and the Timber Trade Federation were awarded second and third place in the FoE awards. Scott for their claims that their forestry work combats the 'greenhouse effect'. The Timber Trade Federation for their publicity indicating that they do not endanger species and further that the timber industry does not destroy rainforests. FoE maintain that both claims are totally untrue. Meanwhile, ICI and Seltzer were jointly awarded the 'Tactical Withdrawal prize'. ICI for their withdrawal of 'environmentally friendly' claims for a household cleaner whose manufacture resulted in pollution. Seltzer for their removal of 'please recycle' labels from drinks cans which were unable to be recycled because of the mix of plastic and aluminium used. The 'Practice what you Preach' award was given to Shell UK for their refusal to clean-up an area of Cornwall which had been polluted by their pesticide Aldrin, whilst at the same time encouraging the public to improve the environment in its 'Better Britain' campaign.

(*ENDS Report* 191 (1990))

INTRODUCTION

As the erstwhile examples in the *Ends Report* 191(1990) indicate, environmental issues affecting businesses, consumers and society at large are *newsworthy*. Notably, as the world accelerates toward the twenty-first century, environmentalists maintain (in an increasingly *visible* manner) that business is responsible and accountable for many of the world's environmental problems (Dermody and Hanmer-Lloyd, 1995a). Many responses of businesses to environmental problems indicate that such charges are merited. During the 1980s and early 1990s there was a proliferation of 'green' claims made by business, some of which were intentionally dishonest and misleading, with the sole aim of keeping their stakeholders quiet (Dermody, 1994; Mayer *et al.*, 1993; Prothero *et al.*, 1994). The examples in the illustration are typical of the claims made by industry during this time, and they were not just restricted to the UK. In the United States, for example, a company launched 'dolphin-friendly' cornflakes in 1990, claiming that because their manufacture caused no threat to dolphins, it was an environmentally-friendly product! The Consumer Protection Agency took a rather grim view of this claim and prevented the company from using the slogan in their advertising campaign (Dermody and Hanmer-Lloyd, 1995b).

While greener advertising is one marked example of the way(s) in which businesses seek to take advantage of environmental trends, other environmental issues increasingly impact on organizational behaviour, and, by implication, marketing communications. The latest advance in marketing conceptual development indicates that *societal marketing* is the name of the game for business development. By definition this concept holds that:

> It is the organization's task to determine the needs, wants, and interests of target markets and deliver the desired satisfactions more effectively and efficiently than competitors *in a way that preserves or enhances the consumers' and society's well being*.

(Kotler, 1997, italics added)

Notably, most large companies have recognized the need for this. For example, Proctor and Gamble has redesigned products, packages and services so that less material or less packaging is needed to achieve the same (if not better) profitability. Pitney Bowes, which at one time spent over $16 million on such processes as hazardous waste disposal, began a programme to eliminate environmental problems even before products were placed on the market (Dechant and Altman, 1994). Dechant and Altman's paper was titled 'Environmental leadership: from compliance to competitive advantage'. Environmental factors, then, are big business. But initial compliance has now become a key to future growth and profitability. In other words, marketing is not just about creating exchanges but also being seen to contribute to the quality of the environment. How businesses operate by means of products, processes, packaging, distribution all impacts on the environment, and thus exercises a manageable communication function. However, this chapter concerns marketing communications in relation to environmental factors. One metaphor or construct for exploring environmental factors is that of 'green advertising'. Much of green advertising appears unfortunately to be founded on deceit and ignorance. Not a good starting point for any business attempting to redress the ecological balance by adopting a more responsible approach to environmental issues.

However, there is cause for hope. Business is increasingly recognizing the strategic importance of environmental responsibility, and some organizations are responding in a thoughtful and effective way, for example through new product development (Dermody and Hanmer-Lloyd, 1994). The problem could therefore be one of communication, and perhaps advertising as a marked element of marcoms in particular. But, this is potentially a minefield. For example, can advertising contribute to the quality of life if it encourages consumption? Consumption, or the processes involved in manufacture and consumption, has [ostensibly] led to many of the environmental problems in the first place through industrial emissions into air, water and land.

This chapter begins by considering the philosophical nature of greener marketing communications. The discussion will then illustrate the ways in which this philosophy has been flouted by the advertising industry in particular. The meanings and terminology of 'green' advertising claims will be examined, culminating in the recognition of the need to acknowledge different shades of green appeals. The chapter will conclude by examining the challenges facing the marcoms industry in the development and implementation of greener persuasion.

GREENER MARCOMS: ENVIRONMENTAL NECESSITY

McDonagh *et al.* (1994) maintain that green communications is:

> the process of information exchange activities between an organisation and its various publics, where the organisation wishes to be perceived as a good corporate citizen acting in a socially responsible manner, initiated and maintained through long term dialogue with those publics.
>
> (McDonagh *et al.*, 1994: 1)

This definition is consistent with Harrison's (1992) views on sustainable communication, considered by some to be a deeper shade of green because it is rooted in the concept of sustainable development – meeting the needs of the present generation without compromising the needs of future generations (Brundtland, 1987). Harrison (1992) defines sustainable communication as:

> a results driven process to be used by the organisation wishing to benefit from the creation of long term relationships with the firm's stakeholders . . . It is continuous, open, interactive; it is consistent, with measurable results, and ever improving.
>
> (Harrison, 1992: 244)

Notably, it the concept of sustainability which is challenging the way(s) business is conducted and just what is [and isn't] communicated to stakeholders (Davis, 1991).

Green marketing activities are necessitous because of the need for companies to display environmental stewardship (Dermody, 1994; Coddington, 1993; Charter, 1992), rather than an ostensible and self-centred pursuit of profit and related goals. This stewardship, in turn, needs to be reflected in organizational marcoms.

Marketing communications in a greener environmental context can therefore be characterized by responsibility, interaction and dialogue. In this respect it is supported by the philosophy of integrated marketing communications which advocates ongoing conversation, results and accountability (Schultz, *et al.*, 1996). Green marcoms, whether or not subdivided into advertising, should therefore possess these attributes to be truly green. Banerjee *et al.* (1995) translate these qualities into more tangible attributes by suggesting that for advertising to be green, it must satisfy at least one of the following environmental criteria:

1 Explicitly or implicitly addresses the relationship between product(s)/service(s) and the surrounding biophysical environment.
2 Promotes a green lifestyle, not necessarily highlighting green products/services.
3 Presents or sustains a corporate image of environmental responsibility.

Thus, greener advertising is more than simply advertising green products and services, there also needs to be an underlying and recognizable organizational commitment to the environment (Dermody, 1994). Expressions of green claims can take many forms, not just in terms of the medium, but also the nature of the language used. This can be illustrated through 'green' advertising claims.

A HISTORY OF GREENER ADVERTISING CLAIMS

Notably, the UK's Advertising Standards Authority (ASA) has warned industry that absolute green claims must not be made in product advertising. In order to clarify this position, the ASA has developed five 'rules' which must be adhered to in the creation of greener advertising

1 **Basis**: claims must be clearly explained and must not omit any significant qualifying information.
2 **Vague claims**: terminology like 'environmentally friendly' must not be used without qualification unless advertisers are able to provide 'convincing evidence' that their product causes no harm to the environment. 'Greener' or 'friendlier' may be permitted provided they can prove their product gives improved environmental performance against a previous or competitor's product.
3 **Scientific uncertainty**: a significant split in scientific opinion or inconclusive evidence about particular product attributes must be reflected in the advertising.
4 **Misleading improvements**: claims that a product has been reformulated to make it safer for the environment must not be used where the product has never had any demonstrable 'adverse' environmental impact.
5 **Extravagant language**: extravagant language and bogus and confusing scientific terms must not be used. If scientific terminology is used, its meaning must be made clear.

(ENDS Report 240 (1995), p. 30)

It appears that these warnings were virtually ignored in the late 1980s and early 1990s as the following examples illustrate.

- BP initiated what could be regarded as the 'darker side of green advertising' during 1990 when it boldly claimed that 'cars running on its unleaded petrol caused no pollution to the environment' (ENDS Report 191 (1990), 16). The ASA cautioned BP for inaccuracy; cars running on unleaded fuel still pollute the atmosphere.
- Peaudouce objected to claims by their competitor Swaddlers in 1989 that 'Togs' nappies were now 'environmentally friendly' and manufactured in a way which 'does not damage the natural world'. The Committee on Advertising Practice (CAP) maintained the claims were an oversimplification and should be amended. In a 'tit-for-tat' manner Swaddlers objected to Peaudouce's nappy advert which challenged other nappies to come clean, implying that chlorine-bleached brands were less environmentally friendly. CAP supported the complaint, arguing that chlorine was not the only factor to be taken into consideration in assessing environmental friendliness. Peaudouce were asked to ensure the claims were not repeated. (ENDS Report 191 (1990))
- In 1993, The Advertising Standards Authority upheld a complaint from Greenpeace against ICI for their advertising claims that a chemical (HFC-134a), used to replace CFCs in refrigerants, was 'ozone friendly'. The advert was placed in a House of Commons weekly magazine just before Ministers were due to participate in international negotiations on the ozone layer in Copenhagen in November 1992. While HFC-134a does not deplete the ozone layer, it is thousands of times more potent than carbon dioxide as a greenhouse gas. (ENDS Report 221 (1993))
- The ASA upheld complaints against Vauxhall Motors in 1993 for a press advertisement which claimed that its Corsa model is 'the greenest car in its class'. The ASA ruled that the evidence provided by Vauxhall on the car's emissions 'did not warrant such a broad and universal claim'. (ENDS Report 224 (1993))
- Saab were called to account by the ASA for their press advertising stating that one of Saab's models 'refreshes the air other cars leave behind' and 'can actually clean city air'. In upholding the complaint from Greenpeace, the ASA maintained that air cannot be considered cleaner if some pollutants are decreased while some are increased as was the case with Saab. Saab subsequently placed the advert in Australia to the condemnation of Greenpeace. (ENDS Report 224 (1993))
- Peugeot Talbot Motors were criticized by Friends of the Earth (FoE) for their press advertising claiming that 'diesel cars traditionally save fuel, save cash and do their bit to help save the planet'. The ASA upheld FoE's complaint that it is misleading to suggest diesel cars provide a benefit to the planet. They advised Peugeot Talbot to avoid any expression of benefit in their future advertising and to ensure that future claims are fully qualified. At the same time, Esso were reprimanded for claiming that diesel fuel is 'environmentally friendly'. (ENDS Report 225 (1993))

The late 1980s and early 1990s saw a dramatic increase in the volume of green advertising messages, 430 per cent growth for green print adverts and 367 per cent for green TV adverts between 1989 and 1990 (Ottman, 1993). All use a variety of different terms to communicate the green attributes of a company, product or service. The plethora of 'green' terms intentionally used in this chapter serves to illustrate the range which can be used – environmental protection, environmental responsibility, environmentally friendly, green, and ecological. Additional claims include 'dolphin-friendly', CFC free, recyclable, recycled, biodegradable, etc. All have been used in the advertising of 'green' products and services. But what do these terms really mean? Are they interchangeable? Do they encourage misleading and meaningless advertising claims? Carlson *et al.* (1993) analysed the believability of green advertising claims and found that only 40 per cent of their sample were unambiguously true; 42 per cent were vague and ambiguous and 18 per cent were either total lies or errors of omission. The Advertising Standards Authority were so concerned with the liberal use of green claims in UK car and fuel advertising (as illustrated above) that they organized a seminar in December 1993 to address the do's and don'ts of motoring advertising (ENDS Report 225 (1993)). Significantly, it is ambiguity, lying and omissions which are giving so-called green advertising a bad name. It is no wonder that Friends of the Earth (FoE) launched their 'Green Con' awards. While environmental regulations attempt to protect consumers from being misled, it would seem that they are confused by the green claims made by industry and as a result are becoming increasingly cynical about green advertising (Mayer *et al.* 1993; Cude, 1991; Abt Associates, 1990), while simultaneously more interested and critical concerning the way(s) businesses interact in the wider environmental setting.

This does not bode well for the future of greener marketing communications. It will remain in the wilderness unless universal definitions are accepted by industry and are acceptable to all stakeholders. It will also undermine the effectiveness of legitimate green claims (McDonagh, 1994; Mayer *et al.* 1993). This concern prompted the Environmental Protection Agency in 1991 to warn:

> If national consensus over the use of these terms is not reached in the near future, we face the danger of losing a valuable tool for educating the public and influencing the production and use of more environmentally orientated products. Consumers may come to distrust or ignore *all* environmental claims.
>
> (The Environmental Protection Agency, 1991: 10, italics added)

The legitimization of green advertising claims is further undermined by consumers' rejection of green advertising in favour of information on packaging as a credible source of environmental information (Abt Associates, 1990). While the eco-labelling scheme has been criticized (Dermody, 1994), it is at least attempting to ensure a level playing field for industry and protect consumers against misleading information. The politics of its implementation is another matter entirely!

The ASA has attempted to address some of these issues through its five rules governing environmental claims, and it could be that they are starting to encourage more legitimate green advertising because the number of complaints about environmental claims received by the ASA up to January 1995 has halved since 1991 (ENDS 240, 1995). While these rules do not go far enough for some, they are a step in the right direction. So what do these claims really mean and are they

219

interchangeable? In order to analyse this question further, let us examine different shades of green in advertising appeals.

SHADES OF GREEN ADVERTISING

Banerjee, *et al.* (1995) classified green advertising into shallow, moderate and deep:

Shallow appeals: vague environmental claims in the advertising, e.g. environmentally friendly

Moderate appeals: claims mentioning specific issues, e.g. recycling, but with limited information on environmental issues relating to the product or service

Deep appeals: adverts focusing specifically on environmental issues and considering them in depth, (e.g. a detailed account of pollution prevention equipment; and/ or environmental behaviours not widely practised)

The illustrations given throughout this chapter certainly come nowhere near 'deep green' advertising. At best they are moderate, with the majority being shallow. It would therefore appear that the different meanings of terminology need to be graded accordingly. Conceptually this grading has been ignored by most marketing professionals and academics (Kilbourne, 1995). The result has been a fragmented and ignorant approach to greener communication culminating in misinformed, misleading and meaningless 'greenish' advertising claims, as illustrated throughout this chapter. What is needed therefore is a framework into which different shades of green marketing communications can be placed. While the work of Banerjee *et al.* (1995) touches on some important issues, it does not address the fundamental questions underpinning different shades of green. For this we must explore the thinking of Kilbourne (1995), who maintained there are indeed different intensities of green which are rooted in different philosophies.

Kilbourne (1995) stresses that in order to understand the nature of green, distinctions need to be made between environmentalism and ecologism, or what Dobson (1990) refers to as 'green' and 'Green'. The complexity of these claims is presented in Figure 13.1.

Figure 13.1 illustrates that these environmental and ecological dimensions are dependent on different political and positional philosophies. The political philosophy embraces the acceptable degree of change and actions necessary to achieve this change. Essentially it is one of considering whether or not political reform is enough. If it is, all necessary change can be achieved through legislation. This 'reformist' position promotes the status quo by accepting the dominant social paradigm. If it is not, radicalism is called for to challenge political reforms which it regards as inadequate to preserve the planet in the long term. Reformism and radicalism are therefore at opposite ends of the political spectrum (Dolbeare and Dolbeare, 1976). Lying midway between these two extremes is 'reform liberalism' offering a modest challenge to the dominant social paradigm through political reform. However, according to Dolbeare and Dolbeare (1976), deeply significant change requires a shift in the dominant ideology; reform liberalism can never achieve this because it attempts to redress the balance through the very measures that have been denounced.

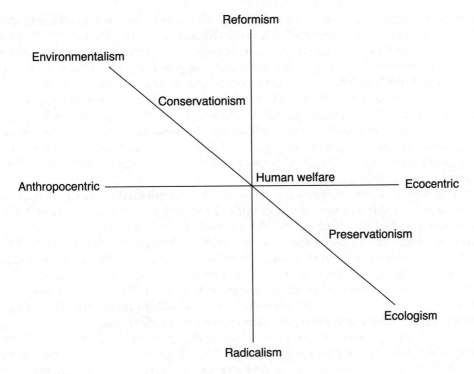

Figure 13.1 Levels of ecological concern.
(Source: Kilbourne, 1995: 9)

The positional philosophy refers to the position in which humans regard themselves in the eco-system in relation to its other inhabitants. Within this perspective the dominant paradigm is one of anthropocentrism (Dobson, 1990; Porrit, 1984; Capra, 1982), which is closely aligned with technocentrism (O'Riordan, 1976) and human centredness (Fox, 1990). All see nature as a servant for human purpose. Ecocentrism is the complete opposite, recognizing that ecology should be valued in its own right rather than as an instrument to be used by mankind. It is acknowledged, however, that ecocentrism will have some elements of anthropocentrism because by definition any product of human rationality is anthropocentric to some extent (Dobson, 1990; O'Riordan, 1976).

Shades of green can therefore be classified as anthropocentric green (environmental) or ecocentric green (ecological) (Kilbourne, 1995), with multiple shades between – conservationism, human welfare, and preservation. It is these which this chapter will now consider.

After environmentalism, resource conservationism is the most reformist and anthropocentric shade of green. It is based on the efficient management of natural resources to ensure their use for future generations – a key philosophy of the Brundtland Report (1987). This perspective is well immersed within the dominant social paradigm where ecological protection merely becomes the management of resources. Ecological diversity and stability, aesthetic and spiritual needs, and the value of non-human life are simply ignored (Kilbourne, 1995; Hayes, 1959). This can be illustrated by consumers who are willing to purchase a detergent which conserves resources through its packaging and composition, providing it washes as effectively as brands which are not based on a 'green' philosophy. In other words, consumers are unwilling to change their attitudes and behaviour unless it is in their best interests to do so (Dermody, 1994). Advertising reflecting this might claim 'performance in a recyclable bottle'! Within this framework, claims like this would be regarded as rather insipid 'green' appeals. While the conservation of resources is clearly important, the inclusion of human welfare moves communication further towards a 'Green' philosophy.

Human welfare ecology argues for the aesthetic and spiritual elements of human life which nature will not be able to provide if the fragile eco-system is destroyed. Within this context, the focus is on the intrinsic rather than economic value of resources, which are implemented in the spirit of reform liberalism. Here the advertising for a detergent might claim 'caring for the planet for future generations to enjoy and caring for your wash'. While this position is still anthropocentric, Kilbourne (1995) argues that ecology can still benefit from human welfare. However, if there is a conflict of interests, mankind will inevitably win (Fox 1990; Rodman, 1983). Preservationism can help reconcile this dilemma.

Central to the preservationist perspective is the preservation of nature from development. Human welfare forms a part of this. If preservation is motivated by spiritual and aesthetic needs then preservation is deemed weak. However, if preservation is motivated by the intrinsic value of nature regardless of its worth to mankind, preservationism is deemed strong. The advertising of Greenpeace falls into this category. With respect to our detergent, it appears to be less appropriate to make individual product claims here. Instead, detergent manufacturers need to communicate their 'true' green credentials. Advertising at this level might claim, 'I have always known we need to care for the earth rather than trying to destroy it. It has meant I have had to make some very tough career decisions. Not anymore though. On Monday I'm joining a company that has a proven track record in helping all of us to preserve the earth's animal and plant species and their natural habitats. I cannot wait for Monday.' A word of caution, however, in labelling claims like this as preservationist: what motives underly them? Human welfare? In which case it is a weak preservationist claim. Or the intrinsic value of nature? If this is so, then the preservationist claim is strengthened. However, how many companies are truly committed to the principles of preservation and ecologism? Like the majority of advertising they are likely to be positioned within the anthropocentric, reformist dimensions of environmentalism.

While preservationism is further down the green spectrum than either human welfare or conservationism, it is still rooted in the anthropocentric perspective because humans still determine which aspects of our environment are worth preserving. It is ecologism at the end of this spectrum which provides an all-embracing view of nature and in this sense is truly 'Green'. So where does this leave the advertising of our green detergent? Kilbourne (1995) sums the position up nicely:

Since this position requires a virtual overthrow of the dominant social paradigm, few, if any, advertisements will be found supporting the position. Major advertisers would view this as virtual economic suicide, and its advocates would see it as so extreme as to be ineffective in promoting their position . . . The theses of these ads are that we cannot consume ourselves out of our over-consumption problem, we cannot techno-fix our way out of problems caused by technology, and nothing ecologically viable can be sustained without global redistribution of wealth.

(Kilbourne, 1995: 16)

Any ecological advertising for a detergent would therefore have to claim that the brand was being withdrawn in the best interests of the planet until it and its consumers truly have no adverse effect on the fragile eco-systems of the earth. Is this the basis for greener marketing communications in the next century?

So, what are the implications for advertising? Can advertising be green? Well, yes and no depending on perspective. It should be clear by now that there are different kinds of green advertising appeals derived from the principles of environmentalism, conservation, human welfare, preservation and ecology. All reflect differing philosophical positions of the sender and the receiver. Environmental messages would be regarded by committed Greens as shallow. Ecological messages would be regarded as too radical by the majority of organizations to take seriously. The result? No environmental improvements. It would therefore appear that the greening of communications, like other elements of the green marketing mix, is an incremental one. This is not to imply there is no urgency; the planet is in crisis now and measures need to be implemented now. However, it is better to work with industry to achieve environmental goals, rather than working against it (Dermody, 1994). True, this is 'reform liberalism' but from a slightly different perspective than that advocated by Dolbeare and Dolbeare (1976). Rather than being perceived as a modest challenge to the dominant social paradigm, view it instead as the first stage in challenging industry to become much more environmentally responsible in all facets of its strategies, policies and operations, including the communication of environmental messages. It is a springboard from which great things are possible and we all have a responsibility to ensure that they are achieved.

This leads to a second issue in considering whether advertising can be green, namely consumption. Kilbourne (1995) argues that over-consumption is a major barrier in moving from environmentalism to ecologism. It is the most difficult challenge marketing will face since the encouragement of consumption is at its core, whether it is products, services or ideas, needs or wants. The majority of advertising encourages consumption, therefore it can never be more than green. The ecological perspective challenges us all, particularly as consumers. It requires us to re-evaluate what we consume, why we consume it and is it worth the cost to the planet? From a psychological perspective this is moving beyond our attitudes and behaviour to more fundamental values. Greenpeace target our values relating to the rights of the planet of which mankind is a part. FMCG advertising targets our values which consider consumption and wealth to be our rights. Clearly then, a reassessment of human value systems is a central element in the paradigm shift which will lead to greener marketing communications.

SUMMARY AND CONCLUSIONS

It is clear that defining green advertising in an increasingly discernible environment is not only complex, but fraught with numerous pitfalls for unwary (or even dishonest) communicators. It is multidimensional in the sense that advertising can evidently possess different shades of green which reflect different philosophical positions ranging from pale green environmentalism to dark green ecologism. It is further characterized by the principles of greener marketing communications which advocate responsibility, interaction and dialogue. For companies displaying an ostensible societal marketing orientation it is more than simply advertising green products and services; they must also reflect environmental stewardship which embraces a commitment from industry to protect the planet or at least contribute to the quality of life in all facets of their strategies and operations. Marketing communications complexity, especially in relation to greener advertising, has largely been ignored or misinterpreted by organizations. In the main, it has been poorly interpreted and as a result outputs have tended to be misleading, meaningless or ambiguous. As a consequence, consumer confidence in green product claims or company claims is low while perception of current practices has been heightened. It would appear therefore that industries' understanding of green advertising in the context of environmentalism may go no further than shallow environmental claims. It is likely that this surface understanding is also reflected in other areas of the marketing communications mix.

Education for practitioners could potentially appear to be central to any future and further greening of advertising. While businesses need to be made aware of the philosophical complexities underlying use of green advertising and their impacts on consumer behaviour, it may be that awareness will come through imposed legislation rather than self-regulation. Consumers, perhaps for the first time in human history, are becoming only too aware of the pollution caused by manufacture and marketing of products detrimental to individual and collective health. They need to start to act in evaluating consumption behaviour in the light of the need for environmental protection and cognitive consistency.

One way, hopefully offered in a spirit of environmentalism, may be to review values which place importance on consumption as the be-all and end-all of existence. Over-consumption or consumption of products detrimental to individual and collective quality of life may be a root cause of the ecological crisis facing the earth. But a far greater root cause is firms acting in environmentally hazardous ways, while simultaneously proclaiming or seeking to proclaim corporate environmental virtues. In other words, consumers, it is felt, appreciate product benefits communicated well. But the communication has to be backed by solid environmental sustainability both as a corporate philosophy and as a set of actionable communicable criteria. In other words, the shade of green reflected is not as important as the actual green actions carried out and communicated by firms. The semantic argument is not as important nor as significant as the actual actions put out by firms. But, it can be argued, well, so what?

Well, the *Worldwatch Magazine* (Source: *The Scotsman*, 7 October 1997: 14) indicates the following:

- Amount of topsoil created by nature each year – 0.4 billion tons. Amount lost to erosion – 25 billion tons.
- Number of species lost to extinction each year during the past 65 million years – one to ten. Number lost in the past year – between 1000 and 10 000.
- Time it takes the human population to use 22 million tons of oil – one day. Time it took the planet to create that energy – 10 000 days.

What these statistics indicate is that most major companies will not in future just be judged on the basis of return on capital invested, share growth ratios, or even sales and profitability. They will also be judged on the basis of what was returned or put into the environment from which business development has been wrested.

While advertising can never be more than pale green if it encourages excess consumption, companies can never be more than pale green if they continue to pollute the earth's environment while maintaining a green profile. Messages may continue to encourage consumers in more responsible ways but they will fail to register in consumer consciousness if businesses do not become more environmentally responsible. This focus on root causes can do much to encourage green advertising to evolve. It can facilitate incremental shifts in thinking, moving from environmentalism to preservationism, the furthest point green advertising is likely to develop unless there is a very fundamental and necessary paradigm shift involving businesses, consumers and government in the United Kingdom and around the world.

DISCUSSION TOPICS

1 What impact do environmental factors have upon marketing communications?
2 Is green communication or advertising necessary? Discuss your response from the context of the societal marketing orientation.
3 Should consumers be positive or negative toward marketing communications' green product claims? Why or why not?
4 Using examples from the daily press or the ASA Monthly Reports, can industries or specific companies be held responsible for making unproven or quasi-proven environmental claims for their products? Explain.
5 Should consumers be encouraged to reconsider their consumption behaviour to facilitate environmental protection? Who do you suggest should be the source of the encouragement?
6 What persuasion strategies, if any, would you suggest to minimize the screening-out of green messages by an audience who do not wish non-green behaviours?
7 Compare the incremental and radical approaches to greening advertising. Which do you consider more appropriate? Why?
8 What issues emerging from the greening of advertising can be applied to other elements of the marketing communications mix? What are the implications for integrated marketing communications?
9 Examine the strategic importance of greener marketing communications. Should further research be undertaken to facilitate the evolution of greener marcoms?

10 Argue for or against the case that the only way forward to environmental sustainability will come about as three groups interact, namely businesses, consumers and government.

CASE STUDY – JMD INTERNATIONAL: A PIONEERING ENVIRONMENTALLY CONSCIOUS COMPANY?

Background

JMD International have been committed to the global need to protect and care for the environment since it was founded in the late 1800s. Their business philosophy is guided by an ecological consciousness embracing the principles of responsibility, social commitment and respect. In the mid-1930s the company's President travelled to Brazil to ensure that the harvesting of palm leaves was not damaging the ecology of the rainforests. In the mid-1970s the company voluntarily phased out CFCs from its aerosol products, 13 years ahead of other companies and 14 years before the Montreal Protocol leading to the global agreement in 1989 to phase out CFCs by the end of the century. In 1990 the company created an Office of Environmental Action World-wide. In the mid-1990s the company reduced volatile organic compounds by 25 per cent; packaging by 25 per cent; waste output from manufacturing by 50 per cent; and increased their use of recycled material in packaging to 50 per cent of total pack content. This commitment was recognized by former President Bush in 1991.

Environmental mission statement

We are committed to respecting and protecting the environment in all our business operations. We want to work with the environment not against it. We will lead the challenge in protecting the planet for future generations to enjoy.

The decision to phase out CFCs

We removed CFCs from our aerosols in the mid-1970s and replaced them with butane. We lost an entire deodorant brand because of this decision. It was the second largest deodorant brand in the UK and a major financial loss because the deodorant market is huge. While it could have been reformulated, the decision was taken that we could not sell it. Aerosols with CFC propellant are a lot heavier than butane. So consumer's being used to the weight of CFCs would have picked up a can with butane in it and thought it was empty, put it back on the shelf and chosen a more weighty competitor's product. Decisions like these obviously cause marketing horrendous problems but that's the sort of commitment we are prepared to make. We have only recently started putting 'no CFCs' labels on our aerosols. Consumers thought they still contained CFCs because we did not label them, which is rather ironic given that our competitors had only taken CFCs out the year before. We were very reluctant to label our products in this way. To us, reformulating or withdrawing products in order to protect the environment is natural. We do not feel the need to congratulate ourselves as our competitors seem to do. We did not want to be associated with their token gestures. At the same time we had totally failed to communicate our commitment to our consumers; they had no idea what our environmental mission is or how we are translating this in our business activities. Our phone lines were red hot with the public asking why we did not do more for the environment. We had a lot of corporate literature which we were failing to distribute. Our silence was hurting us financially but perhaps more importantly it was hurting us in our attempts to become a world leader in protecting the planet for future generations to enjoy. As a result we have added 'no CFC' labels to our aerosols, we have improved our public relations, we distribute corporate environmental information, we have our telephone help-lines where staff are appropriately briefed, we set environmental goals for all our staff, we have a staff environmental ideas system and top management regularly discuss environmental initiatives with staff at all levels of the organization. As for environmental advertising, isn't that a bit tacky? It has been tainted by token gestures, we would rather remain above all that.

(Dermody, 1994)

This case study is based on a real company whose name has been changed for reasons of confidentiality.

REFERENCES

Abt Associates (1990) *Environmental Consumerism in the US.*

Banerjee, S., Gulas, G.S. and Iyer, E. (1995) 'Shades of green: a multidimensional analysis of environmental advertising', *Journal of Advertising*, XXIV(2), Summer.

Brundtland, G. (1987) Our Common Future, *The Brundtland Report*, World Commission on the Environment and Development.

Capra, F. (1982) *The Turning Point*, London: Fontana Famingo series.

Carlson, L., Grove, S.J. and Kangun, N. (1993) 'A content analysis of environmental advertising claims: a matrix method approach', *Journal of Advertising*, 22, September: 27–39.

Charter, M. (ed.) (1992) *Greener Marketing: A Responsible Approach to Business*, Sheffield, UK: Greenleaf Publishing.

Coddington, W. (1993) *Environmental Marketing: Positive Strategies for Reaching the Green Consumer*, New York: McGraw-Hill.

Cude, B.J. (1991) Comments prepared for the U.S. Environmental Protection Agency hearings on the use of the terms recycled and recyclable and the recyclable emblem in environmental marketing claims, Washington DC (13 November).

Davies, J. (1991) *Greening Business Managing for Sustainable Development*, Oxford: Basil Blackwell.

Dechant, K. and Altman, B. (1994) 'Environmental leadership: from compliance to competitive advantage', *Academy of Management Executive*, 8(3): 7–19.

Dermody, J. (1994) 'Guidelines for developing environmentally responsible new products', PhD Thesis, Bristol Business School, University of the West of England.

Dermody, J. and Hanmer-Lloyd, S. (1994) 'Successfully developing environmentally responsible products: the response of UK manufacturers of detergents and household cleaning products', *Proceedings of the Groningen-UMIST workshop*: Meeting the Challenges of Product Development, Manchester.

Dermody, J. and Hanmer-Lloyd, S. (1995a) 'Greening new product development: the pathway to corporate environmental excellence?', *Greener Management International*, Issue 11.

Dermody, J. and Hanmer-Lloyd, S. (1995b) 'Developing environmentally responsible new products: the challenge for the 1990s', in M. Bruce and W. Biemans (eds), *Product Development: Meeting the Challenges of the Design-Marketing Interface*, Chichester: John Wiley.

Dobson, A. (1990) *Green Political Thought*, London: Harper Collins Academic.

Dolbeare, K.M. and Dolbeare, P. (1976) *American Ideologies*, Boston: Houghton Mifflin.

ENDS Report 191 (1990) *Advertising and the Environment: Uneasy Bedfellows*, December, 16–23.

ENDS Report 191 (1990) *Eastern Electricity Wins Green Con Award*, December, 24.

ENDS Report 221 (1993) *ICI Rapped Over Claims for New Refrigerant*, June, 27–28.

ENDS Report 224 (1993) *Firms Fail to Heed ASA Advice on Absolute Green Claims*, September, 30.

ENDS Report 225 (1993) *ASA Acts on Misleading Green Claims for Cars*, October, 27–28.

ENDS Report 240 (1995) *Screws Tighten on Green Claims*, January, 30.

Environmental Protection Agency (1991) Guidance for the use of the terms recycled and recyclable and the recyclable emblem in environmental marketing claims, Notice of Public Meeting, *Federal Register*, 56(191), 2 October, 49992–50000.

Fox, W. (1990) *Toward a Transpersonal Ecology: Developing New Foundations for Environmentalism*, Boston: Shambhala.

Harrison, B.E. (1992) 'Achieving sustainable communications', in P.B. Erdmann (ed.) 'Corporate environmentalism', in *Columbia Journal of World Business*, 27(3 and 4) (Fall–Winter).

Hayes, S.P. (1959) *Conservation and the Gospel of Efficiency*, Cambridge, MA: Harvard University Press.

Kilbourne, W.E. (1995) 'Green advertising: salvation or oxymoron?', *Journal of Advertising*, XXIV(2), Summer.

Kotler, P. (1997) *Marketing Management*, 9th edn, New Jersey: Prentice Hall International, 27–28.

Mayer, R.N., Scammon, D.L. and Zick, C.D. (1993) 'Poisoning the well: do environmental claims strain consumer credulity?', *Advances in Consumer Research*, 20: 698–703.

McDonagh, P. (1994) 'Towards an understanding of what constitutes green advertising as a form of sustainable communication', paper presented at the Doctoral Colloquium of The Marketing Education Group Annual Conference, University of Ulster.

McDonagh, P., Peattie, K. and Prothero, A. (1994) 'Everyone's listening but no-one is talking', *Marketing Education Group Annual Conference*, University of Ulster, July.

O'Riordan, T. (1976) *Environmentalism*, London: Pion Limited.

Ottman, J. (1993) *Green Marketing: Challenges and Opportunities for the New Marketing Age*, Lincolnwood, IL: NTC Business Books.

Porrit, J. (1984) *Seeing Green: The Politics of Ecology Explained*, Oxford: Basil Blackwell.

Prothero, A., McDonagh, P. and Peattie, K. (1994) 'Green marketing communications: dressing windows or opening doors?', *Proceedings of the 25th Marketing Education Group Annual Conference*, University of Ulster, Vol. II, 766–76.

Rodman, J. (1983) 'Four forms of ecological consciousness reconsidered', in D. Scherer and T. Attig (eds), *Ethics and the Environment*, London: Prentice Hall.

Schultz, D.E., Tannenbaum, S.I. and Lauterborn, R.F. (1996) *The New Marketing Paradigm Integrated Marketing Communications*, Chicago, IL: NTC Business Books.

Scotsman, The (1997) 'What a Waste', in Environmental Section, 7 October, 14.

14

MARKETING COMMUNICATIONS RENAISSANCE: A TIME FOR REFLECTION?

Philip J. Kitchen

CHAPTER AIMS

- to analyse significant developments impacting on marcoms from a domestic and global perspective
- to indicate the extent to which these developments could impact on marcom strategies
- to argue the case that these issues constitute a time of 'renaissance' and 'reflection'

ILLUSTRATION: HOW MCDONALD'S TAILORS ITS BRAND IDENTITY TO LOCAL MARKETS (RICHARD COOK)

McDonald's has long enjoyed an ambiguous relationship with consumers outside its US heartland. While it has proved successful at opening up and developing new markets around the world, it has rarely assimilated the local culture well enough to let customers forget it was a US invention.

This remains one of the key challenges facing McDonald's and its two main advertising networks, Leo Burnett and DDB Worldwide. The director on the account at Burnett's London agency, David Kisilesvsky, says: 'The message we get back from focus groups in the UK – and it's the same in many other markets – is that brands like Kellogg's and Heinz which are every bit as American as McDonald's, have become a strong and enduring part of British society. It's got to the point now where most people aren't aware of their American origins. McDonald's hasn't got there – at least not yet.'

However, the diversity of McDonald's worldwide markets means there are as many different marketing challenges facing the fast-food chain as there are languages in which to say 'hamburger'. And, because of McDonald's policy of keeping the hiring, firing and briefing of ad agencies on a local level, each of these problems gets dealt with in a very different way.

Burnett's handles the brand in 18 countries, while DDB – which picked up the $400 million US domestic account in August 1997 – runs McDonald's in 45, according to DDB's international account manager Mark Hans Richer. The result is a widely uneven body of work across the world.

In China, for example, Burnett's uses children who explain to the older generation what McDonald's is all about, just as they are having to explain many of the economic changes sweeping the country. In China's newly regained territory, Hong Kong, children also front the ads, but in a more sophisticted way that uses humour tailored to its more westernized customers.

In stark contrast to newer markets, DDB's job in Australia – which has one of the highest concentrations of outlets per head of population in the world – is to keep the established brand fresh in the mind of its consumers. To this end, DDB decided to reinforce the US credentials of McDonald's by producing a series of award-winning commercials starring dead American stars, such as James Dean or Marilyn Monroe. More recently, it has developed its own theme tune, *MacTime*.

Germany, the second-largest market outside the US, poses a different challenge for DDB. Here, the growth of green issues means menus have a heavy vegetarian content, while the country's prosperous inhabitants demand greater variety than other parts of the world. Thus, a sizeable chunk of advertising effort goes on special promotions, such as vegetarian McNuggets or Oriental Burgers. Again DDB unites with McDonald's theme tune, *McDonald's ist einfach gut* (McDonald's is simply good).

(*Source: Campaign*, 29 August 1997, p. 29, used with permission.)

INTRODUCTION

The marketing methods, strategies and tactics deployed by global, multinational and domestic firms are undergoing rapid and consistent change amounting almost to a renaissance in which old rules, tactics, methods and messages are fragmenting, breaking down and coalescing into new medias, new forms, and with more integrated strategies, tactics and closer alliances with increasingly globalized and integrated agencies. The break-up of old-style mass markets, new technological developments, international and national economic fluctuations, and the proclaimed emergence of global markets which indicates global competition, are impacting strongly on the ways firms develop and apply marketing and, within the domain of marketing – marketing communications. Seven overarching developments are explored with respect to marketing communications. These developments are discussed in line with organizational changes typified by writers such as Toffler and Toffler (1990), McKenna (1991) and Hammer and Champy (1995). The discussion then focuses on development of an integrating structure (see Figure 14.1) that attempts to draw together the growing body of knowledge concerning database marketing, integrated communications strategies and multinational marketing. Almost irrespective of the country of habitation, these developments are illustrated in the opening case vignette. Evidently, McDonald's and its agencies market on a country-by-country basis, including the UK. National headquarters and agencies enjoy a significant degree of autonomy in designing and implementing marcoms strategies. But, is the approach adopted by McDonald's the case for other firms? Are there any other approaches which could be more appropriate? What circumstances proscribe or empower these approaches? The chapter considers developments with references to McDonald's and a further case relating to a US-based service company. The conclusion then links these strands together in considering their impact on national or international marcoms. For marcoms students, this seems to be a 'time of renaissance' in which older ideas, values and ossified structures are being supplanted and replaced by new forms of communication, in a more integrated and structured fashion, with the consumer becoming 'king'.

Developments identified include:

1 Growth in advertising and promotion
2 Emergence of the global consumer
3 Development and importance of integrated communications
4 Direct marketing – a new promotional tool?
5 Database marketing – towards coordinated strategy
6 Internet advertising – a form of promotion?
7 Coordination and control – process vs. output

The chapter discusses these various issues. Admittedly, while some may be conjectural, it is evident that these are vital developments underpinning *the* major marketing mix variable – promotion!

As has been argued elsewhere in this and other texts, the essence of marketing is the use of the strategic/tactical variables of the marketing mix in relation to target markets (Waterschoot and Van Bulte, 1992; Webster, 1992). In discussing the marketing mix it is acknowledged with Shimp (1997) that all four variables impact on consumer choice behaviour and thus all have a communication function. However, we also live in an age where products are increasingly homogeneous, where pricing strategies are fairly uniform, and (notably in the UK) where distribution channels have all the differentiation of a row of detergent packets on a supermarket shelf. In this somewhat lacklustre consumer environment, riddled with organizational restructuring and competitive turbulence, promotion is still charged with the responsibility to move products forward. Marketing communications is the process whereby organizations seek to create commonness of thought and meaning between themselves and individuals and/or intermediaries in the distribution chain or with publics or audiences who could impact on organizational success or failure. This chapter will discuss several of these issues, notably from a domestic and international perspective. Thus, it is acknowledged that global initiatives impact significantly upon domestic marketing communications, not least strategically (as seen in the McDonald's case) but also tactically. The discussion extends beyond the advertising boundary encountered in the illustration to considering other pertinent issues.

GROWTH IN ADVERTISING AND PROMOTION

Few can doubt that advertising has become a powerful and pervasive societal force. From a parochial UK context, data from a number of sources show that the non-personal promotional tools of sales promotion, advertising, marketing public relations, and sponsorship enjoyed an estimated conservative expenditure in 1992 in excess of £10 billion. This estimate is based on advertising expenditure of £7.6 billion (at current prices), sales promotion in 1987 of some £1.5 billion, and public relations (which includes MPR and corporate activities (including sponsorships)) estimated at £0.5 billion with a projected growth rate of 35 per cent a year – i.e. a projected £1.7 billion by 1992 (Advertising Association Pocketbook, 1993; White *et al.*, 1988; Kitchen, 1994). Considering the world's largest market – the USA – indicates that in 1980 advertising expenditures were in the order of $53 billion, while sales promotion was around $49 billion. By 1993 total expenditures on advertising had risen to £139 billion on advertising versus $177 billion on sales promotion. The latter figure reflects worldwide growth in below-the-line activity (Cohen, 1994). In a global sense, advertising expenditure went from $55 billion in 1980 to $170 billion by 1993 (Belch and Belch, 1995; Cohen, 1993). And despite the difficulties with estimating expenditure, further billions were spent on sales promotion, personal selling, direct marketing, event sponsorships and public relations. Japan records a similar profile, saving that less is expended on sales promotion. For 1995 in Japan total advertising expenditure was Yen 3503 billion, compared to Yen 1907 billion for sales promotion (Dentsu Inc., 1996).

Advertising and sales promotion, together with other forms of marketing communications or promotion, form an integral backdrop to economic and social life. Driving forces underpinning growth (Belch and Belch, 1995) are as follows:

1 Ever-increasing costs of advertising (leading to increasing below-the-line activity)
2 Saturated mature markets (i.e. the only way to grow is by taking sales away from competitors)
3 Burgeoning price competition in many markets (divergence of budgets to sales promotion)
4 Fragmentation of media markets (move toward direct mail, sponsorships and MPR)
5 Balance of power shift from manufacturers to retailers plus emergence and increasing sophistication of scanning technology (equates to greater support for short-term tactics, i.e. sales promotion)
6 Growth in database marketing (resulting in more and better targeted direct marketing)
7 Changes in media buying practices (spells potentially the demise of the commission-based system, a dinosaur by any standards; increasingly buyers are stating terms and conditions, among them the need for less expensive alternatives to advertising)
8 Significant organizational restructuring or re-engineering, in the context of increasingly turbulent national, international and global markets

Each and all of these changes are reflective of market dynamics. Increasingly companies need to break through smudge and clutter and deliver pertinent messages in a timely manner to clearly targeted markets. But markets are no longer passive recipients of marketing messages. Today's consumers are sophisticated, streetwise, savvy; and resistant to direct approaches. Thus, while advertising continues to support warm non-rational brand loyalties, increasingly it is the totality of messages through various media that underpin communication or promotional effectiveness. Thus, the birth and rapid development of Integrated Marketing Communications (IMC) and its interrelations with corporate communications spell continued development in terms of emphasis and expenditure on promotional activities.

EMERGENCE OF THE GLOBAL CONSUMER

International marketing has provided for many years a focus for the adaptation of the promotional variable to suit the needs of indigenous national cultures. International marketing implies that marketing must, for example, be coordinated across nation states. But the very word 'international' can imply that a firm is not a global citizen (Keegan, 1995) but operates from a home country. Keegan goes on to argue, quite rightly in this context, that a more appropriate term is 'multinational' or even 'global' as there is nothing foreign or domestic about a world market and global opportunities. But what is meant by a world or global market? Before the Iron Curtain was torn aside the world market was America/Canada, Western Europe or the European Community, and Japan and other nations in the Pacific Rim area (Ohmae, 1985): this was the First World; the Second World was the nations grouped under Comecon; the Third World at that time was the underdeveloped nations. Much of world trade was concentrated in the then First World. Taking the scene forward to 1996, the USA/EC/Japan still constitute a powerful triad that dominates world trade. Notably, many academics in the 1980s followed the lead of Ted Levitt whose milestone article brazenly trumpeted a 'globalization of markets' (Levitt, 1983). According to Levitt, 'The world [was] being driven towards a single converging commonality . . . the emergence of global markets for globally standardized products'.

Levitt quoted Coca-Cola, McDonald's, Levi's and IBM as exemplars of the new global philosophy – 'global corporations who operate with resolute constancy and at low relative costs as if the world were a single largely identical entity'. As seen in the opening case vignette, it is questionable as to whether such an entity ever existed. An answer is a Janus-faced 'yes' and 'no'. 'Yes', there may well be homogeneous segments of demand within heterogeneous cultures to whom global appeals may appeal; and 'no' certain global appeals may be ineffective in persuading potential buyers. Chris Lorenz quoting Kotler (1984) has stated that Levitt was setting the marketing clock back (Lorenz, 1984a, 1984b). The marketing clock implies a movement from mass marketing, to market segmentation, to target marketing and positioning. Baker (1985) suggested cogently that mass marketing be equated with globalization – i.e. bending consumer demand to suit the manufacturer or provider of a good or service. Hout *et al.* (1982), writing well before Levitt, proposed a useful distinction between multi-domestic and global companies:

1 *Multi-domestic* autonomous, independent, some centralization, compete on a market-by-market basis usually involving separate strategies in markets offering different competitive challenges (the Colgate vignette would fall into this category)

2 *Global* Interdependent, centralized strategy, operations centralized or decentralized as needed; responsive to market needs while not compromising the integrity of the global system (the American Express vignette would fall into this category)

A careful reading between the lines of most major textbooks in the international/ global marketing arena (Keegan, 1995; Paliwoda, 1993; Porter, 1986; Czinkota and Ronkainen, 1996) reveals a close conformity with the second of Hout *et al's* alternatives. That is, a firm takes advantage of global opportunities where and when they occur, reaps the advantages of economies of scale in production and experience and learning curve effects, *standardizes when possible and adapts when necessary.* What was described as the First World earlier has now been, or may be soon, joined by China (1.2 billion consumers), Eastern Europe (300 million consumers) and NICs (newly industrialized countries) such as Indonesia, Malaysia, Thailand and Singapore (Saporito, 1993; Jacob, 1993). Despite the dominance of the 'triad' in world trade, growth for the future lies further afield. Such growth opportunities may necessitate a global communications strategy, but more likely a differentiated or localized communications strategy. Differentiated does not necessarily mean messages have to be altered wholesale, but adapted to appeal to identified consumer needs. Inside the UK, Japan, the Czech Republic, or the USA or Singapore – media used, monies spent and creative strategies applied may all have to be adapted. While global consumers exist in the sense of a global need for burgers, jeans, CDs or combine harvesters, those needs still have to be appealed to in the sense of cultural consistency. Either by following a global (unadapted) or differentiated (adapted) strategy, communications and promotion will remain crucial to developing and sustaining national and global market share.

DEVELOPMENT AND IMPORTANCE OF INTEGRATED MARKETING COMMUNICATIONS (IMC)

As discussed in Chapter 7, marketing communications is an area of marketing that provides a unique perspective for looking at the entire field of marketing. This area has tended to be treated as a group of functional activities such as advertising, sales promotion, marketing public relations (MPR), point-of-sale promotion, direct marketing and personal selling. It is, however, only very recently that any serious attempts have been made to integrate these separatist functions together. Robertson (1993) from the Leith Agency in Scotland stated that 'consumers see one brand, but often hear it speaking in different tongues, let alone in variety of tones of voice'. Thus while marketers may long have recognized the idea of interaction and synergy among marketing mix elements, such interaction and synergy has only recently been recognized under the IMC banner. According to Schultz *et al.* (1994), IMC is 'a new way of looking at the whole, or realigning communications from the customer viewpoint . . . a flow of information from indistinguishable sources; . . . it is all "one thing" . . . at least to the customer who sees or hears it'.

The drive for IMC is predicated on many of the same factors underpinning growth in global communications and promotion; namely the shift away from advertising, media market fragmentation, manufacturer/retailer balance of power issues, growth in database technology, and media buying practices; and the dawn of consumer control over what is purchased, and over messages accessed. Success, in the sense of building consumer loyalties and maintaining and building market share domestically, internationally and globally, will come about as firms find the correct blend of

234

promotional tools and programmes, clarify their functions and the extent to which they could be used, and then correlate their application. This in turn suggests that rather than developing specialist programmes via, say, advertising, each promotional element and the various medias to be deployed are analysed from the context of integration. This in turn implies significant changes to be made in current promotional development. Most notably, three types of changes are envisaged:

- *Potential changes in brand management systems* – brand managers have to consider the wider panoply of all promotional elements including sponsorship in terms of their integrative, interactive and synergistic effects. This demands brand managers be involved in all types of promotional activities, not just the tried and tested advertising and sales promotion. This in turn may clash with organizational structure and culture leading to reorganization; turf and budget battles involving replacing functional specialists with promotional generalists; more acceptance of risk by brand managers – i.e. the new, untried, methods; and a need to focus on a wider tranche of promotional educational training (see Schultz, 1994).

- *Potential changes in the interaction between corporate and marketing communications* – Recent years have seen changes in the way(s) in which major companies promote and develop corporate image and identity. At corporate level, communications has differentiated into public affairs, issues management, media relations, corporate advertising, lobbying and government relations, financial relations, publicity and sponsorship. Formerly, with the exception of sponsorship, these were seen to lie within the domain of public relations (Kitchen, 1993). However, public relations has entered a wider field of activity under the heading of corporate communications (Kitchen, 1997). Corporate communications includes organizational communications, managerial communications, AND marketing communications according to van Riel (1995). While not accepting van Riel's argument in relation to marketing communications, it seems evident that *raising a corporate umbrella over all communication activities* is the face of the future. Thus, potentially all communications from all parts of an organization could be systematically planned in terms of their overall communication effects on publics or audiences.

- *Back to media buying practices* – This concerns originators (e.g. manufacturers) and intermediaries (i.e. agencies). According to Crosier (1994) the *advertising agency has existed in relatively unchanged form for 200 years*. However, advertising in response to the environmental circumstance *is changing*. More agencies are expanding, offering below-the-line services and one-stop shops for all promotional needs to potential clients. How to compensate agencies for their services is also under attack. Agency structures (e.g. DDB Worldwide, and Burnett's) are mirroring corporate requirements. Compensation implies what is reasonable in a cultural and historical context AND what is workable or usable in practice. It is argued that there is discord between these two areas. Increasingly, discounting is the norm, in-house buying is becoming more prevalent, and clients are demanding more accountability from promotion – all aspects of promotion! Likewise, return on investment is required, thus underpinning movement away from advertising toward other elements of the promotional mix, and emphasis on the integrative nature of promotional elements (see Chapters 16, 24 and 25).

Each of the above three elements is impinging upon the need for crisper, cleaner, integrated, consistent messages via all media to publics or audiences.

DOES DIRECT MARKETING FORM A NEW PROMOTIONAL TOOL?

Direct marketing, for a long time the Cinderella of promotion, is experiencing a new and sustained period of growth (see Chapter 18). Mintel (1996) report that even though in the early stages of development, expenditure on direct marketing in the European Union (EU) was more than £20 billion and rising, with expenditure in Germany estimated at £7.6bn, followed by France £3.8bn, the UK £2.6bn, Italy £2.2bn, and the Netherlands £2bn. Direct mail activity, a key component of direct marketing, has been increasing markedly in Europe, with the volume of addressed mail doubling from 8466 million items in 1983 to 16708 million items in 1993. In the United States expenditure on direct mail has also risen from $15 500m in 1985 to $27 266 in 1993 (DMA, 1996). Part of this growth arises from the activities of FMCG multinational corporations like Procter and Gamble and Heinz who have in the past been heavy users of above-the-line media, but now are using direct marketing in new ways, formulating direct marketing campaigns (alongside IMC or sponsorship activities) to replace some above-the-line activities (Dwek, 1995).

However, an accurate picture of growth rates is clouded by definitional problems as there is no standard definition of direct marketing. Ogilvy & Mather Direct (1985) suggested direct marketing is 'any activity which creates and exploits a direct relationship between company and customer'. Baier (1985) defined direct marketing as an 'interactive system of marketing which uses one or more advertising media to effect a measurable response and/or transaction at any location'. The key characteristic is measurable response which has been an important factor in the growth of direct marketing. Evans *et al.* (1995) define the elements of direct marketing as including:

- direct mail
- direct response advertising
- telemarketing
- leaflet drops
- inserts
- samples, and
- home shopping.

In practice, direct marketing is a means of communication that can also be used as a channel of distribution. The development of direct marketing in firms can be characterized as progressing through a number of phases, the last of which is the development of database marketing (Fletcher *et al.*, 1991).

1 The sales-oriented phase, in which direct marketing is seen as a channel of distribution to sell low-involvement, low-priced products effectively.

2 The image building phase in which direct marketing is, in a sense, 'a personalized image system': here customers receive regular mailings targeted according to his/her lifestyle or behaviour. Profiles thus built up are used to motivate usage. At this stage, direct marketing, although still incomplete, is used as a medium.

3 The integrated system phase is where the uses of direct marketing as a channel of distribution and as a medium come together for both tactical and strategic purposes. In this stage direct marketing is integrated into the marketing process and database marketing ensures a long-term view of customer relationships.

Hence, development of direct marketing can serve to lead to development of database marketing.

With the growth of direct marketing have come changes in the number and the way direct marketing agencies are organized. Along with the transfer of advertising spend from above to below the line has come the growth of specialist agencies. Fifteen years ago only three or four direct marketing agencies existed in the UK, but now there are more than 70 listed by the British Direct Marketing Association (BDMA). These include not just small agencies, some of whom have grown out of mailing houses, but also the multinational agencies like Ogilvy & Mather and Saatchi & Saatchi who have set up direct marketing subsidiaries (Fletcher *et al.*, 1991).

DATABASE MARKETING – TOWARDS COORDINATED STRATEGY

Database marketing uses the power and reduced cost of computers to access and use customer data in ways not previously possible. While direct marketing is the promotional tool most frequently used in conjunction with a computerized customer database, database marketing is much wider in scope than direct marketing. Database marketing uses technology to drive customer-oriented programmes in personalized, articulated and cost-effective ways (Fletcher *et al.*, 1992).

Database marketing does this by analysing both customer characteristics and purchasing habits, allowing profiles of customers to be built up which can then be matched with other lists and geodemographic databases. These can be used to drive marketing communication strategies. Computer databases allow for greater accuracy in targeting and segmentation than is possible with simple mailing lists or general advertising, although there are still problems with list accuracy.

Ability to handle customer data cost-effectively allows firms to engage in long-term dialogues with existing and potential customers. At its best this may be described as a long-term direct relationship whereby customers buy from the company over many years.

Evidence suggests that use of customer databases is increasing. Heinz, for example, have developed database marketing to counterbalance the power of multiple retailers as they continue to develop own-label brands. Currently, Heinz are spending approximately £12m a year on direct marketing, including upgrading the database of respondents to direct marketing activities. By using direct marketing as a medium, alongside other below-the-line activities, Heinz are able to solve the problem of having to advertise 40 to 50 product lines, too broad a range to support via individual brand advertising. Instead the company advertise the attributes of Heinz in a corporate sense and direct marketing is 'more to do with detailed product information and sales motivation. Direct marketing . . . is . . . the story behind the ads, linking ads to consumers in a personal way' (Marshall, 1995). A significant challenge for companies is to use database marketing as part of branding strategy should this be deemed desirable. Thus television advertising campaigns and sponsorship of worthy (image-related) causes serve to fulfil image objectives while direct marketing acts as an informational vehicle.

It is evident that database marketing not only has the potential to maintain existing products but could also serve to help develop new markets and new products. Thus, many firms may be able to use database marketing strategically and this may facilitate movement away from the earlier distribution or promotional role of direct marketing. Indeed, Shaw and Stone (1988) argue that database marketing has potential in all competitive opportunity areas for information technology identified by Michael Porter, namely:

1 Changing the basis of competition
2 Strengthening customer relationships
3 Overcoming supplier problems
4 Building barriers against new entrants
5 Generating new products

The potential of database marketing to develop new business has now been greatly extended with development of the Internet and other interactive media.

INTERNET ADVERTISING – A FORM OF PROMOTION?

There is no doubt that the Internet is changing the way that clients and agencies formulate promotional strategies. What is more difficult to ascertain is how companies can make effective use of the Internet. The Net is in the early adoption stage (Rogers, 1983; Gatignon and Robertson, 1985) and while it remains to be seen just how it can be used by firms and consumers alike, this new means of communication has tremendous appeal for both business and consumers. In an early study Troiano (1995) estimated that, worldwide, the Internet connects potentially with about 25 million people and that $6 million changed hands on the Net in 1994. Users tend to be male (65 to 90 per cent), 18 to 35 years of age, college/university educated (60 to 80 per cent), white-collar employed (50 to 60 per cent), and affluent (average income between $65 000 and $80 000).

In reviewing adoption of the Net in America, Troiano puts forward the proposition that marketing on the Internet has gone through three phases which have application for other countries. The phases are: feasibility, pre-stalgia and reality.

In the first phase Troiano argues that firms have to give up the idea that cost-per-thousand is the only predictive measure of communication effectiveness in relation to expenditure. In support of Schultz *et al.* (1994) he argues that return on marketing investment will become more important and its measurement is another of the skills international/global firms and agencies will need to learn. While this point is readily acceptable in marketing communications *per se* it is of great significance in the unexplored realms of the Internet.

The second pre-stalgia phase is defined as a longing for that which has not yet been, and is characterized by exaggerated claims which may lead marketers to a situation where use of the Internet becomes an end in itself where 'novelty overwhelms both strategic soundness and user value'.

The third phase is the realistic assessment of interactive marketing and the role of the Internet. Interactive marketing is defined as communicating, promoting and selling in a consumer-controlled, electronic environment. This concept is distinct from advertising and direct marketing because it speaks to a consumer, like advertising; records a response, like direct marketing; *and responds*, in real time. It is more controllable by users than the other intrusive forms of marketing communications, and is in this way highly integrated, though by receivers rather than senders.

In supporting Troiano's view, interactive media are not, as yet, effective channels for purely promotional messages. More sender and user-centric approaches are needed. An example of this is a solution put to American Express to rebuild its customer loyalty amongst a segment of its customers labelled 'TSC/ABTs' (techno-savvy consumers/affluent business travellers). These customers were offered access to account information and a cross-indexed database of travel-related information on thousands of locations which was successfully launched under the name ExpressNeta.

Besides the Internet there are a number of new media which are also interactive. One example of these is the launch of the Vauxhall Vectra which used new media to underline the message that the car is one of the most technologically advanced vehicles on the market. Five new-media ventures were used for the launch. The campaign included a Web site specifically designed for the Vectra; a commercial for interactive TV; touch-screen kiosks; and CD-ROMs sent to dealers and consumers via car and consumer magazines. Notably, the more traditional television advertising carries the World Wide Web address for the Vectra site, and press and posters also carry freephone 0800 numbers for delivery of further requested CD-ROMs.

What is clear is that agencies and clients are only just beginning to understand the plethora of ways the Internet and other forms of new media can be used to interact with consumers. Nevertheless, the Internet is essentially a 'directive' medium not a 'broadcast' one, and as such it seems ill-suited to brand building. That appears to be the role of conventional media advertising in well-known, tried and tested media – like the press, television, radio and posters (Pringle, 1995).

COORDINATION AND CONTROL – PROCESS VERSUS OUTPUT

There has long been a debate about the coordination and control of international campaigns. This is important given that many UK campaigns, i.e. shown on television, are actually coordinated elsewhere. The key issue is whether campaigns should be standardized or locally adapted. Over the past 25 years work by Quelch and Hoff (1986) and Peebles *et al.* (1978), amongst others, have found that neither of the extremes of complete standardization or adaptation was the best solution for the output of international advertising campaigns. However, recently two factors have provided an added stimulus to this debate.

Firstly, there is the rapid economic development of South East Asia and with that the explosion in growth of media, notably the proliferation of satellite television channels. A recent survey by Shao and Waller (1993) investigated American advertising agencies' practices in this region by evaluating 200 Asia-Pacific regional affiliates of American advertising agencies in 11 countries. Their propositions were accepted by the findings from the research. These were that:

- The majority of American advertising agencies would adapt campaigns in order to gain benefits of standardization while paying attention to local differences.
- Legal restrictions and cultural sensitivities would be the leading environmental impediments for agencies operating in the region.

Interestingly, Shao and Waller's research also found that a significantly large number of factors militated against or caused major problems in standardizing or attempting to standardize campaigns in the Asia Pacific area. The most important factors were multiple languages; different ethnic groups; restrictions on importing advertising materials; restrictions on hiring foreigners; legal restrictions on advertising claims; currency exchange limits; and activities of consumer groups. In evaluating the standardization of the sales platform and creative context they found that while some agencies viewed country markets as similar, the majority of agencies recognized differences in national or even in regional preference terms. They revealed a well-founded belief amongst agency personnel that there is need to adapt advertising campaigns to local or regional markets. Shao and Waller concluded that more often than not, most agencies tended to use adaptive approaches. However, only in very few cases did complete customization occur, probably because of high associated costs in creating individual campaigns for each market. Above all, severity of legal restrictions was the major problem that agencies faced. Also apparent were differences in the degree of difficulty of advertising in different countries. Australia and Malaysia were cited as being the most problematic while Japan, Korea and Taiwan were the least problematic.

The second major factor is the development of new media, particularly use of the Internet. An example of a globally organized standardized output is the investment that Levi's have made in a World Wide Web site on the Internet. Levi's set up a global site and coordinated the work of all their European offices. Instead of having a possible 27 sites they have one. Working with various Internet specialists and agencies, Levi's together with their subsidiaries have put together what they term a surf-friendly site where text is almost completely absent from the Home Page, but a grid of icons links the page to seven areas. Three zones are given over to company information: its history, products and commercials. Others are designed to draw in Levi's target audience of 15 to 24-year-olds with 'E-zines' on youth culture and street fashion.

Levi's intend to have more virtual meeting places, where visitors can interact with each other. Also, the company has developed a Valentine service where people can choose a card in a server-composed style, then invite the senders and receivers to view it via e-mail (Summerfield, 1996).

Levi's experience illustrates the dilemma that more and more global advertisers will face. While some global brands like American Express, Levi's, Coca-Cola and Pepsi can contemplate a standardized campaign on a global basis, this is the exception rather than the rule. It seems clear that many problems involved in producing standardized global campaigns are such that the new media, particularly the Internet, will support globally organized but locally adapted campaigns.

ORGANIZATIONAL RE-ENGINEERING: PARADOXICAL PRIMACY

So far, this chapter has argued that changes taking place in the communications environment equate to companies needing to radically rethink coordination and control of communications strategy and tactics to realize potential interactions, synergies and other non-serendipitous benefits associated therewith. For example, McKenna (1991) argued that technology has created feedback loops connecting customers and companies which creates opportunity for firms to adapt more ably to changing consumer and customer needs. Figure 14.1 indicates that global/ multinational firms can now *potentially* use marketing communications to further integrate and synergize marketing communications strategy and tactics.

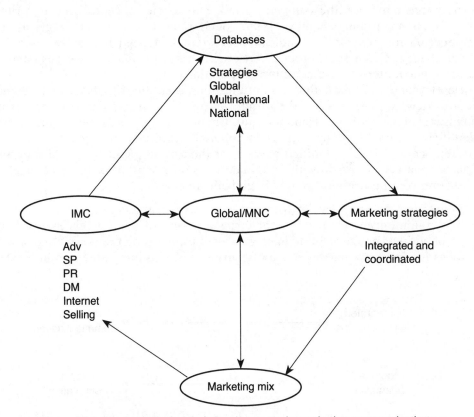

Figure 14.1 The impact of global developments in marketing communications.

Notably, the model outlined in Figure 14.1 is contingent or dependent for its validity on several factors, notably (1) the prevailing domestic, international and global environment; (2) the stages of life cycle in which brands are positioned on a country-by-country basis and the extent to which such brands are globally directed; and (3) the corporate culture of the company with respect to 'global' or 'integrated' communications strategies and tactics. Figure 14.2 suggests that 'reality' for these firms lies along a continuum of communication potentialities and early evidence (Kitchen, 1997b) from empirical research tends to support this.

Few firms would argue or disagree with continuum A in Figure 14.2. Research, either of a secondary or primary nature, would indicate significant movement towards integration. The real issue, however, from the context of this chapter, is whether integration is possible, desirable or actualizable from a multinational or global perspective. From continuum B in Figure 14.2, the expectation is that firms would range along the continuum with relatively few firms with narrow product lines, positioned in terms of globally integrated approaches. Notably the first case vignette would fall to the left of the continuum on both counts from an international marcom perspective, while from a domestic perspective, McDonald's as 'brand' would be coherently integrated.

Notably, however, forces shaping new conditions as to how MNCs/global corporations approach the competitive task have been conceptualized by writers such as Hammer and Champy (1995). Such radical conceptualizations as 're-engineering the corporation' indicate the extent and need for radical organizational change. Often such proposed re-engineering, no matter how desirable or needful, encounters resistance within corporations.

Developments in marketing communications identified in this paper require radical new approaches in the organization and integration of marketing communications globally. Hammer and Champy (1995) and McKenna (1991) identified reasons why organizations do not easily undertake or implement change; further, Schultz (1991) identified reasons for the slow implementation of IMC and database marketing. Broadly, the rationale for slow adoption of these changes in marketing communications in MNC's globally may be:

- *Brand management systems*: For companies that use a brand management system the new communications environment forms a period of painful renaissance from usual business practice. Brand managers focus primarily on their own brands; such focus is often on a narrow range of activities which is antipathetic to integrated

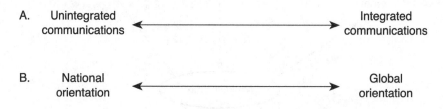

Figure 14.2 Integrated global/multinational communication potentialities.

communications; but often such antipathy is not to do with brands *per se*, but product lines and product mixes. Moreover, brands can develop integrated communications internationally, even globally, but often control for such multi-£$ million brands is not brand management responsibility. Most brand management organizational structures are based on establishing functional specialisms in support of brand management objectives. Budget allocation systems tend to be organized along similar specialization lines such as advertising, sales promotion and direct marketing. Where such conditions prevail, developing IMC becomes difficult if not impossible. Further, most brand managers are inherently risk-averse. The kinds of changes indicated in this chapter imply risk in adopting or sometimes even in considering innovation. The result is that considering IMC implies changes in organizational structure or in the types of decisions, responsibilities and autonomies carried in the hierarchical change of marketing control.

- *Investment justification*: Costs of implementing change are invariably high which in itself acts as a disincentive for multinational/global firms. Integrating marketing communications globally or database marketing represents substantive investments in hardware, software, staff training and personnel development. Further, successful application of global communications activities, however 'success' is evaluated, generates new ideas for additional applications which lead to more investment. Thus, it could be anticipated that attitudes to such investment would vary in terms of domestic, multinational and 'global' communicators (De Mooij, 1994) which further spells implication for agency choice, compensation, and market research and database analysis.

- *Senior management support*: Support for IMC, database marketing, Internet usage, and organizational structure and change has to be led by corporate headquarters. However, executives may well understand the need for such changes, but be forestalled by market dynamics, life-cycle positions or brand market shares in perceivably different markets around the world. Admittedly, the marketing literature is littered with many examples of failure, when corporate will to integrate globally is backed by appropriate resources and implementable campaigns, only to find confusion at the consumer end. A further problem is stated by Bernstein (1984) that 'corporate executives manipulated the world like puppet masters, much of the time blithely unaware that the strings had been cut'.

- *IMC – a long-term goal?* Development of IMC is now being seen as a long-term investment. New technologies acting in support of IMC activities internationally or globally are central to corporate marketing activities and would be appear to be justifiable on the basis of cost reduction and increasing organizational, marketing and brand efficiencies. However, some of the most valuable benefits which the new technologies offer, such as improved customer relations, do not readily figure in optimizable investment equations, as McKenna (1991) points out.

- *The supply infrastructure*: Changes occurring in the communications environment amount to a renaissance. Suppliers of technology for IMC and database marketing face the problem that they have to match needed technologies to user needs and capabilities. But, as Fletcher *et al.* (1991) point out, there is a shortage of good suppliers of databases and analytical software. Moreover, amongst agencies much work is still handled on a project-only basis, suggesting a nascent lack of understanding of IMC and database marketing in an international or global context.

Changes taking place in marketing communications are reshaping the work of communicators and communications as rapidly now as at any time in the history of marketing. Notably, such reshaping faces significant barriers. It is not merely a matter of organizational or managerial will. Many internal and external barriers remain and have still to be tackled. But, as Hammer and Champy (1995) argue, how business was done yesterday does not matter. What is important is how to organize marketing communications today.

SUMMARY AND CONCLUSIONS

Based on the preceding discussion, the following issues are identified as crucial to global marketing communications:

1 Reflecting upon the dynamics of marketing situations – this includes consumer behaviour, client/agency relations, media accessibility, environmental infrastructure (i.e. legal, technological, cultural, economic, situational, competitive, each of which will vary from corporation to corporation and nation to nation) *and* the totality of marketing communications in terms of emphasis and expenditure.

2 The need to recognize homogeneous segments among heterogeneous markets (applies domestically and internationally). For the former, differentiation rather than standardization of promotion would appear to be the norm, with the specific exception of advertising where many attempts are made to integrate internationally and globally. Admittedly, other elements of the promotional mix are integrated nationally, but not internationally.

3 Consideration of the potential and potency of IMC with its concomitant focus on organizational structures; breaking down of boxes and linear arrows; potential relational changes between corporate and marketing communication functions and activities; and changes in media buying practices. To all intents and purposes, the rationale for IMC at national level appears to be inescapable; at an international level, such a drive is again only the norm for advertising *per se* oftentimes in terms of strategy, themes and style rather than 'one sight, one sound, one ad'.

4 Acquiring knowledge and skills in the use of new medias. Interactivity alone demands a new approach to marketing communications. However, new media should not be sought out as a result of 'newness' alone. The tried and tested principles of pre- and post-testing apply in these domains just as much as in long-standing media, if not more so.

5 Understanding the limitations of the Internet, particularly the 'directive' nature of this medium. Nonetheless, such limitations can also be seen as a mechanism to sidestep consumer perceptual filters.

6 Evaluating the potential of database marketing, especially in relation to interactive media. Customer databases can now be linked to the Internet, enhancing the potential of database marketing.

7 Firms should review the provision of agency services, as new service providers allow alternative ways of developing promotional strategies.

Each and all of these areas suggest that as marketers approach the twenty-first century changes in marketing communications and in the promotional mix constitute exciting challenges. The question needs to be asked whether these changes constitute a time of renaissance or a time of reflection. Kitchen (1993b) argued that the late 1980s and early 1990s have been a time of 'renaissance' in the sense that radical changes in the communications mix occasioned by the environment have led to a need for renewal, regeneration and reflection upon marketing communications within the ever-changing constellations or organizational reshaping amidst a turbulent competitive environment. These changes were radically conceptualized by Elliott (1996) in his paper 'Opening boxes and breaking arrows: millennial models of communication'. Each of the preceding elements of our argument underpins a need to re-analyse the worn, dated models of the past. Which boxes need to be opened? Which arrows need to be broken? We suggest the black box between input and output (i.e. the consumer's mind, note the global consumer), the boxes associated with cognitive information processes and hedonic experiential processes, and boxes associated with linearity and rationality in relation to consumer behaviour. For originators and intermediaries similar types of boxes and linear arrows are being broken as new techniques and technologies appear on the communications scene. Further, as media environs become more and more cluttered with the promotional iconography of the twentieth century, as consumer minds become cluttered with the fossilized remains of previous part-absorbed part-remembered promotions, so new ways (probably consumer-led) to break through such clutter and consumer perceptual filters will have to be devised and operationalized. IMC, the Internet and other interactive media, direct marketing and database marketing may constitute just a first few steps in moving marketing communications toward the twenty-first century. Such a renaissance inevitably requires reflection – by marketing management and students alike. For the latter, they will be a new generation of communicators for whom interaction and integration of all communications media inside dynamically responsive organizations will be the perceived norm.

DISCUSSION TOPICS

1 Discuss, in detail, any other developments which you feel are impacting in a major way on either domestic or international marcoms.
2 Critically analyse any one of the developments described in this chapter, citing additional appropriate literature where necessary (i.e. you could use the Internet to access information).
3 Argue for or against the view that for a new generation of communicators 'interaction and integration' of all communications will be the norm.
4 Following Elliott (1996), which boxes need to be opened?, which arrows need to be broken?
5 Using the McDonald's vignette or any other accessed from *Campaign*, what precisely is the cause of a given marcoms approach to a market?

6 Should marcoms vary from company to company or nation to nation?
7 Argue the case that new media (i.e. the Internet, etc.) are plainly irrelevant to most consumer goods manufacturers.
8 Critique the two continuums in Figure 14.2. Choose a selection of companies from the marketing practitioner literature and attempt to position them. What conclusions can be drawn from this?
9 Examine Figure 14.1. Choose a company and evaluate how and in what way(s) these developments impact on marcoms.
10 Is 'reflection' an adequate metaphor in exploring the nature of marcoms developments?

CASE STUDIES

American Express

American Express developed a $100 million campaign in 1994 that covered 30 nations and developed 60 advertisements with the strapline 'places you want to go, people you want to meet'. All advertising generated around the world followed the same formula. Business (presumed celebrity) endorsers expound their (winning) business philosophies and then refer to the indispensability of the American Express Card. These endorsers, for example, include British designer and retailer Sir Terence Conran, founder and managing director of Body Shop International, Anita Roddick, Italian fashion designers, and Japanese innkeepers. Notably such advertising was previously successful in the United States (1993) featuring Toys R Us Chairman Charles Lazarus. The advertising brief obtained by Ogilvy & Mather included the mandate to develop a series of ads that would give travel cardholders the same campaign they see at home but look like a domestic effort to locals.

(*Source:* Czinkota and Ronkainen (1996))

Comments

Notably this campaign was integrated in terms of overarching strategy and campaign design but offered only one component of the promotional mix, namely advertising. Early empirical evidence from interviews conducted with executives from multi-national/global FMCG firms (Kitchen, 1997) indicate that integration internationally is usually, but not always, associated with advertising, with other components of the promotional mix developed nationally. In relation to the example quoted, the approach combines what amounts to national public relations exposure for business endorsers (Body Shop, for example, does not advertise) while reinforcing appropriate imagery for American Express via advertising. Further to the point, the American Express card has long been positioned as a global product. Moreover, earlier experience with American Express revealed the fundamental but important dynamic '*standardize where possible, adapt where necessary*', as seen in the following commentary from an earlier round of American Express ads:

Each of the vignettes were emphasising one major benefit-service of American Express, like 24 hour card replacement, local utility etc. We said to all the local markets that we are going to re-shoot some of the vignettes that looked too American. Most agreed on some vignettes being unsuitable.

So we made a list of replacements and then asked for new ideas. Then we all got together making a list of new vignettes, specifying which market was interested in which vignette. But we ended up with too many vignettes. Therefore, we combined similar scenes. We had . . . one setting . . . instead of three. We had one big meeting with the client and all creatives to reach a final decision on vignettes, sets etc, casting country-by-country. Then we made local offices sign a contract because they change their minds during or after the shooting. It happened with DYKM. Then we had a problem with splitting up costs . . . creatives . . . etc

(Vardar, 1992)

Colgate Palmolive

'Colgate's advertising and marketing in the 1990's will be tailored specifically to local markets and countries; there will be little global advertising. To underscore this point, TV commercials from different countries were shown and no two were alike.'

'Once market penetration and positioning is established in the target country, Colgate moves the product into similar markets in other countries. Product introduction has matched this approach with the introduction of Ajax bathroom spray in France. Once a market is established there (in France), plans are made to extend the product to other market areas. Colgate products such as actibrush plaque-fighting mouth rinse, currently in the UK, France and Brazil, is approved for marketing in Australia and Italy, but not necessarily using the same approach'

(Freeman, 1990; Keegan, 1995)

Comments

Notably with this example a clear and conscious decision was taken at corporate level to act locally with regard to promotional development, at least insofar as advertising is concerned. This does not mean, however, that campaigns developed elsewhere will not be utilized. What it does mean is that national-level executives have greater autonomy to develop promotional activities than their counterparts, say, at American Express. In other words, a scenario very similar to that depicted in the McDonald's vignette.

ACKNOWLEDGEMENTS

Grateful thanks are extended to *Campaign* for permission to use the Macdonald's case vignette.

This chapter was originally published as a paper titled 'Issues Influencing Marcoms in a Global Context', *Journal of Marketing Communications*, Volume 3, No 4, 1997 (with Colin Wheeler).

REFERENCES

Advertising Association Marketing Pocketbook (1993) ASA in conjunction with NTC Publications Limited.

Baier, M. (1985) *Elements of Direct Marketing*, New York: McGraw-Hill.

Baker, M. (1985) 'Globalization vs differentiation as international marketing strategies', *Journal of Marketing Management*, 1: 145–55.

Belch, G.E. and Belch, M.A. (1995) *Introduction to Advertising and Promotion: An Integrated Marketing Communications Perspective*, 3rd edn, London: Richard D. Irwin, 4–5.

Bernstein, D. (1984) *Company Image and Reality*, Eastbourne: Holt, Rinehart and Winston/ The Advertising Association, 23.

Campaign, 'How McDonald's tailors its brand identity to local markets' (Richard Cook), 29 August 1997, 29. Used with permission. Students are encouraged to read the entire article in *Campaign*.

Cohen, R.J. (1993) 'Insider's report – Robert Cohen presentation on advertising expenditures', *McCann Erickson Worldwide*, June, 8.

Cohen, R.J. (1994) 'Ad gain of 5.2% in 93 marks downturn's end', *Advertising Age*, 2 May, 4.

Crosier, K. (1994) in M. Baker (ed.) *The Marketing Book*, Butterworth–Heinemann, Chapter 21.

Czinkota M.R. and Ronkainen, I.A. (1996) *Global Marketing*, Fort Worth: Dryden Press.

De Mooij, M. (1994) *Advertising Worldwide*, London: Prentice Hall, Chapters 7–8.

Dentsu Inc. (1996) *1995 Advertising Expenditures in Japan*, Tokyo, Japan: Dentsu Inc. Corporate Communications Division.

Direct Marketing Association data accessed July 1996.

Dwek, R (1995) *Campaign*, 7 July, 29.

Elliott, R. (1996) 'Opening boxes and breaking arrows: millennium models of communication', keynote paper presented at the *1st International Conference on Corporate and Marketing Communications*, Keele University, Keele, UK: 22–23 April.

Evans, M., O'Malley, L. and Patterson, M. (1995) 'Direct marketing: rise and rise or rise and fall?', *Marketing Intelligence & Planning*, 13(6): 16–23.

Fletcher, K., Wheeler, C. and Wright, J. (1991) 'Database marketing: a channel, a medium or a strategic response', *International Journal of Advertising*, 10(2): 117–27.

Fletcher, K., Wheeler, C. and Wright, J. (1992) 'Success in database marketing: some crucial factors', *Marketing Intelligence & Planning*, 10(6): 18–23.

Freeman, L. (1990) 'Colgate axes global ads: thinks local', *Advertising Age*, 26 November: 1, 59.

Gatignon, H. and Robertson, T.S. (1985) 'A propositional inventory for new diffusion research', *Journal of Consumer Research*, March: 849–67.

Hammer, M. and Champy, J. (1995) *Reengineering the Corporation: A Manifesto for Business Revolution*, London: Nicholas Brealey.

Hout, T., Porter, M.E. and Rudden, E. (1982) 'How global companies win out', *Harvard Business Review*, September/October.

Jacob, R. (1993) 'Where the big brands are blooming', *Fortune*, 23 August, 55.

Keegan, W.J. (1995) *Global Marketing Management*, 5th edn, Englewood Cliffs, NJ: Prentice Hall International, 7–26, 557.

Kitchen, P.J. (1993a) 'Marketing communications renaissance', *International Journal of Advertising*, 12(3): 367–86.

Kitchen, P.J. (1993b) 'Public relations: a rationale for its development and usage within UK FMCG firms', *European Journal of Marketing*, 27(7): 53–75.

Kitchen, P.J. (1994) 'The marketing communications revolution: a Leviathan unveiled?', *Marketing Intelligence and Planning*, 12(2): 19–25.

Kitchen, P.J. (1997a) 'Public relations: a prelude to corporate communications?', Volume 2.1 *Corporate Communications: An International Journal*.

Kitchen, P.J. (1997b) Empirical work with Multinational/Global FMCG Firms with HQs in the United Kingdom, ongoing, completion date end-1998.

Kotler, P. (1984) *Marketing Management*, Englewood Cliffs, NJ: Prentice Hall.

Levitt, T. (1983) 'The globalization of markets', *Harvard Business Review*, May–June.

Lorenz, C. (1984a) 'The overselling of world brands', *Financial Times*, 19 July.

Lorenz, C. (1984b) 'Why new products are going global', *Financial Times*, 16 July.

Marshall, C. (1994) *Campaign*, 23 June: 29.

McKenna, R. (1991) 'Marketing is everything: everything is marketing', *Harvard Business Review*, January–February: 65–69.

Mintel Report (1996) *Direct Mail Developments*.

Ogilvy & Mather Direct (1985) *Direct Marketing: New Opportunities for Business to Business Selling*, London: Ogilvy & Mather.

Ohmae, K. (1985) *Triad Power*, New York: Free Press.

Paliwoda, S. (1993) *International Marketing*, 2nd edn, London: Butterworth–Heinemann.

Peebles, D.M., Ryans, J.K. Jr. and Vernon, I.R. (1978) 'Coordinating international advertising', *Journal of Marketing*, 42 (January): 28–34.

Porter, M.E. (ed.) (1986) *Competition in Global Industries*, Harvard, MA: Harvard Business School Press.

Pringle, H. (1995) *Campaign*, 20 October, 28.

Quelch, J. A. and Hoff, E. J. (1986) 'Customizing global marketing', *Harvard Business Review*, 64 (May–June): 59–68.

Robertson, T (1993) Invited guest lecturer at Communications Seminar, University of Strathclyde.

Rogers, E.M. (1983) *Diffusion of Innovations*, 3rd edn, New York: The Free Press.

Saporito, W. (1993) 'Where the global action is', *Fortune*, Special Issue, Autumn/Winter: 63–5.

Schultz, D.E. (1991) 'Integrated marketing communications', *Journal of Promotion Management*, 1.1: 99–105.

Schultz, D.E., Tannenbaum, S.I. and Lauterborn, R.F. (1994) *Integrated Marketing Communications*, Illinois: NTC Business Books.

Shao, A. T. and Waller, D. S. (1993) 'Advertising standardisation in the Asia Pacific region: what stands in the way?', *Asia Pacific Journal of Marketing and Logistics*, 5(3): 43–55.

Shaw, R. and Stone, M. (1988) *Database Marketing*, Aldershot: Gower.

Shimp, T. (1997) *Advertising, Promotion, and Supplemental Aspects of Integrated Marketing Communications*, Fort Worth: Dryden Press, Chapter 1.

Summerfield, G. (1996) *Campaign*, 23 February, 22.

Toffler, A. and Toffler, H. (1990) *Powershift: Knowledge, Wealth and Violence at the Edge of the 21st Century*, New York: Bantam Books.

Troiano, M. (1995) *Campaign*, 7 July, 30.

Van Riel, C. (1995) *Corporate Communications*, Englewood Cliffs, NJ: Prentice Hall International.

Vardar, N. (1992) *Global Advertising: Rhyme or Reason?* London: Paul Chapman Publishing Limited, 104–5.

Waterschoot, W. and Bulte, C. (1992) 'The Four P classification of the marketing mix revisited', *Journal of Marketing*, 56(4): 83–93.

Webster, F. E. Jnr (1992) 'The changing role of marketing in the corporation', *Journal of Marketing*, 56(4): 1–17.

White, J., Dickson, A. and Myers, A. (1988) *Public Relations Employment and Expenditure in the United Kingdom*, a report for the Institute of Public Relations prepared by the Cranfield School of Management, UK.

15

MARKETING COMMUNICATIONS ACTIVITIES

Graham Hughes

CHAPTER AIMS

- to explore the relationships between communications theory and the development of effective marketing communications strategies
- to discuss the emergence of a new communications mix
- to consider the value of adopting a strategic planning approach to marketing communications
- to look at the organizational roles played in the implementation of marketing communications – internal and external
- to examine the impact of new approaches to media planning and new media opportunities
- to highlight the importance of communications in creating, developing and managing brands

ILLUSTRATION

Recognition of the stages (Figure 15.1) customers go through in making purchase decisions, whether as individuals or as organizational representatives, has long been utilized as a basis for developing marketing communications activities. Understanding consumer and organizational behaviour and attitudes, and the likely effects communications may have, has an increasingly significant importance for all marketing organizations. By utilizing purchase decision making, it is possible to consider examples of the relevance of communications activities at appropriate stages. Further, it is possible to see practical applications of varying elements of the communication mix.

UK-based tour operators such as Thomson, Airtours and First Choice dominate the so-called package holiday sectors. Between them they spent £12+ million on advertising in the UK during 1996 (AC: Nielsen.MEAL). The product involves pre-booking a one- or two-week holiday which includes transport and hotel accommodation, typically to resorts around the Mediterranean. The peak season is during summer, particularly July and August when children are on school vacation. The marketing communications activities of companies involved in these sectors commence anything up to a year in advance of when a holiday may be taken.

Need recognition

↓

Information search

↓

Evaluation of alternatives

↓

Purchase decision

↓

Post-purchase

Figure 15.1 The consumer buying decision process.

Purchasing a holiday of this type is an important consumer decision. It is also one of the most emotive, as the 'wrong' decision has far-reaching consequences in terms of inculcating high levels of dissatisfaction (i.e. cognitive dissonance) for long periods of time, probably until the next holiday is taken.

Marketing communications activity commences with publication of brochures by holiday companies. This coincides with the beginning of the decision-making process as consumers enter the *'need recognition'* phase, namely they begin to think about next year's holidays. Advertising creates awareness and prompts consumers into *'information search'*. These holiday company informational sources are buttressed tangentially by television programmes giving illustrative up-and-down-market examples. These programmes invariably appear during the New Year 'down-time' when consumers are exposed to all the vagaries of UK weather and shorter, colder days.

With most package holidays being sold through high street agents, potential purchasers may collect brochures from such outlets or access them via direct mail. Study of brochures, discussions with sales representatives in the travel agents and word-of-mouth communication with informal sources such as friends provide the basis for *'evaluation of alternative'* destinations. Further reference points include memory search, i.e. accessing previous experiences and knowledge.

The actual 'purchase decision' usually takes place at a travel agent's shop where there is still scope for personal communication and point-of-sale materials. The latter would include data generated by computerized booking systems regarding availability of destinations and flights. After the holiday has been taken, the holiday companies gather information about satisfaction levels which aids in future planning. Such information, along with existing personal information, allows the holiday companies and their agents to build up databases of consumer information which can be utilized for future communication campaigns, including direct marketing. Purchase decisions and consumption may lead to cognitive dissonance, i.e. a feeling of acute psychological discomfort caused by the fact that the accepted alternative may have some negative characteristics which then have to be overcome or allayed.

INTRODUCTION

Understanding and defining 'the customer' is one of the most difficult challenges facing today's marketers. Advances in technology do, to some extent, help the process but in other ways can add further complexities to the task. Permutation of factors influencing purchase behaviour, whether on an individual basis or business-to-business basis, highlights both potential for focused customer targeting and the ability to communicate in a sophisticated manner with selected target audiences.

Concepts which aid in achieving the required level of customer understanding are developing rapidly. These help in allowing identification of critical success factors for effective marketing communications. While the level of understanding will never be perfect, it has in many areas reached a point where patterns of purchase behaviour can be accurately predicted and effectively measured, or at least this is the assumption by many in the marcoms industry.

Table 15.1 gives some indication of the increasingly significant amounts of expenditure on global advertising. Such indicators, combined with forecast increases in other communications activities, suggest that organizations will be striving to maximize the use of the communications 'mix' and improve dispersion, control, integration and measurement. More and more pressure is being exerted on advertising and other integrated agencies to deliver measurable outcomes (i.e. success), and payment by results is replacing (or at least standing alongside) media commission. No longer do agencies have carte blanche to deliver campaigns that might win creative awards, (i.e. Cannes) but do not necessarily achieve commercial success (in terms of behavioural as opposed to attitudinal outcomes). A far more rigorous and critical approach is being undertaken in establishing and measuring communication objectives for every facet of marketing activity, including its integrated totality. A similarly strict approach is being followed for corporate communications activities.

Specification of objectives allows the development of marketing communications activities designed to meet set objectives and control mechanisms to be established

Table 15.1 Global advertising expenditure forecasts

	1995 £bn	1996 £bn	1997 £bn	1998 £bn est.	1999 £bn est.
North America	99	105	110	115	120
Europe	77	82	86	92	97
Asia/Pacific	71	78	85	93	102
Latin America	18	21	23	26	30
Other	5	6	6	7	8
Totals	270	292	310	333	357

(Main media: TV, print, radio, cinema, outdoor – $bn at current prices. *Source*: Zenith Media, London)

for effective measuring of results achieved. This 'planned' approach to marketing communications is not necessarily a guarantee of success but recognizes the importance of communications in achieving overall marketing effectiveness. It also suggests that marketing communications are being viewed with a medium to long-term perspective rather than a narrow short-termist perspective.

Communication is replacing promotion as the key word in depicting the wider range of activities available to organizations to reach their target audiences. Most general marketing texts still use the promotional 'P' heading in discussing this element of the marketing mix. Individual items of a mix consisting largely of advertising, sales promotion, public relations and personal selling are the norm. It is only more recently that attention is focusing on marketing communications from a strategic dimension. Smith, *et al.* (1997) and Linton and Morley (1995) provide input on the strategic role that marketing communications activities play and the importance of taking an integrative approach to their implementation.

Shimp (1997) notes the increasing use of marketing communications to replace promotion management as the collective term for describing such activities. He suggests that the latter description has been most commonly used by marketing educators, while the former has been used by marketing practitioners. Marketing communications, he proposes, is a 'more descriptive and encompassing term'. He also adopts an integrated view toward implementation of marketing communications activities.

COMMUNICATION THEORIES: UNDERPINNING ACTION

Communication requires both senders *and* receivers. Figure 15.2 is a framework for marketing communications activity based on both participants in the communications process.

In marketing communication terms, senders are the organizations marketing products and/or services and the receivers are customers or intermediaries. Successful communication may be based on the premise that the sender has something meaningful to say and that the receiver has an interest in wanting to listen to the message. Marketing communications aim at three primary areas: raising awareness, changing attitudes, and influencing behaviour. In order to achieve any

Communicators	Communications activities	Communications receivers
Organizations	Communications mix	Consumers/clients
Agencies	Media	Individuals
	Planning	Businesses
	Positioning	
	Research	

Figure 15.2 A Framework for marketing communications activity.

degree of success, a detailed understanding is required of who the target customer is and their current level of awareness/understanding, and knowledge of existent attitudes and current behavioural patterns. This information provides the basis for developing appropriate communications that will help achieve organizational objectives. Understanding the customer is the starting point for effective communication activity. From this an understanding can be developed in relation to how the communication process between sender and receiver actually works.

Earlier chapters in this book have indicated how better understanding of customers and consumers can be achieved and how communications between senders and receivers (and vice versa) can work effectively. The chapters following examine the roles of individual components of the communications mix. These components or activities are of crucial significance to either singular or integrated approaches to marketing communications. Consideration is extended here to examples of how customer knowledge has contributed toward marketing success and the ways in which the communications process has been used effectively.

BT's 'It's Good to Talk'

This campaign contained elements of the three main areas in which marketing communications can play a key role, namely awareness, attitude and behaviour. At the consumer level there was a misconception as to the true cost of making calls. Advertising raised awareness by the provision of examples of how much calls actually cost, while simultaneously stimulating call behaviours. This in turn helped change both attitudes and behaviour. Male attitudes toward phone usage had been identified as largely functional and therefore restricted in terms of frequency of use and call duration. In addition to raising awareness with regard to cost, male customers were encouraged to use the phone in more social and family contexts. The series of campaigns were based on extensive research aimed at developing a detailed knowledge of customer attitudes *and* behavioural patterns. National campaigns utilizing TV, press and posters were used to communicate with key targets.

Daewoo

For a Korean company to establish almost a 1 per cent share of the UK car market within its first year of operation was a spectacular achievement. Careful and detailed research into car buyer attitudes and behaviour provided the key platforms for marketing success. The research identified strong dissatisfaction among buyers with the processes of both purchasing and servicing new cars. The marketing communications strategy therefore focused on Daewoo's ability to provide hassle-free purchasing and servicing.

First Direct

Gaining an understanding of customer attitudes towards traditional banking services saw the emergence of a significant new channel for financial services marketing as a whole. First Direct identified that for a significant proportion of the market, there was a decreasing need for transacting business in person at bank premises. Technology provided the systems for the creation of a service that did not require a physical presence in a building and that could provide customers with the ability to do business out of traditional banking hours. The establishment of a 24-hour telephone service transformed the sector. TV and press advertising supported by direct mail and telemarketing were used to demonstrate the ease of switching to the new service and the benefits in improved service.

THE CHANGING MARKETING COMMUNICATIONS MIX

The traditional approach taken by organizations has been to think in terms of *promoting to* target audiences. This has been changing and in many cases the approach that is now being taken is to think more in terms of *communicating with* customers. There has been a shift away from the concept of a promotional mix majoring on advertising and sales promotion activities toward an integrated communications approach which includes not only specific communications activities but also involves recognition of the communicative effects of all marketing activities. Figure 15.3 illustrates the integrative nature of marketing communications activities.

There are a number of factors that have led to a wider perspective being taken towards the role of marketing communications. More and more organizations are developing a customer-focused or relationship-building approach to their marketing. This entails recognition of customers as individuals, even if the company has

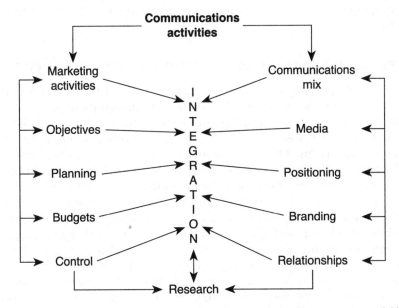

Figure 15.3 An integrative approach to organizing and planning marcom activities.

millions of them. Communications activities are being designed to establish two-way dialogues. This helps the company build knowledge about customers which assists in the future development of marketing strategies. Global companies such as Heinz are building significant databases of customers with whom they communicate by providing product information and incentives and in return collect responses to marketing initiatives which contribute to future planning.

Such activities are based on the adoption of a more direct approach in communicating. Response-based advertising is now almost the norm in print media and increasingly so in broadcast vehicles. In addition, more sophisticated usage and better targeting of direct mail and telemarketing are refocusing direct marketing as a leading communications activity. Indeed, companies are adopting a direct approach to much of their marketing planning, not just in communications.

Media fragmentation, particularly developments in cable and satellite broad-casting, provide new opportunities to target specific market segments. This, combined with technological advancement, provides a host of new ways to communicate with customers, increasingly on an individual level. The Internet is providing exciting opportunities for marketers of all kinds in terms of both providing information and facilitating actual purchases. Retailers are trialling customer ordering via phone, fax and the Net. Evidence of real commercial success using these methods is limited, largely due to the relatively small number of potential consumers who have Internet access.

Terms such as 'above the line' and 'below the line', while still widely used by practitioners, are becoming increasingly less precise in defining the roles of marketing communications activities. While through-the-line, indicating a merging of activities, seems a suitable alternative (it is inadequate as it based on an historical accounting definition), increasingly the 'line' will disappear more and more as advertising agency remuneration focuses on achieving results rather than media commissions.

STRATEGIC PLANNING FOR COMMUNICATIONS EFFECTIVENESS

Strategic business planning and strategic marketing planning have been emerging, albeit slowly in some cases, as key factors in the achievement of organizational success. At a planning level, marketing communication has come yet further down the development path. Considering the expenditure levels, this might be considered to be somewhat surprising. Of course, many large and successful organizations have produced what have been considered to be sophisticated and effective marketing communications. Even so, there have been relatively few who have viewed their communications holistically. Rather there has been a tendency to look at the individual elements of a promotional mix instead of considering the benefits of taking an integrated and strategic approach to communications planning.

How might we define *integrated marketing communications*? Smith *et al.* (1997) provide a definition based on a strategic approach: 'The strategic analysis, choice, implementation and control of all elements of marketing communications which efficiently, economically and effectively influence transactions between an organization and its existing and potential customers, consumers and clients'.

Shimp (1997) provides a definition which highlights the importance of the communications process:

IMC is the process of developing and implementing various forms of persuasive communications programs with customers and prospects over time. The goal of IMC is to influence or directly affect the behaviour of the selected communications audience. IMC considers all sources of brand or company contacts which a customer or prospect has with the product or service as potential delivery channels for future messages. Further, IMC makes use of all forms of communication which are relevant to the customer and prospects, and to which they might be receptive. In sum, the IMC process starts with the customer or prospect and then works back to determine and define the forms and methods through which persuasive communications programs should be developed.

(Shimp, 1997)

Brannan (1995) bases his perspective of integrating marketing communications on the identification of 'a single, core message which leads to one great creative idea which is implemented across everything we do'.

The benefits that can accrue from developing an integrated approach to marketing communications activities centre to a large extent on the value of building long-term relationships with customers. Marketing communications can play a pivotal role in managing such relationships in establishing 'two-way' mechanisms for exchange of information between parties. Consistency of themes or messages leads to a greater depth of recognition and understanding. It is more likely to achieve not only initial impact and awareness but also create platforms for longer-term communications effectiveness. Cost efficiencies might also arise from taking an integrated approach. Using a single agency to control all aspects of marketing communication, particularly in handling such activities on a multi-national basis, can lead to cost savings and also improve control. Another major benefit lies in in linking communications objectives to marketing and central business objectives. This ensures consistency of understanding throughout an organization.

There exist a number of barriers which can prevent or slow down the process toward integration. These barriers are particularly prevalent in those organizations which are resistant to change in all areas, not just in respect of communications activities. The view of marketing communications in these anachronistic firms is one of a support tactical function often managed by external agencies perhaps specializing in one area such as advertising or PR.

Smith *et al.* (1997) provide a planning framework for marketing communications. This is derived from recognized business and marketing planning models (Table 15.2).

ORGANIZED APPROACH TO MARKETING COMMUNICATIONS: INTERNAL/EXTERNAL

The planning frameworks discussed above require a systematic approach when it comes to organization of communications, both internally and externally.

Table 15.2 A planned approach to marketing communications

Situational analysis	Current position, historical trends
Objectives	Business/marketing/communications
Strategy	Target audiences/positioning, Four Ps
Tactics	Communications/media mix
Action	Budgets/timing
Control	Measuring effectiveness

Adapted from Smith *et al.* (1997)

Internally this suggests a central coordination of communications activities. Historically, promotional functions have grown, along with their respective budgets, to established positions of strength. Thus, there is often infighting between advertising and sales promotion and other areas as these areas seek power in the form of larger budgets. Organizations that are now recognizing the benefits of integrating their marketing communications activities take a more holistic view of management structure. While maintaining responsibilities for functional areas, there is someone operating at a senior level to control the communications activity as a whole. Lately, a number of organizations have been advertising for communications 'czars'.

When it comes to organizing external agencies, again some companies are taking a holistic perspective. In some cases this extends to having one agency that is responsible for all communications activities. In others it entails a coordination of specialist agencies operating on a 'team' basis. This is by no means easy to achieve, given the parochial nature of communications specialists, all of whom consider their activities to be superior in achieving results (see Chapter 7).

Jones (1996) provides examples of agencies taking different approaches toward integration of marketing communications. HHCL & Partners work on all aspects of communications for the soft drink Tango brand. This has included TV and radio advertising featuring direct response, sales promotion, direct marketing, PR events, trade marketing programmes and the creation of one of the first consumer product Internet Web sites. Ogilvy & Mather take a different approach to their work on accounts such as IBM and American Express. They utilize separate companies within their own group. Integration can also be achieved by management of different specialist function agencies by clients.

Marketing communications agencies and consultants are by and large still organized on a functional activity basis. A variety of Institutes and Associations represent advertising, direct marketing, public relations, sales promotion, sponsorship and others. While there is some degree of recognition of the benefits of an integrated approach, there is nevertheless a desire for such bodies to protect their own self-interests. The shift toward integration is being driven more by clients rather than their agencies as they seek measurable success from their communications activities as a whole rather than through the individual parts.

MEDIA SELECTION AND PLANNING

Fragmentation of available media has been one of the driving forces toward the integration of marketing communication activities. This has been based on the extension of existing media such as TV and print, but also on the creation of new media opportunities, particularly those arising from technological developments.

Cable and satellite stations have transformed broadcasting, allowing the targeting of niche markets. There has been a proliferation of hobby and lifestyle magazines which also offer specialist targeting. Technology is dramatically affecting the marketing communications business. This is not just in more obvious fields such as computers but also in areas such as printing where complex and high quality direct mail pieces can be constructed.

New life is also being breathed into less fashionable media such as exhibitions, radio, cinema and outdoor. Independent radio now has a limited number of stations broadcasting on a national basis and cinema has become an increasingly popular leisure activity, particularly amongst younger audiences.

Media selection can play a crucial role in achieving communications effectiveness. British consumers are exposed to around 200 messages per day, which means for a message to be seen, heard or read it must be available in appropriate media. The Playtex Wonderbra campaign was so successful not purely for the creativity of the advertisements but also due to the impact created through the use of eye-catching poster sites.

Further examples of creative media usage include the sponsorship of *The Times* newspaper by Microsoft when launching the Windows 95 software. To announce their new corporate structure in 1997, Cable & Wireless booked all the colour positions in broadsheet newspapers on one day and put their messages on a yellow background to create impact.

An understanding of the target audiences and the careful setting of detailed objectives allow the media planners scope to select the most appropriate media opportunities.

DELIVERING COMMUNICATIONS EFFECTIVENESS

How can the success of a marketing communication campaign be measured? This question has bedevilled and challenged marketing communicators for decades, from a client, agency, and academic perspective. Increased sales, market share, improvement in brand awareness, and changes in attitudes or behaviour are all possible dimensions that might be measured.

Exactly what is measured depends on what objectives have been set and what strategies and tactics have been employed to achieve them. The planning processes discussed above recognize the relationship between these key areas. The relationship between the setting of marketing communications objectives and marketing objectives must also be considered when it comes to assessing performance. Product, price or distribution deficiencies can of course render communications efforts worthless.

Developing a better understanding of customers and consumers and the ways in which communications processes work provides a more coherent basis for establishing mechanisms for effectiveness measurement. The relationship between marketing communications activities and sales effects is something of a holy grail for the communicators. The complexities of the communications process and consumer behaviour patterns present a series of challenges to be overcome if the effects of marketing comunications are to be comprehensively understood.

A number of organizations measure viewing, listening and reading statistics of the various available media. More specific research is undertaken by agencies and their clients to provide measures of effectivenss with regard to individual campaigns. Much of this kind of research centres on recall of advertisements being seen, heard or read. The Institute of Practitioners in Advertising have a large databank of case histories which examine the effectiveness of advertising campaigns for a wide variety of brands.

Before summarizing or concluding, it is important to note that each of these marcoms activities is dynamically expansive. The following chapters, 16 through 23, will examine each of the marketing communication or promotional elements in greater detail.

SUMMARY AND CONCLUSION

The relationship between theoretical concepts and the realities of practising marketing communications activities is close. However, there is no guaranteed formula for success. For example, L'eggs (Hanson Corporation) built sales and market share on the basis of advertising and direct mail, the Body Shop based their success on marketing public relations, Avon on in-house party representatives, and Oxford Instruments on personal selling and public relations. However, in relation to the marketing concept, the benefits of attempting to understand the behaviour of customers in purchase decision situations can assist in developing communications which result in demonstrable, measurable outcomes.

In an increasingly competitive environment, communications is playing, and will continue to play, a significant role in achieving marketing performance. This is true not only in the marketing of consumer products and services but also in industrial marketing and business-to-business sectors. Within these scenarios, as expected, differential emphases are placed on elements of the communications mix. It is, however, still an axiomatic requirement to understand the planning, implementation and likely effects of communications activities.

The communications mix has changed considerably over a short period of time. It will continue to change as knowledge of how the communication process works is developed and as new communications opportunities develop. Close attention to the integrative effects of managing communications activities will continue to underpin and improve performance levels from both client and agency perspectives.

Effectiveness measurement techniques will continue to be developed as the pressure on communicators increases to justify continuing high levels of expenditure. Use of new technologies in the communications process and in measuring behavioural outcomes suggests a more interactive approach to marketing communications. This supports the move away from thinking in terms of promoting *to* customers, to communicating *with* them. Arriving at this level of thinking about the application of marketing communications activities may see a quantum leap in performance for those companies prepared to accept the challenge.

DISCUSSION TOPICS

1 Why may marketing organizations' agencies (i.e. particularly advertising agencies) be considering switching attention to either integrated marketing communications or non- traditional approaches?
2 Suggest how organizations may adopt an integrated marketing communications approach. Provide illustrative examples.
3 What factors may influence decisions regarding the selection of marketing communications activities?
4 Illustrate the differences between the way marketing elements *communicate,* and the way promotional elements *promote.*
5 Suggest some examples where media selection has played a significant role in achieving communications effectiveness.
6 Devise an appropriate marketing communications mix for a product of your choice.
7 Delineate and illustrate how marketing communications 'effectiveness' can be evaluated. What roles do objectives play in evaluating effectiveness?
8 Discuss the proposition that communications success can only be achieved by spending large amounts of money.
9 Following Chernatony and Dall-Olmo Riley (1998), how valid is it to argue that well known brands can be 'extended' into any other market sector?
10 Why should advertising, sales promotion, direct marketing and other elements of the communications mix be described as 'functional activities'? What functions do they perform? Are they necessary?

CASE STUDY – CARLING

The beer market and, more noticeably, the lager sectors have undergone major developments in the recent past. This has been reflected in the marcoms domain. Questions such as: who makes the best beer? form an emotive topic for debate wherever in the world you might be! For beer producers, one of their tasks has been to try to persuade consumers that their brands are best. To some extent this has been based on a 'nationalistic' basis. British, Australian, Belgian, American or German? Manufacturers have attempted to use such platforms to enhance their claims. In the UK, of course, there is a 'regional' debate. One of the classic marketing campaigns in recent times has been the launch of Boddingtons, a northern beer, as the national bitter brand for Whitbread. They used the northern connection heavily in positioning the product in the national roll-out.

The lager sectors have seen a shift toward premium branded products. While there has been a gradual shift over a number of years from bitter to lager, the switch to stronger, bottled and canned, individually branded products has been more recent. This has led the major volume brewers such as Bass and Whitbread to take stock of their marketing activities and their use of marketing communications.

Carling Black Label has been the successful volume lager brand produced by Bass for a number of years. It has benefited over time as the switch in consumer preference from bitter to lager has gained momentum. This structural change in the market has been highlighted by an increased demand for lager products by younger drinkers. The shift toward bottled and canned products has been driven by higher consumption of beer at home rather than in pubs and bars.

In terms of marketing communications, Carling Black Label represents one of the most successful uses of advertising to build a brand into a market leader that the sector has ever seen. 'I bet he drinks Carling Black Label . . .' has become one of advertising's most memorable straplines. As the market has changed due to the factors noted above, the Black Label brand has come under pressure and has led Bass to take a critical look at their marketing communications activities. What emerged from this is an illustrative example of a more modernistic approach to communications, moving away from the largely exclusive use of brand advertising towards an integrated marketing communications strategy.

The most notable evidence of the changes that have begun to take place centres on the use of sponsorship as the 'lead' marketing communications activity. This has provided the platform for developing a whole range of communications and marketing initiatives. The sponsorship involves the UK's top football competition which is now well known as the FA Carling Premiership. Carling's communications effectiveness has been further aided by the success of the competition as a whole. Games are attracting increasing gates and a more affluent customer. This latter point is of some significance as the brand attempts to reposition itself as a premium rather than a mass volume brand. As well as linking sponsorship with a range of other communications activities, including advertising and sales promotion, it has also provided an opportunity for other supporting marketing activities. The kit worn by players carries the Carling Premiership logo, as do replica kits sold to fans. Delivery vehicle liveries all make significant reference to the sponsorship. All product packaging is designed to illustrate the links. The competition provides opportunities for corporate hospitality to be provided to trade customers at specific games.

A new, higher-strength lager brand, 'Premier', has recently been launched with the name deriving from the football sponsorship. Most recently Bass have announced that they are dropping the words 'Black Label' from the product in order to focus more specifically on developing the Carling brand identity.

Other sponsorship activities are being developed, for example in the support of rock music events. Carling Premier recently sponsored the tour by the group Supergrass and have organized regionally sponsored pub music competitions.

(Source: Author)

REFERENCES

A.C. Nielsen.MEAL (1997) *IPA data pack – advertising education award 1997/98*, Institute of Practitioners in Advertising, September.

Brannan, T. (1995) *A Practical Guide to Integrated Marketing Communications*, London: Kogan, 13.

De Chernatony, L. and Dall'Olmo Riley, F. (1998) 'Expert practitioners' views on the role of brands: Implications for marketing communications', *Journal of Marketing Communications*, 4(2): 87–107.

Jones, H. (1996) 'United Front', *Marketing Week*, 20 September.

Linton, I. and Morley, I. (1995) *Integrated Marketing Communications*, Oxford: Butterworth–Heinemann.

Shimp, T.A. (1997) *Advertising, Promotion and Supplemental Aspects of Integrated Marketing Communications*, Fort Worth: The Dryden Press, 10–12.

Smith, P., Berry, C. and Pulford, A. (1997) *Strategic Marketing Communications*, London: Kogan Page, 119, 167.

Zenith Media (1996) 'Global advertising expenditure forecasts', *Financial Times*, 16 December, 15.

16

ADVERTISING

Keith Crosier

CHAPTER AIMS

- to define advertising, clearly and unequivocally
- to establish the nature of advertising objectives
- to examine objective-setting in practice
- to assess the implications for measurement of effectiveness
- to examine the relationship between advertisers and audiences
- to evaluate the standard model of how advertising works
- to assess its influence on effectiveness-testing procedures
- to examine the principles and practice of budgeting for advertising
- to explain the processes of creative strategy development and media planning
- to provide a template for the writing of an advertising plan
  and, in general
- to provide a guide to sources of further information

ILLUSTRATION

The short case history which follows illustrates a unique degree of continuity and consistency in British advertising. The direct quotations are taken from an in-house publication, *The BMW Breakthrough: 15 years of BMW Advertising*.

The ultimate driving machine

Until 1979, BMW was a rather exotic niche product in the British car market, sold by concessionaires. If it was generally familiar at all, it would be as one of the makers of that sixties phenomenon, the bubble car. In 1997, the brand's popularity had surpassed that in its home market, and Britain had become the only country in which it was accorded more prestige than Mercedes. It is generally agreed that advertising has been a major contributor to this history of achievement.

In 1980, the company took control of its brand in the UK by setting up BMW (GB) Ltd in Bracknell, and appointed the London advertising agency WCRS. They have held the account ever since, producing 300 press advertisements, 40 television commercials and a series of poster campaigns, which have won an unprecedented number of awards. The relationship is also the source of a famous advertising aphorism, for it was in that year on a visit to Munich headquarters that Robin Wight, the W in WCRS, said 'I would like to interrogate your product until it confesses to its strengths.' The outcome has been a tradition of headlines that distil complex engineering attributes into memorable propositions: the fried egg on the bonnet, the cocktail glass on the cylinder head, the saloon balanced on the windscreen of the coupé, to name only the best known of them.

Salient facts about the brand may surprise the uninitiated. Its UK market share of just over 3 per cent in 1997 was well ahead of Honda's 2.5, and in a quite different league from Mercedes at 1.9, Volvo at 1.8, Audi at 1.6 and Saab at well below 1 per cent. There are curently almost half a million BMWs on British roads; three-quarters of which are the lowly 3-series. The average age of its drivers is 46, rising to 53 for the Compact version, which is especially popular among women and retired men. Despite this, or perhaps because of it, the WCRS creative strategy has generated what Wight calls 'an automotive icon'. It is redolent of 'suave authority' and 'cool restraint', according to style journalist Deyan Sudjic, and demonstrates 'the art of making products that have the characteristics of an English butler', in the words of the famous designer Dieter Rams. This has been achieved by an understated flair which never compromises either the client's house style (the 'roundel' plus the signature line always in capitals, always black and always the BMW Neue Helvetica typeface) or the 'central brand values of exclusivity, advanced technology and performance' (contrasting interestingly with the buyers' own choice criteria of reliability, style and top speed). Only once has an identifiable human being ever featured in the advertising, and that was a small boy.

Media strategy is carefully integrated with the creative imperative. WCRS pioneered the notion of the first double-page spread in Sunday colour supplements as a prime position, and always has the first slot in television commercial breaks. They have recently conceived the idea of 20-second 'television posters'. Unlike conventional cut-down versions of longer commercials, these are intended to be 'read' by the audience just as a 48-sheet poster would be. The overall aim has single-mindedly been to 'communicate the same core values' as the creative strategy.

The challenge for the future will be to maintain the required exclusivity now that a minority marque has become a middle-market brand, and acquired Rover. BMW (GB) knows that consistency and continuity will assume even more importance. As their managing director remarked: 'I very much hope that WCRS will be with us to see what the next fifteen years will bring for BMW.'

WHAT ADVERTISING IS AND ISN'T

Advertising is unique among the ingredients of the marketing communications mix in that it, along with packaging, forms part of the average citizen's everyday life. Most people find their jobs and houses by way of classified advertisements in newspapers. Most, if asked, could almost certainly call to mind television commercials for the breakfast cereal consumed that morning, the brand of toothpaste used, and the model of car driven to work. If a person needs to dispose of an outdated PC or an old bike, a 'small ad' is usually placed. Consequently, everyone has a good idea what 'advertising' is and does not normally ask for it to be formally defined. As a result of familiarity, there are as many definitions of advertising as there are authors who have written on the subject. Here follows yet another:

> communication via a recognizable *advertisement*
> placed in a definable *advertising medium*,
> guaranteeing delivery of an unmodified *message*
> to a specified *audience* in return for a published
> *rate* for the space or time used

The key feature of this definition is that it allows us, by replacing the italicized descriptors with alternatives appropriate to other ingredients of the marketing communications mix, to recognize that advertising belongs to a family of means to a common end and yet to explain just how it differs from its relatives. Their shared aim is, of course, to communicate a message to an audience for a marketing purpose: 'marketing communications' for short.

To discuss comparisons and contrasts with every other family member would be to intrude on other contributors' territory, but one demands special attention here. Many business-to-business marketers use the term 'publicity' to describe what a consumer-product brand manager would call advertising. Furthermore, the word for advertising in three major world languages – French, Portuguese and Spanish – is the direct equivalent of 'publicity'. To confuse the matter even further, commentators routinely describe publicity as 'free advertising' and contrast it with 'paid advertising'. These two marketing communications methods are in fact fundamentally different from one another. A marketing communications manager opting for a *publicity* initiative as part of a marketing public relations campaign, for instance, takes the significant risk that the message of a press release to the news media (generally the advertising media in their other role) will receive an editorial 'spin' and thus be transmitted to the target readership in *modified* form. That cannot happen to an advertisement. If sloppy vocabulary is allowed to obscure the fact that the price of 'paid' advertising buys the control that 'free' publicity sacrifices, the result can be a very risky tactical decision.

It is often assumed that publicity can be 'bought' by taking advertising space in a newspaper or magazine. On the contrary, a strong professional etiquette maintains watertight doors between the editorial and advertising functions. In 1994, *Cosmopolitan* responded firmly to one such allegation from an unexpected source by issuing a statement that 'the marketing manager quoted was incorrect in his/her assumption that spending a significant amount on advertising gives the right to demand editorial coverage . . . [which is] judged purely on its relevance and interest to our magazine's 2.3 million readers'.

WHAT ADVERTISING CAN AND CAN'T DO

Advertising takes a more remote approach to its target audience than many other ingredients of the marketing communications mix, and is thus unlikely to be able to clinch a sale except in the special case of *direct-response* advertisements. It is nowadays generally agreed that its primary role is longer-term brand-building, which it can do by:

- building awareness
- conveying information
- telling a story
- establishing an identity
- creating a predisposition.

Those are general, common aims for advertising as an activity. Specific campaigns need more precise objectives. It is a sound general principle that these should be established as a prelude to planning and implementation. More particularly, assessment of campaign effectiveness depends upon the existence of formal objectives as benchmarks with which measures of performance can be compared. This point will be taken up later. It is therefore disturbing that so many case histories disclose a careless approach to this crucial task, or even hint at post-hoc rationalization.

Workable advertising objectives need to be:

- debated
- explicit
- precise
- specific
- calibrated
- measurable.

The first of these criteria requires that all those with a legitimate interest in the aims of the eventual campaign have an opportunity to influence the content of the objectives during the campaign planning process. That list would include as a minimum: corporate planners; board directors whose portfolio includes advertising; senior managers with executive responsibility for sales, production, distribution and pricing; advertising agency client service managers, account planners and media planners; those who will specify and implement procedures for assessing campaign effectiveness. The second criterion further requires that the outcome of this process of debate is formally recorded and disseminated. That record becomes a vital control document for two purposes in particular. It is a fixed point of reference during subsequent campaign development, serving to keep the process on target and, if necessary, to resolve differences of opinion between client and agency with respect to details of the execution. It is also the starting point for the design of appropriate research methods for pre-testing campaign strategy and post-testing its effectiveness. The explicit objectives derived from debate must be precise in the sense that they are more than vague statements of a general aspiration. An example from a published case history of advertising effectiveness manifestly lacks the required precision: 'to position Black Magic as the ultimate'. It does have value in capturing the overriding strategic *goal* at a time when the brand needed to redefine itself in a changing marketplace, but would have been of no practical use to the interested parties identified above unless elaborated by altogether more precise tactical *objectives*. When precision is lacking in objective setting, this reflects a lack of discipline, creating a vacuum likely to be filled with ambiguous creative media outcomes.

The precise objectives must furthermore be specific in the sense that they are capable of being achieved by the advertising campaign on its own. An example from a published case history of advertising effectiveness requires advertising to: increase consumer awareness; rebuild trade confidence in the brand; motivate and support the trade; increase brand sales; increase market share. To put this criterion in perspective, consider how likely an advertising manager would be to accept sole responsibility for the failure of a campaign to achieve any but the first of those five objectives. In practice, advertising is repeatedly charged with one non-specific task in particular, to raise sales volume apparently single-handedly.

The fourth criterion requires that an objective offers more guidance than 'increase consumer awareness' in the first case example, one which is in fact very commonly encountered in practice. Suppose that it were to be applied to the advertising of this textbook. The task of preparing a brief for campaign development or effectiveness testing would demand answers to the following supplementary questions, at least. Awareness of *what* about it? Among *whom* in particular, and *where*? Increased by *how much*, against what baseline? By *when*? When that degree of precision is absent in practice, unimaginative or downright inappropriate creative and media solutions are apt to fill the vacuum, and test results tend to be equivocal at best.

Lastly, any performance characteristic implied by an advertising objective should ideally be amenable to measurement by realistically available research methods. There are long-established and well-understood research procedures for measuring the change in consumer awareness required by the specimen just cited, for example. The same goes for knowledge of a product's attributes, perceptions of its benefits, attitudes towards acquiring it, intentions to do so, and the like. Practical problems begin to arise when objectives are phrased in such a way as to require the advertising to 'reposition' the product, to modify its 'image', to 'convince' non-users of potential benefits, or to 'induce' trial. Such performance characteristics are difficult to measure, mainly because they are multidimensional. Strategists would do better to concentrate their efforts on more measurable *intermediate* effects, such as perceptions, attitudes and predispositions.

HOW ADVERTISING WORKS

The working definition of advertising takes it as read that the purpose of communicating messages to target audiences is to persuade them to revise negative opinions or renew positive beliefs, and ultimately act accordingly. The very existence of a large and thriving advertising business world-wide implies a belief that advertisements can achieve this effect, at least frequently enough to make the investment of effort and money worthwhile. This raises a crucial question: how do they do so? The answer is by no means straightforward.

The very people who execute advertising campaigns are the least likely to provide an answer. As a respected senior practitioner remarks in a professional guide to best practice, they 'may follow very varied "mental models" but they too seldom articulate them' (Broadbent, 1995). When they do, it is very likely to be recognizable as a member of a family of verbal paradigms proposing that advertisements exert their influence by precipitating a progressive sequence of behavioural responses in the individual. This 'hierarchy of effects' explanation made its appearance in the literature more than 70 years ago. A textbook by a famous American market researcher of the day included a conceptual framework for testing the effectiveness of advertisements, which argued that 'to be effective, an advertisement must be . . . seen, read, believed, remembered, and acted upon' (Starch, 1923). That initiative was closely followed by another practical framework in a textbook, this time offered as a guide to the effective delivery of a sales pitch: the celebrated 'AIDA' (Strong, 1925). It was soon transferred to the formulation of advertising strategy, and interpreted as proposing that successive exposures to an advertising campaign had to move an individual from initial attention to the message through interest in the product and desire for it to eventual action. The title of the model is an acronym composed from the initial letters of those four progressive stages.

After a considerable hiatus, the generic description 'hierarchy of effects' was coined in an article in the influential *Journal of Marketing*, to describe 'a model for predictive measurement of advertising effectiveness' (Lavidge and Steiner, 1961). It proposed a progression from initial awareness through acquisition of knowledge about the product, development of a liking and then a preference for it, to conviction that it should be acquired and eventual action. In the same year, another model intended as a framework for the measurement of effectiveness was published in a monograph for the Association of National Advertisers in New York (Colley, 1961). Bearing the name DAGMAR, an acronym derived from the title of the monograph, it proposes a progression from unawareness to awareness and thence through comprehension and conviction to action. The only further progress in the subsequent three decades has been a relatively little-noticed article with the telling subtitle 'Keeping the hierarchy concept alive' (Preston and Thorson, 1984). This greatly expanded version has at its heart a familiar progression of effects: exposure to the advertisement, followed by awareness of its elements, leading to perception and evaluation of the product, leading in turn to search, trial and adoption. It was the first to separate responses to the advertisement from those to the message and to the product. In the description of AIDA, above, an assumption had to be made that 'interest' and 'desire' relate to the product rather than to the advertisement itself.

Table 16.1 proposes a consolidation of the five paradigms, and could accommodate other family members not reported here. The two left-hand columns arrange the levels of response in a vertical hierarchy and assign labels mostly taken from the established variants. They take different perspectives on the process by describing respectively what the advertisement 'should achieve' and how the audience 'should respond'. For example, it should communicate and the audience should comprehend. These two schemes have historically been mixed together in a single model. The third column relates the new scheme to the generic 'cognitive–affective–conative' (C-A-C) pattern of response to stimuli other than advertisements. Cognitive responses are the outcome of thinking about what is happening, affective responses result from an emotional reaction to the stimulus, and conative responses involve consequent actions. Colloquially, these three levels are summed up by the vividly explanatory 'think–feel–do'.

Table 16.1 A consolidation of the hierarchical models of advertising effect, 1923–84

Performance characteristic	Required response	C-A-C equivalent
Motivation	Action	Do
Persuasion	Conviction	Feel
Empathy	Sympathy	Feel
Communication	Comprehension	Think
Involvement	Interest	Think
Impact	Attention	Think

The hierarchy-of-effects hypothesis has the obvious appeal of being an intuitively reasonable representation of a presumed cause-and-effect relationship, but has in fact been subjected to continuous theoretical criticism (see Schultz and Schultz, 1998) over the past 30 years. This began with a widely reported evaluation of Lavidge and Steiner's model by Palda (1966). Reporting that he could find no conclusive evidence in the literature for the proposition that affective change necessarily preceded conative change, rather than resulting from it, he called into question the very sequence of the hierarchy of effects. Ray (1973) subsequently suggested that three variants could occur in practice: 'learning' (think–feel–do), 'dissonance attribution' (do–feel–think) and 'low involvement' (think–do–feel). A decade later, Ehrenberg (1988) argued that a continuous series of empirical studies in Britain indicated that an 'attention–trial–reinforcement' or ATR paradigm was evident, particularly in the case of certain categories of staple product. The decision to try a new product was arrived at somewhat arbitrarily. Provided the experience was not unsatisfactory, a stable pattern of subsequent reselection developed, during which users deliberately paid attention to advertising for the product in order to rationalize the choice. This would seem to be a fourth variation on the C-A-C theme: do–think–feel.

Palda furthermore reasoned, *a priori*, that progression from one type of response to the next does not mean that the probability of eventual action has necessarily been increased. As he put it, Lavidge and Steiner's model did not represent a true 'hierarchy of prepotency'. A third serious weakness of this standard model is the observation that it is simply descriptive rather than explanatory. That is, it may be able to describe *what* happens in a limited range of circumstances, but certainly cannot explain *why* individuals respond to advertisements in the ways it is hypothesized that they do.

One might expect that these theoretical shortcomings would inhibit practical application of the hierarchy of effects as a framework for decision making. On the contrary, case histories show that campaign objectives are repeatedly couched in terms familiar from Table 16.1. Therefore, and despite comments from elsewhere, it is recognized that AIDA and its kin are still the implicit conceptual underpinning of much of present-day advertising strategy. Indeed, it must be conceded that a deficient but codified basis for objective-formulation is preferable to no common framework at all, or any of the new behavioural variants (see Schultz, 1998). That must remain the case, of course, until marketing academics are able to produce a better model which practitioners can understand and are willing to use. Evidence that this state of affairs is no closer than it ever has been, in Europe at least, is to be found in two authoritative reviews commissioned by the Advertising Association (McDonald, 1992; Frantzen, 1994). If progress towards that better model is in fact made within the shelf life of this book, the impetus is likely to originate in the 'planning' discipline within advertising agencies (see Chapter 4) or from the new behavioural approaches promulgated by Schultz and others.

Two academic approaches to the study of communication in general are familiar within this intellectual wing of the advertising business, but not beyond it: semiotics (see Chapter 9) and discourse analysis. The first originated with the Swiss linguist Ferdinand de Saussure at the turn of the century and has been developed as a means of interpreting how people 'deconstruct' visual symbolism and reconstruct it into their own reality. It remains essentially a specialization of French linguists and philosophers, only one author writing in English having so far devoted a whole textbook to semiotic analysis of advertisements, and that 20 years ago (Williamson, 1978). Discourse analysis is a sub-discipline of applied linguistics, which offers a means of explaining how people pick apart verbal messages and construct from them a personal version of the 'real' meaning. This framework has recently been applied to advertising messages by Cook (1992).

Two accessible texts on the application of semiotics, discourse analysis and other promising theoretical frameworks to advertising are Dyer (1982) and Myers (1994), but neither is yet sufficiently familiar among practitioners to have mounted an effective challenge to the hegemony of the hierarchy-of-effects models.

All the theoretical frameworks described so far treat communication and persuasion at the micro level, in terms of the effect that an advertisement may have on one person. Given that advertising campaigns are almost always directed at target audiences rather than individuals, and also that they are typically consumed in a social context rather than in private, a macro focus would clearly be more appropriate. As Broadbent (1997: 46) puts it, 'people *use* or process messages: the results are not always what the advertiser wants, but are decided by the recipient' (see Chapter 8). Thus, the theory of advertising effect will remain deficient until academics or planners turn their attention to its sociological dimension. The way forward will presumably be to search the literature of politics and media studies for transferable principles of mass communication and propaganda.

Before leaving the important issue of how advertising works, a practical caveat must be added to the theoretical shortcomings. Observation suggests that the formulation of campaign strategy typically proceeds on the tacit assumption that messages and images are conveyed to target audiences by one ingredient of the marketing mix only: 'promotion' among McCarthy's 'four Ps', or what this book calls 'marketing communications'. This is to confuse explicit statements with implicit propositions, and deny the human capacity to construct a personal version of reality from any and all information available. In fact, clear messages can be received from the other three Ps. The specification and packaging of the product or service 'positions' it relative to alternative choices; the price asserts that it is 'exclusive' or 'cheap'; the place at which it is on offer indicates the social standing of a user.

If all four elements of the marketing mix are perceived to be speaking with one voice, *synergy* will occur. That is, the communicative effect of the whole will exceed the sum of its parts. The aim at any stage in the development of a marketing communications campaign can quite simply be to reinforce it with consistent messages. If the perception is that the four are speaking with different voices, the task is altogether more challenging: to cut through the confusing cacophony and have its explicit message prevail over all contradictory implications. A microcosm of this situation can recur within the marketing communications mix, particularly if constituent parts are the responsibility of different individuals and a number of specialist agencies are called in to translate strategy into action. It is therefore crucial that the process of planning an advertising campaign includes an analysis of the whole complex of existing communications, explicit and implicit, into which the target audience will fit the messages delivered by the advertisements. The realistic aim must be to avoid counter-synergy, at least, hence the emphasis in this text on integrated approaches.

DOES ADVERTISING WORK?

Knowing how advertising works in principle is not at all the same thing as knowing how well a given advertisement has worked in practice.

The measurement of performance would pose few problems if advertising were a more precise science. Consider the engineering of a lawnmower motor to meet environmental noise-pollution standards. An *objective* is set: to ensure that the mower's performance justifies a claim of low noise levels in use. A *criterion* is established: that the sound level detectable 10 metres from a mower being operated in normal conditions is no more than, say, 70 decibels. A *measuring instrument* is chosen: an audiometer, to be positioned the required distance from the edge of the test strip. *Results* are recorded: an average reading of 67 decibels. Comparing this figure with the criterion produces the *conclusion* that the objective has been met and performance is therefore acceptable. Alas, advertising is not engineering.

It is evident that practitioners find it difficult to set the kind of objectives that can be converted into quantifiable criteria realistically achieveable by advertising alone. The need to do so is clearly stated in the title of an influential article, reprinted in several anthologies of readings: 'Defining Advertising Goals for Measured Advertising Results' (Colley, 1962). Unfortunately, it has been remembered as the acronym of a model of advertising effect proposed in the text, 'DAGMAR', rather than as a pithy statement of a crucial principle of campaign planning and control. Even when the point is taken, advertising campaigns are often required to produce results which are notoriously difficult to measure, such as a new image, a changed mood, or predispositions to respond positively to other stimuli.

An absence of bespoke criteria forces advertisers to fall back on off-the-peg alternatives. One source of these is the standard technology of social research, notably the repertoire of attitude and opinion scales. The results can be post-rationalized as a measure of predisposition to change behaviour, but the causal link only sounds logical. It has never been proved, and often operates the other way round. Furthermore, it is impossible to relate the magnitude of a change in attitude or opinion to the probability of a change in behaviour. The second main source of second-hand measures is the familiar 'hierarchical models of advertising effect'. Since effectiveness is clearly a measure of effect, the reasoning goes, measure the one according to the other. The problem is that the models in question are, as we have seen, simplistic and flawed. Nevertheless, practitioners routinely use the labels on their hierarchical steps as surrogate 'tests' of effectiveness. Each level in the middle column of Figure 16.1 has its associated 'test': survey-based measures of attention and recall; laboratory tests of interest in the details, popular in the textbooks but strangely elusive in the real world; tests of comprehension of the message, less often conducted than logic would suggest; measures of 'liking' for the execution; 'propensity-to-buy' scales; and, of course, the tracking of sales move-ments, which may or may not have something to do with the advertising. By far the most popular are those furthest removed from the top of the hierarchy.

Until the 'doers' improve their objective-setting skills, the 'thinkers' produce a better model of advertising effect, or both, the assessment of effectiveness will remain a dubious business. Against that background, an excellent account of the many methods used in practice is to be found in Brierley (1995: Chapter 13). As this text and chapter goes to press, it is reported that a research study conducted by the research companies TSMS and Taylor Nelson AGB claims to provide 'conclusive evidence' that television viewers who notice a commercial for a product are more likely to buy it than those who do not. Even this interesting finding begs the question *why*, however.

HOW MUCH TO SPEND?

The scope of an advertising campaign is limited by the financial resources available, particularly for allocation to the buying of media space and time. This constraint can have an indirect but crucial impact on the achievement of the campaign objectives.

The amount of money to be spent in a fixed period, generally a year, is formally defined as the 'advertising appropriation', reflecting the fact that it is *appropriated* from the total funds allocated to the marketing effort. It is as likely to be called the 'budget' in practice, but that could be misleading. Although the colloquial meaning is indeed a sum of money available for a particular purpose, a budget is actually a control mechanism, which describes future sources and uses of funds and sets standards for their cost-effective application to predetermined objectives. This section is concerned with the outcome, not the process.

Textbooks conventionally imply that the size of the appropriation is decided by those who have responsibility for spending it. In fact, this is rarely the case. Twenty years ago, Rees (1977) in Britain and Dhalla (1977) in America independently found that advertising managers or brand managers typically made an initial bid in competition with other claimants on marketing funds, or at least provided specific inputs, but that the decision process was notably hierarchical. The heads of each major function within the marketing division then negotiated for their slice of the pie, and the outcome of that competition was scrutinized at board level, where vested interests might result in further negotiation. Almost invariably, the chief executive retained sole authority for approval of the advertising appropriation, and the decision was duly transmitted down the organization to those who would be answerable for using it productively. The generally political nature of the process was confirmed a decade later in Britain by Piercy (1987).

With that proviso, a considerable number of techniques exist for deciding the amount to be spent on advertising, under a potentially confusing variety of names. In fact, they can be grouped into five categories:

- executive judgement
- internal ratios
- external ratios
- modelling and experimentation
- 'objective-and-task'

The application of executive judgement may seem an unacceptably vague and risky approach to such an important decision, but the other options can be disturbingly illogical and highly inflexible. That being so, the accumulated wisdom and intuition of experienced practitioners may be as useful as any formal 'method'. However, the usual descriptions hardly inspire confidence: 'AYCA' (All You Can Afford), 'notional sum', or the 'affordable' approach.

The best known of the internal ratios is the 'A/S (advertising-to-sales) ratio', which sets the appropriation at a given percentage of either last year's sales or this year's forecast. It has the attraction of being a formula, but suffers the serious conceptual flaw that the ratio itself must be decided before the method can be used. In practice, that is normally done either by executive judgment all over again or by the adoption of industry norms, which may not be appropriate to the particular circumstances. Furthermore, it is potentially disastrous to apply this method when sales have been falling. If the assumption is that advertising can generate sales, then spending a constant ratio of a decreasing amount is hardly the way to go about remedying the situation. As the adage observes, numbers drive out reason.

The most familiar of the external ratios is 'competitive parity', which matches the appropriation to the expected spending of the most significant competitor or the prevailing norm, with the aim of buying a fair 'share of voice' in the general advertising hubbub. This crucially assumes that competitors are behaving rationally or the collective wisdom is correct, or both. The more everyone follows everyone else, the less likely that is to be true. Furthermore, the method takes no account of the need for a new entrant to a market to take the risk of disproportionately heavy expenditure to gain a foothold.

The many proprietary modelling and experimentation procedures are of course only as reliable as the formulae on which they are based, and the average practitioner lacks the mathematical sophistication to evaluate those. Using them is in that case rather like buying a pig in a poke from a magician. For a dispassionate review of what is available, see Broadbent (1997: Chapter 8).

The objective-and-task method has won increasing support in recent years on the grounds that it is more 'logical' because it starts with objectives and then calculates the cost of the tasks required to achieve them, rather than starting with a sum of money and then deciding what to do with it. However, as seen, many advertisers have difficulty in articulating precise and measurable objectives. Furthermore, it does not follow that the means of achieving the objectives will be obvious and the costs unequivocal. Practical guides are apt to conclude with the exhortation to 'estimate the required expenditures', a nasty sting in the tail. Nevertheless, this procedure does force decision makers to be more rigorous in their approach to a disturbingly vague science.

A collective weakness of all the common appropriation-setting methods is their focus on short-run profit maximization at the expense of long-term goals. Indeed, the very convention of annual budgeting can encourage unnecessary revision of existing creative and media strategies. The highly effective thematic continuity of the BMW and British Airways campaigns is the exception rather than the rule.

Surveys show that decision makers typically use two procedures, on average, to arrive at the appropriation. Historically, three have dominated practice. Data collected in Britain and America between 1973 and 1985 showed executive judgment narrowly ahead of the A/S ratio, with objective-and-task in third place and the next most popular far behind (Broadbent, 1989). Since 1986, surveys of practice in the USA, Canada, Britain and a number of other European countries suggest that the order has exactly reversed (e.g. Synodinos *et al.*, 1989). This finding has interesting implications in the light of the comments just made about the pitfalls of applying the objective-and-task method in practice.

DELIVERING THE MESSAGE

This section assumes for convenience that responsibility for delivery of the advertising message to the target audience has been delegated to a conventional *full-service advertising agency*. Other possibilities are to use the services of a separate creative specialist, media specialist or both, or to retain the task in-house. It is in fact unusual for advertisers to do their own creative planning and development and very rare indeed for media planning and buying not to be delegated. As an integral part of the campaign development process, the agency distils from the *client brief* an internal *creative brief* and *media brief*, frameworks for the development of the respective strategies. The corresponding functional departments plan independently at first, and ultimately combine their respective proposals into a single, workable *campaign strategy*. Figures 16.1 and 16.3 are specimens of real-life creative and media briefs.

Creative strategy development

This activity converts the *creative brief* into the *creative executions* that become finished print *advertisements* or radio, television and cinema *commercials*. Authoritative descriptions of the development process, as distinct from executional techniques and outcomes, are elusive. There is neither a British textbook nor a professional monograph dealing specifically with it. Interesting expert discussions of advertising creativity are to be found in two edited collections of papers from the Institute of Practitioners in Advertising (Butterfield, 1997: Chapters 4, 7 and 8) and the Account Planning Group (Cooper, 1977: Chapters 4, 5 and 6), but they do not collectively define the means to the end. The framework which follows reflects a personal view

Job No	Date
Client	Product/Service
Project	Media
Budget £ For	Air Date
Size/Timelength	Account Handler

Background	(What has the client done before? And, how has it worked?)
Target audience	(Be specific. Try to give more than just socio-economic groups. E.g. 'malemalt whisky drinkers', 'housewives who work part-time'.)
Objectives	(What does the client realistically expect the ad to do? This could range from: 'sell 100000 items off the page' to 'Change people's negative attitudes towards the product')
Proposition	(To persuade the target audience that............ In no more than one sentence)
Support	(List any important information that backs up our main message)
Tone	(Accurately define the tone of voice required. E.g., humorous, serious, authoritative, dramatic, etc.)
Desired response	(Imagine a spontaneous quote/reaction. E.g. 'I always thought "Brand X" was a foreign import – I didn't know it was handcrafted locally')
Attitudes	(The more information we have about the consumer's pre-conceived ideas the better)
Mandatories	
Requirement	

Date Issued	Planner/GAD
Due Date	D.A.M.
Time Allowance	Creative Director

Figure 16.1 A typical creative brief.

(*Source*: Original from the Leith Agency; John MacDougall (used with permission), tel (44) 0131-557 5840)

of the creative planning process, drawing upon industry seminars and conversations with practitioners. Summarized in Figure 16.2, it assumes that the advertiser has delegated the task to an advertising agency. The sequence is by no means invariable, and the process may be altogether less methodical in practice.

Creative planning is a team operation involving *account planners* and *account managers*, the '*creatives*' themselves, and a representative of the media function. Its aim is to produce advertising which meets the objectives in the client brief, and outflanks the opposition in doing so. It begins with the identification of specifically creative objectives from guidelines in the brief, including a clear statement of the key messages and target audiences. The next stage is likely to be a 'think-tank'

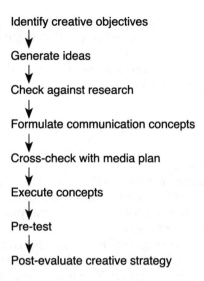

Identify creative objectives

↓

Generate ideas

↓

Check against research

↓

Formulate communication concepts

↓

Cross-check with media plan

↓

Execute concepts

↓

Pre-test

↓

Post-evaluate creative strategy

Figure 16.2 The creative planning process.

session within the creative department, at which the aim will be to 'apply lateral, disruptive thinking to the problem', in the words of a partner in one London agency. This somewhat mystical activity is not explained at all in the advertising literature, but 'brainstorming', 'blue skies groups' and various other techniques are a familiar ingredient of the new-product development process: see, for example, Kotler (1997). It was inspiration by such means that redefined Lucozade as an energy drink for teenagers and the Automobile Association as 'the fourth emergency service'. The raw creative ideas are next subjected to the discipline of scrutiny against a research-based analysis of probable audience responses, typically contributed by the account planner on the team. Survivors are refined into more precise communication concepts, such as that *The Times* is the newspaper for 'changing times' or that travelling by Virgin Atlantic Airways is a way to 'get a life'.

The creative strategy is next matched with the media plan that has been developing in parallel, for there is no point in devising a creative strategy which cannot be executed in the media vehicles capable of reaching the target audience. When compatibility has been achieved, concepts can be converted into creative executions. Evans (1988) provides an expert description of the craft which produces *copy* and *visuals* (words and pictures), then melds them into a finished creative solution, and of the production operations which in turn convert that into advertisements and commercials. Planning teams may take the precaution of pre-testing the outcome on a sample of the target audience and reviewing the strategy in the light of the findings, or may decide to trust the creative development process and back their own judgment. Once the campaign has run, it would be extremely unusual not to conduct a post-test of effectiveness. Findings relevant to creative strategy can be compared with the objectives set at the start of the process, and the conclusions held as an input to the next creative planning cycle.

The lack of published literature on the development process is in marked contrast to the abundance of material on its results, which can yield insights into the planning behind those outcomes. The most useful current source is a series of collections of winning submissions for the Creative Planning Awards (Account Planning Group, 1993, 1995, 1997).

Media planning

This process converts the *media brief* into a *media plan*, specifying the vehicles chosen to deliver the creative strategy to the target audience and the timing of individual *exposures* over the duration of the campaign. The classic British textbook is Broadbent and Jacobs (1984). Beware, however, that the media landscape has changed radically since it was published; the general principles are all that remain valid. There is a thought-provoking review of media planning in a rapidly changing landscape in a 'guide to best practice' from the Institute of Practitioners in Advertising (Butterfield, 1997: Chapter 11), but no textbook-length successor to Broadbent and Jacobs has yet appeared. The framework which follows, summarized in Figure 16.4, draws upon those sources and industry contacts.

Media strategy development, like its creative counterpart, should be a team effort involving *account planners, account managers* and a representative of the creative function, as well as the *media planners* themselves. It is a process of applying objective criteria to the task of allocating the advertising appropriation among the proliferating *media options* available. The aim is to build a *media schedule* that finds the right targets and outflanks the competition, and to do so cost-effectively.

It begins with the extraction from the client brief of specifically media-related objectives and the *media allocation* within the advertising appropriation. The latter

```
* Client:                              * Product:
* Objective(s):
* Who will be the end users?:
* Who will influence the decision?:
* What is the advertising message?:
* Campaign period:
* Budget:
* Regionality:
* Seasonality:
* Commercial length/space size:
* Any constraints:
* Author:                              * Date:
* Others:                              * Date required by:

NB: If possible and applicable, please supply information such as competitors, current
advertising, sales data, creative brief, mandatory requirement, marketing strategy...
```

Figure 16.3 A typical media brief.

(Original from CIA Media Network Scotland: Odile Montfort, (44) 0141-332-3456)

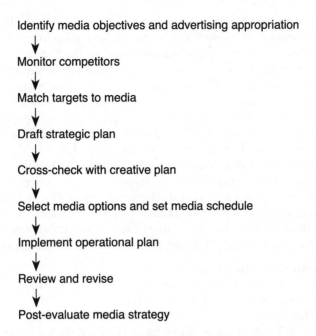

Identify media objectives and advertising appropriation

↓

Monitor competitors

↓

Match targets to media

↓

Draft strategic plan

↓

Cross-check with creative plan

↓

Select media options and set media schedule

↓

Implement operational plan

↓

Review and revise

↓

Post-evaluate media strategy

Figure 16.4 The media planning process.

places a limit on what is practically possible. The former must include a clear 'psychographic' description of the audiences to be reached, for the sophisticated and comprehensive databases built up by industry-wide *media research* over many years can tell planners a great deal about associated *media-consumption characteristics*. The next step is to monitor competitors' media usage, in order to find unoccupied ground in the communication landscape. For example, the agency which launched the Häagen Dazs brand chose the quality press and posters instead of the orthodox medium for ice-cream advertising, television, and thereby caught Unilever off guard for a total investment of less than £500,000.

These preliminaries completed, planners can begin to match audience specifications with the audience-delivery capabilities of the main *media classes*, information which is equally accessible in the media planning network. The national *media mix* in the UK has traditionally been defined as comprising five such classes. They are the so-called 'major media' (press, television, radio, cinema and outdoor), a simplistic categorization which is rapidly becoming outmoded in the face of the well-chronicled 'information explosion'. This issue is explored and the key features of an integrated approach described in Chapter 7. A broad-brush 'strategic plan' can then be prepared, and cross-checked with the creative plan that has been developing in parallel. There is no point in buying a media vehicle which delivers the right audience at a favourable cost if it cannot offer the required creative scope. The BMW case history furthermore makes it clear that the choice of media vehicles can in itself communicate a message which helps the audience to position the brand in its mind.

Once the strategic plan has been debated and agreed, the emphasis shifts to the tactical level. A number of costed media plans and schedules are drawn up, as alternative ways of reaching the target audience within the timescale set by the brief. In practice, the first step towards the choices involved is almost always to feed performance requirements such as 'reach' and 'coverage' into online media selection programs or desktop software packages, the price of both having fallen in recent years to the point that any agency which regularly buys media for its clients must regard computer assistance as an affordable resource. The systems do not make the decisions by themselves, however, for this highly numerate and technologically sophisticated discipline is still highly susceptible to the influence of routine, past experience and industry folklore.

Technological sophistication makes media selection, as distinct from scheduling, appear more complex than it actually is. *Intermedia* and *intramedia* decision making (between and within media classes) is in essence a matter of evaluating available options with respect to a relatively small number of key variables, as follows:

- Target: to whom do we need to talk?
- Message: what do we need to tell them?
- Price: what is the unit cost of space or time?
- Cost: what is the production cost to fill the space and time?
- Creative scope: will the medium allow us to do what we want to?
- Vehicle effect: how will the medium affect the message?
- Audience effect: how does the audience interact with the medium?
- Usability: how easy is it to book and control a campaign?
- Measurability: how easy is it to assess effectiveness?

The outcome of media selection, by whatever means, is a costed operational plan. It is converted into a campaign schedule, in stages, by *media buyers*. These specialists have an encyclopaedic knowledge of 'their' media and the disposition needed to haggle successfully with the hard-nosed representatives of the media 'sales houses' and advertising departments. Bargaining skills are especially important in buying television advertising time, which is effectively auctioned. Although the other media sell their commodity in the normal way, the basic 'rate card' price is subject to a variety of discounts and surcharges. The complexities of media buying are well explained by Brierley (1995: Chapter 8). Because the cost of a schedule reflects deals struck with suppliers, it may vary significantly from the forecast in the operational plan, which is consequently reviewed and if necessary revised at intervals. At the end of the campaign, the planning team will assess the cost-effectiveness of their media strategy, and retain the findings in mind as part of the history influencing each future iteration of the planning cycle.

Examples of media planning in practice can be found in the relevant passages of the winning submissions for the biennial IPA Advertising Effectiveness Awards, published as a series under the generic title Advertising Works (Institute of Practitioners in Advertising, 1981–1997). If the esoteric vocabulary used in those case studies acts as a barrier to understanding the finer points of a particular media strategy, consult the authoritative glossary published by the Media Research Group (1995).

The chicken and the egg

Non-experts encountering the twin disciplines of creative and media strategy formulation sooner or later ask either which 'comes first', or which is the more important of the two. This section has stressed the need to coordinate creative and media strategies at key stages in the respective development processes, to avoid the formulation of incompatible plans. Nevertheless, popular accounts of advertising generally stress the creative aspect. That bias prompted a former Strategic Planning Director of a leading British advertising agency, addressing a recent industry seminar, to set out to 'explode the myth that media is an "add-on" service which lies dormant whilst the brand team are developing creative work . . . and is then called upon to write a plan which delivers the messages to the target audience'. On the contrary, 'a good media brief is as important as a good creative brief. It should excite the planning team into exploring new opportunities to deliver the brand message with impact . . . to be surprised'. In short, the only intellectually proper answer to the popular question is 'it depends', however equivocal that may sound.

PULLING IT ALL TOGETHER: THE ADVERTISING PLAN

Surprisingly, the advertising literature does not provide any more or less standard template for the construction of an overall advertising plan. Figure 16.5 therefore offers a formal framework for the planning, development, implementation and control of an advertising campaign, first proposed as a broader marketing communications plan by Crosier (1994). Integrating the strategic issues discussed in this chapter, it accentuates its role as an action plan by posing a series of questions for the advertising manager or brand manager to answer. This plan will form the basis of the *client brief* to the advertising agency, which is in turn the departure point for the creative and media briefs guiding the planning processes just described.

Filling in the blanks in this pro-forma, it is first of all vital to recognize that providing a statement of the *benefits* the brand can deliver to users will be far more helpful, when the time comes to deliver a brief to the agency, than a strictly internal perspective on the product or service. To do this may be more easily said than done, in practice, for lateral thinking is often required to arrive at answers which will convert into persuasive propositions. A camera is not a sophisticated optical instrument, for instance, but an insurance policy against failing memory. Similarly, a straightforward description of the company or organization needs to be supplemented by a statement about how it wants to be seen by every audience it wants to address. More than that, the plan should ideally explain how it is actually seen. *Identity* is a controllable composite of livery, a trade mark, architecture, product design and so on, which can be faithfully reflected in corporate and brand advertising. *Image*, on the other hand, belongs to individuals in those audiences. Advertising can do no more than influence what they 'imagine' to be true.

Profiles of the audience and the marketplace accompany more obviously controllable variables in Section 1 of the plan, because an advertiser can be selective with respect to the audiences it targets and the market segments it enters. In defining the first of those, *socio-demographic* profiles (such as 'ABC1 males, 18–35,

1 RAW MATERIALS
What are we offering to whom?

1.1 *Product or Service Profile*
Specification: what can it do?
Benefits: what can it offer?
1.2 *Company or Organization Profile*
Specification: what do we do?
Identity: how do we present ourselves?
Image: how are we seen?
1.3 *Audience Profile*
Socio-demographics: who are they, and where?
Psychographics: who do they want to be?
1.4 *Market Profile*
Structure: what does it look like?
Competition: who is there with us?
Dynamics: what's coming?

2 CONSTRAINTS
What is beyond our control?

2.1 *Marketing Mix*
Product policy: what effect on advertising strategy?
Pricing policy: what effect on advertising strategy
'Place' policy: what effect on advertising strategy?
2.2 *Givens*
Precedents: what is traditional?
Mandatories: what is compulsory?
2.3 *Budget*
Appropriation: what funds are available?
Allocations: how and where are they to be spent?
Control: how will cost-effectiveness be monitored?

3 OBJECTIVES
What do we need to achieve?

3.1 *Goals:*   what are the overall, long-term aims?
3.2 *Targets:*   what are the intermediate aims of the plan?
3.3 *Criteria:*   how will communication effectiveness be measured?

4 STRATEGY
How will we achieve our objectives?

4.1 *Communication:*   what do we want to say?
4.2 *Creative:*   how do we want to say it?
4.3 *Media:*   how will we deliver the message to the audience?

5 TIMETABLE
How will our strategy become a campaign?

5.1 *Time scale*   how soon must the objectives be met?
5.2 *Schedule:*   what needs to happen when?

6 IMPLEMENTATION
How will the campaign be managed?

6.1 *Authority:*   who can say yes or no?
6.2 *Responsibility:*   who will coordinate it?
6.3 *Delegation:*   what will be subcontracted?
6.4 *Procedures:*   how will we keep track of progress?
6.5 *Evaluation:*   how will we measure results?

Figure 16.5 The advertising plan.

in the Granada ITV Region') are only the starting point. Recipients of a subsequent brief will find much better clues to meaningful propositions and effective communication vehicles in *psychographic* segmentation schemes, which describe audiences in terms of their patterns of living, self-image and social aspirations. 'Yuppies', 'generation X', and 'empty nesters' are familiar examples of the many *lifestyle* categories in the sophisticated databases maintained by proprietary market research providers, of which ACORN Lifestyles, Mosaic, Sagacity and VALS are the most widely used. They can be cross-indexed for media selection purposes with the analyses of media consumption provided by TGI (Target Group Index), the NRS (National Readership Survey) and others. The key issue with respect to the marketplace which contains the target audience is that an advertising campaign is a future, continuous, evolving activity. It is therefore important to forecast medium-term *changes* in that environment, and plan for contingencies accordingly.

Two of the constraints specified in Section 2 of the plan have already been discussed: messages sent out by the other three Ps of the marketing mix, with which advertising must be consistent, and limits imposed on creative and media strategies by board-level decisions about how much can be spent. The precedents and 'mandatories' it further specifies could be interpreted respectively as historical baggage and client interference in the creative process. On the contrary, preserving enough *continuity* over time and *consistency* from campaign to campaign is the key to sustaining a dialogue with the audience, rather than periodically issuing communiqués. The saga unfolding in a linked series of British television campaigns for Nescafé Gold Blend strikingly demonstrates the former quality, while BMW press advertising shows exactly how the specifying of manadatory elements can achieve a degree of consistency (and continuity) which is quite unique, at least among high-profile national advertisers. Procedures for determining the size of the advertising *appropriation* have already been described. The funds thus available must then be *allocated* to a variety of specific uses, such as the buying of media or paying for ancillary services of one kind and another. The sub-heading *control* reminds us that the very process of budgeting demands accountability for cost-effectiveness in the spending of those allocations. Broadbent (1997) addresses this key theme in an important handbook, *Accountable Advertising*, written for the Incorporated Society of British Advertisers and the Institute of Practitioners in Advertising.

Moving to Section 3, issues related to the setting of goals and targets have been discussed in *What advertising can and can't do*, and the measurement of effectiveness in *Does advertising work?*. Answers to the questions in Sections 4 and 5 will duly become, in a client brief, the starting point for creative development and media planning, the subject matter of *Delivering the message*. The fact that the stated *time scale* is typically a year reflects budgetary conventions, rather than communication logic, and raises two issues. First, the average time-lag between consuming the advertising and consuming the product (or not) may be more than 12 months in particular markets, in which case the objectives set in Section 3 must be realistically attainable within that period or the *measurement time scale* must be different from the campaign duration fixed by the budget. Second, annual planning reviews can in practice encourage deliberate *discontinuity* from year to year and thereby militate against the maintenance of dialogue with the audience. Cases in point are not hard to detect.

Finally, Section 6 specifies important practical parameters in the eventual *management* and *control* of the planned campaign.

SUMMARY AND CONCLUSION

Advertising is the one ingredient of the marketing communications mix which has always been part of everyday life. It nevertheless speaks to its audience less directly than several of the others, and consequently should not normally be expected to clinch the sale. A longer-term brand-building effect is a more realistic expectation. More specific objectives within that general aim are often found in practice to be unsatisfactory when tested against six key requirements listed in this chapter. This has clear implications for subsequent assessment of campaign effectiveness. Typical practitioners furthermore define the expected effect of advertising in terms of a so-called model which will be 75 years old at the millennium, has been subject to continuous conceptual criticism since the 1960s, and takes a view of the advertiser–audience relationship which is far too unilateral for a modern society. Since effectiveness defines the presence or absence of a required effect, this state of affairs also has worrying implications for the measurement of campaign performance. New theory is urgently needed.

What an advertising campaign can achieve depends significantly on the amount available to be spent on it. All textbooks describe a variety of procedures for establishing the budget, reviewed here, but it is likely in practice that managers will be awarded an 'appropriation' from total marketing funds, rather than 'setting the budget' themselves. The campaign strategy which can then be planned comprises 'creative' and 'media' elements. Typically, corresponding sets of specific guidelines are derived from the advertising brief, developed independently by specialist teams, and brought together again to define the message and the messenger. This chapter has described formal frameworks for managing the process efficiently. The advertising brief is in turn a distillation of a formal advertising plan. In the surprising absence of an industry standard, this chapter has concluded by proposing a 20-item template for its construction.

Finally, readers with a particular interest in the practice of advertising will find readable and thought-provoking accounts in two books not so far mentioned: Bullmore (1991) and Fletcher (1992). Both authors are industry gurus. Jeremy Bullmore began his career as a trainee copywriter with the J. Walter Thompson agency and stayed with them for 33 years, as Chairman from 1976 to 1987. He is also a past chairman of the Advertising Association. Winston Fletcher is Chairman of Bozell Europe, a network of advertising agencies in 20 countries, and a past chairman of the Institute of Practitioners in Advertising (IPA). Both are profilic authors and their books are worth reading.

DISCUSSION TOPICS

1 What are the strategic characteristics that distinguish advertising from the other ingredients of the marketing communications mix?
2 Does the Internet qualify as an advertising medium? If so, should its exploitation

be entrusted to advertising agency media and creative specialists, or to cyber-communication experts?

3 Evaluate this real-life suite of advertising objectives for one brand:
- To reverse volume and share decline
- To grow volume sales
- To increase the brand's consumer strengths, including awareness of and trust in the brand; loyalty to the brand; desirability of the brand particularly amongst the young
- To deter competitive launch
- What do you think the brand might be?

4 Assess the relative merits of the main methods for fixing the size of the advertising appropriation.

5 What is the proper role for research in the creative development process?

6 Do computers remove imagination and inspiration from the media planning process? If so, does it matter?

7 Which comes first, creative strategy or media strategy? Why?

8 The slogan *Manchester: we're up and going* and the symbol accompanying it were withdrawn after a very short life, amid widespread criticism. What reasons do you think might explain its failure to achieve what *Glasgow's Miles Better* and Mr Happy did?

9 'The Ad-Fluent Society' was a research report published by the Leo Burnett advertising agency. What does the title suggest about the conclusions that will be drawn within? What are the implications for practitioners?

10 Draft an advertising plan for the BMW Compact.

CASE STUDY

The following vignette is based on a submission to the IPA (Institute of Practitioners in Advertising) Awards for 1986. It described a total marketing communications campaign, over two years, but we concentrate here on the advertising dimension. It will be instructive to read the case against the framework of the advertising plan proposed in this chapter, particularly with respect to objective-setting and effectiveness-measurement. Whatever your conclusions, there is no disputing that the civic slogan it devised became something of a legend in its own lifetime, the influence of which is still felt during the development of corporate advertising for civic organizations elsewhere.

Reshaping the image of a city: How Glasgow became 'Miles Better'

It was in late 1982 that the founder of what was then Scotland's third-largest advertising agency approached the Lord Provost of Glasgow with an idea for a strategy to reverse contemporary perceptions of the city in the rest of Britain and beyond. At that time, media interest in the plight of post-industrial urban conurbations had shaped an unequivocal image of a city on its knees, characterized by multiple deprivation, endemic violence, chronic unemployment, and the steady migration of its citizens to better places. The assumption had long been made (though never actually tested) that this was why vacant factories and offices mostly remained empty, while few tourists visited a city on the edge of the Highlands and a mere half-hour from 'the bonnie, bonnie banks of Loch Lomond'. In fact, the city had always had an imposing centre and acres of green space. It furthermore had a vibrant popular culture, and was also the home of Scottish Opera, the Scottish Ballet and the Royal Scottish National Orchestra. It was already moving forward vigorously on a number of economic and social fronts. The key advertising objective was therefore defined as 'to show target audiences why Glasgow is a better place than it was, and than they think it is'.

The first of those audiences to be tackled was Glaswegians, for it was reasoned that there was little chance of persuading the world beyond if the citizens themselves were not convinced. If they were, however, they could in effect become a sales force for the city, adding considerable leverage to an inevitably modest campaign chest. Fund-raising plus matched financing from the Scottish Development Agency resulted in the City having to meet only 10 per cent of the eventual £450,000 budget. The second key audience, geographically, was South-East England, where 30 per cent of the national population contained 46 per cent of its ABC1 households, according to TGI data, and where negative images were particularly strong.

The whole strategy was built around the proposition that 'Glasgow's Miles Better', backed by the Mr Happy character created by Roger Hargreaves. The slogan deliberately begged the questions *than what* or *than when*, while the symbol hinted that Glaswegians had plenty to be glad about and might even be amused by the misconceptions of outsiders. Indeed, many people misread the caption from the start as 'Glasgow smiles better'. The basic proposition was delivered by outdoor advertising and a variety of sales promotion activities, and the factual foundation explained by a publicity drive and press advertising targeting the 1.1 million ABC1 readers of three Scottish newspapers. By the time the campaign was launched in the south, in late 1984, the findings of baseline research were available to shape a strongly show-and-tell creative strategy, delivered by a burst of advertising in six national magazines. The symbol and slogan were meanwhile to be seen on 400 bus sides in Glasgow and 1000 in London, 200 Glasgow bus shelters, 200 taxi doors in Glasgow and 1500 in London, and 750 London Underground poster sites. They even appeared on Edinburgh bus sides during the Festival.

By mid-1983, Mr Happy had appeared in office and shop windows throughout the city and one car sticker had been distributed for every two citizens, many of whom demonstrated their involvement by taking the scissors to them to add their own word plays to the message. Further afield, however, research in early 1984 showed that Glasgow was still scoring worst of six British cities with respect to four out of six negative image statements, and second-worst on the other two. It did little better with respect to 13 positive statements, and came just behind Liverpool overall. When the research was replicated just less than a year later, responses to the negative statements had improved by 5.8 percentage points on average, and those to the positive ones by 9.6 points. Between 1984 and 1986, the campaign earned a laudatory 20-page review in *The Architect's Journal*, was credited with 'an extraordinary outburst of civic pride' in a six-page analysis by *The Sunday Times*, and featured in *The Economist* and *Wall Street Journal*. The Greater Glasgow Tourist Board reported a 62 per cent increase in enquiries during 1985. A bulletin from the Fraser of Allander Institute expressed the opinion in 1986 that 'the positive images fostered by the Miles Better campaign were a powerful antidote to the negative images which act as a strong deterrent to potential visitors'. In 1990, Glasgow took its turn as European City of Culture, characteristically billing itself as the 'cultural capital of Europe'.

Today, the success of this campaign has been such that outsiders now know far more than they did about Glasgow, and most are surprised that it ever sat so low in the league table of British cities. Meanwhile, several others have followed its slogan-and-symbol lead, but none has yet been able to achieve comparable results.

REFERENCES

Account Planning Group (1993, 1995, 1997) *Creative Planning > Outstanding Advertising*, Vols 1–3, London: The Account Planning Group.

Brierley, S. (1995) *The Advertising Handbook*, London: Routledge.

Broadbent, S. (1989) *The Advertising Budget: The Advertiser's Guide to Budget Determination*, Henley-on-Thames: NTC Publications.

Broadbent, S. (1995) *Best Practice in Campaign Evaluation*, London: Institute of Practitioners in Advertising.

Broadbent, S. (1997) *Accountable Advertising*, Henley-on-Thames: Admap Publications.

Broadbent, S. and Jacobs, B. (1984) *Spending Advertising Money*, 4th edn, London: Business Books.

Bullmore, J. (1991) *Behind the Scenes in Advertising*, Henley-on-Thames: NTC Publications.

Butterfield, L. (ed.) (1997) *Excellence in Advertising: The IPA Guide to Best Practice*, Oxford: Butterworth–Heinemann.

Colley, R.H. (1961) *Defining Advertising Goals for Measured Advertising Results*, New York: Association of National Advertisers.

Colley, R.H. (1962) 'Squeezing the waste out of advertising', *Harvard Business Review*, 40, September/October: 76–88.

Cook, G. (1992) *The Discourse of Advertising*, London: Routledge.

Cooper, A. (ed.) (1997) *How to Plan Advertising*, 2nd edn, London: Cassell.

Crosier, K. (1994) 'Promotion', in M.J. Baker (ed.) *The Marketing Book*, 3rd edn, Oxford: Butterworth–Heinemann, Chapter 21, 491–2.

Dhalla, N.K. (1977) 'How to set advertising budgets', *Journal of Advertising Research*, 17, October: 11.

Dyer, G. (1982) *Advertising as Communication*, London: Routledge.

Ehrenberg, A.S.C. (1988) *Repeat Buying: Facts, Theory and Applications*, 2nd edn, London: Charles Griffin.

Evans, R. (1988) *Production and Creativity in Advertising*, London: Pitman.

Fletcher, W. (1992) *A Glittering Haze: Strategic Advertising in the 1990s*, Henley-on-Thames: NTC Publications.

Franzen, G. (1994) *Advertising Effectiveness: Findings from Empirical Research*, Henley-on-Thames: NTC Publications.

Institute of Practitioners in Advertising (1981–1997) *Advertising Works*, vols 1–9. The current edition is: Duckworth, G. (ed.) (1997) *Advertising Works 9*, Henley-on-Thames: NTC Publications.

Kotler, P. (1997) *Marketing Management, Analysis, Planning, Implementation, and Control*, 9th edn, Englewood Cliffs, NJ: Prentice Hall, Chapter 11, 313–15.

Lavidge, R.J. and Steiner, G.A. (1961) 'A model for predictive measurements of advertising effectiveness', *Journal of Marketing*, 25, October: 59–62.

McDonald, C. (1992) *How Advertising Works: A Review of Current Thinking*, Henley-on-Thames: NTC Publications.

Media Research Group (1995) The MRG *Guide to Media Research*, The Media Research Group, Salisbury, Wilts.

Myers, G. (1994) *Words in Ads*, London: Edward Arnold.

Palda, K.S. (1966) 'The hypothesis of a hierarchy of effects: a partial evaluation', *Journal of Marketing Research*, 3, February: 13–24.

Piercy, N. (1987) 'Advertising budgeting: process and structure as explanatory variables', *Journal of Advertising*, 16(2): 34–40.

Preston, I.L. and Thorson, E. (1984) 'The expanded association model: keeping the hierarchy concept alive', *Journal of Advertising Research*, 24(1) (February/March): 59–65.

Ray, M.L. (1973) 'Marketing communication and the hierarchy of effects', in P. Clarke (ed.) *New Models for Mass Communication Research: Sage Annual Review of Communication Research*, Volume II, Beverly Hills: Sage Publications, 147–76.

Rees, R.D. (1977) *Advertising Budgeting and Appraisal in Practice*, Research Study no. 11, The Advertising Association, London.

Schultz, D.E. and Schultz, H.F. (1998) 'Transitioning marcoms into the twenty-first century', *Journal of Marketing Communications*, 4(1): 9–26.

Starch, Daniel (1923) *Principles of Marketing*, Chicago: A.W. Shaw.

Strong, E.K. (1925) *The Psychology of Selling*, New York: McGraw-Hill.

Synodinos, N.E., Keown, C.F. and Jacobs, L.W. (1989) 'Transnational advertising practice: a survey of leading brand advertisers in fifteen countries', *Journal of Advertising Research*, 29(2) (April/May): 43–50.

Williamson, J. (1978) *Decoding Advertisements*, London: Marion Boyars.

17

THE DYNAMIC ROLE OF SALES PROMOTION

Andreas Laspadakis

CHAPTER AIMS

- to provide a thorough introduction by defining and describing sales promotion
- to evaluate the objectives that companies and retailers have when using this tool and to comment on their interrelationship which determines sales promotion effectiveness
- to consider the growing emphasis of companies towards sales promotion and to explore the major underlying rationale
- to evaluate whether companies are likely to continue to drive sales promotion spending ahead in the future
- to stress the need for a formal planning and decision-making process and to reveal weaknesses and limitations of current sales promotional planning practices
- to comment on the issue of the long-term effectiveness of sales promotion on brand image, consumer loyalty and repeat purchase behaviour and to show that sales promotion can prove as effective as much as disastrous depending on how it is used by companies in the market

ILLUSTRATION

The following case vignette provides significant insights into consumer behaviour in the fast moving consumer goods sector and also indicates how sales promotion can be used for marketing purposes (i.e. product launch).

A self-test of coupon usage

Readers are strongly urged to participate and answer these questions from the perspective of being a regular grocery shopper.

	Yes	No
I pay more for brands with strong emphasis on quality		
I like testing new brands in the market		
I participate in competitions for brands		
If I find a brand that satisfies me I usually do not change it		

Yes   No

When I purchase brands, I always search for best prices and offers
I like switching brands frequently for the sake of variety seeking
When I purchase I usually search for known brand names
I don't mind purchasing own labels as well

These questions form part of recent research carried out in one European Union country in 1995 (MRB, 1995). A national sample of 4000 consumers responded to these questions. The study found that:

- 48 per cent of consumers were willing to pay more for brands with strong emphasis on quality;
- 48 per cent of consumers like testing new brands in the market;
- only 48 per cent had participated in brand competitions in the market;
- 45 per cent of consumers prefer to repurchase brands that satisfy their needs effectively relative to competition;
- 67 per cent of consumers claimed that they always search for better prices and offers available when making purchasing decisions;
- only 30 per cent of consumers like switching brands for the purpose of variety seeking;
- 38 per cent of consumers search for known brand names when making purchasing decisions;
- 22 per cent of consumers only would purchase own labels.

INTRODUCTION

The aim of this chapter is to outline the subject and topic known as sales promotion, which is an important and developing subject of crucial significance to companies – whether producers or retailers – in any sector; it is also an increasingly complex subject mainly due to lack of consistent and commonly shared attitudes concerning the direction and magnitude of its long-term effectiveness on brand image, consumer loyalty and repeat purchase behaviour. Notably, sales promotion forms a significant marketing communications weapon in today's competitive and turbulent markets. Thus, this chapter aims to provide a thorough introduction to sales promotion. To better review the case of sales promotion and provide a sound theoretical framework, four significant topics are evaluated. These are:

- To define and describe sales promotion starting with a formal and general definition. This is crucial as sales promotion is a term often used rather indiscriminately to encompass all promotional activities other than advertising, personal selling or public relations. Unfortunately, sales promotion means exactly what a user intends it to mean, sometimes more and sometimes less than what others may have in mind (Christopher and McDonald, 1995). The overall result is that communication suffers, which eventually undermines the value of sales promotion in today's highly competitive marketing environment. It is therefore crucial at this stage to define and describe sales promotion. In addition, a typology of sales promotion is presented with examples of each type. Closely related, there is a review of why sales promotion exists. The most important objectives companies and retailers have when using this tool are presented. The aim is to show that both parties have different and to some extent conflicting objectives which may considerably undermine sales promotion effectiveness in both the short and the long run.

- To evaluate the growing emphasis in terms of expenditures on sales promotion. Evidence is presented showing its rapid growth at the expense of other elements of the marketing mix and particularly mass media commissionable advertising. The most important underlying factors are explored. The critical issue is to show that these factors reflect changes in the company's uncontrollable macro-environment which implies that these are too far away to control. Apparently, companies need to evaluate and incorporate them into strategies if they are to be strong market players. Whether these factors are likely to continue to drive sales promotion spending ahead in the future is also explored.

- A crucial aspect of sales promotion concerns the planning process. Business planning requires that systematic planning precedes decision making. One would expect that companies undertake formal planning and rigorous pre-testing as well as evaluation of results. Unfortunately, this is not the case as sales promotion still suffers from informal, seat-of-the-pants decision making. Thus, the objective is to stress the importance and the reasons why companies should be more involved and more concerned in sales promotion planning.

- Comment is also made on one of the most critical aspects of sales promotion, that is its long-term effectiveness on brand image, consumer loyalty and repeat purchase behaviour. The aim is to show that sales promotion can do much in terms of diluting long-term brand interests as well as further securing and strengthening them, depending on how effectively these are deployed and what emphasis companies place upon the various sales promotion activities. The overall objective is to show that companies need to adopt a different orientation with sales promotion, a long-term and strategic one that will enable firms to further secure and enhance a brand's long-term interests in the market.

WHAT IS SALES PROMOTION?

Although everyone may have a general understanding of sales promotion, few actually know exactly what it is. As everyone gives his/her own meaning, the ultimate result of this crude usage is that communication suffers (Blattberg and Neslin, 1990; Baker, 1993). Hence, it is crucial to know exactly what is being spoken of when using the term. The literature provides various definitions of sales promotion. Some of these are:

> Sales promotion is a direct inducement or incentive to the sales force, the distributor or the consumer with the primary objective of creating an immediate sale.
>
> (Schultz and Robinson, 1982)

Sales promotion is a diverse collection of incentive tools, mostly short term, designed to stimulate quicker and/or greater purchase of a particular product by consumers or the trade.

(Kotler, 1988)

Sales promotion is a short term inducement to customer buying action.

(Webster, 1981)

Sales promotion are marketing efforts that are supplementary in nature, are conducted for a limited period of time and seek to induce buying.

(Davis, 1981)

These definitions have several common features. They all indicate that the aim is to create an immediate sale or to get the customer to buy now. They imply that sales promotion merely shifts timing of behaviour that would have occurred anyway. Although there is some empirical evidence of this, it may not always be the case. For example, coupons are the quintessential sales promotion tool, yet their focus is more on brand switching or repeat purchasing than on purchase acceleration. Therefore it would be more appropriate to argue that the aim of sales promotion is to have a direct impact on consumer behaviour rather than an immediate one.

Further, these definitions include the descriptor 'short term' which implies that sales promotion effects are only temporary. While sales promotions may take place during a short period of time, this does not mean that effects are only temporary. The direction and magnitude of long-term effects are the subject of intense debate. In addition, the phrase 'short term' may influence companies when allocating their budgets among various sales promotion activities. If effects are perceived as being merely short term, then more emphasis may be given to certain activities known to have a strong short-term sales effect (price cuts), while concentrating less on others which may enhance a brand's long-term interests. Thus, the most appropriate definition is that provided by Blattberg and Neslin (1990) who defined sales promotion as 'an action focused marketing event whose purpose is to have a direct impact on the behaviour of the firm's customers'.

Also, the Institute of Sales Promotion in the UK has provided another equally acceptable definition:

Sales promotion comprises that range of techniques used to attain sales/ marketing objectives in a cost effective manner by adding value to a product or service either to intermediaries or end users, normally but not exclusively within a defined time period.

(Cummins, 1994)

Types of sales promotion

Sales promotion can broadly be classified into three main categories depending on the initiator and the target of the promotion. Retailer and consumer promotions are directed toward the consumer by retailers and companies respectively. The manufacturer also directs trade promotion to retailers. As Figure 17.1 reveals, the ultimate target is the consumer.

Companies' direct sales promotion to their own sales force as incentives to improve productivity should not be omitted. Table 17.1 provides a list of the major sales promotion activities used by companies nowadays.

The most frequently used are price cuts, coupons, displays and feature advertising and/or a combination of them. Following, the interest is to examine the reasons why sales promotion exists.

Sales promotion objectives

Manufacturers and retailers have different and sometimes conflicting objectives with sales promotion. When manufacturers offer trade promotions, they expect that these will persuade retailers to provide added brand support. This might include passing manufacturers' price reductions through to consumers, featuring price cuts in store advertising and displaying products prominently (Quelch, 1982). Thus, trade promotions aim to push products from manufacturers to retailers. On the other hand, the aim of consumer promotions is to create demand for products and therefore pull them from retailers. Manufacturers' specific objectives with consumer promotions are: to increase brand awareness among consumers, to induce brand switching and attract new customers, and to promote purchase acceleration by existing customers (Blattberg and Neslin, 1990).

However, manufacturer objectives are quite different and to some extent conflict with retailer objectives. Retailers very often undertake retail promotions to: generate added store traffic, move excess product inventory, enhance store image, and create an overall perceived price image to attract consumers into the store. Manufacturers need to pay attention to how their objectives interact with those of retailers. Any failure to incorporate the retailer's perspective in their sales promotion plans may have considerable implications upon sales promotion effectiveness if the retailer's support is not achieved.

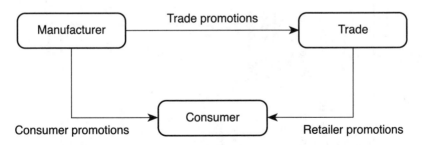

Figure 17.1 A schematic framework of the major types of sales promotion.

Source: Blattberg, R. and Neslin, S. (1990) *Sales Promotion: Concepts, Methods and Strategies*, Englewood Cliffs, NJ: Prentice Hall

Table 17.1 Sales Promotions Activities Depending on the Sector and The Target

Target market	Money		Goods		Services	
	Direct	Indirect	Direct	Indirect	Direct	Indirect
Consumer	Price reductions Dealer loaders Loyalty schemes Incentives Full range buying	Coupons Vouchers Money equivalent Competitors	Free Goods Premium offers Free gifts Trade in offers	Stamps Coupons Vouchers Money equivalent Competitions	Guarantees Group participation Special exhibitions and displays	Cooperative advertising Stamps, coupons Vouchers for services Competitions
Trade		Extended credit Delayed invoicing Sale or return Coupons Vouchers Money equivalent	Free gifts Trial offers Trade-in offers	Coupons Vouchers Money equivalent Competitions	Guarantees Free services Risk reduction schemes Training Special exhibitions Demonstrations	Stamps, coupons Vouchers for services Competitions
Sales Force	Bonus Commission	Coupons Vouchers Money equivalent Competitions	Free gifts	Coupons Vouchers Points systems Money equivalent	Free services Group participation events	Stamps, coupons Points system for services Competitions

Source: Christopher, M. and McDonald, M. (1995) Marketing: An Introductory Text, Macmillan Business.

IMPORTANCE AND GROWTH OF SALES PROMOTION

There is ample evidence to support the statement that sales promotion has grown dramatically. Two decades ago, the advertising to sales promotion ratio was 60/40, while nowadays sales promotion expenditures exceed 75 per cent (Jones, 1990; Donnelley Marketing, 1991; 1993). Clearly the situation in marketing allocations has changed. A feature of even greater importance, at least to the traditional advertising industry, has been the fact that mass media budgets have not grown as fast as demands upon them, which implies that the amount available for advertising has tended to shrink (Bowman, 1986; Marketing Report, 1995). It is evident therefore that sales promotion has grown dramatically, mainly at the expense of mass media. Several factors from the company's uncontrollable macro-environment have contributed to this; these are explored below.

Reasons for the shift from above the line towards sales promotion

1. Balance of power transfer from manufacturers to retailers

The past 30 years have seen a dramatic increase in the scale and power of retailers in most Western economies. It is reasonably argued that four major reasons are responsible for that transfer of power. These are:

- The *abolition of resale price maintenance* (RPM) in 1964 in the UK for most product categories. This represented a significant landmark in the shift of power although pressures for change existed well before the legislation.
- The *growing retail concentration* which is both an effect and a cause of further retail power (British Business, 1988; McGoldrick, 1990; Randall, 1994). Small retailers find it difficult to continue in business and compete with larger chains. The situation is equally competitive for companies which now have to work harder to secure distribution and prominent shelf-space.
- The *spread of private label brands* during the 1980s and subsequently of their market shares (Nielsen, 1980; Clark, 1981; Euromonitor, 1986; Powell, 1992; Quelch and Harding, 1996). Retailers have seen own brands as a way of achieving competitive advantage. The bottom line is that supermarkets now hold four out of the top ten places for advertising expenditure on own label food brands (Bond, 1984; *Marketing Week*, 1995). Over the period 1992–95, retail pressures reduced shelf space for brands by 12 per cent (Sargent, 1995). As own brands become better and better developed, perceived quality distinctions between them and manufacturers' brands become blurred. Apparently, manufacturers should not underestimate their growing role in the market.
- The *advent of optical scanning equipment* gave retailers the opportunity to have immediate knowledge on product sales, advertising and sales promotion effectiveness (*Progressive Grocer*, 1986; Olver and Farris, 1989; Rees, 1992). Retailers were no longer dependent on manufacturers for facts (Piercy, 1983). On the contrary, it gave them power to demand terms of sale (Ody, 1987; Jones, 1987). Thus, it is anticipated that retailers will become more sophisticated and

demanding in their deal terms and manufacturers will have to adapt in order to secure distribution.

2. Stagnating markets and increased brand similarities

Since World War II, consumer goods markets have been maturing and gradually stagnating and during the 1970s the number of stabilized ones overtook those still growing (Jones, 1990). Thus, companies have found it difficult to continue growing and keep profits high. This, coupled with inflationary conditions which kept profits low, meant that companies had to find alternative ways of improving shares (Euromonitor, 1995). A major method was movement of budgets towards sales promotion because of its perceived immediacy in terms of sales impact.

Further, the advent of production technologies led to growing brand similarities which meant that there is less scope to advertise product features effectively (Strang, 1976; Shimp, 1990). In certain product categories (paper towels, soaps) the percentage of those consumers who perceive all brands as alike is as high as 70 per cent (Alsop, 1989). Consequently, consumers are less brand loyal and more likely to rely on price and cost-related incentives (Frankel and Phillips, 1986). Therefore, because real and concrete advantages are often difficult to obtain, many companies have turned to sales promotion which has a more measurable and immediate impact.

3. Reduced advertising efficiency

Advertising effectiveness has been the subject of considerable discussion among academics and practitioners. It is believed that mass media commisionable advertising is no longer as efficient as it once was.

Perhaps the most important reason is the fact that *advertising cost has risen dramatically* (Davidson, 1987; Snoddy, 1988; Kitchen, 1993). The deregulation of the TV medium in most western markets (except the UK), which gave TV channels the ability to set their own rates, made a significant contribution (Boddewyn and Leardi, 1989).

Another major weakness is *media clutter.* Consumers are inundated with so many commercial messages that advertising effectiveness is diminished (Johnson and Cobb-Walgren, 1994). When this is combined with the fact that consumers possess limited capacity for processing and storing information (Bettman, 1979), it can be seen why there is a growing concern over the continued effectiveness of TV as an advertising medium (Cobb, 1985; Jonas, 1996).

Audience fragmentation and receptivity, in particular the erosion of television audiences, is another weakness. Developments such as remote control TV consoles and VCRs have contributed to this (Kitchen, 1993). Even when consumers are actually watching TV, their time may be spent in switching channels (Yorke and Kitchen, 1985), zipping through commercials when materials are pre-recorded, or zapping commercials by fast-forwarding playback (Kitchen, 1986). The development of these facilities has given consumers greater choice of what and when to watch. Audiences could be seen as becoming extremely fractionalized and demassified, making it particularly difficult for advertising to reach them effectively (Kirkham, 1982). Media plans therefore need to reflect these changes, moving from a mass media approach to one that is more personalized and successful (Katz, 1991).

However, this is not to argue against the effectiveness of advertising in the market. Advertising is still the most important tool for image building and its effects tend to last for a long period of time. Companies still need to invest in mass media, however, in a more efficient way, but excessive media support may not be necessary. For example, there is considerable evidence suggesting that returns from advertising are diminishing (McDonald, 1992; Pedrick and Zufryden, 1991; Jones, 1995). Other researchers have concluded that a small number of exposures per household during the week before purchase, may be 'enough', at least for consumer goods markets (Naples, 1979; Simon and Arndt, 1980; Sawyer, 1981; Tellis, 1988; Jones, 1995). Thus, there is an urgent need for companies to re-evaluate current mass media plans and modify to be more effective, efficient and accountable.

4. Demographic changes

Several changes are occurring within the demographic structure of society that have had a profound effect upon consumer behaviour (Lucas, 1986; Poynor, 1987) and subsequently affected the growth and appeal of sales promotion.

The major change is that *population in most economies grew very little* (Lazer, 1987). In the EC, the rate was only 17 per cent over the period 1960–94 (Euromonitor, 1995). Apparently, consumer goods companies can no longer assume that the market will grow around them and market share must be won from competitors.

In addition, the *growth of unemployed people* is becoming an unfortunate and seemingly long-term feature of the market in most countries. A high level of unemployment is coupled with an even higher level of underemployment, with many people obliged to take low-grade, low-paid employment. In the face of shrinking incomes, competition between companies will further intensify in an overall attempt to maintain and increase margins and profits.

A very significant demographic trend is the *growing number of women in employment* (May et al., 1988) which has inevitable effects upon the time available to shop frequently (Walters, 1986) and the time available to watch daytime TV. Consumers' lives have become much busier which implies that consumers are less interested in shopping, more likely to be under time pressure, and less inclined to prepare a shopping list ahead of a store visit. At the same time, there is an increased role for men in shopping as a more equal partner in the shopping process (Shimp, 1990). The ultimate result of these changes is an even higher proportion of unplanned purchases. Consequently, companies concentrate efforts at the point of sale. As the extent of impulse buying appears to increase (Cobb and Hoyer, 1986), in-store promotions have become an integral part of marketing plans as these represent the time and the place at which all the elements of the sale – the consumer, the money and the product – come together (Quelch, 1983).

To summarize, there is ample evidence to support the argument that companies will continue investing heavily in sales promotion which makes critical the need for a different, long-term and strategic orientation. However, given the short-term orientation of most consumer goods companies in the market, it is apparent that sales promotion is still regarded as a 'low status' area and companies do not undertake the necessary steps to ensure maximum control and efficacy of this activity.

SALES PROMOTION PLANNING

Successful usage of sales promotion implies that systematic planning precede formal decision making. Figure 17.2 depicts the fundamental elements of a formal sales promotion planning process and illustrates their application with Domestos Klinex, a leading brand in the detergents category. This framework was derived based on a review of several excellent references in sales promotion, including Schultz and Robinson (1982), Blattberg and Neslin (1990) and Shimp (1990).

The first step involves *environmental analysis*. Brand managers are urged to perform environmental or situational analyses to identify problems and opportunities facing the target brand. Issues that need to be reviewed include brand performance, competitive performance, competitive promotion activity and consumer response to sales promotion. This analysis leads to a determination of the possibilities of using sales promotion as a response to identified problems and opportunities.

The next step involves the *establishment of objectives* in response to the problems identified and opportunities raised by the environmental analysis. The specific objectives set for sales promotion vary according to the type of target market. For example, at the trade level, the objective may be to encourage greater shelf space and feature price cuts in store advertising. At the consumer level, the objective may be to generate trial purchases, encourage repeat purchases and build brand loyalty.

The third step involves *setting the budget*. Preparing detailed event budgets is usually straightforward, once details and desired objectives have been specified. However, given the complexity of sales promotion events, costs can escalate rapidly unless attention is given to all the details of the promotion as well as to the most critical dimensions likely to determine its effectiveness (Schultz and Robinson, 1982).

The fourth step of the planning process involves *development of promotion strategies*. Brand managers need to formulate the most appropriate promotion strategy for accomplishing the marketing objective and to determine which sales promotion technique or combination of techniques will accomplish the designated objectives. Attention needs to be given to the type of market, competitive conditions and cost-effectiveness of each tool. For example, if the objective is to retaliate against competitive promotional activity, then an appropriate strategy would be to use price-offs and coupons to load up consumers, thereby taking them out of the market for a short period of time.

Step five involves *devising tactics, deciding on the time schedule and implementing the campaign*. Creativity and timing are critical aspects given the proliferation of promotional activity in the market. The issue is to build campaigns that break through the tremendous competitive clutter, thereby generating brand awareness and interest at the point of purchase and encouraging brand switching and trial.

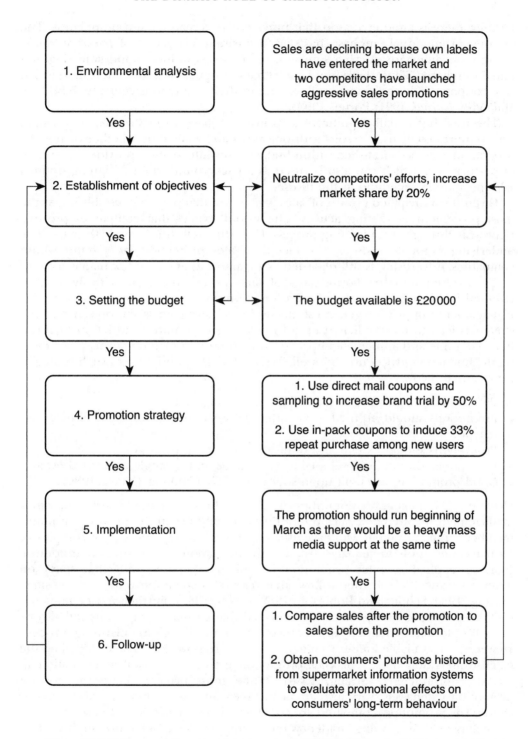

Figure 17.2 Sales promotion planning process and its application to Domestos (right).

Further, there is another reason that urges greater creativity and uniqueness. The growing promotional emphasis has started creating a situation of *promotion clutter*, where companies are offering similar promotions to induce brand switching and initial purchases. Thus, there is a danger that consumers will lose interest, in which case coupons and other media will weaken in their ability to trigger purchase (*The Wall Street Journal*, 1991; Porter, 1993).

The final but equally significant step involves *follow-up and evaluation of results*. This requires comparing results with objectives and evaluating whether or not the programme was accomplished within budget. This information provides a measure of performance which can also be used as a background when designing optimal sales promotion schedules in the future.

Given the anticipated growth of sales promotion that may soon establish it as the most prominent marketing activity, one would expect that companies proceed rigorously through this planning process. Unfortunately, this is rarely the case. The underlying rationale rests on the fact that sales promotion lacks status within companies. Advertising is still regarded as a glamorous area and few managers want to be involved with the boring area of sales promotion. Senior involvement is essential if the company is to adopt a long-term and strategic orientation. Senior management can provide general strategies for achieving goals and objectives. Such strategies lead to more efficient use of marketing expenditures which in turn can have a definite and immediate impact on the promotion planning process as well as on the budgeting procedure followed (Webster, 1981). A brief list of such strategies is presented below:

- Promotions are an integral part of the marketing mix.
- Promotions should be used as an offensive weapon, not merely as a defensive reaction.
- Promotions should extend and reinforce advertising messages.
- Promotions should be developed as campaigns, not as single, unrelated events.
- Good promotions are built upon sound strategic planning (Maier, 1985).

However, such maxims are not universally shared. In the absence of sufficient senior management involvement, sales promotion planning lies in the province of junior members of management who have little experience in one of the most complex of all marketing tools to manage. Apparently, the amount of genuinely innovative thinking applied to sales promotion is limited compared with that spent on advertising and R&D. It then follows that research expenditures will also be small (Strang, 1980; Schultz and Robinson, 1982; Kotler, 1988). Further, most companies do little or no pre-testing. It can be expected that evaluation of results will also be rare. Promotion evaluation is a critical aspect of the entire planning process. However, the available literature suggests that there is weak evidence regarding the extensiveness and quality of sales promotion evaluation as well as evaluation in terms of profitability (Strang, 1980). While most firms evaluate the cost of promotion extensively, very few attempt to measure the profitability of a long- or short-term promotion compared to not doing it at all (Lodish, 1986). Recently, there has been a growing tendency for companies to adopt more sophisticated methods of setting promotional budgets and improve research and evaluation of sales promotion in the market (Heinz, 1991; Holloway, 1991). The bottom line is that companies need to re-evaluate attitudes and policies regarding sales promotion planning. Nowadays, it is crucial for senior management to be more actively involved, as it is for managers to pre-test alternatives and rigorously evaluate results. As there is no reason to suspect that sales promotion should not continue to grow in terms of emphasis and expenditures, it is vital to use it in the best possible long-term brand interests. Sales promotions, like any other communications material, do provide a vehicle for attaining a brand's long-term interests as evaluated below.

LONG-TERM EFFECTIVENESS OF SALES PROMOTION ON BRAND IMAGE, CONSUMER LOYALTY AND REPEAT PURCHASE BEHAVIOUR

The issue of the long-term effectiveness of sales promotion has long been the subject of considerable dispute among academics and researchers in the field, with considerable evidence on each side. Sales promotions can do as much to preserve and enhance a brand's long-term interests as damage them, depending on what emphasis companies place on price and non-price promotions and also on short- and long-term orientations. The available literature reveals the following – quite significant – outcomes concerning this issue.

In the long run, *repeated price promotions weaken the added value produced by advertising* (Ogilvy, 1987; Papalta and Krishnamurthi, 1996). Frequent sales promotions are in effect price reductions which diminish a brand's perceived value and eventually market share (Sargent, 1995). This happens because (a) *price promotions lower consumer reference price levels* which does not drive repeat purchasing once the price returns to its original pre-promotional level because consumers regard the brand as expensive, (b) *consumers attribute low quality to frequently promoted brands* because of their use of price as a surrogate measure of quality, and (c) *consumers become accustomed to and plan purchases based on discount availability.* Eventually consumer loyalty is diluted, brand image weakens in its ability to drive a purchase and is replaced by the availability or not of a price-related incentive.

Trade promotion, which receives by far the lion's share of budgetary appropriations (Broadbent, 1989), *has the weakest long-term effect.* This is attributable to the fact that trade promotion lacks the customary stress on building a consumer franchise that features a brand's competitive benefits or builds warm, non-rational associations with it. These are factors that may encourage consumers to buy goods on a more permanent basis.

Non-price-related sales promotions have much more potential in terms of further strengthening and enhancing brand image in the market. Such activities alter a brand's perceived value and not its cost one, as is the case with price promotions. As long as these activities capitalize upon a brand's values and differential attributes, and with a creative approach in their formulation and implementation, they can do much to support and enhance those long-term interests.

Further, *sales promotion can't be expected to change the attitudes or behaviour of consumers who are already strongly loyal or strongly negative.* Only for consumers who are essentially indifferent to several brands can sales promotions increase the short-term attractiveness of the brand and therefore drive choice. Implications for brand managers are obvious: where strong loyalty exists, there is less scope for sales promotion as in the short term there aren't too many sales to be gained and in the long term there is the risk of losing sales from brand-loyal consumers who become accustomed to promotional availability.

Overall, sales promotion provides an important vehicle for the attainment of a brand's long-term interests. The issue is what emphasis companies place upon the various sales promotion activities (price and non-price related) and whether they employ them in a way that is consistent and integrated with the overall marketing communication objectives. Too much emphasis upon price promotion usually generates a dramatic sales effect but often at the expense of long-term demand as image is diluted and consumer loyalty weakened. On the other hand, non-price promotion may not have equal sales effects in the short run but reinforces and enhances a brand's interests in the long term. Apparently, both activities (price versus non-price) have different objectives (induce brand switching/trial versus reward behaviour) and aim at different consumer segments (price-prone versus loyal consumers). Thus, an evaluation of the consumer base and the relative opportunities to be gained is considered to be a determinant step before engaging in any form of sales promotion in the market.

A long-term and strategic approach is considered to be critical if firms are to take advantage of the long-term potential of sales promotion. This is, however, hardly the case in the market. The dominance of the brand-management structure and reward systems that emphasize short-term sales response rather than slow, long-term growth have contributed largely to that. Evidently this may have considerable negative implications for a brand in the long run as more emphasis is like to be given to price promotions which, apart from the short-term sales effect they may have, do little to support the brand in the long term. Thus a need for a different orientation concerning sales promotion, long term and strategic in nature, becomes pertinent and crucial.

This requires considerable commitment by senior management. In most companies sales promotion decisions fall under the control of junior managers who do not have the experience needed to cope with this marketing tool, which is growing in emphasis and expenditures. Considering also the fact that compensation and job promotion are usually judged based on yearly (or more frequent) sales and profit performance of products under their control, it could easily be assumed that more emphasis is likely to be give to those activities known to have a strong short-term sales effect without any prior consideration as to their long-term effectiveness. Thus, senior management needs to be more involved in the sales promotion planning process. Senior management can stress the need to secure a brand's long-term welfare in the market and establish policies that reflect this direction and may lead to a more efficient use of sales promotion expenditures.

Equally significant is to stress the issue that sales promotion must not be used as a response to weaknesses in other elements of the marketing mix. Unfortunately, this is rarely taken into consideration, as brand managers tend to invest significantly in this activity when sales are falling due to weaknesses in other elements of the marketing mix. Declining sales over an extended period indicate either poor quality performance or the availability of a superior alternative. Sales promotion can in no way reverse the non-acceptance of a no longer desired product. Apparently, only significant investments in product quality can reverse this declining sales trend, but sales promotion on its own is a waste. If consumers perceive the brand as encompassing superior differential attributes against the competition, then they will repurchase it. On the other hand, inferior brands won't survive no matter how often they are in any form of sales promotion. Thus, looking for brand differentiation in product categories characterized by growing brand similarities is the only feasible strategy for securing brand survival and long-term profitability. Apparently, brand managers need to constantly monitor the differential advantages of their marketing mix relative to competing sales propositions by identifying potential weaknesses. Merely investing in sales promotion as a response to these weaknesses is not a proper strategy and won't alter long-term brand position to any significant extent. Thus, there is a great deal of truth in saying that sales promotion is not a cause but a symptom of the many effects for which it is blamed, such as diluting brand image and weakening consumer loyalty.

SUMMARY AND CONCLUSIONS

The aim of this chapter was to outline the subject and topic known as sales promotion which is an important and developing subject of crucial importance to companies. It is also an increasingly complex subject as the term 'sales promotion' is often used rather indiscriminately. Thus, this chapter initially defined sales promotion as 'an action focused marketing event whose purpose is to have a direct impact on the behaviour of a brand's customers'. While most researchers regard sales promotion as a short-term-oriented tool, it was argued that this is not appropriate as the issue of long-term effectiveness has been the subject of considerable discussion as to its magnitude and direction.

Next, it provided an overview of the basic objectives companies and retailers have when using sales promotion. The important issue was that they both have different and to some extent conflicting objectives. This is an aspect that companies need to consider when planning optimal sales promotion schedules.

Then, the focus was on the rapid growth and development of sales promotion and the major underlying reasons. Evidence was provided to support the argument that companies will continue to spend significantly on sales promotion.

Deficiencies arising from current sales promotion planning practices were also explored. Such deficiencies as lack of senior management involvement and limited time and effort spent on pre- and post-evaluation may allow more emphasis on certain activities which, apart from dramatic short-term sales effects, do nothing with regard to the long-term brand benefits in the marketplace. Therefore the need for formal sales promotion planning is pertinent and important if it is to take advantage of the true long-term potential of this activity. A crucial determinant in adopting more formalized sales promotion planning is the involvement of senior management, which can provide general strategies for achieving objectives and may lead to a more efficient use of marketing expenditures which in turn can have a definite and immediate impact on the promotion planning process as well as on the budgeting procedure followed.

The need for formalized sales promotion planning process is further supported by the fact that that sales promotion can do as much to dilute as to enhance a brand's long-term interests in the market. Discrimination was made between price and non-price-related sales promotion activities where the former have potential for damaging a brand's long term interests in the market. On the other hand, non-price sales promotion can further secure and enhance those long-term interests in the market. The rationale lies in the fact that these activities alter a brand's perceived value and not its cost one, as is the case with price promotions. Apparently, companies need to put less emphasis on those activities (price-related) likely to damage long-term interests and more on those likely to enhance and secure those interests. Thus the need for formal decision processes. The need for a sales promotion planning process is supported by the vitality of sales promotion in terms of expenditure and practice. Involvement by senior management is a necessary requirement in adopting more sophisticated planning processes.

DISCUSSION TOPICS

1 The term 'sales promotion' is often used rather indiscriminately to encompass all promotional activities other than advertising, personal selling and public relations. The overall effect is that communication suffers. In your own words, how would you define sales promotion and how would you justify that definition?

2 Sales promotion is growing both in emphasis and expenditures in most western markets. Is this trend likely to be a permanent market characteristic and what factors underpin driving sales promotion spending ahead?

3 Perhaps the most important factor explaining the rapid growth of sales promotion expenditures is the balance of power transfer from consumer goods companies to retail chains which are growing in size and power. In your perception, which are the most appropriate strategies for restoring this balance of power in favour of the manufacturer and its portfolio of brands?

4 The use of formal sales promotion planning processes by consumer goods companies is currently weak and incomplete. Assuming you are a member of senior management, what are the steps you might follow to impose more sophisticated sales promotion planning processes and what are the benefits of this approach?

5 The issue of long-term effectiveness of sales promotion has long been a subject of considerable discussion among academics and practitioners in the field. In your perception, how can sales promotion affect the long-term interests of a brand in the market in terms of brand image, consumer loyalty and repeat purchase behaviour?

6 Assume that you are the brand manager of a well-known brand in the market. Recommend which sales promotion activity should be used to build brand image and strengthen consumer loyalty, and justify your choice.

7 Growing promotional emphasis has started creating a situation of promotion clutter, where companies are offering similar promotions to induce brand switching and initial purchases. There is a danger, therefore, that consumers will

lose interest, in which case coupons and other media will weaken in their ability to trigger purchase. Evaluate the magnitude of this clutter in your market and recommend strategies for overcoming it.

8 Assume that you are the brand manager of a well-known brand in the market. Explain the potential trade-offs between short-term and long-term emphasis you may face and how you expect to use sales promotion as a response.

9 Trade promotion receives the vast majority of sales promotion expenditures in the market. Added retail support and pass-through of the promotion to end consumers is a determinant factor of the effectiveness of trade promotion in the market. Recommend strategies as to how retail support and greater pass-through of promotions to consumers can be achieved.

10 Sales promotion can be broadly divided into two major categories: consumer oriented, and trade oriented, where the former is considered to be the pull emphasis and the latter the push strategy. In your opinion, which are the most critical factors likely to determine the emphasis companies place on the push or pull strategies?

CASE STUDY

Consider that you are the marketing and sales manager of a major fast-moving consumer goods company known for its high-quality reputation. The primary product category in which the company operates is food, but recently strategic plans to expand into another major fast-moving consumer goods category, dairy products, have been developed. After months of planning and testing, the company introduces its new line of milk products.

Within the first year, the new product line achieves a 20 per cent market share which is not sufficient given that the dairy market is an oligarchic one (there are only two players in the market). Its penetration rate is 30 per cent (the percentage of the target market that purchased the brand at least once). Its repurchase rate is 70 per cent (the percentage of first-time triers who repurchased the brand one or more times). This high repurchase rate implies that the new product line has superior differential advantages and attributes that meet consumer needs and wants effectively in the market. Apparently, the task is to increase the penetration rate, in other words to attract more new triers.

As the marketing manager, you are thinking of offering a case allowance to the trade. You expect sales to be 30 000 cases when not employing sales promotion. The case price is £10 and the gross profit contribution is 35 per cent. You are thinking of offering a £1/case allowance in return for expected increased sales of 15 000 during the sales promotional period. Additional administrative costs are estimated to be £10,000. It is therefore up to you to evaluate whether the sales promotion will make any profit at all. Further, determine whether it is actually worth deploying the sales promotion, taking into account the net profitability had the sales promotion not been available.

On the other hand, you are thinking of employing coupons to stimulate brand awareness and consumer interest. The redemption rate varies with the mode of distribution; newspaper coupons are redeemed about 2 per cent of the time, coupons distributed by direct mail about 8 per cent of the time and coupons distributed with the pack about 17 per cent of the time. Experts believe that coupons should provide around 20 per cent saving to be effective and that is what you intend to do. You decide that the most appropriate mode of distributing the coupons is through direct mail. Given the high repurchase rate of 70 per cent, distributing coupons through the pack won't make any significant change in terms of sales generated and therefore you decide to use only coupons distributed by direct mail. If administrative costs are considered to be £20,000 for a circulation of 200 000 coupons, will the sales promotion make any profit for the company? Further, evaluate whether it is actually worth using this sales promotion.

REFERENCES

Alsop, A. (1989) 'Brand loyalty is rarely blind loyalty', *The Wall Street Journal*, 19 October: B1.

Baker, M. (1993) *Basic Marketing*, London: Butterworth-Heinemann.

Bettman, J. (1979) *An Information Processing Theory of Consumer Choice*, Reading, MA: Addison-Welsey Publishing Company.

Blattberg, R. and Neslin, S. (1990) *Sales Promotion: Concepts, Methods and Strategies*, Englewood Cliffs, NJ: Prentice Hall.

Boddewyn, J. and Leardi, M. (1989) 'Sales promotions: practice, regulation and self regulation around the world', *International Journal of Advertising*, 8(4): 374–8.

Bond, C. (1984) 'Own labels vs the brands', *Marketing*, 6(10): 24–7.

Bowman, R. (1986) 'Sales promotion: the 1985 annual report', *Marketing and Media Decisions*, July: 170–4.

British Business (1988) 'DTI retailing inquiry for 1986', *British Business*, 18 March: 29–30.

Broadbent, S. (1989) *The Advertising Budget: The Advertiser's Guide To Budget Determination*, Henley: NTC Publications.

Christopher, M. and McDonald, M. (1995) *Marketing: An Introductory Text*, Macmillan Business.

Clark, I. (1981) *Retailer Branding: Profit Improvement Opportunities*, Richmond: Management Horizons.

Cobb, C. (1985) 'Television clutter and advertising effectiveness', in R.F. Lusch *et al.*, (eds) *AMA Educators' Proceedings*, Chicago: American Marketing Association.

Cobb, C. and Hoyer, W. (1986) 'Planned vs impulse purchase behaviour', *Journal of Retailing*, 62(4): 384–409.

Cummins, J. (1994) *Sales Promotion: How to create and implement campaigns that really work?*, London: Kogan Page Ltd.

Davidson, H. (1987) *Offensive Marketing*, 3rd edn, London: Penguin Books.

Davis, K. (1981) *Marketing Management*, 4th edn, New York: John Wiley.

Donnelley Marketing (1991) 'Ninth annual survey of promotional practices', Stanford, Conn.

Donnelley Marketing (1993) 'Eleventh annual survey of promotional practices' Stanford, Conn.

Euromonitor (1986) 'The own brands report', in P. McGoldrick (1990) *Retail Marketing*, London: McGraw Hill.

Frankel, B. and Phillips, J. (1986) 'Escaping the parity trap', *Marketing Communications*, November: 93–100.

Heinz (1991) 'Heinz: creating, executing and evaluating promotions', MRS 1991 Seminar Paper, 243–8.

Holloway, P. (1991) 'Making promotions work harder', MRS 1991 Seminar Paper, 239–42.

Johnson, R. and Cobb-Walgren, C. (1994) 'Ageing and the problem of television clutter', *Journal of Advertising Research*, 34(4): 54–62.

Jonas, K. (1996) 'Does clutter matter?', *Admap*, 32(3): 14–15.

Jones, G. (1987) 'EPOS and the retailer's information needs' in E. McFadyen (ed.) *The Changing Face of British Retailing*, London: Newman, 22–32.

Jones, P. (1990) 'The double jeopardy of sales promotion', *Harvard Business Review*, 68(5): 145–52.

Jones, P. (1995) *When Ads Work*, New York: Lexington Books.

Katz, H. (1991) 'From mass media to personal media', *Marketing and Research Today*, August: 186–9.

Kirkham, M. (1982) 'The need for VCR research', *Admap*, 18(7): 405.

Kitchen, P. (1986) 'Zipping, zapping and nipping', *International Journal of Advertising*, 5(4): 343–52.

Kitchen, P. (1993) 'Marketing communications renaissance', *International Journal of Advertising*, 12(4): 367–85.

Kotler, P. (1988) *Marketing Management: Analysis, Planning, Implementation and Control*, 6th edn, Englewood Cliffs, NJ: Prentice Hall.

Lazer, W. (1987) *Handbook of Demographics for Marketing and Advertising*, Lexington, MA: Lexington Books, 6.

Lodish, L. (1986) *The Advertising and Promotion Challenge: Vaguely Right or Precisely Wrong?*, New York: Oxford University Press.

Lucas, M. (1986) 'Changing stores to suit the changing customer', in ESOMAR (ed.) *Retail Strategies for Profit and Growth*, Amsterdam: ESOMAR, 59–77.

Maier, J. (1985) 'The big event and the sales promotion campaign', in S.M. Ulanoff (ed.) *HandBook of Sales Promotion*, New York: McGraw-Hill, 429–42.

Marketing Report. (1995) 'Mass media advertising expenditures within Europe', September, 11, weekly magazine published in Athens.

Marketing Week (1995) 'Looking after own-label', 14 July, 25.

May, E., Ress, C. and Salmon, W. (1988) 'Future trends in retailing: merchandise line trends and store trends 1980–1990', in E. Kaynak (ed.) *Transactional Retailing*, Berlin: Walter de Gruyter, 333–48.

McDonald, C. (1992) *How Advertising Works*, The Advertising Association, London: NTC Publishers, McGraw-Hill Book Company.

McGoldrick, P. (1990) *Retail Marketing*, UK: McGraw-Hill Book Company.

MRB (1995) *Consumer Purchasing Behaviour Vs Consumer Lifestyles in Greece*, unpublished data given to the author for the purpose of this chapter.

Naples, M. (1979) *Effective Frequency*, New York: Association of Advertisers.

Nielsen (1980) *Nielsen Study of Private Labels in the Grocery Retail Trade of Europe*, Oxford: A.C. Nielsen.

Ody, P. (1987) 'Creating long term strategy for retailing', *Retail and Distribution Management*, 15(6): 8–11.

Ogilvy, D. (1987) 'Sound the alarm', *International Journal of Advertising*, 6(1): 81–4.

Olver, J. and Farris, P. (1989) 'Push and pull: a one two punch for packaged products', *Sloan Management Review*, 31(1): 53–61.

Papatla, P. and Krishnamurthi, L. (1996) 'Measuring the dynamic effects of promotions on brand choice', *Journal of Consumer Research*, 33(1): 20–35.

Pedrick, J. and Zufryden, F. (1991) 'Evaluating the impact of advertising media plans: a model of consumer purchase dynamics using single-source data', *Marketing Science*, 10(2): 111–30.

Piercy, N. (1983) 'Retailer information power – the channel marketing information system', *Marketing Intelligence and Planning*, 1(1): 40–55.

Porter, A. (1993) 'Strengthening coupon offers by requiring more from the retailer', *Journal of Consumer Marketing*, 10(2): 13–18.

Powell, D. (1992) *Counter Revolution*, London: Grafton.

Poynor, M. (1987) 'The changing consumer', in E. McFayden (ed.) *The Changing Face of British Retailing*, London: Newman Books, 103–13.

Progressive Grocer (1986) *Annual Report of the Grocery Industry*, April 1983 and April 1986, United Kingdom.

Quelch, J. (1982) *Trade Promotion by Grocery Products Manufacturing: A Managerial Perspective*, Report No. 82–106, Marketing Science Institute, Cambridge, MA, August.

Quelch, J. (1983) 'Its time to make trade promotion more productive', *Harvard Business Review*, 61(3): 130–6.

Quelch, J. and Harding, D. (1996) 'Brands versus private labels', *Harvard Business Review*, 75(1): 99–109.

Randall, G. (1994) *Trade Marketing Strategies*, London: Butterworth–Heinemann Ltd.

Rees, A. (1992) 'How Sainsbury as a retailer has become a successful brand', paper given at a *Marketing Week* conference, London, 2 April.

Sargent, J. (1995) 'Brand building in the UK', *Admap*, 31(1): 46–8.

Sawyer, A. (1981) 'Repetition, cognitive responses and persuasion', in R.E. Petty, T.M. Ostrom and T.C. Brock (eds) *Cognitive Responses in Persuasion*, Hillsdale, NJ: Lawrence Erlbaum Associates.

Schultz, D.E. and Robinson, W. (1982) *Sales Promotion Management*, Chicago: Crain Books.

Shimp, T.A. (1990) *Promotion Management and Marketing Communications*, 2nd edn, Philadelphia: The Dryden Press.

Simon, J. and Arndt, J. (1980) 'The shape of the advertising response function', *Journal of Advertising Research*, 20(4): 11–30.

Snoddy, R. (1988) 'Study into cost of TV adverts', *Financial Times*, 26 January, 6.

Strang, R. (1976) 'Sales promotion: fast growth, faulty management', *Harvard Business Review*, 54(4): 115–24.

Strang, R. (1980) *The Promotional Planning Process*, New York: Praeger Publishers, 7.

Tellis, G. (1988) 'Advertising exposure, loyalty and brand purchase: a two stage model', *Journal of Marketing Research*, 25(2): 134–44.

The Wall Street Journal (1991) 'Recession feeds the coupon habit', 20 February, B1.

Walters, D. (1986) 'International consumer trends', *Retail*, 4(3): 41–4.

Webster, F. (1981) 'Top management's concerns about marketing issues for the 1980s', *Journal of Marketing*, 45(3): 51–5.

Yorke, D. and Kitchen, P. (1985) 'Channel flickers and video speeders', *Journal of Advertising Research*, 25(2): 21–5.

18

DIRECT MARKETING

Martin Evans

CHAPTER AIMS

- to explore the reasons for the growth of direct marketing
- to demonstrate how market information is becoming very much more personalized and how this provides direct marketers with a basis for individualized targeting
- to explore the nature and power of marketing databases in a direct marketing context
- to raise topical issues with respect to the strategic role of direct marketing, the 'research versus testing' debate and privacy concerns

ILLUSTRATION: THE CAR DEALER'S DIRECT MARKETING DISCOVERY

A motor car dealer has been on a direct marketing course and discovered that he had much more information about his customers than he previously realized. Before attending the course he was rather reactive in his marketing – waiting for customers to book services/repairs for their vehicles and, apart from some cooperative local advertising with his supplying motor manufacturer, generally waiting for people to come into the showroom. Now he realizes that he can be proactive and understand his customers and potential customers much more – and on an individual basis. He was shown that when a car is purchased he gathers information on the purchaser – name, address, telephone number and, when there is any credit agreement, information on the customer's financial and occupational circumstances is also available. He now sends letters (perhaps backed by telephone calls) asking about the new customer's evaluation of how well he/she was treated during the purchase process, thus potentially starting a relationship with that customer.

Satisfaction surveys can also be used to gather a little more information about the customer – perhaps lifestyle details which could help with the targeting of relevant offers. At regular intervals, he could mail the customer to remind about servicing – and after several 'services' would know the mileage that customer normally did, thus making reminders more timely. He can also send out a timely reminder about when the MOT is needed by checking the purchase date in the log book. At appropriate intervals he could contact the customer individually with news about new car launches and modifications, therefore offering up-selling opportunities for his dealership. Wine and cheese evenings could be arranged for selected customers for appropriate launches. Cross-selling was also possible because he could contact the customer with details of car alarm systems and other accessories. The customer's partner became an important target as well – the second family car might be a used vehicle and targeting for cross- and up-selling was approached in a similar way.

The dealer also became aware of the ages of the couple's children and was able to target them when they reached the age of 17. The customer's business address might be useful for targeting a potential fleet market. An analysis of address locations of customers – perhaps even geodemographically profiled – can be helpful in defining catchment area and where potential customers might live – this can sometimes surprise a dealer who previously thought he knew his market. Likely targets in this catchment area who are not as yet customers could be mailed with invitations to attend launches or other events. The dealer also now has a 'list' which he could sell on to, for example, warranty or 'breakdown' companies. With regular contact a relationship developed and he realized that if he was able to retain this customer – and his or her family – over several years, the 'lifetime value' of their business would be quite significant – and at the same time much cheaper to achieve than trying to recruit new customers.

(*Source*: Author)

INTRODUCTION

Direct marketing is not new conceptually. In Venice in 1498 a book catalogue was published by Aldus Manutius – and William Lucas published a gardening catalogue in England in 1667. A variety of other mail order catalogues and clubs appeared, especially in Europe and the USA through the eighteenth and nineteenth centuries and in fact there was a significant growth in the USA in particular during the 1800s because of rising demand for goods from isolated communities which could be serviced by the improving distribution and postal systems (Institute of Direct Marketing, 1995).

The mail order industry in the UK also grew on the basis, initially, of 'savings clubs' (for example Christmas Clubs) and this was extended to credit availability, so a major motivation in the UK revolved around financial considerations. The development of sophisticated credit referencing can be traced back to this era and is a significant factor in the growth of current direct marketing, as is explored later.

Direct marketing has probably been the most significant development in marketing in recent years. It has contributed to the paradigm shift from transactional marketing based on the 'marketing mix' approach created by Borden (1964) and popularized into the four Ps by McCarthy (1960), to the notion of retention strategies within a relationship marketing context.

There are several reasons for this change and these can be categorized as being either 'demand' for or 'supply' of direct marketing (Evans *et al.*, 1996a). This chapter summarizes these and goes on to explore emerging issues for the direct marketing industry.

DIRECT MARKETING 'DRIVERS'

Demand for direct marketing

Market Changes

Demand-side factors are based on changes in market behaviour and also on changes in the effectiveness of traditional media. In terms of markets, it is clear that fragmentation has taken place. Markets have become demassified and this has been a major trend aiding the growth of direct marketing. This is manifested in greater pluralism within society, evident in the high street where pluralism in clothing styles is observable. The Henley Centre (1978) predicted this trend as far back as the 1970s when they discussed household behaviour as being 'cellular' rather than 'nuclear' – households were beginning to do things together less and less and beginning to behave more independently – families were not eating together as often, having TV and sound systems in their 'own' rooms and, whereas at one time it was typical to have one large 'family sized' packet of Corn Flakes in the kitchen, it was becoming more likely that each household member would have a packet of 'their' cereal in the cupboard.

Other changes have seen the increase in the number of working women, many of whom are joining their male counterparts in seeking time-saving purchasing methods, such as direct mail and telemarketing. Working women are also more independent and contribute to the greater number of smaller households which require narrower targeting. The divorce rate has risen and with it the number of small and single households – affecting both sexes. This also means that more men are deciding which washing powder they will buy and more women are buying cars and pensions for themselves. The continuing trend away from cash as the means of payment to credit, debit and smart cards, through the post and over telephone and Internet cables has enabled purchase behaviour to take place when the customer wants it – 24 hours per day and from the armchair, office phone or even travelling laptop computer.

Less effective traditional promotional media

Companies have become disillusioned with more traditional promotional media over recent years. Market fragmentation has resulted in diminishing audiences for individual media, media costs have soared and consumers are experiencing clutter. Although above-the-line advertising *is* targeted at specific audiences – the audience for a late night Friday show on Channel 4 is unlikely to have the same composition as one for a Wednesday afternoon on BBC2 (or if it has, it might not be in the same frame of mind) – the targeting is still of the 'shotgun' variety rather than the 'sniper's rifle' which is possible through direct marketing. Audiences are fragmenting as more TV channels appear (satellite and cable) along with more newspapers and magazines – all with advertising space to fill. Furthermore, consumers are not helping the advertiser by video recording TV programmes and 'zapping' the commercials (Kitchen, 1986). Direct marketing is seen to have the potential to overcome the difficulty of this 'clutter' because the message can be personalized.

Together the trends have created *demand* for more effective targeting. The *supply* side on the other hand is concerned with changes in information about customers (based on much more sophisticated research) and also on technological improvements which have facilitated the collating and analysis of huge amounts of detailed and personalized information.

Supply of direct marketing

More individualized customer information

In parallel with markets' apparent desire to be treated more as individuals and marketing's desire to find more effective media is the marketer's search for more detailed and personalized information about customers.

This is based, in part, on the relative decline of demographic segmentation variables, due to their lack of explanatory depth and their relatively broad targeting capabilities. The typical market profiling according to age, gender and social grade saw, in the 1980s, parallel profiles in psychographic and geodemographic terms. Indeed the rise of psychographics and geodemographics has added to demographics' decline because of their potential abilities to understand target customers in great detail, even individually, and to be able to target them specifically.

It is a proposition of this chapter that one of the more significant events in moving from generalized customer profiles to more individualized approaches was the commercial availability of the Census and the development of geodemographics from it. From the 1981 UK Census, some 40 census variables were cluster analysed and the emerging clusters of households led to the creation of 39 neighbourhood types. Compare this with one of the leading alternatives of the time – social grade – which classifies the entire population into just six groups on the basis of one variable (occupation of the chief income earner in the household). Whereas such demographic profiles are often based on sample surveys of 1000, the marketing industry now had access to a census of 56 million. Names and addresses cannot be revealed from the census, but the statistics for enumeration districts can. These are groupings of around 170 households. Such data can be linked with the postcode database (there is one postcode for approximately 15 households) and with the electoral register (another database) it is possible to identify individual households and their characteristics.

There are 'me-toos' of the original ACORN system. Richard Webber, who created ACORN, set up one of the newer competitors after he left CACI to join another similar agency, CCN (Consumer Credit Nottingham, but now called Experian, following the link with the American company of that name – and reinforcing the earlier point that one of the origins of direct marketing lay in credit referencing), and developed MOSAIC which analyses the census data together with credit company records and even a database on county court bad debt cases. The basic rationale behind geodemographics is that 'birds of a feather flock together', making neighbourhoods relatively homogenous. An easy criticism in riposte is that 'I am not like my neighbour'. However, geodemographics have proved to be reasonably robust overall. In other European countries similar systems exist, for example under the names Geo Market profile and Omnidata. Several geodemographic companies now operate throughout many European countries, such as Experian (with its MOSAIC brand).

There has been a full geodemographic analysis of the Target Group Index (TGI) which is an annual report in 34 volumes of buyer profiles in most product-markets and based on samples of over 20 000. From this, each geodemographic category's interest in the product concerned can be determined. In fact the TGI sample design is now based on geodemographic categories. In addition, the National Readership Survey is similarly analysed by geodemographics and this can provide readership profiles for media selection purposes.

Table 18.1 shows that although the base source of geodemographic data is the census, there are now many more sources integrated into the analysis. The census in 2001 may have some additional questions relevant to the direct marketer. The following is a selection being tested prior to that census (Rees, 1997):

'Are you in receipt of unpaid personal help?'
'Do you provide substantial unpaid personal help for a friend or relative with any long-term illness, health problems or disability?'
'Does your household's accommodation have a garden or yard?'
'Do you consider you belong to religious group?' (list of categories provided)
'What is your total gross income from all sources?'

These questions could provide some additional data for geodemographics/lifestyle databases; for example, income is a useful measure of potential disposable income, the possession of a garden would be of interest to garden products direct marketers, levels of personal help might be of interest to service providers and the questions

Table 18.1 MOSAIC's data sources.

Census statistics	
Source: OPCS	Socio-economic data
	Housing
	Household and age
Demographic data	
Source: Electoral Registers	Age
	Household composition
	Population movement
Financial data	
Source: Lord Chancellors Office	County Court Judgements
CCN Credit Database	CCN consumer searches
Companies House	Directors
Retail data	
Source: Experian	Accessibility

about religion could be used by church organizations to target individuals – churches are increasingly turning to direct marketing. The 1991 census included a controversial question about ethnic origin; will the questions above prove equally controversial?

Marketing databases

The availability of more individual-specific data coupled with technological facilitators is leading to the targeting of individuals based on what is known of their interests and characteristics. The means for storing and retrieving such individual data is the marketing database and it is this that is at the heart of much direct marketing – not the main focus, because that should be the customer, and neither does the database drive direct marketing, because again it is the market that should provide this impetus.

At a strategic level, decisions will need to be taken with respect to segmentation and targeting. In this sense the marketing database can focus on a whole range of different categories – for example, new prospects, best prospects, loyals and so on; perhaps essentially, these can be boiled down into acquisition or retention strategies.

Once created, the database has a variety of uses. It can clearly be used as a list from which to target customers via direct marketing activity. But in addition it can also provide a wealth of information on the market and on customers and potential customers within it. In this context, the database provides data for both planning and analysis purposes: the database can be analysed for most attractive segments, for campaign planning and predicting campaign response. Strategically, the database can be used for (Shaw and Stone, 1988a): 1) changing the basis of competition, 2) strengthening customer relationships, 3) overcoming supplier problems, 4) building barriers against new entrants, 5) generating new products.

On the other hand, if used merely tactically, the nature of the marketing database does not need to refer greatly to corporate strategy or organizational structure (Cook, 1994). Under such circumstances it is more concerned with 'the next event' than with a longer-term view of customers (Bigg, 1994). Cook (1994) suggests that it is actually more usual for organizations to employ the database at the tactical rather than at the strategic level.

Parkinson (1994) identifies three levels of IT application within marketing. The first is concerned with the management of transactions, the second with profiling, targeting and developing effective direct marketing and the third with marketing productivity analysis, modelling and strategic planning.

If the organization is not truly customer orientated then there will only be a tactical role for the marketing database, but if used strategically, it has a central role to play – as DeTienne and Thompson (1996) imply in their definition of database marketing:

> Database marketing is the process of systematically collecting, in electronic or optical form, data about past, current and/or potential customers, maintaining the integrity of the data by continually monitoring customer purchases and/or by inquiring about changing status and using the data to formulate marketing strategy and foster personalized relationships with customers.
>
> (De Tienne and Thompson, 1996)

Another proposition of this chapter, then, is that the database, if used in a mere tactical way, will also relegate direct marketing itself to a tactical appendage of a broader, more strategic marketing function.

DATA FUSION AND BIOGRAPHICS

With what to 'populate' the database is of course a key question. There are 'off the shelf' databases such as geodemographics from Experian and CACI, lifestyle lists from NDL and CMT and a plethora of mailing lists. Lifestyle questionnaires are constantly expanding due to the increase in the number of sponsored questions added to the questionnaire. Individual companies pay to have a question included that is relevant to their (perhaps very specialized) products. Because answers are personalized, those for whom the company might have a relevant product become known by name and address – and can be further geodemographically profiled via their postcode.

Another interesting development is the linking of lifestyle with geodemographics. In Experian's 'Psyche' profile, every UK postcode is assigned to one of the following groupings:

Self Explorers (11 per cent of UK), Experimentalists (10 per cent of UK), Conspicuous Consumers (18 per cent of UK), Belongers (20 per cent of UK), Social Resisters (12 per cent of UK), Survivors (23 per cent of UK), Aimless (6 per cent of UK!).

There is a plethora of direct marketing lists available for purchase or sharing. Each list is itself a database and most provide names and addresses of those who possess certain characteristics – either profile based or transaction based.

External lists can be rented or purchased (or licensed) and can be of consumer, industrial or international markets. It is generally the case that internal lists will perform better than external ones, but externally acquired lists will be modified on the basis of the company's personal experience, so becoming more tailored to their market requirements. It is also generally true that lists of people who have already shown a willingness to respond will produce better response rates than lists of non-responders.

Sources of lists can be very varied, with some being specially compiled for marketing (though not necessarily for each client company) and some being a result of other marketing activity. Examples of the latter would include lists compiled from magazine subscribers, store card applicants, attendees at exhibitions, responders to DRTV advertisements, mail order, telephone and direct mail responders.

Take a hypothetical consumer list – one based on consumers who have purchased from a mail order catalogue. Lists of names and addresses could be provided for each of the product categories serviced by the catalogue: photography, car accessories, gardening, hi-fi, fashion, health aids and so on – individual categories can usually be bought and often run to several hundred thousand names. There will usually be other profiling factors included from the original purchase from the catalogue, such as age, gender, payment method, marital status, home ownership and income. Many of the last-mentioned factors are derived from customers' applications to the catalogue for credit arrangements – again reinforcing the credit referencing origins of database marketing. Recency of purchase is another factor and is a major determinant of response rates.

There are also in-house sources of data from which to populate the database. For example there are customer records, results from sales promotion campaigns (coupons, competitions etc.), also from market research and from *transactional* data – the latter being one of the major growth areas for database population.

Retailers are capturing transactional data at point of sale via loyalty card schemes – for example, Tesco, Safeway and Sainsbury. By late 1996 Tesco had analysed their customer database and identified 5000 different segments – each of which was targeted differently. Their aim at that time was to be literally one-to-one by 1999! The company analysing the Tesco data is DunnHumby, and Clive Humby (1996a) describes the interrogation of data and states that it is not worth including 'everything'. There is always the danger of 'paralysis by analysis'! Humby goes on to suggest that 'it is not the detailed transaction data that is of interest, but patterns in transactions, such as an increasing balance over time of the range of products purchased' (1996b). He also highlights the problem that the industry has over a lack of staff to fill the IT–Marketing gap.

If geodemographics was a significant catalyst in marketing database development, *transactional* data is now providing a yet more dramatic impetus. For example, an inspection of a retail loyalty scheme database revealed, for a certain Mrs 'Brown', her address and a variety of behavioural information including: she shops once per week, usually on a Friday, has a baby (because she buys nappies), spends £90 per week on average and usually buys two bottles of gin every week (Mitchell, 1996). By knowing what individual consumers buy, the retailer might be able to target them with relevant offers while the consumer saves money in the process. If a 'relationship' develops, the retailer is moving from the more expensive 'acquisition' to the much cheaper 'retention' of consumers – and several writers advocate this in times of low industry growth (Rossenberg and Czepiel, 1989; Barlow, 1992; Donovan, 1996).

Now that transactional data is at the heart of many databases, overlaid with a multitude of profile data, we are perhaps moving into the era of *biographics* – the fusion of profile and transaction data. Figure 18.1 shows some of the typical sources of data for fusion into biographical profiles.

Indeed, 'data matching is the key because it bridges sources' (di Talamo, 1995); the ability to match names, addresses, purchasing behaviour and lifestyles all together onto one record allows companies to build a picture of someone's life. Database linking occurs on two levels. Firstly, on an industry level census data, geodemographics and lifestyle data build up a broad picture of the population – ideal for segmentation purposes. Secondly, at the individual company level, matching this data to credit history, actual purchasing behaviour, media response, and the recency, frequency and monetary (RFM) value of purchases can potentially describe one's life. In addition to leading to the identification of volume segments and best prospects, the RFM information also contributes to the calculation of 'lifetime value' – another of the direct marketer's cornerstone measures. 'Lifetime' is perhaps something of an overstatement – it doesn't mean the lifetime of the customer, but rather a designated period of time during which they are a customer of an organization. In 1997 the DMIS found that 53 per cent of a sample of companies matched their internal customer record data with external geodemographics and 57 per cent with external lifestyle profiles (DMIS, 1997).

Often it is very useful to be able to picture, geographically, what the database information tells us. The key to this is address and postcode because from this there are geographical information systems (GIS) which allow any linked database to produce map overlays. Another application of GIS-linked data is in the citing of posters for direct response advertising, based on the profile of the neighbourhood or even the profile of 'through' traffic (Leggit, 1997). A related software solution is offered by The Data Consultancy (Drivetime Software) because this calculates drive times as *isochrones* (the distance one can drive in a given time along roads).

However, fusion doesn't always take place; in studies by Long *et al.* (1992), it was suggested that synergy is needed between marketing, operations, information technology and database literacy before the power of such systems will be unleashed in practice. In a follow-up study a clear message emerges, namely a call for organizations to 'move away from using technology to do things to customers, to doing things with customers by giving the customer a voice in the process of building relationships' (Long *et al.*, 1992).

In a variety of empirical research studies (Evans *et al.*, 1996b; Patterson *et al.*, 1996; O'Malley *et al.*, 1997) consumers have expressed concerns over the lack of privacy of their personal details – '1984' it may not be but the privacy issue clearly needs constant vigilance.

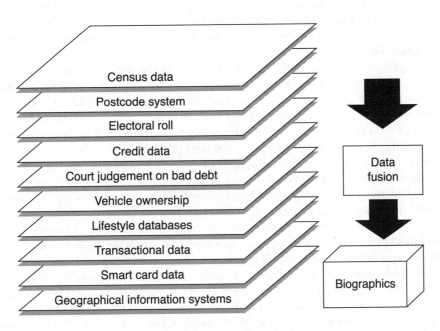

Figure 18.1 Layers of database marketing.

DATA MINING

Data mining refers to the digging around in databases in a relatively unstructured way with the aim of discovering links between customer behaviour and almost any variable that might potentially be useful.

Direct marketers have tried a variety of unusual or unexpected areas in which to mine. For example, some have examined consumers' individual biorhythms and 'star signs' as predictors of their purchasing patterns and others have linked their transactional and profile data with meteorological databases to predict, perhaps months ahead, what demand there might be for ice cream or woolly sweaters – and from whom!

Another example of data mining is afforded by the linking with a GIS database to target as specifically as a newspaper round! This is usually around 150–200 households and by linking transactional data with lifestyle, geodemographics and panel data, a very accurate picture of individual buying patterns emerges. The newspaper round – or milk round – can be used for door drops or direct mail as well as for local catchment area analysis. This has been formalized by Unigate which has advertised a doorstep delivery service based on MOSAIC geodemographic profiles at local level. In addition to product delivery they offered a delivery service for samples and vouchers and a delivery and collection service for questionnaires.

A number of dedicated tools are available for analysing databases. One such 'product' is VIPER – a rather aggressively branded piece of software developed by Brann Software. This tool allows very fast linking and analysis of different databases. Figure 18.2 demonstrates a VIPER-processed query on a lifestyle database, linked with a geodemographic database and a geographical information system (GIS). The questions asked might have been: select those (name and address) who claim to be readers of the *Sun*, like to play bingo, drink above-average quantities of lager and live in South Wales.

The graphical printout combines data from all of the databases interrogated, and shows in topographical form where these people live and also in tabular form the actual names and addresses of the individuals concerned. VIPER is not the only database interrogator on the market but it does reflect the sort of capability that is now available – the speed with which the analysis is completed is indeed impressive – and on what is now a relatively standard desktop PC.

Database 'data' becomes 'information' when we identify the 'recency, frequency and monetary value' (RFM) of customer orders. Recency – just knowing they have purchased in the past is important but not sufficient; companies are probably less interested in those who bought in 1984 but not since. Frequency – a one-off purchase may also make a customer less attractive (depending, of course, on the product-market in which a company operates). So knowing how often customers buy is an important measure. Monetary value – small orders are usually less attractive than larger ones, so this is yet another measure of significance. Indeed, marketers are increasingly concentrating on their 'better' customers – those who have the highest monetary value (and frequency) of purchase, and are segmenting on the basis of 'volume' because in this way they are more cost-effective, because they concentrate on those who bring greater returns. Vilfredo Pareto's theory of income distribution has been transferred and borrowed by direct marketers to support the proposition that 80 per cent of sales come from just 20 per cent of customers – in many markets the ratio can be even more polarized (95:5 is not uncommon). The Pareto principle is often quoted by direct marketers and is certainly relevant to this discussion of RFM analysis. RFM analysis clearly, by the nature of the variables involved, means that transactional data must be tracked by the database – actual purchase history is needed.

As a summary of this section, the author suggests that transactional data, fused with profiling data, will produce the new biographics and this will be the basis of marketing databases over the next few years.

RESEARCH VS. TESTING

A final theme of this chapter concerns a related aspect of the use of the database in direct marketing, namely what might be described as an over-reliance on testing at the expense of more traditional market research.

The direct marketing industry is able to conduct experiments by selecting samples from different lists and monitoring response rates in order to identify the

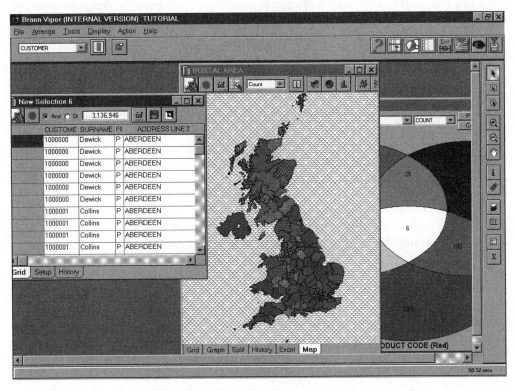

Figure 18.2 VIPER database interrogation.

(Reproduced with kind permission of *Brann Software*.)

better performing lists. Different direct mail 'creative' can be tested on sub-samples and the version which produces stronger response rates can be rolled out.

With colleagues, the writer conducted some market research into consumer attitudes toward direct marketing (Evans *et al.*, 1997) and in interviews, some of the older women, in particular, declared that they received substantial quantities of direct mail on behalf of charities. They also said that this was not 'junk mail' because it was of interest to them – the matching of 'causes' with their own interests was very accurate. They were so moved by the direct mailing that they felt it important to donate – and they did just this. As far as the direct marketer is concerned, this 'response' reinforces the donors' status on the database and they will be targeted again – and probably by related charities who are likely to share lists.

The point which the writer feels it is important to add is that in 'research' the women went on to say that they were barely able to afford to donate, but felt they 'had to' and were almost in tears over the issue. The reaction of the direct marketing industry was 'but it worked' – such reliance on mechanistic testing at the expense of more insightful research is submitted here as being an issue that the industry would do well to address. Although this targeting might 'work' in the short term, what problems might be being stored up for the future – not only when the 'targets' decide 'enough is enough' and refuse to donate any more and 'bin' all subsequent mailings, but even if they merely spread ill will about the charities' direct marketing approach?

This issue can be taken further and related back to the data fusion concept. Much database data, such as transactional and profiling data, provides valuable information on who is buying what, when, how and where, but it is market research that can get beneath the surface even further and discover reasons 'why' behaviour is as it is.

As a result, some direct marketers are linking their databases with market research data. In this way, for example, consumer panels are linked with geodemographic or lifestyle databases in '*T-Groups*'. The 'T' means that 'horizontally' database data provides tremendous breadth of data over millions of consumers but the 'vertical', from market research, provides greater depth of information.

The point, then, is that direct marketing has much to gain from turning to more traditional market research – not as a substitute for the highly measurable and accountable testing methodology, but to create a valuable 'gestalt'.

However, a related issue is raised by Fletcher and Peters (1996) with respect to the use of market research data to populate databases. The main problem is one of using marketing research data for selling purposes (selling under the guise of research; SUGGING). The Market Research Society has long outlawed this practice but has now compromised over the issue by having dual codes of conduct for the two 'reasons' for data collection. The concerns will not go away, however, and the direct marketing and marketing research industries probably have more work to do to resolve these conflicts.

SUMMARY AND CONCLUSIONS

This chapter has discussed some of the reasons for the growth in direct marketing – market fragmentation, database advances and the recognition by marketers of the need for marketing to be better targeted.

Several propositions have emerged. First, that *geodemographics* provided the first revolution in market profiling because they raised the stakes from sample surveys of 1000 based on very few profiling characteristics (age, gender, occupation) to the census of 56 million based on 60 census variables and a variety of overlaying factors.

Secondly, the future will be dominated by *transactional* data, overlaid by geodemographic, lifestyle and other *profiling* data, via *data fusion*, producing databases of *biographical* information for understanding, analysing and targeting individual customers (whose own buying behaviour has become increasingly individualistic) and this is moving towards *mass customization*.

This 'biographical' analogy is perhaps analogous with the Domesday Book, for which, in the UK in medieval times, William the Conqueror collected personal information (though rather more brutally than the database industry of today does!) about each of his subjects. In this sense we have seen the birth of what might be termed 'Domesday Marketing' (Evans, 1994). This raises a variety of ethical issues concerning the acquisition and use of personal data – whether these issues produce Orwellian concerns or not is probably a personal matter, but the direct marketing industry must continue to research and address the privacy issue and this is the third proposition submitted here.

The fourth proposition is that direct marketing will always be a tactical appendage if an integrated strategic approach is not adopted in the use and role of the marketing database.

The final proposition is that direct marketers, by over-relying on response rates and testing, is in danger of being accused of short-termism because the reasons behind 'response' or 'non-response' are not being studied as fully as the mere fact of response or non-response. Even the Institute of Direct Marketing itself can be criticized here – in a recent mailing to its members it stated 'we've been accused . . . of drowning the marketing profession in mailings, inserts and leaflets, too many of them looking interchangeable . . . (but) the programme always made its response targets' (Smith, 1997).

DISCUSSION TOPICS

1 Why has direct marketing grown so dramatically over recent years?
2 What are geodemographics and what is their significance to the direct marketing industry?
3 What can transactional data provide the direct marketer?
4 Discuss the role of the marketing database, strategically and tactically.
5 What are 'RFM' measures and 'lifetime values' and what is their value to direct marketers?
6 What is data fusion? Provide examples of how data is being linked and then used by direct marketers. What might be future examples of data fusion?

7 How significant is the privacy issue for direct marketers and their targets? What should the industry do about consumer concerns, if anything?

8 What are the advantages and disadvantages to both marketer and customer of focusing – via the Pareto Principle – on the 'best' customers?

9 What is the 'testing vs. research' issue and how should it be addressed?

10 How do you see the future of direct marketing? Will it be a short-lived fad or will most marketing include a 'direct' element of some kind?

CASE STUDY – SPINNING THE WHEEL OF FORTUNE WITH DIRECT MAIL

Washing machines that grind to a halt can mean more than a trip to the local launderette. Repair bills may soar above the cost of the appliance itself, leaving a frustrated family not only exposing its dirty laundry in public but suffering financially too. That's why Norwich Union Direct, a limb of the 6000-strong financial services giant, decided to be the first to exploit the gap in the market for an alternative to extended warranties offered by retailers of consumer durables.

Direct mail played a major part in the marketing campaign to promote Appliance Breakdown Cover (ABC), Norwich Union Direct's competitive insurance policy covering all major domestic appliances. Indeed their strategy – which also embraced advertising on TV, radio and in the national press – won their advertising agency third place in the coveted Direct Marketing Awards. Research conducted after the one month campaign found that 17 per cent of all adults had heard there had been a new entrant in the appliance breakdown market. Andrew Jackson, Norwich Union Direct's head of marketing, explained how direct mail proved effective in raising ABC's profile among buyers of white and brown goods. He said: 'The results of targeted direct mail have improved significantly over the recent past and gone are the days of the single digit response to a campaign. It's still underused in the UK, though, since there continues to be a large number of haphazard, "confetti" mailings. Using databases intelligently and sustaining a dialogue with customers is fundamental to marketing success.'

Andrew outlined the reasons for creating ABC in the first place. He said: 'Manufacturers' warranties on domestic appliances usually last only a year, while the extended insurance that's available in the shops is both expensive and offered only for a limited period.' 'It's a real burden for the customer financially, with the cost of the cover usually bolted on to the credit price of the product – on which he is already paying interest – plus a liability to pay 17.5 per cent insurance tax on the warranty,' he added.

Norwich Union Direct's solution was to provide the customer with a hassle-free service for all non-moveable cooking, cleaning, preserving and entertainment goods in the home. ABC is a simple service that has the added attraction to the customer of no excess to pay. Andrew explained: 'Before we launched the promotion, research had shown that two propositions would turn people on: the first was a money-saving one; the second was a hassle-free proposition. It revealed two distinct types of buyer and mirrored the classic Henley Centre division between those who spend money to save time and those who spend time to save money by shopping around.' Direct mail was crucial to reaching Norwich Union Direct's 110 000 existing customers, each of whom received an eight-page A5 colour brochure detailing the benefits of ABC. 'We were able to be very focused by converting our claims experience to finely target the brochure at those people who would find this product attractive. Thousands responded to the mail shot which easily outperformed the usual response rates to financial services products,' Andrew recalled.

As a major customer of Royal Mail, Norwich Union Direct was able to negotiate generous discounts to substantially reduce distribution costs for the direct mailing through the local Royal Mail account manager, Mike Batt. Other benefits included Royal Mail's sophisticated Mailsort facilities which allowed Norwich Union Direct to stagger the mailing over a four-week period so it was not swamped with customers' responses all at once. Due to the insurance company's buoyant experience of direct mail, it plans to use this proven method to maximum effect in future marketing campaigns.

(Reproduced with kind permission of *The Reputation Managers*)

REFERENCES

Barlow, R. (1992) 'Relationship marketing – the ultimate in customer services', *Retail Control*, March: 29–37.
Bigg, A. (1994) 'Techno tactics', *Campaign*, 8 July, 37–8.
Borden, N. (1964) 'The concept of the marketing mix', *Journal of Advertising Research*, June: 2–7.
Cook, S. (1994) 'Database marketing: strategy or tactical tool?', *Marketing Intelligence and Planning*, 12(6): 4–7.
DeTienne, K.B. and Thompson, J.A. (1996) 'Database marketing and organizational learning theory: toward a research agenda', *Journal of Consumer Marketing*, 13(5): 12–34.
di Talamo (1995) cited by Reed, 'Jumping on the Bandwagon', *Marketing Week*, 24 March, 25–6.
Direct Mail Information Service (1997) 'Consumer databases: a study of external lists and in-house database usage'.
Donovan, J. (1996) 'The true price of loyalty', *Marketing Week*, Customer Loyalty insert, 8 February, XI–XIII.
Evans, M. (1994) 'Domesday marketing', *Journal of Marketing Management*, 10(5): 409–31.
Evans, M., O'Malley, L. and Patterson, M. (1996a) 'Direct mail and consumer response: an empirical study of consumer experiences of direct mail', *Journal of Database Marketing*, 3(3): 250–61.
Evans, M., O'Malley, L. and Patterson, M. (1996b) 'Direct marketing communications in the UK: a study of growth, past, present and future', *Journal of Marketing Communications*, 2(1): 51–65.
Evans, M., O'Malley, L., Patterson, M. and Mitchell, S. (1997) 'Consumer reactions to supermarket loyalty schemes', *Journal of Database Marketing*, 4(4): 307–20.
Fletcher, K. and Peters, L. (1996) 'Issues in consumer information management', *Journal of the Market Research Society*, 38(2): 145–60.
Henley Centre (1978) *Planning Consumer Markets*, London.
Humby, C. (1996a) 'Digging for information', *Marketing*, 21 November, 41–2.
Humby, C. (1996b) 'Opening the information warehouse', *Marketing*, 18 September, 34–7.
Institute of Direct Marketing (1995) *Marketing Planning: Strategy, Planning and Analysis*, Module 1, 1-3-05.

Kitchen, P. (1986) 'Zipping, zapping and nipping', *International Journal of Advertising*, 5, 343–52.

Leggit, D. (1997) 'Putting posters on the map', *Marketing*, 3 July: 23–5.

Long, G., Angold, S. and Hogg, M. (1992) 'Who am I?', *Marketing Education Group Conference Proceedings*, Salford, July.

McCarthy, E.J. (1960) *Basic Marketing*, Homewood IL: Irwin.

Mitchell, A. (1996) Interview transcribed from BBC Radio 4 'You and Yours', January.

O'Malley L., Patterson, M. and Evans, M. (1997) 'Intimacy or intrusion? The privacy dilemma for relationship marketing in consumer markets', *Journal of Marketing Management*, 13: 541–59.

Parkinson, S. (1994) *Computers in Marketing*, London: Butterworth–Heinemann, 18–19.

Patterson, M., Evans, M. and O'Malley, L. (1996) 'The growth of direct marketing and consumer attitudinal response to the privacy issue', *Journal of Targeting, Measurement and Analysis for Marketing*, 4(3): 201–13.

Rees, P. (1997) 'ESRC/JISC questionnaire to users of census data: views about the 2001 census of population', Summer.

Rossenberg, L.J. and Czepiel (1989) 'A marketing approach for customer retention', *Journal of Consumer Marketing*, 45.

Shaw, R. and Stone, M. (1988a) 'Competitive superiority through database marketing', *Long Range Planning*, 21(5): 24–40.

Shaw, R. and Stone, M. (1988b) *Database Marketing*, Guildford: Gower.

Smith, G. (1997) Letter to IDM members, 4 September, 1.

19

PERSONAL SELLING: MANAGEMENT AND ORGANIZATION

Bill Donaldson

CHAPTER AIMS

- to consider the role of personal selling as part of the marketing communications mix
- to clarify the role of personal selling and different types of selling
- to stress the importance of effective sales force management
- to analyse decisions relating to the organization of personal selling in terms of type, structure, size and deployment
- to assess future needs and likely direction of the personal selling effort

ILLUSTRATION

The following case indicates how the role of personal selling is changing as part of the communications and marketing mix as used by one FMCG company.

Kraft General Foods plc restructures its sales force

In 1992, Kraft General Foods plc decided to change their sales force in a very radical way, which totally changed the role of the salesperson and involved complete restructuring of their sales operations. At that time the sales force was reduced from just under 300 people to a mere 24. The traditional role of calling on individual supermarket accounts, independent grocers and corner shops at a local level throughout the UK was replaced in favour of a small number of 'account managers' who were responsible for dealing with major supermarket chains, large wholesalers and other buying groups with centralized ordering procedures.

The rationale for this transformation was the ambition of the company to pursue a modern marketing programme as a customer-focused business and improve their competitive position by knowing their customers' needs and working closely with key buyers. In addition, the company wanted a sales force that would be cost-efficient and maximize their profits through promotional effort and organization. This transformation was dictated by their major customers (e.g. Tesco, Sainsbury) who wanted to deal with suppliers on a centralized, large-order basis and not on a store-by-store basis with frequent stock-outs and multiple delivery problems. Kraft had maintained the previous system to control the way price promotions, new product stocking and merchandising were presented to end users. The market had moved away from this localized approach to a new buyer behaviour based on the needs of large organizations and automated ordering and stocking procedures. Kraft decided that the costs of maintaining a sales and merchandising presence at local level was too high and outweighed the benefits gained by the company or its customers. The business from independent small retailers and wholesalers did not generate sufficient revenue to cover costs and sustain an adequate level of profitability. The new sales operation operated with 24 key account managers and a new improved customer ordering and help service based on an expanded telemarketing operation from head office.

(*Source:* Donaldson, 1998)

INTRODUCTION

The development of marketing communications, as an integrated discipline within marketing, brings salespeople to the front stage of current developments, since salespeople have direct, face-to-face contact with customers. Key academics and sales professionals, recognizing this importance, suggest that the sales profession is undergoing a transformation and that this process, already started, will gather momentum as the year 2000 approaches. These changes will enhance the profile of the sales function, promote best practice in the area of personal selling, and drive improvements in the professionalism and competencies of salespeople. However, unless there is strategic insight into what this transformation entails, guidelines cannot be provided for the development of the discipline and the profession at the start of the new millennium.

The reason why this new perspective, integrating sales and other forms of communication, is so urgent arises from more complex supply chains, fewer and larger purchase points, availability and use of IT in customer contact operations, relative increased costs of labour, and the continuing internationalization of business in the global market economy. These factors contribute positively to the need for more efficient exchange and communication systems between firms and their customers. This need for an effective sales force is predicated by increases in the costs of acquiring new customers, the need to retain the existing customer base and stimulate the purchasing power of those customers already on the books.

In this chapter the role of personal selling is examined as part of the marketing communications mix. Different types of selling and the development of a relationship-based approach (see Chapter 23) are considered. The search for effective and efficient management of sales operations is justified and a review of forms, types and different sales force structures is made. Issues of sales force size and methods of deployment are also considered. Conclusions are made on key aspects of managing sales now and in the future.

THE ROLE OF PERSONAL SELLING

Personal selling is personal contact with one or more purchasers for the purpose of making a sale. To be effective, marketing managements need to integrate personal selling with other promotional elements, with other organizational functions such as distribution and production and with the customer and competitive structures prevailing in the market. The importance of personal selling is such that expenditure on the sales force usually exceeds the budget for all other marketing communications activities added together, with the exception of advertising in fast-moving consumer goods companies' promotion. Personal selling has several interrelated roles within the communications mix. The information role is part of a two-way process whereby information about the company's product or offer needs to be communicated to existing and potential customers and, in the reverse direction, customers' needs are correctly interpreted and understood by management. Salespeople impart knowledge about products or services which provide benefits to customers and also a range of information on promotional support, finance, technical advice, service and other elements which contribute to customer satisfaction. Salespeople are also the face-to-face contact between purchasers and the company and for good reason are referred to as 'the eyes and ears of the organization' since senior management's customer contact may be limited.

A second role salespeople must fulfil is persuasion. The importance of correctly identifying customers' needs and market opportunities can never be over-stated. Nevertheless, in competitive markets prospective customers are usually faced with an abundance of choice. As a result, adoption of the marketing concept can be no guarantee of competitive advantage. Purchasers will have to be convinced that their needs have been correctly identified by the company and that the offer provides benefit over any other firm. Salespeople are part of this process through persuasion and service.

A third role is relationship building and salespeople must initiate, build and develop relationships between the firm and its customers. Owing to their boundary-spanning role, the sales force of a company has traditionally been a vital link between the firm and its customers (Cravens *et al.*, 1992) and a prime platform for communicating the firm's marketing message to its customers and the voice of the customer to the firm. In the high tech, nano-second nineties it is easy to overlook the importance of personal relationships and how interaction with customers has changed, if at all. Sales management practices need to be re-engineered to maximize the sales force potential.

The nature of the personal selling task is continuing to change in that selling to customers has been replaced by cooperating with customers. The goals and objectives for the salesperson have also changed from achieving or exceeding target, selling X products in Y period and maximizing earnings, to that of building repeat business with the firm's existing and potential customer base. The emphasis has shifted from 'closing' the singular sale to creating the necessary conditions for a long-term relationship between the firm and its customers that breeds successful sales encounters in the long-run. This shift renders obsolete many of the currently available sales management practices and the sales philosophy and culture that has driven the development of the sales management field for decades. It also questions sales performance measures based on individual criteria and sales management practices which reflect recruitment, training and rewards based on sales volumes rather than relationship performance. The role of the salesperson seems to have moved away from traditional aggressive and persuasive selling, to a new role of 'relationship manager' (Crosby *et al.*, 1990). Also, in practice, we are witnessing a tendency to change the sales lexicon from sales force to sales counsellors, professional representatives or sales consultants (Manning and Reece, 1992; DeCormier and Jobber, 1993). Perhaps the title changes are designed to facilitate the transition of the sales force's tasks from selling to advising and counselling, from talking to listening, and from pushing to helping as suggested by Pettijohn *et al.* (1995). This transition is not only a matter of title. The new reality of relationship marketing directs salespeople and sales managers to develop long-lasting relationships with their customers based on mutual trust and commitment (Morgan and Hunt, 1994).

The most significant difference between selling and other elements in the marketing communications mix is personal contact. The need for this personal contact will vary depending on such factors as the scale of risk, size of investment, type of customer, frequency of purchase, newness of product and many other factors. In some situations the information or persuasion role can be achieved by impersonal means of communication, particularly advertising. Advertising is impersonal, indirect and aimed at a mass audience, whereas selling is individual, direct and much more adaptable. With advertising the message is more limited, cheaper per contact but unidirectional, relying on a pull approach rather than personal selling which is two-way, but employs a push strategy and is relatively expensive per contact. These differences are highlighted in Table 19.1.

In most exchanges, except direct response campaigns, it is unlikely that a sale can be made without first establishing a personal contact. This is the primary role of personal selling. While selling skills are always important, it is worthwhile to distinguish between different types of selling, such as transaction and relationship

Table 19.1 Communication choice: comparing personal selling and advertising

Personal selling	Advertising
Individual directionality	Mass audience directionality
Personal, direct contact	Impersonal, indirect contact
Highly adaptable	Fixed format
Working in depth	Working in breadth
Two-way	One-way
Direct feedback	Organized feedback (MIS, Market Research)
Expensive per contact	Relatively inexpensive (cost per 1000 criteria)
Push effect	Pull effect

selling, and between new business and service selling. In the case of one-off transactions, salesmanship is often the reason a sale is made or not and therefore gives rise to hard sell techniques. In some cases these techniques seem to be the opposite of marketing, as characterized by double glazing, timeshare and second-hand car salespeople where customer dissatisfaction and post-cognitive dissonance levels are unacceptably high. In these direct selling situations the task of the salesperson is to provide prospective buyers with information and other benefits, motivating or persuading them to make buying decisions in favour of the seller's product or service. In other situations, salespeople are involved with regular rather than one-off customers where repeat business is both the aim and the norm and it is more appropriate to think of exchange as a continuing relationship, not merely that of making a sale. This form of exchange is characterized by buyer and seller being known to each other, by business being lost rather than won and by forms of joint cooperation in the exchange relationship. Other forms of communication must support this activity.

It is also important to distinguish between new business selling and maintenance selling. In a new business situation the salesperson has to identify worthwhile prospects, identify the influences and decision makers within the buying unit and, by establishing a relationship based on the identification of customer needs, problem solving and shared values, build up a rapport with prospects and customers. This type of salesperson has to match his or her offer to the buyer's real needs and motivate prospects to change. Further, this change has to materialize into an initial order and, finally, the salesperson has to convert the initial purchase into repeat ordering behaviour. This is a time-consuming, difficult job.

Most people in selling are employed selling existing products to existing customers. This type of selling, service selling, requires different skills and a different approach to that of the new business or development salesperson. Here the task is to consolidate existing customers, to preserve and expand the volume of business these customers do and maintain inertia in the buyer–seller exchange relationship. Service salespersons know their customers very well, know their customers' business, have access to a number of personnel in the buying organization, and seek to maintain the status quo and continue the favoured buyer–supplier relationship. A salesperson's tasks might include taking orders, product display, advice to distributors, advice to users and specifiers, after-sales service, complaint handling, collecting payment, stock management, training customers' staff, and many other activities.

THE ROLE OF SALES MANAGEMENT

Sales management is the management process of directing strategy, organizing tactics and implementing policies which fulfil the firm's sales, marketing and corporate objectives. This is achieved by means of influencing subordinates to be more efficient and effective. The job of the sales manager is not to sell but to achieve sales through subordinates. Managing a sales force is different to selling. Put simply, sales managers need to establish the role salespeople can be expected to perform, the tasks to be accomplished and the means to achieve their sales objectives. Three problems hamper sales managers. First, the high cost of personal selling. The average cost of a salesperson in the UK is £49,400 per annum (Donkin, 1997). Secondly, only about 20–30 per cent of a salesperson's time is face-to-face with customers (other time is driving, administration, call preparation, merchandising, etc.). Thirdly, customer buying is changing, becoming more professional, efficient and increasingly automated and centralized. The danger may be that with the passage of time and maturity in product markets the sales force become courtesy callers rather than salespeople and this is an expensive resource for this purpose. An amusing way to describe salespeople is to refer to them as inter-organizational boundary spanners but this is exactly what they are and what makes their management both challenging and difficult. As a result, increasing the productivity of salespeople is a necessary, and important, managerial activity.

THE ORGANIZATION OF THE SALES FORCE

Having decided on the role salespeople will play, management must select and organize individuals into an effective sales force by deciding on the type, the structure and the size of their operation and on how best to deploy their salespeople and allocate them to customers and prospects. These are the issues to which we now turn.

Agents vs. direct sales force

The first issue is whether to use manufacturers' representatives (agents) or to employ a direct sales force. The high proportion of marketing expense accounted for by direct sales costs, the relatively fixed nature of these costs and the low face-to-face selling time have encouraged a reappraisal of how sales forces operate (Anderson, 1985). Management have traditionally been wary of acknowledging this choice, instead preferring to alter training or remuneration or to change deployment or other features when problems arise. There is some evidence that contracting out the sales function, similar to the trend to subcontract many non-core activities, may be a viable alternative to the high cost of a national direct sales force (Brown-Humes, 1997; Fites, 1996).

Traditionally, agents have been used where the market is new, such as exporting, where the company has lacked adequate resources or where tradition has encouraged this practice, e.g. printing and publishing. However, a sales force of service callers has become something of a luxury item and serious consideration should be given to using highly motivated independent agents. The independent agent whose survival and prosperity depend on his or her sales performance may be a realistic alternative. Such people can be used where a number of complementary products are sold to the same customer, as with computer software, the food broker, category manager or financial services advisor. The agent requires less training, will already have established a relationship with customers and prospects and is only paid when sales are made. Supervision, recruitment and training costs will be much less and turnover in personnel will be significantly lower. They are also unlikely to transfer to the competition. As markets extend yet fragment, the local knowledge of an agent may be a significant advantage if it brings continuity and greater customer knowledge.

Generally, a direct sales force would be preferred where there is high investment, specialized products and a need to control the selling situation because of uncertainty in the market or environment in which the company operates. If sales performance is difficult to evaluate and non-selling activities such as technical advice and goodwill are likely to be important, a direct sales force is more likely.

Sales force structure

A second organizational task is to decide how to structure the sales force to achieve the best, most productive result which meets customer needs. There are six concepts to be borne in mind when designing an organizational structure:

- Organizational structure should be marketing-oriented
- Organizations should be designed for activities, not people
- Clearly defined responsibility and maximum possible delegation of authority
- A reasonable span of control
- Organizations should be stable yet flexible
- Organizations should be balanced and coordinated in the activities to be performed

Inevitably, there will be some conflict between organizational and sales objectives and between management and individuals as to the best way to organize selling effort. The sales force organization will achieve best results where duplication of effort is eliminated, where internal conflicts are minimized and where cooperation is maximized. This is not easy. The sales manager must:

- set clearly defined objectives;
- specify the role of salespeople and the tasks to be performed;
- group activities into specific jobs with clear authority and responsibility;
- assign personnel to these jobs;
- provide effective coordination and control.

Geographical specialization is the traditional and most widely used type of sales organization. In this type of structure each salesperson is responsible for all tasks, all products and all existing and prospective customers within a geographical area. It is most appropriate in larger rather than smaller organizations, where there is a widely spread customer base, rather than only a few, where regional variations are more important than national standards and where personal contact between buyer and seller is frequent rather than occasional. The advantages of a geographical split are likely to be that travel time and expense are lower. Each salesperson can build good customer and area knowledge which itself is a motivating factor in that salespeople manage their territory. There is less confusion since multiple calling on a single customer is avoided; customers know who is the point of contact. Additionally, management control and evaluation are more easily administered. These advantages are important but the complexity of today's selling job and the dynamics of the business environment may require specialization. The need to specialize in product or customer, the need to use experts to meet customers needs and the problem of using low-level personnel for key management decisions do exist. Further, while control is straightforward, overhead costs may rise as more layers of management evolve.

Product specialization would appeal where a company has product lines which differ in technical complexity, end users and profitability. Each salesperson can then attain the necessary expertise in product knowledge to handle different customer requirements more effectively. Companies who take over or merge with others sometimes continue to operate separate sales forces. Also, the case for expertise with a new product may require specialist development salespeople. With this type of organization, problems arise with duplication of effort and multiple calling on one customer. This requires management to promote cooperation between salespeople with minimum conflict and confusion as to who does what job.

Market specialization is not yet a popular type of sales organization in UK industry but there has been a trend in some industries for sales organizations to organize by customer or prospect. Implementation of the marketing concept would suggest that the most appropriate form of specialization is that based on customers. Where market segmentation policies can be applied it is sensible to operate the sales force by specializing on the respective segments. Grouping of customers into suitable classifications means salespeople can develop customer expertise, and implement marketing policy and programmes. In dynamic, innovative markets the information exchange process may require this form of specialism. In other cases, too much specialization will result in excessively high selling costs.

Combined methods. The advantages and disadvantages of the three previous methods encourage many firms to seek systems of organization which combine the benefits of specialization with reduced selling costs. The increasing complexity of the selling job in dynamic, changing markets gives impetus to this organizational dilemma. The problem still remains of how to deploy salespeople to achieve sales objectives. Several more recent developments in sales force organizational structure must be considered:

- *Key account selling.* A newer form of market-based organization may split customers into key accounts, different channel members or by industry type. There is no doubt in several markets, particularly food, DIY and household goods, that the disproportionate effect of major customers' control of the market necessitates specialist sales treatment. This in turn affects the job to be done by salespeople on the ground at branch level. A separate merchandising sales force may be used to call on branches rather than to sell to buyers. In some markets such as office equipment, a junior sales force establishes contact and evaluates prospects. The Kraft Foods case typifies this dilemma. The traditional sales role of calling on individual accounts at a local level is replaced in favour of a small number of account managers dealing with the head offices of the major supermarkets and the major wholesale chains. This combination of key account selling and boosting inside sales and customer service was considered to be the most appropriate organization for most grocery product companies in the 1990s.
- *Telesales.* The application of the 80/20 rule can also mean that large numbers of customers account for a relatively small proportion of sales. An inside sales force

or telemarketing operation may be used to complement the outside sales force for specific tasks. The most obvious advantage of telemarketing is the ability to target specific contacts quickly at much lower cost than a personal sales call. Telemarketing can also be used to prospect, qualify and service accounts, not only as an order-taking vehicle. Customers who are small, marginal or geographically remote can be handled more efficiently than in person. Telemarketing can be used:

- as a low-cost substitute for personal selling; one estimate suggests that five to six personal calls can be replaced with 30 long telephone calls at one-tenth the cost (Stone and Wyman, 1986)
- to supplement personal selling calls
- to reinforce a direct mail campaign
- to offer guidance and advice on product usage or as a complaint vehicle for customers.
- *Team selling*. Based on successful implementation in 'high tech' selling and 'big ticket' items, a recent development has been the emergence of team selling whereby the salesperson is supported in negotiations by technical, operations, financial specialists, or others, as appropriate. This approach has extended to other markets as the advantages of relationship building between supplier and buyer, or intermediary, becomes apparent. For example, Proctor and Gamble (Kumar, 1996), recognizing that 80 per cent of sales come from a number of key accounts, have developed business teams whose sole responsibility is to sell the whole product range for one key customer. In some cases this team have offices within their customer's head office, for example Walmart.
- *Information technology (IT)*. A related but separate issue has been the impact of IT on sales operations (Singh, 1997; Singh *et al.*, 1997). The ability to obtain, store, analyse and retrieve large amounts of information quickly and cheaply has given innovative sales organizations a competitive edge (Meredith, 1997). It enables the firm to collect data from dispersed and diverse sources such as prospects, customers, distribution channels, company sources and salespeople themselves. If relevant information can be drawn together, formatted, stored, retrieved and manipulated into meaningful sales support information that is relevant, timely and cheap then sales force productivity will improve. This applies not only in administration and reporting but in assisting in routing, call scheduling and other forms of time management.

Sales force size

Having decided the most appropriate structure and combination of selling approaches, decisions have to be taken on how many people are needed to achieve objectives. Sales management problems are complex and solutions seldom permanent. In determining sales force size the temptation to look for a simple, universal formula should be avoided. The type of sales organization will affect the size of the sales force, particularly the degree of specialization considered appropriate. The nature of the selling task between development and service selling will be fundamental. Other aspects of the selling task will be affected by the time required to be spent on activities such as:

- demonstration/presentation
- negotiating on price
- explaining company policy
- providing information on competitors, customers
- dealer support programmes
- stock checking
- display work
- complaint handling
- credit problems
- prospecting for new business
- report writing.

These activities should be part of the salesperson's job description, being included to reflect their importance to the firm. This importance will in turn affect whether six or 16 calls per day is possible. Questions about sales force size will also depend on company objectives, company resources and on competitive or other environmental factors. Neither can issues of sales force size be divorced from the form of organization, the method of specializing and territory allocation.

The traditional approach to determining sales force size was based on one of three methods. The work load method is a composite figure made up from the total work time available, the allocation of this time to sales tasks and the time spent with each customer or prospect, usually on the basis of size of sales revenue per account. It is the most commonly used technique in UK sales management (Donaldson, 1998). With this approach each salesperson should have a similar work load in terms of size of accounts, number of calls and travel time. It is rarely the case that accounts can be distributed evenly so that travel time in some areas will eventually be much greater than in others. Other weaknesses in this approach may be that larger accounts may not be those with the highest potential in the future. If potential is used these may not be the most profitable if costs of servicing the account are higher or a less profitable product mix is taken. The most serious problem is the simplistic assumption that quantity equals quality. Each account and each salesperson will be different in quality, a factor not incorporated in this method. Put simply, different call frequencies (and time per call) may yield higher sales and profits.

A second method is to determine size on an estimate of sales potential for the company's products (sales forecast) based on management objectives and a desirable market share. If each salesperson performs to their job description an average productivity level per person can be calculated. Some allowances should be made for the loss of someone leaving, say 10 per cent per annum. Part of the problem with this method is the accuracy in estimating each variable, particularly average productivity. The accuracy of such an average is influenced by the effects of someone leaving, the lead time for a replacement to become established and the effects of cross-selling between salespeople in different areas. It assumes a rather static market position when most companies will experience growing or declining sales productivity and perhaps regional variations within an overall sales forecast.

The third method, the incremental method, suggests that the sales force should be expanded as long as additional sales revenue exceeds additional costs. Intuitively, this makes good business sense but this method is also flawed. First, there is the difficulty of estimating incremental revenues, and costs can be quite daunting. Second, this approach over-simplifies the economics of selling by assuming the product mix is uniform, that extraneous factors can be correctly assessed in advance in each area, that the costs of selecting/recruiting/dismissing salespeople can be accurately predicted and that other forms of promotion such as advertising have an equal effect on all prospects. It is unlikely these assumptions will prevail. The simplicity of sales responding to personal selling effort where all other factors are constant is simply not tenable. The dynamic nature of markets, coupled with economic growth or decline patterns, distorts the calculations of the effectiveness of salespeople in terms of a sales response function. Seasonal, cyclical and competitive fluctuations create market uncertainty with a possible danger of over-staffing leading to cost inefficiencies. Third, companies may compound these problems by adding salespeople as long as profits are positive. The important weakness here is that salespeople become the result of sales rather than the creators of sales. Finally, the incremental method fails to take account of, or alternatively dismisses, the effects of differing abilities, knowledge, skills and aptitude of salespeople.

Therefore, the three most popular methods of determining sales force size all have weaknesses. Management should take account of these different approaches, but as a result of their inherent problems, should also consider methods which combine good organizational practice with sound territory planning and which incorporate flexible management and lean organizational structures. This is considered next.

Territory deployment

The final organizational issue and a key determinant of performance is territory management. It would be wrong to isolate organization, especially sales force size, from territory management or to suggest suitable territories can be determined and evaluated without studying other determinants of performance such as salesperson ability, distribution, economic conditions or marketing effectiveness. Nevertheless, sales territories are established to facilitate effective sales force operations. This is achieved by allocating a number of present and potential customers within a given area to a particular salesperson. The benefits of sales territories are:

- more thorough coverage of the market
- clearer definition of an individual's responsibilities
- more specific performance evaluation
- reduced selling expense
- better fit between sales resources and customer's needs
- helps the salesperson by improving job clarity.

To establish sales territories, management must decide on the basic unit, evaluate the number of accounts and sales potential, analyse salesperson workload, design the basic territories and assign salespeople to these territories. The optional territory design is achieved where:

- territories are easy to administer
- sales potential is relatively easy to estimate
- travel time and expense are minimized
- equal sales opportunity is provided across customers and prospects
- work load is equalized.

The aim of good territory design is more effective use of the salesperson's time. The most significant improvements can be achieved by salespeople being more disciplined and professional by better planning of work, less calling on unqualified or unimportant prospects, more use of the telephone, including making appointments, and more systematic paperwork. Various attempts have been made to model the territory allocation problem. CALLPLAN (Lodish, 1971) was one of the first attempts and today there are many computer software packages available, based on these original concepts, which can assist with sales force time management problems. Whatever model is used, research confirms that the most significant factor in territory sales performance is to put the effort where sales potential is greatest. Territory design on the basis of anything other than potential (e.g. work load, historical rule of thumb) will be less efficient (Ryans and Weinberg, 1979; Singh, *et al.*, 1997).

SUMMARY AND CONCLUSION

The importance of personal selling to the achievement of company marketing objectives, and to the efficiency of the exchange process, must not be under-estimated. Salespeople provide information on their products and services, use persuasion and salesmanship to obtain and sustain a competitive advantage and are responsible for building a relationship between a supplier and its customers. These activities are fundamental to both customer satisfaction and the competitiveness of the firm. Sales managers should be clear as to whether salespeople are employed to win new business or service existing customers. While these tasks are not mutually exclusive, they do require different skills and perhaps separate organizational solutions. The job of the sales manager is to achieve sales targets through subordinates. This involves decisions on whether to employ direct salespeople or use independent agents, or a combination of both. They must decide and manage a suitable sales structure on the basis of geographic, product or customer specialization, or by a combination of these. The use of key account salespeople, telesales, team selling and information technology should be used in an efficient combination to ensure the productivity of the sales force is maximized. Various ways of determining sales force size can be recommended but by recruiting the most suitable people, training them effectively and, most of all, motivating the sales force to work to their full potential, sales force performance and company prosperity will be enhanced.

DISCUSSION TOPICS

1 Review the strategic decisions taken by Kraft in the opening case in this chapter and appraise the circumstances which led to this upheaval in sales operations.

2 Make a list of the differences between the role of the key account salesperson and the role of the traditional salesperson at Kraft Foods.

3 Most firms employ their own sales force but under what circumstances might the use of outside agents be preferred to a direct sales force?

4 Discuss the view that the single most untapped source of productivity in sales operations is the more efficient allocation and deployment of people to sales tasks.

5 Critically appraise the use of the telephone in sales operations.

6 Most sales organizations are organized on a traditional hierarchical style based on geographical or product divisions or both. Assess the merits and drawbacks of these organizational forms.

7 Assume the position of a new sales manager for a consumer products firm organized along conventional lines. Make recommendations to your managing director for a more customer-focused sales operation incorporating database marketing, key account management and telemarketing.

8 'Supplier–customer relationship management makes the traditional role of the salesperson redundant'. Discuss.

9 Discuss the most appropriate methods of determining the size of the sales force.

10 Outline the trends and changes you expect to see emerging which will affect the management of sales operations after the year 2000.

CASE STUDY – AGM ASSOCIATES

Fiona Green, Business Development Executive at AGM Associates, was feeling pretty good. AGM, a specialist exhibition, conference and marketing services agency, had just successfully pitched for a prestigious car account. This involved a number of sales conferences, dealer training events and sponsorship activities used as part of the car company's marketing programme. The services offered by the agency involve the design, coordination and implementation of these conferences and events.

Following the pitch by AGM, the car company employed them to organize a large-scale training conference for their most important dealers some six months ahead. The conference was to be held in Southern France over four days and attended by 70 international delegates. As a prestigious marque these delegates represented the main dealerships in Europe for the car company.

Initially things went well. Several new ideas were introduced by AGM which the client found to be acceptable, such as the use of time schedules, test car driving and hotel activities. The agency was able to display its dedication to the project, showing its creative and innovative approach yet reflecting a high taste and quality service. Having chosen the hotel and reviewed the test track facility, the clients were happy with the arrangements the agency had been making.

Owing to internal problems at the car company, the initial brief for the conference had to be changed. In particular, the date was moved forward one week which necessitated several important changes and caused considerable extra work for the agency. Although there was daily contact between client and agency at this stage, the main focus for both was on producing a satisfactory end result. Some of the changes that had to be made were mostly at the logistical level. Times of arrival for delegates, hotel requirements, organization of the test track and other social events had to be rescheduled. This was complicated and labour intensive but when the event took place it proved to be a considerable success in terms of content, smooth running and general enjoyment of the delegates. On return, however, the agency reported that there had been several problems which had proved costly to resolve. The agency presented its bill which was way in excess of the original figure quoted and it came as a severe shock to the client. The client demanded a detailed breakdown of costs, most of which turned out to be labour charges, and saw the actions of the agency in meeting the crisis to have been opportunistic behaviour. As a result, the relationship between client and agency was severed and all future business cancelled.

1 Analyse the different stages in this relationship and identify how the problems which later arose might have been avoided.
2 What lessons can be learned about relationship selling from this case?

(*Source*: Donaldson, 1998)

REFERENCES

Anderson, E. (1985) 'The salesperson as outside agent or employee: a transaction cost analysis', *Marketing Science*, 4, Summer: 234–54.

Brown-Humes, C. (1997) 'Staff to go as Eagle Star disband direct sales team', *Financial Times*, 13 November, 10.

Cravens, D., Grant, K., Ingram, T., LaForge, R. and Young, C. (1992) 'In search of excellent sales organizations', *European Journal of Marketing*, 26(1): 6–23.

Crosby, L.A., Evans, R.K. and Cowles, D. (1990) 'Relationship quality in services selling: an interpersonal influence perspective', *Journal of Marketing*, 54, July: 68–81.

DeCormier, R.A. and Jobber, D. (1993) 'The counselor selling method: concepts and constructs', *Journal of Personal Selling and Sales Management*, 23(4): 39–59.

Donaldson, B. (1998) *Sales Management: Theory and Practice*, 2nd edn, Basingstoke: Macmillan.

Donkin, R. (1977) 'Life after the salesman dies', *Financial Times*, 15 August, 9.

Fites, D.V. (1996) 'Make your dealers your partners', *Harvard Business Review*, Mar/April: 84–95.

Kumar, N. (1996) 'The power of trust in manufacturer–retailer relationships', *Harvard Business Review*, Nov–Dec: 92–106.

Lodish, L.M. (1971) 'CALLPLAN: an interactive salesman's call planning system', *Management Science*, 18(4): 11.

Manning G.L. and Reece B.L. (1992) *Selling Today: An Extension of the Marketing Concept*, 5th edn, Boston, MA: Allyn & Bacon.

Meredith, S. (1997) 'We have the technology', *Marketing Business*, Chartered Institute of Marketing, UK, 43–6.

Morgan R.M. and Hunt S.D. (1994) 'The commitment-trust theory of relationship marketing', *Journal of Marketing*, 58 (July): 20–38.

Pettijohn, C., Pettijohn, L. and Taylor, A. (1995) 'The relationship between effective counselling and effective behaviors', *Journal of Consumer Marketing*, 12(1): 5–15.

Ryans, A.B. and Weinberg, C.B. (1979) 'Territory sales response', *Journal of Marketing Research*, 16, November: 453–65.

Singh, J. (1997) *SoftWorld Survey of Sales and Marketing Technology*, London: Interactive Information Services.

Singh, J., Verbeke, W. and Rhodes, G.K. (1997) 'Do organisational practices matter in role stress processes: a study of direct and moderating effects for marketing-oriented boundary spanners', *Journal of Marketing*, 60, July: 69–86.

Stone, B. and Wyman, J. (1986) *Successful Telemarketing: Opportunities and Techniques for Increasing Sales and Profits*, Lincolnwood, IL: NTC Business Books.

20

MARKETING PUBLIC RELATIONS

Philip J. Kitchen and Ioanna Papasolomou

CHAPTER AIMS

- to analyse the emergence of marketing public relations (MPR)
- to consider the marketing perspective of public relations
- to consider the view of PR as a complement to marketing
- to analyse the extent to which marketing and PR can be seen as corporate allies or adversaries
- to explore the emergent MPR concept, definitional issues, consider MPR in the marketing mix, and indicate whether MPR is a distinct new discipline, and how it can be used in practice

ILLUSTRATION: MERE TACKLES INTERSPORT DRIVE TO UNIFY BRANDING (KAREN DEMPSEY)

Sports retailer Intersport . . . hired Cheshire-based agency Mere Communication to speed up its PR in the competitive sports retail market. Intersport is a buying and marketing group which represents 360 independently owned shops throughout the UK. The majority carry Intersport branding. Mere aims to raise the profile of the brand so that the Intersport shops can compete more effectively with chains such as Allsports, JJB Sports, and JD Sports.

'It is trying to change from a group of retailers to a retail group' said Mere MD Tony Tighe.

Mere won a three-way pitch to handle the trade and consumer PR account. The consultancy will work closely with Manchester-based Sass Panayi, Intersport's recently appointed advertising agency, in orchestrating a fully coordinated marketing campaign.

Mere will run a heavyweight media relations campaign in the national consumer press, including media competitions to 'improve the position of the brand and build football to the stores' said Tighe. Some competitions may be built around next year's football World Cup. It will also carry out a major internal communications campaign as part of its new emphasis on being a 'retail group'.

Intersport has stores across Europe, Japan, and the US although the PR account is limited to the UK.

(*Source*: *PR Week*, 15 August 1997, p. 2, used with permission.)

INTRODUCTION

Whether MPR, as proclaimed by Harris (1993), can legitimately be seen as a separate marketing or PR discipline is controversial. Some marketing authors have suggested that MPR be part of the marketing discipline, while some PR academics argue that MPR is merely another attempt by marketers to 'hijack' PR, by incorporating it into the promotional mix. Despite the academic furore, firms will simply continue to do whatever is best to communicate to target audiences, markets and publics as depicted in the Intersport vignette. PR can be, and often is, used for marketing as well as for other communication purposes.

One area of controversy concerns the delineating respective roles of the two functions. PR is frequently classified alongside advertising and promotion and that is why marketers believe that PR is or should be part of marketing and managed as a marketing activity. This view represents the marketing perspective of PR. The views of PR practitioners and academics suggest that PR activities can be distinguished from those of marketing (see Kitchen, 1997) and from that perspective, marketing and PR may serve different functions. However, it is not the intent of this chapter to subsume PR within a dominant marketing function but simply to indicate ways in which PR might be used in a marketing communications context either as a stand-alone activity or in an integrated approach.

However, this chapter does address a major and important issue: whether MPR has the potential to be a new approach to the practice of PR in the context of marcoms. The chapter explores this question by first reviewing the marketing literature concerning the relationship between marketing and PR. This review is important in relation to MPR, since examination of the relationship between the two disciplines provides a backdrop to the issue involved. Whether marketing PR is likely to become a marketing management discipline may depend on reasons behind the debate as well as the controversy between the marketing and PR disciplines. Arguments are then presented concerning the marketing perspective of PR. Then consideration is given to the perspective advanced by White (1991), where PR can be seen as a corrective and complement to marketing, before considering ways practitioners can work together to help organizations reach communication goals, in essence enabling the marketing and PR disciplines to be corporate allies. Some of the broader issues concerning MPR, its emergence, definition, growth, usage and rationale can then be tackled in a more robust fashion. The chapter is then summarized and concluded.

THEORETICAL BACKGROUND

Many organizations have, of necessity, in order to maintain or develop competitive differential advantage, elevated marketing to a dominant position. Marketing is treated as the most important commitment within an organization (Cohen, 1991) in order to create exchanges that satisfy individual and organizational objectives. This dominant paradigm suggests that the other major communication discipline, namely PR, may be, and often is, subsumed under the marketing function (Kitchen and Moss, 1995; Kotler and Mindak, 1978), and may be accorded a lower organizational priority. This does not mean that PR is subservient to marketing as indicated by many writers (e.g. Bernstein, 1988; Gage, 1981; Kreitzman, 1986). However, substantive evidence has been presented indicating that there is confusion concerning the boundaries between PR and marketing. For example, an increasing number of articles have been presented in which marketing communications and PR practices are recognized as increasingly integrating and converging concepts (Goldman, 1988; Merims, 1972; Novelli, 1988). The purpose of these articles was to give emphasis to the emergence of the concept of PR in the marketing support context, but instead they reflected a growing tendency for PR and marketing to be seen as converging disciplines in both professional and academic circles. This trend is supported by the emergence of the concept of marketing public relations (MPR) – a term which appeared in both the marketing and PR vocabularies in the 1980s. Kotler (1991) described MPR as:

> a healthy offspring of two parents: marketing and PR. MPR represents an opportunity for companies to regain a share of voice in a message-satiated society. MPR not only delivers a strong share of voice to win share of mind and heart; it also delivers a better, more effective voice in many cases.
>
> (Kotler, 1991a)

The growth of MPR and its acceptance as a valuable or even essential marketing tool is widespread. Companies assign PR specialists to product marketing teams and engage PR firms to help them get mileage from product introductions, keep brands strong throughout product life cycles, and defend products at risk (Harris, 1993).

Harris (1993) ventured to argue, in a highly readable and widely acceptable text, that the 1980s witnessed MPR emerging as a distinctive new promotional discipline which comprised specialized application techniques supporting marketing activities. He suggested, and few would disagree, that MPR is a separate practice from corporate PR, and that it will move closer to marketing. According to Harris (1993), corporate PR will remain a function concerned with company relationships with all publics. However, MPR and CPR will maintain a necessary strategic alliance. Gage (1981) indicated that MPR has become one of the fastest-growing segments of the PR field, a finding supported by Kitchen and Proctor (1991). PR, in its undifferentiated form, is also getting increasing interest in the marketing and business media. On 13 March 1989, *Advertising Age* ran a forum titled 'PR on the offensive'. In the same year a cover story in *Adweek*'s 'Marketing Week' section declared that 'the new PR is used virtually everywhere', and advised its readers to 'stir some PR into their communications mix'. Finally, the academic community is showing greater interest in PR (Kitchen, 1993a). A number of American (Harris, 1993) and British (Kitchen, 1993b) universities are responding to the growing demand for business leaders trained in PR and for PR practitioners trained in business.

Despite this growing acceptance of public relations in marketing, the question needs to be tackled: Does MPR have the potential to be a new marketing management discipline? To explore this question it is first necessary to investigate the marketing perspective of PR.

342

THE MARKETING PERSPECTIVE OF PUBLIC RELATIONS

Various writers, as indicated previously, pointed to the use of public relations for marketing purposes, or its relevance to marketing communications. White (1991), for example, in his authoritative PR textbook, states that Kotler, a leading American commentator on marketing practice, supports the view that public relations is part of marketing and serves as an aid to customer relations. When marketers consider options for marketing communications, public relations is often bracketed with advertising and other forms of general marcoms promotional purposes. In 1988, Kotler described public relations as 'another important communication/promotion tool'. He also stated that PR has been the least-utilized tool, but it has great potential for building awareness and preference in the marketplace, repositioning products, and defending them. From a marketing perspective, public relations is being incorporated into the marketing communications mix. They suggest that marketers may be in a better position to plan how to achieve desired responses from target audiences or publics than public relations people since very often the company's objective is to influence a public, and this is best done by considering the problem in terms of exchange theory and not simply communications theory. Extension of this argument may suggest that marketers should take over the PR function.

While PR undoubtedly can be, and is, used for promotional purposes, its real role extends to establishing 'understanding' between an organization and those publics that have either a potential or actual interest in it. According to Lancaster and Massingham (1988), various arguments and academic debate already cited have probably arisen from the fact that even though many organizations consider and implement 'publicity' as part of overall marketing activity, they do not usually have a separate PR department, which coordinates the various promotional activities that fall under the PR label, and have as an aim to build trust and understanding by open communication. In these smaller organizations PR is often supportive of, and directly responsible to, the marketing function. But is this true in larger organizations?

Cohen (1991) further classifies PR alongside advertising and promotion. To Cohen the main objectives of advertising and publicity are to make the product or service known to potential buyers and present it in the most favourable way, in comparison to competitive offerings. He further quotes PR as publicity, an opinion which reflects the American tendency to label PR loosely as 'publicity'! This view does not take into consideration the fact that PR may have a different role to fulfil apart from creating awareness, i.e. in considering the case of new product development. PR may perform a distinctive supportive role over and above the one performed by advertising and promotion. PR can also communicate through the press, television and radio the fact that the company has launched something new to the target market, and thus it contributes to the product launch in a tactical sense. But, PR also satisfies a corporate function, that of informing a wide range of interested publics extending beyond immediate exchange partners.

There is, however, a tendency found in the marketing management literature of attempts made to assign public relations to an inferior technical role under the stewardship of marketing (Grunig 1992). Specifically, Shimp and Delozier (1986) saw public relations and publicity essentially as activities that 'serve to supplement media advertising, sales, and sales promotion in creating product awareness, building favorable attitudes toward the company and its products, and encouraging purchase behaviour'. Stanley (1982) saw public relations, publicity, and institutional advertising as part of a company's sales promotion effort which, in turn, is part of the marketing mix. Schwartz (1982) argued that public relations is but another form of 'consumer-oriented sales promotion' with a mission to build or shape the 'image' of a business in its support of sales promotion efforts under the control of marketing. McDaniel (1979), in turn, asserted that 'public relations, like personal selling, advertising, and sales promotion, is a vital link in a progressive company's marketing communications mix', and, further, that 'public relations complements the role of advertising by building product/service credibility'.

However, efforts to bring PR activity under the jurisdiction of marketing management make no reference to any empirical or conceptual base to support this opinion (Gruning, 1992). Generally a naive marketing perspective of PR promotes a reductionistic view of PR, that clearly implies the efforts of many marketing textbook authors to bring PR activity under the jurisdiction of marketing mangement, diminishing the PR discipline into a strategy and a tactical function. Figure 20.1 presents a descriptive model of the marketing perspective of PR.

As illustrated in the figure, the marketing perspective of PR suggests that public relations be incorporated as an extra element within the promotional mix to

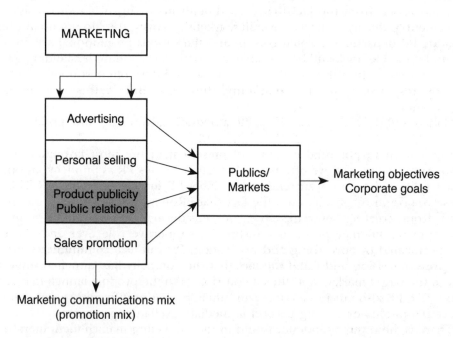

Figure 20.1 A descriptive model of the marketing perspective of PR.

influence current or potential audiences, markets or publics, in order to achieve marketing objectives and subsequently, corporate goals. Marketing is seen as the dominant communications function, whereas public relations can be seen merely as a promotional tool. Unsophisticated acceptance of marketing dominance ignores the volatile and hostile environment in which organizations function. Further, subsuming PR in this way also ignores the fact that non-marketing problems cannot be solved by marketing management methods and techniques. This means that PR extends beyond marketing, without decrying marketing's dominant role in creating exchanges. Thus PR can be seen as a corrective and complement to marketing in many circumstances.

PR: a corrective and complement to marketing

PR can play an expanded role in marketing. PR activities, in many circumstances, can complement an organization's marketing objectives. For example, a number of PR techniques were used to sustain and develop Dunhill Holdings' brand names in order to build brand awareness, to communicate the range of the company's products, and to position the Dunhill brand as one offering outstanding quality; thus contributing to the company's overall marketing effort. Notably deployed PR techniques in this case were also used for corporate as well as marketing functions by using media relations and financial PR programmes (White, 1991). British Airways also used the PR function as a complement to marketing activities. Specifically, British Airways used PR and internal communication techniques to bring about organizational change, improve the company's approach to customer service, and support the company's move into the private sector (White, 1991).

Seitel (1992) suggests that even though in the past marketers treated PR as an ancillary part of the marketing mix and promoted their products and services heavily through advertising and merchandising, gradually a change began to occur within these traditional notions, mainly for the following reasons:

- Consumer protests about both product value and safety and government scrutiny of product claims began to shake historical views of marketing.
- Product recalls generated recurring and recurrent headlines.
- Ingredient scares began to occur regularly.
- Advertisers were asked to justify their messages in terms of social needs and civic responsibilities, not just product benefits.
- Rumours about particular companies are rapidly spread by national and international media.
- The media has continuously criticized the image of companies and industries.

Thus, PR has an important role to play with respect to direct support to a firm's marketing activities. One task is to keep its publics informed about new-product development. In addition, PR can also 'prepare the ground for marketing activity by explaining policy changes', for example in updating distribution strategy. Also, PR can be a method of offering a public explanation or apology.

Lancaster and Massingham (1988) stipulate that while the success or failure of PR strategy will depend on how well the marketing functions are carried out, marketing and PR are essentially complementary and working together should produce a *synergistic* effect on *total company operations*. Marketing and PR must work closely together to achieve the corporate aims of the company. PR has the potential to aid marketing at a tactical level, but one cannot be substituted for the other. Furthermore, Black (1993) says that PR ideas and skills play a valuable part in certain marketing processes, such as creating value, as perceived by other parties.

PR as a complement to marketing provides information and, also, techniques of communication used in PR are available to marketing, and can be used in support of product and sales promotion. These communication techniques fall under the description of marketing communication when used in marketing. In fact, by building important relations and contributing to the central relationship with customers, PR can help to develop a social environment in which marketing activities are more likely to be effective. Similarly, PR's contribution as a corrective to the marketing approach is based on the fact that the perspective on which the practice is based is broader than the marketing perspective. PR can raise questions which the marketing approach, with its focus on the market, products, distribution channels and consumers, and its orientation towards growth and consumption, cannot. Therefore, what Friend (1986) said, under this perspective, may be true:

> Working in support of marketing, PR has a primary function to *promote*. It also has to *protect* and *project*. This requires PR thinking across the full spectrum of an organization's operations, or a series of irreconcilable differences and conflicts will invariably arise.
>
> (Friend, 1996, italics added)

Thus, many authors have pointed to the use of PR for marketing purposes (i.e. Bernstein, 1988; Kotler, 1988b; Gage, 1981; Kreitzman, 1986) and to its relevance to marketing communications (i.e. Novelli, 1988; White, 1991; Goldman, 1988; Merims, 1972). In particular, Bernstein (1988) postulates halfheartedly that PR will inherit the marketing communications world by having the other elements of marketing communications under its dominance. Kotler (1989b) says that the part of PR function named as MPR carries out marketing activities. Thus, marketing and PR form the major, but by no means mutually exclusive communication functions in organizations.

MARKETING AND PR: CORPORATE ALLIES

A number of current developments presage a closer working relationship between marketing and PR in the future. Marketing practitioners are very likely to increase their appreciation of PR's potential contributions to marketing products, because they are facing a real decline in the productivity of other promotional tools (Kotler, 1988: 655–8, 661):

- Advertising costs continue to rise while the advertising audiences reached continue to decline.
- Increasing clutter reduces advertising impact.

- Sales promotion expenditures continue to climb.
- Sales force costs continue to rise.

PR efforts may well enable desired results in solving market-type problems (Kitchen, 1993b). Pure PR problems can be solved through marketing's strong propensity for analysis, planning, implementation and control. For many years, each discipline and practice has operated in a quasi-independent spirit. If the academic argument is believable, marketing practitioners have attempted to subsume PR within a dominant marketing function whereas PR practitioners' attitude towards the marketing discipline is one characterized by hostility. But, 'divorce' between the two communication types would be a fatal mistake as both have direct impact on organizational ability to achieve communication objectives.

Such objectives (Kotler, 1989b) are first, survival, second, to make good financial returns, and third, to deliver values and satisfactions to customers and other stakeholders. These are independent goals which can be achieved through the management of the value delivery process shown in Figure 20.2 (Kotler, 1989b).

Company management must choose the customers and values they want to serve, provide the values, and communicate these values effectively to target customers. Much of this process is marketing-led. Kotler (1989b), indicates that the company needs skilled marketers who can identify market opportunities, create appropriate products, and price, distribute, promote and service these products. Friend (1986b) says that it is the PR professional's job to be part of the management team which develops the overall marketing strategy and positioning of a new or existing product, service or brand. The PR professional should bring to that team a combination of perspectives, an understanding of how the team sees the brand, how it wishes it to be seen, how it can be seen, and how it will be seen in the context of the overall reputation of the organization.

The recent emergence of the term MPR perhaps no more than revives the existing debate in both the marketing and PR literatures on whether PR is, or should be, part of marketing and managed as a marketing activity. The main issue concerning the MPR concept is whether it is a new PR discipline separate from corporate PR, or whether it is a new marketing management discipline (Kitchen and Moss, 1995).

Kotler (1989) believes that PR or at least the part called Marketing Public Relations (MPR), manages a miscellaneous set of communication/promotion activities that marketing practitioners normally neglect or lack the skill to handle. He specifically named these activities the 'pencils' of PR, namely:

CHOOSE THE VALUE			PROVIDE THE VALUE				COMMUNICATE THE VALUE			
Customer Segmentation Value Needs	Market Selection Focus	Value Positioning	Product Development	Pricing	Sourcing Making	Distributing Servicing	Sales Force	Sales Promotion	Advertising	Public Relations

Figure 20.2 The value delivery system.

1 **Publications**
2 **Events**
3 **News**
4 **Community relations**
5 **Identity media**
6 **Lobbying**
7 **Social investments**

Each of these activities creates and communicates value and therefore helps in the customer-creation and satisfaction process. Even then, PR may be seen only as a marketing tool. This opinion supports one of the five possible views of the relation between marketing and PR shown in Figure 20.3, namely B (Kotler and Mindak, 1978).

The current view of interaction between marketing and PR is that practitioners manage distinct activities, which despite the relative independence in which they are performed, share interrelations (Kotler, 1989). For example, PR practitioners are responsible for news management and despite the fact that marketing practitioners may want to advise on the news strategy, PR personnel retain final responsibility in this area. Similarly, in matters that fall under the jurisdiction of marketing, i.e. price setting and distribution policies, PR practitioners may want to make suggestions; however, marketing practitioners have primary responsibility in these matters.

Even though both disciplines perform distinct activities Kotler (1989b), they share commonalities, which can be carried out by the MPR function (Figure 20.4). MPR manages a miscellaneous set of communication/promotion activities that marketing practitioners lack the skill to handle. Similarly, Harris (1993) stipulates that the MPR practice is separated from the general practice of corporate PR. MPR may thus move closer to marketing, and corporate PR (CPR) may remain a management function concerned with the company's relationships with its publics. Despite this separation, MPR and CPR will remain closely allied. Such 'alliance' brings needful cooperation and integration between the marketing and PR functions. MPR will not, however, be managed by CPR (Kitchen and Moss, 1995) despite efforts by PR practitioners to capitalize on the boundary obfuscation issue. Therefore:

1 From a marketing perspective, MPR is a new approach to the practice of PR which is closely related to marketing.

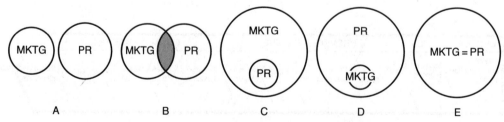

Figure 20.3 Models of possible relationship between marketing and public relations.

Figure 20.4 Spheres of responsibility for marketing and PR.

2   From a naive PR perspective, the concept of MPR is an attempt by marketeers to 'hijack' PR, incorporating it as an extra element within the promotional mix (as we have seen, the argument is much more sophisticated).

Despite the ongoing debate, which may never be fully resolved, many organizations have achieved successful integration of the two disciplines within their managerial structures. Figure 20.5 illustrates what could be considered an operationalizable model.

As the argument has indicated, the model suggests that even though marketing and PR are independent, they are also interdependent and interrelated disciplines. As Kotler (1989b) suggested, each discipline encloses a distinct set of independent activities, i.e. marketing is responsible for market assessment and PR is responsible for community relations. At the same time, some PR activities – the pencils of PR – (Kotler, 1989b; Harris, 1993) are shared by both disciplines.

MARKETING PUBLIC RELATIONS (MPR)

In proclaiming the emergence of MPR, Harris (1993) argued that MPR is a new promotional discipline which comprises specialized application techniques supporting marketing activities. Kotler (1989a), Professor of Marketing at Northwestern University's Kellogg School of Management, remarked that 'MPR in the future can only go one way: up'. Kotler further stated that: 'PR is moving into an

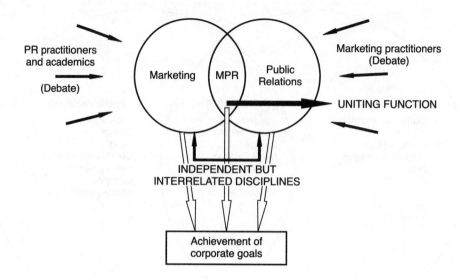

Figure 20.5 The descriptive model of the ideal relationship between marketing and PR disciplines.

explosive growth stage because companies realize that mass advertising is no longer the answer; . . . organizations are merging PR into marketing ending a long-lasting love/hate relationship'.

Various surveys to try to identify the degree of awareness toward MPR by the business sector have been carried out. One survey that documented increasing awareness and use of MPR was conducted by Duncan (1985). This surveyed 286 *Advertising Age* subscribers who held marketing and advertising positions with client organizations (Duncan, 1985). Among the key findings were the following (reported by Harris, 1993):

1 MPR was perceived as being effective in a variety of areas that were traditionally the responsibility of advertising.
2 MPR was thought to be especially effective in building brand awareness and brand knowledge.
3 There were no areas in which the majority of clients said MPR would not be effective.
4 The importance of MPR had increased over the previous five years and was expected to continue to increase. The main reasons given were mainly that marketers are becoming more sophisticated and that MPR:
   (a) is made cost-effective by increases in media advertising costs;
   (b) breaks through clutter;
   (c) complements advertising (increases the credibility of messages);
   (d) is proving itself.

MPR can also add value in the marketing domain by (Harris, 1993):

- Positioning companies as leaders and experts
- Introducing new products
- Cultivating new markets
- Extending advertising reach
- Breaking through commercial clutter
- Gaining exposure for products that cannot be advertised to consumers
- Influencing opinion leaders

Gage (1981) said that MPR had become one of the fastest-growing segments of the PR field. Indeed, there are many signs that MPR has come of age. Firstly, *PR has become a big and profitable business*. During 1980 an article in *PR News* stated: 'The proven power of PR and its cost effectiveness in contrast to advertising motivated the advertising industry to add PR departments to their operations in order to help alleviate its financial woes.'

Shandwick PLC, the first worldwide, publicly owned PR company, has become the largest of all PR firms, with annual fee billing of $180 million (Shandwick PLC, 1989). Even though, Shandwick retained its crown as leader of the UK pack in 1991 its income dropped 18 per cent to £26.6 million – a decline which indicates declining income levels in some areas of the UK PR industry, i.e. business-to-business marketing (*UK Top 150 – PR Consultancies*, 1992). In 1993, the *UK Top 150 – PR Consultancies* magazine showed Shandwick still maintaining its position at number one in the UK rankings for the sixth year in succession; however, its income declined somewhat. The 1994 *PR Week – Top 150 PR Consultancies* had Shandwick in the first position of the UK rankings. The 3 per cent fall in income at Shandwick belies the fact that the company increased its profits in every quarter of 1993 from a 12 per cent jump in the first quarter to 20 per cent by the year end. Overall, each head of staff made a profit of £9,000 during the year which was helped by a 10 per cent growth in fee income in the third quarter, resulting in a total fee income for 1993 of £22,812,000. Exploration of what Shandwick *does* on behalf of clients indicates significant marketing emphasis.

Secondly, *MPR is the largest and fastest-growing segment of a fast-growing industry.* A study of the world market for PR services, conducted by Shandwick (1989), estimated that 20 per cent of the fee income of PR firms throughout the world is generated by PR for consumer products. In fact, 70 per cent of the business handled by PR firms is marketing-related, with the remaining 30 per cent distributed among corporate, governmental, environmental and financial billing (Harris, 1993).

Thirdly, *companies have recognized the growing importance of MPR with bigger budgets and fatter paychecks.* MPR now 'leads all PR disciplines with its rapidly increasing importance, and PR marketing skills are in greater demand than ever before' (Cantor Concern, 1989). Robert Dilenschneider (1988), president and CEO of Hill and Knowlton, one of the largest worldwide public relations agencies, says: 'the million-dollar worldwide program, almost unheard of ten years ago, is now experienced with increasing regularity'.

PR is getting increasing interest in the marketing and business media. On 13 March 1989, *Advertising Age* ran a forum titled 'PR on the Offensive' led by Robert

Dilenschneider. Additionally, in 1989, *ADWEEK's Marketing Week,* cover story on 'The New Public Relations' declared that 'the new PR is used virtually everywhere'.

Last, but not least, *the academic community is showing greater interest in PR.* Universities are responding to the growing demand for business leaders trained in PR and for PR practitioners trained in business as opposed to generic communications (Harris, 1993).

TOWARD AN MPR DEFINITION

What is MPR? Definitions and interpretations vary widely. While PR experts cannot agree what MPR is, they all agree what it is not – free advertising. Carl Byoir & Associates, USA 'work very hard to eliminate that misconception' (Gage, 1981). According to Harris (1993), the designation (MPR) arose in the 1980s because of the need to distinguish the specialized application of PR techniques that support marketing from the general practice of PR. According to Harris (1993), MPR has grown rapidly and pragmatically to meet the opportunities of a changing marketplace. In the process, it has borrowed and amalgamated thinking from traditional PR, marketing, advertising and research. The issue of defining MPR is complicated by the fact that there are many definitions of both marketing and PR.

Harris (1993), superseding Black (1952), believes that MPR can be defined more precisely than the larger concept of PR because of its relevance to marketing, especially in helping an organization meet its marketing objectives. He suggests the following definition:

> MPR is the process of planning, executing and evaluating programs that encourage purchase and consumer satisfaction through credible communication of information and impressions that identify companies and their products with the needs, wants, concerns, and interests of consumers.
>
> (Harris, 1993)

Moreover, Shimp (1993) gave the following definition:

> It is the more narrow aspect of PR which involves an organization's interactions with consumers or with other publics (such as governments) regarding marketing matters (like safety). In short, it is the marketing-oriented aspect of PR.
>
> (Shimp, 1993)

According to Kotler (1988), it can contribute to the following tasks:

- Assist in the launch of new products (e.g. Cabbage Patch Kids).
- Assist in repositioning a mature product (e.g. New York City).
- Build up interest in a product category (e.g. milk, egg, cheese consumption).
- Influence specific target groups (e.g. sponsorship of local community activities).
- Defend products that have encountered public problems (e.g. Johnson and Johnson and Tylenol).
- Build the corporate image in a way that projects favourably on its products (e.g. Lee Iaccoca and the image of Chrysler Corporation).

As the power of advertising somewhat weakens, due to rising media costs, increasing clutter and smaller audiences, marketing managers may turn to MPR.

MPR IN THE MARKETING MIX

According to Harris (1993), MPR is a promotional option that rounds out the marketing mix and adds value to advertising campaigns. While it cannot substitute for advertising, it can make advertising work harder. In many cases, MPR is launched in conjunction with an advertising and marketing campaign. It complements other marketing efforts, but serves a distinct and unique purpose, often giving a product, service or market added credibility, exposure and newsworthiness. Specifically, in some MPR efforts, one of the objectives is to enhance a product's credibility and to position its marketer not only as a good business, but as a company that has a genuine concern for people – one that uses its resources and know-how to make life better for them (Gage, 1981). Kitchen and Proctor (1991), in a series of depth interviews with major UK FMCG firms, found that use of MPR helps achieve marketing objectives, although there was ambiguity concerning effective measurement. Gumm, in an early (1978) paper, claimed that 'MPR can be proven to be a valuable addition to the marketing mix'. Similarly, Kitchen (1993a), says:

> Latterly, advertising, sales promotion, and personal selling have undergone difficulties in relation to achievement of cost-effective communication objectives . . . the emergence and application of MPR in the communications mix may be playing a more significant complementary role in business organizations facing a more turbulent competitive environment.
>
> (Kitchen, 1993a)

As the power of advertising may weaken as a result of of cost, clutter, audience receptivity or media inflation; as criticism is levelled at sales promotions in terms of sales effects and profits; and as sales forces diminish in size due to retail concentration and key account selling, firms could practically consider MPR alongside the other promotional tools.

Several UK case histories, e.g. the relaunch of Beechams Brylcreem, the PR effort supporting the 'garden city' concepts, and the repositioning of Glasgow as a city of culture, illustrate that MPR has been used alongside traditional marketing communications tools or alone to achieve marketing and/or corporate goals. In the US market, Kotler (1988a) identifies several examples of the use of MPR: new product launch (Cabbage Patch Kids) and influencing specific target groups (neighbourhood events, e.g. McDonalds) (Kitchen and Proctor, 1991).

The above examples are given to illustrate that MPR can be used either alone or in conjunction with other communication mix tools to achieve marketing objectives. In fact, some firms have utilized PR in a marketing sense, usually by working with and alongside highly experienced PR agencies. The key point to be derived from this is that MPR in some firms appears to be working alongside or in a complementary manner to other elements in the communications mix. It is also noticeable that there may be some interaction with its more important relation: Corporate Public Relations (CPR). This schism of opinions suggests that it may indeed be difficult to define MPR and provide a definite answer to the issue of its legitimacy.

MPR: A DISTINCT DISCIPLINE?

Harris (1993) claims that the term MPR is used to distinguish this field from the broader one of PR. However, this opinion seems to suggest fission sometime in the future; that is, the split-off of marketing-support PR from other PR activities that define the corporation's relationships with its non-customer publics. The corporate public relations function may, however, well remain a corporate management function, whereas MPR may become a marketing management function. In this situation, the mission of CPR would be to support corporate objectives, and the mission of MPR would be to support marketing objectives. MPR practitioners would become marketing associates, and their career paths would be directed toward marketing management. CPR practitioners would continue to report to top management (Harris, 1993).

Harris (1993) recognizes that a close working relationship needs to be maintained between the CPR and MPR disciplines, not only because of the similarity of skills and experience, but also because of the need to integrate marketing objectives with corporate objectives. Relationships with government on all levels, for example, significantly affect the environment in which the company markets its products, as do the company's public positions on a variety of existing and emerging issues that affect the public as consumer. While there is evidence of a move towards closer integration of corporate and marketing messages, and hence the need for closer cooperation between marketing and PR practitioners, this trend alone does not support the argument for a further subdivision of the PR function in the way advocated by Harris. Such division of responsibilities would create potential for confusion and possible conflict between the messages communicated to an organization's various shareholder audiences without necessarily bringing any recognizable communications benefits. However, Cutlip, *et al.* (1985), acknowledge that: 'in practice PR specialists are many times called upon to help in the marketing effort by writing publicity stories and arranging media coverage for new products' but they believe that because some view publicity in the same way as 'public relations', product publicity may be a source of some confusion between the marketing and PR functions.

The above view, according to Harris (1993), fails to draw the needed distinction between MPR and CPR. It specifically assigns PR a limited role of issuing new-product press releases, whereas no recognition is given to the increasing role of MPR in maintaining markets for mature products and in winning consumer confidence for companies and products through sponsorship of and involvement in events and endeavours that consumers, market influencers and sellers care about. Therefore, Kitchen and Moss (1995) claim:

> In order to help resolve the question of whether the concept of MPR has a legitimate claim to be a new discipline, it is necessary to seek answers to a number of important questions. Where is or should the dividing line between

marketing and PR be drawn? Is there, in fact, a dividing line? . . . Perhaps most important, does the concept of 'MPR' merely obfuscate two relatively straightforward disciplines?

(Kitchen and Moss, 1995)

Despite the variability of opinions concerning the legitimacy of MPR, it is evident that the concept has a wide range of uses from which many benefits may be derived, justifying the contribution of MPR to an organization's successful implementation of promotional tools.

USING MPR

This section will present and discuss different uses of MPR by referring to case histories in which the effective use of MPR led to organizations achieving their marketing and corporate objectives. Initially, the discussion will refer to the use of MPR in the introduction of new products. One worldwide success was the Sony Walkman. The product was positioned as a powerful, portable, high-quality sound-reproducing personal entertainment vehicle. Sony first aroused public interest by giving Walkmans to Japan's leading musicians, teen idols and magazine editors. In the USA the name 'Walkman' was timely, coinciding with the boom in walking, running and jogging for which it became standard equipment. Massive resultant publicity was heard around the world and the product became a 'runaway' success despite its price-skimming strategy (Harris, 1993).

As has already been mentioned earlier in this chapter, companies have been using the MPR concept in a variety of situations. Table 20.1 presents certain case histories in relation to the multi-use role of MPR and illustrates the benefits that organizations obtain from its use.

MPR's value in growing brands, sustaining mature brands and supporting declining brands is less universally understood than its use in introducing new products (Harris, 1993). However, while MPR may lack the ability of reminder advertising to reach the consumer with measured frequency, it can often exceed the benefits of advertising by providing marketers with the opportunity to extend the reach of advertising and capitalizing on the credibility factor to build brand loyalty. As a result, its role in relaunching, revitalizing, repositioning and sustaining mature and even declining brands may be ultimately of even greater value to the company than the quick and dramatic hit that can be achieved in publicizing new products. The case history of the Peanut Advisory Board illustrates the effective use and valuable benefits of MPR in repositioning mature products and 'extending' their life cycles.

Among the MPR roles which are acknowledged by companies are those of contributing in building consumer trust and positioning a company in the market as a help provider. As Kenneth Lightcap (1984), vice president of corporate communications of Reebok International, says, MPR has the potential to be used as a positioning tool by companies. In Lightcap's view, it is essential that companies gradually build up impressions to publics over time, in order to gain a lasting impression that will induce consumers to value the company's products and be more

Table 20.1 Using marketing public relations

Used for	Cases	Benefits from the use of MPR
Introducing new products	The Sony Walkman	• Received massive publicity • Product's huge global success • In 10 years' time, sales exceeded 50 million devices
	The new Lean Cusine range	• 90% brand awareness amongst the slimmer group • 80% brand awareness amongst consumers • Consistent high media visibility.
Promoting mature products	USA Peanut Advisory Board (PAB)	• 6% increase in peanut butter consumption • Effective repositioning of the product.
Winning consumer trust	McDonald's Trust Bank (San Ysidro, California)	• The company received credit by the media • Received hundreds of positive letters from the public
Celebrating special occasions	Barbie's 30th birthday	• Massive publicity
	Hasbro's G.I. Joe's 25th birthday	• Massive publicity
	Bugs Bunny's 50th birthday	• Massive publicity
Sponsoring public service programs	'We Care About New York' campaign	• 12,000 New Yorkers participated • 700 clean-up events • 12 million media impressions
Sponsoring good causes	Tang march across America for MADD	• Extensive media coverage • 13% increase of Tang consumer purchases during the six-month march
Sponsoring sports	Waste Management Cleans Up at Calgary	• Extensive media coverage Massive publicity

Source: Harris (1993)

receptive to product publicity. Companies that establish themselves as 'caring' and help-giving organizations are those that eventually earn consumer loyalty and trust, and subsequently secure their 'societal' image in a highly competitive trade world. McDonald's is one of the companies that have adopted this philosophy, i.e. giving something back to society. In fact, MPR can successfully attract and focus attention on products by celebrating a special occasion. In this way it can revitalize interest in old products or continuously retain the interest of the public in a brand's products or services. Mattel, Hasbro and Warner Brothers are among those companies that have effectively implemented the tactics that MPR applies in order to gain publicity.

Among the many uses of MPR is cause-related marketing. The concept of cause-related marketing is the following: buy a company's product and it will make a donation on your behalf to some worthy cause. These sponsorships not only raise money for good causes, but they are also good business. One of the best examples of the role of MPR in cause-related marketing is the Tang March Across America for MADD (Mothers Against Drunk Drivers). Finally, MPR played a significant role in the sports marketing boom. 'Waste management cleans up at calgary' is a case history that illustrates how the concept of MPR provides a variety of benefits and merits, if a company that is involved in the sports industry recognizes and accepts its use as a promotion tool.

SUMMARY AND CONCLUSIONS

The unique features and different situations identified in the case material discussed delineate the concept of MPR as one which substantially adds the dimension of credibility to companies and their products. It has the power of maintaining brand franchises either by providing information and service to the consumer, and identifying the brand with causes that consumers care about, or by sponsoring high-visibility events that excite consumers.

However, even if the value of MPR as a set of PR techniques and tools has been acknowledged by the business sector globally and it has been assigned to many uses, its value as a concept and its place in either the marketing or PR literature is still debated. Based on latent research carried out by Kitchen and Papasolomou (1997), MPR does not yet have a legimate claim to be either a new public relations or marketing management discipline. But the use of MPR within a company's promotional activity is acknowledged. As a concept, MPR requires integration with other promotools in order to be effective. Thus it can be argued that many firms utilize MPR, it is not a new subject, it appears to be cost-effective and credible to marketers, PR specialists and their respective clusterings of appropriate support agencies. Whether MPR will develop to the status of a fully fledged marketing management discipline is debatable. But it does extend beyond semantics or simply relabelling an old aspect of marcoms.

DISCUSSION TOPICS

1 Why should PR fit into the 'more inclusive and more important marketing function'?
2 Consider Figure 20.1. Is this a simplification of the issues involved?
3 Explore the dynamics of Figure 20.5. Is the backdrop debate merely about semantics or does the debate have real implications for marketing and PR?
4 Using a brand of your choice, illustrate how MPR has helped the brand to 'succeed' (information from *PR Week* or *Campaign* can be used as background material).
5 Where does MPR actually belong? To marketing or corporate communications?
6 Discuss the contribution of MPR to the success of a firm's marketing communications programme.

7 Should all firms have an MPR programme? Discuss.

8 Justify the view taken by some PR academics that PR is not about marketing.

9 Do you think the debate identified within the marketing and PR literatures is likely to affect the future of MPR? Discuss.

10 Does MPR have the legitimacy to be a separate marketing management discipline?

CASE STUDY – KODAK SHARPENS ITS FOCUS ON CHINA THROUGH O&M PR (JEMIMAH BAILEY)

Kodak has appointed Ogilvy and Mather PR to run its consumer marketing communications programme in China. O&M has worked with the film giant on a corporate brief for eighteen months. Its contract has now been extended to include support for consumer branding, new product launches, sponsorship, and events.

Kodak's decision to appoint O&M follows the consolidation of its worldwide advertising with Ogilvy and Mather Worldwide at the end of June [1997].

The advertising agency, sister company to the PR firm, took over responsibility for Kodak's traditional film and camera products from fellow WPP agency J. Walter Thompson. It already handles corporate branding, digital and applied imaging products, photofinishing, retail services, and single-use cameras.

'Most people who are buying PR services at the moment are multinationals who want to deepen their roots in China' said Scott Kronick, MD for O&M in Beijing. He added that firms are keen to explore opportunities in the 'second tier' of Chinese cities including Shenyang, Chengdu, and Wuhan.

The trend away from project-based work, towards more comprehensive campaigns, is signalled in another O&M win, with computer giant IBM. O&M won the brand building *and* corporate account after a three-way pitch.

'This work will include support for executive visits to China and product launches' said Kronick.

(*Source: PR Week*, 18 July 1997, p. 5, used with permission.)

This chapter is based on two pieces of work. The first is the PR perspective of MPR which is tackled in Kitchen, P.J. (1997) *Public Relations: Principles and Practice*, International Thomson Business Press, see chapters 13 and 14. Also see Kitchen, P.J. and Papasolomov, I. (1997) 'Marketing Public Relations: Conceptual Legitimacy or Window Dressing?' *Marketing Intelligence and Planning*, Volume 15, 2, pp. 71–84. Grateful acknowledgements are extended to these two sources.

REFERENCES

Bernstein, J. (1988) 'PR in top communication role', *Advertising Age*, 28 November, 59.

Black, G. (1952) *Planned Industrial Publicity*, Chicago: Putnam, 3.

Black, S. (1993) *The Essentials of Public Relations*, London: Kogan Page Ltd, 40–1.

Cohen, W.A. (1991) *The Practice of Marketing Management*, New York: Maxwell Macmillan, 503–6.

Cutlip, S.M., Center, A.H. and Broom, G.M. (1985) *Effective Public Relations*, Englewood Cliffs, NJ: Prentice Hall, 89.

Dilenschneider, R. (1989) 'PR on the offensive: Bigger part of marketing mix', *Advertising Age*, 60, 13 March, 20.

Duncan, T. (1985) *A study of how manufacturers and service companies perceive and use MPR*, Muncie, Ind.: Ball State University.

Friend, C. (1986a) *Public relations and marketing – the synergy and the separation*, written for the Institute of Public Relations, 1–2.

Friend, C. (1986b) *Public relations – not just puffering and nonsense*, Institute of Marketing, 8.

Friend, C. (1994) Letter to Dr Philip J. Kitchen, Department of Management, Keele University, expressing her opinions concerning the place of Public Relations in the Marketing Mix, 7 November, 1.

Gage, T.J. (1981) 'PR ripens role in marketing', *Advertising Age*, 5 January, 10–11.

Goldman, T. (1988) 'Big spenders develop newspaper communications', *Marketing Communications*, 13(1): 24.

Grunig, J.E. (1992) *Excellence in Public Relations and Communication Management*, Hillsdale, NJ: Lawrence Erlbaum Associates Publishers, 357–90.

Gumm, J. (1978) 'Public relations is a primary element in Beech-Nut food's marketing program', *Advertising Age*, 6 February, 39.

Harris, T. (1993) *The Marketer's Guide to PR: How Today's Companies are using the New Public Relations to Gain a Competitive Edge*, New York: John Wiley and Sons.

Kitchen, P.(1993a) 'Public relations: A rationale for its development and usage within UK fast-moving consumer goods firms', *European Journal of Marketing*, 27(7): 367, 379–84.

Kitchen, P. (1993b) 'Towards the integration of marketing and public relations', *Marketing Intelligence and Planning*, 11(11): 15–21.

Kitchen, P.J. (1997) *Public Relations: Principles and Practice*, London: International Thomson. The PR perspective of MPR is tackled more rigorously in this volume, see Chapters thirteen and fourteen.

Kitchen, P.J. and Moss, D. (1995) 'Marketing and public relations: The relationship revisited', *Journal of Marketing Communications*, 1(2): 7–11.

Kitchen, P.J. and Papasolomou, I.C. (1997) 'Marketing public relations: conceptual legitimacy or window dressing?', *Marketing Intelligence and Planning*, 15(2): 71–84.

Kitchen, P.J. and Proctor, R.A. (1991) 'The increasing importance of public relations in FMCG firms', *Journal of Marketing Management*, 7: 359–60.

Kotler, P. (1988) *Marketing Management*, Englewood Cliffs, NJ: Prentice Hall, 655–56, 661.

Kotler, P. (1989) 'Public relations versus marketing: Dividing the conceptual domain and operational turf', a position paper prepared for the Public Relations Colloquium, San Diego, January 24, 1–11.

Kotler, P. (1991) *Marketing Management*, 9th edn, Englewood Cliffs, NJ: Prentice Hall, 621–48.

Kotler, P. and Mindak, W. (1978) 'Marketing and public relations', *Journal of Marketing*, 42(4), October: 13–20.

Kreitzman, L. (1986) 'Balancing brand building blocks', *Marketing*, 13 Nov, 43–6.

Lancaster, G. and Massingham, L. (1988) *Marketing Primer*, London: Heinemann Professional Publishing, 125–28.

Lightcap, K. (1984) 'Marketing Support', In B. Cantor, *Experts in action: Inside public relations*, New York: Longman, Inc., Chapter 8.

McDaniel, C. (1979) *Marketing: An Integrated Approach*, New York: Harper and Row, 455.

Merims, A.M. (1972) 'Marketing's stepchild: Product publicity', *Harvard Business Review*, 36(5), Nov/Dec: 107–13.

Novelli, W.D. (1988) 'Stir some PR into your communications mix', *Marketing News*, 22, 5 December, 19.

PR Week – UK Top 150 PR Consultancies (1994) 'Mixed fortunes for the top ten', Haymarket publication, 28 April, 37.

PR Week – UK Top 150 PR Consultancies (1993) Haymarket publication.

PR Week – UK Top 150 PR Consultancies (1992) 'Tougher all round for the top ten', Haymarket publication, 30 April, 27.

PR Week (1997) 'Mere tackles intersport drive to unify branding' (Karen Dempsey), 15 August, 2. Used with permission.

PR Week (1997) 'Kodak sharpens its focus on China through O&M PR' (Jemimah Bailey), 18 July, 5. Used with permission.

Schwartz, G. (1982) 'Public relations gets short shrift from new managers', *Marketing News*, 15 October, 8.

Seitel, F.P. (1992) *The Practice of Public Relations*, New York: Maxwell Macmillan, 6–7, 273–91.

Shandwick PLC (1989) *The public relations consultancy market worldwide*, Autumn, study published by the company.

Shimp, T.A. (1993) *Promotion Management and Marketing Communications*, Philadelphia: Harcourt Brace and Co, 587, 590–3, 604.

Shimp, T.A. and Delozier, M.W. (1986) *Promotion Management and Marketing Communications*, New York: Dryden, 493–94.

Stanley, R.E. (1982) *Promotion: Advertising, Publicity, Personal Selling, Sales Promotion*, 2nd edn, Englewood Cliffs, NJ: Prentice Hall.

White, J. (1991) *How to Understand and Manage Public Relations*, London: Business Books, 95–109.

21

SPONSORSHIP

Janet Hoek

CHAPTER AIMS

- to analyse the evolution and development of sponsorship management
- to consider cognitive and behaviourist perspectives on sponsorship
- to discuss evaluation of sponsorship activities
- to examine emerging ethical and legal issues affecting sponsorship management
- to present a research agenda designed to enhance future sponsorship management practices

ILLUSTRATION

The following vignette, quoted from *AdMap* (December, 1996) highlights the rapid development of sponsorship over recent decades.

Revenues from the 1966 World Cup Final amounted to just over £2 million (£20 million in today's equivalent). Money generated from the ticket sales alone of the Euro 96 final totalled around £55 million. And this was only the tip of the iceberg. Sponsorship deals were estimated to be worth around £50 million, the sales of licensed goods fetched a further £120 million, and on top of this, TV rights amounted to £45 million. Sponsoring sports events is big business.

Likewise sponsorship of Euro 96 was a multi-million pound business. Eleven companies officially sponsored the event: Canon, Carlsberg, Coca-Cola, Fujifilm, JVC, Mastercard, McDonald's, Opel/Vauxhall, Philips, Snickers and Umbro. Each of these sponsors paid £3.5 million for the exclusive rights to sell their products inside the stadia and to advertise on the perimeter boards around the pitch, which were seen by a cumulative TV audience of 6.9 billion people around the world. It is estimated that, collectively, sponsors spent an additional £100 million on further advertising and marketing efforts.

Most of the sponsors invested in posters and TV, and to a much lesser extent, in the national press. This was probably because the press packages on offer were less attractive and innovative, and also because of the belief that those who follow sport in their newspaper are more down-market.

And let us not forget that, in addition to the official sponsors, there were official suppliers, like Sema, BT and Microsoft, who paid UEFA to supply their goods and services free of charge estimated to cost in the region of £10 million.

INTRODUCTION

Although a comparatively new promotion tool when compared to more traditional vehicles, such as advertising, sponsorship already accounts for a sizeable proportion of some companies' overall promotion budgets, and many expect this figure to rise further (see Javalgi *et al.*, 1994; Meenaghan, 1996; Lee *et al.*, 1997). From its origin as a form of corporate philanthropy, patronage designed to do little more than foster senior managements' interests, sponsorship has evolved into a sophisticated and highly competitive promotion activity (Mescon and Tilson, 1987; Gross *et al.*, 1987; Witcher *et al.*, 1991). Meenaghan (1991a) clearly recognized the financial return expected of sponsorship when he defined it as 'an investment in cash or kind, in an activity, in return for access to the exploitable commercial potential associated with this activity' (p. 36).

Unlike corporate patronage which simply entails donating money or other supplies to a beneficiary with no expectation of a return (other than the beneficiary's gratitude), sponsorship is a commercial transaction where both parties anticipate a financial return. The beneficiary clearly receives direct funds, while the sponsor's expectations are ultimately measured in terms of consumers' behaviour. Under sponsorship arrangements, both parties will normally have clearly defined outcomes which they believe the sponsorship will achieve.

Yet, despite sponsorship's burgeoning popularity, aspects of its management remain poorly charted, and it remains without a rigorous theoretical framework (Gardner and Shuman, 1987). Early research suggested that, while managers set clear sponsorship objectives, few evaluated the outcome of their investment (see Meenaghan, 1991a; Witcher *et al.*, 1991). Indeed, Bowey (1988) described sponsorship evaluation as '*notoriously difficult*' (p. 75), and Farelley *et al.*(1997) noted that, even in the more sophisticated North American market, there was a lack of attention given to performance measures. In general, while some studies have noted increases in the proportion of managers undertaking systematic evaluations, a surprising proportion of managers still rely on ad hoc procedures, such as informal client feedback (see also Marshall and Cook, 1992). This lack of evaluation may be a direct consequence of sponsorship's rather flimsy theoretical framework: if academics and practitioners are not sure how sponsorship works, evaluation becomes a task which is at best complex, and at worst, too difficult to contemplate.

This chapter begins by reviewing the work already undertaken to describe and classify aspects of sponsorship management. This review is important, since it enables both an assessment of progress to date and an analysis of the assumptions on which the research is based. These assumptions are explored further in terms of cognitive information processing models and behaviour modification theory. Although the former have dominated the marketing communication and promotion literature, the latter offer an alternative, and arguably more robust, perspective from which to explain and predict sponsorship's effects. The two different models are also used to examine sponsorship's likely effects on consumers and, on the basis of this, current evaluation procedures are themselves critically evaluated and alternatives are suggested.

In addition, the chapter discusses recent developments which have complicated sponsorship management. Specifically, the phenomenon known as ambush marketing is examined, as are methods for dealing with this, and assessing its likely effects on consumers' behaviour.

The chapter concludes by proposing a research agenda which both builds on the progress to date and highlights a series of questions which require detailed attention before sponsorship's full potential as a promotion tool can be exploited.

EVOLUTION OF SPONSORSHIP

Meenaghan (1991a) documented the rapid development of sponsorship and suggested that this may be attributable to regulatory changes, particularly those affecting alcohol and tobacco promotions (see also Meerabeau *et al.*, 1991; Witcher *et al.*, 1991). Mescon and Tilson (1987) suggested that more fundamental changes in government policies, namely a decline in funding of more discretionary activities, had led to sponsorship becoming a vital component of some cultural and sporting groups' budgets. Meenaghan (1996) also compared sponsorship favourably to advertising when he commented on the increasing costs and clutter of mass media advertising. He also noted sponsorship's status as a global communications medium which, he suggested, can simultaneously reach quite disparate audiences, transcending language and cultural barriers (see also Parker, 1991). In addition, Meenaghan (1991b) suggested that pursuit of sports, leisure and cultural activities has become an increasingly important element of some consumers' lifestyles, making sponsorship an ideal medium for reaching people.

However, despite the advantages over other promotion disciplines which Meenaghan argued sponsorship offers, he noted that its acceptance and employment by managers had been limited by perceived disadvantages. Among the reasons offered for this was the suggestion that sponsorship remains confused with philanthropy and appears an unknown quantity, especially when compared with advertising and other more established promotion disciplines. Whether these issues have seriously impeded uptake of sponsorship opportunities remains a moot point, given the rapid growth in sponsorship he and others have documented.

Irrespective of the barriers noted by Meenaghan, an increasing number of managers have used sponsorship to achieve communication objectives (although Thwaites (1995) reported that only two-thirds of the managers he surveyed set specific objectives). Awareness and media coverage were frequently cited goals in earlier studies (Abratt *et al.*, 1987), but were augmented, and in some cases supplanted, by image and attitudinal goals in subsequent studies (Gardner and Shuman, 1987; Armstrong, 1988; Witcher *et al.*, 1991; Scott and Suchard, 1992; Meenaghan, 1994; Hansen and Scotwin, 1995; Meenaghan, 1996). Meenaghan (1991b) noted that sponsorship can work at both a brand and a corporate level to achieve awareness and image goals, and numerous anecdotal examples have been used to support such claims (see Speed and Thompson (1997), for example). Internal goals, such as fostering staff morale, rewarding staff achievements and providing corporate hospitality have also featured amongst some companies' objectives (Shuman, 1986, cited in Rajaretnam, 1994; Marshall and Cook, 1992).

Some researchers have noted that managers also set behaviourally oriented goals, such as sales (see Gardner and Shuman, 1987; Scott and Suchard, 1992; Hoek, *et al.*, 1993; Hansen and Scotwin, 1995). Although Thwaites (1995) reported that sales objectives were not a high priority among the managers he surveyed, he noted that: 'It is clear from the high rankings given to both potential and existing customers that the attraction and retention of business is an underlying motive' (p. 156). Arguably, all marketing activity is designed to prompt or maintain behaviour patterns and while only a comparatively small proportion of managers may specify direct behavioural outcomes, those who set intermediary goals presumably do so in the belief that these are in some way precursors to the behaviour patterns they wish to see.

In addition to examining the types of objectives set, researchers have also examined the audiences reached via sponsorships. Crowley (1991) argued that early researchers concentrated excessively on what he described as the 'what effects' factor rather than [on] 'to whom' aspects of objectives (p. 10). His comment was addressed by Speed and Thompson (1997) who classified sponsorship objectives according to the group at whom the sponsorship was directed. Figure 21.1 combines suggestions made by a number of researchers about the objectives and recipients of sponsorship communications.

Figure 21.1 indicates the diverse range of audiences and objectives set for sponsorship, and, if sponsorship is to achieve these objectives, its popularity is hardly surprising. However, the studies documenting managers' use of sponsorship have been largely descriptive and few have undertaken any assessment of how well sponsorship fulfils managers' expectations. When discussing managers' apparent reluctance to evaluate their sponsorships, Thwaites (1995) detected: 'either a lack of confidence in the validity and relevance of current theory or possibly insufficient knowledge of how these prescriptions can be implemented effectively' (p. 161; see also McDonald, 1991, pp. 32–33). To assess sponsorship's effectiveness, it is first necessary to examine how it works; the following section addresses this question by examining sponsorship within the context of both a cognitive and a behaviourist framework.

HOW DOES SPONSORSHIP WORK?

Considerable debate over how advertising works is ongoing and there has been surprisingly little work into the relationship between advertising and sponsorship, and the different roles they may play in shaping or maintaining consumers' behaviour (Hansen and Scotwin, 1995). Hastings (1984) noted that while the precise content of advertising can be specified, managers have less control over when, where and how the media might feature sponsorship activity. Meenaghan (1991b) also discussed these differences and argued that because sponsorship is largely a 'mute, non-verbal medium' (p. 8), it should be used in conjunction with traditional advertising. Failure to do so, he suggested, would mean full exploitation of the purchased rights could not be guaranteed and this would leave open the opportunity for competitors to sabotage the sponsorship (Meenaghan, 1994, 1996).

Meenaghan argued that effective sponsorship was reliant on advertising support, a point developed by Witcher *et al.* (1991), who suggested that sponsorship is simply

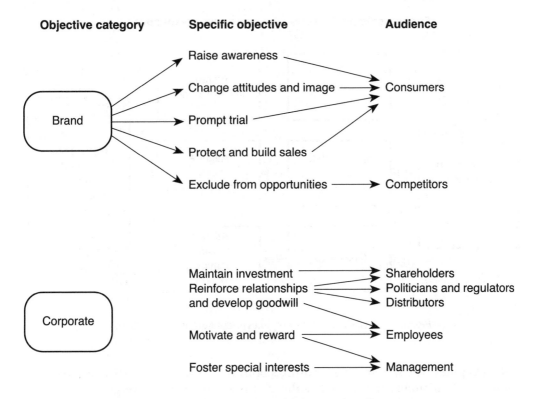

Figure 21.1 Sponsorship objectives and audiences.

another form of advertising. Given that sponsorship is seen either as analogous to, or dependent on, advertising, it is logical to examine how theories of advertising might be used to explain, predict and measure sponsorship's effects.

Marketing communication literature is dominated by cognitive information processing models which posit consumers as rational decision makers who seek and evaluate information before making choices. Whether or not this has been explicitly acknowledged by managers, many appear to have implicitly, at least, adopted this model when setting sponsorship objectives. This model is consistent with the heavy emphasis on awareness and attitudinal goals and also with the belief that these variables foster behaviour. One of the only attempts to adapt cognitive information processing models to suit sponsorship's characteristics attribute a central role to various attitude components, as Figure 21.2 demonstrates. Lee *et al.*'s variation on the AIDA model posits attitude towards the event, towards the promotion of the event, and towards behavioural intention as at the core of sponsorship's effects on consumers.

However, despite the widespread acceptance of cognitive models, trenchant criticism of them has emerged. Ehrenberg's (1974) ATR model uses behaviourist principles to posit a quite different pathway that specifically considers the role of repeat purchase, which Ehrenberg argued is the determinant of marketing success

365

Sponsorship perspective   **Consumer perspective**

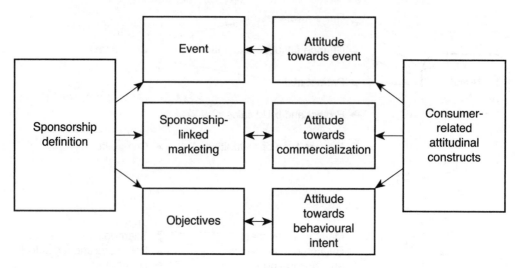

Figure 21.2 Sponsorship perspective, consumer perspective.

(see also Jones, 1990). Table 21.1 outlines both the ATR and the AIDA models and compares their similarities as well as the points at which they diverge.

Although both models commence with awareness, the role attributed to advertising in fostering awareness varies. Whereas the AIDA model posits advertising as having a key role in creating the awareness that finally culminates in behaviour, the ATR model suggests advertising has only a minor role in the early stages. Instead Ehrenberg suggests that advertising's chief function is to reinforce behaviour consumers have already performed, in order to maximize the probability of repeat purchase.

Ehrenberg also criticized the causal sequence depicted in the AIDA model, and those like it, and suggested that the image objectives set for many advertising campaigns were more likely to be realized after usage experience than developed before it. Subsequent work, examining belief attributes and usage behaviour, supported Ehrenberg's arguments.[1]

Table 21.1 AIDA and ATR models

AIDA	ATR
Awareness	Awareness
Interest	Trial
Desire	Reinforcement
Action	

In summary, although the debate over how advertising and sponsorship works can hardly be described as resolved, the empirical research to date favours the ATR model, which is more parsimonious, directly measurable, and displays greater conformity to principles of empirical generalisations (Barwise, 1995).

In one of the only studies to examine sponsorship in the context of the ATR model, Hoek *et al.* (1997) used a pre-post methodology in which respondents viewed either advertising or sponsorship stimulus material. According to Ehrenberg (1974) consumers tend to perceive advertising for the brands [they] are already buying (p. 32), thus Hoek *et al.* hypothesized that the stimulus material would have little or no effect on either the evaluative beliefs or the purchase probabilities of users or non-users. The data supported this hypothesis and Hoek *et al.* concluded that the behaviourist-based ATR model accommodated their findings more easily than did the more cognitively oriented AIDA model. In addition, the results were entirely consistent with the wider context of work into descriptive and evaluative attributes (see Bird and Ehrenberg, 1970; Barwise and Ehrenberg, 1985).

Crimmins and Horn (1996) used the AIDA model to argue that sponsorship fulfils a persuasive role, analogous to, but less direct than, that played by advertising. However, their claim that 'sponsorship improved the perception of a brand by flanking our beliefs about the brand and linking the brand to an event or organisation that the target audience already values highly' (p. 12) uses the behaviourist theory of respondent conditioning, not the cognitive theory of persuasion, to establish how sponsorship works (see also Hansen and Scotwin, 1995, p. 176). Similarly, Javalgi *et al.* (1994) noted the presence of operant conditioning (or reinforcement) when they noted that sponsorship may enhance corporate image 'if the company has a good image before the sponsorship' (p. 57).

Overall, while sponsorship clearly creates awareness, there is, as yet, no evidence that awareness, and the subsequent development of descriptive belief attributes, will prompt trial. The evidence to date suggests that sponsorship may create descriptive beliefs, through the pairing implicit in respondent conditioning, but that, more generally, it works in a similar way to advertising, as a form of operant conditioning that serves to maintain behaviour patterns. Thus McDonald (1991) argued: 'As more people have the sponsorship brought to their notice by publicity, they are *reminded* of something they already approve of; it is brought to the front of their mind. It does not follow that anybody's mind has been *changed* about the company because of the sponsorship' (p. 33).

These conclusions, while tentative and unreplicated, suggest that sponsorship, like brand advertising, is unlikely to generate sales increases. If improved sales are sought, managers could consider linking sponsorship to direct behavioural outcomes, through the use of competitions (with FMCGS) or other lead-generating activities (with durables and services).

SPONSORSHIP EVALUATION

Several researchers have noted that, although sponsorship objectives have been well documented, research into sponsorship evaluation has remained, at best, haphazard (see Witcher *et al.*, 1991; Quester, 1997). Indeed, Speed and Thompson (1997) concluded that 'models identifying factors that influence a sponsorship's success lag far behind those seen in other area of promotion' (p. 266). Although Javalgi *et al.* (1994) noted that evaluation may not be undertaken because the sponsorships satisfy personal rather than commercial objectives, most researchers agree that evaluation is imperative, especially given the scale of investment now occurring. Thwaites (1995) concluded that: 'measures of exposure, awareness, image, sales effectiveness and guest hospitality are possible' (p. 152), but noted that 'objectives often appear to be imprecise and are not developed in a form that allows subsequent evaluation' (p. 161). Clearly some debate over the extent and viability of evaluation research exists, and the remainder of this section examines the work undertaken to assess sponsorship's effectiveness.

Media audits

Although sponsorship requires advertising support, the fact that news coverage of the sponsored event itself is at the discretion of the media means it also has elements in common with public relations activities. Perhaps not surprisingly, therefore, one method of evaluation has entailed a straightforward analysis of media coverage (Abratt *et al.*, 1987; Parker, 1991; Marshall and Cook, 1992). However, this measure is analogous to using the frequency with which an advertisement has screened as a measure of advertising effectiveness. Clearly the number of insertions is not a measure of exposure, nor does it indicate whether any change in behaviour has occurred. While apparently straightforward and objective, media audits have very limited practical usefulness (see also Meenaghan, 1994; Crimmins and Horn, 1996).

Awareness measures

The natural progression from a media-centred measure is to one which recognizes that any marketing communications' success depends, at least to some extent, on whether it is noticed. Awareness has long been a popular variable in the assessment of advertising, for two reasons. First, awareness is simple and inexpensive to measure; recall studies can be conducted quickly and make few demands on either researchers or the respondents they interview. More cynically, awareness is regarded as highly responsive to levels of advertising intensity. From a political perspective, the marked changes in awareness scores that traditionally occur during an advertising campaign provide an obvious demonstration of the campaign's effect.

Researchers have measured a variety of different awareness variables, including awareness of the event itself, as well as awareness of the event sponsors and any sub-branding that may also have been undertaken (these measures are preferable to brand recall, since this may not be attributable to the sponsorship itself.) That sponsorship can produce marked increases in awareness has been well documented (see Sandler and Shani, 1993), although recent commentators have noted a number of variables which mediate consumers of sponsorship (see d'Astous and Bitz, 1995, for a discussion of this work).

Yet whether measurement of awareness variables also offers insights into a campaign's effectiveness remains a contentious question (see Javalgi *et al.*, 1994) . According to the AIDA model, high levels of awareness are an important prerequisite for interest, the next variable in the sequence proposed. The ATR model also commences with awareness, although Ehrenberg sees advertising as playing only a minor role in creating this and suggests that word of mouth and in-store exposure are largely responsible for creating awareness.

Thus while both models include awareness, they differ in the role and importance assigned to this variable. Some insight into this is afforded by research exploring the relationship between awareness and actual behaviour, which has suggested the link is tenuous (Haley and Baldinger, 1991). Nor has the direction of causality been clearly established. If, as Barwise and Ehrenberg (1985) have argued, the belief attributes consumers associate with brands depend largely on their experience of those brands, it seems logical to surmise that awareness may also have two components which parallel the descriptive and evaluative belief attributes Barwise and Ehrenberg discussed. That is, people may have a superficial awareness of brands they have seen featured somewhere, but this awareness, like descriptive attributes, is neither a precursor to, nor a consequence of, usage behaviour. By contrast, consumers may have a sophisticated awareness of brands because they have used them and have some knowledge of them. This latter form of awareness is consistent with Ehrenberg's argument that consumers: 'tend to perceive advertising for the brands [they] are already buying and repetitive advertising allows the habit to continue to operate in the face of competition' (1974: 32).

This reasoning implies that simple measures of awareness may provide little insight into the effectiveness of sponsorship (or advertising). The finding, that changes in awareness are poorly correlated with changes in sales, is at odds with the AIDA model, but is consistent with the ATR model, and with our wider knowledge of belief attributes and usage behaviour. However, this knowledge in turn implies that the awareness may vary across users and non-users, and that studies which do not collect usage information may provide little practical guidance.

Furthermore, knowledge of these theoretical developments as they affect advertising suggests that changes in awareness are likely to be simply changes in respondents' descriptive knowledge, and, since there is no evidence that changes in this type of knowledge are related to subsequent purchase behaviour, the value of fostering and measuring this type of awareness must surely be queried. Given that awareness features prominently as a core objective of many sponsorships, this reasoning raises some doubts about the uses to which sponsorship is put, as well as the methods used to evaluate it.

Image and attitude

Examination of the literature relating to sponsorship evaluation also suggests that image and attitudinal variables are popular objectives (see Abratt and Grobler, 1989; Parker, 1991; Javlagi *et al.*, 1994; Stipp and Schiavone, 1996, for example). Javalgi *et al.* (1994) investigated whether consumers who were aware of a firm's sponsorships viewed that firm more favourably and found that, while some elements were viewed more favourably, this was not consistently the case. Similarly inconclusive was a test of whether companies who understood sponsorship had a better image than those who did not. Hansen and Scotwin (1995) noted improved awareness following sponsorship, but found few attitudinal improvements, a result they attributed to the limited information conveyed by sponsorship.

D'Astous and Bitz (1995) specifically investigated the relationship between sponsorship characteristics and consumers' perceptions and found, among other things, that sponsorships that were not overtly commercial tended to be viewed more favourably, and that favourability was further enhanced if consumers were interested in the sponsored event. These findings are unsurprising, yet while they may confirm widely held beliefs, they offer no insights into how these perceptions may be managed, or, more importantly, how they affect consumers' purchase behaviour.

Whereas d'Astous and Bitz employed a variety of scenarios in their study, Stipp and Schiavone's study addressed very similar questions, but was located specifically within the context of the 1992 Olympics. Their results, that sponsorship of the Olympics improved the sponsor's image, are also largely predictable, if only on the grounds that few companies deliberately engage in activities likely to detract from their corporate profile. Yet the behavioural consequences on these image improvements were deemed 'beyond the scope of this research' (p. 23), and the question of greatest interest to managers was thus ignored.

Rajaretnam (1994) had earlier criticized studies such as these for adopting an overly short-term perspective. He claimed that longer-term measures were necessary to address the true effects sponsorship may have on an organization's image or positioning. Rajaretnam's case study of one Indian firm found marked long-term improvements in awareness, corporate image and brand preference. However, promising though these results may appear, the study did not include a discussion of other mix activities which may have affected these variables, nor have the results been replicated. More importantly, although brand preference (arguably a proxy for purchase behaviour) improved, the study did not report any attempts to assess the effects of this on sales.

The use of awareness, image and preference variables in evaluation is consistent with the AIDA model, but is contrary to the increasing body of work which suggests that attitudinal or interest variables may also be consequences of usage experience (Barwise and Ehrenberg, 1985), and with the wider body of psychological literature which also documents attitude–behaviour inconsistencies (see Foxall, 1983; East, 1997). Until further work has explored the direction of causality (if indeed this exists), it would seem prudent to avoid relying on attitudinal measures to predict sales behaviour.

Persuasion and preference

Rajaretnam's (1994) examination of brand preference went beyond consideration of attitudinal variables alone, and other researchers have also examined variables that have a stronger behavioural dimension; of these, persuasion has received the most detailed attention.

According to Crimmins and Horn (1996), sponsorship is a form of indirect persuasion which works though the strength and duration of the sponsorship link, the gratitude felt due to this link, and perceptual changes that may have occurred. To investigate these components of persuasion, Crimmins and Horn measured awareness and found that it was critically dependent on the level of advertising support and the time period over which this support was present. Gratitude was measured as a crude form of loyalty or brand-switching to the sponsor's brand. However, instead of assessing actual behavioural data, Crimmins and Horn used only levels of agreement to attitude statements, whose link to actual behaviour is tenuous. Likewise, the measures of perception were not specifically linked to behaviour. While it may be a source of corporate pride to be ranked more highly than competitors on the basis of perception, shareholders are unlikely to be impressed if these rankings do not correspond to improvements in market share or profitability.

Lee *et al.* (1997) also used a series of attitude statements as the basis of a factor analysis from which three factors, corresponding to attitude towards the event, promotion of the event, and behavioural intention, were extracted. However, the findings presented suffered from two problems: one analytic and one theoretical. First, nowhere are the Eigen values of the retained factors reported, nor is there any discussion of the proportion of total variance explained by these factors. Even if this information was satisfactorily provided, there is no evidence that these variables are directly related to behaviour. Although Lee *et al.* recommended that future research address this question, efforts directed at addressing the same question in the context of advertising have done little to establish the existence of the posited relationship.

Behavioural measures

If sponsorship is undertaken to achieve behavioural outcomes, it would seem logical to measure the behaviours thought to be affected. Yet such measures are complicated by both theoretical and practical considerations. First, numerous authors have acknowledged that sales are affected by more than advertising, sponsorship, or any other promotional variable that may have been employed in a given campaign. In other words, sales are a function of many variables, and the belief that sales can be predicted on the basis of promotion activity alone ignores the plethora of variables thought to affect purchase behaviour.

Even if this argument is not accepted, the ATR model implicitly suggests that advertising (and by implication, sponsorship) reinforces behaviour. If this is true, the sales results managers should expect would be no more than maintenance of the status quo, in line with the primarily defensive role accorded to advertising by the ATR model.

The difficulties, either logical, practical, or both, in using awareness, image or behaviour as an indication of sponsorship effectiveness inevitably raise the question of whether sponsorship can be evaluated (and may explain why so few managers appear to undertake any formal research). Rather than dismissing this key management question as too difficult, it seems logical to reconsider whether sponsorship can be managed in such a way that behavioural measures are made more accessible.

One such method is to link the sponsorship directly to some form of sales activity, typically a sales promotion. For example, some manufacturers of confectionery bars have used special packaging to denote their sponsorship of key events. Collection of a pre-specified number of packages has become a prerequisite for entry into competitions, and entrants have been effectively conditioned to expect to have to attach bar codes to their entry.

Where sponsorship has been associated with both an event and the media coverage of that event, sponsors have also run phone-in competitions, which have usually required entrants to display some knowledge of the sponsor, and for which the prize has been donated by the sponsor. Although the need for respondents to know some details of the sponsor means little more than that awareness measures can be assessed, the value of these associated promotions lies in the sales office leads that can be generated. For this reason, these promotions are typically undertaken by service or consumer durables organizations.

However, not every sponsorship will offer an opportunity for direct behavioural links such as these to be established. In these cases, it may be necessary to foster intermediate variables. While managers have already sought to affect variables thought to mediate behaviour (awareness and image), the empirical evidence linking these to behaviour has remained contradictory, and some would argue illusory. Examination of the ATR model suggests that trial, itself a behaviour, may be a more satisfactory measure than awareness or image.

While supermarket shoppers or browsers are thoroughly familiar with product trial promotions, such as demonstrations, the ambit for such promotions goes well beyond FMCGS. Publishers who sponsor conferences trial new software and texts, while collecting business cards that serve as leads for future sales opportunities. Wineries and breweries also sponsor events in return for exclusive rights as suppliers. It would seem that opportunities such as these, which have a clear emphasis on usage experience with the sponsoring brand, usually supported by some kind of data collection, offer opportunities for behavioural monitoring which relatively few companies currently exploit.

In summary, evaluation is arguably the most important phase of any promotion campaign and there is no reason why it should not also be so for sponsorship. However, the variables currently assessed in the sponsorship research that is undertaken seem unlikely to offer managers specific guidance about the success of a campaign, or about how sponsorship generally could be better managed in the future. To obtain this information, managers may find it more helpful to consider these objectives in terms of cueing or reinforcing behaviour, and to relate their sponsorship to specific sales promotion activities which enable some assessment of behavioural consequences.

LEGAL AND ETHICAL DILEMMAS

A full assessment of sponsorship's effectiveness has been limited by the difficulties managers have found when evaluating it. This problem emerges again in the context of ambush marketing, a growing ethical and legal problem that has affected sponsorship. This term appears to have first been coined in the mid-1980s, in response to competitive clashes which occurred between Kodak and Fuji, during the 1984 Los Angeles Olympic Games (Sandler and Shani, 1989). Meenaghan (1994) defines ambush marketing as: 'The practice whereby another company, often a competitor, attempts to deflect some of the audience attention to itself and away from the sponsor' (p. 72).

In practice, ambushing may involve any number of blatant or more covert activities ranging from sponsoring a team competing in an event sponsored by a competitor, through to purchasing media time and space around the reporting of an event sponsored by a competitor. Perhaps not surprisingly, sponsors have been irked by this practice, especially when they have invested heavily in the actual sponsorship rights. Event owners have also reacted strongly against ambushers, in the belief that failure to do so would threaten the integrity of their causes and lead to a decline in the sponsorship investment on which they depend.

Meenaghan (1994 and 1996) set out anti-ambushing checklists which prescribed actions sponsors should consider taking to maximize their sponsorship exposure and protect their investment from ambushing. These lists have two key themes which relate to contractual and promotion support decisions. First, Meenaghan advocated ensuring that sponsorship contracts do not leave open the possibility that competitors could procure rights to sponsor sub-categories of the event. Second, he suggested that sponsors dominate the media and ensure that competitors have no opportunity to exploit any advertising opportunities that might be associated with media coverage of the event (a point made also by Lee *et al.*, 1997).

Adoption of Meenaghan's suggestions clearly entails considerable expense and, although researchers have for some time noted that sponsorship activities require mass marketing support, Meenaghan's advice requires sizeable promotion budgets to ensure purchase and full support of the sponsorship rights. From the event owner's perspective, the apparent need to take these steps will almost inevitably diminish the pool of potential sponsors, as those who cannot afford to protect their sponsorship in this way may instead invest in other promotional activities. Meenaghan's advice is clearly preventative as it advocates closing a number of loopholes previously left open and exploited by ambushers. However, while these steps may make overt ambushing more difficult, Meenaghan himself noted that ambushers have employed increasingly creative tactics. Given this, managers also need to ensure that their planning arrangements include both preventative steps and remedial measures.

Yet while it seems widely agreed that some companies embark on a deliberate and carefully orchestrated programme of activities designed to disrupt a competitor's sponsorship and create confusion amongst consumers, others seem to transgress accidentally. Quester (1997) summarized this predicament: '. . . it is also conceivable that some degree of "ambush" may result from less purposeful activities or even, in some cases, simply from consumers' inaccurate information processing' (p. 4). Thus, while ambush marketing may be undertaken deliberately, at least in some cases it would appear to occur almost irrespective of the alleged ambushers' activities.

Unfortunately, an unambiguous method of establishing whether deception has occurred as a result of ambushing activities, and what damage this has caused, has not yet been documented. Thus although several organizations and event owners claim to have observed or experienced ambushing tactics (deliberate or accidental), the effects of alleged ambushing on consumers remain largely unexplored.

Sandler and Shani (1989) undertook one of the first studies to explore consumers' understanding of ambush tactics. Using the 1988 Winter Olympic Games as the vehicle for their study, they identified a range of product categories and, within each of these, collected details of the official sponsor, the alleged ambusher and two other companies. They compared the average number of correctly identified sponsors with the average number of incorrectly recalled ambushers and concluded that a significantly higher proportion of official sponsors were correctly associated with the sponsorship. By comparison, ambushers' scores did not vary significantly from those of the other companies within the category (who apparently did not undertake any promotions that could be construed as ambushing). Yet while Sandler and Shani concluded that ambushers received no greater benefit from their activities than did non-ambushers, they also noted that in only four of the seven categories examined were official sponsors identified more frequently than other organizations. From this, they suggested that purchase of sponsorship rights alone was insufficient to ensure association of the sponsoring brand with the event, and noted that recognition as an official sponsor was more likely to follow if additional promotions were undertaken to publicize the sponsorship.

Although this study began to address the question of overriding importance to managers interested in obtaining remedies – the effect any alleged ambushing had on consumers – the key variables examined were recall and recognition, which shed little light on the behavioural implications of ambushing activities. Investigation of this latter question requires a further appraisal of how ambushing might be expected to work, as well as a reconsideration of the research procedures used to investigate alleged ambushing. The following section discusses these issues in detail.

A RESEARCH AGENDA

This review of sponsorship's development and the research undertaken into the management of sponsorship activities has highlighted two distinct areas which merit more detailed research attention. The first of these is the vexing question of sponsorship evaluation. While a limited amount of work has been conducted in this area, many have yielded to the temptation to regard this issue as too troubling and complex.

Almost all of the sponsorship research that has been undertaken has adopted a cognitive-information processing perspective and, while this work may have further elucidated various attitude components and the interrelationships between these, it has not illuminated the relationship between sponsorship and behaviour. This failure to address the most important question to managers, coupled with the increasing level of criticism directed at this approach, must surely raise questions about the value and logic of pursuing this research direction.

An alternative which merits serious attention uses a behaviourist framework and places greater emphasis on the outcomes of sponsorship, and correspondingly less on the processes thought to mediate these outcomes. With comparatively few exceptions, researchers have agreed that sponsorship raises awareness, but while the cognitive model assumes that this fosters attitudinal changes, the behaviourist-based model attempts to link this to trial behaviour. At present, few reported studies into sponsorship routinely collect details of respondents' brand usage behaviour, and few sponsorships make explicit provision for trial-prompting activities. Collection of brand repertoire details would enable some assessment of the direction in which awareness worked. That is, if consumers who used the sponsoring brand were more aware of the sponsorship than non-users, the sponsorship would appear to reinforce behaviour rather than serve as the basis of an as yet unperformed purchase. However, if awareness levels were similar across usage groups, the awareness may be simply a descriptive belief attribute which bears little relationship to usage behaviour.

Whether the accumulation of descriptive belief attributes does foster trial is, as yet, unexplored. This question will require the incorporation of specific mechanisms, such as those discussed earlier, into sponsorship. Without these, sponsorship evaluation will remain limited to a bland investigation of awareness, attitudes (image) and possibly preferences, with no real understanding of the relationship between these variables and consumers' behaviour. The variety of formats which sponsorship can take, and the direct interaction with audiences, live and media-delivered, offer great opportunities for the incorporation of trial prompting mechanisms, and the consistent use and evaluation of these would appear to offer great potential for examining the behavioural consequences of sponsorship.

If, like advertising, sponsorship also plays a key role in reinforcing consumers' behaviour, the overt behavioural consequences would be less profound, since reinforcement would simply maintain the status quo. Yet, even here, opportunities for more behaviourally oriented research exist. If sponsorship can increase the chances of repeat purchase (a measure of loyalty), improve a brand's position in consumers' repertoire hierarchy, or decrease churn (the substitution of one brand for another in a brand repertoire), it would also help achieve critical management objectives. Examination of panel data which combined details of respondents' purchase behaviour and leisure activities would enable preliminary investigations into these questions.

A more particular subset of evaluation research is the issue of ambush marketing, or, more specifically, the effects this activity may have. While many Western countries have statutes prohibiting the promulgation of misleading or deceptive claims, a clear procedure for establishing the existence of incorrect beliefs, and their relationship to alleged ambushing practices, has yet to be developed. More importantly, the effects of ambush marketing on consumers' behaviour remain largely unknown.

Preston's (1994) work into misleading advertising examined respondents' interpretations of various advertising claims. A similar methodology which explored the literal and implied claims contained in sponsorship promotions could establish the presence of misleading claims and the proportion of respondents who detected these. However, while the establishment of misleading claims may help address the first question, it does not provide any indication of the extent to which an alleged ambusher should be held responsible for these views. This decision would need to be dealt with on a case-by-case basis, depending on the specific circumstances associated with each situation.

The question of the behavioural consequences of these beliefs is more problematic, but could be addressed by using choice modelling techniques to isolate the effects competing claims have on consumers' likely purchase behaviour. While there are some obvious problems with this approach (namely the artificiality of the research conditions), the findings would, nevertheless, offer some insight into the relationship between respondents' beliefs and behaviour. If there was a strong correlation between non-users' beliefs and projected behaviour, this would provide some support for the cognitive information processing model of sponsorship. Conversely, if only weak correlations existed, further questions would need to be raised about the model. If the results of consumers' projected choices were inconsistent with current market shares, they could provide a means of quantifying the damage caused by the misleading claims, and thus a basis for calculating any reparations.

The research agenda outlined above has deliberately focused on issues of evaluation, since a consistent theme amongst the papers discussed is the general paucity of research in this area. Underlying the research suggestions is a clear theoretical framework, which, if rigorously tested and evaluated, will clarify how sponsorship works and deepen our understanding of what it can achieve.

SUMMARY AND CONCLUSIONS

Sponsorship has grown rapidly over the past two decades and there is widespread agreement that this trend will continue. However, this growth has not been paralleled by an understanding of how sponsorship works. Although managers' sponsorship objectives are frequently ambitious, and range from awareness through to sales growth, systematic evaluation remains the exception, rather than the rule.

This chapter argues that the cognitive information processing model on which managers and researchers have implicitly relied is unsatisfactory, for reasons which have been well documented over the past 25 years. An alternative framework which draws heavily on Ehrenberg's ATR model is proposed and evaluated. While the logic of this model is superior to that of cognitive information processing models, and while the empirical support for the ATR model is growing, it has still to be applied consistently to sponsorship. For this reason, a detailed research agenda is also proposed. The research programme outlined not only incorporates behavioural measures into sponsorship evaluation, but also explores the consequences of an increasingly common sponsorship problem: ambush marketing. Although it is arguably unethical to sabotage a competitor's sponsorships, ambush marketing has become more prevalent and presents managers and the courts with some difficult questions which researchers have yet to address fully.

Sponsorship practices have been fully described, analysed and summarized, and it is now time for researchers to adopt a more evaluative perspective and to address directly the question of greatest management importance: what effect does sponsorship have on consumers' behaviour?

DISCUSSION TOPICS

1 Given the stated need to support sponsorship with a heavy advertising programme, how realistic are predictions that sponsorship's rapid growth will continue? How likely is it that sponsorship will become an option available only to those companies with large promotion budgets?

2 Snickers and Gillette were both major sponsors of the 1994 Soccer World Cup. Consider the audiences these manufacturers could have reached via their sponsorship and evaluate the logic of their investment.

3 Examine Table 21.1 and contrast the AIDA and ATR models. Comment critically on their relevance to sponsorship research.

4 How valid is Crowley's criticism that researchers have concentrated excessively on what managers do rather than on who their sponsorships reach and affect?

5 Consider the case for and against the use of awareness as a measure of sponsorship's effectiveness.

6 Discuss the potential impediments which inhibit the measurement of sponsorship's effect on behaviour. To what extent do you think these impediments can be overcome?

7 Meenaghan (1994) asked whether ambush marketing was an imaginative or an immoral practice. Develop arguments in support of both options.

8 Select a recent sponsorship and consider how it might have included more behavioural-oriented elements. How would you revise this campaign, should it be run again in the future?

9 Suggest how sponsoring organizations should minimize their exposure to ambushing practices.

10 To what extent should sponsorship deliver specific behavioural outcomes?

CASE STUDY – THE FINE ART OF DOING BUSINESS – AND MAKING THE CLIENT FEEL GOOD (SOURCED FROM RESEARCHPLUS, JUNE 1997, PP. 8–10.)

At the Tate Gallery, exhibition sponsorship alone is now worth significantly more than £1m per year. The Tate undertakes regular research to provide an attractive service to current sponsors and to collect information to help attract new ones. This case documents promotion of the Cézanne exhibition which was sponsored by Ernst & Young.

Promotion of the Cézanne exhibition (8 February to 28 April 1996) started early, as did the Tate's monitoring of awareness of the forthcoming events and its sponsors among Tate visitors. In November 1995, just 8 per cent were aware that Ernst & Young was about to sponsor at the Tate, yet once the exhibition started 54 per cent of visitors to the gallery recognized Ernst & Young as a sponsor.

Awareness of Cézanne was so high that 34 000 tickets were booked before the exhibition even opened in London. PR, all of which credited the sponsor, included

TV coverage in *Omnibus*, a radio programme, editorials in the press, press trips to the Cézanne exhibition in Paris in third quarter 1995, followed by a trip to the artist's studio in Aix-en-Provence, *Sunday Times* competitions, poster promotions and the *Funday Times* competitions for children, advertisements in the *Financial Times*, posters on London buses and London Underground, even a Prêt-à-Manger Cézanne-wich tabletop promotion in London outlets of the Café Rouge restaurant chain and Harvey Nichols shop front windows. Again the Tate pushed for Ernst & Young crediting and an independent media evaluation valued Ernst & Young's media credits at £500,000.

Ernst & Young's primary objective was high-quality corporate hospitality, achieved by entertaining 5500 clients and contacts on 44 occasions during the 12 weeks of the exhibition. Furthermore, the Tate was able to demonstrate to Ernst & Young the popularity of the sponsorship: Cézanne was the most popular exhibition in the Tate Gallery's history, with a total attendance of 408 688 visitors. Fifty four per cent of visitors recognized Ernst & Young as sponsors at the gallery. Of these, 71 per cent identified them as sponsors of the Cézanne exhibition.

NOTE

1 Barwise and Ehrenberg (1985) suggested that the belief attributes consumers held about different FMCG brands depended largely on their usage of those brands. Although they noted deviations from this pattern, where a higher than expected proportion associated certain attributes with brands, this association bore less relationship to usage than it did to heavily promoted brand features. The key point is that while advertising and other promotions can create awareness, this may have no relationship with usage behavior. The assumption that awareness will eventually lead to purchase is not, therefore, supported by empirical evidence.

REFERENCES

Abratt, R., Clayton, B. and Pitt, L. (1987) 'Corporate objectives in sports sponsorship', *International Journal of Advertising*, 6(4): 299–311.

Abratt, R. and Grobler S. (1989) 'The evaluation of sports sponsorship', *International Journal of Advertising*, 8(4): 351–62.

Armstrong, C. (1988) 'Sports sponsorship: A case study approach to measuring its effectiveness' *European Research*, 16(2): 97–103.

Barwise, T. (1995) 'Good empirical generalisations', Centre for Marketing Working Paper No. 95–602, London Business School, United Kingdom.

Barwise, T. and Ehrenberg, A. (1985) 'Consumer beliefs and brand usage', *Journal of the Market Research Society*, 27(2): 81–93.

Bird, M. and Ehrenberg, A. (1970) 'Consumer attitudes and brand usage', *Journal of the Market Research Society*, 12(4): 233–47.

Bowey, S. (1988) 'Editorial', *European Research*, 16(2): 85.

Crimmins, J. and Horn, M. (1996) 'Sponsorship: From management ego trip to marketing success', *Journal of Advertising Research*, 36(4): 11–21.

Crowley, M. (1991) 'Prioritising the Sponsorship Audiences', *European Journal of Marketing*, 25(11): 11–21.

D'Astous, A. and Bitz, P. (1995) 'Consumer evaluation of sponsorship programmes', *European Journal of Marketing*, 29(12): 6–22.

East, R. (1997) *Consumer Behaviour: Principles and Applications in Marketing*, UK: Prentice Hall.

Ehrenberg, A. (1974) 'Repetitive advertising and the consumer', *Journal of Advertising Research*, 14(2): 25–34.

Farelley, F., Quester, P. and Burton, R. (1997) 'Integrating sports sponsorship into the corporate marketing function: an international comparative study', *International Marketing Review*, 14(3): 170–82.

Foxall, G. (1983) *Consumer Choice*, London: Macmillan.

Gardner, M. and Shuman, P. (1987) 'Sponsorship: An important component of the promotion mix', *Journal of Advertising*, 16(1): 11–17.

Gross, A., Traylor, M. and Shuman, P. (1987) 'Corporate sponsorship of arts and sports events' 40th *ESOMAR Marketing Research Congress Proceedings*, Montreux, Switzerland, 535–62.

Haley, R. and Baldinger, A. (1991) 'The ARF copy research validity project', *Journal of Advertising Research*, 31(2): 11–32.

Hansen, F. and Scotwin, L. (1995) 'An experimental enquiry into sponsorship: What effects can be measured?', *Marketing and Research Today*, August: 173–81.

Hastings, G. (1984) 'Sponsorship works differently from advertising', *International Journal of Advertising*, 3(2): 171–6.

Hoek, J., Gendall, P. and Sanders, J. (1993) 'Sponsorship management and evaluation: Are managers' assumptions justified?', *Journal of Promotion Management*, 1(1): 53–66.

Hoek, J., Gendall, P., Jeffcoat, M. and Orsman, D. (1997) 'Sponsorship and Advertising: A comparison of their effects', *Journal of Marketing Communications*, 3(1): 21–32.

Javlagi, R., Traylor, M., Cross. A. and Lampman, E. (1994) 'Awareness of sponsorship and corporate image: An empirical investigation', *Journal of Advertising*, 23(4): 47–58.

Jones, J.P. (1990) 'Advertising: Strong force or weak force? Two views an ocean apart', *International Journal of Advertising*, 9(3): 233–46.

Lee, M., Sandler, D. and Shani, D. (1997) 'Attitudinal constructs towards sponsorship', *International Marketing Review*, 14(3): 159–69.

Marshall, D. and Cook, G. (1992) 'The corporate sports sponsor', *International Journal of Advertising*, 11(4): 307–24.

McDonald, C. (1991) 'Sponsorship and the image of the sponsor', *European Journal of Marketing*, 25(11): 31–8.

Meenaghan, T. (1991a) 'The role of sponsorship in the marketing communication mix', *International Journal of Advertising*, 10(1): 35–47.

Meenaghan, T. (1991b) 'Sponsorship – Legitimising the medium', *European Journal of Marketing*, 25(11): 5–10.

Meenaghan, T. (1994) 'Point of view: Ambush marketing – immoral or imaginative practice?', *Journal of Advertising Research*, 34(3): 77–88.

Meenaghan, T. (1996) 'Ambush marketing – a threat to corporate sponsorship', *Sloan Management Review*, 38(1): 103–13.

Meerabeau, E., Gillett, R., Kennedy, M., Adeoba, J., Byass, M. and Tabi, K. (1991) 'Sponsorship and the drinks industry in the 1990s', *European Journal of Marketing*, 25(11): 39–56.

Mescon, T. and Tilson, D. (1987) 'Corporate philanthropy: A strategic approach to the bottom line', *California Management Review*, 29(2): 49–61.

Parker, K. (1991) 'Sponsorship: The research contribution', *European Journal of Marketing*, 25(11): 22–30.

Preston, I. (1994) *The tangled web they weave: Truth, Falsity and Advertisers*, Wisconsin: The University of Wisconsin Press.

Quester, P. (1997) 'Awareness as a measure of sponsorship effectiveness: the Adelaide Formula One Grand Prix and evidence of incidental ambush effects', *Journal of Marketing Communications*, 3(1): 1–20.

Rajaretnam, J. (1994) 'The long-term effects of sponsorship', *Marketing & Research Today*, February: 62–74.

Sandler, D. and Shani, P. (1989) 'Olympic sponsorship vs ambush marketing: Who gets the gold?', *Journal of Advertising Research*, 29(4): 9–14.

Sandler, D. and Shani, D. (1995) 'Sponsorship and the Olympic Games: The consumer perspective', *Sports Marketing Quarterly*, 2(3): 38–43.

Scott, D. and Suchard, H. (1992) 'Motivations for Australian expenditure of sponsorship', *International Journal of Advertising*, 11(4): 325–32.

Speed, R. and Thompson, P. (1997) 'Developing a model of the determinants of sports sponsorship impact', paper presented at the *1997 European Marketing Academy Conference*, Warwick Business School, UK, May 20–3.

Stipp, H. and Schiavone, N. (1996) 'Modelling the impact of Olympic sponsorship on corporate image', *Journal of Advertising Research*, 36(4): 22–8.

Thwaites, D. (1995) 'Professional football sponsorship – Profitable or profligate?', *International Journal of Advertising*, 14(2): 149–64.

Witcher, B., Craigen, J., Culligan, D. and Harvey, A. (1991) 'The links between objectives and function in organisational sponsorship', *International Journal of Advertising*, 10(1): 13–33.

22

THE INTERNET (INTERNATIONAL CONTEXT)

Jim Hamill and Philip Kitchen

'The global information superhighway may be mainly hype today. Tomorrow it will be an understatement.'

(Negroponte, 1995)

CHAPTER AIMS

- to examine the revolutionary impact of the Internet on international marketing communications
- to identify the key strategic and marketing management issues involved in implementing effective Internet-supported marketing communications strategies
- to argue the case for greater recognition of the Internet in marketing communications teaching and research

ILLUSTRATION: AXIS COMMUNICATIONS (http://www.axis.se)

This case provides a good example of the way in which one organization has successfully used the Internet to develop a global brand and to build relationships with geographically dispersed customers at low cost.

Headquartered in Lund, Sweden, Axis Communications Inc. develops and manufactures a range of products designed to support network-centric computing. The company's 'flagship' products – the StorePoint CD Network CD-ROM Server, the NetEye 200 Network Camera and print servers – are part of the first wave of innovative network and Web appliances designed to increase productivity by enabling users to access and share computer resources more efficiently. Axis' proprietary Thinserver Technology enables users to more easily share peripherals on heterogeneous networks with state-of-the-art, cost-effective connectivity alternatives. The company, which currently employs 200 people, has experienced an average annual sales growth of 43 per cent since its foundation in 1984 (1995/1996 – $49 million) and has an installed base of 500 000 products worldwide. Major customers include 'Fortune 500' companies such as Ford, GM, AT&T, Pepsi, ABC News, Microsoft, GE, Boeing – and many medium-sized organizations worldwide. The rapid growth of the company has been, to a large extent, dependent on the establishment of 'strategic technology relationships' with customers and with leading hardware vendors and software developers such as Hewlett-Packard, IBM, Canon, Fujitsu, Sony, Xerox, Microsoft, Netscape, Oracle and Sun. Maintaining good relationships and communications with their existing customer base is vital for Axis.

Despite its success, Axis remains a relatively small company in global terms and this has created two major challenges. First, how to support the existing global customer base. Second, how to achieve greater global brand awareness and increased sales volume on a small promotion budget compared to major global competitors.

Axis sees the Internet as providing a low-cost solution to both problems and one which is highly relevant to the changing nature of procurement in the IT industry. The benefits of using the Internet to support customer relationships and to achieve global brand development are explained clearly on the company's Web site which states:

> Buyers' mindsets are increasingly getting younger and they want to play a more active role in acquiring information about our products. They do not want advertising stuffed down their throats as in more traditional methods of promotion. Network managers are intelligent and there is no reason to push them. That's why the Web is an ideal means of reaching this audience and once we get them to visit us on the Web, business becomes self generating. The more they know, the more they will want to know and we will build a relationship with our users instead of feeding them sales pitches. The Web provides an ideal channel for achieving this interactivity and feedback at low cost.

The content of Axis' Web site, which has become centrally important to its global marketing strategy, includes full and comprehensive product information; sales contacts by region; corporate news (annual reports, press releases etc.); a 'What's New' section (e.g. new product developments); and a Jobs Vacant section. The site is fully interactive and the company relies heavily on e-mail to support existing customers and to develop relationships with new customers and resellers. An innovative feature of the Web site is the Axis Electronic Newsletter which is sent on request to all subscribers. This provides a very low-cost method of communicating new product and technology information to existing and potential customers around the world. The Web site supports rather than replaces the company's existing international distribution strategy with the ultimate aim of developing a virtual community of customers, distributors, resellers, suppliers, etc. in order to develop the Axis brand globally.

(Source: Jim Hamill, 1998)

INTRODUCTION

Rapid technology change, especially in Information Technology, is having a revolutionary effect on the study and practice of marketing as we move towards the new millennium (see Figure 22.1). Many of the fundamental tenets of mainstream marketing are being called into question and new paradigms will be required to explain marketing realities in the emerging 'digital age'. Some of the most important emerging trends include:

- The growing importance of electronic commerce, especially in business-to-business marketing.
- Levelling of the corporate 'playing field' and the more rapid internationalization of small- and medium-sized enterprises made possible through effective Internet marketing.
- Innovative approaches to market segmentation and the move towards 'one-to-one' marketing.
- New developments in market research and marketing information systems using electronic communications, data mining techniques, and the Web.
- The changing role of marketing intermediaries, with IT facilitating direct buyer/ seller relationships.
- The growing importance of virtual communities and electronic networks.
- New approaches to marketing communications, promotion and advertising.
- Changing power relationships between customer and supplier; innovative, 'digital' approaches to customer service and support.
- The impact of IT on market structure, conduct and performance.
- New, customer-driven approaches to product development incorporating IT.

This chapter examines the revolutionary impact of the Internet on the study and practice of international (by definition the Internet *is international in scope*, hence the need to tackle the subject from an international prospective) marketing communications and the key strategic and management issues facing firms in developing effective Internet-supported marketing communications strategies. The main argument developed is that the Internet is no longer a 'fad' or the preserve of computer 'nerds' and 'techies'. It has become an indispensable international marketing tool. Especially for small- and medium-sized enterprises (SMEs), effective Internet marketing can provide a low-cost 'gateway' to global customers. The Internet, however, provides a fundamentally different environment for international marketing communications. New strategic approaches and a 'digital' mindset are required to be successful. This has major implications for marketing communications educators. Much of what is taught at university level may already be outdated; fundamental reassessment of the results of past research may be necessary and new marketing communications paradigms may have to be developed to take account of the electronic age (see Hoffman and Novak, 1996b; Quelch and Klein, 1996; Hamill, 1997; Hamill and Gregory, 1997). Many of the fundamental tenets on which most marketing communications research and teaching is based are called into question by the growing popularity of Internet marketing. A major research initiative is required to improve our understanding in this area, especially the extent to which the 'Net' provides a 'gateway' to global markets for SMEs. In the absence of such an initiative, mainstream academic literature on marketing communications, which (maybe because of the speed of innovation) has largely ignored the Internet, will no longer accurately describe the reality of international business (nationally or internationally). As international marketing educators, we need to ensure that they

- 'Commercialisation of the WWW will revolutionise the study and practice of international marketing as we move towards the new millennium' (Quelch and Klein, 1996; Hamill 1997a&b)
- 'The speed with which things are moving on the web is stunning and punishment is proving swift for those who don't understand it' (Tapscott, 1996).
- 'Agent, broker, distributor and even retailer – anybody with these job titles ought to be doing some serious career planning' (Tapscott, 1996).
- 'On the web, marketing is not about selling – but about buying. It is the customer who decides . . . . Selling on the Internet is unlike anything that companies have had to deal with before. It requires new techniques and new approaches . . . . Companies should forget today's theories of mass-marketing and start to segment their customer base. By using web site feedback and intelligent databases companies can target specific customer groups with tailored offerings . . . . Having immediate access to customer data at any place and at any time will radically change the traditions of service and distribution' (Molenaar, Interactive Marketing: The End of Mass Marketing, 1996).
- 'The Internet is not about mass marketing and mass markets. It's about people – individuals with unique aspirations, needs, desires and cultural backgrounds. It's not as much a mass market of 60 million people as it is 60 million markets, each containing one person' (Vassos, 1996)
- 'The global information superhighway may be mainly hype today. Tomorrow it will be an understatement' (Negroponte, 1996).
- 'Most of today's corporations are structured for an age that is gone. But attempts at "business reengineering" have met with failure more often than success. Executives around the world are asking what comes next?'. The next giant step in the evolution of the corporate world is the building of corporations that take full advantage of the cyberspace revolution – agile, virtual, global, cybernetic corporations: cybercorps for short – fluid and fast learning so that they do not need to be periodically reengineered. The age of traumatic business reengineering will be replaced by an age of corporations designed to constantly evolve' (Martin, 1996).
- 'All economic growth is fuelled by technological development and the growth created by the networking of the world's millions of computers will be staggering. The more you understand the Net, the more you will be able to participate in the growth' (Hammond, 1996).
- 'Over the next decade, businesses worldwide will be transformed. Intranets will revolutionize the way companies share information internally, and the Internet will revolutionize how they communicate externally. Corporations will redesign their nervous systems to rely on the networks that reach every member of the organization and beyond into the world of suppliers, consultants and customers' (Bill Gates, 1996)

Figure 22.1 The Internet and international marketing communications.

(*Source*: Jim Hamill)

understand the strategic importance of the Internet; are familiar with the range of communications tools available; and have developed the necessary 'hands-on' skills required to make effective use of the Internet in marketing, including the design and marketing of corporate Web sites. This can be achieved through using Web-based teaching and assessment methods and by ensuring that all marketing communications programmes include formal training in the strategic and marketing management applications of the Internet.

The chapter comprises four main sections:

- Section 1 provides a brief overview of the origins, growth and evolution of the Internet as background to the remainder of the chapter. One of the main issues discussed is 'netiquette', an understanding of which is critically important to successful Internet-supported marketing communications.

- Section 2 examines the distinctive characteristics of marketing communications on the Internet; the main differences between Internet and traditional marketing communications mediums; and the various tools available. The Internet and World Wide Web are not the same thing and effective marketing communications on the Net requires an integrated approach combining non-Web Internet communications, Web-based communications, and traditional approaches.
- Section 3 indicates the changing power relationships potentially occasioned by the emergence and dynamic growth of the Internet.
- Section 4 examines Web-site design and marketing, with consideration extended to emergent pricing scenarios.

An extensive bibliography is given at the end of the chapter together with a list of hypertext links to supporting online material. Reflecting the interactivity of the new medium, the authors welcome e-mail comments on the chapter: *jimh@market. strath.ac.uk*, or *p.kitchen@qub.ac.uk*.

THE INTERNET: ORIGINS, GROWTH AND EVOLUTION

Connectivity

The key to understanding the Internet is the concept of connectivity. The capability of even the most expensive PC is extremely limited when operated on a 'stand-alone' basis. Essentially, it is a word and data processing device whose use remains largely internal to the office in which it is located. When networked to other PCs, however, it becomes a very powerful communications and information search vehicle. Networks may take the form of LANs (Local Area Networks such as the internal e-mail systems operated by most large offices) and WANs (Wide Area Networks linking offices in different localities). Increasingly, cities and regions are connecting into MANs (Metropolitan Area Networks). The most exciting form of networking and the one with the greatest business potential is the Internet.

What is it?

Simply speaking, the Internet is a network of interlinked computers throughout the world operating on a standard protocol which allows data to be transferred between otherwise incompatible machines. The word itself simply means a 'network of networks'. Participants on the 'Net' include individuals, companies, governments, universities, research establishments and many others. Any form of data can be transfered over the 'net', including text, graphics, video, software, voice, etc. Estimates of the number of computers linked to the Internet become dated very quickly. In 1996, approximately 10 million host computers were thought to be connected.

Origins, growth and evolution: 'If you know the history'

The origins of the 'Net' date back to the early 1970s when the US Defense Department established the Advanced Research Projects Agency (ARPAnet) to link various military and research institutions. One of its major achievements was the development of a standard protocol which allowed dissimilar computer systems to communicate. This protocol, known as TCP/ IP (Transmission Control Protocol/ Internet Protocol), remains the most commonly used on the 'Net' today. During the late 1980s, the National Science Foundation (NSF) used the ARPAnet technology to expand its own NSFNET – a high speed backbone network linking campuses and research centres to NSF's supercomputers.

The original users of the Internet were predominantly government sponsored or university sponsored researchers. Public interest exploded in the early 1990s as the 'Net' was opened up to other groups, including individuals and companies. Full commercial Internet connections became available in 1991 with the establishment of the Commercial Internet Exchange Association, whose aim was to encourage greater business participation. This led to a proliferation of commercial sites which remains the fastest growing part of the 'Net' today. Commercialization resulted in a major clash of cultures between original users (mainly researchers), who emphasized the free exchange of information, and new, corporate users emphasizing the commercial opportunities available. The clash of cultures, however, was short lived and marketing on the Internet has now become a generally accepted part of the WWW as long as proper 'Netiquette' is observed.

There can be little doubt that the Internet will transform international business as we approach the new millennium. There are an estimated 60 million individuals and organizations currently linked to the 'Net', with connectivity growing at an average of 10 per cent per month. Estimates of connectivity levels by the year 2000 range from a low of 200 million to a high of 500 million. The Internet is becoming truly global in scope. While the largest percentage of active users still reside in the US, recent years have witnessed a rapid growth in connectivity levels in Europe and Asia. The 'Net' can no longer be considered a 'fad' or the preserve of 'techies' and 'computer nerds'. The development of effective Internet marketing strategies has become essential to maintaining international competitive advantage in an increasingly online world.

There are, of course, certain negative effects deriving from such a rapid growth in Internet usage. In particular, concerns have been expressed about 'Internet gridlock', i.e. too many users online at the same time leading to clogged up telephone lines and very slow download times. The development of faster modems (56k versions) and the massive capital investments currently being made in global telecommunications infrastructure will ensure that this is a short-term problem.

Demographics

Rapid Internet growth has been accompanied by the emergence of a brand new industry – the publication of Internet Demographic Surveys. As can be seen from the extensive links provided below, numerous such surveys have been published in recent years, often with conflicting results. Two important conclusions, however, are not in dispute. First, Internet use is growing rapidly (e.g. the NOP Survey shows a growth rate of 60 per cent per annum in the UK during 1995/1996). Second, the demographics of Internet users are changing, albeit slowly, with an increase in the number of female and older users.

It is worth checking out some of the survey sites, paying particular attention to the methodology involved and the most important survey results. A detailed comparison of the various surveys would be a useful assignment for a Market Research class.

A warning: observe 'Netiquette'

The Internet (especially e-mail, newsgroups and listserv – see later) comes complete with a culture of use referred to as 'netiquette'. For example, some groups allow direct advertising but most do not. Observing proper 'netiquette' is not an option; it is a 'must do'. Failure to follow guidelines will not only create an adverse reputation; it could also lead to a company being 'flamed' or at worst 'blacklisted' (see Blacklist of Internet Advisors). Promoting your company to groups must be done carefully and users should be aiming to contribute positively to group discussions, thereby building up an image as a reputable organization. When joining a group, you should pay particular attention to the guidelines posted to you when subscribing, and it is often a good idea simply to read messages for a month or so before actively becoming involved. This will allow greater familiarity with the list culture.

MARKETING COMMUNICATIONS AND THE INTERNET

This section examines the marketing communications tools available on the Internet and the 'digital mindset' required to be successful. The main argument developed is that effective marketing communications on the Internet requires a much wider perspective than the simple design and development of a corporate Web site. The multimedia capabilities of the WWW has encouraged many companies to adopt a 'build it and they will come' strategy. Most have quickly discovered that this approach is entirely inappropriate to cyberculture. The Internet is not a mass marketing or selling medium. It is a communications medium. Proactive use of non-Web tools such as e-mail and the proper use of Usenet and Listserv groups are essential to building up electronic relationships and to effective marketing communications. A new Internet marketing 'mindset' is required; one that emphasizes mutual help, support and the establishment of long-term relationships, as opposed to the 'hard' sell approach. A unified approach is required whereby non-Web communications tools are used to support and promote the company's overall international marketing strategy.

Marketing communications tools: The Internet provides various tools for improving communications with the different actors in the firm's international network, including e-mail; Usenet; Listserv; Internet Relay Chat; MOOS and MUDS; video conferencing; interactive Web sites etc. The first three of these are the 'workhorses' of effective Internet marketing communications and are discussed here. Issues relating to the design and marketing of Web sites are examined in Section 4.

E-mail: E-mail is the most widely used and best known Internet communications tool and has a number of advantages over more traditional forms of communications such as the telephone, postal (snailmail) and fax systems most commonly used by companies. It is a more cost-effective method, especially when large distances are involved, and does not rely on real-time presence, which is a particular advantage when different time zones are involved. It is a very reliable and flexible method since graphics, drawings etc. can be transferred as well as text. Individuals may become more rather than less communicative using e-mail, which is best seen as supporting rather than replacing personal, face-to-face relationships.

Strategic use of e-mail is critical, e.g. build up e-mail mailing list.

Usenet/Newsgroups: Newsgroups are on-line discussion forums on topics of particular interest to subscribers. There are more than 12 000 such groups covering an extremely broad range of subjects – many serious, but others trivial. In terms of format, a newsgroup reads like a string of messages associated with a particular line (thread) of discussion. Participants (subscribers) can choose to read the messages, reply, pose questions or start a new line of discussion.

Effective use of newsgroups is critically important to successful Internet marketing – both as a source of information and as a means of communication. The very large number of groups which exist means that there will be online discussions taking place relevant to most products and services. Proactive use of online discussion groups can be an important source of primary market research (information) and an excellent way of promoting the company and its Web site to clearly defined target audiences.

Listserv: Lists are a combination of e-mail and newsgroups. When messages are posted to discussion groups, subscribers must visit the site to read or reply to the various messages. On a Listserv, messages are automatically e-mailed to all subscribers. Newsgroup subscribers may visit only occasionally; listserv subscribers recieve messages automatically in their personal e-mail boxes. Listserv comes in two forms – unmoderated or moderated. In the latter, an individual is responsible for reviewing postings to ensure that they fit with the group's scope. Over one million individuals are known to subscribe to Listserv groups covering an extremely broad range of topics. E-mail, usenet, listserv and interactive Web sites are the main marketing communications tools available on the Internet. It is now generally recognized that the Internet provides a fundamentally different environment for international marketing communications (Hoffman and Novak 1996b; Quelch and Klein, 1996; and Hamill).

Two of the strongest proponents of this view are Hoffman and Novak and the pioneering work being conducted by the Project 2000 Group at Vanderbilt University. In a series of papers available on the Project 2000 web site (http://www2000.ogsm.vanderbilt.edu/papers.html), Hoffman and Novak argue that the World Wide Web possesses unique characteristics which distinguish it in important ways from traditional commercial communications environments.

The main distinctive feature of the Web emphasized by Hoffman and Novak is that it is a hypermedia computermediated environment (CME). In other words, the Web allows users of the medium to provide and interactively access hypermedia content, and to communicate with each other. Such interactivty contrasts with traditional marketing communications models for mass media (e.g. Lasswell, 1948; Katz and Lazarsfeld, 1955) which holds that mass communication is a one-to-many process whereby a firm transmits content through a medium to a large group of consumers. The key feature underlying all models of mass media effects is that there is no interaction present between consumers and firms. The new model underlying marketing communications in a hypermedia CME like the Web (Hoffman and Novak, 1995) is a many-to-many mediated communications model in which consumers can interact with the medium, firms can provide content to the medium, and, in the most radical departure from traditional marketing environments, consumers can provide commercially oriented content to the medium. In this mediated model, the primary relationships are not between sender and receiver, but rather with the CME with which they interact. In this new model, information or content is not merely transmitted from a sender to a receiver, but instead, mediated environments are created by participants and then experienced.

Because the World Wide Web presents a fundamentally different environment for marketing activities than traditional media, conventional marketing activities are being transformed, as they are often difficult to implement in their present form. This means that in many cases, these marketing activities have to be reconstructed in forms more appropriate for the new medium. This process of transformation and reconstruction of marketing and communication activities in information-intensive environments has been noted by numerous researchers (e.g. Glazer, 1991; Reid, 1991; Blattberg *et al.*, 1994; Stewart and Ward, 1994; Venkatesh *et al.*, 1993; van Raaij, 1993).

Most important from a marketing perspective, however, is the manner in which the Web transforms the marketing function. For example, the many-to-many communication model turns traditional principles of mass media advertising (based on the onetomany communication model) inside out, rendering application of advertising approaches which assume a passive, captive consumer difficult, if not impossible (Hoffman and Novak, 1994). Thus, marketers must reconstruct advertising models for the interactive, many-to-many medium underlying the Web in which consumers actively choose whether or not to approach firms through their Web sites, and exercise unprecedented control over the management of the content they interact with. Informational and image 'Internet presence sites' (Hoffman, *et al.*, 1995) provide examples of such new forms of Web-based advertising.

While Hoffman and Novak focus mainly on interactivity, there are several other distinctive features of marketing communications on the Web, especially in the context of the internationalization of SMEs. Quelch and Klein emphasize the wider dimensions. Nonetheless, the research being undertaken by the Project 2000 Group makes a particularly important contribution to the literature on Internet marketing. The Project, which is being coordinated by the Owen Graduate School of Management, Vanderbilt University, is a five-year sponsored research effort devoted to the academic study of the marketing implications of 'commercialization of hypermedia computer-mediated environments' including the Internet and WWW. The Project's Homepage (http://www2000.ogsm.vanderbilt.edu/) contains a number of very interesting papers relevant to the theme of this chapter. These include papers concerned with the Internet's impact on buyer–seller relationships (Steinfield, *et al.*, 1995); the Internet and network organizations (Nouwens and Bouwan, 1996); financial services marketing on the Internet (Crede, 1996); commercial opportunities and challenges of the WWW (Hoffman and Novak, 1995); the Internet and marketing intermediaries (Sarkar *et al.*, 1995); and various market research reports covering Internet size, growth, the number and demographics of users etc. (Kalsbeck and Novak, 1996). Overall, the group poses the fundamental question of whether new marketing paradigms are required in an era of increasing electronic commerce (Hoffman and Novak, 1996b).

Although we are beginning to see the emergence of more serious academic studies covering Internet based marketing, there has been little attempt to examine the specific role of the 'Net' in the internationalization of SMEs, the main focus of this paper. Only the study by Quelch and Klein (1996) has addressed this issue. The authors argue that the Internet will revolutionize the dynamics of international commerce and, in particular, lead to the more rapid internationalization of SMEs. The WWW will reduce the competitive advantages of scale economies in many industries, making it easier for small companies to compete on a worldwide basis. Global advertising costs, as a barrier to entry, will be significantly reduced as the Web makes it possible to reach a global audience more cheaply. Small companies offering specialized niche products will be able to find the critical mass of customers necessary to succeed through the worldwide reach of the Internet. Overall, the authors argue that the Internet's low-cost communications permits firms with limited capital to become global marketers at an early stage in their development.

A number of other international marketing implications of the Internet are identified. First, the 'Net' will lead to the increasing standardization of prices across borders, or at least, to the narrowing of price differentials as consumers become more aware of prices in different countries. Second, the Internet, by connecting end-users and producers directly, will reduce the importance of traditional intermediaries in international marketing (i.e. agents and distributors). To survive, such intermediaries will need to begin offering a different range of services. Their value-added will no longer be principally in the physical distribution of goods but rather in the collection, collation, interpretation and dissemination of vast amounts of information. The critical resource possessed by this new breed of 'cybermediary' will be information rather than inventory. Third, the Internet will become a powerful tool for supporting networks, both internal and external to the firm. Fourth, the 'Net' is an efficient new medium for conducting worldwide market research, e.g. gaining feedback from customers; establishing on line consumer panels; tracking individual customer behaviour etc.

Deriving from the 'pioneering' work summarized above, the proposition developed in this chapter is that the Internet can provide SMEs with a low-cost 'gateway' to global markets by helping to overcome many of the barriers or obstacles to internationalization commonly experienced by small companies. An Internet connection can substantially improve communications with actual and potential customers, suppliers and partners abroad; generate a wealth of information on market trends and developments worldwide; provide an 'ear to the ground' on the latest technology and R&D; and be a very powerful international promotion and sales tool. These applications arise against a background where 'Net' access is becoming cheaper, the range of services available is multiplying daily and, with the advent of new hardware and software, the computer know-how required to '*surf the net*' is now within the grasp of even the most 'techno-phobic' executive. What is needed is a guide to identify strategic uses of the Internet, whether from a multinational or SME perspective. Evidently, such a guide will (at the least) comprise three principal applications of the Internet in international marketing, including network communications, market intelligence, and global sales promotion. Intended targets would include all of the actors in a firm's network, including foreign customers, agents, distributors, partners, goverments, R&D institutions etc. The variety of tools available for implementing Internet-based international marcom strategies, including e-mail and other forms of online communications, information search and retrieval software, and the establishment of company Web sites, will also need identification from a sender *and* receiver perspective. In addition to Web site applications, the extent to which marketing objectives can be deveoped *via* the Web need to be considered. Embryonically, they can be envisaged as in Figure 22.2.

CHANGING POWER RELATIONSHIPS

Glazer (1991) notes that in the presence of higher information intensity, channel power shifts in favour of consumers and a breakdown occurs in formal distinctions between producer and consumer. In the information-intensive Web environment, the firm is no longer broadcasting a single communication to many consumers, but in effect tailoring its communications according to consumers' varied interests and needs. This is currently implemented through the unique process of network navigation in which the consumer chooses what information (if any) to receive from the firm. Thus, marketers must begin to examine the manner in which these more collaborative communication efforts should proceed.

These shifts in channel power hold important implications for consumer participation in the marketing process. For example, consumers may collaborate not only in idea generation and product design, but also in the marketing

---

In addition to Web-site applications such as network communications, market intelligence, and global sales promotion, a *good* Web site can contribute to achieving multiple marketing communications tasks and objectives including:

- Advertising
- Corporate visibility
- Brand name recognition
- Public relations
- Press releases
- Corporate sponsorship
- Direct sales
- Customer support
- Technical assistance
- Online sales

Figure 22.2 Web-site marketing objectives.

communication effort itself. This is because interactivity on the Web gives consumers much greater control of the message. Such control may manifest itself in startlingly new ways: for example, it is feasible that consumers interested in purchasing big-ticket durables such as cars or appliances will broadcast their interest and solicit open bids from different firms (Cutler, 1990). Similarly, Digital has enjoyed success with their innovative programme of making the Alpha AXP computer systems available to potential customers for 'test drive' over the Web (Jarvenpaa and Ives, 1994).

The limitations of relying on old paradigms become apparent when considering the 'more is better' logic implicit in current approaches to measuring consumer activity on sponsored-content Web sites. Driven by traditional mass media models, 'hit' and visit counting methods implicitly seek to achieve unstated mass audience levels, since in traditional media, 'advertising effectiveness' is tied to ratings or circulation models where larger numbers are preferred. Yet on the Web, advertising effectiveness can be explicitly tied to customer response and the possibility exists of developing new measurement systems that capture the value of a single consumer's visit and subsequent response in new and innovative ways.

New bases for market segmentation will also be needed for Web-based marketing efforts because consumers vary in their ability to achieve flow. Research can determine the variables that relate to a consumer's propensity to enter the flow state and such information can be used to develop marketing efforts designed to maximize the chances of the consumer achieving flow. Since 'repeat purchase', that is, repeat visits to a particular Web site, will be increased if the environment facilitates the flow state, the marketing objective on the first visit (i.e. 'trial') will be to provide for these flow opportunities. Pricing strategy is an emergent and extremely relevant, but under-researched area. To an extent, pricing models or issues can be conceptualized as in Figure 22.3.

- **CPM** – main pricing model – cost per thousand – the price charged for displaying an ad one thousand times. Used in traditional advertising and most common on the Web.

- **Click-through** – pay per click-through when a visitor to a site clicks on the advert and is taken to the advertiser's own Web site.

- **Flat fee** – a set amount charged monthly or yearly – associated with premium placements.

- **Pay per viewer** – charges advertisers every time a viewer interacts with their brand – involves offering users money and other incentives to read advertisements and participate in interactive experiments with the advertiser's brand. Users can get paid for visiting the advertiser's site and completing short surveys.

- Other innovative payment schemes include **pay per purchase** and **auctions**.

Figure 22.3 Conceptualization of pricing issues.

WEB SITE DESIGN AND MARKETING

The most visible aspect of a company's Internet marketing communications strategy is the organization's Web site (see Table 22.1 for advertising data for 10 UK Web sites). Management guidelines covering the design, content and effective marketing of company Web sites are presented in this section. In discussing these issues, it is important to note that a good Web site can achieve multiple marketing objectives in addition to direct selling online. These were illustrated in Figure 22.2.

Table 22.1 Advertising data for 10 Web sites

Company	URL	Traffic per month	Target audience	Advertising
Yahoo!	www.yahoo.co.uk	22–24m	General Internet user	Banners, keyword searches, content sponsorship
Excite	Excite.co.uk	9m	Ditto	Banners, sponsorship
Infoseek	www.infoseek.com/uk	4m	Ditto	Ditto
British Telecom	www.yell.co.uk	3m	Ditto	Banners, micros, classifieds
Global Online Directory	www.altavista.telia.com	2.4m	Ditto	Banners, keywords searches, directory sections
Associated New Media	www.plus.co.uk	2.4m	Ditto	Banners, classifieds, competitions, microsites, sponsorship
Scoot	www.scoot.co.uk	Over Im	Everyone who wants to buy something	Banners, sponsorship
News International	www.the-times.co.uk and www.Sunday-times.co.uk	11.3m	73% of users are ABC1, 54% aged 25–44, 27% over 45	Banners, sponsorship
Microsoft Network	Www.msn.co.uk	9m	The UK population	Banners, sponsorship, microsites, promotion
Telegraph Group	Www.telegraph.couk	7.5m	60% are aged 25–44, 84% male, 35% are senior/middle management or IT professionals	Banners, targeted by editorial section (business & personal finance, sport, lifestyle, Connected supplement etc), competitions, sponsorship, microsites, classified, screensavers, online retailing (hosting of secure transactions)

The key to achieving these benefits is a well-designed site and effective marketing of the site to ensure a large number of 'hits'.

According to Ellsworth and Ellsworth (1994), successful business Web sites have a number of common characteristics as shown in Figure 22.4.

Good Web site design is an art rather than a science and should be delegated to html/design experts. However, it is crucially important that Web site designers operate within clearly defined marketing guidelines. From a marketing perspective, five important elements of good Web site design can be identified and these are summarized below in the 'Nifty' model of site design where the letters stand for Navigation, Interactivity, Functionality (or features), Test, and Your Customers or Visitors.

Navigation: As stated by Sterne (1995), electronic information can be difficult to navigate. Without proper signposts, it is very easy for the visitor to your site to get lost, frustrated, turn around and leave disgruntled. This could make a Web site for marketing a disaster. Good Web sites should have clear signposts on each page and a clear menu structure at the start.

Interactivity (including feedback): Most Internet marketing authors agree that a Web site is not something that people read, it's something that they do. In this respect, a Web site represents a completely different communications medium to printed information which is read in a largely passive manner. Ellsworth and Ellsworth (1996), for example, argue that the Web is an interactive medium and requires structures, visuals etc. different from marketing in the mass media. Sterne (1995) argues that the Internet is not a broadcast medium; it is a multidirectional communications medium.

If visiting a Web site is an activity, then effective use needs to be made of the various tools available for encouraging viewer interaction. These should include hypertext links where appropriate; an e-mail reply facility; and the use of comment forms. The last two can be an invaluable source of customer feedback and market research.

Functionality/Features: This refers to the specifics of page design or authoring and covers a variety of issues too numerous to discuss in detail here. On Web site content, Wilson in his 'Web Marketing Today Newsletter', 12 December 1996, states:

- Adding your sig. file to your e-mail
- Effective use of your e-mail mailing list
- Announcing and promoting your Web site in relevant newsgroups
- Announcing and promoting on relevant lists
- Submitting your Web site to search engines
- Submitting to 'What's New'
- Establishing cross-links with other sites, especially directories
- Using electronic newsletters
- Creating your own listserv or discussion group
- Using banner advertising on high traffic sites
- Integrating your electronic promotion with more traditional marketing communications mediums

Figure 22.4 Web site promotion and marketing department.

Real estate brokers tell us of three important factors in appraising a particular piece of property. They are, in this order, location, location, location. Translate to marketing your business on the Web and these become content, content, content. That could mean high quality graphics, or streaming audio, or interactive on-line games. For business Web sites, it usually means information.

Sterne (1995) reinforces this point by arguing that the key to successful Web site development is value-added marketing. This is an issue that many individuals and organizations have difficulty in understanding or accepting as it basically means giving something away for nothing. The Internet was born and grew up in a 'gift economy' – one where researchers freely exchanged information. Despite recent commercialization, 'gift economy' culture still drives much of the 'Net's development. Offering something of value free (normally information) will prove your company's worth as a vendor. Delivering exceptional service and valuable products or information (i.e. value-added marketing) before making the sale is crucially important to successful Internet marketing.

Test: You should test your Web site locally before posting it on the Internet to ensure coherence and that all links are working and are up to date. You should also test your site immediately after posting it on the Web and try to look at it using different browsers and machines.

Your Customers/Visitors: Many of the points discussed above can be restated by emphasizing the need to adopt a customer-oriented approach to Web page design and content. Your Web site needs to provide the type of information demanded by customers; be friendly in terms of navigation and download times; allow adequate scope for feedback and interactivity; be regularly updated etc. Web site marketing has been adequately summarized in poetic form by Sterne:

Web Site Marketing

Shout it from the roof tops. Write it in the sky.
Promote until your budget pops, until they all surf by.
Announce in proper newsgroups. Mail directly through the post.
Fire up the sales troops. Televise the most.
A 1-800 number won't get you any calls.
Unless you advertise it and paint it on the walls.
Put it on your letterhead. Put it on your cards.
A web site will be left for dead unless it's known on Mars.
Your web site can be funny, pretty, useful, crisp and clean,
But if you don't promote it, its message won't be seen.
(Source: Sterne: message posted to the inet-marketing@einet.net discussion group,
18 April 1995)

Ellsworth and Ellsworth (1994) argue that Web-based marketing must be an integrated part of an overall marketing plan which encompasses the Web, the larger Internet, and non-Internet strategies. The latter two are essential to proper marketing and promotion of the company's Web site.

SUMMARY AND CONCLUSIONS

In sum, it can be argued that the traditional one-to-many model, with its attendant implications and consequences for marketing theory and practice, has only limited utility in emerging many-to-many media like the World Wide Web, and that a new marketing paradigm is required for this communication medium. In this paradigm, new rules of cooperation and competition can emerge in which marketers focus on playing an active role in the construction of new standards and practices for facilitating commerce in the emerging electronic society underlying the Web.

The Web as both medium and market is more likely to be successful if it frees consumers from a traditionally passive role as receivers of marketing communications, gives them much greater control over the search for and acquisition of information relevant for consumer decision making, and allows them to become active participants in the marketing process. Firms have the opportunity to reap the benefits of this innovation in interactivity by being closer to the customer than ever before. For this area of study there needs to be much wider evaluation of the implications of the Internet for the study and practice of marketing communications. There is an emergent case for new pardigms to explain the realities of marketing communications in an 'age of computerization and digitalization'.

DISCUSSION TOPICS

1 Summarize the main issues involved in Internet marketing communications.
2 Evaluate the key findings of at least one recent Internet demographic study.
3 Discuss the main benefits of using e-mail as a strategic marketing communications tool.
4 For a product or service of your own choice, identify relevant newsgroups where potential customers could be found. Summarize the 'netiquette' of each group.
5 Repeat the above for listserv groups.
6 Critically evaluate five Web sites from a marketing-oriented perspective.
7 Spend some time using the search engines. Examine the extent to which search engine advertising varies with respect to keywords used.
8 Evaluate alternative pricing models for Web advertising.
9 To what extent do you agree with the view that Internet marketing represents a fundamental paradigm shift in marketing communications theory and practice?
10 E-mail me (jimh@market.strath.ac.uk) with your comments on this chapter.

CASE STUDIES

Amazon.com (*http://www.amazon.com*)

Amazon.com is one of the Web's most successful commercial sites. It is an online retailer of books which claims to be the largest bookstore in the world holding more than 2.5 million titles. The success of the site has been such that second quarter (1997) online sales exceeded $27 million. The company has accumulated 610 000 customer accounts (an increase from 340 000 in 1996) and went public in 1997 with a very successful $50 million share offering. Proceeds from the share offer are being used to aggressively extend the company's customer base and brand image.

Although one of the most successful examples of electronic commerce, Amazon.com is much more than an online bookstore. It is a virtual community of book lovers and provides a good example of the way in which effective use of the full range of Internet marketing communications tools can build brand and customer loyalty. The site includes an easy-to-use search and browse facility to find books by title, author, subject or by ISBN; Web-based credit card payment and direct shipping to customers; regular book reviews; a readers' book review section where visitors to the site are encouraged to submit their own reviews; book excerpts; author summaries; etc. One of the innovative and most useful features of the site from a communications and customer loyalty perspective is the automated search agent nicknamed 'Eyes'. Visitors to the site can register to be kept up to date with newly published books by author or subject. Once registered, they automatically receive e-mail messages informing them of newly published books in their chosen area. For example, someone registering to be kept informed of new books published using the key word 'Internet' would regularly receive the following message direct into their e-mail account:

Hello from Amazon.com Books!

As you requested, we are notifying you of new books matching the following criteria:

     subject words include 'internet'

The new books are listed at the end of this message. If you're interested in any of these books, you can order them online at *http://www.amazon.com/.*

Your most humble automated search agent,

    Eyes
    Amazon.com Books
    http://www.amazon.com/

There would then follow a full list of Internet books published since the last e-mail message.

Comments

Amazon.com is one of the Net's most quoted success stories. Its success has been built around a loyal customer base developed and supported by the full range of Internet communications tools available. Amazon.com is not an online book shop. It is a 'virtual community' of book lovers. The brand and customer loyalty developed makes it difficult for new entrants to compete.

Sausage Software (*http://www.sausage.com*)

Sausage Software Ltd is an Australian company which produces world-class Internet tools. One of its main products is the HotDog Web Editor which makes it easy to publish information on the WWW. The first version of HotDog was officially released for sale on 29 June 1995. Since then, it has become one of the best selling HTML Editors with more than 50 000 users in 120 countries. The product has received highly favourable reviews from the Internet community and has often been cited as the best product of its kind. Major customers include US and other overseas government departments, Fortune 500 companies and major universities throughout the world. In 1996, the company earned more than A$2m in software revenues.

The company makes extensive use of the Internet in all of its activities from new product development through sales to customer support and service with the Web site acting as the focal point for this.

> First, we ask the 'Net community what kind of software it wants. Then, we let the 'Net community test our software and suggest improvements to make it more useful. Finally, we make free evaluation copies of our software available on our Web site. We're not like other software companies, who see 'Net software as just another product range. We believe in the 'Net: it's early days yet, but we are now on the brink of a major paradigm shift – something that will fundamentally change the world we live in. For the first time, 'little people' have a true voice, and an opportunity to share their views with millions of others around the world.
>
> The experience of Sausage Software demonstrates the opportunities that the Internet offers for newcomers to business. When you consider the implications of communication between scores of millions of people around the world and realize that the network is growing every month, the business possibilities are enormous. The ability to act quickly is one of Sausage Software's greatest strengths. Selling over the Net means we can bring fresher, hotter new technology to the market sooner than any traditional retail-based company. All of our software is available anytime you want it, from our Web site; just download a free, fully functional evaluation copy and try it to your heart's content! The Net is our main distribution medium.
>
> (Adapted from the Sausage Software web site *http://www.sausage.com*)

Comments

The Sausage case study shows the way in which small and medium-sized companies can use the Net as a powerful global marketing tool. Sausage describes itself as a 'totally wired company'; a company that makes Internet software 'on the Net, by the Net and for the Net'. The HotDog HTML Editor is marketed and distributed almost entirely over the Net with royalty payments for software distributed in this way accounting for more than 90 per cent of total revenue.

Cygus Technology (*http://www.cygtel.com*)

Cygus Technology is a small telecommunications systems integration company based in Fredericton, New Brunswick. The company has been in operation for eight years and employs a staff of 20. Cygus was a pioneer in using the Internet to support its business and has been online since 1993. Initially the company's Web site was established to improve communications and customer support to existing clients rather than to promote or market the company in global markets. The site, however, has proved very useful in stimulating new business enquiries. The Net has become an integral part of the day-to-day running of the company and to its future strategy. The company makes use of the full range of Internet business applications, including e-mail communications, ftp and video conferencing with customers around the world; market research and intelligence; competitor analysis; establishing trade leads and enquiries; savings on long-distance telephone calls and travel, etc. An intranet has been developed to improve internal communications and team work.

Comments

As a small company, Cygus believes that the Internet has put them on a 'level playing field' allowing them to communicate effectively with actual and potential customers regardless of location. Total investment in building and maintaining the site is estimated at Cdn 25,000. In the past two and a half years, an additional one million US dollars of business has been generated directly from its Net presence; a significant return on the initial investment made. The US market has taken off and now accounts for 60 per cent of their business compared to 25 per cent previously. Other markets include Argentina, Mexico and Kuwait, where a recent contract was won for a computerized audio dispatch system.

REFERENCES

'Blacklist of Internet Advertisers', http://math.www.uni.paderborn.de/-axel/BL/blacklist.html

Blattberg, R.C., Glazer, C.R. and Little, J.D.C. (1994) *The Marketing Information Revolution*, Boston: HBS Press.

Crede, A. (1996) 'Electronic commerce and the banking industry: the requirement and opportunities for new payment systems using the Internet', Special Edition of the *Journal of Computer Mediated Communication*, 1(3), December, *http://jcmc.huji.ac.il/vol1/issue3/crede.html*

Cutler, B. (1990) 'The fifth medium', *American Demographics*, 12(6) 24–9.

Ellsworth J.H. and Ellsworth M.V. (1996) *Marketing on the Internet – Multimedia Strategies for the WWW*, New York: John Wiley (*http://www.oak-ridge.com/orr.html*).

Gates, W. (1996) *The Way Ahead*, New York: Viking Books.

Glazer, R. (1991) 'Marketing in an information-intensive environment: strategic implications of knowledge as an asset', *Journal of Marketing*, 55, October: 1–19.

Hamill, J. (1997) 'International marketing education and the Internet', working paper, Department of Marketing, University of Strathclyde.

Hamill, J. (1997) 'The Internet and International Marketing', on-line modules for MSc International Marketing, Marketing Department, University of Strathclyde [http://web.uk.online.co.uk/Members/jim.hamill/topic1.htm].

Hamill, J. and Gregory, K. (1997) 'Internet marketing in the internationalisation of UK SMEs', *Journal of Marketing Management*, Special Edition on Internationalisation (J. Hamill, ed.), 13(1–3), Jan–April.

Hammond, R. (1996) *Digital Business: Surviving and Thriving in an On-line World*, Hodder & Stoughton (*http://www.hammond.co.uk/digitalbusiness*).

Hoffman, D.L. and Novak, T.P. (1994) 'Commercializing the information superhighway: are we in for a smooth ride?', working paper, Vanderbilt University (*http://www2000.ogsm.vanderbilt.edu/smooth.ride.html*).

Hoffman, D.L. and Novak, T.P. (1995) 'Marketing in hypermedia computer-mediated environments: conceptual foundations', working paper, Vanderbilt University (*http://www2000.ogsm.vanderbilt.edu/cmepaper.revision.july11.1995/cmepaper.html*).

Hoffman, D.L. and Novak, T.P. (1996b) 'New metrics for new media: toward the development of Web measurement standards', working paper, Vanderbilt University (*http://www2000.ogsm.vanderbilt.edu/novak/web.standards/webstand.html*).

Hoffman, D.L., Novak, T.P. and Chatterjee, P. (1995) 'Commercial scenarios for the Web: opportunities and challenges', *Journal of Computer-Mediated Communication*, 1(3), December, available at *http://www.ascusc.org/jcmc/voll/issue3/hoffman.html*

Jarvenpaa, S. and Ives, B. (1994) 'Digital Equipment Corporation: The Internet Company (A)', CoxMIS Cases, Edwin L. Cox School of Business, Southern Methodist University. [http://www/cox.smu.edu/mis/cases/home.html]

Kalsbeck, B. and Novak, T.P. (1996), 'Internet use in the United States: 1995 baseline estimates and preliminary market segments', Project 2000 working paper, 12 April, *http://www2000.ogsm.vanderbilt.edu/*

Katz, D. and Lazarsfield, P.F. (1955) *Personal Influence*, Glencoe: The Free Press.

Lasswell, H.D. (1948) *Power and Personality*, New York: Norton.

Martin, C. (1996) *The Digital Estate: Strategies for Competing, Surviving and Thriving in an Internetworked World*, London: McGraw-Hill.

Molenaar, C. (1996) *Interactive Marketing: The End of Mass Marketing*, London: Gower Publishing Company.

Negroponte, N. (1996) *Being Digital*, London: Vintage Books.

Nouwens, J. and Bouwman, H. (1996) 'Living apart together in electronic commerce: the use of information and communication technology to create network organizations', Project 2000, *Journal of Computer-Mediated Communication*, 1(3), December, available at *http://shum.huji.ac.il/jcmc/vol1/issue3/hoffman.html*

Quelch, J.A. and Klein, L.R. (1996) 'The Internet and international marketing', *Sloan Management Review*, Spring: 60–75.

Reid, E.M. (1991) 'Electropolis: communications and community on Internet Relay Chat', Honours thesis, University of Melbourne, Department of History [URL: *gopher://wiretap.spies.com/00/Library/Cyber/electrop%09%09%2B*].

Sarkar, M.B., Butler, B. and Sreinfeld, C. (1995) 'Intermediaries and cybermediaries: a continuing role for mediating players in the electronic marketplace', in R.R. Dholakia and D.R. Forrin (eds) *Proceedings from Conference on Telecommunications and Information Markets*, October, 82–92.

Steinfield, C., Kraut, R. and Plummer, A. (1995) 'The impact of electronic commerce on buyer–seller relationships', *Journal of Computer-Mediated Communication*, 1(3), December, available at *http://shum.huji.ac.il/jcmc/vol1/issue3/hoffman.html*

Sterne, J. (1995) *World Wide Web Marketing: Integrating The Internet Into Your Marketing Strategy*, New York: John Wiley (*http://www.targeting.com*).

Stewart, D.W. and Ward, S. (1994) 'Media effects of advertising', in B. Jennings and D. Zillman, (eds) *Media Effects, Advances in Theory and Research*, Hillsdale, NJ: Lawrence Earlbaum Associates.

Tapscott, D. (1996) *Digital Economy: Promise and Peril in the Age of Networked Intelligence*, McGraw-Hill (*http://www-mitpress.mit.edu/bookstore/nonpress/digecon.html*)

Van Raaij, W.F. (1993) 'Postmodern consumption', *Journal of Economic Psychology*, 14(3): 541–63.

Venkatesh, A., Sherry, F., Jnr. and Firat, A.F. (1993) 'Postmodernism and the marketing imaginary', *International Journal of Research in Marketing*, 10(2): 215–23.

Wilson, T. (1996) in *Web Marketing Today Newsletter*, 12 December [http://www.wilsonweb.com]

Other useful references

Activ/Media (1996) 'Case studies of successful online marketers', *http://www.activmedia.com/Casestudies.html#details*

Aldridge, R. (1995) 'Putting your business on the web'.

Barnatt, C. (1995) *CyberBusiness: Mindsets for the Wired Age*, Chichester: John Wiley.

Benjamin, R. and Wigand, R. (1995) 'Electronic markets and virtual value chains on the information superhighway', *Sloan Management Review*, Winter: 62–72.

CommerceNet/Nielsen (1995) 'The CommerceNet/Nielsen Internet demographic survey: executive summary', 30 October, CommerceNet Consortium/Nielsen Media Research, available at *http://www2000.ogsm.vanderbilt.edu/paper_list.html*

Cronin M.J. (1994) *Doing Business on the Internet*, New York: Van Nostrand Reinhold.

Cronin M.J. (1995) *Doing More Business on the Internet*, New York: Van Nostrand Reinhold.

Cronin M.J. (1996a) *The Internet Strategy Handbook: Lessons from the New Frontier of Business*, Boston: Harvard Business School Press.

Cronin M.J. (1996b) *Global Advantage on the Internet*, New York: Van Nostrand Reinhold.

De Angelis, M. (1996) 'Marketing on the Internet'.

Department of Trade and Industry (1993) 'Information society initiative', *http://www.isi.gov.uk*

Dinsdale, A. (1995) 'The do's and don'ts of online marketing', *http://www.netrex.com/business/dosdonts.html*

Donaton, S. (1994) 'OK to put ads on the Internet, but mind your Netiquette', *Advertising Age*, 65(18), 3–62.

Elderbrock, D. and Borwankar, N. (1996) *Building Successful Internet Businesses*, IDG Books (*http://www.idgbooks.com/idgbooksonline/*).

Ellsworth J.H. and Ellsworth M.V. (1994) *The Internet Business Book*, New York: John Wiley.

Emery, V. (1995) *How to Grow your Business on the Internet*, Coriolis Books (*http://www.emery.com*).

FIND.SVP (1996) 'The American Internet user survey: new survey highlights', *http://www.findsvp.com/findsvp/index.html/tige7ba*

Gupta, S. and Pitkow, J. (1995) 'Consumer survey of WWW users: preliminary results from 4th survey', *http://www.umich.edu/~sgupta/hermes/*

Hagel, J. and Armstrong, A.G. (1997) *net.gain: expanding markets through virtual communities*, Harvard Business School Press (*http://www.hbsp.harvard.edu/netgain*)

Hardy, H.E. (1993) 'History of the Net'.

Hobbes, R. (1996) 'Internet timeline v2.4a', *On the Internet, Journal of the Internet Society*, March/April: also at *http://info.isoc.org/guest/zakon/Internet/history/HIT.html*

Hoffman, D.L. and Novak, T.P. (1994) 'Wanted: Net Census', *Wired*, 2(11): 93–4.

Hoffman, D.L. and Novak, T.P. (1995) 'The CommerceNet/Nielsen Internet demographics survey: is it representative?', Project 2000 note, 12 December, *http://www2000.ogsm.vanderbilt.edu/surveys/cn.questions.html*

Hoffman, D.L. and Novak, T.P. (1996a) 'Marketing in hypermedia computer-mediated environments: conceptual foundations', *Journal of Marketing*, July.

Hoffman, D.L. and Novak, T.P. (1996b) 'A new marketing paradigm for electronic commerce', Project 2000 working paper, 19 February, *http://www2000.ogsm.vanderbilt.edu/*

Hutmik, R. (1996) 'The viability of web marketing and sales'.

International Business Resources on the WWW, *http://ciber.bus.msu.edu/busres.htm*

Jim, S. (1995) *World Wide Marketing: Integrating the Internet into your Marketing Strategy*, Chichester: John Wiley.

Kiam, A. (1995) *Making Money on the Internet: Complete Beginners Guide*, Harrogate: Net Works.

Kimball, J.G. (1993) 'Association to fight advertising on the internet', *Business Marketing*, 78(11): 14.

Krol, E. (1992) *What's Allowed on the Internet, The Whole Internet Catalogue and User's Guide*, O'Reilly and Associates Inc.

Levinson, J.C. and Rubin, C. (1995) *Guerrilla Marketing in the Internet: A Complete Guide to Making Money On-Line*, London: Piatkus.

Littman, J. (1993) 'Commerce on the Internet: the digital goldrush', *UnixWorld*, December 42–9.

Lottor, M.K. (1996) 'Internet domain survey'.

Martin, C. (1997) *The Digital Estate: Strategies for Competing, Surviving and Thriving in an Internetworked World*, McGraw-Hill (*http://www/mcgraw-hill.com/digitalestate*).

Netpost, (1996) '1995 Tenagra Awards for Internet marketing excellence announced', *http://www.netpost.com/awards95.html*

Network Wizard (1996) 'Internet domain survey', January, *http://www.nw.com/zone/WWW/report.html*

Poon, S. and Swatman, P.M.C. (1995) 'Small business alliances: a framework for Internet-enabled strategic advantage', Monash University, Department of Information Systems, *Working Paper 25/95*, July.

Poon, S. and Jevons, C. (1997) 'Internet-enabled international marketing: a small business perspective', *Journal of Marketing Management*, Special Edition on Internationalisation (J. Hamill, ed.), 13(1–3), Jan–April.

Project 2000 (1996) *http://www2000.ogsm.vanderbilt.edu/*

Tartan Shopping Mall (1996) *http://www.ibmpcug.co.uk/~ecs/mall/malla.html*

US Department of Commerce (1996) *http://www.stat-usa.gov/*

Vassos, T. (1996) *Strategic Internet Marketing*, Que Books; author's Web site at (*http://www.webdiamonds.com/~webdiamonds*); *Strategic Internet Marketing* Web site at (*http://www.mcp.com/que/desktop os/int market/*).

Verity, J.W., Hof, R.D., Baig, E.C. and Carey, J. (1996) 'The Internet: how it will change the way you do business', *Business Week*, 14 November: 80–8.

23

RELATIONSHIP MARKETING

Fiona Cownie

CHAPTER AIMS

- to further enrich the conceptual framework which underpins marketing communications
- to provide the context for the emerging relationship marketing paradigm
- to reflect upon the role of trust and commitment within relationship marketing
- to explore the opportunities for relationship marketing within the consumer sector
- to evaluate the contribution of an understanding of personal relationships to relationship marketing
- to provide illustrations of relationship marketing concepts within the UK charity sector

ILLUSTRATION

The following case vignette demonstrates the move to a relationship marketing approach within the charity sector, and illustrates the need for marketing communications to stimulate involvement within the relationship.

A Giving Relationship (Eddie Gibb)

Retailers may be making a big noise about their own loyalty schemes, but in the charity sector that kind of relationship marketing has always been at the heart of good fundraising. As a rule of thumb, enlisting a new donor generally costs around the same amount as their first donation, and for some charities recruitment even runs at a loss.

Clearly, it only makes sense to spend that kind of money if there is a reasonable chance of securing repeat business, and this is where relationship marketing becomes not just important but absolutely central to the fundraising effort. Sophisticated database techniques are being used more often by charities to segment their donor lists, which allows for better targeting of the mailshots. If a donor is a one-a-year, only-at-Christmas type, that doesn't mean you give up on them for the rest of the year, but it may be wise, nonetheless, not to include them on every single mailing.

The trick is maximising the 'value' of donors without appearing to squeeze them until the pips squeak. 'Donor fatigue' is a term that has been bandied about in the charity world for some time.

Whilst most fundraisers agree that it is generally used to excuse an unsuccessful appeal, there must come a point where even the most generous and altruistic of people simply switch off.

'We always try to find some involvement device that allows the donor to express more than financial support' says Angela Walledge, client services manager at Amherst Direct Marketing, which won a Direct Marketing Association award for its Great Ormond Street Hospital fundraising appeal last year. 'We found that mailings and appeals based on research or specific aspects of the hospital's work were less successful than something which let people become personally involved with the children'.

The paper-chain appeal, which invites donors to send a personal message to the children on a link of the chain hung up in the hospital during the Christmas period, has been so successful that it is likely to run for a third year. Amherst has called this desire to participate in a charity's work beyond simply donating money the 'duality of response'. 'People say "make me feel special but don't spend money doing it" which is quite a tough proposition' says Walledge.

(Source: Marketing, 4 July 1996, used with permission)

INTRODUCTION

Bagozzi (1995) encapsulates the thinking of many marketing academics and practitioners – that a relational approach lies at the heart of marketing. There is some disagreement about the stage relationship marketing is at. Sheth and Parvatiyar (1995) and Gronroos and Strandvik (1997) perceive it to be at an early stage of development; while Berry (1995), who originated the term relationship marketing, considers the discipline to have reached maturity. What is agreed is that regardless of whether relationship marketing is an emergent or developed discipline, it is worthy of further development and research. Indeed, entire editions of the *European Journal of Marketing, Journal of Marketing Management* and the *Journal of the Academy of Marketing Science* have recently devoted special issues to the study of relationship marketing.

As a new marketing paradigm, relationship marketing offers further enrichment of the conceptual framework underpinning marketing communications. Hutton (1996) perceives relationship marketing and marketing communications to be interconnected; the purpose of marketing communications being the creation of relationships. While direct marketers and public relations practitioners are arguably at the forefront of incorporating relationship marketing concepts, the collaborative dimension of relationship marketing offers much in the explanation and analysis of sponsorship activity. Furthermore, trust, which lies at the heart of relationship marketing, is clearly a critical issue for advertising. Sales promotion, typically a short-term activity, can be effectively integrated into long-term relationship-orientated communications; and personal selling, arguably for many years the epitome of relationship marketing, has much to contribute to a relationship-building strategy.

This chapter will provide a review of pertinent literature and concepts concerning relationship marketing. A wide variety of sectors claim to have embraced the concepts of relationship marketing including financial services, airlines, retailers, high profile FMCG operators and charities (Buttle, 1996). This chapter focuses on just one of these sectors in an attempt to provide depth of application and understanding. The opening illustration and end-of-chapter case study provide illumination of the application of relationship marketing within leading UK charities, and this theme continues throughout the chapter.

RELATIONSHIP MARKETING

Relationship marketing has been hailed as a new approach to replace or exist alongside traditional transaction marketing (Brodie *et al.*, 1997; Gronroos, 1994; Christopher *et al.*, 1991; Buttle, 1996; Berry, 1995). The choice between relational and transactional approaches will be driven by opportunities for profitability (Gronroos, 1997).

From transactional to relational marketing

Progression from transactional to relational partnerships is demonstrated in Figure 23.1. Ganesan (1994) claims that it is the customer's time orientation, distinct from the longevity of the relationship, which defines the location of a partnership on the spectrum. Movement down the spectrum can be achieved by making long-term commitments to relationships with offers of quality, service and innovation, and by so doing, extending the customer's expectancy of future interactions. Such long-term relationships offer sustainable competitive advantage to marketers, which many firms may currently overlook. This is strongly supported by the work of Kay (1993) who sees a network of relationships, termed as 'architecture', as a key distinctive capability which, when applied in a relevant market, delivers sustainable, appropriable competitive advantage and ultimately added value for the company. Hunt (1997) claims that relationship development to complement existing organizational competencies should be incorporated within the strategic planning process. Both Hunt (1997) and Brodie *et al.* (1997) identify the need to establish a relationship portfolio. Relationships have become strategic.

While the spectrum of relationships illustrated in Figure 23.1 is developed for a business-to-business exchange, the underlying framework can be applied to buyer–seller partnerships within the consumer sector. To illustrate this within the charitable sector, 'high-street' donors to charity might reside at the transaction end, while lifetime members of a charity would be placed alongside buyer–seller partnerships demonstrating an emphasis on mutuality of interest. Strategic alliances are unlikely to be developed between donor and charity, although arguably the use of covenants could be perceived to represent a step towards such an alliance. Charities might, however, develop strategic alliances with each other as the American Heart Association, Multiple Sclerosis Society and Arthritis Association have done in order to share resources (Conway, 1996), or indeed cause-related marketing alliances may be formed with other corporate partners (Andreasen, 1996).

Stage in relationship		Characteristics of relationship
		discrete, short-term, mechanical, little
Transactions	low	commitment
Repeated transactions	↑	
Long-term relationships	│	
Buyer–seller partnerships	expectancy of	
Strategic alliances (including joint ventures)	future interaction │	
Network organizations	↓	
Vertical integration	high	on-going, complex, highly personal, characterized by complete trust and discretion

Figure 23.1 Spectrum of marketing relationships.

(*Source*: developed from Webster, 1992, Ganesan, 1994 and Barnes, 1994)

DEFINING RELATIONSHIP MARKETING

Despite the relative youth of relationship marketing, there appears to be a general consensus of opinion on the essence of its definition from an academic context, although Barnes (1994) claims that academics and practitioners use the term in different ways.

Early definitions focused on the structural and social bonds inherent in relationship marketing, with the implication that these bonds would form barriers to entry (to reduce competition and choice) and exit (to retain customers). However, Berry (1983) sees such a preclusive bonding approach to be contrary to the underlying concept of relationship marketing. More recently these bonds have been considered to represent a move towards a state of partnership between buyer and seller, and academics have realized that bonds must be supplemented by deeper feelings associated with humanistic relationships (Hutton, 1996) in order to generate a genuine marketing relationship. Barnes (1994) suggests that essentially both partners must be willing participants and must find the relationship experience satisfying: this might be manifest in a feeling of mutual ownership demonstrated in talk of 'my partner'. Indeed mutuality, the degree of congruence between the partners' evaluations, is a critical element of relationship marketing (Smith and Barclay, 1997; Berry, 1995; Wilson, 1995).

Gronroos (1994, p. 9) sees the purpose of relationship marketing as 'to establish, maintain and enhance relationships with customers and other partners at a profit, so that objectives of the parties involved are met. This is achieved by a mutual exchange and fulfillment of promises.' Those objectives might be, for the buyer, customer satisfaction via the purchase of a quality offering, and for the seller, increased profitability via enhanced customer loyalty (Evans and Laskin, 1994). Clearly there is a link between the two parties' objectives as increased customer satisfaction is a key driver of customer loyalty.

In essence then, relational elements can enhance performance outcomes. This does not necessarily imply altruistic behaviour, rather that self-interest is considered over the long rather than short term. Over such a time frame, maximization of self-interest may partly result from the success of one's relational partner and the ability of the partnership to confront higher levels of risk and potential reward.

Exchange within relationship marketing

Gronroos' (1994) definition of relationship marketing encompasses the concept of exchange. Traditionally exchange has been used in the context of discrete rather than ongoing events; however, relational exchange within the domain of relationship marketing reflects the essential idea that each exchange takes into account both the past and the anticipated future (Davies, 1995; Ganesan, 1994). Indeed the relational exchange must focus on a present and future informed by past experiences. Hutton (1996) proposes the need for a re-evaluation of the exchange perspective in favour of a more humanistic approach relating to issues of trust and commitment, suggesting that this is critical to what he calls 'Integrated Relationship Marketing Communications' (see Chapter 7).

TRUST

Doney and Cannon (1995) note that trust is pivotal to marketing theory and practice. The concept of trust is certainly central to personal relationships and thus to relationship marketing. Ganesan (1994), Morgan and Hunt (1994), Doney and Cannon (1995) and Smith and Barclay's (1997) writing reflect this. Ganesan (1994, p. 1), suggests that 'trust is necessary for the perception of a fair division of the pie of resources in the future'. Three vital points arise from this: first, trust is about equity, not necessarily actual equity, but perceived equity; second, trust is about looking ahead, as suggested above, using past and present behaviours to inform an understanding of what might be in the future; and third, trust is essentially about the allocation of scarce resources such as time, money, and product benefits, the very things which stimulate the use of coercive or reward power in dysfunctional partnerships. Trust reduces conflict and increases satisfaction between collaborative partners (Doney and Cannon, 1995). Trust is all about *confidence* in a partner.

Conceptually, trustworthiness comprises two elements: credibility and benevolence (Doney and Cannon, 1995, Ganesan, 1994). Credibility is rooted in belief in a partner's expertise to perform a task effectively and reliably; benevolence is a belief that a partner's intentions and motivations are beneficial to both parties when new circumstances arrive for which a specific commitment has not been made. Ganesan (1994, p. 3) notes that this second dimension can exist when the 'objective credibility . . . is less than perfect'. This may be as a result of competing demands within the partner's performance or support network, or due to circumstances out of the partner's control. To illustrate within the charity sector, a donor might give money in expectation of its direction towards relief in Ethiopia, but the incidence of a natural disaster might result in the money being used to support emergency action in another country. Benevolence is a signal of the donor's support of the intention of the charity.

Andaleeb (1992) calls these two dimensions of trust 'ability' and 'motive', and suggests that the dimensions provide four categorizations of trust: bonding, hopeful, unstable and distrust (Figure 23.2).

Sheaves and Barnes (1996) argue that repeat encounters are a prerequisite of trust and that trusting relationships are only possible within sectors which involve a high risk for customers in the short term or necessitate long-term obligation on behalf of the company. Arguably charities may meet these requirements, as donors must risk their donation (there are no guarantees of its destination or effectiveness) and charities make long-term obligations to life members and indeed those who bequeath legacies. Game theory (Kay, 1993) offers a useful conceptual perspective on the need for repeated iterations to allow the development of expectations of future behaviour and thus trust. If these repeated iterations are not from the same partners, then players must see themselves as part of a larger group playing iteratively. To illustrate, a member of the National Trust visiting an historic building on holiday might avoid acting opportunistically (perhaps shouting within a silent area), not because they were likely to repeat the same visit, but because their actions would have an impact on future visitors, a collective of which they perceived themselves to be a part.

Morgan and Hunt's (1994) Commitment–Trust Theory identifies trust as one of two key mediating variables within a relationship (Figure 23.3). Morgan and Hunt further suggest that commitment and trust are key requisites within a relationship as they encourage partners to work at preserving the relationship via cooperation, to favour long- rather than short-term alternatives, and to enter potentially high risk situations because of a belief that their partner will avoid opportunistic behaviour. Ganesan (1994) sees trust as enhancing commitment to a long-term orientation by increasing confidence that short-term inequities will be resolved over time, reducing transaction costs and reducing the perception of risk associated with opportunistic behaviour.

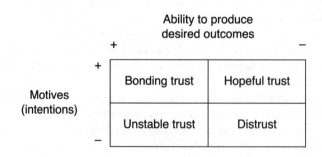

Figure 23.2 A framework for categorizing levels of trust.

(*Source*: Andaleeb, 1992, p. 12)

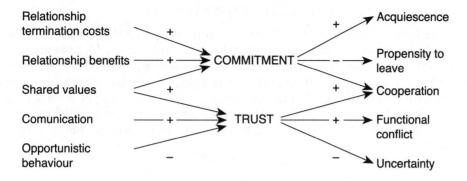

Figure 23.3 Commitment–Trust Theory.
(*Source*: Morgan and Hunt, 1994)

Doney and Cannon (1995) suggest that trust can be built between the customer and the supplier organization and /or the customer and any representative of the organization. To illustrate, a representative of the NSPCC periodically visits members with legacies donated to the charity (Roff, 1997). Clearly this contact is selective, focusing on high value members. Doney and Cannon's (1995) research indicates that members will assess the level of trust they place in the charity as a whole and the representative. While the introduction of a nominated representative from a charity provides opportunities for trust-building, with those opportunities come demands on the nature and action of that representative.

COMMITMENT

Morgan and Hunt (1994) cite Moorman *et al.*'s (1992) definition of commitment as 'an enduring desire to maintain a valued relationship'. For Wilson (1995, p. 337) commitment is 'the desire to continue the relationship and to work to ensure its continuance'. This corresponds with Ganesan's (1994) concept of long-term orientation. Both indicate an attitudinal state ('a desire') relating to intended behaviour ('to maintain'). The concept of commitment is derived from social exchanges such as marriage; arguably one partner within a marriage can be committed to the union even if it breaks down, illustrating the attitudinal dimension of commitment. The important point is that commitment to a partnership implies that the partner is prepared to work at it, that is, to invest scarce resources (time, money) and avoid alternative partners, in order to perpetuate the partnership's existence. Commitment implies a degree of vulnerability. Morgan and Hunt (1994) argue that commitment is central to relationship marketing as it distinguishes social from economic exchange. Commitment is about trying to make things work better and for longer.

TRUST AND COMMITMENT

Morgan and Hunt's (1994) Commitment–Trust model posits that commitment and trust are the cornerstones of functional marketing relationships. Morgan and Hunt (1994) argue that the vulnerability implied by commitment (the sacrifice of independence for interdependence) demands a partnership based on trust, as trust facilitates confidence in the future. Interestingly the results of Ganesan's (1994) empirical work showed that only one dimension of trust, that of credibility, proved to be a significant predictor of long-term orientation (commitment) within a relationship.

Critical issues

A number of critical issues exist regarding Morgan and Hunt's model. There is no indication of the relative influence of the input variables in generating commitment and trust, nor of the likely balance of outputs (for example, does increasing trust produce an equal increase in functional conflict and cooperation?). The model does not consider the affect of relationship expectations on input and output variables; indeed, while relationship benefits are a key factor, to what extent can these be considered as actual benefits or the difference between expected and actual benefits? While both Morgan and Hunt's (1994) and Ganesan's (1994) work suggest that trust feeds into commitment, Ganesan notes that it is possible that the reverse is happening, that is, a long-term orientation (commitment) produces trust (and dependence).

Shared values are posited as a key input variable, impacting both commitment and trust. Wilson (1995) considers shared values to be appealing but rather too broad to be effectively operationalized. He suggests that an alternative measure might be the degree to which partners share the same goals, that is, mutuality of goals, rather than attempting to measure values and norms.

Morgan and Hunt's (1994) model suggests a structure for marketing relationships. Evans and Laskin (1994) claim that relationship marketing is a continuous process dependent on customer feedback. Communication could thus be seen as critical, acting as both an input and output to marketing relationships and thus providing the opportunity for the development and maintainence of dialogue between the partners (Figure 23.4). Whereas communication acts as an input of trust, it may be an output of commitment as committed partners develop the need and desire to communicate with each other.

Such a mechanism would contribute to an understanding of relationships as dynamic entities with life cycles; they can grow in strength (enhanced interdependence delivering improved mutual benefits) or they can wither and dissolve. Wilson (1995) suggests that a series of relational variables, including commitment, trust, cooperation, social bonds and mutuality of goals, have varying roles to play during the relationship life cycle. They may start as active, that is, needing the attention of management resources, but may pass into a latent phase in which little attention is required for the successful management of the relationship. Reflecting this variation, communication, while always essential, will vary in content by relationship stage.

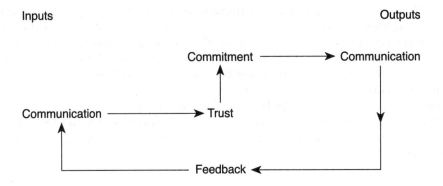

Figure 23.4 Communication as an input and output of trust/commitment.

RELATIONSHIP MARKETING WITHIN THE CONSUMER SECTOR

The development of sophisticated databases has in part driven the interest of practitioners in the implementation of relationship marketing within the consumer sector (Buttle 1996; Webster, 1992; Sheth and Parvatiyar, 1995). Berry (1995) comments that the database facilitates the efficient performance of key tasks critical to relationship marketing within the consumer service sector:

- Tracking buying
- Customization
- Integration of multiple services
- Providing a two-way communication channel
- Minimizing service errors
- Augmenting the core offer
- Personalizing service encounters.

The role of the database within relationship marketing is, however, the source of some debate. Within the charity sector, computer power is considered to be critical for the development of relationships (Taylor and Mitchell, 1996). Copulsky and Wolf (1990) claim that the database is key as it allows a differentiated message to be transmitted to the consumer and allows lifetime value to be tracked. However, Hogg et al. (1993) are critical of companies which use databases established without customer consent to build relationships. Humanistic relationships would respect issues of privacy and confidentiality, which Hogg et al. (1993) argue are compromised in such an approach to relationship marketing. Barnes (1994) suggests that the database misses the point of understanding the relationship and Hutton (1996) considers the very concept of lifetime value or share of customer as contrary to the essence of relationships. Barnes (1994, p. 565) emphasizes that caring is the essence of the customer relationship: 'some authors view the establishment of a database as a precursor to the development of a customer relationship. What is missing in this view is any evidence of caring about the customer.'

While Robin (1995) claims that relationship marketing is now possible in most businesses, academics have been slow to research its applicability within the consumer sector. Authors consider the origins of relationship marketing to lie within industrial and service markets (Payne *et al.*, 1995; Aijo, 1996), and are only now putting forward suggestions regarding its conceptual development within consumer markets (Christy *et al.*, 1996).

While Morgan and Hunt's (1994) model of a marketing relationship provides a useful starting point for the analysis of consumer relationships, further insights can be gained from a consideration of consumer behaviour, personal and social relationships.

Integrating consumer behaviour and relationship marketing

'Relationship marketing addresses the basic human need to feel important.'
(Jackson, 1993, cited in Berry, 1995 p. 238)

Sheth and Parvatiyar's (1995) analysis of relationship marketing within the consumer sector concluded that consumers' involvement is due to personal, social and institutional influences. Their investigation centred around understanding what motivates consumers to become loyal. The fundamental axiom upon which their analysis was built was that consumers actually seek (rather than accept) choice reduction by engaging in relationships. Sheth and Parvatiyar (1995) suggest that this desire for choice reduction enables the consumer to simplify purchasing, reduce perceived risk, maintain cognitive consistency and retain a state of psychological comfort. As Bitner (1995, p. 250) puts it, 'Staying in a relationship . . . serves to simplify one's life . . . frees up time for other concerns and priorities.'

Sheth and Parvatiyar (1995) identify the role of social relationships within relationship marketing:

Sociological theories of consumer behaviour suggest that consumers reduce choice to comply with group norms. Such compliance is motivated by the consumer's desire to develop a close relationship with the group, to attain the benefits of socialisation and the rewards associated with social compliance, and to avoid conflict and punishments associated with non-compliance of norms. Consumers also reduce choice in order to fulfill aspirations and reduce perceived risk. They have a desire to be socially connected and give credence to information that has strong social ties. Those who have a greater social orientation are likely to be more relationship orientated than the others.

(Sheth and Parvatiyar, 1995, p. 261)

Thus social relationships form a key driver for relationship marketing between certain marketers and consumers. Insights into social and personal relationships thus provide further underpinning for a study of consumer relationships.

LEARNING FROM PERSONAL RELATIONSHIPS

Sheaves and Barnes (1996) draw on the work of McCall (1970) and Clark and Mills (1979) in order to understand the range and form of personal relationships, and emphasize the importance of understanding that relationships are unique to a set of partners.

McCall (1970) suggests that social relationships in which members view themselves as sole members of a common collectivity can be subdivided into formal and personal relationships (Figure 23.5). Formal relationships involve a relationship essentially between two roles, whereas personal relationships engage the people themselves within the relationship. Sheaves and Barnes (1996) suggest that company–customer relationships may evolve from a formal to a personal nature when the level of personal contact between partners is high. Clearly personal relationships do not necessarily reflect entirely positive emotions: close personal relationships embrace both positive and negative emotions, but the trust inherent within a functional relationship should allow negative to be negotiated by positive.

Clark and Mills (1979) make a further distinction between relationship types – exchange and communal (Figure 23.6). The essential difference between the two is reflected in the level of obligation required further to an exchange of benefits. In exchange relationships, benefits are given with the expectation of the receipt of benefits in return. In communal relationships 'the assumption is that each individual is concerned about the welfare of the other; the exchange of benefits is based on the needs of the other, not on the anticipation that benefits will be received in return' (Sheaves and Barnes, 1996, p. 225)

Sheaves and Barnes (1996, p. 226) suggest that the distinction between communal and exchange relationships is very relevant from the marketing perspective:

> The basic nature of a customer–business relationship implies that it is an exchange relationship only. A customer deals with a firm because of his or her desire/need for the good or service that the firm is offering. The firm attempts to build a relationship with the customer in order to secure present and future revenue. Any interactions that take place between the two are performed with the expectation of receiving comparable benefits in return. Furthermore, given that the expectation of an equal exchange of benefits inhibits the formation of a communal relationship, it may seem that

Figure 23.5 Formal and personal relationships.
(*Source*: McCall, 1970)

413

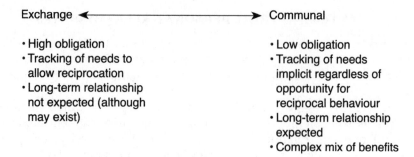

Figure 23.6 Exchange and communal relationships.
(*Source*: Clarke and Mills, 1979)

converting an exchange-orientated customer–firm relationship to a communal relationship would be a very difficult task.

(Sheaves and Barnes, 1996, p. 226)

As communal relationships involve benefits above tangible goods and services, and within the charitable sector donors rarely expect an equal exchange for their gift, it is arguable that charities could be considered to display communal relationships. Donors can exhibit genuine concern for the charity, particularly when it is in difficulty (for example, the demise of anti-fur charity Lynx), thus, provided the charity itself is reciprocating this concern, arguably Sheaves and Barnes' (1996) comments are less applicable for relationship marketing within this sector.

If a matrix is constructed (Figure 23.7), bringing together communal and exchange relationships with formal and personal relationships, it is possible to see that charities have the ability to move into the high relationship potential quadrant, particularly if they engage in high levels of personal contact with donors.

SOCIAL SUPPORT

Sheaves and Barnes (1996) argue that social support is another key dimension of relationships which marketers need to consider. Social support is able to provide key

	Communal	Exchange
Formal	Medium relationship potential Charities may be here	Low relationship potential
Personal	High relationship potential Charities may move here	Medium relationship potential

Figure 23.7 Matrix of Relationship Type.

benefits in the form of the reduction and control of uncertainty, an increase in self-acceptance through enhanced self-esteem, and social integration providing relationships within the larger community. These benefits can be considered to be part of the complex benefits involved in communal relationships.

Social support has been further subdivided into strong and weak ties, the latter of which should particularly interest marketers. Whereas strong ties represent the links within family and marital relationships and close friendships, weak ties cover the links with those who lie beyond the network of friends and family. Weak ties describe relationships that lack the frequency and intimacy of contact associated with relationships with friends and family. Adelman *et al.* (1987) identify the distinctive functions and contextual features of weak ties as:

Functions of weak ties:

- Extending access to information, goods and services
- Allowing social comparison with dissimilar others
- Facilitating low-risk discussion of high-risk topics
- Fostering a sense of community

Contextual features of weak ties:

- Exist within a more restricted range of contexts than most strong ties
- Exist within a restricted temporal context
- Are not dependent on face-to-face contact

Weak ties are good news for marketers. They indicate that consumers might be more readily accepting of relationships with some of their suppliers in order to gain the benefits that weak ties can provide. To illustrate, the elderly might be one group particularly keen to develop weak ties, to complement or replace strong ties which may be diminishing, for example those with their previous employer and work colleagues. Possibly this is a group for whom the strength of both strong and weak ties is changing. Marketers may be able to build weak ties into strong ties in order to balance the reduction in the strength of some strong ties and in doing so revalidate self-esteem and provide new opportunities for social integration within the larger community.

There may then be opportunities for businesses to provide an interpersonal service in order to strengthen weak ties. However, such an approach carries with it responsibilities which centre on trust and commitment. Adelman *et al.* (1994) argue that by providing social support, service providers take on the moral obligation not to exploit the customer's trust in a way that would be harmful. Thus the use of social support within relationship development requires a commitment from the service provider to act appropriately. Yet again, mutual trust and commitment are identified as key attributes of a marketing relationship.

THE USE AND ABUSE OF RELATIONSHIP MARKETING CONCEPTS

While analysis of the literature emphasizes that the concepts of trust, commitment and mutual benefit lie at the heart of relationship marketing, many marketers could arguably be considered to be conducting marketing strategies under the guise of relationship building, but without a commitment to these central concepts. While trust is considered to be a critical issue for marketers (e.g. a 1997 Henley Management Report ranked the Kelloggs corporate brand very highly in terms of trust), commitment is often confused with the repeat purchasing associated with frequent flyer plans and retailer loyalty cards. In part, this confusion seems to stem from the misapprehension that relationship marketing is the equivalent of direct marketing, and that the database is at the core of the relationship. As has already been discussed, the database can be considered to be a key component of a relationship-building strategy, but as a means to an end. Direct mail, representing one-to-one communication, also has a role to play, but again as a facilitator of commitment, trust and mutual benefit, not an end in itself. Thus short-term behavioural measures of success should be supplemented by relationship-orientated evaluation. While communication is critical to relationship marketing, there are many other facets to the marketing relationship, as demonstrated by Morgan and Hunt (1994). Misunderstanding of relationship marketing carries with it not just the risk of the setting of inappropriate marketing and communication objectives, but also the risk of denigrating the existing marketing relationship in the eyes of the consumer. While charities have been used as the focus of application within this chapter, there are marketing practices within this sector which could be considered to abuse the relationship concept, for example the rejection of trust building in favour of the short-term benefits of multiple asks. Such approaches carry the risk of deterioration of the donor–charity relationship.

Direct marketing has a significant role to play within relationship marketing, but so too do other marketing communications disciplines as demonstrated in Table 23.1. No matter which techniques are adopted, honesty must permeate the relationship-building process. Relationship marketers must recognize the implications of relationship building on their own behaviour way beyond the messages disseminated within marketing communication activity. True relationship orientation should exist within the organization's culture and corporate identity.

SUMMARY AND CONCLUSION

The chapter has provided a review of the literature on relationship marketing, with a particular focus upon pertinent issues to marketing strategies within the consumer sector. The charitable sector has been used to illustrate relationship marketing issues, but clearly the concepts are applicable across a wide variety of sectors in which long-term orientation is considered beneficial.

Implications for marketing communications are clear. Within sectors and segments identified to be appropriate for a relational approach (and not all are appropriate), the ultimate aim for marketing communications is to provide a one-to-one dialogue between the focus company and its stakeholders, centred around building a relationship founded on mutual trust and commitment. Direct marketing and public relations have a particularly clear role to play in establishing and maintaining this dialogue (see Table 23.1), but their integration with advertising, sponsorship, personal selling and even sales promotion strategies, which are developed with the core relational strategy at their heart, will help underpin effective, long-term, profitable, mutually rewarding relationships.

Table 23.1 Relationship marketing and marcoms: key issues across the disciplines

Marcoms discipline	Relevant issues
Direct marketing	• Database: – Opportunity to establish dialogue – Recording of relationship data – Privacy issues • Direct mail – Short-term behavioural measures to be supplemented by relationship-orientated evaluation
Public relations	• Recognition of range of stakeholder interests • Need to build mutual understanding • Long-term approach
Advertising	• Provides required reassurance within target audience • Vital to build trust • Opportunity to integrate with dialogue-building mechanisms
Sales promotion	• Integration of sales promotion into long-term relationship • Opportunity for reward
Sponsorship	• Opportunity for understanding collaboration between sponsor and sponsored • Need to recognize internal relationships • Opportunity to reduce ambush marketing activity
Corporate identity	• Recognizes the multi-faceted requirements of communication and thus relationship building • Relationship orientation should permeate corporate culture and identity
Personal selling	• Opportunity to develop trust • Dialogue/dyads • Long-term personal contact preferable

DISCUSSION TOPICS

1 Identify consumer market segments which you believe would be particularly open to relational approaches. Justify your suggestions.
2 Provide examples of two offerings (within the product–service continuum) for which a relationship marketing approach would be appropriate.
3 Similarly, provide examples of two offerings for which you feel a relationship marketing approach would be inappropriate.
4 Explore the particular opportunities and challenges which face relationship marketers within the charitable sector.
5 Identify the range of stakeholders the RNLI could sensibly communicate with on a relational basis (see case study).

6 Reflect upon the opportunities and limitations a marketing database provides for consumer relationship marketing.

7 Evaluate the extent to which advertising and public relations can contribute to the generation and maintenance of trust between company and consumers.

8 Evaluate the potential contribution of sales promotion in the development of commitment between company and consumers.

9 Apply the collaborative principles of relationship marketing to the development of television programme sponsorship.

10 What can personal selling and relationship marketing learn from each other?

CASE STUDY – INCORPORATING A RELATIONSHIP MARKETING APPROACH WITHIN THE RNLI'S MARKETING COMMUNICATIONS

The RNLI, Britain's third largest charity (Mintel, 1996), embraces relationship marketing as an underpinning concept for its marketing communications. The RNLI is committed to building a relationship with its members based upon commitment and trust, and in so doing, aims to achieve membership retention levels and lifetime values which surpass those of comparable charities.

The relationship marketing approach chosen by the RNLI recognizes the benefits of segmenting members into groups with similar reasons for belonging to the charity. In doing this, marketing communications can be more accurately targeted to meet the diverse needs of RNLI members. Different membership packages are offered to different segments:

- **Stormforce** is a branded membership especially designed for younger members under the age of 10 years. The aim of this category of membership is to build awareness of the RNLI, sowing the initial seeds of a long-term relationship with members.
- **Shoreline** is the standard membership offer with a membership fee of £15. Shoreline members tend not to be sea users, indeed many, when asked, express a fear of the sea, and a consequent admiration of the courage of the lifeboat men who undertake risk in order to save the lives of others.
- **Offshore** is a different membership package which at £40 targets sea-users themselves, yachtsmen in particular, people who may be motivated to join the RNLI as self-protection or as protection of others with whom they share a particular affinity.
- Shoreline or Offshore members may wish to extend their commitment to the RNLI by becoming **Governors**. Their commitment is expressed in a far higher fee of £50 per year or a one-off payment of £1,000 (Life Governors) and higher levels of involvement, for example by partaking in voting at AGMs or membership of committees.

The RNLI offers this choice of membership channels, and their marketing communications provides members with further opportunities to choose the type of relationship they wish to adopt with the RNLI. This is best expressed within the welcome pack for new members in which a menu of communication approaches is provided from which members can select to suit their own requirements. Clearly it is vital for the RNLI to pursue the membership approach selected by the members in order for the trust essential to successful marketing relationships to be engendered between charity and member.

The RNLI recognizes that while the database is integral to its relationship marketing approach, it does not define the extent of relationship marketing. Public relations activity, particularly that involving reportage of rescues, is sensitive to the need to build and nurture relationships with members, potential members and critical internal customers such as the lifeboat crew themselves. News releases are therefore judged in terms of content and tone in order to further the trust and commitment between the RNLI and its stakeholders.

To summarize, the RNLI recognizes how an understanding of the nature and range of relationships it can develop with its members can support successful marketing communications. The aim is always one-to-one communication, and while this is currently possible in high value categories such as legators, the development of a marketing-orientated relational database and an enhanced understanding of the type of relationship members desire to develop with the charity will facilitate future success within marketing communications activity.

(*Source*: RNLI, used with permission)

REFERENCES

Adelman, M., Ahuvia, A. and Goodwin, C. (1994) 'Beyond smiling: social support and service quality', in R.T. Rust (ed.) *Service Quality : new directions in theory and practice*, Thousand Oaks, CA: Sage, 139–71.

Adelman, M.B., Parks, M.R. and Albrecht, T.L. (1987) 'Beyond close relationships: support in weak ties in T.L. Albrecht and M.B. Adelman (eds) *Communicating Social Support*, Newbury Park, CA: Sage, 126–47.

Aijo, T.S. (1996) 'The theoretical and philosophical underpinnings of relationship marketing', *European Journal of Marketing*, 30(2): 8–17.

Andaleeb, S.S. (1992) 'The trust concept: research issues for channels of distribution', *Research into Marketing*, 11: 1–34.

Andreasen, A.R (1996) 'Profits for nonprofits: find a corporate partner' *Harvard Business Review*, 74(6), Nov–Dec: 47–59.

Bagozzi, R. (1995) 'Reflections on Relationship Marketing in Consumer Markets' *Journal of the Academy of Marketing Science*, 23(4): 272–77.

Barnes, J. (1994) 'Close to the customer: but is it really a relationship?', *Journal of Marketing Management* 10(7): 561–70.

Berry, L. (1983) 'Relationship marketing', in L. Berry, G. Shostack and G. Opah (eds) *Emerging Perspectives on Services Marketing*, Chicago: American Marketing Association, 25–8.

Berry, L. (1995) 'Relationship marketing of services – growing interest, emerging perspectives', *Journal of the Academy of Marketing Science*, 23(4): 236–45.

Bitner, M. (1995) 'Building service relationships: it's all about promises', *Journal of the Academy of Marketing Science*, 23(4): 246–51.

Brodie, R., Coviello, N., Brookes, R. and Little, V. (1997) 'Towards a paradigm shift in marketing? An examination of current marketing practices', *Journal of Marketing Management*, 13(5): 383–406.

Buttle, F. (ed) (1996) *Relationship Marketing: Theory and Practice*, London: Paul Chapman Publishing.

Christopher, M., Payne, A. and Ballantine, D. (1991) *Relationship Marketing*, Oxford: Butterworth–Heinneman.

Christy, R., Oliver, G. and Penn, J. (1996) 'Relationship marketing in consumer markets', *Journal of Marketing Management*, 12(1–3), Part C: 175–87.

Clark, M. and Mills, J. (1979) 'Interpersonal attraction in exchange and communal relationships', *Journal of Personality and Social Psychology*, 37(1): 12–24. (Cited by Sheaves and Barnes, 1996).

Conway, T. (1996) 'Relationship marketing within the not-for-profit sector', Chapter 13 in P. Buttle (ed.) *Relationship Marketing*, London: Paul Chapman Publishing, 170–87.

Copulsky, J. and Wolf, M. (1990) 'Relationship marketing: positioning for the future', *Journal of Business Strategy*, 11(4): 16–20.

Davies, J.C. (1995) 'Dependency, self interest and relationship marketing: a view of the nature of exchange', *Journal of Marketing Theory and Practice*, 3(4): 17–23.

Doney, P. and Cannon, J. (1995) 'An examintion of the nature of trust in buyer–seller relationships', *Journal of Marketing* 61(2): 35–51.

Evans, J.R. and Laskin, R.L. (1994) 'The relationship marketing process', *Industrial Marketing Management*, 23(5): 439–52.

Ganesan, S. (1994) 'Determinants of long-term orientation in buyer–seller relationships', *Journal of Marketing*, 58(2), April: 1–19:

Gronroos, C. (1994) 'From marketing mix to relationship marketing: Towards a paradigm shift in marketing', *Management Decision*, 32(2): 4–20.

Gronroos, C. (1997) 'Value driven relationship marketing: from products to resources and competencies', *Journal of Marketing Management*, 13(5): 407–19.

Gronroos, C. and Strandvik, T. (1997) 'Editorial', *Journal of Marketing Management*, 13(5): 341.

Hogg, M., Long, G., Hartley, M. and Angold, S. (1993) 'Touch me, hold me, squeeze me, freeze me: Privacy – the emerging issue for relationship marketing in the 1990s', *Proceedings of the 1993 Annual Conference of the Marketing Education Group*, Loughborough University, July, 504–14.

Hunt, S. (1997) 'Competing through relationships: grounding relationship marketing in resource–advantage theory', *Journal of Marketing Management*, 13(5): 431–45.

Hutton, J. (1996) 'Integrated relationship marketing communications: a key opportunity for IMC', *Journal of Marketing Communications*, 2(3): 191–9.

Jackson, D. (1993) 'The seven deadly sins of financial services marketing . . . and the road to redemption', *Direct Marketing*, 55(11): 43–45 (cited by Berry, 1995).

Kay, J. (1993) *Foundations of Corporate Success*, Oxford: Oxford University Press.

McCall, G. (1970) 'The social organisation of relationships', in G. McCall, M. McCall, N. Denzin, G. Suttles and S. Kurth, (eds) *Social Relationships*, Chicago: Aldine, 3–34 (cited by Sheaves and Barnes, 1996).

Moorman, C., Zaltman, G. and Deshpande, R. (1992) 'Relationships between providers and users of market research: the dynamics of trust within and between organisations', *Journal of Marketing Research*, 29(3): 314–28 (cited by Morgan and Hunt, 1994).

Morgan, R. and Hunt, S. (1994) 'The commitment–trust theory of relationship marketing', *Journal of Marketing*, 58(3): 20–38.

Payne, A., Christopher, M., Clark, M. and Peck, H. (1995) *Relationship Marketing for Competitive Advantage*, Oxford: Butterworth–Heinneman.

Robin, D. (1995) 'Comment. Exchange, perception of value and relationship marketing: applying the basics to the future', *Journal of Marketing – Theory and Practice*, 3(4): 38–40.

Roff, S. (1996) 'The ultimate relationship', paper delivered at Relationship Marketing for Charities Conference, London, 25 February 1996.

Sheaves, D. and Barnes, J. (1996) 'The fundamentals of relationships: an exploration of the concept to guide marketing implementation', *Advances in Services Marketing and Management*, 5: 215–45.

Sheth, J. and Parvatiyar, A. (1995) 'Relationship marketing in consumer markets: antecedents and consequences', *Journal of the Academy of Marketing Science*, 23(4): 255–71.

Smith, B. and Barclay, D. (1997) 'The effects of organisational differences and trust on the effectiveness of selling partner relationships', *Journal of Marketing*, 61(1): 3–21.

Taylor, S. and Mitchell, M. (1996) 'Building donor relations: Enter database marketing', *Nonprofit world*, 14(6): 22–4.

Webster, F.E. (1992) 'The changing role of marketing in the corporation', *Journal of Marketing*, 56(4): 1–17.

Wilson, D. (1995) 'An integrated model of buyer–seller relationships', *Journal of the Academy of Marketing Science*, 23(4): 335–45.

24

THE RELATIONSHIP AMONG ADVERTISERS, AGENCIES, MEDIA, AND TARGET AUDIENCES

Keith Crosier

CHAPTER AIMS

- to describe how the advertising business is organized, at the macro level
- to explain and assess the possible working arrangements [and circumstantial merits] within that overall framework
- to provide an overview of advertising media, and identify sources for further reading
- to suggest how advertisers ought to set about choosing an advertising agency to work with
- to establish audience attitudes to advertising and advertisements
- to provide an overview of how advertising is regulated, and identify sources for further reading

ILLUSTRATION

The short case history which follows is a fictionalized account of a real situation, featuring a very different kind of advertiser from the fast-moving consumer goods manufacturers and high-street service providers that routinely feature in case examples of working relationships in the business.

University of Dalriada

The University of Dalriada was created by a merger between a long-established, top-flight technological institution and a regional college of commerce in 1964. By 1996, it had more postgraduates than any other university in Atlantica, old or new, and was the second biggest overall in the country. National higher education policy had meanwhile doubled the number of universities by granting that status to existing polytechnics which met the necessary criteria, and participation in degree-level higher education had risen from 10 per cent of the population to 30 per cent. Dalriada's strategic planners responded to this radically changed landscape by placing a high priority on: proactively competing for students beyond their traditional recruiting grounds in Northern Atlantica; de-emphasizing the university's technological bias without diminishing its excellent reputation for research and teaching in science and engineering; and building awareness of its distinguished history before 1964.

A working party was formed, to carry out a marketing audit and recommend a strategy. Chaired by one of the university's senior officers, it drew its members from the offices with responsibility for external affairs, development, research and consultancy services, enterprise ventures, schools liaison and alumni relations, and from the marketing specialization in the business faculty. With regard to marketing communications, the findings were that the key messages were directed at a considerable number of distinct audiences, and that almost every ingredient of the marketing communications mix was used in the process at some time. The university had a very small in-house advertising agency, and used an external agency to place staff recruitment advertising, but work was otherwise commissioned on a rather ad hoc basis from a number of suppliers. The working party recommended the establishment of a coordinated working relationship with a full-service advertising agency.

After surveying the relatively small number of Atlantican advertising agencies not already retained by rival institutions, it invited 30-minute 'credentials presentations' from the two agencies already working on parts of the account, plus five others: one with full service capabilities but a strong specialization in recruitment advertising, another with a strong public relations division, a 'through-the-line' specialist in integrated marketing communications, a mid-order conventional agency, and one with a particularly strong creative reputation. The contenders presented during the course of one day to a panel of three members of the working party, who were surprised by the variation in content and quality. It proved relatively easy to choose a shortlist of three, to be invited to return with proposed solutions to particular communication and positioning challenges. The whole account would be awarded to the one which demonstrated the best understanding of the university's aspirations, of the nature of the marketplace in which it was competing, and of the main target audiences' communication expectations. Circumstances intervened, and that final stage remains to be completed.

THE ADVERTISING SYSTEM

This system consists of a set of relationships among four parties. The definition of advertising given at the start of Chapter 16 describes *advertisers* as marketing communicators who use advertising *media* as their channel of communication with target *audiences*, thereby identifying three of the four. What it does not indicate, however, is that they routinely conduct their dealings with various '*media owners*' via *advertising agencies*. Figure 24.1 summarizes the full range of working relationships that consequently exists. If it seems that a logically possible arrow has been omitted, linking advertisers with audiences direct, re-read the second sentence of this paragraph; that would be defined as a different ingredient of the marketing communications mix.

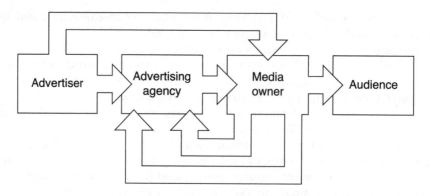

Figure 24.1 The structure of the advertising business.

ADVERTISERS

The way in which firms typically organize and integrate their advertising function has changed twice in the past half-century, and examples of at least three structures can be found in practice today.

The oldest arrangement was to have an Advertising Department headed by a specialist *advertising manager*, often called 'publicity manager' in firms marketing industrial or business-to-business products. The department's role was normally defined almost wholly in terms of support for the sales function. As this emphasis on selling was supplanted by the marketing orientation, specialists in particular marketing functions tended to be replaced by generalist *brand managers*, who counted advertising among several operational responsibilities and called upon [their] advertising agencies to provide specialist expertise. The distinction can perhaps be visualized as substituting a horizontal structure for a vertical one. In response to very rapid recent change in the advertising environment, the 'vertical' manager has reappeared among firms operating in particularly competitive markets, who need to be sure that their creative and media strategies take advantage of every new opportunity. Given the current emphasis on 'integrated marketing commu- nications' (see Chapter 6), their responsibility will no longer be for a single discipline such as advertising, but rather for a range of activities across the marcoms mix, which the job title will reflect in one way or another (e.g. a 'communications czar'). The collective interest of all managers whose remit includes advertising is represented by the *Incorporated Society of British Advertisers* (ISBA), a proactive organization with a continuous programme of professional development and a wide range of publications on key aspects of advertising practice. Table 24.1 lists the top ten advertisers and brands in the UK in terms of total adspend.

ADVERTISING AGENCIES

As early as the start of the nineteenth century, proliferation of newspapers, magazines and poster sites was making it very difficult for advertisers to keep track of the unit

Table 24.1 Top advertisers and brands (UK), 1996

Advertiser	Adspend in £ million	Brand	Adspend in £ million
BT	114.0	McDonald's	26.6
Ford	69.6	BT: Friends and Family	22.2
Vauxhall	63.2	Currys	21.8
COI*	61.1	Renault Mégane	20.4
Proctor & Gamble (P&G)	59.6	Sainsbury's	18.8
Renault	54.9	BT Product Range	17.6
Peugeot	48.7	Peugeot 406	16.7
P&G Health and Beauty	44.3	Nissan Primera	15.1
Nissan	43.9	Ford Escort	14.3
Van den Berghs Foods	42.7	Barclaycard	14.2

* The government, in the form of the Central Office of Information
(*Source*: *The Advertising Statistics Yearbook 1997*, The Advertising Association, London)

cost of space in all the media options available, deal efficiently with the many contractors involved in the booking of a nation-wide campaign, or effectively check that advertising had in fact been placed in the spaces and sites ordered, at prices quoted. This situation provided an obvious opportunity for entrepreneurial intermediaries to set up in business. The first of these, describing themselves as 'advertising agents', acted as expert consultants to advertisers and charged a *fee* for their services. A second wave of 'space brokers' bought advertising space in bulk, speculatively, and resold it in lots to advertisers at a *marked-up* price. By mid-century, the brokers were buying at a fixed discount and selling at a published list price. In the 1880s, they began to prepare clients' advertising as well as placing it, subsidizing the cost of this additional service from '*media commission*'. The financial consequences of these historical precedents are explained and discussed in Chapter 25.

As the twentieth century began, the two ancestors of what is now one of the world's largest advertising agencies were already employing 100 and 67 staff in London. By that yardstick, both would still be in the British top fifty. Their clients were the consumer-goods manufacturers whose businesses were booming in the new age of mass production: Bovril, Colman's, Dewar's, Ever-Ready, H. Samuel, Mackintosh's and Rowntree's. The shape and scale of the present-day '*full-service advertising agency*' had thereby been established more than a hundred years ago, and has changed only in detail since. The progress to maturity of this service industry is indicated in Britain by the existence of a thriving professional association, the *Institute of Practitioners in Advertising*. As well as the expected range of services to its 200-odd member agencies, it has since 1981 run the bi-annual *IPA Effectiveness Awards* and published the winning submissions under the generic title *Advertising Works*. These are thoroughly documented case histories of the cost-effective use of advertising, as distinct from the abundant awards for creative campaigns which may or may not have achieved advertisers' objectives.

In the period of economic reconstruction after the Second World War, the major agencies in London were American multinationals which had allowed themselves to become slow-moving behemoths. Sensing the lack of creative originality in particular, break-away teams set up the so-called '*hot shops*' or 'boutiques' which characterized the 1960s in Britain and America. Saatchi & Saatchi, later to become the biggest conventional advertising agency in the world, began its life as one such in 1970. Conventional agencies have since reclaimed the creative territory, and no single-minded specialists of any significance remain. Meanwhile, dissatisfaction with the planning and buying of media in full-service agencies led to a second wave of break-aways. As it became apparent that these '*media independents*' were routinely securing volume discounts which could be passed on to their clients, a steady flow of advertisers handed that role over to them while leaving the rest of the full-service account where it was. As the volume of their bookings thereby increased, so did their price-negotiating leverage. Several agencies retaliated by setting up devolved media-buying operations to compete in the open market, which have since been dubbed 'media dependents', or by forming strategic alliances. The upshot has been that media independents and quasi-independents have flourished to the extent that the most successful of them are now bigger businesses than the largest full-service advertising agencies, as Table 24.2 shows. They are collectively represented by the *Association of Media and Communication Specialists (AMCO)*.

The five *operational functions* and two *planning functions* identifiable in the typical structure of a modern full-service advertising agency are symbolized in Figure 24.2.

The **creative** and **media** functions are responsible for converting the client's *brief* into an *advertising campaign* by, respectively: devising *creative strategies* and specifying the finished *advertisements or commercials*; devising *media strategies* and booking the resultant *media schedule*. Chapter 16 describes the processes by which these tasks are achieved, in the section 'Delivering the Message'.

Production is the function which converts the output of the creative department into what the audience eventually hears and sees, for example by turning a script into a radio commercial or a finished layout into a magazine advertisement. Some of this work will be carried out in-house, but such complex operations as the shooting of a television commercial or the printing of a large roadside poster will necessarily be delegated to specialists, subcontracted and supervised by the production department.

Evans (1988) provides an expert account of the production function, but many details have been rendered obsolete by the pace of change in information technology during the intervening decade. In particular, it has outmoded the process by which 'roughs' or 'scamps' hand-drawn by 'visualizers' were transformed into high-quality 'finished artwork', which a 'paste-up artist' married with the result of 'photo-typesetting' to produce the 'masters' required by the printer. Today, Apple Mac operators set to work on the scamps, using suites of typefaces and graphics software with such self-explanatory names as 'freehand', 'illustrator' and 'photo-shop', to produce an image on disk that can be digitally transformed into the necessary 'bromide' photo-transparency or transmitted direct to the printer via the ISDN data-transmission network.

Traditional 'studio skills' are not totally redundant, however, for agencies still present material for client approval in the form of artwork pasted-up on boards or

Table 24.2 Top advertising agencies and media buying specialists (UK) 1996

Name	Status	Billings* in £ million
Zenith Media	Media dependent	554.3
TMD Carat	Media independent	400.7
The Media Centre	Media dependent	357.7
BMP DDP	"	311.1
AMV BBDO	Full service agency	306.8
J. Walter Thompson	"	278.2
Ogilvy & Mather	"	254.6
BMP DDB	"	237.0
Mediapolis	Media dependent	233.0
CIA Medianetwork	"	230.4
New PHD	"	227.7
Universal McCann	"	220.8
The Network	"	211.2
Media Com	"	210.9
DMB&B	Full service agency	186.9
Publicis	"	186.5
M&C Saatchi	"	175.0
Media Business Group	Media independent	174.6

* The total sum the agency or independent spent in that year on behalf of its client for all services provided.
(*Source*: *The Advertising Statistics Yearboook 1997*, The Advertising Association, London)

made up into dummies of printed pieces. It is more practical to hand such material round the participants in a meeting than to have them look at a computer screen, and easier for most people to visualize the finished product.

Traffic is a low-profile function of absolutely crucial importance. Given the sheer number of often complex operations that have to take place between the completion of planning and the appearance of the required advertising at the right time in the right places, every agency must devise a control system to guard against the obvious scope for the whole campaign to be jeopardized by a simple mistake somewhere in the detail. The 'traffic managers' who implement it need to be natural project managers, with all the unglamorous skills that description implies: scheduling, progress-chasing, record-keeping, coordinating and negotiating – not to mention dogged persistence. Undeservedly unmentioned in 'credentials presentations' and unseen during visits to the agency, they are the mortar that makes a wall from a pile of bricks.

Account handling is the agency's *client-service* function, 'account' being the word traditionally used to define one piece of business given to an agency by its client. Typical account handling departments are markedly hierarchical, staffed by teams of account executives, account managers, account supervisors and account

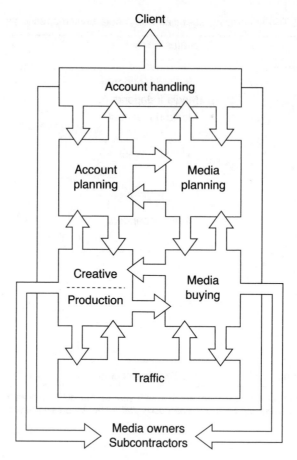

Figure 24.2 The key functions in an advertising agency.

directors. Though they are often disparaged as 'bag carriers' or 'the suits' (because no one else below board level in a typical agency wears one), it should be obvious that they need to be much more than well-dressed messengers if they are to carry out their responsibilities effectively. Indeed, theirs is a pivotal role in the whole agency–client relationship, as seen shortly.

Account planning is a 'thinking' discipline, rather than a 'doing' function. Originating in two London advertising agencies in the late 1970s, it remains something of a British specialization. For example, the agency which pioneered the discipline in America some years later staffed its Account Planning Department entirely with expatriates, and the trade press there has ever since speculated that 'British-style' planning may at last produce the hoped-for renaissance of creativity in domestic advertising.

The goal is to bring to bear on the development of effective advertising campaigns an understanding of consumers, audiences, markets and society, gained by combining available general theory with appropriate specific research. The description thus disguises the fact that it is, in effect, creative planning. This may have been a deliberate ploy to reduce the likelihood of conflict with the people who actually have the ideas and execute the concepts, and are likely to believe that the creative process is intuitive and personal, not amenable to design by committee or interpretation by researchers. It is perhaps these very tensions in an internal working relationship which have kept the account planning discipline in a prolonged adolescence, not yet really widespread in smaller or less sophisticated advertising agencies. On the other hand, the existence of an active *Account Planning Group*, a series of published case histories (Account Planning Group, 1993, 1995, 1997), a handbook edited on its behalf (Cooper, 1997) and what is in effect a house journal for account planners, *Admap*, suggest that it will continue to make an important intellectual contribution to the practice of advertising, at the cutting edge at least. Meanwhile, the tendency has been to shorten the description to 'planning'.

Media planning is the discipline the first advertising agencies offered to the advertisers of the time, and has responded to a second explosion of media choice some two centuries later. The expansion and fragmentation of television and radio in particular presents media planners with both problems and opportunities. Their role is to apply the abundance of industry research data at their disposal to the task of finding the most cost-effective means of delivering the advertiser's message to the required target audiences. The section on *Media Owners* will briefly survey the rapidly changing media environment and the main research services available, recommending further reading as required. It may strike an outside observer as odd that account planning and media planning have not merged into a single planning discipline. It is probably their distinct and highly specialized research requirements which have so far kept them clearly separate in typical agencies, but current opinion among leading practitioners suggests the need for closer integration (McDonald, 1995; O'Donoghue, 1997). Media planners are supported by an active Media Research Group, publishers of an invaluable 'guide to media research suitable for complete beginners . . . and comprehensive reference source for others whose job entails the frequent use of research based data' (McDonald and Monkman, 1995).

MEDIA OWNERS

These are the organizations which hold the rights to the sale of advertising space and time. In Britain, the media mix they collectively offer to advertisers is conventionally defined as comprising five 'major media'. Table 24.3 shows the share of total national advertising expenditure held by each of these in seven countries. It is clear that every national mix actually consists of two major categories and three distinctly minor ones. The extent and nature of the variation is interesting, but the reasons too complex to discuss further here. Although the table shows cinema as an unavailable option in the USA, Belch and Belch (1998, p. 429) report that it is in fact 'increasing quickly (to the dismay of many) . . . commercials shown before the film and previews, with both local and national sponsorships, have almost replaced cartoons'.

In the UK, the pattern of *media share* among the first three areas in the mix has remained pretty stable over the past quarter-century. Radio and cinema have both

Table 24.3 Media share* in selected countries, 1995

	France %	Germany %	Italy %	Spain %	Japan %	USA %	UK %
Press	47.4	69.0	38.1	47.5	39.6	51.8	59.5
Television	33.0	22.4	57.6	37.4	41.5	35.5	32.7
Poster	11.6	3.5	2.6	4.5	13.7	1.1	3.7
Radio	7.4	4.1	1.6	9.8	5.1	11.6	3.3
Cinema	0.6	1.0	–	0.8	–	–	0.7

* Percentage of total national advertising expenditure allocated to each medium.
(*Source*: *Advertising Statistics Yearbook*, 1997, Advertising Association)

increased theirs steadily during the 1990s, but from a very small base. They remain very small media in absolute terms. The fact that both are nevertheless labelled 'major' implies the existence of an uncertain number of even more 'minor' media. Surprisingly, no author uses the term, let alone defining them explicitly, but the list would include videotext, tethered balloons, 'ad-trailers', parking meters, matchbooks, shopping bags, performance programmes, and many other transient opportunities for advertising.

In the necessarily brief review of the UK media mix which follows, italics have the special purpose of indicating that a description is elaborated in the encyclopaedic *Macmillan Dictionary of Marketing and Advertising* (Baker, 1998). Additionally, Smith (1993) provides an authoritative account of the options available at that time, concluding with a case history of the high-profile Häagen-Dazs magazine advertising campaign. Brierley (1995) offers a business analysis of the media marketplace, with thumbnail sketches of six media owners, and a thorough account of industry research as a 'trading currency'. Readers interested in the US situation should refer to Belch and Belch (1998, Chapters 10–13).

Press, with almost twice the media share of the next largest, owes its size to its composite make-up. It is conventionally split into five categories: the *regional press* and *local press* (*paid-for titles* and *freesheets*), which together accounted for just over a third of total expenditure in the medium in 1996; the *national press*, contributing just over a quarter; 27 sub-categories of 'business and professional magazine' (paid-for titles and *controlled circulation publications*), at somewhat less than a fifth; 'directories', at about an eighth; and nine sub-categories of 'consumer magazine', accounting for precisely a tenth of the total share. This already fragmented medium will present an even greater challenge to media planners of the twenty-first century, as the new '*e-zines*' and online versions of existing newspapers proliferate. They are, however, well provided with reliable research data for all but the smaller titles in each sub-category, on which to base allocation decisions within the medium. *Circulation*, the average number of titles sold per issue, is defined by *ABC* and *VFD* figures; *readership*, the average number of people reading an issue, normally larger, is obtained from *NRS* and *JICREG* data. A ready-made *readership profile* of larger-circulation titles can be found in *BRAD*, which lists circulation and readership figures, a 'profile index' and two measures of coverage, cross-indexed by gender, age, social class and 'main shopper' status.

Commercial **television** is the most expensive medium, in terms of both *air time* and production costs. It shares the total viewing audience on a more or less 50–50 basis with the BBC. Though attracting only half the advertising revenue that the press as a whole does, it in fact takes almost as much as newspapers of all kinds, and more than the other three categories together. Taking that fact with the undoubted impact of moving images in colour with sound, it should come as no surprise that national advertisers seem to treat television as the prime advertising medium rather than runner-up. It currently comprises the 14 regional *ITV* stations on Channel 3, national Channels 4 and 5, morning-only GMTV, six of the 26 cable channels and 33 of the 56 satellite services originating in the UK. Significant developments in *digital television* impending in early 1998 are expected to add hundreds of new terrestrial and satellite stations. In short, this medium will soon be as fragmented as the press already is. Media planners faced with this daunting choice among costly options have access to raw data or computed statistics from 'audience measurement' and 'audience appreciation' surveys commissioned by *BARB*, providing a reliable picture of viewer presence during any programme, but not necessarily of their *attention* during commercial breaks. Time is bought from *sales houses*, not from the media owners individually.

The **poster** medium is conventionally divided into two categories, separating *poster sites* seen mainly by motorists and public transport users from the rest. The descriptions 'outdoor', 'transport' and 'poster' itself are used rather inconsistently to make the distinction, which is based on the audience's different relationship with the medium in each case. The first category consists of a variety of spaces available in and on buses and taxis, in train, bus and underground stations; 10 second mainly comprises outdoor sites for ten standard *poster sizes*. BRAD further identifies 'venue' sites (sports and athletic stadia, golf courses, exhibition halls, hospitals, washrooms) and 'specialized' sites (hot-air balloons, blimps and airships, aeroplane-towed banners, supermarket trolleys). 'Billboard' is the American term for a conventional outdoor site. Three large 'contractors' own roughly half the total number of sites in Britain, media buyers often dealing with them through specialist intermediaries. *Coverage* and *frequency* data for 73 000 poster sites are available from *POSTAR*, for London bus and underground campaigns from TDI: see *outdoor*.

Commercial **radio** is the least expensive medium, in terms of both *air time* and production cost. It came late to Britain, the first government-sanctioned domestic station starting to broadcast in 1973. Ten years later, there were 40 *ILR* stations on air, and by 1990 a hundred. Nevertheless, a stubbornly low media share earned radio the nickname 'the two per cent medium', and it singularly failed to win advertising for national brands. Three events in 1992 marked a sea-change in its fortunes: the setting up of the national *INR* network, the *Radio Advertising Bureau* and the *RAJAR* audience measurement system. By 1996, this once moribund medium comprised 196 local, five regional and four national stations. It shares listening exactly 50-50 with the BBC, but takes at least 60 per cent in every age group up to the mid-forties. The audience profile has attracted such national brands as Dixons, Coca-Cola, McDonald's and Carphone Warehouse. Media share has reached 4 per cent, and it is the fastest growing of the major media. The structure of the medium will change radically again after 1998, with the arrival of *digital radio*. Time is bought mainly through five *sales houses* collectively representing the individual media owners.

As the **cinema** audience shrank from 19 million admissions a week in the 1940s to 70 million annually 40 years later, its media share collapsed from almost 4 per cent to only 0.4 in 1989. When the media owners at last responded constructively by improving programmes and accommodation, and started to build *multiplexes*, audience figures rose for the first time in half a century. The 100 million per year barrier was broken in 1993, industry research showing the audience to be significantly more up-market than the general population and to contain very nearly twice as many young adults. In research experiments commissioned by the *Cinema Advertising Association* in 1992 and 1997, recall scores for a cinema commercial were between five and ten times higher than an identical television commercial screened simultaneously. Advertisers attracted to this revitalized medium include three brewers, two distillers, Levi's and DeBeers. Despite a media share still no greater than 0.7 per cent in 1996, it occupies a well-protected niche. 'Space' on the 2200-odd screens in the UK is bought from one of only two authorized 'contractors'.

Notably absent as yet from published lists of major and minor media are what might be termed **cybermedia**: messages on the Internet and banners or pages on the World Wide Web. This is a potentially powerful business-to-business marcoms medium, at present something of a cross between advertising and direct marketing (see Chapter 22). Almost 30 per cent of British businesses were connected to the Net in 1996 and all but 5 per cent of the laggards were expected to have joined them within a year, according to the *Financial Times* (cited in Baker, 1998). The potential for reaching consumer audiences will take longer to develop. A prominent British market research company estimated that the net had achieved a 'household penetration' of only 2 per cent in Britain in 1995, which translates to no more than 400 000 home computers linked up. Its survey further showed that almost two-thirds of current Internet users were under 35, while *Campaign* magazine reported that 95 per cent were male. Research figures from the USA show that the British are the heaviest users of the World Wide Web in Europe, presumably because the English language dominates its content. Extrapolated and interpreted, they suggest that no more than 220 000 UK households visited a Web site in 1996. Despite undoubted eventual potential, cybermedia are not yet a mass-market rival to any of the established major media. Belch and Belch (1998, pp. 457–65) provide a useful up-to-date review, concluding with a list of advantages and disadvantages; and Chapter 22 reports later data.

WORKING RELATIONSHIPS

It is a truism that all service industries are 'people businesses', but one which nonetheless emphasizes the crucial role of interpersonal relationships in the effective management of advertising campaigns.

Client and agency

It is generally accepted that more than three quarters of total annual advertising expenditure in the UK passes to media owners via advertising agencies or specialist media-buying agencies. This does not quite mean that three campaign schedules in every four have been booked by an advertising agency, for a large number of small advertisers account for the quarter that is spent direct, but it does indicate that client–agency working relationships are a major feature of the advertising business.

An observer with no knowledge of historical precedents might well be surprised that advertisers seem so ready to relinquish *control*, by delegating responsibility to a third party, over activities as vital as campaign planning and implementation. However, to keep it in-house would demand substantial investment in the professional *expertise* required to generate effective creative and media solutions. Even if an advertiser were willing to match the very high salaries commanded by the individual possessors of those skills, it could prove difficult to lure them from their natural habitat in advertising agencies. Furthermore, it would be even harder to keep them motivated. Typically, they would be working sporadically on a limited variety of projects, whereas at an agency their time would be fully occupied on work for a number of clients. The advertiser would be left paying for expensive, under-employed and unenthusiastic human assets; much better instead to buy a share in a pool of talent managed and motivated by someone else. Moreover, an agency could approach the task free of the insider's preconceptions, and bring to bear lateral thinking derived from experience in applying the basic disciplines across a range of situations.

The decision to trade off *control* against *cost* is normally clinched by the fact that clients do not have to pay large fees for this time-sharing arrangement. A recent industry survey in Britain showed that media owners contribute more than two-thirds of a typical full-service advertising agency's total earnings, in the form of sales commission, not the 'clients' who are happy to call it 'our agency'. In the case of media-buying specialists, the figure is normally 100 per cent. Chapter 25 explains the mechanism and consequences of this somewhat paradoxical payment system.

The onus for maintaining the agency–client relationship in good working order is borne mainly by the agency's *account handling* function. An especially vital task is to help refine the advertiser's brief for a new campaign, to interpret it from the agency perspective, and to play a major part in translating it into separate creative and media briefs. As explained in Chapter 16, these set in motion the corresponding phases of campaign planning and development. It is then the account handler's task to deliver and justify an agency's campaign proposal to a client. Many iterations of the process may take place before everything is agreed, and there is considerable scope for tension among the parties concerned.

Thereafter, routine maintenance of the relationship depends on the ability to divide time, and indeed loyalty, between employer(s) and client(s) who employ the employer. It is for that reason that Figure 24.2 depicted the account handling function straddling the agency's organizational boundary. As an Account Manager memorably explained it to a class of students: 'Whenever I'm at the client's office, I must be the agency's man; back at the agency, I have to be the client's man.' The best exponents are thus diplomats, negotiators, facilitators, coordinators, organizers, and more besides. The worst spend their time 'ferrying messages back and forth between agency and client with all the interpretational skills of a yo-yo' (Mayle, 1990).

However effectively account handlers deliver client service, this particular working relationship tends to be shorter lived than is the norm in other professions. Briggs (1993) reports evidence that more than three-quarters of them last less than 10 years.

Agency and media owner

Once the client has approved the agency's media strategy, *media buyers* set to work to convert that into a cost-effective *media schedule*: a pattern of spaces and time slots in a variety of vehicles over a period of time. The price structure in media owners' *rate cards* is notoriously complex, balancing surcharges for fixed dates, special positions and the like against discounts for series bookings and sheer volume. In response to supply and demand, the price paid can vary substantially from the figure on paper. Indeed, television rate cards are in practice no more than a statutorily required departure point for bargaining. Effective media buying thus requires an encyclopaedic knowledge of the media mix and haggling skills.

Whereas the client–agency working relationship is normally collaborative, this one is often adversarial.

The two arrows in Figure 24.1 which point from right to left symbolize the fact that media owners do not wait passively for orders from media buyers. It was in the 1830s that a New York newspaper responded to proliferating options for advertisers by hiring 'advertisement solicitors' to sell the commodity proactively. Later called 'space salesmen', they nowadays sell either time or space, and are as likely to be female as male. In making their sales pitches, these *media sales representatives* typically deploy an array of facts and figures extracted from industry-wide research programmes by in-house research managers. A rigorously observed convention of the business is that they do not make a sales call on an advertiser without informing the agency handling the account, and that the advertiser does not respond by placing an order direct. This is to protect advertising agencies from loss of the *media commission* which is a large part of their total revenue (see Chapter 25).

Advertiser and media owner

It has already been noted that media orders placed direct by advertisers account for less than a quarter of total advertising expenditure in Britain. The comparatively unsophisticated smaller advertisers who choose to operate in this way have to deal with the variety of booking options generally available, the complexity of most pricing structures, the potentially baffling figures produced in sales pitches as evidence of cost-effectiveness, and the hard-bargaining ethos of typical media sales departments. It is therefore not surprising that this particular relationship often turns out to be a one-sided one, in which the advertiser buys a *package* rather than building a specific media schedule from the details of a formal plan.

Advertiser and audience

Opinion leaders – such as some journalists, social commentators, politicians and academics – will often express a negative attitude towards advertising. They may suggest that it is: a business cost that drives up prices; a 'barrier to entry' against would-be competitors, reducing consumer choice; an appeal to the emotions, not the sense of reason; a malign influence on popular culture; the paymaster of the information media; or, a force that makes people buy things they don't need and shouldn't want. Practitioners and business analysts have ready counter-arguments, of course, but the opinion of the audience at whom advertisements are directed is perhaps the most important issue. (NB: this is a different view to that put forward in Chapter 8; readers may be interested to compare these two perspectives.)

The Advertising Association has commissioned nine large-scale replicated surveys of public attitudes since 1961. In the most recent of these, 5 per cent of the sample chose 'advertising' from a list of a dozen general social topics as one of those they talked most about with their friends; 3 per cent said they felt strongly about it, and the same proportion felt something should be done about it. Asked to rate their approval or disapproval of the same abstract concept on a five-point scale, 16 per cent took the chance to register a negative opinion. On a similar scale of liking or disliking for the visible manifestations, 18 per cent expressed negative feelings about television commercials, 12 per cent about posters and 10 per cent about press advertisements. The survey report concludes that ordinary people in Britain overwhelmingly accept the existence of an advertising industry and enjoy its output. Nevertheless, advertisers 'should never become complacent about public attitudes . . . advertising is far too much in the public eye (and in its ears) for the industry to let its standards fall' (Advertising Association, 1996).

It was argued in Chapter 16 that most individuals in a modern Western society are well able to resist the supposed power of advertisers to manipulate them. The audience in general is furthermore protected from dishonest and untruthful advertising by a formal system of direct legislation, statutory regulation and self-regulation.

More than a hundred pieces of legislation can affect advertisers in some way. Both television and radio advertising are further controlled by the statutory duty of the *Independent Television Commission* and the *Radio Authority* to ensure that commercials are pre-cleared for broadcast against the *ITC Code of Advertising Standards and Practice and Advertising and Sponsorship Code* respectively. Non-broadcast advertising (including that on CD-ROM and the Internet) is subject to regulation by an industry-funded body, the *Advertising Standards Authority (ASA)*, which judges public complaints about advertisements against the relevant part of its *British Codes of Advertising and Sales Promotion*. All three codes are distributed so widely throughout the industry that no advertiser or agency could credibly claim ignorance of their prohibitions and guidelines. All cinema commercials must be pre-cleared by the *Cinema Advertising Association*, those of 30 seconds or longer additionally requiring a certificate from the *British Board of Film Classification*. Thereafter, they are subject to the ASA's code. For further details of the enforcement mechanisms and an account of harmonized regulation within the European Union, refer to the 'advertising control' entry in the *Macmillan Dictionary of Marketing and Advertising* (Baker, 1998).

If the client–agency and agency–media relationships can be thought of as respectively collaborative and adversarial, that between advertiser and audience is perhaps conversational.

SELECTING AN ADVERTISING AGENCY

As stated earlier, most client–agency relationships last less than 10 years. The productive collaboration between BMW and their agency, described in the 'illustration' case history in Chapter 16, is the exception rather than the rule. One obvious way to reduce the probability of a premature rift is to take as much care as possible over the selection process preceding the start of the relationship. This section therefore proposes an appropriately systematic approach to that key task, summarized in Figure 24.3. It is described from the point of view of a prospective client actively searching for a suitable partner, whereas the Lakeland Cycles case history features an agency soliciting a potential client. In practice, the former situation is far more common than the latter.

Analogies with courtship and marriage characterize the relatively few discussions of agency selection in the literature: see, for instance, White (1993). Apart from trivializing an important decision, they propose as a framework a process which is normally far more emotional than rational, and by no means always successful. Conversely, most people would think the checklists and competitions in the procedure which follows an unacceptably dispassionate approach to the choosing of a spouse.

Step 1, formally defining what will be required of the agency, often falls victim in practice to the false doctrine: 'cut the cackle and get down to business'. To avoid the necessary intellectual effort would prejudice the outcome at the very outset, for this crucial step is the source of decision criteria needed three times during the process. **Step 2** is in effect window shopping. Sources of this preliminary information include the trade press, a range of directories, the World Wide Web, and the informal grapevine within the business. The *Institute of Practitioners in Advertising* (IPA) will provide a list of suitable agencies, in exchange for a profile of the advertiser and a statement of its requirements. Promotional videos, prepared by agencies to a standard specification, can be viewed anonymously at the premises of the *Advertising Agency Register*. The owner of Lakeland Cycles undertook none of these sensible preliminaries. **Step 3** is to draw up a pool list of agencies who seem capable of meeting the criteria defined at Step 1. How many it contains should reflect a pragmatic judgement about span of attention at the next stage. In the University of Dalriada case, it included two 'incumbents' and five others.

At **Step 4**, the advertiser goes public for the first time by inviting 'credentials presentations' from those agencies, and can expect approaches from others not in the list, as the grapevine goes into action and the trade press probably reports the move. The professional convention is that the presenting agencies do not respond to this invitation, provided it is specific, with speculative campaign plans and a full-blown pitch for the business. Instead, they typically provide a 'philosophy statement', staff profiles, a client list, 'showreels' of television and cinema commercials, 'radio reels', dossiers of print work, and some case histories. It is a

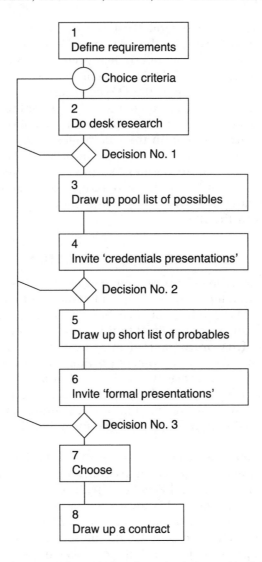

Figure 24.3 A systematic procedure for selecting an advertising agency.

moot question whether the presentations should take place at the agencies, in which case a general impression of their working ethos may be an additional benefit, or on home ground, where there is less risk of being overwhelmed by a practised presentation team. They should certainly be seen by a panel, as in the Dalriada case, not an individual. This is first so that an isolated decision maker is not as vulnerable to pressure as the owner of Lakeland Cycles was, and second so that **Step 5** will be the result of informed debate, structured by the criteria defined in Step 1.

Step 6 is to invite survivors on the resulting shortlist to make a 'formal presentation', which will in all other circumstances be more graphically called the 'pitch for the business'. A leaflet on 'best practice in the management of the pitching process', issued jointly by the IPA and the *Incorporated Society of British Advertisers* (ISBA), is unequivocal about how many pitches should be invited: 'Decide on a list of three agencies – four if the incumbent is involved . . . Don't be seduced into lengthening the list.' At **Step 7**, the choice criteria are consulted for the last time, and the decision is made. Until quite recently, the contract required by **Step 8** of Figure 24.3 was likely to be nothing more than a handshake, imitating the 'gentlemen's agreements' common in the true professions. The transformation of successful agencies from small partnerships into large listed companies has fortunately brought with it more businesslike practices. Advertisers and agencies entering a working relationship today can reduce the likelihood of damaging arguments later by adopting *Some Suggested Provisions for Use in Agency/Client Agreements*, published by the IPA.

SUMMARY AND CONCLUSION

The advertising system is made up of four parties. Advertisers typically delegate responsibility for the development and implementation of their campaign plans to advertising agencies. The agencies in turn buy advertising space and time from media owners, create the advertisements to fill it, and commission associated work from subcontractors. They are organized in a distinctive way to deliver this 'full service' to their clients. The media owners provide a diverse range of advertising opportunities, backed by a considerable body of industry research into their performance in delivering target audiences. The audience consumes the output voluntarily and is generally positive about advertising, unlike many opinion leaders. Relationships among the four parties range from collaborative to potentially adversarial.

The necessarily limited description account of the business given here can be supplemented, if necessary, by first-hand accounts in three books by practitioners: Mayle (1990), Bullmore (1991) and Fletcher (1992). Peter Mayle, best known as the author of *A Year in Provence*, started his advertising career as a copywriter and retired from it as a creative director at the multinational BBDO agency after 13 years in London and New York. His style is by far the most irreverent, but the picture he paints is utterly recognizable. Jeremy Bullmore also started out as a copywriter. Unusually for this business, he stayed with the J. Walter Thompson agency for the whole of his 33-year career, as chairman from 1976 to 1987. Winston Fletcher is the present chairman of Bozell Europe, a network of agencies in 20 countries, and past chairman of the IPA. These two are both regular writers on advertising topics, and always a good read.

DISCUSSION TOPICS

1 Is it time for advertisers to abandon tradition, and start taking responsibility themselves for campaign planning?
2 Should the 'account planning' discipline in advertising agencies embrace both creative and media planning?

3 Assess the statement by a marketing director in the automotive services sector that 'too often, account executives are an unnecessary extra link in the chain of communication'.

4 How might the UK media mix be redefined for the twenty-first century?

5 Why does the text describe the relationship between advertising agency and media owner as potentially adversarial?

6 The title page of a book written by a British journalist in 1988 says 'The Want Makers: lifting the lid off the world advertising industry – how they make you buy'. How much truth is there in these assertions?

7 Assess the approach taken by the University of Dalriada to the task of selecting an advertising agency.

8 How do you think Paul Olloman will answer Mo Gupta's question, and why?

9 How would you rewrite the Lakeland Cycles case history, to make it an example of best practice?

10 What are advertising agencies for?

CASE STUDY

Like the University of Dalriada case history, this vignette deals with a situation far removed from the stereotype of sophisticated brand managers with a clear idea of advertising strategy, briefing experienced account managers from famous agencies, which duly produce prize-winning television campaigns familiar to everyone by virtue of the exposure the client's budget could buy. The details have been changed, but the action is real.

Lakeland Cycles

'I take it you would like us to proceed, rather than thinking to yourself, "I can't stand the thought of working with these guys; I must leave".' Paul Olloman, owner of Lakeland Cycles, had spent the past hour listening to a pitch for his business at the Dunsmore Gupta McDonald advertising agency and then having lunch with two of the partners. Mo Gupta was now asking him to make up his mind.

Lakeland Cycles was in its third year of hand-assembling mountain bikes and 'hybrid' touring bicycles from good quality imported components at a factory unit in a light industrial estate near Kendal, on the edge of the Lake District. It was a high-skill, low-volume operation; Paul Olloman had previously worked at an engineering research laboratory. 'DGM' had started in business at about the same time, as a break-away from a top-50 London agency. Its offices were in a Thames-side warehouse development. A cycling enthusiast in the agency had noticed that Lakeland's product line was attracting favourable reviews in the trade press, visited their stand at an outdoor activities exhibition, and suggested that Mo Gupta should invite them to an 'exploratory meeting' at the agency.

Accepting the invitation, Paul Olloman agreed that, 'having got so far and done what we've done literally by the seat of our pants, we do now need advice'. During the morning's presentation, he had met the agency's partners and learnt that DGM would always 'tell a client what he needs to know, not what he wants to hear' and had 'never lost a client by telling him strictly the truth'. The agency built creative strategy round a single 'residual image', identified by 'concept synthesis', and concentrated on making it 'the one piece of information that the human mind can retain from any one piece of communication at any time', so that money allocated to advertising would be spent more effectively. As an example, he had been taken through a case history of DGM's work for a major supplier and installer of domestic swimming pools. The target market was defined as 'affluent AB householders on the edge of major conurbations', the relative roles of the husband and wife in the decision to make such a radical purchase were explored, possible motivations were identified, and the key proposition eventually emerged that a swimming pool could 'enable you to become something of a social centre'. Advertisements had run in lifestyle magazines.

Paul Olloman had seized the chance to pose a vital question: 'But how can you do anything really effective for an operation with as low product volumes as ours?'. Mo Gupta had responded that it wasn't so much a question of how the agency could sell his product, as whether the two of them could work together towards that end.

DGM's planner had then joined the meeting, to report the findings of an informal survey. Lakeland Cycles were admired by those who had bought from them, and had the potential to 'own a lucrative niche in a crowded market', but needed to be much more widely known. The way to achieve that objective would seem to be to concentrate all communication on the Fellmaster ZX, an orthodox but very highly engineered off-road model that had already been ridden to victory by Lakeland's technical director in a handful of trials and competitions. It should be advertised as the 'ultimate riding machine', four-figure price and all. Every opportunity to win further accolades should be pursued, and all successes vigorously publicized. When enthusiastic mountain bikers visited the showroom or the Web site which DGM would create, 'they would find to their pleasure that there were other Fellmasters that looked the same but were quite a lot cheaper', and would decide that no one but themselves would spot the difference.

That was the point at which Mo Gupta had announced that a table was awaiting them at a restaurant nearby.

REFERENCES

Account Planning Group (1993, 1995, 1997) *Creative Planning > Outstanding Advertising*, Vols 1–3, London: The Account Planning Group.

Advertising Association (1996) *Public Attitudes to Advertising 1996*, London: The Advertising Association.

Baker, M.J. (1998) *Macmillan Dictionary of Marketing and Advertising*, London: Macmillan.

Belch, G. and Belch, M. (1998) *Advertising and Promotion: An Integrated Marketing Communications Perspective*, 4th edn, New York: McGraw-Hill.

Brierley, S. (1995) *The Advertising Handbook*, London: Routledge: Chapters 7 and 9.

Briggs, M. (1993) 'Why ad agencies must change', *Admap*, January: 22.

Bullmore, J. (1991) *Behind the Scenes in Advertising*, Henley-on-Thames: NTC Publications.

Cooper, A. (ed.) (1997) *How to Plan Advertising*, 2nd edn, London: Cassell.

Evans, R.B. (1988) *Production and Creativity in Advertising*, London: Pitman, Parts 2 and 3.

Fletcher, W. (1992) *A Glittering Haze: Strategic Advertising in the 1990s*, Henley-on-Thames: NTC Publications.

McDonald, C. (1995) 'The role and purpose of media planning', Chapter 1 in C. McDonald and M. Monkman (eds) *The MRG Guide to Media Research*, Salisbury, Wilts: Media Research Group, 1.

McDonald, C. and Monkman, M. (eds.) (1995) *The MRG Guide to Media Research*, Salisbury, Wilts: Media Research Group.

Mayle, P. (1990) *Up the Agency*, London: Pan Books.

O'Donoghue, D. (1997) 'Account planning and media planning', Chapter 8 in A. Cooper (ed.) *How to Plan Advertising*, 2nd edn, London: Cassell, 121.

Smith, P.R. (1993) *Marketing Communications: An Integrated Approach*, London: Kogan Page: Chapter 11.

White, R. (1993) *Advertising: What it is and how to do it*, 3rd edn, London: McGraw-Hill, Chapter 4.

25

THE ARGUMENT FOR ADVERTISING AGENCY REMUNERATION

Keith Crosier

CHAPTER AIMS

- to explain the complicated system of conventions and calculations governing the process by which advertising agencies are paid for their services
- to explain why a historical curiosity has proved so robust
- to identify the significant consequences
- to analyse controversy surrounding its application in practice
- to evaluate a widely proposed alternative to the dominant method
- to identify typical current remuneration arrangements

ILLUSTRATION

This short case history concerns a particularly controversial aspect of the way in which advertising agencies are remunerated, which is explained in full in the main text.

The Jingle Kings on crusade

The Allen Brady & Marsh advertising agency was best known in the 1980s for 'that's the wonder of Woolies' for Woolworths and 'this is the age of the train' for British Rail. Rod Allen, who had a grand piano in his office, and Peter Marsh, a former actor with a penchant for white suits, had earned themselves the sobriquet *The Jingle Kings of EC4*.

The agency had its serious side, however. In 1982, it placed the following four-page advertisement in *Campaign* magazine to launch a crusade, on behalf of the whole business, against threats to one of the very cornerstones of professional practice:

'ABM won't let it crumble'
The pursuit of excellence or the pursuit of expedience?
ABM deplores the attacks on the 15% commission system. It is the only system that can adequately fund the true full service agency.

And the full service agency is the industry's most valuable resource.

The full service advertising agency is under attack.

Certain advertisers are putting pressure on agencies to cut the normal 15% commission.

And some agencies are giving in.

ABM says this is suicidal.

Agency profits are already slender.

Cut the commission and you cut the service the agency provides to its clients.

Inevitably, the agency's focus of attention is no longer directed to providing the best possible service; it is directed to providing whatever service *it can afford.*

This is the difference between the pursuit of excellence and the pursuit of expedience.

A risk business

The true full service agency is not a supplier.

It is a business partner.

It takes risks of a high order based on notional billings which will not necessarily be forthcoming.

Such a partner demands a reward that reflects such risks and allows for reinvestment in the future.

That basic reward is the 15% commission.

It has become the yardstick of all agency remuneration.

At ABM we are the premier example of the true full service agency.

We are also the most successful gatherer of new business.

We are constantly taking business from other agencies – including the largest ones.

In every case we find the service we give our clients is significantly greater in all aspects.

We assign a greater number of talented people together with a greater depth and range of service.

Moreover we find that these clients do in fact need this deep level of service.

To fund this service, we operate exclusively on the basis of the 15% commission system.

Fees are added where appropriate.

The 15% commission system allows us to deploy a full width of talent and capability against a single client meeting.

This enables a multitude of problems to be explored and resolved with only one client representative present.

These problems can range across Creative, Media, Promotion, Packaging, Research, Sales Force Organisation, Distribution and all aspects of agency service.

This adds up to the maximum economy and effective deployment of that client's time.

The agency provides the manpower that the client would have to provide if he were funding, developing and servicing that requirement from his own resource.

This method of compensation permits us to provide our clients with a service impossible under any other system. And permits us to reinvest at a satisfactory level.

(In fact, ABM reinvests all its profit. We do not pay management monies to Chicago or New York. We do not pay dividends to shareholders. We plough it all back into the business.)

Why 15%?

The commission system is akin to democracy or marriage.

It's not totally explainable but it works.

The commission system takes both client and agency through the heights and the troughs.

It frees us from the halting and wasteful taxi-meter principle and allows us to deploy generous resource on our clients' behalf on our own initiative.

It enables us to concentrate singlemindedly on defining and solving advertising problems without the stultifying effect of constant renegotiation.

The first recorded practice of this system was in 1819 when advertising agencies were principally media brokers.

At that time the commission percentage was 10%.

Gradually the agencies' services to their clients grew.

And as the services grew so did the commission percentage.

It levelled out at 15%.

The test of time

This figure was agreeable to both parties.

And it is a figure that has stood the test of time.

Many years of its application – and extensive discussion and experimentation in both America and Europe – have served only to emphasise its validity.

It is significant that even the 15% figure allows agencies an average of less than 2% net profit to turnover before tax, for reinvestment. (Source: IPA Annual Analysis of Agency Costs. 1981 Edition.)

Yet without reinvestment no agency – or any other business – can survive.

Principals at law

An agency is a principal at law.

We are legally liable for all money we spend on our clients' behalf.

Yet of every £100 we spend for a client we receive only £15 as income. And of those £15 we end up with less than £2 as a net profit.

To put this in perspective, the profit to an agency from a £1 million television campaign is less than the cost of one national 30 second peak television spot.

By no stretch of the imagination is this reward unreasonably high.

We believe a sound agency must have the 15% of the gross cost if it is to handle and capably spend the 85% on its clients' behalf.

If an agency does not receive that compensation, undesirable practices may arise in order to pump up income.

The COI threat

One of the advertisers attacking the commission system is the Central Office of Information.

John Bessant, the COI's Director of Advertising, is quoted in the March edition of *Newstime* as saying:

'Our objective is to spend as little as we can, consistent with good work. We are now having discussions with individual agencies and there will be adjustments to the present system.'

The impossible dream

We believe the COI is seeking the impossible dream.

Spending as little as you can is *never* consistent with good work.

Inevitably when an advertiser's stated priority is to spend as little as he can, then whether he likes it or not the work will deteriorate.

Unofficial subsidies

We believe that if the COI achieves this objective there will be an unpleasant side effect: COI work could be subsidised by the incumbent agency's other clients.

The honeyed words that lead to diminished profitability and diminished standards are familiar to the ear.

They invariably conjoin a cost cutting exercise with a higher sounding objective to show that the speaker is fair and true.

In this instance the honeyed words are: 'consistent with good work'.

Face to face dialogue we have had with the COI on the issue bears the supposition out.

Arm twisting

No-one knows better than ABM the way government works behind the scenes to 'twist arms'.

Could it be that the COI is in receipt of this arm twisting? Could it be that it has received a specific remit and the remit is 'cut costs'?

It is in the public interest that such question should be asked.

At ABM we do not intend to cut our costs at our clients' expense or at the expense of our own profitability or ability to invest.

Off the list

When the COI mooted their revision to the remuneration system of agencies, ABM took them off the list of prospects with whom we would like to work.

Indeed when ABM was recently approached by the COI so that an inspection could take place, ABM reiterated its trading procedures and practices and its adherence to the 15% commission system.

In fact, we declined to see them except on such a trading basis.

Mr Bill Claggett, Vice President for Advertising and Marketing Services of the Ralston Purina Company at the Marketing Week Conference on 'The Commission System' held in May 1979:

'Cost cutting should not be permitted if it seriously dilutes the quality of the agency service we receive. The money we save in reducing the relatively minor amount of dollars spent in agency commission can certainly be negated by a few share points decline in the market place.'

The lessons of history

History depressingly repeats itself.

Time and time again when a company permits a customer to cut the just level of compensation then that company either cuts the service it gives or goes out of business or both.

ABM will not cut the service it gives.

ABM will not cut the commission it receives.

Eyeball to eyeball

At ABM our advertising stands eyeball to eyeball with the consumer. So does our philosophy with our clients.

We believe that the demise of the commission system would lead to fewer agencies, inferior agencies and poorly serviced clients.

We are committed to a healthy advertising industry which will aid Britain's course for economic recovery.

ABM stands firmly by its philosophy, the Pursuit of Excellence, and the compensation system that allows it to flourish.

A year later, ABM resigned the £3.5 million B&Q account, because an agreement had been demanded which would reduce even further a profit margin already pared to the bone by the particular demands of retail advertising. The agency was at the time the country's sixth largest; not long after, it was no longer in business. It would be rough justice indeed if that were the result of their brave manifesto, however self-righteous its tone.

THE COMMISSION SYSTEM

The financial convention which the ABM advertisement defended in fact remains virtually unchanged today. The *media commission system of advertising agency remuneration* is an anachronism, but one with remarkable powers of survival. Ignorance of its complicated workings would leave a serious gap in the knowledge of anyone aspiring to genuine familiarity with the working relationship between advertisers and their agencies (the non-financial aspects of which are dealt with in Chapter 24).

There are two key words in the full description just given of what is generally called simply 'the commission system': *media* and *remuneration*. The first establishes the crucial fact that advertisers are reimbursed for the services they deliver to advertisers by the media owners, not by the advertisers themselves. This is an obvious paradox, requiring explanation. The second key word hints that agencies do not earn 'income' or receive 'revenue' in quite the same way as conventional businesses. The preferred American description, 'compensation', carries the same implication.

Media commission

Chapter 24 explains, in the section *Advertising Agencies*, that nineteenth-century proliferation of media choice provided an obvious opportunity for entrepreneurs to offer a problem solving service to the advertisers of the time. One group speculatively bought advertising space in bulk, and resold it in lots to advertisers at a marked-up price, along with 'free' advice on choice and frequency. By mid-century (ABM say as early as 1819), media owners had recognized their value as main customers, and were allowing them a fixed discount. What have always been called 'space brokers' thus became in effect *commission*-earning *sales agents* to the media owners. Shortly thereafter, in America, an index of all media owners' unit prices was published. The system thereby became transparent: brokers took to charging advertisers the list price; advertisers could check that it was exactly what they would have had to pay the media owner in any event. The latter were pleased to have work taken off their hands at no charge, the former content to subsidize the service actually given out of their commission discount.

The nineteenth-century space brokers imperceptibly evolved into twentieth-century advertising agencies. For instance, the records show that *Charles Barker*, who had acted as an intelligence agent for the Duke of Wellington, established himself as a space broker in London in the memorable year of 1812. A hundred and eighty years later, Charles Barker plc had advertising agencies in London, Birmingham, Edinburgh and Glasgow. Today, after a series of complex mergers and buy-outs, the founder's surname lives on within the BNB Resources group, in Barkers Recruitment Advertising and the Barkers Communications regional network. All descendants of the space brokers are still remunerated by a *media commission* discount that has since stabilized at 15 per cent, except in the case of some smaller newspapers and magazines, which offer only 10 per cent. Advertisers still check the price the agencies charged them for space, and now time, bought on their behalf against a published list, *BRAD* (British Rate & Data), a printed and online compendium of every media owner's *rate card*.

EXAMPLE 25.1

Client ABC delivers a brief to agency XYZ, and in due course approves XYZ's proposed media schedule. One item is a package of poster sites with a total '*rate card cost*' of £10,000. XYZ makes the booking, and sets about preparing the posters to occupy the spaces.

The campaign starts, and the media owner renders an invoice to XYZ for £10,000 minus *media commission* at 15% = £8,500. XYZ settles by the due date in the media sales contract, to avoid a reduction in the commission discount. It meanwhile bills ABC £10,000, the package price verifiable in BRAD.

Two special conditions need to be met if this system of remuneration is to work properly: that media owners restrict the 15 per cent discount to advertising agencies; and that only bona fide agencies receive it.

Non-expert observers often find it hard to believe that a media owner would in fact dare to refuse a demand for direct commission from an advertiser with the spending muscle of BT (£113,991,000 in 1996) or Kelloggs (£63,150,000), but the twin forces of historical precedent and professional etiquette have so far maintained that feature of the system intact.

For a long period in the history of the media commission system, the media owners collectively awarded 'recognition' to agencies that met certain criteria. A complex set of arguments precipitated by the appearance of 'media independents' in the 1970s (see Advertising Agencies, Chapter 24) resulted in the abandonment of a universal and exclusive 'recognition agreement'. The details are thoroughly reviewed by Brierley (1995, pp. 65–8). Nevertheless, media owners' sales contracts still require agencies to qualify for commission. For instance, those buying television time have to meet the criteria of the Independent Television Association's *Agency Registration and Credit Listing Committee*.

The Restrictive Practices Act of 1976 and an Office of Fair Trading (OFT) ruling in 1978 both declared this whole system of remuneration a monopolistic and anti-competitive business practice, the Sherman Anti-Trust Act having already done likewise in the USA in 1955. Yet it remains the norm in both countries today, despite uninformed assertions to the contrary, as survey evidence reported in the Fees section of this chapter demonstrates. Its inherent robustness derives mainly from the simple facts that it is easy to understand, easy to apply, and consistent, but also from vested interests. Media owners much prefer to deal with a relatively small number of large and regular customers – advertising agencies – than with a much greater number of sporadic and comparatively small ones – advertisers. Furthermore, they can exercise a particular form of financial control over agencies, as explained in the next section. Advertisers, too, are more likely to support the system than to undermine it, for they can put considerable pressure on their agency to absorb costs and subsidize extra services out of their media commission, 'as they always have', and suspect that a properly costed direct payment to the agency would cost them more than a commission-free open market. Only the advertising agencies, at the centre of the whole system, are disadvantaged by the system. The next section explains how.

Bad debts and cash-flow problems

Clearly, the successors to the space brokers are not exactly correct in describing themselves as *agencies* working for *clients*. Nor are they any longer sales agents to the media owners, however. In 1917, the legal case of Tranter versus Astor (Lord Astor, the publisher) established that British advertising agencies act as independent *principals*. That ruling was re-affirmed exactly 40 years later by Emmett versus DeWitt. Since principals enter into contracts on their own behalf, a crucial consequence of these rulings is that the 'agency' takes the financial risk. If it buys advertising space or time but its 'client' fails to reimburse it, for whatever reason, it remains liable for the *bad debt*. If a client has defaulted on account of bankruptcy, its agency will usually be low on the list of creditors. ABM was right to place so much emphasis on risk, though the advertisement does not exactly explain why.

A further consequence of the media commission system is a less dramatic but nonetheless insidious financial problems for agencies. If they do not settle media invoices by the due date, which is as early as two weeks *before* the advertising actually runs in the case of television time, the media owners begin to impose a progressive reduction in the percentage of the commission discount. This is a strong incentive to any agency to pay up promptly. However, its clients will adhere to the normal business practice, which is to settle up before the end of the month following the date of the invoice, at best, and quite possibly to wait for a statement or two before finally paying the bill. It is unlikely that they will consider any charge acceptable until they have seen evidence that their advertising has appeared (or is at least guaranteed to, if it is a television campaign) so pre-payment cannot be realistically expected. Meanwhile no realistic sanction against late payment is available to the agency; indeed, it risks antagonizing a valuable client by pressing for payment too firmly or frequently. Therefore, even if it renders its own invoice as early as it can, there will be a collection interval between payment to the media and reimbursement by the advertiser. Advertising agencies operate under constant threat of a cash-flow crisis.

The system which ABM defended so vigorously seems to work to an agency's disadvantage rather than in its interest, on the evidence so far.

Top-up fees

In the 1880s, the Philadelphia agency N W Ayer added *creative* advice and execution to the *media* advice and buying which had been subsidizing the cost from its media commission, and thereby set another potentially problematic precedent for later 'full-service' advertising agencies. A quirk of fate brought it together in a transatlantic merger with the first space broker, to form Ayer Barker. That venerable name, like its partner's, finally disappeared in a welter of mergers and de-mergers in the early 1990s.

During the first half of the twentieth century, developments in media drove production costs far above the levels with which Ayer had contended. Poster sites became much larger; the aspirations of cinema advertisers were raised beyond projected versions of static advertisements on theatre safety curtains; magazines and then newspapers began to print in colour; and then there was television. The price of space and time did not rise commensurately, for the media owners would thereby have priced themselves out of business, and agencies thus found themselves meeting escalating production costs out of commission that increased only with general price inflation and the extent to which they could persuade advertisers to spend more on advertising. Meanwhile, creative people were demanding ever higher salaries for their increasingly specialized skills. It had become clear that agencies with ambitious clients could no longer survive on media commission alone.

A new convention duly evolved, in the piecemeal manner that characterizes this outwardly dynamic but inwardly conservative business, that certain consequential costs could be charged direct to the client. They include studio fees, for example, but the list is far from definitive. A report on remuneration practices throughout Europe simply remarks that: 'The range of services provided at no charge will depend on each individual relationship. Where non-commissionable Agency services are charged (work done within the Agency), this is normally done on the basis of a prior estimate' (European Association of Advertising Agencies, 1994, p. 21). These are the fees 'added where appropriate' that the ABM advertisement mentions nonchalantly in passing.

Marking up

The increasing sophistication and cost of media production processes have also resulted in agencies routinely subcontracting some of them. On the basis of likely usage, they could hardly be expected to invest in a printing plant capable of handling poster work, for instance, nor to pay the salary of a top-flight commercials director. For the same general reasons that their client employs them, they in turn buy a share in outside expertise. Furthermore, logical extension of the full-service concept has led to agencies commissioning such non-advertising work as market research, packaging design, sales promotions or telesales campaigns on the client's behalf.

Another industry convention has evolved that these particular kinds of cost are not simply passed on. A guidance document published by the IPA says 'consideration will need to be given to which of the following items will be charged for', appends a list which contains such diverse items as 'photography and model fees' and 'printwork', and recommends a clause in the agency contract to the effect that the client will pay 'the net cost of all these materials and services purchased for you, plus X% of such net cost' (Institute of Practitioners in Advertising, 1986). Thus a standard *mark-up* is routinely added to the agency's *buying price* in order to arrive at its *selling price* to the client. This convention replaces the obvious alternative of accumulating actual on-costs and adding a notional handling fee.

The key point about this standard, constant percentage is that it produces an equation which makes the agency's revenue the same as it would have been if the supplier's bill had in fact been discounted by 15 per cent. In other words, it derives absolutely directly from the media commission convention. The question is, what is the mark-up that equates to that discount?

EXAMPLE 25.2

Client ABC instructs agency XYZ to supply promotional calendars at a competitive price. XYZ finds a capable supplier at a favourable price, and places the order. The supplier delivers the goods and invoices the agency £850. XYZ invoices ABC, adding enough to £850 to be the equivalent of having received a 15% discount.

We know from Example 25.1, moving the decimal point, that the eventual charge has to be £1,000. The required mark-up is therefore £150. Our calculator tells us that 150 is 17.6470% of 850. Rounding off, we conclude that the amount of XYZ's invoice to ABC needs to be the amount of the supplier's invoice plus 17.65%.

To double-check the equation: $(0.1765 \times 850) + 850 = 1000.025$, which is quite close enough.

So XYZ renders an invoice to ABC for £1,000.03, in practice rounded down to £1,000, which reimburses the price paid on ABC's behalf and compensates XYZ for the work it did in arranging and delivering this instance of a full-service extra.

Thus, the 'X%' referred to in the contract clause suggested by the IPA is 17.65 per cent. This remarkably precise figure is confirmed by the European Association of Advertising Agencies (1994, p. 21): 'In addition to the Agency retaining 15% on the gross media billings, it is normal practice for all production and other outside purchases which are billable to be charged at cost plus 17.65%.'

Rebating

One crucial consequence of all advertising agencies being remunerated in the same way is that they are restricted in their efforts to compete with one another largely to the non-price dimensions of the service they offer. However, as a ploy to win new business or to retain a client showing signs of moving elsewhere, some will offer 'commission rebating' deals. That is what ABM say they will never do, in an impassioned attack on rebating which manages not to use the term itself. Alternatively, the impetus may come from the client, as in the case of the 'COI threat' that figures so prominently in the ABM advertisement.

This mechanism is regularly described by the trade press and textbooks in terms implying that it works in a way which is in fact impossible. Press reports say agencies have agreed to 'hand back' some of their commission to a client. ABM speak of 'pressure on agencies to cut the normal commission'. Yet the commission, as discussed, is not a payment but a privilege discount on a published list price, given to agencies by media owners. It follows, then, that agencies cannot do the 'cutting', that there is no actual sum of money to be 'handed' to anyone, and that it could in any case be handed 'back' only to the party who allowed it in the first place. Furthermore, there would be no incentive to the client in the agency receiving a reduced commission discount from the media owner.

Textbooks are not immune to illogical descriptions of the process. A recent American example claims that few advertisers there 'still pay a 15% commission' and that, consequently, 'the agency's fee is less than 15 per cent'. Advertisers do not 'pay' commission and their 'fees' are, as seen, either a top-up amount rather than a proportion of something else or a mark up of 17.65 per cent, not 15 per cent. Such mistakes are not simply careless, but downright misleading. Beware!

EXAMPLE 25.3

Agency XYZ offers a 3% *commission rebate* to client ABC.

It subsequently buys advertising time costing £10,000 on ABC's behalf, and in due course receives an invoice from the media owner for £8,500. XYZ in turn renders an invoice to ABC for £10,000 minus 3% = £9,700.

XYZ thereby earns £9,700 minus £8,500 = £1,200 instead of £1,500.

The 'rebate' is in fact a second discount in the transaction, which *has the effect of* reducing the agency's commission earnings. 'Commission rebating' is an entirely inaccurate description, for the 15 per cent discount from the media owners remains intact.

This practice is perennially controversial. Indeed, it was one of the motives for setting up a forerunner of the IPA, some 60 years before ABM took their stand against it. The key reason for concern is the effect on the bottom line of an agency's profit-and-loss account. On the face of it, the 3 per cent discount is hardly generous. Shoppers would not see it as a bargain at the sales, and traders will often take off 5 per cent for cash in hand. However, three is a fifth of 15 per cent. XYZ's apparently minor concession to ABC will thus have brought about a 16.7 per cent reduction in profit margin on that particular transaction. At the same time, the media owner's revenue is exactly the same as it would have been without rebating, and ABC is £300 better off.

Given that an advertising agency's net profit before tax is typically around 2 per cent of turnover, according to the survey reported in the ABM advertisement, and seldom if ever more than 5 per cent according to current general opinion, it should come as no surprise that so many have landed themselves in a serious financial predicament by practising rebating. On the other hand, it has to be conceded that others have, like ABM, suffered equally by losing clients as a result of refusing to do so.

An agency which does rebate must make up for loss of revenue in some way, such as by: cutting corners on creative work for the client; recommending unnecessarily expensive media schedules; proposing more add-on services; claiming more top-up fees; reducing the level of account handling service; or cross-subsidizing from other accounts. Clients who demand rebates thus commit themselves to a game of swings and roundabouts. Furthermore, smaller advertisers will suffer most when rebating is widespread. If an agency enters into a rebating arrangement with a powerful client, standards will be maintained on that account at the expense of the less valuable ones in the agency's portfolio. The net outcome can only be long-term damage to the advertising business as a whole.

It seems clear enough that there is a compelling case against commission rebating, but there is a counter-argument. The crux is the amount paid to media owners in any particular case. The creative and administrative effort an agency must put into a £10 million national television campaign is not a hundred times greater than that required for a £100,000 poster campaign, let alone a thousand times more than would be demanded by £10,000-worth of advertising in local newspapers. Yet the corresponding commission earnings are £1.5 million, £15,000 and £1,500. On this basis, it is not unreasonable to expect agencies to be satisfied with a level of recompense that diminishes pro-rata as spending increases. If an agency arranges that by charging a client less than the list price of media bought, this logic says, it has merely reduced its service charge to an amount commensurate with the work actually done. The debate is likely to continue.

Meanwhile, in France, a parliamentary bill proposed in 1992 that advertising agencies should actually be agents to advertisers, not principals, and that media owners should pay all discounts of any sort direct to advertisers. In other words, the media commission system would disappear altogether and agencies would be remunerated (presumably) by client fees. A year later, the *Loi Sapin* legislation included amendments reprieving media commission but requiring financial dealings among the three parties to be more transparent than before in a number of ways. A pan-European survey conducted during 1993 found that French advertisers were the most likely to support commission against fees (along with German and Japanese), and that French agencies were the most likely to rebate (European Association of Advertising Agencies, 1994). Plus ça change.

THE FULL-FEE ALTERNATIVE

Although 'space brokers' such as Charles Barker are the identifiable ancestors of modern advertising agencies, it is known that other entrepreneurs had already been selling general expertise to advertisers at a price. They did not buy from the media owners speculatively or in bulk, but earned their living entirely from their fees. After the middle of the nineteenth century, this mode of operation was swamped by the media commission convention. In recent years, however, journalists and other commentators have regularly asserted that payment by fee has made a comeback to the extent that the commission system is 'dying', if not already dead. In 1993, a new advertising agency closely identified with the Advertising Woman of the Year for 1990 proclaimed that it would be 'dispensing with the traditional commission-plus-fees system' in favour of a single fee reflecting 'values and a cost around the development of ideas in advance of advertising execution'. The trade press reported a sceptical reaction from the client side of the fence: 'On the evidence presented so far, I'm not convinced that anything really new is on offer.'

The fee system has the obvious attraction that it reflects the pragmatic realities of the 'agency–client' relationship rather than the legal reality that the agency is in fact a principal in a contractual relationship with the media. However, the commission system has four strong characteristics in its favour: it has a historical pedigree; it is a standard practice; it is generally understood in the business; it is easily put into practice. Furthermore, advertisers and media owners both have a vested interest in its retention. The former suspect that any fee arrived at by a calculation of overheads, production costs and profit margins would come to more than 15 per cent of media bills plus chargeable extras. The latter appreciate the control it gives them over their own cash flow, as explained in the section *Bad debts and cash-flow problems*. The net outcome is considerable inertia in the system.

If an agency nevertheless challenged the status quo, it would face a number of pragmatic obstacles to implementation of a full-fee arrangement:

- Media owners would still give it the commission discount, automatically.
- The fee would need to be calculated carefully, and reviewed periodically.
- A new internal data-handling system would probably be needed.
- The fee would either have to be based on forecasts, or received in arrears.
- It would have to be renegotiated at each new budget period.
- Clients would exert strong downward pressure ('rebating' again, in effect).
- Agencies would get into price wars.

So far, institutional inertia and perceived procedural problems have combined forces to overcome the philosophical superiority of a fee payment system. Thirty years ago, media commission accounted for three-quarters of advertising agency revenue, according to the Institute of Practitioners in Advertising. Ten years ago, stockbrokers James Capel said that 'the proportion of agency income sourced purely from fees' was 30.5 per cent. Table 25.1 presents the results of a pan-European survey of practice in 1992, conducted during 1993 (European Association of Advertising Agencies, 1994). The relevant findings are that the much heralded full-fee remuneration system accounted for only 18 per cent of all responses from 16 multinational 'network advertising agencies', slightly higher than the figure of 16 per cent in a comparable survey three years before. (On the face of it, the difference

Table 25.1 Agency Remuneration Practices in Europe

Method	% of agencies using in 1989	% of agencies using in 1992
Fixed commission	60	49
Rebated commission	16	17
Fixed fees	16	18
Actual cost plus margin	3	3
Commission plus fees	3	5
Other arrangements	2	8

(*Source*: extracted from European Association of Advertising Agencies (1994), pp. 5–7)

represents a third of an agency.) All forms of remuneration involving media commission were collectively practised by 71 per cent, compared with 78 per cent in 1989. Reports of its death are, as they say, highly exaggerated.

The report also concluded that advertisers with variable advertising expenditure from one year to the next tended to pay their agencies fees, whereas a relatively stable pattern correlated with arrangements that included a substantial commission component. High-spending advertisers were apparently content for their agencies to be remunerated mainly by media commission (presumably so that pressure to rebate could be exerted).

SUMMARY AND CONCLUSION

The commission system of advertising agency remuneration is an anachronism with remarkable powers of survival. Under its terms, an advertising agency is paradoxically rewarded by a commission discount from media owners for most of the total service it renders to an advertiser. Direct fees are additionally charged for some internal services, and the price of subcontracted work is marked up by an amount that is arithmetically related to the media commission discount. The system operates to the advantage of advertisers and media owners, not agencies. The misleadingly named 'commission rebating' is a competitive ploy which weakens agencies even further. Despite popular opinion to the contrary, there is no real evidence that a full-fee system of remuneration is gaining ground significantly.

The predicted death of the commission system will require a seismic force in business, which seems likely in Britain only if the IPA, ISBA and half-a-dozen bodies representing media owners can find common ground and agree terms.

WORKSHEET

In lieu of the customary *Discussion Topics* and *Case Study*, there now follow six practical exercises, by means of which to test personal achievement of the learning objectives listed at the start of this Chapter. ABC and XYZ do not correspond to their namesakes in the worked examples given earlier. Answers are given after the references (no cheating!).

Exercise 1

The ABC Agency places media orders on behalf of its client XYZ to a total rate-card value of £66,224.

1.1   Calculate the amount ABC pays the media owners concerned, in total, showing your workings.

1.2   Explain how the agency profits from the transaction.

Exercise 2

2.0   Identify five key assumptions you must have made in the course of Exercise 1 (come back to this exercise, if necessary).

Exercise 3

Client XYZ directs ABC to carry out a before-and-after attitude survey among the target audience for a forthcoming campaign. ABC subcontracts the task to the DEF market research company, and receives an invoice for £10,997 with their final report.

3.1   Calculate the amount ABC should charge XYZ when it delivers DEF's findings to them, showing your workings.
3.2   Is there any difference between £10,997 and your answer to 3.1? If so, why?
3.3   What is the correct term for that difference?

Exercise 4

XYZ suspects ABC of over-charging them by invoicing £18,500 for a full-page space in the *Radio Times*.

4.0   How can they find out if they're right or wrong, without confronting ABC?

Exercise 5

In 1997, the total 'billings' of ABC Advertising were £38.6 million. This defines the total amount they were instructed to spend by their client throughout the course of the year.

5.1   Estimate the value of the media commission they received over the year, showing your assumptions and calculations.
5.2   Estimate the amount they paid to subcontractors for non-advertising services, showing your workings.

Exercise 6

Under pressure from XYZ, which is their largest client, ABC agrees to a two-and-a-half per cent commission rebate during 1997. By the end of the year, they will have spent £16 million on buying poster sites, television time and space in the major women's magazines.

6.1   How will XYZ receive this rebate?
6.2   What fraction of their commission revenue will ABC thereby sacrifice?

REFERENCES

Brierley, S. (1995) *The Advertising Handbook*, London: Routledge, Chapters 7 and 9.
European Association of Advertising Agencies (1994) *Client/Advertising Agency Partnerships in the New Europe*, Henley-on-Thames: NTC Publications.
Institute of Practitioners in Advertising (1986) *Some Suggested Provisions for Use in Agency/Client Agreements*, London: Institute of Practitioners in Advertising.

ANSWERS TO THE WORKSHEET EXERCISES

Exercise 1

1.1   66,224 minus [15% of 66,224] = 66,224 − 9,933.60 = 56,290.40 = £56,290 to the nearest pound, before VAT. It's very unlikely that firms dealing in tens of thousands of pounds would bill one another to the nearest penny.

1.2   By charging XYZ the full rate-card price: as simple as that.

Exercise 2

2.0.1   That ABC qualifies for the current equivalents of *recognition*; if not, it is ineligible for the media commission discount.

2.0.2   That ABC is paying the standard *rate card cost*. There might have been *surcharges* (e.g. for specifying a particular page, or a specific time of day) or *discounts* (e.g. for volume bookings).

2.0.3   That the commission is 15 per cent in all cases. Some magazines and regional or local newspapers offer only 10 per cent, but 15 is the overwhelming norm.

2.0.4   That ABC pays the media invoices promptly enough to avoid the commission rate being reduced as a penalty for late payment.

2.0.5   That XYZ doesn't default altogether, leaving ABC to pay the bills itself, as the *principal* in the contract with the media owners.

Exercise 3

3.1   10,997 plus [17.65% of 10,997] = 10,997 + 1940.97 = £12,937.97, or £12,938 to the nearest pound.

3.2   Because of the *convention* that ABC deserves to be recompensed for the incidental costs and staff time involved in setting up and managing this subcontracted service. A second *convention* is that this is achieved by XYZ paying a surcharge which brings the price of the service up to what it would have been if £10,997 were the amount paid after a discount of 15 per cent from the supplier. Thus, 12,937.97 minus [15% of 12,937.97] = 12,937.97 − 1940.70 = 10,997. 27, which gets the value back to where it started, give or take a few pence.

3.3   The *mark-up*.

Exercise 4

4.0   By looking up the *rate-card cost* in BRAD (*British Rate & Data*). The price is in fact correct; advertising is expensive.

Exercise 5

5.1   Notice that the description of *billings* does not define the figure as money spent on media buying only, which is in line with normal usage in the business. A convenient assumption, based on data in the text, would be that media commission typically accounts for about 70 per cent of an agency's total billings, the remainder being made up of *mark-ups* on non-media subcontracted services (such as the one in Exercise 3) and *fees*. Thus, the commissionable portion of their billings can be estimated as 70 per cent of the total, or £27,020,000. Making the same further assumptions as in Exercise 1, total commission over the year would be 15 per cent of that amount, which is £4,053,000.

5.2   Since there is no evidence how much of the other 30 per cent was mark-ups and how much was fees, you can either make an assumption or state your answer as 'less than'. The non-commissionable total is £11.6 million, or £11,580,000.

Exercise 6

6.1   In the form of a *discount* on the invoices they receive from ABC for the media time and space bought on their behalf.

6.2   Two and a half per cent is a *sixth* of 15 per cent.

26

MEASURING THE SUCCESS RATE: EVALUATING THE MARKETING COMMUNICATIONS PROCESS AND MARCOM PROGRAMMES

Douglas R. Eadie and Philip J. Kitchen

CHAPTER AIMS

- To present a model to evaluate the marcoms process and its unique functions
- To consider evaluation from a strategic perspective in the planning and execution stages
- To suggest ways in which marketing research could interact with marcoms planning and execution in the marcoms process

ILLUSTRATION: 'PUTTING A VIMTO SMILE ON THE NATION'S FACE'

The strategy

'What we came up with initially was the Vimto smile. What Vimto's research among loyal drinkers told us was that drinking Vimto gives you a feeling of inner contentment and brings back happy memories of childhood. Even adults who had not grown up with it said the same. In addition to the 'smiley' feeling Vimto gives you, when you drink Vimto cordial you are left with a purple smile around your mouth – just like a smile.

'Once we had decided on the Vimto Smile, we felt we should attach it to a person or a celebrity to be the vehicle for the campaign. Purple Ronnie, the cartoon poet, internationally famous for his greetings cards, was perfect. His name echoes the product and he embodies two of Vimto's core values – he is both an individual and he is completely carefree. Best of all, he is very popular with teenagers and as he has never been involved with advertising before, Vimto could 'own' him completely.

'The next step was to take the advertising to research groups which consisted of cordial purchasers and drinkers – mums and young children and carbonate drinkers – teenagers. They agreed with everything we had already thought – that Purple Ronnie appeals to the inner child in everyone and has the innate inoffensive humour of children. They also loved the risqué nature of the ads – children could identify with the cheeky humour and mums knew it was just the kind of harmless, playground fun that they remembered from their own childhood and could still appreciate' (Mark Humphreys, Account Planning Director at Cheetham Bell)

What really thrilled us was that loyal users loved the ads and so did those who had never tasted Vimto. We had achieved exactly what we set out to do – retain the existing customer base and appeal to new consumers, including the tricky teenage group.

Television advertisements were shown in Summer (1997) and were supported with tabloid advertising, 48 sheet poster sites, and limited edition Purple Ronnie packaging on all the product variants.

We wanted to get everyone talking about the campaign and we certainly caused a stir. Purple Ronnie's Summer poem was the first commercial 'botty burp' on TV! Our tactical advertising was also very influential. For example, on the day the *Sun* started its 'Silicon-free Page Three' campaign, a Vimto Purple Ronnie poem about cosmetic surgery appeared on the same page.

The results

The response to the advertising was phenomenal with nearly two and a half million more people buying the drink according to independent researchers, Audience Selection. Since the start of the campaign brand awareness increased by a massive 50%. 20% more people claim they will definitely buy Vimto and a quarter more now describe Vimto as a 'fun brand'.

These changes clearly show that advertising, coupled with other forms of promotional activity have clearly created a massive amount of brand awareness and interest. While the campaign was a complete departure from anything done by Vimto before, marketing management believe that the secret to 'success' was that the ads clearly stood out in one of the noisiest most cluttered market places around. Viewers remembered the TV adverts after seeing them once – where simultaneously they found it difficult to remember other soft drink brands' ads. Not only was Purple Ronnie recalled, but also the brand he was endorsing.

Notably, quality – both of the product and the promotion is what clearly increased volume sales. No benefits can accrue if products or promotion miss the mark, irrespective of £m's expended. For Vimto, promotion – spearheaded by advertising – was exactly right. As a result the company witnessed an increase in sales volume of 33% from Summer 1997 to December.

(*Source*: 'Putting a Vimto Smile on the Nation's Face', Vimto Soft Drinks, in *CIM Executive Briefing*, Northern Region, Chartered Institute of Marketing, Leeds, p. 4, used with permission.)

INTRODUCTION

As seen in the above case vignette, the marketing communications process is an ongoing attempt by companies to creatively match company resources with the needs, wants and desires of target markets to create exchanges that satisfy. This chapter seeks to evaluate how successful or otherwise marketing communications as a process can be, and to indicate how to evaluate individual marcoms programmes. Almost inevitably, an understanding of how research methods are used in the marcoms domain will serve to provide useful insights into this subject.

Marketing research can be defined as 'the function which links the consumer, customer, and public to the marketer through information. This information is used to identify and define marketing opportunities and problems; generate, refine, and evaluate marketing actions; monitor marketing performance; and improve understanding of marketing as a process' (Tull and Hawkins, 1993). As seen throughout this text, evaluating target audiences prior to, during, and after exposure to promotional messages is crucial for firms to grow and develop. From the perspective of the initial case vignette in conjunction with the Tull and Hawkins definition, evaluation of promotion as a process, and in terms of its individual components, can be viewed from a pragmatic problem-solving perspective, with information serving as a guide to develop strategic marcoms options and facilitate decision making. Implicit within this developmental process is the need not only to understand target audiences and the factors which shape and modulate their attitudinal responses, but also the requirement to utilize methodologies that take into consideration marcoms decision-making processes. From this perspective, evaluation of marcoms can in essence provide a matching process in terms of discerning 'best fit' criteria between senders, messages, medias and receivers while simultaneously providing scope for analysis of encoding, decoding, response, feedback and noise (Kotler, 1997). The two main areas from an evaluation perspective are *promotional research* and *media research*. As seen in the Vimto case, prior to developing a promotional message spearheaded by advertising, it was necessary to understand the potential effects of the communication in relation to specific target audiences. Promotional research is concerned with the message and content, and has attracted significant interest. Media research, while sometimes subsumed under the broader heading, is concerned with channel(s) selection and has received less attention (Bovee *et al.*, 1995). This chapter focuses on evaluation as a crucial element in continuous and ongoing interactions with target audiences.

THE EVALUATION MODELS

The research models encompassed by the evaluative process are conceptualized in Figures 26.1 and 26.2. Typically, these figures represent the decision-making sequence that marketers may go through in developing and evaluating a promotional campaign and the research methods that are available to inform the types of decisions involved at each stage. The models do not, and cannot, provide an approach for effective promotion, nor do they address the issue of how promotion works. What they do do is recognize that promotion can work in different ways in terms of objectives, messages and media and hence may require appropriate research methodologies to drive their development and lead to effective evaluation.

Both figures are intended as a research-based evaluative model born out of a necessity to make decisions oriented to consumer need and organize efficient allocation of research resources. Both these applications are of significant value in planning promotional campaigns. Two general points can be noted. One, the model represents an ideal research scenario, but limited planning cycles and budgets usually lead to some type of compromise. This can lead to 'telescoping' or the use of one piece of research to inform a number of stages in the decision-making process. For

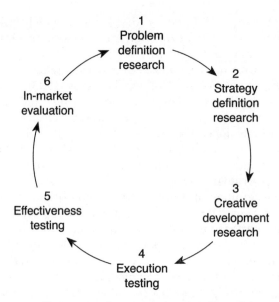

Figure 26.1 Promotional research model.

example, research delayed until the creative development phase may be used to inform strategic and tactical decisions. Secondly, and as highlighted in Chapters 4 and 5, the model is not intended to act as a substitute or proxy for marcoms decision making. In this sense, given limited understanding of how both creativity and marcoms *actually work*, promotional research can, at best, aim to reduce the uncertainties involved in creating and applying marcoms. From a managerial perspective, research can be seen as a disastrous substitute for judgement, since effective marketing communications emerges not just from insight generated from research, but also the creativity, judgement and knowledge base of the people involved (Bovee *et al.*, 1995). Given the recognized need to exercise judgement, use of promotional research methods to guide such judgement needs to be handled with great sensitivity, particularly where the merits of a creative approach are being argued, and a creative team have committed extensive time and energy to the process.

From a marcoms perspective, most firms place significant emphasis on all six stages in order to maximize returns on production, and media investments. Admittedly, the sixth stage is regarded as the most difficult, especially from an advertising, sponsorship or marketing public relations perspective as so many other variables can intervene. For these reasons, evaluating promotional performance is perhaps the most important, yet most unsettled, area of marketing communications. The model presented in Figures 26.1 and 26.2 is dependent for application upon managerial decision making in relation to what to measure?; whether or not to test?; when to test?; and which test is best? For details of the tests involved for each area of promotion, Burnett's (1993) text is a useful starter, though most authors fall short of measuring promotional outcomes from an integrated perspective – i.e. involving all elements of the marketing mix (see Chapter 7).

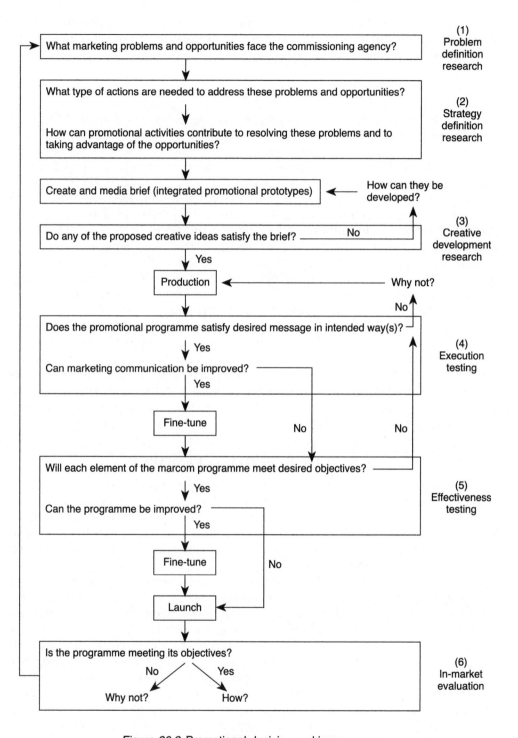

Figure 26.2 Promotional decision-making process.

However, if the model is taken as an idealized conceptualization, as descriptive, not prescriptive, then there is a basis for effective evaluation of both the process and each individual component.

PROBLEM DEFINITION RESEARCH

Problem definition research, sometimes referred to as formative research, typically aims to provide an objective knowledge base for strategic decision making and, in so doing, to avoid a purely reactive approach to such decision making (Flay and Burton, 1990; Atkin, 1990). This area of research/evaluation is considered by marketers to be the most important stage in the marcoms process, on the grounds that effectiveness of decisions taken at later stages of a campaign development are dependent on the decisions that precede them. In promotional terms, this can mean, for example, that brilliant adverting execution will be of little value if the advertising is trying to send the wrong message to the wrong people.

One way to avoid inappropriate messages being sent to the wrong target group is to commission exploratory consumer research. Although not necessarily inappropriate, a more effective way forward, particularly where familiarity with the topic area is limited, is to first conduct an environmental analysis (see Chapters 5, 8 and 13). This involves analysing both internal and external environments. This may mean revising existing business policy or marcoms approaches policy and consolidating what is already known about the topic by assimilating and analysing secondary data and consulting with experts on the topic area. This analysis can then be used as a framework to develop proposals for research with consumers and professionals as appropriate, in order to address identified gaps in knowledge or pursue areas of particular interest.

STRATEGY DEFINITION RESEARCH

Having defined the dynamics of the problem, strategy definition research builds on these findings by identifying and assessing available options for intervention. This stage usually requires a combination of secondary and primary research methods, the former to identify, where available, tested strategies which may be applicable, and the latter, to explore with stakeholders the suitability, feasibility, acceptability and affordability of proposed strategies.

Specifically regarding marketing communications, strategy definition research can be of value at two levels of decision making. Firstly, it addresses the key question, what role does marcoms have?, should it be an independent exercise?, for example involving, say, advertising, or should a more integrated programme be developed involving all promotional mix elements? Evidence presented within this text suggests that marcoms is more likely to be effective when developed in an integrated fashion which in turn can have a more significant impact when combined possibly with corporate or public relations activities, including community level interventions, particularly when changes sought are of a complex nature (see Vimto case vignette; and Redman *et al.*, 1990; Bettighaus, 1988; Pasick and Wallack, 1989; Drobis, 1997–8; Schultz, 1997–8; Schultz, 1998; van Raaij, 1998).

Research can address the question of which strategy will maximize effectiveness. To do this requires answering a number of questions which include: what are the communication objectives?; what is the central campaign message and tone of voice?; who is the target audience?; which media provide the best combination of coverage and reach, and are best suited to carrying the message?; what developmental and evaluation procedures should be built into the programme?; and what budget and time frame is required to achieve desired outcomes?

Setting objectives

When arriving at a preferred strategy, the ability to determine its effectiveness once implemented requires the setting of appropriate aims and objectives. Failure to set objective criteria and standards of judgement *before* the campaign runs can result in subjectivity creeping into later stages of evaluation (Elliott, 1990). This task is central to the strategic decision-making process but has been fiercely debated for many years in the commercial sector (Flay and Burton, 1990; Atkin, 1990). This debate has tended to centre round the problems of attributing outcomes to the marcom components of the marketing plan. With the noted exception of direct response adverting campaigns, personal selling and sales promotion, behavioural or sales effects can be difficult to attribute to advertising, sponsorship or marketing public relations, since ultimate brand choice is dependent on other variables such as price, product performance and availability (the non-promotional variables of the marketing mix). Traditionally, therefore, where outcome measures have been taken, these have typically focused on measuring intermediate effects such as campaign exposure, recall and appreciation of messages, and impact on brand recognition and attitude. These problems of attribution are a continuing issue in the field of integrated marketing communications, despite its seeming desirability, since behaviour can be affected by so many other factors. However, given the significant challenge of modifying or changing behaviour, the effects, say, of advertising, on its own for example, in many cases is likely to be negligible. As a result, outcome measures tend to focus on intermediate effects, which include: raising discussion and debate; prompting requests for information; increasing awareness and salience of health topics; changing knowledge and beliefs; and reinforcing existing attitudes and behaviour (Pasick and Wallack, 1989; Schlinger, 1976). Setting specific objectives in each of these areas probably provides, for the time being, the best means by which to manage future integrated approaches to marcoms and its evaluation.

Commissioning

The research commissioning process is particularly significant at both the problem and strategy definition stages, since the development of methodologies that enable marketers to set appropriate objectives and to design strategies that will achieve them is concerned not only with issues of research design, but also with the means by which generated data can be successfully integrated into decision-making and planning processes. Thus, the ultimate value of research in this area is dependent on the ability of the commissioning agency to utilize research findings to help inform and guide marcoms strategy. Achieving this requires not only analytical skills but also management skills in incorporating into decision making the different insights that external agencies can bring to the task. Such agencies might include independent research consultants and, where appropriate, advertising, public relations, direct marketing and other agency account planners. Central to managing their input is developing a shared understanding between the agencies involved of their respective roles and responsibilities, and in clarifying at the outset research aims and objectives and how these will contribute to development of ultimate marcoms strategy. Where commissioning agencies require research to go beyond the presentation of findings and their possible implications for future action, to actually applying the data to setting objectives and developing strategy, it is essential that the researcher be equipped to undertake this task through access to the appropriate information and personnel. Commissioning agencies purchasing this latter type of product can usefully draw distinctions between consultancy and research, the ultimate value of which can be dependent on the knowledge base and expertise of the research consultancy awarded the contract. Significantly, it is important to recognize that defining the problem and identifying a strategy to address it are two separate tasks, since failure to do so can result in subjectivity influencing strategy selection. Where operational constraints mean that problem and strategy definition research are conducted simultaneously or overlap, then sharing and comparing findings from the two data collection exercises as they emerge is vital if strategy is to address identified need.

The outcome of the problem and strategy definition phase would typically be to set in motion a number of interlocking initiatives, each developing different aspects of the proposed intervention, which together provide a cohesive marcoms strategy. This chapter now goes on to examine the procedures used in marketing that are peculiar to developing marcoms.

CREATIVE DEVELOPMENT RESEARCH

Creative development research, sometimes referred to as concept or proposition testing, is research undertaken to guide the message component of a communication strategy. It is conducted once the strategy has been agreed and some initial creative ideas have been generated, but before any finished advertising, for example, is produced, and should not be confused with pre-testing, which is research undertaken on advertising that is ostensibly complete. Hence, in this sense, while much of pre-testing is concerned with assessing communication and offering guidance on aspects of execution, creative development research aims to assess the extent to which core creative ideas are capable of gaining the desired response from an audience and building an understanding of the responses that arise so that it is possible to see how to develop and improve those ideas (Stewart-Hunter, 1990). Thus, it is not simply concerned with testing creative ideas and approaches, but also using these as stimuli to develop hybrids. This can result in undertaking several stages of fieldwork, if this is possible, before an appropriate concept and mode of communication can be determined. This approach illustrates the mediating role of research, with the audience responding to the views and assumptions of the advertiser encapsulated in the proposed advertising approach and the advertiser, in turn, responding to the audience's own views and the factors that shape them, in the form of revised proposals. For this reason, this type of research is more appropriately described as a developmental than a testing procedure. For this process to be effective, however, requires a range and variety of creative options to stimulate consumer feedback. Researching only one creative idea runs the risk of 'rail-roading', with respondents opting to promote it in the absence of any alternatives against which it can be compared and its relative value assessed.

This process of building an understanding of the target audience and the factors that shape it is of value in virtually all aspects of message construction. There are, however, a number of methodological issues that need to be considered, most notably, how to obtain feedback on ideas which essentially exist within the mind of personnel within, say, an agency's or company's creative department. The problem is commonly solved by developing marcom prototypes, in advertising, sometimes referred to as 'roughs', to convey creative ideas. Developing prototype materials for press and poster is relatively straightforward; however, with moving media such as television and cinema, the prototype options are more diverse, ranging from simple scripts with written descriptions of the intended action and storyline, through to the development of sophisticated animatics and photomatics which convey the visual sequence and soundtrack on video-tape at the actual pace of the proposed production. The choice of prototype can vary according to available time and resources, and the complexity of the creative ideas. Yet, all prototypes, no matter what their production qualities, can, if handled with sensitivity, act as useful stimuli for examining audience relationships with the problem area. Crucially, although all prototypes, in using some degree of elaboration in order to convey the concept, can provide feedback on aspects of communication, it is vital to bear in mind that the primary purpose of this type of research, at least at the early stages, is to examine the appeal and relevance of creative ideas and *not* necessarily the methods of communicating them. However, as ideas are distilled and refined, greater emphasis can be given to specific aspects of communication at the latter stages of the creative development phase.

Practitioners using these research procedures need to guard against the risk of miscommunication posed by using prototypes, where the translation of the creative idea in the mind of the respondent is less 'controllable' than with finished material (Butterfield, 1990). This can lead to judgements as to the value of creative ideas varying in accordance with individual respondents' interpretation of the creative's intention. At the most fundamental level, there is a risk of respondents rejecting, say, an advertising or marketing public relations approach on the grounds of the prototype materials' low production qualities, a particular problem with creative ideas that are dependent on factors such as image and humour which can require higher production qualities in order for them to be fully understood and appreciated.

To avoid these pitfalls, qualitative focus groups are normally used since the interactive approach allows researchers to identify and compensate for variations in interpretation and to actively use these variations as stimuli to establish alternative conceptual approaches. In addition to identifying variations in interpretation, the group dynamic can be used to tap into consumer creativity and language, both of which are of value in guiding subsequent execution.

Finally, consideration might also be given to the management implications of conducting this type of research. Considerable underlying tensions exist in this area of decision making, with commissioners concerned to ensure that highly creative approaches are not adopted at the expense of achieving the desired communication outcomes, while personnel within an agency's creative department are understandably concerned that research does not serve to stifle and undermine the creative process. These tensions are compounded by the convergence of what has been described as two distinct cultures: 'the logical, deductive, realistic, evaluative approach of the researcher and the more intuitive, lateral, impersonistic and subtle approach of creative persons' (Butterfield, 1990). The role of the commissioning agency is to harness and combine these skills. This requires particular sensitivity, with the decision as to who conducts the research crucial. Two developmental routes are typically taken – either give responsibility for development to agency account planners or commission an independent research agency to support the creative process. Although the independent researcher is often better positioned to bring a greater degree of objectivity to decision making, the account planner is often more familiar with the requirements and limitations of the advertising, and is better equipped to translate research findings into a form that will be of assistance to the creative team. One solution to capitalizing on the strengths of both researcher and account planner is to adopt a 'team' approach; commissioning an independent research agency with the appropriate range of skills to conduct research at all stages of campaign development. This can serve to build both familiarity with the problem area and trust between team members; however, to maintain the integrity of the research, care needs to be taken to ensure that the creative ideas and resulting campaign remains the property of both the advertising and commissioning agencies. Crucially, commissioning research to act as an arbiter between agencies and commissioners, when disagreements emerge over the most appropriate creative approaches, almost invariably serves to worsen relations and undermine any trust that has been built up. At the very least, commissioners are best served by agreeing a programme of research with the agencies at the strategy definition phase.

EXECUTION TESTING

Research and evaluation methods in this area of decision making are concerned primarily with assessing the communication properties of marcoms programmes which to all intents and purposes are ostensibly finished. Hence it involves research with marcoms prototypes with production qualities consistent with the finished product. The type of research commonly applied at this stage of development is pre-testing techniques.

Pre-testing, variously termed copy or treatment testing, is often used loosely to refer to *all* research conducted prior to placement of marketing communications in various media, hence it is not uncommon to hear it used when referring to procedures that fall within the domain of creative development. However, whereas creative development research is primarily concerned with identifying the creative idea capable of delivering the communication objective, pre-testing techniques used at this stage of development aim to assess whether the early promise of the creative idea, demonstrated at the creative development phase, has been realized in the finished product. In this sense, it is perhaps best regarded as the concluding phase of creative development research, concerning itself with aspects of execution and communication as opposed to core concepts and ideas (see Figure 26.3).

The function of pre-testing at this stage is both confirmatory and diagnostic: assessing the extent to which creative ideas and modes of communication are represented in 'finished' production and, where problems emerge, establishing possible solutions. In effect, providing information that will enable decision makers to 'fine-tune' a finished integrated approach, should this be desirable. Two methods of enquiry are commonly applied: focus groups and semi-structured interviews. The focus group procedures applied here are similar to those used at the creative development phase. Semi-structured interviews, in this context, are conducted face-to-face with individual members of the target audience and last up to 20 minutes. Unlike focus groups, the specific questions and sequence are prescribed beforehand and are designed to assess specific features of advertising, or other marcoms activities, such as comprehension, tone and communication. Open-ended questioning is also incorporated to establish and examine problems with execution. While focus group techniques provide greater depth and diagnostic capabilities, semi-structured interviews enable some degree of quantification which can help to ensure subjectivity does not creep into decision making. In this respect, semi-structured interviews are perhaps of greater value when execution testing results are used to guide the decisions surrounding whether or not to proceed to a full campaign launch. Automated techniques designed to expose audiences to, say, advertising, under controlled conditions and to measure physiological response to stimuli also have a role to play in this area of research, in measuring issues such as

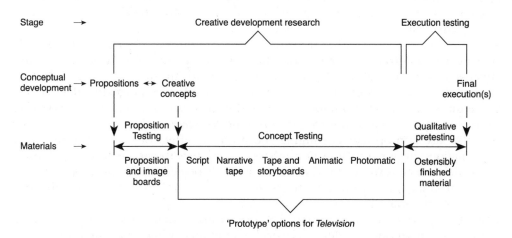

Figure 26.3 Marcoms content development research: an advertising illustration.

intelligibility and arousal. However, their application is specific to certain types of advertising, even though conceptually they can also be applied to other promotional mix variants.

Crucially, although execution testing does help to ensure the finished product realizes the potential of the core creative idea, it does not assess the probable outcome of the proposed campaign in relation to its intended objectives. This is the task of effectiveness testing.

EFFECTIVENESS TESTING

In marketing communications and especially advertising, a variety of research techniques are employed to *predict* outcomes, including quantitative pre-testing and area testing techniques. Both techniques are concerned primarily with providing guidance on what advertisements or campaign formulations to proceed with, a valid focus for research resources given the significant proportion of the promotional budget being spent on purchasing media space and air time for advertising.

Quantitative pre-testing methods, although widely accepted in North America, have attracted much attention in the UK, with their application being fiercely debated. Like pre-testing methods designed to test execution, the research is undertaken with ostensibly 'finished' material prior to media placement. Although testing procedures vary in accordance with media vehicles, research is normally undertaken in a public venue such as a hotel or public hall, typically located in an urban centre, where a representative sample of the target audience can be selected from passers-by. Purpose-designed testing facilities are now becoming more commonplace. The test procedure and follow-up interview, which together last up to 15 minutes, typically attempt to simulate and measure natural exposure to the marcoms, for example by placing a test advertisement amongst other ads with similar production qualities. Unlike execution testing, a test advertisement, for example, is not normally disclosed, at least at the outset. Since response is based upon a single exposure, the technique is limited to assessing short-term effects.

Quantitative pre-testing perhaps reflects the more conventional notion of a 'test', in the sense that marcoms is evaluated using predetermined 'action standards' that have evolved out of similar tests previously conducted on other comparable approaches and based on measures that have been observed to correlate with effectiveness in the real world (Stewart-Hunter, 1990). In this sense, effectiveness is predicted on the basis of what is commonly referred to as normative data. These procedures have raised a number of methodological issues which are too varied to address in the context of this chapter but tend to relate to the need for normative data that are appropriate to gauging the probable effect of the campaign under examination and for measures that reliably correlate with success in the real world and which are consistent with the test campaign's objectives (McDonald, 1993).

Area testing, like quantitative pre-test techniques, employs experimental designs, but differs in certain important respects. Whereas quantitative pre-tests attempt to simulate exposure under what have been described as laboratory conditions, area tests involve exposure under real-world conditions, where matched areas and samples can be exposed to different campaign formulations and results compared.

Although area testing is significantly more expensive and time consuming than quantitative pre-testing, as a precursor to a full launch it can have certain important benefits. Most notably, it is able to measure the cumulative effect of multiple exposures over a period of time and, by testing variations in message content and media plan, is capable of isolating message and media effects and of comparing the effectiveness of different campaign formulations. It can also provide a useful dress rehearsal opportunity, ironing out teething problems before proceeding to a full launch. However, it is considered more suitable for evaluating outcomes than process since its dependence on panel samples and the need to take repeat measures of campaign awareness and effect over time can result in detailed questioning artificially sensitizing respondents to the campaign under examination. With this in mind, it has been noted that if improvements are to be made in the design of future campaigns, it is not only important to measure the effects campaigns can bring about but also to gain an understanding of how a singular or plural [integrated] stimulus led to observed effects (Elliott, 1990). As a result, collecting supplementary qualitative post-testing and tracking survey data to fill this gap in the process can be a worthwhile task. Budget and time scales are likely to act as delimiting factors. Finally, although it is possible for marketing communicators to conduct independent quantitative pre-tests and area tests, many specialist research agencies offering syndicated services have evolved to meet demand for this type of research product.

IN-MARKET EVALUATION

Whereas effectiveness testing procedures can use experimental designs to predict the cause and effect relationship between marcoms and consumer behaviour, when evaluating in-market effectiveness planners are restricted to using descriptive data to infer these relationships. As a result, the ability of in-market techniques employed at this stage are designed to measure intermediate effects, such as campaign recall and message and brand perception and awareness, since these effects can be more reliably attributed to individual communication elements. Only in those instances where communications are specifically designed to prompt immediate action, as is typically the case with direct response advertising, sales promotions and direct mailing, is it possible to relate behavioural effects directly to communications.

A vast array of evaluative techniques and approaches can be deployed at the post-launch stage. These include *post-testing techniques, snapshot surveys, pre-post designs* and *tracking studies.* The decision to evaluate and the mix of techniques ultimately employed is dependent on a variety of factors. These include the level of risk involved, specific information needs, company culture, communications objectives and resource constraints.

Post-testing involves the application of qualitative methods, typically focus groups, to provide detailed feedback and insight into how marcoms have been received once exposed to competitor activity and other wider environmental factors. They therefore offer an opportunity to check the reliability of earlier developmental work and to identify and diagnose unforeseen problems. The richness of the data provided can also act as a stimulus for directing future campaign activity.

471

Snapshot surveys evaluate short-term impact by measuring campaign recall, recognition, communication, appreciation and behavioural intentions. In many ways, they employ the same techniques and measures as those used in qualitative pre-testing, ultimately relying on normative data derived from the evaluation of previous campaigns to assess performance. Their value is therefore dependent upon access to comparable data sets.

Pre-post designs take regular measures of market activity using panel data to map consumer purchasing patterns over a specified period, thus enabling planners to infer the probable impact of campaign activity. They therefore provide a means of equating the long-term effect of marcoms on overall market performance. They do not, however, provide the data necessary to explain how these effects or outcomes have been brought about. As a result, they have a role in ensuring accountability and in monitoring market performance against competitors but their capacity to contribute to learning and to providing insight into how marcoms work is limited. The gap in the process can in part be provided by tracking studies, probably the most resource intensive of the techniques discussed here.

By examining the intervening variables between exposure and brand purchase, *tracking studies* trace the cause and effect link between the two, thus explaining how the communications have worked (Elliot 1990). They therefore provide what are often referred to as 'in-person' data or cognitive measures of the mediating aspects of campaign performance – advertising recall, message communication, brand attitude and awareness, purchase intention etc. Like pre-post designs they employ a longitudinal methodology taking repeat measures over time, thus are able to establish long-term effects. However, unlike their counterparts, tracking studies do not rely upon panel data but instead continually renew the sample in order to avoid biasing responses. Although resource intensive, when supplemented by regular sales data, tracking methodologies probably provide the most comprehensive means of evaluating campaign performance.

SUMMARY AND CONCLUSIONS

Much of the published material evaluating marketing communications activities has taken the form of summative evaluations – measuring outcomes and the processes by which these have been arrived at. This reflective use of research has contributed much to the literature on what marcoms might achieve but its impact on campaign design has been cumulative and gradual. Marketing research, as practised, focuses on operational aspects of campaign management by addressing the many uncertainties that decision makers typically have to deal with from a campaign's inception, through its development, to its implementation and evaluation. Both have valuable contributions to make from an evaluative perspective. More specifically, summative evaluations and marcoms research findings generated by previous media-based programmes can have a crucial role to play in defining the potential value of, and where appropriate a new role for, marcoms, especially at the strategy definition phase, while creative development and testing procedures can be used to guide the strategy implementation. Recent excellent examples in the field of AIDS prevention, of how insight developed from

472

the application of advertising research to earlier campaigns can be used to guide subsequent campaign strategy development, illustrate how activities developed in the commercial realm have implication and resonance in a non-commercial setting (Hasting *et al.* 1987; Hastings and Scott, 1987). Of course, there is already a well-established literature in the wider commercial sector (see Ramond, 1976; Lavidge and Steiner, 1961; Schreiber and Appel, 1991; Donius, 1985; Broadbent, 1975; Blattberg and Neslin, 1990). Providing detailed illustrations of how the model as a whole can be applied and adapted to match prevailing company agendas within the usual structural constraints is not within the scope of this book, although examples of these processes have been published elsewhere (Eadie and Davies, 1992; Leather, 1988).

At a more significant and fundamental level, this chapter has suggested that 'measuring the success rate' depends on continuous and ongoing evaluation of the entire process of marketing communications, together with evaluation integrated approaches. Inevitably, the focus of such evaluation depends on that which has gone before; the time-honoured tested procedures of behavioural or attitudinal criteria. It seems almost certain that such mechanisms will continue to be used in the future, but as the balance of power moves from companies to distributors to consumers in the marcoms transitioning process (see Schultz, 1998) leading to the twenty-first century, such mechanisms may be replaced by pure behavioural data.

We conclude this chapter by suggesting that the potential contribution of marketing research to marcoms evaluation is dependent on that research becoming part of a marcoms strategic planning process. This interdependence between marcoms strategy and marcoms research, *throughout the process*, appears to merit much-needed deliberation by researchers, commissioners and academic writers in this subject domain as an enhanced understanding of this issue would undoubtedly be of significant benefit to the effective development of integrated or unintegrated marcoms programmes in the next century.

DISCUSSION TOPICS

1 Explore the rationale behind the use of the Vimto 'smile' from a consumer research angle.
2 Indicate how you would go about evaluating potential communications for:

Timex watches
Sinclair CV trike
Black and white televisions
Multi-media computer/television

3 Why is it important to evaluate target audiences before, during, and after exposure to promotional messages?
4 Is is really necessary that firms engage in ongoing and continuous interactions with target audiences?
5 Examine the promotional process research model (Figures 26.1 and 26.2). Are any elements missing? Which?

6 How would you build on Figure 26.2? Is in-market effectiveness evaluation more or less important than the preceding evaluations? If so, does the figure need expanding?

7 Assuming the process in Figures 26.1 and 26.2 is followed, is this likely to lead to more effective communications?

8 Can 'effectiveness' serve as a proxy for 'success'? Or are these merely semantic distinctions?

9 Using Figure 26.3, and accessing whatever literature may be available, can this figure be adapted from its advertising foci, and used for other promotional elements? If so, make an attempt at redrawing/redrafting the model.

10 Indicate, in your view, why an integrated approach may be more difficult to measure than an advertising approach.

CASE STUDY

In 1994, the national agency responsible for coordinating health promotion in Scotland, the Health Education Board for Scotland, commissioned problem definition and creative development research to guide its contribution to European Cancer Week. The initial problem definition stage involved conducting a literature review of intervention strategies and a qualitative study to explore consumer attitudes towards cancer prevention. The latter indicated that, although the majority took the view that the individual had some control over health, there was considerable fatalism surrounding the ability of the individual to prevent cancer when viewed as a generic disease. After considering the strategic issues raised by the research, it was decided to continue with a media-based campaign aimed at challenging the fatalistic attitudes surrounding the disease and reinforcing existing knowledge on how to prevent specific cancers. To achieve this, it was proposed using a combination of press advertising to communicate detailed information regarding specific cancers and preventive measures, and outdoor poster advertising to promote the central campaign message that the risk of developing some cancers can be reduced through changes in personal behaviour. An initial stage of creative development research, involving six focus groups, aimed to examine the chosen communication strategy and to assess the creative idea which proposed using a Tarot card theme to trigger consideration and debate on the issues of fatalism and control. This research was instrumental in guiding development in two key areas. Firstly, it indicated that using conventional press display advertising, combined with detailed copy, was an inappropriate means of communicating detailed information on a low involvement issue such as cancer. It was subsequently decided to develop an information booklet for distribution via general practices. Secondly, it confirmed that the Tarot theme had the potential to address the intended aims of the campaign. However, it also indicated that its effectiveness was dependent upon the audience identifying the Tarot imagery and relating it to the campaign slogan, 'Don't Leave it to Fate'. A second stage of creative development research, involving a further six focus groups, was subsequently commissioned to explore reaction to aspects of execution and communication. This confirmed that enhancing the campaign slogan, 'Don't Leave it to Fate' and using stylistic techniques to improve communication of the Tarot imagery could, if successfully implemented, combine to improve communication of the campaign message. In addition, research also suggested that the salience of the message could be improved by altering the slogan to 'Don't Leave it *All* to Fate'. The research was also able to provide detailed guidance on ways of modifying the test advertisements to improve communication of the specific, secondary, cancer prevention messages and to explore consumer response to the booklet format and proposed copy. Operational constraints meant there was insufficient time to test the final executions prior to the launch of the campaign which was to coincide with European Cancer Week.

ACKNOWLEDGEMENTS

Grateful acknowledgements are extended to J.N. Nichols (Vimto) PLC for permission to use materials about the Vimto brand published in CIM *Executive Briefing*.

This chapter adapts an advertising research model originally developed for managing the use of research in the development of social advertising programmes (Eddie and Smith, 1995). The authors would like to express their gratitude to the Health Education Board for Scotland for granting permission to use their work in cancer prevention as case material.

REFERENCES

Atkin, C.K. and Wallack, L. (1990) 'Mass media information campaign effectiveness', In: R.E. Rice and W.J. Paisley (eds) *Public Communication Campaigns*, Sage Publications, 1990.

Bettinghaus, E.P. (1988) 'Forum: a mass media campaign – using the mass media in smoking prevention and cessation programs: an introduction to five studies', *Preventive Medicine*, 17: 503–9.

Blattberg, R.C. and Neslin, S.A. (1990) *Sales Promotion: Concepts, Methods, and Strategies*, Englewood Cliffs, NJ: Prentice-Hall, see chapter 39.

Bovee, C.L., Thill, J.V., Dovel G.P. and Wood, M.B. (eds) (1995) *Advertising Excellence*, International Edition, London: McGraw-Hill.

Broadbent, S. (1979) *Spending Advertising Money*, London: Business Books.

Burnett, J.J. (1993) *Promotion Management*, Boston, MA: Houghton Mifflin, see chapter on 'Measuring Promotional Performance', 602–45.

Butterfield, L. (1990) 'Creative development research, in D. Cowley (ed.) *How to Plan Advertising*, London: Cassell.

Donius, J.F. (1985) 'Market tracking: a strategic reassessment and planning tool', *Journal of Advertising Research*, February/March: 15–19.

Drobis, D.R. (1997–8) 'Integrated marketing communications redefined', *Journal of Integrated Communications*, 8: 6–10.

Eadie, D.R. and Davies, J.K (1992) 'Researching communication approaches to heart disease prevention', *Health Education Journal*, 51(2): 90–3.

Eadie, D.R. and Smith, C. (1995) 'The role of applied research in public health advertising: some comparisons with commercial marketing', *Health Education Journal*, 54: 367–80.

Elliott, J. (1990) 'Campaign Evaluation', in D. Cowley (ed.) *How to Plan Advertising*, London: Cassell.

Flay, B.R. and Burton D. (1990) in R.E. Rice and W.J. Paisley (eds) *Public Communication Campaigns*, Sage Publications, 1990.

Hastings G.B., Leathar, D.S. and Scott, A.C. (1987) 'AIDS publicity: some experiences from Scotland', *British Medical Journal*, 294: 48–9.

Hastings, G.B. and Scott, A.C. (1987) 'AIDS Publicity: pointers to development', *Health Education Journal*, 46(2): 58–9.

Kotler, P. (1997) *Marketing Management*, 9th edn, Englewood Cliffs, NJ: Prentice-Hall.

Lavidge, R.J. and Steiner, G.A. (1961) 'A model for predictive measurements of advertising effectiveness', *Journal of Advertising Marketing*, October: 59–62.

Leather, D.S. (1988) 'The development and assessment of mass media campaigns: the work of the Advertising Research Unit: IV. "Be all you can be" case history – Parts 1 and 2', *Journal of the Institute of Health Education*, 26(1 & 2): 6–12, 85–93.

McDonald, C. (1993) (ed.) *How Advertising Works*. Oxfordshire: NTC Publications Limited.

Pasick R.J. and Wallack. L. (1989) 'Mass media in health promotion: a compilation of expert opinion', *International Quarterly of Community Health Education*, 9(2): 89–110.

Ramond, C. (1976) *Advertising Research: The State of the Art*, New York: Association of National Advertisers.

Redman, S., Spencer, E.A. and Sanson Fisher, R.W. (1990) 'The role of mass media in changing health-related behaviour: a critical appraisal of two models', *Health Promotion International*, 5(5): 85–101.

Schlinger, M.J. (1976) 'The role of mass communication in promoting public health', *Advances in Consumer Research*, 3: 302–5.

Schreiber, R.J. and Appel, V. (1991) 'Advertising evaluation using surrogate measures for sales', *Journal of Advertising Research*, December: 27–31.

Schultz, D.E. (1997–8) 'The evolving nature of integrated marketing communications', *Journal of Integrated Communications*, 8: 10–16.

Schultz, D.E. (1998) 'Transitioning marcoms into the 21st century', *Journal of Marketing Communications*, 4(1).

Stewart-Hunter, M. (1990) 'Testing Advertisements', in D. Cowley (ed.) *How to Plan Advertising*, London: Cassell.

Tull, D.S. and Hawkins, D.I. (eds) (1993) *Marketing Research: Measurement and Method*, 6th edn, Englewood Cliffs, NJ: Prentice-Hall.

van Raaij, F. (1998) 'Interactive communication and consumer power and initiative', *Journal of Marketing Communications*, 4(1).

27

DEVELOPING A RESEARCH FRAMEWORK: GUIDELINES FOR DISSERTATIONS

Andy Lowe

CHAPTER AIMS

- to provide an overview of the main research design options
- to explain the implicit and explicit assumptions behind research design strategies
- to outline guidelines which will help researchers to write good research proposals
- to indicate how novice researchers might perfect their research proposal

ILLUSTRATION: DESIGNING A RESEARCH APPROACH

The following major research issues have been derived from a literature review concerning factors affecting marketing communications from a global perspective:

(a) developments in marketing communications from an international/global perspective are contingent upon prevailing environmental circumstances;
(b) these circumstances reflect either
   – internal organizational culture
   – external market considerations;
(c) that where marketing communications are perceived by executives to be 'globally integrated' this may relate to a singular element of the promotional mix;
(d) that as firms move from an international to a global perspective this will affect how their marketing communications are organized and executed.

   (*Source*: Kitchen, P.J. (1997–8) unpublished research project; quoted with permission)

Question: After reading the chapter determine which research approach would be best suited to tackling these research issues.

INTRODUCTION

This chapter is designed to help novice researchers develop confidence and gain expertise in understanding the main research methodological options available. Following a brief discussion of the implicit and explicit philosophical assumptions, novice researchers are given practical guidance on how to write a research proposal and, if necessary, ensure it is adequately funded.

WHAT IS RESEARCH?

There is no more to research than *systematic application of appropriate methodology to a problem.* The more systematic a candidate is in executing a chosen methodology in any given research project, the more likely it is that the work will be of relevance to those whom the research addresses. All systematic research methods have the potential to yield useful results. It does not really matter which research method is being used; providing it does not violate the tenets of orthodoxy and is appropriate to the problem central to the research, interesting interpretations will be forthcoming. The real challenge is to understand which type of research method is best suited to which type of problem.

Certain types of research problems are more suited to particular research approaches. Where there is already considerable agreement about the nature of the main issues in a particular context then deductive research is to be preferred. In circumstances where very little is known then inductive research is more appropriate. The ideal research plan or design is to begin with inductive research, establish what the issues are, and then to conclude with deductive research.

OVERVIEW OF THE MAIN RESEARCH DESIGN OPTIONS – DIFFERENT TYPES OF RESEARCH DESIGN?

The short answer to this question is that there are only two. The long answer is that there are hundreds. The reason why there is no straightforward answer to such a direct question is because superficially there appear to be two main kinds of research: *deductive and inductive.* The reality is that the issue is not so clear cut because deductive research has elements of induction, and inductive research relies on the logic of deduction. Deductive research adopts the researcher's own agenda as the point of departure and seeks to prove or disprove an hypothesis. Deductive research appears to be quite difficult to some because it often involves learning more about statistical analysis. However, in a way deductive research is relatively straightforward because it involves remembering a series of well-documented procedures. Inductive research appears to be easy because most of the research methods used by this approach are simply listening and watching other people's behaviour. Those with experience of inductive research explain that is it often much more difficult to do than deductive research because the researcher himself has to act as arbiter and interpreter in creating interpretative frameworks. This is a highly creative process to which everyone is not emotionally and intellectually suited. Inductive research seeks to generate an hypothesis by discovering the agenda of those being researched. The reason why there is also a longer answer is because there is no such thing as pure deduction or pure induction. Deductivists choose their own research hypotheses. They claim this is done after having completed a rigorous review of the literature. Since researchers are free to read whatever they wish the choice in reading will be largely based on whatever influences the researchers and on their own individual preferences. This is an intuitive and inductive process. Once the primary data has been collected, analysed and synthesized it has to be interpreted. Interpretation is an inductive process. In inductive research, once data has been generated, it has to be analysed and synthesized; these are deductive processes. It is therefore very misleading to believe that either pure deduction or pure induction actually exists. All that one can say is that the main research emphasis is either deductive or inductive.

The challenge for novice researchers is to see beyond the bigotry of dedicated deductivists or inflexible inductivists and adopt a research design which best addresses the research question most effectively and also is intellectually and intuitively most attractive to the researcher. Ideally the best research design is both deductive and inductive. However, this requires more resources in terms of time, finance and research skills than most individual research projects ever have. The researcher should understand at the outset what kind of research emphasis the research is likely to take, deductive or inductive.

ASSUMPTIONS UNDERLYING THE TWO MAIN RESEARCH DESIGN OPTIONS

Deductive research

Deductive research begins with the researcher's own agenda in the form of a series of statements or hypotheses which are then either proved or disproved by the research evidence. This type of research approach has its origins in French philosophy as championed by Comte (1853). He believed that there can be no real knowledge but from that which is based on observed facts. This statement contains at least two main assumptions: firstly, that reality is external and objective; secondly, that knowledge is only of importance if it is based on observations of external reality. Deductive research also goes by several other names; they include positivism and quantitative research. This argument is further developed in Easterby-Smith *et al.* (1990). Implications for those wishing to do deductive research are as follows:

1 *Independence*: the observer is independent of what is being observed.
2 *Value-free*: the choice of what to study, and how to study it, can be determined by objective criteria rather than by human beliefs or interests.
3 *Causality*: the aim of the social sciences should be to identify causal explanations and fundamental laws that explain regularities in human social behaviour.
4 *Hypothetic-deductive*: science proceeds through a process of hypothesizing fundamental laws and deducing what kinds of observations will demonstrate the truth or falsity of these hypotheses.
5 *Operationalization*: concepts need to be operationalized in a way which enables facts to be measured quantitatively.
6 *Reductionism*: problems as a whole are better understood if they are reduced to the simplest possible elements.
7 *Generalization*: in order to be able to generalize about regularities in human and social behaviour it is necessary to select samples of sufficient size.
8 *Cross-sectional analysis*: such regularities can most easily be identified by making comparisons of variations across samples.

The eight implications of deductive research shown above form the basis of the criteria normally applied to deductive research. The issue of research criteria is an important one because if a researcher is using a methodology which is not widely used within a particular academic discipline, it is likely that the research will be misunderstood and subsequently under-valued. For instance, in the area of academic market research, in most of the mainstream journals, there is a general resistance to findings extrapolated from inductive research (this is slowly changing, *pace* see occasional articles in the *Journal of Marketing*). Largely, this is because of a historical research tradition stemming from the disciplines of economics and psychology. Notably, both these disciplines are heavily reliant on deductive research traditions.

Structural characteristics of deductive research

A research project with a deductive emphasis will have, when it is written, five main, clearly recognizable, sections or segments:

1 *Literature review* which includes both a summary and critical evaluation of secondary data in the substantive area and also includes an exposé, or definition of gaps in the literature. (Often the research plans to address one or more of these 'gaps' or previously untackled areas.)
2 *Explanation of the Research Method*: definition of the main method used, detailed explanation of the research instruments used, and justification of the research approach adopted. Sometimes, but not always, there is an explanation of the research methods not utilized and the reasons why they are inappropriate in [the] given context.
3 *Findings/results*: analysis and synthesis of the primary data.
4 *Discussion*: interpretation/evaluation of the findings, and an explanation of how the findings 'explain' the original research questions or hypotheses.
5 *Recommendations*: for different constituencies; research, policy makers, methodologists, guidance for future research, caveats concerning the limitations of the adopted approach.

This tends to be the orthodox structure for deductive research. As will be shown later, inductive research follows a quite different structure, and care must be taken to clearly indicate to those evaluating a research project just what is the main research emphasis of the research being undertaken. Otherwise the research may be victimized/castigated by methodological bigotry. For further discussion on this aspect of research design see Murray and Lowe (1995).

Inductive research

This type of research is based on the assumption that theoretical explanations of the world we live in can best be achieved by seeking to explain social phenomena which already exist in abundance around us. Unlike deductive research, this approach uses subjectivity as an important resource to be mobilized in the pursuance of understanding. The inductive research researcher should go directly to the real world and generate data so that the implicit patterns of the human world can be understood and then explained. This means that the inductive researcher has to be able to translate, decode, interpret and explain rather than measure the frequency of instances occurring. Inductive researchers do not merely collect data, they also generate it. In the generation of data, researchers must decide, by using initiative, intuition and subjectivity, what to focus on, and what to leave alone. One of the leading philosophers who promulgated this perspective was Popper (1959). He demonstrated that it was logically inconsistent for deductivists to claim to have exclusive access to fundamental scientific laws. The basis of his argument is that deductive research relies on verification as the final proof of a scientific theory. Instead Popper demonstrates that real scientific advances are made when researchers use falsification in preference to verification. *Inductive* research is also known as *qualitative research* and *phenomenological research.* Inductive research is widely used in academic disciplines such as sociology and anthropology, although with increasing incursions made by business and management studies, including marketing (with marketing communications as a subdivision thereof) (see Kitchen, 1993, 1997).

One of the most powerful forms of inductive research is the 'grounded theory' research method. This approach was discovered in the 1960s by Glaser and Strauss (1967). The author has had the privilege of working with Strauss on a number of projects in recent years [Lowe and Glazer (1995), which included a video on the subject in 1997 (Lowe and Glaser, 1977)]. A succinct resumé of this method, approved by Strauss, is to be found in Lowe (1996). In common with all inductive methods, grounded theory begins with the agenda of those being studied. It seeks to discover and explain the main issues of concern in the context of the research rather than imposing the researcher's own agenda on those being studied. This can be a little unnerving to the novice researcher because the inductive researcher does not have the safety net of the preliminary literature review from which to extract ideas and general themes. Instead the researcher goes directly into the context of the research in order to discover the main issue of concern of those being studied. After following the orthodox tenets of the research method being used, inductive researchers generate their own theory from the data which has been generated. One of the main implicit assumptions of all inductive research is that the world is socially integrated. Patterns of behaviour exist whether they are researched or not. It is the inductive researcher's task to discover these patterns by emergence rather than forcing a preconceived agenda on the data.

The main criteria by which inductive research should be judged are as follows:

1 *Fit:*. do the research concepts adequately explain the data which the theory purports to express?
2 *Workability:* do the concepts generated by the research begin to account for how the main concern of those in the study is being continually resolved?
3 *Relevance:* how relevant is the research for people involved in the study?
4 *Modifiability:* how capable is the theory of incorporating new concepts from data which is generated after the completion of the research by others?

Structural characteristics of inductive research

A research project with an inductive emphasis will have, when it is written, the following seven main sections:

1 *Pre-understanding*: containing a summary of the author's previous exposure to the subject area. Includes an overview of the author's own subjective influences which are likely to affect the generation and interpretation of the research data.
2 *Pilot Study*: a primary data generation phase to obtain a better understanding of the main issues of concern amongst those being studied.
3 *Refinement of research objectives*: dialogue between the pilot study indicators and the author's own subjective understanding which leads to a more focused research agenda.
4 *Outline of the chosen research design*: description of the chosen research method, including explanation of the research procedures used, and justification of the chosen research method.
5 *Explanation of generated data*: analysis and synthesis of the data generated.
6 *Data Interpretation and Comparative Literature Review*: a succinct interpretation of the data is followed by a comparative literature review.
7 *Recommendations*: policy guidelines or indicators for the different constituencies of the research community, policy makers and others.

Comparison between deductive and inductive approaches

One of the key differences between the deductive and inductive structural characteristics is that of the position and role of the literature review. Deductive research begins with the literature review whereas inductive research concludes with it.

Whichever type of research method is going to be used in a research project, there are some general guidelines which are used to determine the quality of the research project. Although they will have different meanings in deductive and inductive research designs, the overall categories of analysis have structural similarities:

- *Reliability*: how confident can those reading the research project be that if a similar research project were to be repeated the same results would be obtained?
- *Validity*: what evidence is there for those evaluating the research project that the results are credible? Are the research findings merely logically plausible, or are there special types of corroboratory evidence which makes the reader have greater confidence in the research?
- *Bias*: the question here is not: is the research biased? Everything is biased! Rather, how have the explicit and implicit biases been dealt with? Have they simply been ignored or glossed over?
- *Usefulness or value*: to whom is this research of use or value? Unfortunately much academic research in marketing suffers from its inability to be operationalized by those it may be intended to help or advise. Good research should not only be academically rigorous but also useful to the marketing practitioners it is designed to inform.

- *Relevance*: in disciplines such as marketing there is an overriding responsibility for research to be seen as relevant to those in the context of the research. All too often much academic research is only of relevance to others engaging in research activities themselves.

WRITING AN EFFECTIVE RESEARCH PROPOSAL

Whatever the adopted methodology, there are some general guidelines which will help novice researchers to be more effective in communicating their ideas to those in control of resources. The research proposal should contain the following main sections:

1 A statement of the main research objectives.
2 An indication of the area of study and an explanation of the context in which the research is to be set.
3 Summary of previous research in the same area [where appropriate].
4 An indication of how and in what way(s) the work will relate to previous research [where appropriate].
5 Clarification of the underlying assumptions of the research proposal.
6 Indication of the possible values of the research outcomes to different constituencies.
7 A detailed research design which includes what the intent of the research is, how it can be operationalized, and why the chosen or recommended method is especially appropriate for the type of problem selected.
8 Indication of a detailed resource plan which includes the financial, technical and human resources needed for successful completion.
9 Production of a detailed time plan indicating the key points in the research project, especially when feedback will be given to the sponsor (or sponsors) of the research project.
10 Explanation of the type of dissemination strategy to be adopted once the research has been completed (if necessary).

In addition to the above, novice researchers should ask the following questions:

- *What is the story I am telling?* All research projects are written by people with very different backgrounds and interests and this impacts on the perspective which will be given to each research project. By giving the story in the context of the issues shown above, this may help would-be sponsors of the research to become more personally interested in a given proposal. It will also force the researcher to be more honest, transparent and open about motivations for interest in a specific research topic.
- *Who are the audience(s) to which the research proposal is being addressed?* The researcher has to decide whether the research proposal is a plea for finance, recognition, moral or intellectual support, or rather more straightforwardly, simply gaining the approval of his or her research supervisor or supervisory committee. Occasionally the need may arise to write different research proposals for the same project, as it may be aimed at different audiences. For instance, academic funding bodies will

place more emphasis on the academic credibility of the research design, whereas practitioners will more interested in the utility of the research outcomes.

- *Why does it matter?* Readers and evaluators of research proposals are likely to be very busy and the last thing they want to do is read a rather dull and ordinary proposal, or alternatively read a proposal which is plainly lacking in the basic elements of desirable form and structure. It can be argued that the researcher has a duty to readers (and indeed themselves) to make the proposal interesting, from a both a readability and structural perspective.

- *Why now and why me?* By the time the research proposal is written there is already a sense of knowledgeability in relation to the chosen subject area. This can be demonstrated by injecting a sense of urgency into the research proposal, by explaining consequences of the research not taking place (especially when applying for research funding). In particular, researchers are advised to make a point of communicating [any] unique qualities or skills possessed which will enable the research outcomes to be achieved.

The researcher should also bear the following in mind:

- *Perfecting the research proposal:* where possible, research proposals should never be written in isolation. Often, there are many other highly experienced people whose advice, assistance or critical comments may enhance the probability of successful research progression.

- *Allow sufficient time:* constructing a *good* research proposal is time consuming. Time spend in reconnaissance is rarely wasted. Before beginning detailed development of a proposal it may be worthwhile to investigate other successful proposals, where these are available in the public or borrowable domain. Scanning previously acceptable proposals may assist in generating funds, where necessary, or submitting a successful proposal. Learn by the effort of others before submitting anything. This has now become much easier because all the governmental research bodies have their own Web sites (for example, see: ESRC"www.esrc.ac.uk/home.html"). Where dissertation or thesis proposals need to be written, it is crucial to access any or all literature, either internal or external to the appropriate research domain. Nothing is more frustrating than having to rewrite a proposal for academic research over and over again; notably, for externally funded research, there is no *second chance.*

- *Consider all opportunities for financial help:* in addition to the usual governmental research bodies there are a number of specialist charitable organizations who have research foundations who may well be able to offer financial resources. Obtaining money from the corporate sector is possible but it is wise not to oversell any possible research outcomes and to be honest about time scales. One of the most useful techniques in obtaining funds is called 'snowballing'. This happens when a initial modest amount of money is gradually increased by attracting more funds from other bodies who can be persuaded to collaborate. Often, firms related to your topic area may be interested in sponsoring some or all of the project, but the question of what's in it for them *must be thought through before approaching any firm.*

- *Discuss the proposal*: wherever possible enter into dialogue with experienced research professionals, including collegues, in advance of submitting anything. It is especially important when seeking external funds that the research agendas of these organizations are understood in relation to your own project.
- *Justify all financial requirements of the proposal*: it is not sufficient merely to give an indication of financial requirements relating to a given project. Expenditures need to be justified. This is necessary for all kinds of reasons. One of the less obvious reasons is that the more meticulous one is in explaining requirements, the more it gives a number of positive messages to would-be sponsors. Firstly, it demonstrates that the researcher is not profligate and can be trusted. Secondly, it indicates that the researcher has a firm intellectual grasp of the nature of the project to be embarked upon. Finally, it is simply just more professional.

When researchers consider they have produced a comprehensive research proposal, it is worth asking the following questions just to make sure:

1 Is the problem clearly formulated?
2 Are appropriate objectives established, stated and justified?
3 Is there a well-thought-through research design included?
4 Is there any evidence of innovation being used?
5 Are any ethical issues dealt with openly and honestly?
6 Are any other potential difficulties anticipated?
7 Are *all* potential users of the research identified?
8 Is a clear dissemination strategy given? (where necessary)
9 Is the proposal presented in clear simple English and with a form and structure appropriate to the circumstances?
10 Is there a summary and conclusion in the written document?

It is mistake to get derailed by the circular arguments as to which research method is the best one to use. Instead, focus on two other aspects: (1) the nature of the problem; and, (2) extent of the researcher's abilities, talents, skills and temperament. Certain types of problems are best suited to deducive research and others to inductive research. Since all research contains elements of both methodological approaches, purists may miss the point entirely. To do good research demands a firm intellectual grip of the nature of the research problem and a deep understanding of one's own emotional and intellectual capabilities.

SUMMARY AND CONCLUSION

As stated earlier, never write a research proposal in isolation. Look at the work of other [successful] researchers and find out what they have done previously. Ask the advice of experienced people, and they may offer to critically evaluate your effort prior to submitting the research proposal to a supervisor/sponsor/group. If researchers remember that the journey is more important than the destination then not only should some interesting research be carried out, but also one's own potentially blinkered mindset may be altered or expanded.

DISCUSSION TOPICS

1 What kind of problems will be most amenable to research?
2 In which circumstances is it more sensible to delay the literature review until some primary data has been collected, analysed and synthesized?
3 Is there an ideal research design which could be used in all situations?
4 How can the novice researcher avoid being intimidated by the established literature in a given field of enquiry?
5 Why is it important to begin writing from the moment the research commences?
6 What are the most important aspects of a research proposal?
7 How can one discover which of the two main research approaches a novice researcher might emotionally be disposed toward in order to develop sound research skills?
8 What are the different roles pilot studies can play in the research process?
9 When is it appropriate to use a research design with
   – an inductive emphasis?
   – a deductive emphasis?
10 Which is of more importance: the identification of a relevant research problem or the accomplishment of sound research skills?

CASE STUDY – THE CONSUMER EFFECT

Changing life styles continue to influence the way consumers think and behave. Pressures on their time and finances, increased mobility, and greater awareness of health affect the way people shop. Consumers are more discerning and value conscious than ever before . . . .

Effects . . . on the trade

Consumer demand for new and different leisure products and different leisure pursuits is transforming the leisure industry. The dominance of the local pub, for so long the automatic venue for an evening out, is being challenged by a diverse range of activities and venues. Consumers today have a greater choice of leisure options than ever before.

In direct contrast, diversity in the retail sector is declining as consumers do more of their shopping in supermarkets. The Institute of Grocery Distribution claims that, excluding the Co-op, the leading 10 supermarkets have increased their share of the grocery retail market by 11% since 1990 and now account for 58%. With a market share of 13%, Tesco has replaced Sainsbury as the UK's No1 grocery retailer. The growing dominance of supermarkets has led to a decline in the number of specialist retail shops and places independent outlets under continuous pressure.

As a result, neighbourhood stores are staying open longer and the traditional distinctions between outlets are becoming blurred. CTN's, groceries, and forecourt shops are all stocking similar products and competing for the same business. With stamps and newspapers deregulated and lottery tickets available in all outlet types, the right to sell alcohol is one of the few remaining differentiating factors. Even this will soon be a thing of the past as forecourt shops are obtaining licences to add beers, wines, and spirits to their offer. Soft drinks play an increasingly important role in these outlets, appealing as they do to both the impulse and the take-home shopper.

Convenience is the key benefit offered by smaller outlets. Generally located near the home or workplace, they enable shoppers needing fewer purchases to make them more quickly and meet the growing need for 'top-up' shopping. For older and single people they are particularly significant and their profile could grow as households and older people account for a larger proportion of the population. This fact has not been missed by supermarkets which are continuing to invest in their own convenience offer with high street stores like Tesco Metro and Tesco Express forecourt shops, putting traditional neighbourhood retailers under even greater pressure.

Effects . . . on product development

Although the under-25s consume 63% of all soft drinks sold, the increasing number of older people in the market has led to the introduction of numerous brands, designed to appeal to the more sophisticated drinkers. Many of these are still drinks, some fruit-based, some herbal. Most use natural ingredients and appeal to consumers' increased health awareness.

These drinks have generated much media attention. However, their penetration remains limited and Snapple, Oasis, and Fruitopia together account for just 0.8% of all soft drink retail sales.

Consumer emphasis on heath and fitness is also driving the launch of a number of products in the sports and energy sector.

However, for the foreseeable future at least, adults and teenagers alike will continue to drink more mainstream brands than anything else. Increased health awareness will ensure that no-sugar, full-flavour drinks and packaged water continue to grow.

Effects . . . on packs and packaging

Just as consumer trends drive the development of new products, they are also behind the development of new packaging. Most soft drinks are available in a range of different sizes and packaging innovation is important in maximising their appeal. Independent market research for Britvic in supermarkets demonstrates that consumers are suprisingly loyal to their preferred package types. For example, 83% of people buying cans never buy any other kind of pack.

Consumers are increasingly drinking while on the move and demand for resealable bottles is growing faster than for any other pack type. For example, Coca Cola has invested heavily in a resealable version of its nostalgic contour bottle, while Virgin has followed with the Pammy. Pepsi's answer combines aesthetic and practical consideration with the UK launch of the slam, a branded bottle shape already available in the USA.

(*Source*: Britvic Soft Drinks, *The Soft Drink Industry Report 1996*, Britvic Soft Drinks Limited, Chelmsford, used with permission)

Questions

1 Discuss how research could be developed for either:
   (a) a soft drink manufacturer/bottler/distributor, or
   (b) the teenage market for soft drinks.
2 Illustrate any marketing communications implications derived from the case.

REFERENCES

Comte, A. (1853) *The Positive Philosophy of Auguste Comte*, trans. H Martineau, London: Trubner.

Easterby-Smith, M., Thorpe, R. and Lowe, A. (1990) *Management Research*, New Bury Park CA: Sage.

Glaser, B.G. and Strauss, A.L. (1967) *The Discovery of Grounded Theory: Strategies for Qualitative Research*, New York: Aldine.

Kitchen, P.J. (1993) *Public Relations: It's Use and Development in UK Fast Moving Consumer Goods Firms*, University of Keele, unpublished PhD thesis.

Kitchen, P.J. (1997) 'Developing a research framework: inductive vs deductive?', Chapter 15 in *Public Relations: Principles and Practice*, London: International Thomson Business Press, pp. 272–82.

Lowe, A. (1996) 'An explanation of grounded theory,' Swedish School of Economics and Business Administration, Helsinki, Finland, *working paper*, Series 336.

Lowe, A. and Glaser, B.G. (eds) (1995) 'The potential of grounded theory for the development of relationship marketing', in *Grounded Theory 1984 to 1994*, CA: Sociology Press.

Lowe, A. and Glaser, B.G. (1997) Conversations with Barney Glaser concerning Grounded Theory , video tape, published by SHEFC and Stirling University Press.

Murray, R. and Lowe, R (1995) 'Writing and dialogue for the PhD', *Journal of Graduate Education*, 1(2): 103–24.

Popper, K. (1959) *The Logic of Scientific Discovery*, London: Hutchinson.

28

ROLE AND FUNCTION: PRINCIPLES AND PRACTICE REVISITED

Philip J. Kitchen

CHAPTER AIM

- to provide a summary and conclusion to the text

ILLUSTRATION: TRANSITIONING MARCOMS INTO THE TWENTY-FIRST CENTURY

I have chosen to conclude the text with the abstract from Don and Heidi Schultz' paper. This paper, published in Volume 4.1 of the *Journal of Marketing Communications* (1998), represents, in my view, some of the clearest thinking on the subject of marketing and marketing communications. This is especially relevant as we near the end of a decade of radical, consistent and ongoing change, coupled with one of the fiercest competitive national, international and global environments ever witnessed. As businesses of all kinds stand on the threshold of a new century, it will be the marketing communications discipline, creativity, expertise, and application which will sustain firms in maximizing profitability, market share and growth potentials. To quote Don and Heidi:

> Currently, marketing and marketing communication just don't work like they once did. They aren't revered as they once were. They don't demand the attention and concern of top management as they did just a few short years ago. In fact, in many major firms, both marketing and marketing communications are being challenged by the very persons who have traditionally been their champions. For example, Sir Dominic Cadbury, President, Cadbury Schweppes, addressing a meeting of the Chartered Institute of Marketing (CIM) in the UK said: 'A fixation with advertising and agencies makes it unsurprising that marketing has a struggle to be taken seriously in the boardroom . . . , and . . . the notion of marketing as a source of competitive advantage is regarded with suspicion'. This is even more interesting when considering that Cadbury was installed, with due honours, as President of CIM just a few short months before.
>
> Cadbury does not stand alone in his concern. Marketing and particularly marketing communication appear to be not just under scrutiny. They are

being seriously questioned in board rooms around the world. Quite a unique situation when one considers, we are entering what many consider to be the 'information age'.

There is, however, little question, marketing and marketing communication are in transition. It is our belief that this transition is driving the need for a new view of how marketing, communication, and marketing communication programmes are planned, developed, and implemented. Our belief is that integration can provide a solution. By this, we mean the broad array of activities and functions that influence and impact the dynamic flow of information between the organization and its stakeholders, i.e. customers, prospects, shareholders, employees, and other critical audiences. It is no longer relevant to think of such [presumed] independent activities as advertising or [marketing] public relations or sales promotion or even 'above-the-line' or 'below-the-line' activities. Nor is it appropriate to limit the responsibility of marketing communication solely to traditional outbound channels of communication. Those are old concepts and old issues. Ones which do not and cannot fit the needs of 21st century organizations, nor 21st century customers, consumers, or prospects. They don't fit for they were developed for a marketplace which no longer exists. They were developed for organizations that no longer drive businesses. They were developed for media systems which are no longer dominant. They were developed for management which is no longer in place. Indeed, marketing and marketing communication are in transition. And it is this *transition* that is bedevilling marketing and communication managers around the world.

(*Source*: Schultz, D.E. and Schultz, H. (1998) 'Transitioning marketing communication into the 21st century', *Journal of Marketing Communications*, 4(1). Quoted with permission)

A start to this final chapter is deliberately focused on some of the major issues impacting marketing communications and its satellite industries. Currently, both marketing and marketing communications are facing difficulties and problems of how to take advantage of integrated approaches in a world characterized by increasingly streetwise, savvy, sophisticated consumers to whom power is being transferred. Yet, of many courses in marcoms available in the United Kingdom, few are moving rapidly to an integrated approach; few are establishing strategic workable alliances with advertising associations or integrated agencies. And yet, the job pages in all major media resound with ads for marketing communication specialists, preferably with some type of experience. For qualified, presumed able, graduates in marketing-related disciplines (*pace – marcoms*) opportunities seem to be available as never before.

The textbook commenced by indicating that it was necessary to *target customers and consumers via communications in an integrated fashion* to inform, persuade and remind them of the firm, its products, services and/or ideas. A key concept was that products, services and ideas are differentiated via communication (using any or all promotional mix elements) to appeal to and attempt to satisfy targeted needs, wants and desires of target markets. Through the textual structure of the book we have traversed theoretical foundations, change engine scenarios, functional activities, organizational interactions and research dimensions. Marketing communications is undergoing rapid and diverse change with regard to what the subject constitutes, how it works, and its relevance, meaning and pertinence to modern business organizations. It is now evident that marketing communications is an exciting contemporary, still emergent, subject area with many avenues of exploration, multiple skills, tactics and strategies to offer businesses. The following points, derived from previous chapters, are apposite:

- Change and variability in audience(s), environment, messages, medias, monies and measurements equate to marketing communications as one of the most absorbing and vibrant fields of study and practice for the twenty-first century.
- Marketing communications is not a slow-moving monolithic or anachronistic subject. It is marked with responsibility (*ergo promotion*) for moving products, services and ideas *forward*. It is the essence of what marketing is, or purports to be.
- Marcoms has a marked history and pedigree. Current practice is based on historical precedent *and* environmentally adaptive circumstance.
- Planning, though necessary, can be viewed as *ex-post facto* tidying. From an integrated perspective, planning has to view customers and consumers as partners in the planning process and not just targets to be reached with communications.
- Notably, and in line with the point above, effective and efficient analysis at *all* marcom stages (i.e. planning and implementation) will remain the foundation, irrespective of how much the environment changes.
- Both structural and cultural aspects of organizations can impact on marcoms design and implementation.
- Integrated marketing communications will continue to be the norm from a corporate and agency perspective. Virtually all marcoms texts will move towards an integrated approach from a tactical subject perspective and in terms of book structure. Yet, there is still much theoretical work to be done, in the explosive technological environment faced by twenty-first century consumers.
- People are decoding messages in very different ways. Advertising will continue to be the most visible of all marcoms functions and, despite audience and media fragmentation, will continue to be utilized *alongside* integrative functions old and new.
- Semiotics and the semiotic boundary will continue to offer valuable and insightful perspectives in marcom meaning-making. All semiotic analysis should be viewed from an audience/target market perspective.
- Rationality, logic and systematic decision making are not an appropriate paradigm for describing consumer decision making. Hedonism, experientialism and emotions are just as likely to play a crucial role in decision making, for products are purchased not so much for what they are, or what they do, but also *what they mean.*
- Persuasion is the essence of marcoms, and Petty and Cacioppo's model of receiver involvement undoubtedly has established relational parameters which may help underpin future research initiatives.

491

- Consumers are now considering and acting upon not just product and brand knowledge, but are also seeking to understand what companies behind the brands *actually do*. Firms will be judged not just on the basis of what they produce, but also upon what they put back into the environment they have wrested business development from.

- The past decade particularly seems to have been a period of *renaissance*, sparking off new innovative approaches in the light of changing environmental circumstances. This in turn has led to major changes and developments in each of the tactical areas of promotion, i.e. *advertising, sales promotion, direct marketing, personal selling, marketing public relations, sponsorship,* and the increasingly important *Internet* and *relationship marketing*. All of these areas are closely juxtaposed and integrated in order to deliver or share messages effectively in a coherent and cost-effective manner.

- However, perennial questions concerning relationships between advertisers, media and agencies, and the way(s) in which agencies are to be remunerated for their services, simply refuse to die down or go away. These issues will continue to be of relevance even within technologically integrated systematization of marcoms approaches. Issues of how to measure success or evaluate effectiveness, as witnessed in so many chapters of this text, is a subject that, doubtless, the keenest practitioner and academic minds will continue to tackle.

- For students and practitioners undertaking research in the marcoms domain, the next decade holds significant promise. Marcoms will, it is hypothesized, continue to be the essence of successful marketing, or the art of creating satisfactory exchanges. The themes identified in this text, either in a singular or pluralistic sense, need to be robustly tackled by research methods old and new. The findings from these yet-to-be-published studies will underpin the field of marcoms in the early years of the twenty-first century.

SUMMARY AND CONCLUSIONS

This textbook has sought to tackle numerous issues and questions relating to marketing communications as we approach the twenty-first century. It has tried to deliver the knowledge and skills and to help develop ability in the marketing communications domain. This has been done by the information provided in the text, the readings, end-of-chapter questions for discussion, and case vignettes. However, the field of marketing communications in an integrated sense is expanding almost exponentially. Students and practitioners should see this text not only as a *starting point* for their continued study of the discipline and its many subdivisions, but as a useful and ready source of reference material. Remember, in Chapter 1, readers were urged to become contemporary, dynamic and knowledgeable about marketing communications. The latest information has been derived from the academic and practitioner literature to underpin development of this text.

It is hoped that studying the book has been enjoyable and interesting, and that it will serve to provoke further learning. As you now come to the end of what may be the first phase of your learning/experience curve in marketing communications, it is hoped that your further studies or practices in marketing communications will be reflected in future editions of the text.

REFERENCE

Schultz, D.E. and Schultz, H. (1998) 'Transitioning Marketing Communication into the 21st Century', *Journal of Marketing Communications*, 4(1).

BIBLIOGRAPHY

A.C. Nielson. MEAL (1997) *IPA DATA PACK – ADVERTISING EDUCATION AWARD 1997/98*, Institute of Practitioners in Advertising, September.

Aaker, A. and Myers, D. (1982) *Advertising Management*, 2nd edn, New Jersey: Prentice Hall.

Aaker, D.A. (1995) *Strategic Marketing Management*, 4th edn, New York: John Wiley & Sons.

Aaker, D.A. and Myers, J.G. (1992) *Advertising Management*, 4th edn, Englewood Cliffs, NJ: Prentice Hall.

Abelson, R. (1972) 'Are attitudes necessary?', in B.T. King and E. McGinnies (eds) *Attitudes, Conflict, and Social Change*, New York: Academic Press.

Abratt, R. and Grobler, S. (1989) 'The evaluation of sports sponsorship', *International Journal of Advertising*, 8(4).

Abratt, R., Clayton, B. and Pitt, L. (1987) 'Corporate objectives in sports sponsorship', *International Journal of Advertising*, 6(4).

Abt Associates (1990) *Environmental Consumerism in the US*.

Account Planning Group (1993, 1995, 1997) *Creative Planning > Outstanding Advertising*, Vols 1–3, London: The Account Planning Group.

Activ/Media (1996) 'Case studies of successful online marketers', *http://www.activmedia.com/ Casestudies.html#details*

Adelman, M., Ahuvia, A. and Goodwin, C. (1994) 'Beyond smiling: social support and service quality', in R.T. Rust (ed.) *Service Quality: new directions in theory and practice*, Thousand Oaks, CA: Sage.

Adelman, M.B., Parks, M.R. and Albrecht, T.L. (1987) 'Beyond close relationships: support in weak ties', in T.L. Albrecht and M.B. Adelman (eds) *Communicating Social Support*, Newbury Park, CA: Sage.

Admap (1983) Editorial, January.

Advertising Association (1996) *Public Attitudes to Advertising 1996*, London: The Advertising Association.

Advertising Association Marketing Pocketbook (1993) ASA in conjunction with NTC Publications Limited.

Agrawal, J. and Kamakura, W.A. (1995) 'The economic worth of celebrity endorsers: an event study analysis', *Journal of Marketing*, 59(3).

Aijo, T.S. (1996) 'The theoretical and philosophical underpinnings of relationship marketing', *European Journal of Marketing*, 30(2).

Aldridge, R. (1995) 'Putting your business on the web' *http://eightsea.com/eightsea/bigweb.html*

Allport, G.W. (1935) 'Attitudes', in C. Murchison (ed.) *Handbook of Social Psychology*, Vol. 2, Worcester, MA: Clark University Press.

Alsop, A. (1989) 'Brand loyalty is rarely blind loyalty', *The Wall Street Journal*, 19 October.

Ambler, T. (1996) *Marketing from Advertising to Zen*, London: Pitman.

American Marketing Association (1985) 'AMA board approves new definition', *Marketing News*, 1 March.

Andaleeb, S.S. (1992) 'The trust concept: research issues for channels of distribution', *Research into Marketing*, 11.

Anderson, E. (1985) 'The salesperson as outside agent or employee: a transaction cost analysis', *Marketing Science*, 4, Summer.

Andreasen, A.R. (1996) 'Profits for nonprofits: find a corporate partner', *Harvard Business Review*, 74(6), Nov–Dec.

Andrews, J.C. and Shimp, T.A. (1990) 'Effects of involvement, argument strength, and source characteristics on central and peripheral processing of advertising', *Psychology and Marketing*, 7(3).

Andrews, L.W. and Gutkin, T.B. (1994) 'Influencing attitudes regarding special class placement using a psychoeducational report: An investigation of the Elaboration Likelihood Model', *Journal of School Psychology*, 32(4).

Ansoff, I. (1965) *Business Strategy*, London: Penguin.

Anthony, P. (1994) *Managing Culture*, Buckingham: Open University Press.

Archer, B. (1996) 'Reality v blue-chip advertising', *The Times*, 14 August.

Archer, B. (1996) 'Why consumers are switching off', *The Times*, 30 October.

Argyle, M. (1972) *The Psychology of Interpersonal Behaviour*, Harmondsworth: Penguin.

Armstrong, C. (1988) 'Sports sponsorship: A case study approach to measuring its effectiveness', *European Research*, 16(2).

Armstrong, S. (1996) 'Catch 'em young', *The Sunday Times*, 12 May, Culture supplement.

Assael, H. (1993) *Marketing: Principles and Strategy*, 2nd edn, Fort Worth: Dryden Press.

Atkin, C.K. and Wallack, L. (1990) 'Mass media information campaign effectiveness', In R.E. Rice and W.J. Paisley (eds) *Public Communication Campaigns*, Sage Publications.

Atkinson, J. (1984) 'Manpower Strategies for Flexible Organisations', *Personnel Management*, August.

Bagozzi, R. (1995) 'Reflections on Relationship Marketing in Consumer Markets', *Journal of the Academy of Marketing Science*, 23(4).

Bagozzi, R.P. (1986) *Principles of Marketing Management*, Chicago: Science Research Associates.

Baier, M. (1985) *Elements of Direct Marketing*, New York: McGraw Hill.

Baker, K. and Knight, R. (1998) 'Keeping track of the titles', *The Bookseller*, 21 November.

Baker, M. (1985) 'Globalization vs differentiation as international marketing strategies', *Journal of Marketing Management*, 1.

Baker, M. (1993) *Basic Marketing*, London: Butterworth–Heinemann.

Baker, M.J. (ed) (1985) *Macmillan Dictionary of Marketing and Advertising*, London: Macmillan.

Baker, M.J. (ed) (1998) *Macmillan Dictionary of Marketing and Advertising*, London: Macmillan.

Banerjee, S., Gulas, G.S. and Iyer, E. (1995) 'Shades of green: a multidimensional analysis of environmental advertising', *Journal of Advertising*, XXIV(2), Summer.

Barlow, R. (1992) 'Relationship marketing – the ultimate in customer services', *Retail Control*, March.

Barnatt, C. (1995) *CyberBusiness: Mindsets for the Wired Age*, Chichester: John Wiley.

Barnatt, C. and Starkey, K. (1994) 'The emergence of flexible networks in the UK television industry', *British Journal of Management*, 5(4).

Barnes, J. (1994) 'Close to the customer: but is it really a relationship?', *Journal of Marketing Management*, 10(7).

Baron, R.A., Baron, P. and Miller, N. (1973) 'The relation between distraction and persuasion', *Psychological Bulletin*, 80.

Barthes, R. (1968) *Elements of Semiology*, trans. A. Lavers, New York: Hill and Wang.

Barwise, T. (1995) 'Good empirical generalisations', Centre for Marketing Working Paper No. 95–602, London Business School.

Barwise, T. and Ehrenberg, A. (1985) 'Consumer beliefs and brand usage', *Journal of the Market Research Society,* 27(2).

Bass F.M. (1969) 'New product growth model for consumer durables', *Management Science,* 13(5).

Beard, F. (1996) 'Integrated marketing communications: new role expectations and performance issues in the client–agency relationship', *Journal of Business Research,* 37(3).

Belch, G. and Belch, M. (1998) *Advertising and Promotion: An Integrated Marketing Communications Perspective,* 4th ed., New York: McGraw-Hill.

Belch, G.E. and Belch, M.A. (1995) *Introduction to Advertising and Promotion: An Integrated Marketing Communications Perspective,* 3rd edn, Chicago, IL: Irwin.

Belk, R.W. (1975) 'Situational variables and consumer behaviour', *Journal of Consumer Research,* 2, December.

Belk, R.W. (1988) 'Possessions and the extended self', *Journal of Consumer Research,* 15, Sept.

Bell, M.L. and Emery, C.W. (1971) 'The faltering marketing concept', *Journal of Marketing,* 35(3) October.

Benedixen, M.T. (1993) 'Advertising effects and effectiveness', *European Journal of Marketing,* 27(10).

Benjamin, R. and Wigand, R. (1995) 'Electronic markets and virtual value chains on the information superhighway', *Sloan Management Review,* Winter.

Berger, A. (1987) 'What is a Sign? Decoding Magazine Advertising, Semiotics of Advertisements', in L. Henny (ed.), special issue of *International Studies in Visual Sociology and Visual Anthropology,* 1: Vol. 7 (20).

Berlo, D.K. (1960) *The Process of Communication,* New York: Holt, Rinehart and Richardson.

Bernstein, D. (1984) *Company Image and Reality,* Eastbourne: Holt, Rinehart and Winston/The Advertising Association.

Bernstein, J. (1988) 'PR in top communication role', *Advertising Age,* 28 November.

Berry, L. (1983) 'Relationship marketing', in L. Berry, G. Shostack and G. Opah (eds) *Emerging Perspectives on Services Marketing,* Chicago: American Marketing Association.

Berry, L. (1995) 'Relationship marketing of services – growing interest, emerging perspectives', *Journal of the Academy of Marketing Science,* 23(4).

Bertrand, D. (1988) 'The creation of complicity: a semiotic analysis of an advertising campaign for Black and White Whiskey', *International Journal of Research in Marketing,* 4(4).

Bettinghaus, E.P. (1988) 'Forum: a mass media campaign – using the mass media in smoking prevention and cessation programs: an introduction to five studies', *Preventive Medicine,* 17.

Bettman, J.B. (1979) *An Information Processing Theory of Consumer Choice,* Reading, MA: Addison-Wesley.

Bevan, J. and Jay, J. (1989) *The New Tycoons: Becoming Seriously Rich at 40,* London: Simon and Schuster.

Bigg, A. (1994) 'Techno tactics', *Campaign,* 8 July.

Bird, M. and Ehrenberg, A. (1970) 'Consumer attitudes and brand usage', *Journal of the Market Research Society,* 12(4).

Bitner, M. (1995) 'Building service relationships: it's all about promises', *Journal of the Academy of Marketing Science,* 23(4).

Black, G. (1952) *Planned Industrial Publicity,* Chicago: Putnam Publishing.

Black, S. (1993) *The Essentials of Public Relations,* London: Kogan Page.

Blacklist of Internet Advertisers, http://math.www.uni.paderborn.de/-axel/BL/blacklist.html

Blattberg, R.C. and Neslin, S.A. (1990) *Sales Promotion: Concepts, Methods, and Strategies,* Englewood Cliffs, NJ: Prentice Hall.

Blattberg, R.C., Glazer, C.R. and Little, J.D.C. (1994) *The Marketing Information Revolution,* Boston: HBS Press.

Bloom, A. (1987) *The Closing of the American Mind,* Harmondsworth: Penguin.

Bloor, G. and Dawson, P. (1994) 'Understanding professional culture in organizational context', *Organization Studies,* 15(2).

Boddewyn, J. and Leardi, M. (1989) 'Sales promotions: practice, regulation and self regulation around the world', *International Journal of Advertising*, 8(4).

Bond, C. (1984) 'Own labels vs the brands', *Marketing*, 6(10).

Borden, N. (1964) 'The concept of the marketing mix', *Journal of Advertising Research*, June.

Boush, D.M., Friestad, M. and Rose, G.M. (1994) 'Adolescent skepticism toward TV advertising and knowledge of advertiser tactics', *Journal of Consumer Research*, 21 (June).

Boutie, P. (1994) 'Who will save the brands?', *Communication World*, 11(7).

Bovee, C.L., Thill, J.V., Dovel G.P. and Wood, M.B. (eds) (1995) *Advertising Excellence*, international edn, London: McGraw-Hill.

Bowey, S. (1988) 'Editorial', *European Research*, 16(2).

Bowman, R. (1986) 'Sales promotion: the 1985 annual report', *Marketing and Media Decisions*, July.

Bradmore, D. (1996) *Competitive Advantage: Concepts and Cases*, Englewood Cliffs, NJ: Prentice Hall.

Brandenburger, A.M. and Nalebuff, B.J. (1995) 'The Right Game: Use Game Theory to Shape Strategy', *Harvard Business Review*, July–August.

Brannan, T. (1995) *A Practical Guide to Integrated Marketing Communications*, London: Kogan Page.

Brierley, S. (1995) *The Advertising Handbook*, London: Routledge.

Briggs, M. (1993) 'Why ad agencies must change', *Admap*, January.

Brignull, T. (1996) 'Big bang, little impact', *The Guardian*, 12 February, media supplement.

Brindle, D. (1997) 'Rise in single households takes toll on wedding bells', *The Guardian*, 30 January.

British Business (1988) 'DTI retailing inquiry for 1986', *British Business*, 18 March.

Broadbent, S. (1979) *Spending Advertising Money*, London: Business Books.

Broadbent, S. (1989) *The Advertising Budget: The Advertiser's Guide to Budget Determination*, Henley-on-Thames: NTC Publications.

Broadbent, S. (1995) *Best Practice in Campaign Evaluation*, London: Institute of Practitioners in Advertising.

Broadbent, S. (1997) *Accountable Advertising: A Handbook for Managers and Analysts*, Henley-on-Thames: NTC Publications.

Broadbent, S. and Jacobs, B. (1984) *Spending Advertising Money*, 4th edn., London: Business Books.

Brodie, R., Coviello, N., Brookes, R. and Little, V. (1997) 'Towards a paradigm shift in marketing? An examination of current marketing practices', *Journal of Marketing Management*, 13(5).

Brown, A. and Starkey, K. (1994) 'The effect of organizational culture on communication and information', *Journal of Management Studies*, 31(6), November.

Brown, M. (1997) 'Long Knives and High Drama', *The Guardian*, 14 July.

Brown, P. and Scase, R. (1994) *Higher Education and Corporate Realities*, London: UCL Press.

Brown, S. (1995) *Postmodern Marketing*, London: International Thomson Business Press.

Brown-Humes, C. (1997) 'Staff to go as Eagle Star disband direct sales team', *Financial Times*, 13 November.

Brownlie, D. and Spender, J. (1995) 'Managerial judgement in strategic marketing: some preliminary thoughts', *Management Decision*, 33(6).

Bruell, E. (1986) 'He: this is an okay (lovely) analysis (emotional investigation) of our words (deepest corridors of meaning)', *Chicago Tribune*, 31 December, Sec. 7.

Brundtland, G. (1987) *Our Common Future*, The Brundtland Report, World Commission on the Environment and Development.

Bryman, A. (1986) *Leadership and Organizations*, London: Routledge and Kegan Paul.

Bryman, A. (1996) 'Leadership in Organizations', in S. Clegg, C. Hardy and W. Nord (eds) *Handbook of Organization Studies*, London: Sage.

Buller, D.B. (1986) 'Distraction during persuasive communication: A meta-analytic review', *Communication Monographs*, 53.

Bullmore, J. (1991) *Behind the Scenes in Advertising*, Henley-on-Thames: NTC Publications.

Burki, P. (1997) *The Internet and International Marketing Communications*, unpublished MSc. dissertation, University of Strathclyde.

Burnett, J.J. (1993) *Promotion Management*, Boston, MA: Houghton Mifflin Co.

Burns, A.C., Biswas, A. and Babin, L.A. (1993) 'The operation of visual imagery as a mediator of advertising effects', *Journal of Advertising*, 21, June.

Burns, T. (1977) *The BBC. Public Institution and Private World*, London: Macmillan.

Burns, T. and Stalker, G.M. (1961) *The Management of Innovation*, London: Tavistock.

Butterfield, L. (1990) 'Creative development research', in D. Cowley (ed.) *How to Plan Advertising*, London: Cassell.

Butterfield, L. (ed.) (1997) *Excellence in Advertising: The IPA Guide to Best Practice*, Oxford: Butterworth–Heinemann.

Buttle, F. (ed) (1996) *Relationship Marketing: Theory and Practice*, London: Paul Chapman Publishing.

Buttle, F.A. (1995) 'Marketing communication theory: What do the texts teach our students?', *International Journal of Advertising*, 14(4).

Cacioppo, J.T., Petty, R.E., Kao, C.F. and Rodriguez, R. (1986) 'Central and peripheral routes to persuasion: An individual difference perspective', *Journal of Personality and Social Psychology*, 51(5).

Calfee, J.E. and Ringold, D.J. (1994) 'The seventy percent majority: enduring consumer beliefs about advertising', *Journal of Public Policy and Marketing*, 13 (Fall).

Callinicos, A. (1989) *Against Postmodernism: A Marxist Critique*, Cambridge: Polity.

Campaign (1989) 'Report on top advertisers and brands', 4 May.

Campaign (1997) '50 Ways to Launch a Car', report, 22 August.

Campaign (1997) 'ASA Clears Lee Jeans of Work of Offence', 14 November.

Campaign (1997) 'Cars – the ad bonanza', 22 August.

Campaign (1997) 'How McDonald's Tailors its Brand Identity to Local Markets', 29 August.

Campaign (1997) 'How to get contract publishing out of the Dark Ages', report, 12 September: 12.

Campaign (1997) 'Levi Rethink Spawns Review', 7 November.

Campaign (1997) 'Tesco's One-Stop Shop', 19 September.

Campaign (1997), 21 November, reference to University of Leicester.

Campbell, C. (1987) *The Romantic Ethic and the Spirit of Modern Consumerism*, Oxford: Basil Blackwell.

Capra, F. (1982) *The Turning Point*, London: Fontana Famingo series.

Carlson, L., Grove, S.J. and Kangun, N. (1993) 'A content analysis of environmental advertising claims: a matrix method approach', *Journal of Advertising*, 22, September.

Carter, M. (1993) 'Zap! That's another £1m down the tube', *The Independent*, 12 May.

Carter, M. (1996) 'You saw the ad and bought the dress. But what about the hatchback?', *The Independent*, 7 September, shopping supplement.

Carter, M. (1997) 'Harry's game', *The Independent*, 4 February, tabloid section.

Carter, M. (1997) 'Youth advertising? Just cool it', *The Independent*, 3 March.

Cartwright, D. (1949) 'Some principles of mass persuasion', *Human Relations*, 2(1).

Castle D. (1997) *Grocer*, 18 January.

Caywood, C., Schultz, D. and Wang, P. (1991) 'Integrated Marketing Communications: A Survey of National Goods Advertisers', unpublished report, Medill School of Journalism, Northwestern University, June.

Chaiken, S. (1987) 'The heuristic model of persuasion', in M.P. Zanna, J.M. Olson and C.P. Herman (eds) *Social Influence: The Ontario Symposium*, Vol. 5, Hillsdale, NJ: Lawrence Erlbaum.

Channon, C. (ed.) (1989) *20 Advertising Case Histories*, second series, London: Cassell.

Chapman, S. and Egger, G. (1983) 'Myth in Cigarette Advertising and Health Promotion', in H. Davis and P. Walton (eds) *Language, Image, Media,* Oxford: Blackwell.

Charter, M. (ed.) (1992) *Greener Marketing: A Responsible Approach to Business,* Sheffield: Greenleaf Publishing.

Christopher, M. and McDonald, M. (1995) *Marketing: An Introductory Text,* Macmillan Business.

Christopher, M., Payne, A. and Ballantyne, D. (1991) *Relationship Marketing,* Oxford: Butterworth–Heineman.

Christy, R., Oliver, G. and Penn, J. (1996) 'Relationship marketing in consumer markets', *Journal of Marketing Management,* 12(1–3), Part C.

Cialdini, R.B. (1987) 'Compliance principles of compliance professionals: Psychologists of necessity', in M.P. Zanna, J.M. Olson, and C.P. Herman (eds) *Social Influence: The Ontario Symposium,* Vol. 5, Hillsdale, NJ: Lawrence Erlbaum.

Clark, I. (1981) *Retailer Branding: Profit Improvement Opportunities,* Richmond: Management Horizons.

Clark, M. and Mills, J. (1979) 'Interpersonal attraction in exchange and communal relationships', *Journal of Personality and Social Psychology,* 37(1).

Clark, T.M. (1981) *The Distributive Trades in the Common Market,* London: HMSO.

Clausewitz, Carl von (1832, 1968 edn) *On War,* trans. Col. J.J. Graham, ed. Col. F.N. Maude, London: Penguin.

Cleveland, C.E. (1989) 'Semiotics: determining what the advertising message means to the audience', *Advertising and Consumer Psychology,* (3).

Clifton, R. (1995) 'Do we need another article about women?', *Admap,* September.

Cobb, C. (1985) 'Television clutter and advertising effectiveness', in R.F. Lusch *et al.,* (eds) *AMA Educators' Proceedings,* Chicago: American Marketing Association.

Cobb, C. and Hoyer, W. (1986) 'Planned vs impulse purchase behaviour', *Journal of Retailing,* 62(4).

Coddington, W. (1993) *Environmental Marketing: Positive Strategies for Reaching the Green Consumer,* New York: McGraw-Hill.

Cohen, M.D., March, J.G. and Olsen, J.P. (1972) 'A garbage can model of organizational choice', *Administrative Science Quarterly,* 17.

Cohen, R.J. (1993) 'Insider's Report – Robert Cohen Presentation on Advertising Expenditures', *McCann Erickson Worldwide,* June.

Cohen, R.J. (1994) 'Ad gain of 5.2% in 93 Marks Downturn's End', *Advertising Age,* 2 May.

Cohen, S. (1980) 'Training to understand TV advertising: Effects and some policy implications', paper presented at the American Psychological Association convention, Montreal, September.

Cohen, W. A. (1991) *The Practice of Marketing Management,* 2nd edn, Basingstoke: Macmillan.

Cohen, W.A. (1991) *The Practice of Marketing Management,* 2nd edn, New York: Maxwell Macmillan.

Colley, R.H. (1961) *Defining Advertising Goals for Measuring Advertising Results,* Association of National Advertisers.

Colley, R.H. (1962) 'Squeezing the waste out of advertising', *Harvard Business Review,* 40, September/October.

Collins English Dictionary and Thesaurus (1993) Glasgow: Harper Collins.

Collins, C.D. (1987) 'Ad Images and Iconography', in *Semiotics of Advertisements,* L. Henny (ed), special issue of *International Studies in Visual Sociology and Visual Anthropology,* 1.

CommerceNet/Nielsen (1995) 'The CommerceNet/Nielsen Internet demographic survey: executive summary', 30 October,

CommerceNet Consortium/Nielsen Media Research, available at *http://www2000.ogsm. vanderbilt.edu/*

Comte, A. (1853) *The Positive Philosophy of Auguste Comte,* trans. H. Martineau, London: Trubner.

Constanzo, P.J. (1996) 'Teach IMC technology to future marketers', *Marketing News,* 30(2), 15 January.

Conway, T. (1996) 'Relationship marketing within the not-for-profit sector', in F. Buttle (ed.) *Relationship Marketing*, London: Paul Chapman Publishing.

Cook, G. (1992) *The Discourse of Advertising*, London: Routledge.

Cook, S. (1994) 'Database marketing: strategy or tactical tool?', *Marketing Intelligence and Planning*, 12(6).

Cooper, A. (ed.) (1997) *How to Plan Advertising*, 2nd edn, London: Cassell.

Cooper, R.G. and Kleinschmidt E.J. (1986) 'New products: What separates the winners from the losers', *Journal of Product Innovation Management*, 4(3), September.

Cope, N. (1994) 'Black cabs make the switch to the colour of money', *The Independent*, 17 January.

Copulsky, J. and Wolf, M. (1990) 'Relationship marketing: positioning for the future', *Journal of Business Strategy*, 11(4).

Coulson-Thomas, C. (1991) 'Customers, Marketing and the Network Organization', *Journal of Marketing Management*, 7(3).

Coupland, D. (1991) *Generation X, Tales for an Accelerated Culture*, London: Abacus.

Cowley, D. (ed.) (1991) *Understanding Brands By Ten People Who Do*, London: Kogan Page.

Craik, F.I.M. (1979) 'Human memory', *Annual Review of Psychology*, 30.

Cramp, B. (1996) 'Reading Your Mind', *Marketing*, 22 February.

Crane, D. (1972) *Invisible Colleges and Social Circle: A Sociological Interpretation of Scientific Growth*, Chicago, IL: University of Chicago Press.

Cravens, D., Grant, K., Ingram, T., LaForge, R. and Young, C. (1992) 'In search of excellent sales organizations', *European Journal of Marketing*, 26(1).

Crede, A. (1996) 'Electronic commerce and the banking industry: the requirement and opportunities for new payment systems using the Internet', special edition of the *Journal of Computer Mediated Communication*, 1(3), December, *http://shum.huji.ac.il/jcmc/vol1/issue3/hoffman.html*

Crimmins, J. and Horn, M. (1996) 'Sponsorship: From management ego trip to marketing success', *Journal of Advertising Research*, 36(4).

Croft, R., Dean, D. and Gandersee, C. (1996) 'Interactive or Hyperactive: Advertising on the Internet' in *Proceedings of the 1st International Conference on Corporate and Marketing Communications*, edited by P.J. Kitchen, University of Keele, Keele, UK, April.

Cronin, M.J. (1994) *Doing Business on the Internet*, New York: Van Nostrand Reinhold.

Cronin, M.J. (1995) *Doing More Business on the Internet*, New York: Van Nostrand Reinhold.

Cronin, M.J. (1996) *Global Advantage on the Internet*, New York: Van Nostrand Reinhold.

Cronin, M.J. (1996) *The Internet Strategy Handbook: Lessons from the New Frontier of Business*, Boston: Harvard Business School Press.

Crosby, L.A., Evans, R.K. and Cowles, D. (1990) 'Relationship quality in services selling: an interpersonal influence perspective', *Journal of Marketing*, 54, July.

Crosier, K. (1994) 'Promotion', in M.J. Baker (ed.) *The Marketing Book*, 3rd edn, Oxford: Butterworth–Heinemann.

Crowley, M. (1991) 'Prioritising the Sponsorship Audiences', *European Journal of Marketing*, 25(11).

Cude, B.J. (1991) Comments prepared for the US Environmental Protection Agency hearings on the use of the terms recycled and recyclable and the recyclable emblem in environmental marketing claims, Washington DC, 13 November.

Cummins, J. (1994) *Sales Promotion: How to create and implement campaigns that really work?*, London: Kogan Page Ltd.

Culligan, K. (1995) 'Word-of-mouth to become true measure of ads', *Marketing*, 9 February.

Cushman, A. (1988) '"New" element in marketing mix makes headway', *Marketing News*, 19 December.

Cutler, B. (1990) 'The fifth medium', *American Demographics*, 12(6).

Cutlip, S.M., Center, A.H. and Broom, G.M. (1985) *Effective Public Relations*, 7th edn, Englewood Cliffs, NJ: Prentice Hall.

Czinkota, M.R. and Ronkainen, I.A. (1996) *Global Marketing*, Fort Worth: Dryden Press.

Daft, R.L. and Buenger, V. (1990) 'Hitching a Ride on a Fast Train to Nowhere: The Past and Future of Strategic Management Research', in J.W. Frederickson (ed.) *Perspectives on Strategic Management*, New York: Harper and Row.

Danesi, M. (1993) *Messages and Meanings: An Introduction to Semiotics*, Toronto: Canadian Scholar's Press.

D'Astous, A. and Bitz, P. (1995) 'Consumer evaluation of sponsorship programmes', *European Journal of Marketing*, 29(12).

Davidson, H. (1987) *Offensive Marketing*, 3rd edn, London: Penguin Books.

Davidson, M.P. (1992) *The Consumerist Manifesto: Advertising in Postmodern Times*, London: Routledge.

Davies, J. (1991) *Greening Business Managing for Sustainable Development*, Oxford: Basil Blackwell.

Davies, J.C. (1995) 'Dependency, self interest and relationship marketing: a view of the nature of exchange', *Journal of Marketing Theory and Practice*, 3(4).

Davis, K. (1981) *Marketing Management*, 4th edn, New York: John Wiley.

Dawson, S. (1994) 'Changes in the distance: professionals reappraise the meaning of management', *Journal of General Management*, 20(1), Autumn.

Day, G.S. (1984) *Strategic Marketing Planning The Pursuit of Competitive Advantage*, St Paul, MN: West Publishing Company.

Daymon, C. (1997) *Making Sense of Meridian. A Cultural Analysis of Organisational Life in a New Television Station*, unpublished PhD thesis, University of Kent at Canterbury.

De Angelis, M. (1996) 'Marketing on the Internet', *http://www.netresource.com:80/itp/repel1116.html*

De Chermatony, L. and Dall'Olmo Riley, F. (1998) 'Expert practitioners' views on the role of brands: Implictaions for marketing communications', *Journal of Marketing Communications*, 4(2).

De Mooij, M. (1994) *Advertising Worldwide*, 2nd edn, New York: Prentice Hall.

Deal, T. and Kennedy, A. (1982) *Corporate Cultures. The Rites and Rituals of Corporate Life*, Reading, MA: Addison-Wesley.

Dean, D., Price, L. and Croft, R. (1997) 'TV-based retailing in Britain', *Proceedings of 2nd International Conference on Marketing and Corporate Communications*, RUCA Antwerp, April.

Dechant, K. and Altman, B. (1994) 'Environmental leadership: from compliance to competitive advantage', *Academy of Management Executive*, 8(3).

DeCormier, R.A. and Jobber, D. (1993) 'The counselor selling method: concepts and constructs', *Journal of Personal Selling and Sales Management*, 23(4).

Deighton, J. (1992) 'The consumption of performance', *Journal of Consumer Research*, 19 (December).

Denes-Raj, V. and Epstein, S. (1994) 'Conflict between intuitive and rational processing: when people behave against their better judgement', *Journal of Personality and Social Psychology*, 66(5).

Dentsu Inc (1996) *1995 Advertising Expenditures in Japan*, Dentsu Inc Corporate Communications Division, Tokyo, Japan.

Department of Trade and Industry (1993) 'Information society initiative', *http://www/isi./gov.uk/*

Dermody, J. (1994) 'Guidelines for Developing Environmentally Responsible New Products', PhD Thesis, Bristol Business School, University of the West of England.

Dermody, J. and Hanmer-Lloyd, S. (1994) 'Successfully Developing Environmentally Responsible Products: The Response of UK Manufacturers of Detergents and Household Cleaning Products', Proceedings of the Groningen-UMIST workshop: Meeting the Challenges of Product Development, Manchester, UK.

Dermody, J. and Hanmer-Lloyd, S. (1995) 'Developing Environmentally Responsible New Products: The Challenge for the 1990s', in M. Bruce and W. Biemans (eds.) *Product Development: Meeting the Challenges of the Design-Marketing Interface*, Chichester: John Wiley.

Dermody, J. and Hanmer-Lloyd, S. (1995) 'Greening new product development: the pathway to corporate environmental excellence?', *Greener Management International*, Issue 11.

DeTienne, K.B. and Thompson, J.A. (1996) 'Database marketing and organizational learning theory: toward a research agenda', *Journal of Consumer Marketing*, 13(5).

Dhalla, N.K. (1977) 'How to set advertising budgets', *Journal of Advertising Research*, 17, October.

di Talamo (1995) 'Jumping on the Bandwagon', *Marketing Week*, 24 March.

Dichter, E. (1960) *The Strategy of Desire*, Garden City, NY: Doubleday.

Dickson, P.R. (1994) *Marketing Management*, New York: Dryden Press.

Dilenschneider, R. (1989) 'PR on the offensive: Bigger part of marketing mix', *Advertising Age*, 60, 13 March.

Dinsdale, A. (1995) 'The do's and don'ts of online marketing', *http://www.netrex.com/business/dosdonts.html*

Direct Mail Information Service (1997) 'Consumer databases: a study of external lists and in-house database usage'.

Direct Marketing Association dated accessed July 1996.

Dobson, A. (1990) *Green Political Thought*, London: Harper Collins.

Dolbeare, K.M. and Dolbeare, P. (1976) *American Ideologies*, Boston, MA: Houghton Mifflin.

Donaldson, B. (1998) *Sales Management: Theory and Practice*, 2nd edn, Basingstoke: Macmillan.

Donaton, S. (1994) 'OK to put ads on the Internet, but mind your Netiquette', *Advertising Age*, 65(18).

Doney, P. and Cannon, J. (1995) 'An examination of the nature of trust in buyer-seller relationships', *Journal of Marketing*, 61(2).

Donius, J.F. (1985) 'Market tracking: a strategic reassessment and planning tool', *Journal of Advertising Research*, February/March.

Donkin, R. (1977) 'Life after the salesman dies', *Financial Times*, 15 August.

Donnelley Marketing (1991) 'Ninth annual survey of promotional practices', Stanford, Conn.

Donnelley Marketing (1993) 'Eleventh annual survey of promotional practices' Stanford, Conn.

Donovan, J. (1996) 'The true price of loyalty', *Marketing Week*, Customer Loyalty insert, 8 February.

Drobis, D.R. (1997–8) 'Integrated marketing communications redefined', *Journal of Integrated Communications*, 8.

Duckworth, G. (1997) *Advertising Works 9: Papers from the IPA Advertising Effectiveness Awards*, Institute of Practitioners in Advertising, Henley-on-Thames: NTC Publications.

Duffy, M.F. and Eagle, L.C. (1997) *Inaugural Advertising Effectiveness Awards: Winner's Casebook*, Auckland, New Zealand: Profile Publishing.

Duncan, T. (1985) *A study of how manufacturers and service companies perceive and use MPR*, Muncie, Ind.: Ball State University.

Duncan, T. (1993) 'Integrated Marketing? It's Synergy' *Advertising Age*, 64, 8 March.

Duncan, T. (1995) 'The Concept and Process of Integrated Marketing Communication', *Integrated Marketing Communications Research Journal*, 1(1), Spring.

Duncan, T. and Caywood, C. (1996) 'The Concept, Process, and Evolution of Integrated Marketing Communications', in Thorson, E. and Moore, J. (eds) *Integrated Communications: Synergy of Persuasive Voices*, Hillsdale, NJ: Lawrence Erlbaum4.

Duncan, T. and Everett, S.E. (1993) 'Client Perceptions of Integrated Marketing Communications', *Journal of Advertising Research*, 33(3), May–June.

Dwek, R. (1995) *Campaign*, 7 July.

Dwek, R. (1997) 'So is this Evolution or Revolution?', *Marketing*, 27 February.

Dyer, G. (1982) *Advertising as Communication*, London: Routledge.

Dyer, W. (1985) 'The cycle of cultural evolution in organizations', in R.H. Kilmann, R. Saxton, Sherpa and Associates (eds) *Gaining Control of the Corporate Culture*, San Francisco, CA: Jossey-Bass.

Eadie, D.R. and Davies, J.K (1992) 'Researching communication approaches to heart disease prevention', *Health Education Journal*, 51(2).

Eadie, D.R. and Smith, C. (1995) 'The role of applied research in public health advertising: some comparisons with commercial marketing', *Health Education Journal*, 54.

Eagly, A.H. and Chaiken, S. (1984) 'Cognitive theories of persuasion', in L. Berkowitz (ed.) *Advances in Experimental Social Psychology*, Vol. 17, New York: Academic Press.

Eagly, A.H. and Himmelfarb, S. (1974) 'Current trends in attitude theory and research', in S. Himmelfarb and A. Eagly (eds) *Readings in Attitude Change*, New York: Wiley.

East, R. (1997) *Consumer Behaviour: Principles and Applications in Marketing*, UK: Prentice Hall.

East, R. and Wilson, G. (1989) 'Sales promotion versus advertising: the debate sharpens', published in the *Annual Proceedings of the MEG Conference*, ed. L. Moutinho.

Easterby-Smith, M., Thorpe, R. and Lowe, A. (1990) *Management Research*, Newbury Park, CA: Sage.

Eco, U. (1976) *A Theory of Semiotics*, Bloomington, IN: University Press.

Eco, U. (1984) *Semiotics and the Philosophy of Language*, London: Macmillan.

Eco, U. (1986) 'Towards a Semiological Guerilla Warfare', in *Travels in Hyperreality*, trans. W. Weaver, London: Pan Books.

Economist, The (1996) 'Which half? Which advertisements work?', 339, 8 June.

Edelman, D. (1989) 'PR on the offensive: we can do better than ads', *Advertising Age*, 13 March.

Ehrenberg, A. (1974) 'Repetitive advertising and the consumer', *Journal of Advertising Research*, 14(2).

Ehrenberg, A.S.C. (1988) *Repeat Buying: Facts, Theory and Applications*, 2nd edn, London: Charles Griffin.

Eiser, J.R. (1981) *Attitudes in Psychology*, Exeter University Press.

Elam, K. (1988) *The Semiotics of Theatre and Drama*, London: Routledge.

Elderbrock, D. and Borwankar, N. (1996) *Building Successful Internet Businesses*, IDG Books (*http://www.idgbooks.com/idgbooksonline/*).

Elliott, J. (1990) 'Campaign Evaluation', in D. Cowley (ed.) *How to Plan Advertising*, London: Cassell.

Elliott, P. (1977). 'Media Organizations and Occupations: an Overview', in J. Curran, M. Gurevitch and J. Woollacott (eds) *Mass Communication and Society*, London: Edward Arnold.

Elliott, R. (1996) 'Opening Boxes and Breaking Arrows: Millennium Models of Communication', keynote paper presented at the 1st International Conference on Corporate and Marketing Communications, Keele University, Keele, 22–23 April.

Elliott, R. and Ritson, M. (1997) 'Poststructuralism and the Dialectics of Advertising: Discourse, Ideology, Resistance', in S. Brown and D. Turley (eds) *Consumer Research: Postcards From the Edge*, London: Routledge.

Ellsworth, J.H. and Ellsworth, M.V. (1994) *The Internet Business Book*, New York: John Wiley.

Ellsworth, J.H. and Ellsworth, M.V. (1996) *Marketing on the Internet – Multimedia Strategies for the WWW*, New York: John Wiley (*http://www.oak-ridge.com/orr.html*).

Emery, V. (1995) *How to Grow your Business on the Internet*, Coriolis Books (*http://www.emery.com*).

ENDS Report 191 (1990) *Advertising and the Environment: Uneasy Bedfellows*, December.

ENDS Report 191 (1990) *Eastern Electricity Wins Green Con Award*, December.

ENDS Report 221 (1993) *ICI Rapped Over Claims for New Refrigerant*, June.

ENDS Report 224 (1993) *Firms Fail to Heed ASA Advice on Absolute Green Claims*, September.

ENDS Report 225 (1993) *ASA Acts on Misleading Green Claims for Cars*, October.

ENDS Report 240 (1995) *Screws Tighten on Green Claims*, January.

Engel J.F., Blackwell R.D. and Miniard P.W. (1993) *Consumer Behaviour*, Florida: Dryden Press.

Engel, J.F., Warshaw, M.R. and Kinnear, T.C. (1994) *Promotional Strategy: Managing the Marketing Communication Process*, Homewood, IL: Richard D. Irwin.

Englis, B. and Solomon, M.R. (1996) 'Using Consumption Constellations to Develop Integrated Communications Strategies', *Journal of Business Research*, 37(3).

Environmental Protection Agency (1991) 'Guidance for the use of the terms recycled and recyclable and the recyclable emblem in environmental marketing claims', Notice of Public Meeting, Federal Register, 56, No.191, October 2nd.

Euromonitor (1986) 'The own brands report', in P. McGoldrick (1990) *Retail Marketing*, London: McGraw Hill.

European Association of Advertising Agencies (1994) *Client/Advertising Agency Partnerships in the New Europe*, Henley-on-Thames: NTC Publications.

Evans, J.R. and Berman, B. (1988) *Marketing*, 3rd edn, London: Collier Macmillan.

Evans, J.R. and Berman, B. (1990) *Marketing*, 4th edn, London: Maxwell Macmillan.

Evans, J.R. and Berman, B. (1994) *Marketing*, 5th edn, New York: Macmillan.

Evans, J.R. and Berman, B. (1997) *Marketing*, 7th edn, New York: Macmillan.

Evans, J.R. and Laskin, R.L. (1994) 'The relationship marketing process', *Industrial Marketing Management*, 23(5).

Evans, M. (1994) 'Domesday marketing', *Journal of Marketing Management*, 10(5).

Evans, M., O'Malley, L. and Patterson, M. (1995) 'Direct marketing: Rise and Rise or Rise and Fall?', *Marketing Intelligence and Planning*, 13(6).

Evans, M., O'Malley, L. and Patterson, M. (1996) 'Direct mail and consumer response: an empirical study of consumer experiences of direct mail', *Journal of Database Marketing*, 3(3).

Evans, M., O'Malley, L. and Patterson, M. (1996) 'Direct marketing communications in the UK: a study of growth, past, present and future', *Journal of Marketing Communications*, 2(1).

Evans, M., O'Malley, L., Patterson, M. and Mitchell, S. (1997) 'Consumer reactions to supermarket loyalty schemes', *Journal of Database Marketing*, 4(4).

Evans, R. (1988) *Production and Creativity in Advertising*, London: Pitman.

Farelley, F., Quester, P. and Burton, R. (1997) 'Integrating sports sponsorship into the corporate marketing function: An international comparative study', *International Marketing Review*, 14(3).

Fazio, R.H., Roskos-Ewoldsen, D.R. and Powell, M.C. (1994) 'Attitudes, perception, and attention', in P.M. Niedenthal and S. Kitayama (eds) *The Heart's Eye: Emotional Influences in Perception and Attention*, San Diego: Academic Press.

Feldman, L.P. (1971) 'Societal adaptation: a new challenge for marketing', *Journal of Marketing*, 34(2), July.

Feshback, N.D. (1980) 'The child as psychologist and economist: Two curricula', paper presented at the Amercian Psychological Association convention, Montreal, September.

Festinger, L. (1957) *A Theory of Cognitive Dissonance*, Stanford, CA: Stanford University Press.

Festinger, L. and Maccoby, N. (1964) 'On resistance to persuasive communications', *Journal of Abnormal and Social Psychology*, 68.

FIND.SVP (1996) 'The American Internet user survey: new survey highlights', http://www.findsvp.com/findsvp/index.html/tige7ba

Fishbein, M. and Ajzen, I. (1975) *Beliefs, Attitude, Intention, and Behaviour: An Introduction to Theory and Research*, Reading, MA: Addison-Wesley.

Fites, D.V. (1996) 'Make your dealers your partners', *Harvard Business Review*, Mar/April.

Fitzgerald-Bone, P. and Jantrania, S. (1992) 'Olfaction as a cue for product quality', *Marketing Letters*, 3, July.

Flay, B.R. and Burton D. (1990), in R.E. Rice and W.J. Paisley (eds) *Public Communication Campaigns*, Sage Publications, 1990.

Fletcher, K. and Peters, L. (1996) 'Issues in consumer information management', *Journal of the Market Research Society*, 38(2).

Fletcher, K., Wheeler, C., and Wright, J. (1991) 'Database Marketing: A Channel, a Medium Or A Strategic Response', *International Journal of Advertising*, 10(2).

Fletcher, K., Wheeler, C., and Wright, J. (1992) 'Success in Database Marketing: Some Crucial Factors', *Marketing Intelligence and Planning*, 10(6).

Fletcher, W. (1992) *A Glittering Haze: Strategic Advertising in the 1990s*, Henley-on-Thames: NTC Publications.

Fletcher, W. (1996) 'The end of advertising as we know it?', *Admap,* January.

Fletcher, W. (1997) 'The IPA Effectiveness Awards: Time to Move Forward?' *Admap,* 32(8), September.

Flusfeder, D. (1998) 'The Soft Sell', *The Guardian Weekend,* 14 March.

Forkan, J. (1983) '._._. Along with toys', *Advertising Age,* 5 December.

Fournier, S. and Guiry, M. (1993) 'An emerald green Jaguar, a house on Nantucket, and an African safari: wish lists and consumption dreams in materialist society', *Advances in Consumer Research,* 20.

Fox, W. (1990) *Toward a Transpersonal Ecology: Developing New Foundations for Environmentalism,* Shambhala, Boston.

Foxall, G. (1983) *Consumer Choice,* London: Macmillan.

Foxall, G. (1989) '*Marketing Innovations and Customers*', *The Quarterly Review of Marketing,* Autumn.

Foxall, G.R. (1984) 'Consumers' intentions and behaviour: a note on research and a challenge to researchers', *Journal of the Marketing Research Society,* 26(3).

Frank, J.D. (1963) *Persuasion and Healing,* New York: Schocken Books.

Frankel, B. and Phillips, J.W. (1986) 'Escaping the parity trap', *Marketing Communications,* November.

Franzen, G. (1994) *Advertising Effectiveness: Findings From Empirical Research,* Henley-On-Thames: NTC Publications.

Freedman, J.L. and Sears, D.O. (1965) 'Warning, distraction, and resistance to influence', *Journal of Personality and Social Psychology,* 1.

Freeman, L. (1990) 'Colgate Axes Global Ads: Thinks Local', *Advertising Age,* 26 November.

Frey, N. (1988) 'Ninth annual advertising and sales promotion report', *Marketing Communications,* August.

Friedan, B. (1971) *The Feminine Mystique,* London: Gollancz.

Friend, C. (1986) *Public relations – not just puffering and nonsense,* Institute of Marketing.

Friend, C. (1986) *Public relations and marketing – the synergy and the separation,* written for the Institute of Public Relations.

Friend, C. (1994) Letter to Dr Philip J. Kitchen, Department of Management, Keele University, expressing her opinions concerning the place of Public Relations in the Marketing Mix, 7 November.

Friestad, M. and Wright, P. (1994) 'The persuasion knowledge model: how people cope with persuasion attempts', *Journal of Consumer Research,* 21 (June).

Fry, D. and Fry, V.L. (1986) 'A Semiotic Model for the Study of Mass Communication', in M. McLaughlin (ed) *Communication Yearbook 9,* Beverly Hills, CA: Sage.

Gabriel, Y. and Lang, T. (1995) *The Unmanageable Consumer,* London: Sage.

Gage, T.J. (1981) 'PR ripens role in marketing', *Advertising Age,* 5 January.

Gagliardi, P. (1986) 'The creation and change of organizational cultures: a conceptual framework', *Organizational Studies,* 7(2).

Ganesan, S. (1994) 'Determinants of long-term orientation in buyer-seller relationships', *Journal of Marketing,* 58(2), April.

Gardner, L. (1997) 'Wave riding, ads and lasses', *The Guardian,* 5 April.

Gardner, M. and Shuman, P. (1987) 'Sponsorship: An important component of the promotion mix', *Journal of Advertising,* 16(1).

Gardner, M.P. (1985), 'Mood states and consumer behaviour: a critical review', *Journal of Consumer Research,* 12, December.

Gates, W. (1996) *The Way Ahead,* New York: Viking Books.

Gatignon, H. and Robertson, T.S. (1985) 'A Propositional Inventory for New Diffusion Research', *Journal of Consumer Research,* March.

Gay, V. (1988) 'Clutter is ad pollution', *Advertising Age,* October.

Geis, M. L. (1982) *The Language of Television Advertising,* New York: Academic Press.

Gelinas-Chebat, C. and Chebat, J-C. (1992) 'Effects of two voice characteristics on the attitudes toward advertising messages', *Journal of Social Psychology,* 132(4).

Glaser, B.G. and Strauss, A.L. (1967) *The Discovery of Grounded Theory: Strategies for Qualitative Research,* New York: Aldine.

Glazer, R. (1991) 'Marketing in an information-intensive environment: strategic implications of knowledge as an asset', *Journal of Marketing,* 55, October.

Gliniecki, A. (1993) 'Writer hopes to strike gold with tale of coffee lovers', *The Independent,* 8 February.

Goffee, R. and Scase, R. (1995) *Corporate Realities. The Dynamics of Large and Small Organisations,* London: Routledge.

Goldberg, M.E. and Hartwick, J. (1990) 'The effects of advertiser reputation and extremity of advertising claim on advertising effectiveness', *Journal of Consumer Research,* 17 (September).

Goldman, T. (1988) 'Big spenders develop newspaper communications', *Marketing Communications,* 13(1).

Goodyear M. (1991) 'Five Stages of Advertising Literacy, why different countries respond to different levels of sophistication', *Admap,* 54(3), March.

Govoni, N., Eng, R. and Galper, M. (1986) *Promotional Management,* Englewood Cliffs, NJ: Prentice Hall International.

Grayson, K. and Vehill, K. (1997) 'How does advertising mean what it does? The impact of "real consumers" in commercials', unpublished, London Business School Working Paper Series.

Greenwald, A.G. (1968) 'Cognitive learning, cognitive response to persuasion, and attitude change', in A. Greenwald, T. Brock and T.Ostrom (eds) *Psychological foundations of attitudes,* New York: Academic Press.

Gregory, K. (1983) 'Native-view paradigms: multiple cultures and culture conflicts in organizations', *Administrative Science Quarterly,* 28.

Grein, A.F. and Gould, S.J. (1996) 'Globally Integrated Marketing Communications', *Journal of Marketing Communications,* 2(3).

Griffith, V. (1997) 'Black consumers enter the arena', *Financial Times,* 2 June.

Gronroos, C. (1994) 'From marketing mix to relationship marketing: Towards a paradigm shift in marketing', *Management Decision,* 32(2).

Gronroos, C. (1997) 'Value driven relationship marketing: from products to resources and competencies', *Journal of Marketing Management,* 13(5).

Gronroos, C. and Strandvik, T. (1997) 'Editorial', *Journal of Marketing Management,* 13(5).

Gross, A., Traylor, M. and Shuman, P. (1987) 'Corporate sponsorship of arts and sports events', *40th ESOMAR Marketing Research Congress Proceedings,* Montreux, Switzerland.

Grunig, J.E. (1992) *Excellence in Public Relations and Communication Management,* Hillsdale, NJ: Lawrence Erlbaum.

Guardian, The Supplement Section, 14 March 1998.

Guardian, The Weekend Section, Flusfeder, D, 'The Soft Sell', 14 March 1998.

Guiltinan, J.P. and Paul, G.W. (1994) *Marketing Management: Strategies and Programs,* New York: McGraw Hill.

Gumm, J. (1978) 'Public relations is a primary element in Beech-Nut food's marketing program', *Advertising Age,* 6 February.

Gupta, S. and Pitkow, J. (1995) 'Consumer survey of WWW users: preliminary results from 4th survey', *http://www.umich.edu/~sgupta/hermes/*

Hackley, C. and Kitchen, P. (1996) 'Ethical Perspectives on the Postmodern Communications Leviathan', Proceedings of the annual conference of the Marketing Education Group, Strathclyde University, Scotland, UK., July, (CD-ROM).

Hackley, C. and Kitchen, P.J. (1997) 'Ethical Concepts for a Phenomenology of Marketing Communications', in G. Moore (ed.) *Business Ethics: Principles and Practice,* Sunderland: Business Education Publishers.

Hagel, J. and Armstrong, A.G. (1997) *net.gain: expanding markets through virtual communities*, Harvard Business School Press (*http://www.hbsp.harvard.edu/netgain*)

Hale, E. (1997) 'Levi's Rethink Spawns Review', *Campaign*, 7 November.

Haley, R. and Baldinger, A. (1991) 'The ARF copy research validity project', *Journal of Advertising Research*, 31(2).

Hamill, J. (1997) 'International marketing education and the Internet', working paper, Department of Marketing, University of Strathclyde.

Hamill, J. (1997) 'The Internet and International Marketing', on-line modules for MSc International Marketing, Marketing Department, University of Strathclyde [http://web.u-k.online.co.uk/Members/jim.hamill/topic1.htm].

Hamill, J. and Gregory, K. (1997) 'Internet marketing in the internationalisation of UK SMEs', *Journal of Marketing Management*, Special Edition on Internationalisation (J. Hamill, ed.), 13(1–3), Jan–April.

Hammer, M. and Champy, J. (1995) *Reengineering the Corporation: A Manifesto for Business Revolution*, London: Nicholas Brealey.

Hammond, R. (1996) *Digital Business: Surviving and Thriving in an On-line World*, London: Hodder & Stoughton (*http://www.hammond.co.uk/digitalbusiness*).

Hanan, M. (1982) *Key Account Selling*, AMACOM, New York.

Handy, C. (1985) *Understanding Organizations*, 3rd edn, London: Penguin.

Handy, C. (1990) *The Age of Unreason*, London: Arrow Books

Hansen, F. (1995) 'Recent Developments in the Measurement of Advertising Effectiveness: The Third Generation', *Marketing and Research Today*, November.

Hansen, F. and Scotwin, L. (1995) 'An experimental enquiry into sponsorship: What effects can be measured?', *Marketing and Research Today*, August.

Hardy, H.E. (1993) 'History of the Net', *ftp://umcc.umich.edu/pub/users/seraphim/doc/nethis8.txt*

Harris, T. (1993) *The Marketer's Guide to PR: How Today's Companies are using the New Public Relations to Gain a Competitive Edge*, New York: John Wiley and Sons.

Harrison, B.E. (1992) 'Achieving Sustainable Communications', in P.B. Erdmann (ed.) *Corporate Environmentalism*, in *Columbia Journal of World Business*, 27(3/4) (fall–winter).

Hass, R.G. and Grady, K. (1975) 'Temporal delay, type of forwarning and resistance to influence', *Journal of Experimental Social Psychology*, 11.

Hastings, G. (1984) 'Sponsorship works differently from advertising', *International Journal of Advertising*, 3(2).

Hastings, G.B. and Scott, A.C. (1987) 'AIDS Publicity: pointers to development', *Health Education Journal*, 46(2).

Hastings G.B., Leathar, D.S. and Scott, A.C. (1987) 'AIDS publicity: some experiences from Scotland', *British Medical Journal*, 294.

Hawtree, C. (1996) 'Books: Visions with the lights off', *The Independent*, 10 Feb.

Hayes, S.P. (1959) *Conservation and the Gospel of Efficiency*, Cambridge, MA: Harvard University Press.

Hebdige, D. (1979) *Subculture: The Meaning of Style*, London: Methuen.

Heinz (1991) 'Heinz: creating, executing and evaluating promotions', MRS 1991 Seminar Paper.

Henley Centre (1978) *Planning Consumer Markets*, London.

Henley Centre: Planning for Social Change, cited in *Marketing*, 23 October 1996.

Heppner, M.J., Good, G.E., Hillenbrand-Gunn, T.L., Hawkins, A.K., *et al.* (1995) 'Examining sex differences in altering attitudes about rape: A test of the Elaboration Likelihood Model', *Journal of Counseling and Development*, 73(6).

Herman (eds) *Social Influence: The Ontario Symposium*, Vol. 5, Hillsdale, NJ: Lawrence Erlbaum.

Hersey, P. and Blanchard, K.H. (1988) *Management of Organizational Behavior: Utilizing Human Resources*, Englewood Cliffs, NJ: Prentice Hall.

Hersey, P., Blanchard, K. and Johnson, D. (1996) *Management of Organizational Behaviour: Utilizing Human Resources*, 7th edn, New Jersey: Prentice Hall.

Hill, D. (1997) 'It's a mad, mad, ad world', *The Observer*, 28 December, *Business* supplement.

Hirschman, E.C. (1982) 'Ethnic variation in hedonic consumption', *Journal of Social Psychology*.

Hirschman, E.C. and Holbrook, M.B. (1982) 'Hedonic consumption: emerging concepts, methods and propositions', *Journal of Marketing*, 46, Summer.

Hobbes, R. (1996) 'Internet timeline v2.4a', *On the Internet, Journal of the Internet Society*, March/April: also at http://info.isoc.org/guest/zakon/Internet/history/HIT.html

Hoek, J., Gendall, P. and Sanders, J. (1993) 'Sponsorship management and evaluation: Are managers' assumptions justified?', *Journal of Promotion Management*, 1(1).

Hoek, J., Gendall, P., Jeffcoat, M. and Orsman, D. (1997) 'Sponsorship and Advertising: A comparison of their effects', *Journal of Marketing Communications*, 3(1).

Hoffman, D.L. and Novak, T.P. (1994) 'Commercializing the information superhighway: are we in for a smooth ride?', working paper, Vanderbilt University (*http://www2000.osgm.vanderbiltd.edu*).

Hoffman, D.L. and Novak, T.P. (1994) 'Wanted: Net Census', *Wired*, 2(11).

Hoffman, D.L. and Novak, T.P. (1995) 'Marketing in hypermedia computer-mediated environments: conceptual foundations', working paper, Vanderbilt University (*http://www2000.osgm.vanderbiltd.edu*).

Hoffman, D.L. and Novak, T.P. (1995) 'The CommerceNet/Nielsen Internet demographics survey: is it representative?', Project 2000 note, 12 December, *http://www2000.ogsm.vanderbilt.edu/*

Hoffman, D.L. and Novak, T.P. (1996) 'Marketing in hypermedia computer-mediated environments: conceptual foundations', *Journal of Marketing*, July.

Hoffman, D.L. and Novak, T.P. (1996) 'A new marketing paradigm for electronic commerce', Project 2000 working paper, 19 February, *http://www2000.ogsm.vanderbilt.edu/*

Hoffman, D.L. and Novak, T.P. (1996) 'New metrics for new media: toward the development of Web measurement standards', working paper, Vanderbilt University (*http://www2000.osgm.-vanderbilt.edu*).

Hoffman, D.L., Novak, T.P. and Chatterjee, P. (1995) 'Commercial scenarios for the Web: opportunities and challenges', *Journal of Computer-Mediated Communication*, 1(3), December, available at *http://shum.huji.ac.il/jcmc/vol1/issue3/hoffman.html*

Hogarth-Scott, S., Wilson, K. and Wilson, N. (1996) 'Do Small Businesses Have to Practice Marketing to Survive and Grow?', *Market Intelligence and Planning*, 14(1), January.

Hogg, M., Long, G., Hartley, M. and Angold, S. (1993) 'Touch me, hold me, squeeze me, freeze me: Privacy – the emerging issue for relationship marketing in the 1990s', *Proceedings of the 1993 Annual Conference of the Marketing Education Group*, Loughborough University, July.

Holbrook, M.B. (1980) 'Some preliminary notes on research in consumer esthetics', *Advances in Consumer Research*.

Holbrook, M.B. (1981) 'Integrating compositional and decompositional analyses to represent the intervening role of perceptions in evaluative judgements', *Journal of Marketing Research*, 18, February.

Holbrook, M.B. (1995) *Consumer Research – Introspective Essays on the Study of Consumption*, Newbury Park, CA: Sage.

Holbrook, M.B. and Hirschman, E.C. (1982) 'The experiential aspects of consumption: consumer fantasies, feelings, and fun', *Journal of Consumer Research*, 9, September.

Holloway, P. (1991) 'Making promotions work harder', MRS 1991 Seminar Paper.

Houston, F.S. (1986) 'The marketing concept: what it is, and what it is not', *Journal of Marketing*, April, 48(1).

Houston, M.J., Childers, T.L. and Heckler, S.E. (1987) 'Picture-word consistency and the elaborative processing of advertisements', *Journal of Marketing Research*, 24, November.

Hout, T., Porter, M.E. and Rudden, E. (1982) 'How Global Companies Win Out', *Harvard Business Review*, September/October.

Hovland, C., Janis, I. and Kelley, H.H. (1953) *Communication and Persuasion*, New Haven: Yale University Press.

Howard, J.A. and Sheth, J.N. (1969) *The Theory of Buyer Behaviour*, New York: Wiley.

Huang, M.H. (1997) 'Exploring a new typology of emotional appeals: basic, versus social, emotional advertising', *Journal of Current Issues and Research in Advertising*, 19(2), Fall.

Hughes, S. (1997) 'Good ad, bad ad', *The Independent*, 17 November, media supplement.

Humby, C. (1996) 'Digging for information', *Marketing*, 21 November.

Humby, C. (1996) 'Opening the information warehouse', *Marketing*, 18 September.

Hume, S. (1988) 'Coupons score with consumers', *Advertising Age*, 15 February.

Hunt, S. (1997) 'Competing through relationships: grounding relationship marketing in resource–advantage theory', *Journal of Marketing Management*, 13(5).

Hutmik, R. (1996) 'The viability of web marketing and sales', *http://musieb.marist.edu/~kwp/ @http/thesis.html*

Hutton, J. (1995) 'Integrated Marketing Communications and the Evolution of Marketing Thought', paper presented at the American Academy of Advertising Annual Conference, March, and forthcoming in the *Journal of Business Research*.

Hutton, J. (1996) 'Integrated relationship marketing communications: a key opportunity for IMC', *Journal of Marketing Communications*, 2(3).

Iacobucci, D., Grayson, K. and Ostrom, A. (1994) 'Customer satisfaction fables', *Sloan Management Review*, 35(4).

Independent, The (1993) 'Instant coffee, instant fame', 3 February.

Independent, The (1993) 'Woman as head of the house? Shock! Horror!', Lambert, A. *The Independent, Living* Supplement, 1 April.

Independent, The (1994) 'When you wish upon a star ...', 27 December, media supplement.

Independent, The (1996) 'Boots: Visions with the lights off', Hawtree, Co., *The Independent*, 10 Feb.

Institute of Direct Marketing (1995) *Marketing Planning: Strategy, Planning and Analysis*, Module 1.

Institute of Practitioners in Advertising (1981–1997) *Advertising Works*, vols 1–9. The current edition is: Duckworth, G. (ed.) (1997) *Advertising Works 9*, Henley-on-Thames: NTC Publications.

Institute of Practitioners in Advertising (1986) *Some Suggested Provisions for Use in Agency/Client Agreements*, London: Institute of Practitioners in Advertising.

International Business Resources on the WWW, *http://ciber.bus.msu.edu/busres.htm*

Jackson, D. (1993) 'The seven deadly sins of financial services marketing ... and the road to redemption', *Direct Marketing*, 55(11).

Jackson, R. and Wang, P. (1994) *Strategic Database Marketing*, Lincolnwood, IL: NTC Publishing.

Jacob, R. (1993) 'Where the Big Brands Are Blooming', *Fortune*, 23 August.

Jakobson, R. (1974) *Main Trends in the Science of Language*, New York: Harper and Row.

Janis, I.L. (1954) 'Personality correlates of susceptibility to persuasion', *Journal of Personality*, 22.

Jarvenpaa, S. and Ives, B. (1994) 'Digital Equipment Corporation: The Internet Company (A)', CoxMIS Cases, Edwin L. Cox School of Business, Southern Methodist University. [http://www/cox.smu.edu/mis/cases/home.html]

Javlagi, R., Traylor, M., Cross. A. and Lampman, E. (1994) 'Awareness of sponsorship and corporate image: An empirical investigation', *Journal of Advertising*, 23(4).

Jim, S. (1995) *World Wide Marketing: Integrating the Internet into your Marketing Strategy*, Chichester: John Wiley.

Johnson, G. (1988) 'Rethinking Incrementalism', *Strategic Management Journal*, 9.

Johnson, R. and Cobb-Walgren, C. (1994) 'Ageing and the problem of television clutter', *Journal of Advertising Research*, 34(4).

Jonas, K. (1996) 'Does clutter matter?', *Admap*, 32(3).

Jones, G. (1987) 'EPOS and the retailer's information needs' in E. McFadyen (ed.) *The Changing Face of British Retailing*, London: Newman.

Jones, H. (1996) 'United Front', *Marketing Week*, 20 September.

Jones, J.P. (1990) 'Advertising: Strong force or weak force? Two views an ocean apart', *International Journal of Advertising*, 9(3).

Jones, J.P. (1990) 'Ad spending: maintaining market share', *Harvard Business Review*, January–February.

Jones, J.P. (1990) 'The double jeopardy of sales promotions', *Harvard Business Review*, September–October.

Jones, P. (1990) 'The double jeopardy of sales promotion', *Harvard Business Review*, 68(5).

Jones, P. (1995) *When Ads Work*, New York: Lexington Books.

Journal of Marketing Communications (1996) special edition devoted to Integrated Marketing Communications, 2(3), guest edited by Don Schultz.

Journal of Marketing Communications (1998) published by Routledge, volume 4.1 is devoted to new technology and developments in marketing communications.

Junu, B.K. (1993) 'Databases Open Doors for Retailers', *Advertising Age*, 64, 15 February.

Kahneman, D., Slovic, P. and Tversky, A. (eds) (1982) *Judgement Under Uncertainty: Heuristics and Biases*, New York: Cambridge University Press.

Kaikati, J.G. (1987) 'Celebrity advertising: a review and synthesis', *International Journal of Advertising*, 6.

Kalitka, P. (1996) 'The Equaliser vs Competitive Intelligence', *Competitive Intelligence Review*, 7(1), Spring.

Kalsbeck, B. and Novak, T.P. (1996) 'Internet use in the United States: 1995 baseline estimates and preliminary market segments', Project 2000 working paper, 12 April, *http://www2000.ogsm.vanderbilt.edu/*

Kapferer, J.N. (1997) *Strategic Brand Management* , 2nd edn, London: Kogan Page.

Karpf, A. (1997) 'Read all about me', *The Guardian*, 30 May, G2T supplement.

Katz, E. (1960) 'The functional approach to the study of attitudes', *Public Opinion Quarterly*, 24.

Katz, E. and Kahn, R. (1978) *The Social Psychology of Organizations*, 2nd edn, New York: John Wiley.

Katz, E. and Lazarsfield, P.F. (1955) *Personal Influence*, Glencoe: The Free Press.

Katz, H. (1991) 'From mass media to personal media', *Marketing and Research Today*, August.

Kay, J. (1993) *Foundations of Corporate Success*, Oxford: Oxford University Press.

Keegan, W.J. (1995) *Global Marketing Management*, 5th edn, New Jersey: Prentice Hall International.

Kiam, A. (1995) *Making Money on the Internet: Complete Beginners Guide*, Harrogate: Net Works.

Kiely, M. (1993) 'Integrated Marketing: Way of the Future or Ghost from the Past?', *Marketing (Australia)*, February.

Kilbourne, W.E. (1995) 'Green Advertising: Salvation or Oxymoron?', *Journal of Advertising*, XXIV(2), Summer.

Kimball, J.G. (1993) 'Association to fight advertising on the internet', *Business Marketing*, 78(11).

Kincaid, W.M. Jnr (1985) *Promotion: Products, Services, Ideas*, 2nd edn, Columbus, OH: Charles E. Merrill Publishing Co.

Kirkham, M. (1982) 'The need for VCR research', *Admap*, 18(7).

Kitchen, P.J. (1986) 'Zipping, zapping and nipping', *International Journal of Advertising*, 5(4).

Kitchen, P.J. (1993) 'Marketing Communications Renaissance', *International Journal of Advertising*, 12(4).

Kitchen, P.J. (1993) *Public Relations: Its Use and Development in UK Fast Moving Consumer Goods Firms*, University of Keele, unpublished PhD thesis.

Kitchen, P.J. (1993) 'Public relations: a rationale for its development and usage within UK FMCG firms', *European Journal of Marketing*, 27(7).

Kitchen, P. (1993) 'Towards the integration of marketing and public relations', *Marketing Intelligence and Planning*, 11(11).

Kitchen, P.J. (1994) 'The Marketing Communications Revolution: A Leviathan Unveiled?', *Marketing Intelligence and Planning*, 12(2).

Kitchen, P.J. (1996) Quotes from unpublished letters from leading UK academics, and CEO's in UK Public Limited Companies.

Kitchen, P.J. (1997) 'Developing a research framework: inductive vs deductive?', Chapter 15 in *Public Relations: Principles and Practice*, London: International Thomson Business Press.

Kitchen, P.J. (1997) 'Public Relations: A Prelude to Corporate Communications?', *Corporate Communications: An International Journal*, 2(1).

Kitchen, P.J. (1997) *Public Relations: Principles and Practice*, London: International Thomson Business Press.

Kitchen, P.J. (1997) 'Was Public Relations a Prelude to Corporate Communications?', *Corporate Communications – An International Journal*, 2(1).

Kitchen, P.J. (1997) Empirical work with Multinational/Global FMCG Firms with HQs in the United Kingdom, ongoing.

Kitchen, P.J. and Moss, D. (1995) 'Marketing and public relations: The relationship revisited', *Journal of Marketing Communications*, 1(2).

Kitchen, P.J. and Papasolomou, I.C. (1997) 'Marketing public relations: conceptual legitimacy or window dressing?', *Marketing Intelligence and Planning*, 15(2).

Kitchen, P.J. and Proctor R.A. (1991) 'The Increasing Importance of Public Relations in UK FMCG Firms', *Journal of Marketing Management*, 7(5).

Kitchen, P.J. and Schultz, D.E. (1997) 'Integrated marketing communications: what is it, and why are companies working that way?', in *New Ways for Optimising Integrated Communications*, ESOMAR, The Netherlands.

Kitchen, P.J. and Wheeler, C. (1997) 'Issues influencing marcoms in a global context', *Journal of Marketing Communications*, 3(4).

Klinger, E. (1971) *Structure and Functions of Fantasy*, New York: Wiley-Interscience.

Kneale, D. (1988) 'Zapping of TV ads appears pervasive', *Wall Street Journal*, 25 April.

Knights, D. and Morgan, G. (1991) 'Strategic Discourse and Subjectivity: Towards a Critical Analysis of Corporate Strategy in Organisations', *Organization Studies*, 12(2).

Kotler, P. (1972) 'A generic concept of marketing', *Journal of Marketing*, 36(2), April.

Kotler, P. (1984) *Marketing Management*, Englewood Cliffs, NJ: Prentice Hall.

Kotler, P. (1986) 'Megamarketing', *Harvard Business Review*, 64(2).

Kotler, P. (1988) *Marketing Management*, 6th edn, Englewood Cliffs, NJ: Prentice Hall.

Kotler, P. (1989) 'Public relations versus marketing: Dividing the conceptual domain and operational turf', a position paper prepared for the Public Relations Colloquium, San Diego, January 24.

Kotler, P. (1991) *Marketing Management, Analysis, Planning, Implementation and Control*, 7th edn, Englewood Cliffs, NJ: Prentice Hall International.

Kotler, P. (1993) *Marketing Management*, 6th edn, New Jersey: Prentice Hall.

Kotler, P. (1997) *Marketing Management, Analysis, Planning, Implementation, and Control*, 9th edn, Englewood Cliffs, NJ: Prentice Hall.

Kotler, P. and Levy, S.J. (1969) 'Broadening the concept of marketing', *Journal of Marketing*, 33(3), January.

Kotler, P. and Mindak, W. (1978) 'Marketing and public relations', *Journal of Marketing*, 42(4), October.

Kreitzman, L. (1986) 'Balancing brand building blocks', *Marketing*, 13 November.

Kroeber-Riel, W. (1979) 'Activation research: psychobiological approaches in consumer research', *Journal of Consumer Research*, 5, March.

Krol, E. (1992) *What's Allowed on the Internet, The Whole Internet Catalogue and User's Guide*, O'Reilly and Associates Inc.

Krugman, D.M. *et al.* (1994) *Advertising: Its Role in Modern Marketing*, 8th edn, New York: Dryden Press.

Krugman, H. (1965) 'The impact of television advertising: learning without involvement', *Public Opinion Quarterly*, 29.

Krugman, H. (1969) 'The learning of consumer likes, preferences, and choices', in F.M. Bass *et al.* (eds) *Applications of the Sciences in Marketing Management*, New York: J. Wiley and Sons.

Krugman, H. (197I) 'Brain wave measures of media involvement', *Journal of Advertising Research*, 11, February.

Kudos Productions (1997) 'The Remote Controllers', Channel 4 TV, 29 December.

Kuhn, T.S. (1964) *The Structure of Scientific Revolutions*, Phoenix: University of Chicago Press.

Kumar, N. (1996) 'The power of trust in manufacturer–retailer relationships', *Harvard Business Review*, Nov–Dec.

Lacher, K.T. (1994) 'An investigation of the influence of gender on the hedonic responses created by listening to music', *Advances in Consumer Research*, 21.

Lacher, K.T. and Mizerski, R. (1994) 'An exploratory study of the responses and relationships involved in the evaluation of, and intention to purchase new rock music', *Journal of Consumer Research*, 21, September.

Lambert, A. (1993) 'Woman as head of the house? Shock! Horror!', *The Independent*, 1 April, *Living* supplement.

Lancaster, G. and Massingham, L. (1988) *Marketing Primer*, London: Heinemann Professional Publishing.

Lancaster, G. A. and Taylor, C.T. (1986) 'The Diffusion of Innovations and their Attributes', *The Quarterly Review of Marketing*, Summer.

Langer, E. (1978) 'Rethinking the role of thought in social interaction', in J. Harvey, W. Ickes and R. Kidd (eds) *New Directions in Attributional Research*, Vol. 2, Hillsdale, NJ: Erlbaum.

Lannon, J. (1996) 'Integrated Communications from the Consumer End', *Admap*, 32(11), February.

Lasch, C. (1979) *The Culture of Narcissism*, New York: Norton.

Laspadakis, A. (1997) 'The Dynamic Role of Sales Promotion in the Greek FMCG Sector', University of Strathclyde, MPhil dissertation, unpublished.

Lasswell, H.D. (1948) *Power and Personality*, New York: Norton.

Lavidge, R.J. and Steiner, G.A. (1961) 'A model for predictive measurements of advertising effectiveness', *Journal of Advertising Marketing*, 24, October.

Lazer, W. (1987) *Handbook of Demographics for Marketing and Advertising*, Lexington, MA: Lexington Books.

Le Boutiller, P. (1995) 'Creating car advertising for women', *Admap*, September.

Leach, E. (1976) *Culture and Communication: the logic by which symbols are connected – an introduction to the use of structuralist analysis in social anthropology*, Cambridge: Cambridge University Press

Leather, D.S. (1988) 'The development and assessment of mass media campaigns: the work of the Advertising Research Unit: IV. 'Be all you can be' case history – Parts 1 and 2', *Journal of the Institute of Health Education*, 26(1 & 2).

Leavis, F.R. and Thompson, D. (1933) *Culture and Environment*, London: Chatto and Windus.

Lee, M., Sandler, D. and Shani, D. (1997) 'Attitudinal constructs towards sponsorship', *International Marketing Review*, 14(3).

Leggit, D. (1997) 'Putting posters on the map', *Marketing*, 3 July.

Levinson, J.C. and Rubin, C. (1995) *Guerrilla Marketing in the Internet: A Complete Guide to Making money On-Line*, London: Piatkus.

Levitt, T. (1960) 'Marketing myopia', *Harvard Business Review*, July/August.

Levitt, T. (1983) 'The Globalization of Markets', *Harvard Business Review*, May-June.

Levy, S.J. (1980) *The symbolic analysis of companies, brands, and customers'*, Albert Wesley Frey Lecture, Graduate School of Business, University of Pittsburgh, PA.

Lightcap, K. (1984) '*Marketing Support*', in B. Cantor *Experts in action: Inside public relations*, New York: Longman, Inc.

Lindblom, Charles (1959) 'The Science of Muddling Through', *Public Administration Review,* xix(2), Spring.

Linton, I. and Morley, I. (1995) *Integrated Marketing Communications,* Oxford: Butterworth–Heinemann.

Littman, J. (1993) 'Commerce on the Internet: the digital goldrush', *UnixWorld,* December.

Lodish, L. (1986) *The Advertising and Promotion Challenge: Vaguely Right or Precisely Wrong?,* New York: Oxford University Press.

Lodish, L.M. (1971) 'CALLPLAN: an interactive salesman's call planning system', *Management Science,* 18(4).

Lofman, B. (1991) 'Elements of experiential consumption: an exploratory study', *Advances in Consumer Research,* 18.

Long, G., Angold, S. and Hogg, M. (1992) 'Who am I?', *Marketing Education Group Conference Proceedings,* Salford, July.

Lord, K.R., Lee, M-S. and Sauer, P.L. (1995) 'The combined influence hypothesis: Central and peripheral antecedents of attitude toward the ad', *Journal of Advertising,* 24(1).

Lorenz, C. (1984) 'The Overselling of World Brands', *Financial Times,* July 19.

Lorenz, C. (1984) 'Why New Products Are Going Global', *Financial Times,* July 16.

Lottor, M.K. (1996) 'Internet domain survey', *ftp://ftp.nw.com/pub/zone/*

Loudon, D.L. and Della Bitta, A.J. (1993) *Consumer Behaviour,* New York: McGraw-Hill.

Lowe, A. (1996) 'An explanation of grounded theory,' Swedish School of Economics and Business Administration, Helsinki, Finland, *working paper,* Series 336.

Lowe, A. and Glaser, B.G. (1997) Conversations with Barney Glaser concerning Grounded Theory, videotape, published by SHEFC and Stirling University Press.

Lowe, A. and Glaser, B.G. (eds) (1995) 'The potential of grounded theory for the development of relationship marketing', in *Grounded Theory 1984 to 1994,* CA: Sociology Press.

Lucas, M. (1986) 'Changing stores to suit the changing customer', in ESOMAR (ed.) *Retail Strategies for Profit and Growth,* Amsterdam: ESOMAR.

Luck, D.J. (1969) 'Broadening the concept of marketing – too far', *Journal of Marketing,* 33, July.

Lundberg, C. (1985) 'On the feasibility of cultural intervention', in P. Frost *et al.* (eds) *Organizational Culture,* Newbury Park, CA: Sage.

Lutz, K.A. and Lutz, R.J. (1977) 'Imagery-eliciting strategies: review and implications of research', *Advances in Consumer Research,* 5.

Lutz, R.J. (1996) 'Some General Observations about Research in IMC', in Moore, J. and Thorsen, E. (eds) *Integrated Communications: Synergy of Persuasive Voices,* New Jersey: Lawrence Erlbaum Associates.

Maier, J. (1985) 'The big event and the sales promotion campaign', in S.M. Ulanoff (ed.) *HandBook of Sales Promotion,* New York: McGraw-Hill

Manning G.L. and Reece B.L. (1992) *Selling Today: An Extension of the Marketing Concept,* 5th edn, Boston, MA: Allyn & Bacon.

March, J.G. and Olsen, J.P. (1976) *Ambiguity and Choice in Organization,* Bergen, Norway: Universitetforlaget.

Marketing Pocketbook (1985, 1986, 1987, 1988, 1989, 1990) Contain *Campaign*'s data, compiled by MEAL, The Advertising Association.

Marketing (1995) 'Marketing-Nielsen Biggest Brands', 16 March.

Marketing (1996) see reference to Henley Centre, 23 October.

Marketing Report. (1995) 'Mass media advertising expenditures within Europe', September, 11, weekly magazine published in Athens.

Marketing Week (1995) 'Looking after own-label', 14 July.

Marshall, C. (1994) *Campaign,* 23 June.

Marshall, D. and Cook, G. (1992) 'The corporate sports sponsor', *International Journal of Advertising,* 11(4).

Martin, C. (1997) *The Digital Estate: Strategies for Competing, Surviving and Thriving in an Internetworked World*, New York: McGraw-Hill (*http://www/mcgraw-hill.com/digitalestate*).

Martin, J. (1992) *Cultures in Organizations: Three Perspectives* New York: Oxford University Press.

Martin, J. (1996) *Cybercorp: the New Business Revolution*, AMACOM, (*http://128.197.190.184/stupro/martin*).

Martin, J., Sitkin, S. and Boehm, M. (1985) 'Founders and the Elusiveness of a Cultural Legacy' in P. Frost, L. Moore, M.R. Louis, C. Lundberg and J. Martin (eds) *Organizational Culture*, Beverly Hills, CA: Sage.

Maslow, A.H. (1968) *Toward a Psychology of Being*, 2nd edn, Princeton, NJ: Van Nostrand.

May, E., Ress, C. and Salmon, W. (1988) 'Future trends in retailing: merchandise line trends and store trends 1980–1990', in E. Kaynak (ed.) *Transactional Retailing*, Berlin: Walter de Gruyter.

Mayer, R.N., Scammon, D.L. and Zick, C.D. (1993) 'Poisoning the Well: Do Environmental Claims Strain Consumer Credulity?', *Advances in Consumer Research*, 20.

Mayle, P. (1990) *Up the Agency*, London: Pan Books.

Mazur, L. (1996) 'Follow the Leader', *Marketing*, 29 February.

Mazur, L. and Hogg, A. (1993) *The Marketing Challenge*, Wokingham: Addison-Wesley and The Economist Intelligence Unit.

McAlister, A., Perry, C., Killen, J., Slinkard, L.A. and Maccoby, N. (1980) 'Pilot study of smoking, alcohol and drug abuse prevention', *American Journal of Public Health*, 70.

McCabe, D. (1998) 'The Future is (Dayglo) Orange', *The Bookseller*, 20 February.

McCall, G. (1970) 'The social organisation of relationships', in G. McCall, M. McCall, N. Denzin, G. Suttles and S. Kurth (eds) *Social Relationships*, Chicago: Aldine.

McCann, P. (1997) 'Britons shun advertising overkill', *The Independent*, 18 October.

McCarthy, E.J. (1960) *Basic Marketing*, Homewood IL: Irwin.

McCarthy, E.J. (1981) *Basic Marketing: A Managerial Approach*, 9th edn, New York: Richard D. Irwin.

McDaniel, C. (1979) *Marketing: An Integrated Approach*, New York: Harper and Row.

McDonagh, P. (1994) 'Towards an Understanding of What Constitutes Green Advertising as a Form of Sustainable Communication', paper presented at the Doctoral Colloquium of The Marketing Education Group Annual Conference, University of Ulster.

McDonagh, P., Peattie, K. and Prothero, A. (1994) 'Everyone's Listening But No-one Is Talking', Marketing Education Group Annual Conference, University of Ulster, July.

McDonald, C. (1991) 'Sponsorship and the image of the sponsor', *European Journal of Marketing*, 25(11).

McDonald, C. (1992) *How Advertising Works: A Review of Current Thinking*, Henley-on-Thames: NTC Publications.

McDonald, C. (1993) (ed.) *How Advertising Works*, Oxfordshire: NTC Publications Limited.

McDonald, C. (1995) 'The role and purpose of media planning', Chapter 1 in C. McDonald and M. Monkman (eds) *The MRG Guide to Media Research*, Salisbury, Wilts: Media Research Group.

McDonald, C. and Monkman, M. (eds) (1995) *The MRG Guide to Media Research*, Salisbury, Wilts: Media Research Group.

McDonald, M.B. (1984) *Marketing Plans: How to Prepare Them: How to Use Them*, Oxford: Chartered Institute of Marketing, Heinemann.

McDonald, P. (1991) 'The Los Angeles Olympic Organizing Committee: Developing Organizational Culture in the Short Run', in M. Jones, M. Moore and R. Snyder (eds) *Inside Organizations*, Newbury Park, CA: Sage.

McGoldrick, P. (1990) *Retail Marketing*, London: Prentice Hall.

McGuire, W.J. (1964) 'Inducing resistance to persuasion: Some contemporary approaches', In L. Berkowitz (ed.) *Advances in Experimental Social Psychology*, Vol. 1., Academic Press.

McGuire, W.J. (1976) 'Some internal psychological factors influencing consumer choice', *Journal of Consumer Research*, 4, March.

McGuire, W.J. and Papageorgis, D. (1961) 'The relative efficacy of various types of prior belief-defense in producing immunity against persuasion', *Journal of Abnormal and Social Psychology*, 62.

McIntosh, A. and Wheble, A. (1997) 'The Myth of Fragmentation' *Admap*, 32(11), December.

McKenna, R. (1991) 'Marketing is Everything: Everything is Marketing', *Harvard Business Review*, January–February.

McKitterick, J.B. (1957) 'What is the marketing management concept?', in F.M. Bass (ed.) *The Frontiers of Marketing Thought and Action*, American Marketing Association.

Media Research Group (1995) *The MRG Guide to Media Research, Salisbury, Wilts:The Media Research Group*.

Meenaghan, T. (1991) 'The role of sponsorship in the marketing communication mix', *International Journal of Advertising*, 10(1).

Meenaghan, T. (1991) 'Sponsorship – Legitimising the medium', *European Journal of Marketing*, 25(11).

Meenaghan, T. (1994) 'Point of view: Ambush marketing – immoral or imaginative practice?', *Journal of Advertising Research*, 34(3).

Meenaghan, T. (1996) 'Ambush marketing – a threat to corporate sponsorship', *Sloan Management Review*, 38(1).

Meerabeau, E., Gillett, R., Kennedy, M., Adeoba, J., Byass, M. and Tabi, K. (1991) 'Sponsorship and the drinks industry in the 1990s', *European Journal of Marketing*, 25(11).

Meller, Paul (1991) 'Midland Takes a Simpler Tack', *Marketing*, 8 August, 2.

Meredith, S. (1997) 'We have the technology', *Marketing Business*, Chartered Institute of Marketing, UK.

Meredith, W. and Twyman, A. (1997) 'BARB – Wired for the Future?', *Admap*, 32(11), December.

Merims, A.M. (1972) 'Marketing's stepchild: Product publicity', *Harvard Business Review*, 36(5), Nov/Dec.

Mescon, T. and Tilson, D. (1987) 'Corporate philanthropy: A strategic approach to the bottom line', *California Management Review*, 29(2).

Messaris, P. (1997) *Visual Persuasion, The Role of Images in Advertising*, Newbury Park, CA: Sage.

Metz, C. (1974) *Film Language – a Semiotics of the Cinema*, New York: Oxford University Press.

Micklethwaite, J. (1990) 'A survey of the advertising industry: the proof of the pudding', *The Economist*, 9 June.

Midgley C. and Withworth, D. (1996) 'Adverts take centre stage in Christmas video sales battle', *The Times*, 23 November.

Miles, R. and Snow, C. (1986) 'Network Organizations: New Concepts for New Forms', *California Management Review*, 28(3), Spring.

Miller, C. (1994) 'Celebrities hot despite scandal', *Marketing News*, 28(7).

Miller, D.W. and Marks, L.J. (1992) 'Mental imagery and sound effects in radio commercials', *Journal of Advertising*, 21, December.

Mills, C.W. (1959) *The Sociological Imagination*, New York: Oxford University Press.

Mintel Report (1996) *Direct Mail Developments*.

Mintzberg, H. (1978) 'Patterns in Strategy Formulation', *Management Science*, 24(9).

Mintzberg, H. (1983) *Structure in Fives*, Englewood Cliffs, NJ: Prentice Hall.

Mintzberg, H. (1987) 'Crafting Strategy', *Harvard Business Review*, July/August.

Mintzberg, H. (1989) *Mintzberg on Management: Inside Our Strange World of Organizations*, New York: The Free Press, MacMillan.

Mintzberg, H. (1994) *The Rise and Fall of Strategic Planning*, New York, London: Prentice Hall.

Mintzberg, H. and McHugh, A. (1985) 'Strategy Formation in an Adhocracy', *Administrative Science Quarterly*, 30.

Mintzberg, H. and Waters, J.A. (1982) 'Tracking Strategy in an Entrepreneurial Firm', *Academy of Management Journal*, 6.

Mintzberg, H. and Waters, J.A. (1985) 'Of Strategies, Deliberate and Emergent', *Strategic Management Journal*, 6.

Mintzberg, H., Raisinghani, D. and Theoret, A. (1976) 'The Structure of Unstructured Decision Processes', *Administrative Science Quarterly*, 21.

Mintzberg, H., Quinn, J.B. and Ghoshal, S. (1995) *The Strategy Process*, European edn, London: Prentice Hall.

Misra, S. and Beatty, S.E. (1990) 'Celebrity spokesperson and brand congruence: an assessment of recall and affect', *Journal of Business Research*, 21.

Mitchell, A. (1996) Interview transcribed from BBC Radio 4 'You and Yours', January.

Mitchell, A. (1997) 'Star Gazing', *Marketing Business*, June.

Mitchell, A.A. (1983) 'Cognitive processes initiated by advertising', in R.J. Harris (ed.) *Information Processing Research in Advertising*, Lawrence Erlbaum Associates.

Molenaar, C. (1996) *Interactive Marketing: The End of Mass Marketing*, London: Gower.

Moorman, C., Zaltman, G. and Deshpande, R. (1992) 'Relationships between providers and users of market research: the dynamics of trust within and between organisations', *Journal of Marketing Research*, 29(3).

Morgan, G. (1997) *Images of Organization*, 2nd edn, Thousand Oaks, CA: Sage.

Morgan, R.M. and Hunt, S.D. (1994) 'The commitment–trust theory of relationship marketing', *Journal of Marketing*, 58(3).

Morris, M. and Pitt, L. (1994) 'The Organization of the Future: Unity of Marketing and Strategy', *Journal of Marketing Management*, 10(7).

Mosely, F. (1995) 'Whose Line Is It Anyway?' *The Drum*, Glasgow, October.

MRB (1995) *Consumer Purchasing Behaviour Vs Consumer Lifestyles in Greece*, unpublished data given to the author for the purpose of this chapter.

Mueller, B. (1996) *International Advertising-Communicating Across Cultures*, California, London: Belmont.

Mumby, D.K. and Putnam, L.L. (1992) 'The Politics of Emotion: A Feminist Reading of Bounded Rationality', *Academy of Management Review* 17(3).

Murray, R. and Lowe, R. (1995) 'Writing and dialogue for the PhD', *Journal of Graduate Education*, 1(2).

Myers, G. (1994) *Words in Ads*, London: Edward Arnold.

Naples, M. (1979) *Effective Frequency*, New York: Association of Advertisers.

Nasuretti, R. (1997) 'P&G, seeing shoppers confused, overhauls marketing', *Wall Street Journal Europe*, 20 January.

Negroponte, N. (1996) *Being Digital*, London: Vintage Books.

Netpost (1996) '1995 Tenagra Awards for Internet marketing excellence announced', *http://www/netpost.com/awards95.html*

Network Wizard (1996) 'Internet domain survey', January, *http://www.nw.com/zone/WWW/report.html*

Neumann, J. von and Morgenstern, O. (1944) *The Theory of Games and Economic Behaviour*, Princeton: University Press.

Nielsen (1980) *Nielsen Study of Private Labels in the Grocery Retail Trade of Europe*, Oxford: A.C. Nielsen.

Nielsen, A.C. (1982) *Nielsen Researcher. Annual Reviews of Grocery Trading*, London: Nielsen.

Nouwens, J. and Bouwman, H. (1996) 'Living apart together in electronic commerce: the use of information and communication technology to create network organizations', Project 2000, *Journal of Computer-Mediated Communication*, 1(3), December, available at *http://shum, huji.ac.il/jcmc/vol1/issue3/hoffman.html*

Novelli, W.D. (1988) 'Stir some PR into your communications mix', *Marketing News*, 22, 5 December.

Novelli, W.D. (1989–1990) 'One-Stop Shopping: Some Thoughts on Integrated Marketing Communications', *Public Relations Quarterly*, (Winter).

Novotny, M. (1989) 'Best Laid Plans vs. Reality', *Public Relations Journal,* 5(9), September.

Nowak, G. and Phelps, J. (1994) 'The Integrated Marketing Communications Phenomenon: An Examination of its Impact on Advertising Practices and its Implications for Advertising Research', *Journal of Current Issues and Research in Advertising,* 16(1).

Nutt, P.C. (1984) 'Types of Organizational Decision Processes', *Administrative Science Quarterly,* 29.

O'Barr, W. M. (1994) *Culture and the Ad. – Exploring Otherness in the World of Advertising,* Boulder, CO: Westview Press.

Obermiller, C. and Atwood, A. (1990) 'Feelings about feeling-state research: a search for harmony', *Advances in Consumer Research,* 17.

O'Donoghue, D. (1997) 'Account planning and media planning', Chapter 8 in A. Cooper (ed.) *How to Plan Advertising,* 2nd edn, London: Cassell.

O'Donohoe, S. (1997) 'Raiding the postmodern pantry: advertising intertextuality and the young adult audience', *European Journal of Marketing,* 31(3/4).

Ody, P. (1987) 'Creating long term strategy for retailing', *Retail and Distribution Management,* 15(6).

Ogilvy & Mather Direct (1985) *Direct Marketing: New Opportunities for Business to Business Selling,* London: Ogilvy & Mather.

Ogilvy, D. (1983) *Ogilvy on Advertising,* London: Pan Books.

Ogilvy, D. (1987) 'Sound the alarm', *International Journal of Advertising,* 6(1).

Ohmae, K. (1985) *Triad Power,* New York: Free Press.

Ohmae, K. (1989) 'The Global Logic of Strategic Alliances', *Harvard Business Review,* 67 (March–April).

O'Keefe, D.J. (1990) *Persuasion: Theory and Research,* London: Sage.

Oliver, R.L., Robertson, T.S. and Mitchell, D.J. (1993) 'Imaging and analyzing in response to new product advertising', *Journal of Advertising,* 22, December.

Olver, J.M. and Farris, P.W. (1989) 'Push and pull: A one-two punch for packaged products', *Sloan Management Review,* Fall.

O'Malley, L., Patterson, M. and Evans, M. (1997) 'Intimacy or intrusion? The privacy dilemma for relationship marketing in consumer markets', *Journal of Marketing Management,* 13.

Organ, D.W. and Greene, C.N. (1981) 'The Effects of Formalization of Professional Involvement: A Compensatory Process Approach', *Administrative Science Quarterly,* 26(2).

O'Riordan, T. (1976) *Environmentalism,* London: Pion Limited.

Ottman, J. (1993) *Green Marketing: Challenges and Opportunities for the New Marketing Age,* Lincolnwood, IL: NTC Business Books.

Palda, K.S. (1966) 'The hypothesis of a hierarchy of effects: a partial evaluation', *Journal of Marketing Research,* 3(1), February.

Paliwoda, S. (1993) *International Marketing,* 2nd edn, London: Butterworth–Heinemann.

Papageorgis, D. and McGuire, W.J. (1961) 'The generality of immunity to persuasion produced by pre-exposure to weakened counterarguments', *Journal of Abnormal and Social Psychology,* 62.

Papatla, P. and Krishnamurthi, L. (1996) 'Measuring the dynamic effects of promotions on brand choice', *Journal of Consumer Research,* 33(1).

Parente, D., Vanden Berg, B., Barban, A. and Marra, J. (1996) *Advertising Campaign Strategy: A Guide to Marketing Communications Plans,* Orlando, FL: Dryden Press.

Parker, K. (1991) 'Sponsorship: The research contribution', *European Journal of Marketing,* 25(11).

Parker, M. (1995) 'Working Together, Working Apart: Management Culture in a Manufacturing Firm', *The Sociological Review,* 43(3), August.

Parkinson, S. (1994) *Computers in Marketing,* London: Butterworth–Heinemann.

Pascale, R.D. (1984) 'The Real Story Behind Honda's Success', *California Management Review,* XXVI(3).

Pasick R.J. and Wallack. L. (1989) 'Mass media in health promotion: a compilation of expert opinion', *International Quarterly of Community Health Education,* 9(2).

Patai, R. (1977) *The Jewish Mind*, New York: Charles Scribner's Sons.

Patterson, J. and Kim, P. (1991) *The Day America Told the Truth*, New York: Plume.

Patterson, M., Evans, M. and O'Malley, L. (1996) 'The growth of direct marketing and consumer attitudinal response to the privacy issue', *Journal of Targeting, Measurement and Analysis for Marketing*, 4(3).

Payne, A., Christopher, M., Clark, M., and Peck, H. (1995) *Relationship Marketing for Competitive Advantage*, Oxford: Butterworth–Heinneman.

Pedrick, J. and Zufryden, F. (1991) 'Evaluating the impact of advertising media plans: a model of consumer purchase dynamics using single-source data', *Marketing Science*, 10(2).

Peebles, D.M., Ryans, J. K. Jr., Vernon, I. R. (1978) 'Coordinating International Advertising', *Journal of Marketing*, 42, January.

Pegram, R.M. (1972) *Selling and Servicing the National Account*, New York: Conference Board.

Penner, L.A. and Fritzsche, B.A. (1993) 'Magic Johnson and reactions to people with AIDS: A natural experiment', *Journal of Applied Social Psychology*, 23(13).

Perfect, T. and Heatherley, S. (1996) 'Implicit memory in print ads', *Admap*, January.

Perloff, R.M. (1993) *The Dynamics of Persuasion*, New Jersey: Lawrence Erlbaum.

Peters, T. and Waterman, R. (1982) *In Search of Excellence*, New York: Harper and Row.

Pettigrew, A. (1977) 'Strategy Formulation as a Political Process', *International Studies of Management and Organization*, VII(2).

Pettigrew, A. (1979) 'On studying organizational cultures', *Administrative Science Quarterly*, 24(4).

Pettijohn, C., Pettijohn, L. and Taylor, A. (1995) 'The relationship between effective counselling and effective behaviors', *Journal of Consumer Marketing*, 12(1).

Petty, R.E. (1977). 'A Cognitive Response Analysis of the Temporal Persistence of Attitude Changes Induced by Persuasive Communications', unpublished doctoral dissertation, Ohio State University, Columbus, OH.

Petty, R.E. and Brock, T.C. (1981). 'Thought disruption and persuasion: Assessing the validity of attitude change experiments', in R.E. Petty, T.M. Ostrom and T.C. Brock (eds) *Cognitive Responses in Persuasion*, Hillsdale, NJ: Lawrence Erlbaum.

Petty, R.E. and Cacioppo, J.T. (1977) 'Forewarning, cognitive responding, and resistance to persuasion', *Journal of Personality and Social Psychology*, 35.

Petty, R.E. and Cacioppo, J.T. (1983) 'Central and peripheral routes to persuasion: Application to advertising', in L. Percy and A. Woodside (eds) *Advertising and Consumer Psychology*, Lexington, MA: Lexington Books, D.C. Heath.

Petty, R.E. and Cacioppo, J.T. (1986) *Communication and Persuasion: Central and Peripheral Routes to Attitude Change*, New York: Springer-Verlag.

Petty, R.E., Cacioppo, J.T. and Schumann, D. (1983) 'Central and peripheral routes to advertising effectiveness: The moderating role of involvement', *Journal of Consumer Research*, 10.

Petty, R.E., Ostrom, T.M. and Brock, T.C. (1981) 'Historical foundations of the cognitive response approach to attitudes and persuasion', in R.E. Petty, T.M. Ostrom and T.C. Brock (eds) *Cognitive Responses in Persuasion*, Hillsdale, NJ: Lawrence Erlbaum Associates.

Phelps, J., Plumley, J. and Johnson, E. (1994) 'Integrated Marketing Communications: Who is Doing What?' in K.W. King (ed) *Proceedings of the 1994 Conference of the American Academy of Advertising*, University of Georgia, Athens, GA.

Pierce, C.S. (1975) 'Some Consequences of Four Incapabilities', *Journal of Speculative Philosophy*, 2, in Pierce, C.S. (1975) *Collected Papers of Charles Sanders Pierce*, ed. C. Hartshone, P. Weiss, A.W. Burks. Cambridge, Harvard.

Piercy, N. (1983) 'Retailer information power – the channel marketing information system', *Marketing Intelligence and Planning*, 1(1).

Piercy, N. (1987) 'Advertising budgeting: process and structure as explanatory variables', *Journal of Advertising*, 16(2).

Piercy, N. and Morgan, N. (1990) 'Organisational Context and Behavioural Problems as Determinants of the Effectiveness of the Strategic Marketing Planning Process', *Journal of Marketing Management*, 6(2).

Poffenberger, A.T. (1925) *Psychology in Advertising*, New York: Shaw.

Poon, S. and Jevons, C. (1997) 'Internet-enabled international marketing: a small business perspective', *Journal of Marketing Management*, Special Edition on Internationalisation (J. Hamill, ed.), 13(1–3), Jan–April.

Poon, S. and Swatman, P.M.C. (1995) 'Small business alliances: a framework for Internet-enabled strategic advantage', Monash University, Department of Information Systems, *Working Paper 25/95*, July.

Popcorn, F. (1991) *The Popcorn Report*, London: Arrow Books.

Popper, K. (1959) *The Logic of Scientific Discovery*, London: Hutchinson.

Porrit, J. (1984) *Seeing Green: The Politics of Ecology Explained*, Oxford: Basil Blackwell.

Porter, A. (1993) 'Strengthening coupon offers by requiring more from the retailer', *Journal of Consumer Marketing*, 10(2).

Porter, M.E. (ed) (1986) *Competition in Global Industries*, Harvard Business School Press.

Powell, D. (1992) *Counter Revolution*, London: Grafton.

Poynor, M. (1987) 'The changing consumer', in E. McFayden (ed.) *The Changing Face of British Retailing*, London: Newman Books.

PR Week – UK Top 150 PR Consultancies (1992), Tougher all round for the top ten, Haymarket publication, 30 April.

PR Week – UK Top 150 PR Consultancies (1993), Haymarket publication.

PR Week – UK Top 150 PR Consultancies (1994), Mixed fortunes for the top ten, Haymarket publication, 28 April.

PR Week (1997) 'Kodak sharpens its focus on China through O&M PR' (Jemimah Bailey), 18 July.

PR Week (1997) 'Mere tackles intersport drive to unify branding' (Karen Dempsey), 15 August.

Preston, I. (1994) *The tangled web they weave: Truth, Falsity and Advertisers*, Wisconsin: The University of Wisconsin Press.

Preston, I.L. and Thorson, E. (1984) 'The expanded association model: keeping the hierarchy concept alive', *Journal of Advertising Research*, 24(1), February/March.

Pringle, H. (1995) *Campaign*, 20 October.

Progressive Grocer (1986) *Annual Report of the Grocery Industry*, April 1983 and April 1986, United Kingdom.

Project 2000 (1996) *http://www2000.ogsm.vanderbilt.edu/*

Prothero, A., McDonagh, P. and Peattie, K. (1994) 'Green Marketing Communications: Dressing Windows or Opening Doors?', Proceedings of the 25th Marketing Education Group Annual Conference, University of Ulster, Vol. II.

Quelch, J. and Harding, D. (1996) 'Brands versus private labels', *Harvard Business Review*, 75(1).

Quelch, J. (1983) 'Its time to make trade promotion more productive', *Harvard Business Review*, 61(3).

Quelch, J.A. (1982) *Trade Promotion by Grocery Products Manufacturers: A Managerial Perspective*, Report No. 82–106, Cambridge, MA: Marketing Science Institute, August.

Quelch, J.A. and Hoff, E.J. (1986) 'Customizing Global Marketing', *Harvard Business Review*, 64 (May–June).

Quelch, J.A. and Klein, L.R. (1996) 'The Internet and international marketing', *Sloan Management Review*, Spring.

Quelch, J. (1982) *Trade Promotion by Grocery Products Manufacturing: A Managerial Perspective*, Report No. 82–106, Marketing Science Institute, Cambridge, MA, August.

Quester, P. (1997) 'Awareness as a measure of sponsorship effectiveness: the Adelaide Formula One Grand Prix and evidence of incidental ambush effects', *Journal of Marketing Communications*, 3(1).

Quinn, J.B. (1980) *Strategies for Change*, Homewood, IL: Irwin.

Radio 4, *Sunday Programme*, 22 March 1998.

Rajaretnam, J. (1994) 'The long-term effects of sponsorship', *Marketing and Research Today*, February.

Ramond, C. (1976) *Advertising Research: The State of the Art*, New York: Association of National Advertisers.

Randall, G. (1994) *Trade Marketing Strategies*, London: Butterworth–Heinemann Ltd.

Rapp, S. and Collins, T. (1987) *Maxi-Marketing*, New York: McGraw-Hill.

Rapp, S. and Collins, T.L. (1994) *Beyond Maxi-marketing*, New York: McGraw-Hill.

Ray, M.L. (1973) 'Marketing communication and the hierarchy of effects', in P. Clarke (ed.) *New Models for Mass Communication Research: Sage Annual Review of Communication Research, Volume II*, Beverly Hills: Sage Publications.

Ray, M.L. (1982) *Advertising and Communication Managment*, Englewood Cliffs, NJ: Prentice Hall.

Rayport, G.F. and Sviokla, J.G. (1994) 'Managing and Marketspace', *Harvard Business Review*, November/December.

Redman, S., Spencer, E.A. and Sanson Fisher, R.W. (1990) 'The role of mass media in changing health-related behaviour: a critical appraisal of two models', *Health Promotion International*, 5(5).

Redmond, W. H. (1996) 'Product disadoption: Quitting smoking as a diffusion process', *Journal of Public Policy and Marketing*, 15(1), Spring.

Rees, A. (1992) 'How Sainsbury as a retailer has become a successful brand', paper given at a *Marketing Week* conference, London, 2 April.

Rees, P. (1997) 'ESRC/JISC questionnaire to users of census data: views about the 2001 census of population', Summer.

Rees, R.D. (1977) *Advertising Budgeting and Appraisal in Practice*, Research Study no. 11, The Advertising Association, London.

Reid, E.M. (1991) 'Electropolis: communications and community on Internet Relay Chat', Honours thesis, University of Melbourne, Department of History [URL:*gopher://wiretap.-spies.com:70/00/Library/Cyter/electrop.txt*].

Rhine, R.J. and Severance, L.J. (1970) 'Ego-involvement, discrepancy, source credibility, and attitude change', *Journal of Personality and Social Psychology*, 16.

Rice, R.E. and Paisley, W.J. (eds) (1990) *Public Communications Campaigns*, Sage Publications.

Richards, A. (1995) 'First Direct set for a TV Return', *Marketing*, 26 January.

Ries, A. and Trout, J. (1986) *Marketing Warfare*, New York: Mcgraw-Hill Marketing Series, International Edition.

Riley, M.W. and Riley, J.W. (1959) 'Mass Communication and the Social System', in R.K. Merton, L. Broom and L. Cottrell (eds) *Sociology Today: Problems and Prospects*, New York: Harper.

Roberts, M.L. and Berger, P.D. (1989) *Direct Marketing Management*, Englewood Cliffs, NJ: Prentice Hall.

Robertson, T. (1993) Invited guest lecturer at Communications Seminar, University of Strathclyde.

Robertson T.S. (1967) 'The Process of Innovation and the Diffusion of Innovation', *Journal of Marketing*, January.

Robertson, T.S. and Rossiter J.R. (1974) 'Children and commercial persuasion: an attribution theory analysis', *Journal of Consumer Research*, 1 (June).

Robertson T.S., Zielinski J. and Ward S. (1984) *Consumer Behaviour*, Glenview, IL: Scott Foresman.

Robin, D. (1995) 'Comment. Exchange, perception of value and relationship marketing: applying the basics to the future', *Journal of Marketing – Theory and Practice*, 3(4).

Rodman, J. (1983) 'Four Forms of Ecological Consciousness Reconsidered', in D. Scherer and T. Attig (eds) *Ethics and the Environment*, Prentice Hall, Inc.

Roff, S. (1997) 'The ultimate relationship', paper delivered at Relationship Marketing for Charities Conference, London, 25 February 1996.

Rogers, E.M. (1995) *Diffusion of Innovations*, 4th edn, New York: Free Press.

Rogers, E.M. (1996) *Communications Technology: The new media in society*, New York: Free Press.

Rose, P.B. (1996) 'Practitioner Opinions and Interests Regarding IMC in Selected Latin American Countries', *Journal of Marketing Communications*, 2(3).

Ross, E.A. (1908) *Social Psychology: An Outline and a Source Book*, New York: Macmillan.

Rossenberg, L.J. and Czepiel, P. (1989) 'A marketing approach for customer retention', *Journal of Consumer Marketing*.

Rossiter, J.R. (1982) 'Visual imagery: applications to advertising', *Advances in Consumer Research*, 9.

Rossiter, J.R. and Percy, L. (1978) 'Visual imaging ability as a mediator of advertising response', *Advances in Consumer Research*, 5.

Rossiter, J.R. and Percy, L. (1987) *Advertising and Promotion Management*, New York: McGraw-Hill.

Ryans, A.B. and Weinberg, C.B. (1979) 'Territory sales response', *Journal of Marketing Research*, 16, November.

Sanders, S. (1995) 'Celebrity name game', *Discount Store News*, 34(10).

Sandler, D. and Shani, D. (1995) 'Sponsorship and the Olympic Games: The consumer perspective', *Sports Marketing Quarterly*, 2(3).

Sandler, D. and Shani, P. (1989) 'Olympic sponsorship vs ambush marketing: Who gets the gold?', *Journal of Advertising Research*, 29(4).

Santilli, P.C. (1983) 'The informative and persuasive functions of advertising: A moral appraisal', *Journal of Business Ethics* 2.

Saporito, W. (1993) 'Where the Global Action Is', *Fortune*, Special Issue, Autumn/Winter.

Sargent, J. (1995) 'Brand building in the UK', *Admap*, 31(1).

Sarkar, M.B., Butler, B. and Sreinfeld, C. (1995) 'Intermediaries and cybermediaries: a continuing role for mediating players in the electronic marketplace', in R.R. Dholakia and D.R. Forrin (eds) *Proceedings from Conference on Telecommunications and Information Markets*, October.

Sathe, V. (1985) *Culture and Related Corporate Realities*, Homewood IL: Richard D. Irwin.

Sawyer, A. (1981) 'Repetition, cognitive responses and persuasion', in R.E. Petty, T.M. Ostrom and T.C. Brock (eds) *Cognitive Responses in Persuasion*, Hillsdale, NJ: Lawrence Erlbaum Associates.

Saynor J. (1998) 'The Insult', *The Observer*, 28 January.

Schab, F.R. (1991) 'Odor memory: taking stock', *Psychological Bulletin*, 109(2).

Schein, E. (1983) 'The role of the founder in creating organizational cultures', *Organizational Dynamics*, 12(1).

Schein, E. (1985) 'How culture forms, develops and changes', in R. Kilmann *et al.* (eds) *Gaining Control of the Corporate Culture*, San Francisco, CA: Jossey-Bass.

Schein, E. (1985) *Organizational Culture and Leadership*, San Francisco, CA: Jossey-Bass.

Schein, E. (1992) *Organizational Culture and Leadership*, 2nd edn, San Francisco, CA: Jossey-Bass.

Schlinger, M.J. (1976) 'The role of mass communication in promoting public health', *Advances in Consumer Research*, 3.

Schneider, W. and Shiffrin, R.M. (1977) 'Controlled and automatic human information processing: Detection, search and attention', *Psychological Review*, 84.

Schramm, W. (1948) *Mass Communications*, Urbana, IL: University of Illinois Press.

Schramm, W. (1955) *The Process and Effects of Mass Communications*, Urbana IL: University of Illinois Press.

Schramm, W.D. (1971) 'How communication works', in W.D. Schramm and D.F. Roberts (eds) *The Process and Effects of Mass Communication*, Urbana, IL: University of Illinois Press.

Schreiber, R.J. and Appel, V. (1991) 'Advertising evaluation using surrogate measures for sales', *Journal of Advertising Research*, December.

Schroer, J.C. (1990) 'Ad spending: growing market share', *Harvard Business Review*, January–February.

Schultz, D.E. (1987) 'Above and below the line: Growth in sales promotion in the United States', *International Journal of Advertising*, 6(1).

Schultz, D.E. (1991) 'Integrated Marketing Communications: The Status of Integrated Marketing Communications Programs in the US Today', *Journal of Promotion Management*, 1(1).

Schultz, D.E. (1993) 'Integrated Marketing Communications: Maybe Definition is in the Point of View', *Marketing News*, 18 January.

Schultz, D.E. (1996) 'Integrating the Organization's Information Resources', *Marketing News*, 30(15).

Schultz, D.E. (1996) 'Is IMC Finally Becoming Mainstream?', *Marketing News*, 30(14), 1 July.

Schulz, D.E. (1996) 'The inevitability of integrated communications', *Journal of Business Research*, 37(3).

Schultz, D.E. (1997–8) 'The evolving nature of integrated marketing communications', *Journal of Integrated Communications*, 8.

Schultz, D.E. and Martin, D.G. (1979) *Strategic Advertising Campaigns*, Chicago, IL: Crain Books.

Schultz, D.E. and Robinson, W. (1982) *Sales Promotion Management*, Chicago: Crain Books.

Schultz, D.E. and Schultz, H. (1998) 'Transitioning marketing communication into the 21st Century', *Journal of Marketing Communications*, 4(1).

Schultz, D.E., Martin, D.G. and Brown, W. (1984) *Strategic Advertising Campaigns*, Chicago, IL: Crain Books.

Schultz, D.E., Tannenbaum, S.I. and Lauterborn, R.F. (1992) *Integrated Marketing Communications: Pulling It Together and Making It Work*, Chicago, IL: NTC Business Books.

Schultz, D.E., Tannenbaum, S.I. and Lauterborn, R.F. (1994) *Integrated Marketing Communications*, Chicago, IL: NTC Business Books.

Schultz, D.E., Tannenbaum, S.I., and Lauterborn, R.F. (1996) *The New Marketing Paradigm Integrated Marketing Communications*, Chicago, IL: NTC Business Books.

Schumacher, T. (1997) 'West Coast Camelot: The Rise and Fall of an Organizational Culture', in S. Sackmann (ed) *Cultural Complexity in Organizations. Inherent Contrasts and Contradictions*, Thousand Oaks, CA: Sage.

Schwartz, G. (1982) 'Public relations gets short shrift from new managers', *Marketing News*, 15 October.

Scotsman, The (1997) 'What a Waste' in Environmental Section of the Scotsman Newspaper, 7 October.

Scott, C.G. and Ambroson, D.L. (1994). 'The rocky road to change: Implications for substance abuse programs on college campuses', *Journal of American College Health*, 42(6).

Scott, D. and Suchard, H. (1992) 'Motivations for Australian expenditure of sponsorship', *International Journal of Advertising*, 11(4).

Sebeok, T. (1976) *Contributions to the Doctrine of Signs*, Bloomington, IN: Indiana University Press of America.

Sebeok, T. (1985) 'Pandora's Box: How and Why to Communicate 10,000 Years into the Future', in M. Blonsky (ed.) *On Signs*, Baltimore: John Hopkins University Press.

Sebeok, T.A. (1991) *A Sign is Just a Sign*, Bloomington, IN: University Press.

Seitel, F.P. (1992) *The Practice of Public Relations*, New York: Maxwell Macmillan.

Shandwick PLC (1989) *The public relations consultancy market worldwide*, Autumn, study published by the company.

Shannon, C. and Weaver, W. (1962) *The Mathematical Theory of Communication*, Urbana, IL: University of Illinois Press.

Shao, A.T. and Waller, D.S. (1993) 'Advertising Standardisation in The Asia Pacific Region: What Stands in the Way?', *Asia Pacific Journal of Marketing and Logistics*, 5(3).

Shaw, R. and Stone, M. (1988) 'Competitive superiority through database marketing', *Long Range Planning*, 21(5).

Shaw, R. and Stone, M. (1988) *Database Marketing*, Aldershot: Gower.

Sheaves, D. and Barnes, J. (1996) 'The fundamentals of relationships: an exploration of the concept to guide marketing implementation', *Advances in Services Marketing and Management*, 5.

Sheehan, R. (1965) 'The Way they think at TRW', In I. Ansoff (1965) *Business Strategy*, London: Penguin.

Shepard, R.N. (1978) 'The mental image', *American Psychologist*, 33, February.

Sherif, M. and Sherif, C.W. (1967) 'Attitude as the individual's own categories: the social judgement-involvement approach to attitude and attitude change', in C.W. Sherif and M. Sherif (eds) *Attitude, Ego-involvement, and Change*, New York: Wiley.

Sherry, J.F. (1987) 'Advertising as a Cultural System', in J. Umiker-Sebeok (ed) *Marketing and Semiotics*, Berlin: Mouton.

Sheth, J. and Parvatiyar, A. (1995) 'Relationship marketing in consumer markets: antecedents and consequences', *Journal of the Academy of Marketing Science*, 23(4).

Sheth, J.N., Gardner, D.M. and Garrett, D.E. (1988) *Marketing Theory: Evolution and Evaluation*, New York: John Wiley and Sons.

Shiffrin, R.M. and Atkinson, R.C. (1969) 'Storage and retrieval processes in long-term memory', *Psychological Review*, 76, 23 March.

Shimp, T.A. (1993) *Promotion Management and Marketing Communications*, 3rd edn, Fort Worth TX: Dryden Press.

Shimp, T.A. (1996) 'The Inevitability of Integrated Communications', *Journal of Business Research*, 37(3).

Shimp, T.A. (1997) *Advertising, Promotion and Supplemental Aspects of Integrated Marketing Communications*, Fort Worth, TX: Dryden Press.

Shimp, T.A. (1997) *Advertising, Sales Promotion, and Other Aspects of Integrated Marketing Communications*, 4th edn, Orlando, FL: Harcourt, Brace, Jovanovich International Edition.

Shimp, T.A. and Delozier, M.W. (1986) *Promotion Management and Marketing Communications*, New York: Dryden.

Shimp, T.E. (1990) *Promotion Management and Marketing Communications*, 2nd edn, Philadelphia: The Dryden Press.

Shocker, A.D., Srivastava, R.K. and Ruekert, R.W. (1994) 'Challenges and Opportunities Facing Brand Management: An Introduction', *Journal of Marketing Research*, Spring.

Simon, H. (1957a) (1965 edn) *Administrative Behaviour*, New York: Free Press, McMillan.

Simon, H. (1957b) *Models of Man: Social and Rational*, New York: John Wiley, London: Chapman & Hall.

Simon, H. (1977) *The New Science of Management Decision*, Englewood Cliffs, NJ: Prentice Hall.

Simon, J. and Arndt, J. (1980) 'The shape of the advertising response function', *Journal of Advertising Research*, 20(4).

Singer, J.L. (1966) *Daydreaming: An Introduction to the Experiential Study of Inner Experience*, New York: Random House.

Singh, J. (1997) *SoftWorld Survey of Sales and Marketing Technology*, London: Interactive Information Services.

Singh, J., Verbeke, W. and Rhodes, G.K. (1997) 'Do organisational practices matter in role stress processes: a study of direct and moderating effects for marketing-oriented boundary spanners', *Journal of Marketing*, 60, July.

Skolnik, R. (1993) 'The Emerging Firm of the '90s', *Public Relations Journal*, March.

Slater, M.D. and Rouner, D. (1996) 'Value-affirmative and value-protective processing of alcohol education messages that include statistical evidence or anecdotes', *Communication Research*, 23(2).

Sloan, J.R. (1994) 'Ad Agencies Should Learn the Facts of Life', *Marketing News*, February 28.

Smith, B. and Barclay, D. (1997) 'The effects of organisational differences and trust on the effectiveness of selling partner relationships', *Journal of Marketing*, 61(1).

Smith, G. (1997) Letter to IDM members, 4 September.

Smith, P., Berry, C. and Pulford, A. (1997) *Strategic Marketing Communications*, London: Kogan Page.

Smith, P.R. (1993) *Marketing Communications: An Integrated Approach*, London: Kogan Page.

Smith, S.M. and Shaffer, D.R. (1991) 'Celerity and cajolery: Rapid speech may promote or inhibit persuasion through its impact on message elaboration', *Personality and Social Psychology Bulletin*, 17(6).

Snoddy, R. (1988) 'Study into cost of TV adverts', *Financial Times*, 26 January.

Snyder, M. (1987) *Public Appearances/Private Realities: The Psychology of Self-Monitoring*, New York: W.H. Freeman.

Snyder, R. (1988) 'New Frames for Old. Changing the Managerial Culture of an Aircraft Factory', in M. Jones, M. Moore and R. Snyder (eds) *Inside Organizations. Understanding the Human Dimension*, Newbury Park, CA: Sage.

Solomon, M.R. and Englis, B.G. (1994) 'Observations: the big picture: product complementarity and integrated communications', *Journal of Advertising Research*, Jan–Feb.

Sparkman, Jr., N. and Austin, L.M. (1980) 'The effects on sales of colour in newspaper advertisement', *Journal of Advertising*, Fourth Quarter.

Speed, R. and Thompson, P. (1997) 'Developing a model of the determinants of sports sponsorship impact', paper presented at the *1997 European Marketing Academy Conference*, Warwick Business School, UK, May 20–23.

Stanley, R.E. (1982) *Promotion: Advertising, Publicity, Personal Selling, Sales Promotion*, 2nd edn, Englewood Cliffs, NJ: Prentice Hall.

Starbuck, W.H. (1985) 'Acting First and Thinking Later: Theory versus Reality in Strategic Change', in J.M. Pennings and Associates *Organizational Strategy and Change*, San-Francisco, CA: Jossey-Bass.

Starch, D. (1923) *Principles of Marketing*, Chicago, IL: A.W. Shaw.

Steele, C.M. (1988) 'The psychology of self-affirmation: sustaining the integrity of the self', in L. Berkowitz (ed.) *Advances in Experimental Social Psychology*, 21, San Diego, CA: Academic Press.

Steele, C.M. and Liu, T.J. (1983) 'Dissonance process as self-affirmation', *Journal of Personality and Social Psychology*, 45.

Steinfield, C., Kraut, R. and Plummer, A. (1995) 'The impact of electronic commerce on buyer–seller relationships', *Journal of Computer-Mediated Communication*, 1(3), December, available at *http://shum.huji.ac.il/jcmc/vol1/issue3/hoffman.html*

Stern, B. (1995), 'Consumer myths: Frye's taxonomy and the structural analysis of a consumption text', *Journal of Consumer Research*, 22 (September).

Sterne, J. (1995) *World Wide Web Marketing: Integrating The Internet Into Your Marketing Strategy*, New York: John Wiley (*http://www.targeting.com*).

Stewart, D.W. (1996) 'Market-Back Approach to the Design of Integrated Communication Programmes: A Change in Paradigm and a Focus on Determinants of Success', *Journal of Business Research*, 37(3).

Stewart, D.W. and Ward, S. (1994) 'Media effects of advertising', in B. Jennings and D. Zillman (eds) *Media Effects, Advances in Theory and Research*, Hillsdale, NJ: Lawrence Erlbaum.

Stewart-Hunter, M. (1990) 'Testing Advertisements', in D. Cowley (ed.) *How to Plan Advertising*, London: Cassell.

Stipp, H. and Schiavone, N. (1996) 'Modelling the impact of Olympic sponsorship on corporate image', *Journal of Advertising Research*, 36(4).

Stone, B. and Wyman, J. (1986) *Successful Telemarketing: Opportunities and Techniques for Increasing Sales and Profits*, Lincolnwood, IL.: NTC Business Books.

Strang, R. (1976) 'Sales promotion: fast growth, faulty management', *Harvard Business Review*, 54(4).

Strang, R. (1980) *The Promotional Planning Process*, New York: Praeger Publishers.

Strong, E.K. (1925) *The Psychology of Selling*, New York: McGraw-Hill.

Summerfield, G. (1996) *Campaign*, 23 February.

Swanson, G.E. (1978) 'Travels through inner space: family structure and openness to absorbing experiences', *American Journal of Sociology*, 83, January.

Synodinos, N.E., Keown, C.F. and Jacobs, L.W. (1989) 'Transnational advertising practice: a survey of leading brand advertisers in fifteen countries', *Journal of Advertising Research*, 29(2) (April/May).

Takada, H. and Jain, D (1991) 'Cross-National Analysis of Diffusion of Consumer Durable Goods in Pacific Rim Countries', *Journal of Marketing*, 55(2), April.

Tapscott, D. (1996) *Digital Economy: Promise and Peril in the Age of Networked Intelligence*, McGraw-Hill (*http://www-mitpress.mit.edu/bookstore/nonpress/digecon.html*)

Tartan Shopping Mall (1996) *http://www.ibmpcug.co.uk/~ecs/mall/malla.html*

Tavassoli, N.T., Shultz II, C.J. and Fitzsimons, G.J. (1995) 'Program involvement: are moderate levels best for ad memory and attitude toward the ad?', *Journal of Advertising Research*, September/October.

Taylor, S. and Mitchell, M. (1996) 'Building donor relations: Enter database marketing', *Nonprofit world*, 14(6).

Teather, D. (1995) 'Stars bring unknown risk to endorsement', *Marketing*, 6 July.

Tellis, G. (1988) 'Advertising exposure, loyalty and brand purchase: a two stage model', *Journal of Marketing Research*, 25(2).

The Wall Street Journal (1991) 'Recession feeds the coupon habit', 20 February.

Thomas, H. (1986) 'A modest success', *Marketing*, 13 November.

Thomas, R. (1919) *Commercial Advertising*, LSE Studies of Economic and Political Science, London and New York: G.P. Putnam and Sons Ltd.

Thompson, K. and Luthans, F. (1990) 'Organizational Culture: A Behavioral Perspective', In B. Schneider (ed) *Organizational Climate and Culture*, San Francisco, CA.: Jossey-Bass.

Thwaites, D. (1995) 'Professional football sponsorship – Profitable or profligate?', *International Journal of Advertising*, 14(2).

Tidd, J., Bessant, J. and Paritt, K. (1997) *Managing Innovations*, Chichester: Wiley.

Times, The, (1998) 12 March.

Toffler, A. and Toffler, H. (1990) *Powershift: Knowledge, Wealth and Violence at the Edge of the 21st Century*, New York: Bantam Books.

Towsey, R. and Strickland, G. (1975) 'EDP systems in retailing, the practice and the philosophy', *Retail and Distribution Management*, January/February.

Trapp, R. (1993) 'Viewers drink in lager mystery', *The Independent on Sunday*, 12 September, Business supplement.

Treneman, A. (1997) 'Why teaching is sexy in the States', *The Independent*, 26 March.

Troiano, M. (1995) *Campaign*, 7 July.

Tull, D.S. and Hawkins, D.I. (eds) (1993) *Marketing Research: Measurement and Method*, 6th edn, Englewood Cliffs, NJ: Prentice Hall.

Tversky, A. and Kahneman, D. (1974) 'Judgement under uncertainty: Heuristics and biases', *Science*, 185.

Tylee, J. (1997) 'ASA clears Lee Jeans work of offence', *Campaign*, 14 November.

Umiker-Sebeok, J. (ed.) (1987) *Marketing Signs: New Directions in the Study of Signs for Sale*, Berlin: Mouton.

Umiker-Sebeok, J., Cossette, C. and Bachand, D. (1988) 'Selected Bibliography on the Semiotics of Marketing', *Semiotic Enquiry*, 8(3).

Unnava, H.R. and Burnkrant, R.E. (1991) 'An imagery processing view of the role of pictures in print advertisements', *Journal of Marketing Research*, 28, May.

Urban C. L. and Hauser J.R. (1993) *Design and Marketing of New Products*, 2nd edn, Englewood Cliffs, NJ: Prentice Hall.

US Department of Commerce (1996) *http://www.stat-usa.gov/*

Van Maanen, J. and Barley, S. (1984) 'Occupational Communities: Culture and Control in Organizations', In B. Staw and L. Cummings (eds) *Research in Organizational Behaviour,* Vol. 6, Greenwich, CT: JAI Press.

Van Raaij, W.F. (1993) 'Postmodern consumption', *Journal of Economic Psychology,* 14(3).

van Raaij, W.F. (1998) 'Interactive communication and consumer power and initiative', *Journal of Marketing Communications,* 4(1).

Van Riel, C. (1995) *Corporate Communications,* Prentice Hall International.

Van Riel, C. (1995) *Principles of Corporate Communication,* London: Prentice Hall.

van Riel, C. and Balmer, J.M.T. (1997) 'Corporate identity: the concept, its measurement and management', *European Journal of Marketing,* 31(5 & 6).

Vardar, N. (1992) *Global Advertising: Rhyme or Reason?,* London: Paul Chapman.

Varey, R. (1995) 'A Model of Internal Marketing for Building and Sustaining a Competitive Service Advantage', *Journal of Marketing Management,* 11(1).

Vassos, T. (1996) *Strategic Internet Marketing,* Que Books;, author's Web site at (*http://www/ webdiamonds.com/~webdiamonds*); *Strategic Internet Marketing* Web site at (*http://www.mcp.com/ que/desktop os/int market/*).

Venkatesh, A., Sherry, F., Jnr. and Firat, A.F. (1993) 'Postmodernism and the marketing imaginary', *International Journal of Research in Marketing,* 10(2).

Venkatraman, M.P. and MacInnis, D.J. (1985) 'The epistemic and sensory exploratory behaviours of hedonic and cognitive consumers', *Advances in Consumer Research,* 12.

Verity, J.W., Hof, R.D., Baig, E.C. and Carey, J. (1996) 'The Internet: how it will change the way you do business', *Business Week,* 14 November.

Waldrup, J. (1994) 'Advertising that counts', *American Demographics,* 16(5).

Walter, P. and Hughes, S. (1997) 'Good ad, bad ad', *The Independent,* 13 October, media supplement.

Walters, D. (1986) 'International consumer trends', *Retail,* 4(3).

Wardle, J. (1995) 'The good, the bad, and the ugly', *Admap,* September.

Waterschoot, W. and Bulte, C. (1992) 'The Four P Classification of the Marketing Mix Revisited', *Journal of Marketing,* 56(4).

Webb, P.H. (1979) 'Consumer initial processing in a difficult media environment', *Journal of Consumer Research,* 6, December.

Webb, P.H. and Ray, M.L. (1979) 'Effects of TV clutter', *Journal of Advertising Research,* 19, June.

Webster, F. (1981) 'Top management's concerns about marketing issues for the 1980s', *Journal of Marketing,* 45(3).

Webster, F. E. Jnr (1992) 'The Changing Role of Marketing in the Corporation', *Journal of Marketing,* 56(4).

Wegener, D.T. and Petty, R.E. (1996) *Effects Of Mood On Persuasion Processes: Enhancing, Reducing, And Biasing Scrutiny Of Attitude-Relevant Information,* Mahwah, NJ: Lawrence Erlbaum.

Wells, W.D. (1988) 'Lectures and dramas', in P. Cafferata and A. Tybout (eds.) *Cognitive and Affective Responses to Advertising,* Lexington, MA: D.C. Heath.

Wernick, A. (1991) *Promotional Culture – Advertising, Ideology and Symbolic Expression,* London, Newbury Park, CA: Sage.

Whelan, M. (1996) 'Why Youths have Zero Interest in Banks Messages', *Marketing,* 12 December.

White, J. (1991) *How to Understand and Manage Public Relations,* London: Business Books.

White, J., Dickson, A. and Myers, A. (1988) *Public Relations Employment and Expenditure in the United Kingdom,* a report for the Institute of Public Relations prepared by the Cranfield School of Management, UK.

White, P.H. and Harkins, S.G. (1994) 'Race of source effects in the Elaboration Likelihood Model', *Journal of Personality and Social Psychology,* 67(5).

White, R. (1993) *Advertising: What it is and how to do it,* 3rd edn, London: McGraw-Hill.

Whittaker, J.O. (1967) 'Resolution of the communication discrepancy issue in attitude change', in C.W. Sherif and M. Sherif (eds) *Attitude, Ego-involvement, and Change,* New York: Wiley.

Wicker, A. (1971) 'An examination of the "other variable" explanation of the attitude-behavior inconsistency', *Journal of Personality and Social Psychology,* 19.

Williams, R. (1993) 'Switched-on advertisers ready for a rave', *The Independent on Sunday,* 25 April.

Williamson, J. (1978) *Decoding Advertisements,* London: Marion Boyars.

Wilson, D. (1995) 'An integrated model of buyer-seller relationships', *Journal of the Academy of Marketing Science,* 23(4).

Wilson, T. (1996) in *Web Marketing Today Newsletter,* 12 December [http://www.wilsonweb.com]

Witcher, B., Craigen, J., Culligan, D. and Harvey, A. (1991) 'The links between objectives and function in organisational sponsorship', *International Journal of Advertising,* 10(1).

Wolter, L. (1993) 'Superficiality, Ambiguity Threatens IMC's Implementation and Future', *Marketing News,* 27, 13 September.

Wood, W. and Kallgreen, C.A. (1988) 'Communicator attributes and persuasion: Recipients' access to attribute-relvant information in memory', *Personality and Social Psychology Bulletin,* 14.

Wright, P. (1973) 'The cognitive processes mediating acceptance of advertising', *Journal of Marketing Research,* 10.

Wright, P.L. (1975) 'Consumer choice strategies: simplifying vs. optimizing', *Journal of Marketing Research,* 11, February.

Wynne-Jones, R. (1997) 'Rise of the pick'n'mix family', *Independent on Sunday,* 26 October, 5.

Yates, K. (1996) 'First Direct Reveals Humorous Film', *Campaign,* 30 August.

Ybema, S. (1997) 'Telling Tales: Contrasts and Commonalities Within the Organization of an Amusement Park – Confronting and Combining Different Perspectives', In S. Sackmann (ed.) *Cultural Complexity in Organizations. Inherent Contrasts and Contradictions,* Thousand Oaks, CA: Sage.

Yeshin, T. (1997) *Marketing Communications Strategy 1996–97,* Oxford: The Chartered Institute of Marketing, Butterworth–Heinemann.

Yorke, D. and Kitchen, P. (1985) 'Channel flickers and video speeders', *Journal of Advertising Research,* 25(2).

Young, E. (1989) 'On the Naming of the Rose: Interests and Multiple Meanings as Elements of Organizational Culture', *Organization Studies,* 10(2).

Young, M. and Steilen, C. (1996) 'Strategy bases Advertising Selection: An Alternative to "Spec" Presentations', *Business Horizons,* 39(6), November/ December.

Young, R.F. and Greyser, S.A. (1982) *Cooperative Advertising: Practices and Problems,* Cambridge, MA: Marketing Science Institute.

Zanjonc, R. (1980) 'Feeling and thinking: preferences need no inferences', *American Psychologist,* 35, February.

Zenith Media (1996) 'Global advertising expenditure forecasts', *Financial Times,* 16 December.

Zikmund, W.G. and D'Amico, M. (1996) *Marketing,* 5th edn, New York: West Publishing Company.

Zimbardo, P.G. and Leippe, M.R. (1991) *The Psychology of Attitude Change and Social Influence,* New York: McGraw-Hill.

Zotos, Y., Lysonski, S. and Martin, P. (1992) 'Elaboration Likelihood Model and locus of control: Is there a connection?', *Psychological Reports,* 70(3, Pt 2), Spec Issue.

Zuckerman, M. (1979) *Sensation-Seeking: Beyond the Optimal Level of Arousal,* Hillsdale, NJ: Lawrence Erlbaum.

INDEX

ABM, 442–446
Above-the-line, 295
ACORN, 260
Adoption and Diffusion
  see chapter 12
  adoption process, 194
  behavioural type stages, 194
  brands, 190
  change, 189
  communication channels, 201–202
  diffusion process, 191–194
  diffusion elements, 197
  distribution patterns of diffusion, 192
  early market entrants, 202
  ideal innovator types, 193
  later market entrants, 202
  macro and micro models, 194
  marketing communications management,
    207–208
  micro models and marketing, 196
  social system, 204–205
  time, 206–207
Advertisers, 424
Advertising, 9, 24
  also see chapters 16, 24, 25
  benefits of, 25–26
  budget determination, 273–275
  business, 424
  campaigns, 69, 260, 267, 285–287
  codes, deconstructing, 141–45
  consumer use, 126
  cultural crossover, 127–129
  customization and control, 122
  defined, 265–266
  different from marketing, 12
  does it work, 272–273
  ecological, 223
  efficiency, 296–297
  entertaining, 124–125
  expenditure, 24, 25, 273

global forecasts, 251
green issues, 215, 217
growth, 231–233
how it works, 268–272
informative, 125–126
integrated programme, 14, 103
Internet, 238–239
irritant, 122
noise/clutter, 119–120
objectives, 268, 272–273
plan, 281, 282, 283
postmodernism, 1, 3
print, 26
radio, 26
restraining factors, 231–233
selling, comparison to, 328
system, 423
television, 25–26
time limit (UK TV), 127
what it can and cannot do, 266–268
women and, 118–119
Advertising Agencies
  see chapters 16, 24, 25
  comments on, 424–429
  full service, 275
  remuneration/compensation, see chapter
    25
  selecting, 436–438
  working relationships, 432–436
Advertising Industry, 129
Advertising Standards Authority (ASA),
  15–16, 218
AGM Associates, 337
AIDA, 269, 366
Airtours, 250
Alphabites, 147
AMAZON.COM, 396–397
American Express, 246
Analysis,
  see chapters 5 and 27

data sources, 64–65
  need for, 59
  ongoing, 65–66
Attention, 24
  selective, 161
Attitudes, 163
  affect referral, 166
  persuasion, 173–176
  receiver involvement, 173–176
Audi, 106–107
Audience, 22,
  also see, Chapter 8
  and, markets 126
  demassified, 296
  demographics, 114
  families, 115–116
  fragmentation, 115–116, 296
  in marketing communications, 114
  power, 119
  receptivity, 196
Australian Meat and Livestock Corporation,
    172–173
Australian National Tobacco Campaign,
    184–185
Axis Communications, 381–382

B&Q, 446
Bacardi, 31
Barbican, 32
Barbie, 356
Beecham, 32
Below-the-line, see chapter 17
Birds Eye/Walls, 147
Black Magic, 267
BMW, 18, 264, 275, 279
Bodyshop, The 9, 260
BP, 218
Brand similarities, 296
Branding, 39
  innovation, 190
  strategy, 41
Brand Management,
  system, changes in, 235, 242
British Airways, 275
British Telecom (BT), 129, 205, 254
Britvic 55, 32
Brylcream, 353
Bugs Bunny, 356

Cabbage Patch Kids, 30, 32, 352
Cable and Satellite TV, 259
Cable & Wireless, 259
Cadbury, 29
Campaign Strategy, 275

Cannes, 252
Car marketing, 18–19
Carling Black Label, 261–262
Castlemaine XXXX, 151
Celebrity endorsers, 143
CFC's, 226–227
Channels, 22
Chrysler, 30–31, 352
Cinema, 259, 432
Clutter, 296
  see also 'noise'
Coca Cola, 233
Cointreaux, 49
Colgate-Palmolive, 247
Commission system
  see chapter 25
  bad debt and cashflow, 449
  full fee alternative, 453
  marking-up, 450–451
  media commission, 447
  practices (Europe), 454
  rebating, 451–453
  top-up fees, 449–450
  worksheet examples, 455–458
Communication,
  models, 48 (see also 'hierarchy of effects'
    and 'AIDA')
  process, see chapter 19
  theories, 253–254
Competitive advantage, 61
Competition, 21, 62–63
Consumers
  as pawns, 8
  as sceptics, 123
  decision buying process, 251
  decision making, 165–166
  demographic changes, 297
  global, 233–234
  models, 62
  power and initiative, 8
  reality, 129
  relationship marketing, 411–412
  retail effects, 486–487
  streetwise, savvy, sophisticated, 232
  thinking and feeling, 158–160
  understanding, 62–64
  youth as, 112
Contract Publishing, 35
Co-op, 486
Corporate Communications
  also see, chapter 20
  and planning, 47
  and marcoms, 235
CPM/HEM Models, see chapter 10
  spectrum of, 157

Creative
brief, 275–276
creativity, 129
executions, 275 (see companies cited)
planning process, 277
Cyberspace,
see chapter 22
Cygus Technology, 399

Daewoo, 19, 254
Daihatsu, 18, 47
DAGMAR, 269, 272
Database marketing, 314
coordinated strategy, 237
phases of, 236–237
Decoding, 23
Demand, 21
Diffusion, see chapter 12
Direct marketing, 11
see, chapter 18
and car dealers, 309–310
datafusion and biographics, 315–317
data mining, 318
demand, 311
layers of, 317
new promotion tool, 236
relationship marketing, see chapter 23
research vs testing, 319
supply of, 312–313
underlying factors, 311
Dirty Angels, 168
Dissertations,
see chapter 27
Domestos, 299

Eastern Electricity, 214
Effectiveness, 256–258, 259–260, 267
and IPA, 280
testing, 470–471
Elaboration Likelihood Model (ELM)
see chapter 11
ability, 178
central route, 176
discussion and critique, 182–183
elaboration, 177
motivation, 177
peripheral route, 177
Encoding, 23
also see chapter 9
Entertainment,
need for, 124–125
Environment
see chapters 6, 7, 8, 13
over-use, 225
pollution, 224

Evaluation,
see chapter 26
in market 471–472
Exchange, 8
Exhibitions, 259

Feedback, 23
Financial Services, 129
First Choice, 250
First Direct, 22, 47, 255
Flora Margarine, 129
Flyfishing, 129
Ford Maverick, 19
Foster's Lager, 162
Four P's (see marketing mix)
Fragmentation, 25
Friends of the Earth, 214, 218
Functional activities, 3, 9–15

Generation X, 112, 117
disillusioned and cynical, 117
Glasgow, 30, 285–287, 350
Global Marketing Communications
development, 236–237, 241
coordination/control issues, 239–241
standardized/adapted, 239–240
advertising expenditure forecasts, 252
Gold Blend, 49, 128
Greater London Council, 146
Green
communications defined, 216
sustainable defined, 216
shades of (in advertising), 220
level of ecological concern, 221
Green Con Awards, 214–215
Greening
environmental necessity, 216
advertising claims, 217–218
Greenpeace, 214, 218, 223

Häagen Dazs, 279
Halifax PLC, 22
Health Education Board for Scotland, 474–75
Hedonic Experiential Model,
see chapter 10
Heinz, 237
Heuristics, 166, 181–182
Hierarchy of Effects Models, 67–69, 269–270
Hofmeister Lager, 147
House of Commons, 258

IBM, 233
ICI, 218
Identity and Image,
advertising, 281

Information processing
  see chapter 10
Innovation
  see chapter 12
  behavioural impact of innovators, 198
  branding, 199–200
  diffusion of, 190–191
Institute of Sales Promotion (UK), 292
Integrated, 13
Integrated Marketing Communications (IMC)
  see chapter 6
  agencies, 98–104
  and advertising, 103
  and planning, 66–68, 255
  as promotional management, 13–14
  background/history, 91,
  barriers to, 101
  budgets and time, 102
  communication elements, 97
  defined, 93, 257
  development and importance, 234–236
  empirical studies, 90, 93–105
  global significance, 91
  long term goal, 243
  management fad, 90, 103
  meaning of, 98, 104
  measurement/evaluation, 99, 103–104,
    105
  and, new technology, 105
  and, PR
  prevalence, 91
  reactions to definition, 95, 100–101,
    104–105
  schools of thought, 92
  synergy (lack of), 104
Internal communications, 77
Internet
  see chapter 22
  advertising, 238–239
  background, 382–384
  changing power relationships, 391
  cybermedia advertising, 432
  forms of electronic communication,
    12–13
  and, marketing communications, 387–391
  origins, growth, evaluation, 385–386
  website design and marketing, 393–395
Intersport, 340–341
Involvement, 24
  uninvolvement, 25
Institute of Grocery Distribution, 486
Institute of Practitioners in Advertising (IPA)
  and advertising effectiveness, 280
  awards, 51, 280
  database, 260

Jingle Kings, 442
JMD International, 226–227
Johnson & Johnson, 30, 352

Kelloggs Co, 29
Kraft Dairy Foods, 325
Kodak, 358

L'Eggs, 260
Lean Cuisine, 260
Lee Jeans, 15–16
Leeds Liquid Gold, 40
Levi Strauss, 5–6, 156, 240
Lifestyles
  Acorn, 261, 312
  Mosaic, 261, 313
  Sagacity, 261
  VALS, 261
Little Harry, 128
Lung Ads, 185–186

Magazines, 18
Market
  fragmentation, 28
  market share, 28
  saturation, 28
  stagnation, 296
Market Research Society, 320
Marketing
  change, 230–231
  concept, 21
  defined, 20
  different from advertising, 12
  distinct from marcoms, 19
  dynamic nature, 19
  evaluation of, 20
  Four P's (marketing mix), 21, 31, 91,
    271–272, 291, 353
  generic concept, 20
  and, MPR, 341
  origins, 20
  and, PR, 346–349
  and, selling, 21
  and, semiotics, 140
  warfare, 31
Marketing Communications
  audience, 114–115
  defined, 2
  elements, 24–32
  evaluating, see chapter 26
  explained, 2, 22–24
  framework for, 253
  greening, 216
  importance, 7
  and, Internet, 387–389

models, 22–23, 48, 119, 121, 194
network and structure, 76–77
in, new millennium, 489–490
organizational context, see chapter 6
and, planning, see chapter 4
and, promotion, 6
relationship marketing, 417
renaissance, see chapter 14
role and function, 5–16
and, semiotics, 140
two-way, 9, 22
Marketing Management
  and marcoms, 19, 58, 207–210
Marketing Public Relations (MPR)
  see chapter 20
  advantages, 33
  brilliance, 47
  credibility, 31
  defined and explained, 10, 30–32, 352
  descriptive model, 350
  distinct discipline, 354–355
  explosive nature, 12
  growth, 350–351
  integration, 32
  and, marketing, 346–349
  and, marketing mix, 353
  marketing perspective of PR, 343
  PR, as corrective to marketing, 345
  relationship with corporate PR, 30
  theoretical background, 341–342
  and, 'unmentionable products', 32
  using MPR, 355
Marlboro, 159
Mars, 24
Matchbox Cars, 32
McDonald's, 229, 233, 353
Meaning
  see semiotics, chapter 8
Measurement
  see chapter 8, and 26
  creative development research, 466–467
  effectiveness testing, 470–471
  evaluation models, 461–463
  execution testing, 468–469
  in-market evaluation, 471–472
  promotional decision making process, 463
  promotional research model, 462
  problem definition research, 464
  strategy definition research, 464–466
Media
  see chapter 8
  brief, 275, 278
  buying systems, 235
  clutter, 296
  inter/ intra, 280

mix, 279
owners, 429–432
selection and planning, 258, 278–280
Memory
  short term/long term, 164
Mercedes, 265
Message, 22, 23
  see chapter 11
  attitudes, 163
  comprehension and acceptance, 162–164
  deconstruction of codes, 142
  design and delivery, 173, 275
  fantasy, 161
  green, 218–219
  need states, 163
  retention, search retrieval, 164–165
  semiotics, 138
  sexuality, 161
Microsoft, 44, 259
Midland Bank, 39, 41
Millennium
  new, 123
  and marcoms, 489–490
Mr Happy, 286

National Film Board of Canada, 45
Nestlé, 24
Netiquette, 387
New York City 352, 356
New Zealand
  cheese promotions, 57–58
  road safety, 70
Nissan Almeira, Primera, Micra 18–19
Noise, 23
  advertising, 119
  semiotics, 138
Norwich Union Direct, 322

Olympic Games, 81
One Foot in the Grave, 129
Orange, 89–90
Organizational
  approach to marcoms, 258, 259
Organizational Architecture
  of text, 3
Organizational re-engineering, 241
Organizational Structure
  see chapter 6, 8, 15
  boundaries, 77
  consensus, 81
  culture, 80–81, 83
  flexible forms, 79–80
  leadership, 79–81
  marcom implications, 83
  scenarios, 75

Outdoor, 259
Oxford Instruments, 260

Peaudouce, 218
Pedigree Petfoods, 24
Peperami, 128
Persuasion
  see chapters 10, 11
  and, behaviour, 175
  information processing, 160–161
  self, 175
Peugeot, 18, 218
Personal Selling
  see chapter 19
  callplan, 336
  compared with marketing, 328
  defined, 10, 29–30
  role of, 327–329
  sales force organization typologies, 330–331
  sales force structure, 331–333
  sales force size, 333
  and, sales management, 329–330
  territorial deployment, 335
Pillsbury Toaster Packets, 128
Planning
  see chapter 4
  academic view, 41–43
  and, analysis, see chapter 5
  assumptions, 43
  codification of strategy, 49–50
  evaluative nature, 44–45
  formal cycle, 46
  formulation/implementation, 44
  and, IMC, 257, 258
  leaders, and, 44
  left brain/right brain, 51–52
  logical cascade, 47
  and, magic, 41, 51
  media, 278
  models, 60
  objectives, 61
  and, organizations, 48–49
  practitioner's view, 50
  problem solving, 43
  rationality, 43
  research evidence, 43–45
Playtex Wonderbra, 259
Point-of-Sale, 12
Posters, 18, 431
Postmodernism
  and society, 113
Press, 430
Proctor & Gamble Co, 6, 24, 26, 215
Product
  see Marketing (Four P's)

meaning, 159
Product Publicity
  see MPR,
  as 'marketing stepchild', 30
Promotion
  integrated, 13
  mix, 13
  and, MPR
  see chapters 1, 2, 3
  why needed, 22
Promotional Management
  advertising programme, 14

Radio, 18, 26, 259, 431–432
Rate Card, 280
Receiver, 23
Reception, 25
Reebok, 355
Relationship Marketing
  see chapter 23
  background and history, 404–405
  consumer sector, 411
  commitment, 409–410
  defined, 406–407
  and, direct marketing, 416
  learning from, 413
  and, marcoms, 417
  social support, 414–415
  trust, 407–408
  use and abuse of, 415
Research
  see chapters 26, 27
  dimensions, 3
  see, dissertations
  programmes, 40–41
  defined, 478
  design options, 478–479
  underlying assumptions, 479
    deductive 479–480
    inductive, 480–482
    comparison between deductive and
      inductive, 482
  writing a research proposal, 483
Response, 23, 270
Retailing, 27, 316, 403
Remote control, 123
  see video recorders
Rolex, 131
Royal Mail, 322–323
Royal National Lifeboat Institution (RNLI),
    418–419
Rover, 18

Sales
  as function, 10

see personal selling
vertical marketing systems, 29
Sales Promotion, 10, 26–29,
    see chapter 17
    advantages, 27
    attractiveness, 11
    coupons, 289–290
    defined, 27, 290–292
    demographic changes, 296–297
    development, 27–28
    effectiveness, 301
    effects, 29
    expenditure, 27
    importance/growth, 295–296
    objectives, 293
    planning process, 298–299
    price/non-price, 302–303
    'push' and 'pull', 27
    schematic framework, 293
    strategies, 28
    tactical counterpoint to advertising, 27
    two schools of thought, 28
    typologies, 292–293
Segmentation,
    70's style, 111
    90's style, 112
Semiotics
    see chapter 9
    advertising perspective, 271
    analysis, 140–141
    boundary, 136
    intertextuality, 140–141
    and, marketing, 139
    meaning-making, 138–139
    message, 138
    noise, 139
    origins and scope, 136–138
    and, signs 137, 142
    terms, 138–140
Sender, 23
Social systems, 204–206
Source, 22
    credibility, 176
Sponsorship
    see chapter 21
    AIDA/ATR models, 366
    evaluation of, 363–364, 367–371
    how it works, 364

legal/ethical issues, 372–374
objectives and audiences, 365–367
perspectives, 366
research agenda, 374–376
Strategy and Planning, 45, 49–50
    boldness/innovativeness, 46–47
    described, 50
    for marcoms effectiveness, 256–259
    systematic development, 415–416

Tang, 356
Tate Gallery, 377–378
Television, 18, 26, 31
    ad spend, 431
    demassification, 26
    fragmentation, 25–26
    industry, 124
    and, marketing warfare, 31
Tesco Stores, 316, 486
    clubcard, 1–2
Texas Instruments, 107–108
Theoretical foundations, 3
Thomson, 250
Times, The, 277
Tylenol, 30, 352

Unilever, 279
Union Jack, 153

Vauxhall Motors, 218
Vector, 40
Verbal information, 158–159
Video recorders (VCR's)
    and, remote control, 123, 296
Vimto, 459–460
Virgin Atlantic, 277
Volvo, 18, 265

Windows 95, 258
Women
    and advertising, 118–119
World Cup Final, 361
World Wide Web
    see chapter 22
    websites, 240

Youth market
    70's style, 111–112